MEDICAL TYPING AND TRANSCRIBING

Microcassette Transcriber   Sony BM-840

MARCY OTIS DIEHL, BVE, CMA-A, CMT
Instructor
Medical Typing, Medical Transcription, Medical Office
Management, Medical Terminology, Medical Insurance
Billing
Grossmont Community College
El Cajon, California

MARILYN TAKAHASHI FORDNEY, CMA-AC, CMT
Formerly Instructor of Medical Insurance,
Medical Terminology, Medical Machine Transcription
and Medical Office Procedures
Ventura College, Ventura, California

Chapter opening illustrations by Gail Niebrugge

W.B. SAUNDERS COMPANY
A Division of Harcourt Brace & Company
Philadelphia London Toronto Montreal Sydney Tokyo

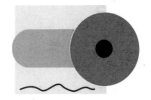

MEDICAL TYPING AND TRANSCRIBING
Techniques and Procedures

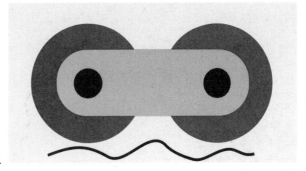

third edition

W.B. SAUNDERS COMPANY
A Division of
Harcourt Brace & Company

The Curtis Center
Independence Square West
Philadelphia, Pennsylvania 19106

Library of Congress Cataloging-in-Publication Data

Diehl, Marcy Otis.

   Medical typing and transcribing; techniques and procedures/Marcy Otis Diehl, Marilyn Takahashi
Fordney; chapter opening illustrations by Gail Niebrugge. — 3rd ed.

    p.   cm.

Includes bibliographical references.

Includes index.

ISBN 0–7216–3479–6

   1. Medical secretaries. 2. Typewriting. 3. Dictation (Office practice) 4. Medical writing.

I. Fordney, Marilyn Takahashi.   II. Title.

[DNLM: 1. Medical Records—problems. 2. Medical Secretaries—problems. 3. Nomenclature
—Problems. W 18 D559m] R728.8D47   1991

652.3′26—dc20

DNLM/DLC   909152

Editor: Margaret M. Biblis
Designer: W. B. Saunders Staff
Production Manager: Ken Neimeister
Manuscript Editor: W. B. Saunders Staff
Illustration Coordinator: Cecilia Kunkle
Cover Designer: Ellen M. Bodner

MEDICAL TYPING AND TRANSCRIBING: Techniques and Procedures, Third Edition   ISBN 0–7216–3479–6

Printed in the United States of America

Last digit is the print number: 9   8   7   6

To my students, whose anticipation and excitement for this exciting field have inspired and delighted me.
    M.O.D.

To my sister Toni, whose dedication in helping the deaf to communicate has been an inspiration.
    M.T.F.

Preface

It is with much excitement, pride, and satisfaction that we have assembled this third edition of *Medical Typing and Transcribing: Techniques and Procedures.* In fact, beginning with the new cover design and all the way back to additional appendices, there are many new ideas and interesting changes. Advances in the technology of equipment, educational methodology, and new medical diseases and procedures have led to the decision that it was time for a new edition. Each chapter has been reviewed by three different experts so that improvements in the way of changes, deletions, insertions, and so forth in the content and format could be considered. We are very grateful that we received helpful critiques. Additional material has been incorporated encompassing hospital protocols, and additional exercises have made independent study (with the answers provided at the end of the chapter) easier. For those teaching institutions using individualized instruction or a modular approach, Appendix E provides the answers to the practice tests and Appendix F provides performance evaluation sheets for review tests. The pages are perforated and the instructor may elect to remove them before the course begins, or if the instructor wants the student to have access to these answers and sheets, they can remain in the textbook. An instructor's guide is a complete syllabus and is available for the chapter review exercises or additional exercises that have no answers provided in the text. The review exercises or additional exercises should be carefully discussed with the guidance of the teacher. Three difficult chapters have a complete synopsis at the end of the chapter facilitating quick referencing of rules. Owing to the explosion of reference books in the last five years for medical transcriptionists, Appendix C has been greatly updated and expanded.

This text is designed for the secretarial student who plans to major in medical transcription, seeking eventual employment in a private physician's office, clinic, or hospital or to be self-employed and free-lance. There continues to be a serious shortage of medical transcriptionists resulting from the problems of training qualified medical typists, the increase in the quantity of dictation due to longer reports and a larger number of diagnostic studies, and the demand by hospitals for quality reports. It is an appropriate text for a first-semester medical typing class after completion of a medical terminology course. The legal secretary and court reporting student will also find it a useful introduction to medical terms and practices.

We have designed the book so that it can be used in the community college or vocational-technical institute, for in-service training in the hospital or private medical office, or in extension programs. It can also be used for independent home study if no formal classes are available in the community. The textbook can also be used by practicing medical or legal assistants who want to upgrade their skills but are unable to attend class. Finally, the book serves as a reference for the working medical or legal transcriptionist.

All the material included in the exercises is authentic medical dictation. The facts in the examples have been altered only to the extent necessary to prevent identification of the cases or parties involved. No evaluation of medical practice, nor medical advice, nor recommendations for treatment are to be inferred from our selections.

Basic English rule books and style manuals form the backbone of the rules and guidelines. We found disagreement among the various medical journals and style manuals, with some suggested forms being out of touch with current medical writing. Medical journals and medical transcripts were reviewed extensively to ascertain present practice. Some techniques for medical typing were not defined by any manuals, so the instructions governing these were based on general English guidelines and on what appears in print. For instance, you may have seen the word *x-ray* written as *xray, X-ray, x-ray,* or *X ray.*

Furthermore, some purists use *roentgenogram* for the noun form and *x-ray* for the verb form only. (This was correct at one time.) However, noun or verb, *x-ray* is the currently accepted correct form.

Objectives introduce each chapter to let the student and instructor know exactly what will be taught. The instructor may test with these objectives in mind to see how well they have been met. We have also incorporated handy hints that we have learned over the years in our careers, as well as information shared by students and colleagues during our years of teaching. An instructor's guide, available for use with this text, assists in the establishment of a transcription course and gives the teacher some ideas on how to use the text as an adjunct to an existing class.

A series of three audiotapes designed to provide the student with practice in medical transcription is available. The tapes consist of 60 medical reports, letters, and chart notes using a variety of voices just as various physicians might dictate. Transcription can be attempted after completing Chapters 1 to 7. Initially, the letters are dictated slowly with some punctuation and paragraphing indicated. Later in the program, reports are dictated at a more natural dictating speed, and students are asked to employ their own skills in paragraphing and punctuation. These tapes are excellent for a beginning student, and then as the student advances, "live" dictation by physicians in your locale is important before the student attempts to obtain employment. These audiotapes may be obtained from the publisher of this textbook.

As a result of this textbook, we have coauthored a handy reference book that has been well received by the working transcriptionist. It is entitled *Medical Transcription Guide: Do's and Don'ts.* In fact, we have discovered that many students seem to enjoy having this book for reference also, and it may be obtained from the publisher of this book.

Lastly, there is Joy, our transcriptionist, who appears at the beginning of each chapter to help put a smile on the face of our readers.

MARCY O. DIEHL
San Diego, California

MARILYN T. FORDNEY
Oxnard, California

Acknowledgments

Credit for the production of this text is owed to many persons, including our husbands, families, and friends, who gave encouragement, advice, and understanding of the priority it had on our time.

We are thankful to the reviewers of each of the chapters who gave us concrete and extremely helpful criticisms:

Jerri Adler, AA, CMA, CMT, *Lane Community College, Eugene, Oregon.*

Judith E. Bertram, *Alexandria Technical College, Alexandria, Minnesota.*

Jane L. Bragg, *Gateway Technical College, Racine, Wisconsin.*

Lana L. Bublitz, MA, *Gateway Technical College, Racine, Wisconsin.*

Kathy Cadile, *California Paramedical Technical College, Riverside, California.*

Carol Chambers, *Mohawk College of Applied Arts and Technology, Hamilton, Ontario, Canada.*

Janet L. Fisk, RN, *Santa Rosa Junior College, Santa Rosa, California.*

Sharon Lee Frank, RN, *Anoka Technical College, Anoka, Minnesota.*

Ginny Hancock-Stefan, CMA, AAS, *William Rainey Harper College, Palatine, Illinois.*

Vicki S. Sanders, CMA, *University of Alabama at Birmingham, Birmingham, Alabama.*

Janet Stiles, BSN, CMA-C, *El Centro College, Dallas, Texas.*

Sharon Tauke, MA, *Art Kirkwood Community College, Cedar Rapids, Iowa.*

Carol Warden-Tamparo, CMA-A, PhD, *Highline Community College, Des Moines, Washington.*

We gratefully acknowledge the members of our local chapters of the American Association for Medical Transcription and the members of the California Association of Medical Assistant Instructors (CAMAI) who contributed suggestions over the years for improving the text and have been supportive in this project from its outset in 1979.

We are most indebted to many individuals on the staff of the W. B. Saunders Company for their participation in making this text a reality. We wish to express particular appreciation to Margaret Biblis, Senior Acquisitions Editor, her assistant, Charles Keenan, and the Developmental Editor, Martha Tanner. Our thanks go also to Ken Neimeister, Production Manager.

Special acknowledgment is given to the artists who assisted in the cover design and graphic illustrations shown throughout this text: Ellen Bodner, who created the cover on a Macintosh, and Joan Wendt, designer, both of the W. B. Saunders Company; and Gail Niebrugge, Graphic Illustrator, Glennallen, Alaska.

We are grateful to Carol Chaney, Senior Medical Transcriptionist at Camarillo State Hospital, and Joan Marie Griffin, Psychiatric Counselor, for assisting us in preparing the psychiatric report section of this textbook.

We wish to acknowledge the Joint Commission on Accreditation of Healthcare Organizations for always being there to answer our many questions so promptly.

In addition, we received many valuable suggestions and much help from Jean Morgan, CMT, San Luis Obispo General Hospital, Jayme Tuskan, RRA, Lompoc District Hospital, Marq Priesel, Toronto, Ontario, Canada, and Reiko Dimon.

We appreciate the help from many students, whose questions and criticism while working with the material have been very constructive.

Numerous equipment and supply companies were kind enough to cooperate by supplying photographs and descriptive literature of their products. Their names will be found throughout the text.

Contents

The Medical Transcriptionist's Career, Including Ethical and Legal Responsibilities

OBJECTIVES

After reading this chapter and working the exercises, you should be able to

1. identify the background and importance of medical records.
2. explain the skills a transcriptionist must possess and know why terminology is so vital.
3. calculate the speed to strive for in transcribing.
4. identify opportunities for the physically challenged transcriptionist.
5. assemble a reference notebook.
6. list some general references available to the transcriptionist.
7. define and explain the purpose of a medical report or record.
8. define privileged and nonprivileged information.
9. enumerate the guidelines for release of information from both the private medical office and the hospital.
10. explain the importance of subpoenas for patient records.

INTRODUCTION

Welcome to an exciting and vitally important career field. We hope that this text will assist you in maintaining an eager interest and excitement about the course of study you are undertaking as well as provide you with a strong foundation as a medical transcriptionist. This text has been designed to speed the beginner transcriptionist (who already knows how to type) on his or her way to proficiency. The more skills you bring with you, the faster you will progress. At the same time, we hope you will begin to experience the fascination and appreciation for medicine that working medical transcriptionists have come to enjoy.

The recording of diseases and injuries goes back many centuries, as shown by hieroglyphics on the walls of the Egyptian tombs. Our first medical terms depicted treatments or remedies in the form of prescriptions. As shown in Figure 1–1, the picture of the bone looks perhaps like a tree with branches, and the

1

 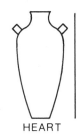

BONE   HEART

FIGURE 1–1.

heart is depicted as a vessel of some type. This communication has helped bridge the gap between ancient and modern civilizations. Part of the joy of being a transcriptionist is in knowing that you are the modern communicator in the medical field.

When you have completed your course of study, you will be prepared to seek employment in a variety of medical settings or become a self-employed transcriptionist. The private physician's office and the hospital are both exciting and interesting places to work, and the duties and responsibilities of an employee in these settings offer a real challenge for the modern career transcriptionist. Although transcribing correspondence, reports, and other medical documents will be your prime responsibility, you may find that there are other interesting business duties. For instance, in the physician's office you may be responsible for processing insurance claims or assisting in patient care. In the hospital, you could work in the medical records department as a full-time transcriptionist or as a part-time transcriptionist with some records management duties. Other hospital departments that require the skills of medical transcriptionists are Radiology, Pathology, Outpatient Surgery, Admissions, Business, and Executive.

Public health clinics, school health facilities, private insurance agencies, specialized typing and transcription agencies, large legal firms, military medical departments, and governmental agencies also offer challenging opportunities for the professional transcriptionist. Medical research is conducted in many settings, and this particular field may offer you, again, the opportunity to participate in what is going on as well as to record it. You might decide to work for a private transcribing service. In this setting, you could be working on several different accounts, and each may have different criteria.

You will always be working with others who have chosen the field of medicine in some similar way, and you will find that you are a vital part of the team wherever you are employed; therefore, it is important that you also learn to respect and appreciate the duties of the other personnel with whom you work. To avoid confusion, let's discuss further the difference between

a medical typist, medical transcriptionist, and medical secretary.

1. A *medical typist* is a professional who
   a. sets up medical records and accounting forms.
   b. prepares letters from drafts using proper mechanics.
   c. does "light" transcribing of letters and chart notes.
   d. completes workers' compensation and state disability forms.
   e. writes letters to follow up insurance claims, order supplies, collect monies, and so forth.
   f. responds to requests for data from life insurance companies.

2. A *medical transcriptionist* is a professional who
   a. possesses excellent typing and word processing skills.
   b. is highly skilled and knowledgeable about human anatomy, physiology, and pathophysiology.
   c. has excellent spelling, editing, and proofreading skills.
   d. has a good command of English grammar, structure, and style.
   e. has a thorough knowledge of medical terminology used in medical and surgical procedures, drugs, instruments, and laboratory tests.
   f. is an indispensable assistant to physicians and surgeons in producing medical reports, which become permanent records of medical, scientific, and legal value.

3. A *medical secretary* is a professional who
   a. possesses a mastery of all medical business office skills (appointment making, telephone procedures, accounting, insurance claim completion, collection of accounts, banking, payroll, mail processing, filing, patient records, office maintenance).
   b. has knowledge of medical terminology as well as excellent grammar skills.
   c. demonstrates the ability to assume responsibility without direct supervision.
   d. exercises initiative and judgment.
   e. makes decisions within the scope of assigned authority.
   f. writes letters over own signature or that of his or her employer.
   g. abstracts medical records and reports.
   h. edits and revises documents for the employer.

Because medicine is ever changing and because people and their problems are interesting, we can assure you that you will never get bored. Because of the heavy load of paperwork in the medical field that must be completed on a personal basis, you know that you will never be replaced by a machine. In fact, the demand for medical business personnel is increasing.* There is no age limit, provided that you work proficiently and maintain an acceptable standard of performance. The salary for high-quality professionals is excellent, depending on your experience and locality, of course.

You can be your own boss if you wish: many successful transcriptionists work out of their own homes, work at night, work part-time, or do freelance work to suit the hours they want. However, this involves more responsibility since you will have to learn to set up your own business, obtain accounts, advertise and market your service, and so forth.

Medical transcription is both an exacting science and an artistic accomplishment. It is important to have a combination of skills, including the formatting of medical documents, spelling, proofreading, knowledge of medical terminology, and typing, and a firm background in English grammar, structure, and style. The successful medical transcriptionist has accuracy and speed; a broad knowledge of anatomy; and a thorough knowledge of medical, surgical, drug, and laboratory terms; in addition, the medical transcriptionist knows how to use all the standard reference materials, including the medical dictionary.

As you proceed through the exercises in this text, you will become more aware of terms that may sound alike but are spelled differently because of their location in different parts of the body. For English-speaking persons, Greek terms are sometimes more difficult to spell and Latin ones easier. You will learn how to make Greek and Latin words plural, since they are pluralized differently from English words. In Chapter 8, you will find exercises that will help you to use the dictionary effectively. In the chapters that follow, you will also be introduced to the equipment used in transcribing, such as typewriters, stenotype machines, transcribing machines, word processors, voice synthesizers, and photocopiers. Other practice sets will develop your skills in punctuating and capitalizing, in using abbreviations, and in typing symbols. Your profession will become more rewarding as your understanding of medical terminology grows.

It is also important for the medical transcriptionist to understand the ethical implications of handling medical records. Experience in medical transcription brings with it the ability to interpret, translate, and edit medical dictation for content and clarity as well as the ability to use deductive reasoning and detect medical inconsistencies in dictation.

In today's world, medical records have proved to be a vital key in patient care and medical research. If the records are kept neatly, thoroughly, and accurately, and if one is prompt in recording the data, they help the physician in the treatment of the patient as well as aid in future research on diseases and their management. As you will learn later in this chapter, properly kept records can eliminate medicolegal problems. Occasionally, records are seen by attorneys, employers, other physicians, insurance companies, and courts, so we cannot overemphasize the importance of keeping them correctly. An efficient system of keeping records can even allow the physician more time for patients. Therefore, the medical transcriptionist becomes an important figure in recordkeeping.

The good transcriptionist types material that makes sense to him or her or asks the dictator by flagging the section for clarification. That is why it is important for you to understand medical terminology. Learning the component parts of medical terms (prefixes, suffixes, and roots) enables the transcriptionist to spell and pronounce words he or she may never have encountered.

TRANSCRIPTION SPEED

Unless copy is perfect, speed is worthless. You should always strive for accuracy. At the same time, your pay often will be based on the number of pages, characters, or lines typed, so speed also becomes a skill to work toward. However, some employers pay by the hour or provide a monthly salary. Opinions vary in regard to how many lines per hour a superior secretary should transcribe. A production norm in one situation cannot be applied to another because of a wide range of variables, such as type of hospital (local community, large metropolitan, university teaching medical center); type of dictators (medical students, residents, foreign-speaking, regional accent); type of equipment (electronic typewriters, correcting electrics, word processors, computer-linked equipment); additional duties besides transcription; resource materials available; definition of a "line" or other measure of production (words, keystrokes by page, characters typed per day); and standards of quality. One suggested goal is 100 lines per hour, using a 6-inch line as the average. A 15-minute tape averages about 150 lines, and a 30-minute tape averages from 300 to 400 lines, depending on the speed of the dictator. As all experienced transcriptionists know, speed and accuracy come together only with constant practice.

---

* The U.S. Department of Labor projects a faster than average employment growth in the health occupations between 1988 and 2000.

1 – 1: TIMED TYPING TEST

Take a timed typing test to see what your typing speed is at the beginning of the course. Your instructor may also wish to time you with familiar work as well as unfamiliar work. Keep this typing speed score because you will compare it at the end of the course when you complete Timed Typing Test 17 – 4. On the following pages is a timed typing segment. This can be dictated by the instructor to obtain a timed transcription or it can be used by simply looking at it while typing to obtain typing speed and accuracy. A quick-scoring chart for typing speed and accuracy is included. Directions for its use are given at the bottom of the chart.

Directions:

1. Type the copy line for line, making a return at the end of each printed line. Do not type the numbers.

2. Time yourself for five minutes. When the time is up, finish the line you are on and mark the spot.

Scoring:

3. The number in the right margin next to this line tells you how many words you must type according to the average word-length formula. Write that number down.

4. Now go to the quick-scoring chart and follow the directions at the bottom of it to obtain your typing speed and grade.

The following article is reprinted from Marcy Diehl's President's Message which appeared in the August 1983 San Diego Chapter, AAMT Newsletter.

```
                       CRITICISM                                        2
Criticism first became a subject for conversation in my life about     15
21 years ago when I went to work for a prominent San Diego thoracic    28
and cardiovascular surgeon.  During the course of the interview, he    41
asked me if I were able to take criticism gracefully.  Well, I was     54
stumped.  No one had ever ASKED before; they had just handed it out,   68
and I really didn't know how gracefully I had accepted what I'd had    81
so far.  It sort of depended on who was dishing it out, I guess.  I    94
thought about my response, worrying that my prospective job somehow   107
hinged on what I said one way or the other.  I felt he would have     120
liked for me to say something like "Oh, I love criticism," or even    133
"I never need it!"  Evidently I gave the right answer, however (he    146
did hire me), when I replied, "Well, I guess we'll have to find out,  159
won't we?"  This answer implied to him that he would hire me and that 173
we would both see how his criticism and my acceptance of it went      186
along.                                                                187
```

But I was now on the alert. I was forewarned that criticism was, in   201
fact, a big possibility, and I worked very hard against the day when   215
"we" would find out how gracefully I could accept it. I really didn't   229
know where it would come from, either--gosh, there were a lot of   242
possibilities; the day seemed fraught with them.   251
This was just the first day.   256
By the second day, I found out. That was the day my first transcripts   270
were returned. Large permanent blue-black ink circles covered the   283
many carefully prepared documents. It was hard to be graceful when I   297
looked at the ruination of a half-day's labors (actually, half a   310
night, too, as I had spent long hours at home researching unfamiliar   324
words in Dorland's). "Oh, well," I said offhandedly before he could   338
say anything, "it's back to the typewriter with these, I see."   350
We had weeks of that, and I was getting discouraged; still graceful, I   364
presume, but discouraged. The errors were becoming fewer and fewer,   378
but that didn't seem to help much, since I wanted them to disappear.   392
It was harder and harder to face up to them somehow, now that I was   405
feeling more secure in the job. Grace was wearing thin. He never   418
said anything. I never said anything; I just retyped. A lot.   430
Now two things happened. The surgeon's wife came in to the office on   444
Saturday morning when he proofread and busily marked up my work. She   458
watched, appalled. Monday morning shortly after I arrived for work,   472
she called "to see how you're taking it." "Fine," I said. She was   486
relieved, and reported that she had talked to him about it, feeling   500
that he had been too harsh. "Well, she won't learn if I don't teach   514
her, and she's worth teaching." I learned about grace that day. He   528
took his precious time to teach and to help me. He had a B.S. in   541
journalism and knew his Greek and Latin roots to a fine degree as well.   555
I was pretty much humbled by his constant criticism, his love of   568
perfection, and his belief in my potential for growth.   578
All of our lives we are both subjected to and the dispensers of   590
criticism. If we can remember to accept it with the spirit in   602
which it is given, realizing it took some time to critique our   614
performance and that it was done because of our ultimate potential,   628
we then must accept it not only with grace but also with thanks.   641
Secondly, we must try to remember to give our criticism only with   654
graciousness, knowing that we can help someone in whom we see the   667
potential for personal or professional betterment, and not criticize   681
to showcase our own skills. If we cannot criticize fairly, with   694
love and in private, then we need to withhold it.   704

We wish to thank Jolly F. Griggs of Ventura College in Ventura, California, for allowing us to share with you his chart.

QUICK-SCORING CHART FOR TYPING SPEED AND ACCURACY
For 5-Minute Writings

Strokes	Words	WAM	Figures = NWPM		ERRORS				Letters = ACCURACY				
			0	1	2	3	4	5	6	7	8	9	10
750	150	30	30	28	26	24	22	20	18	16	14	12	10
800	160	32	32	30	28	26	24	22	20	18	16	14	12
850	170	34	34	32	30	28	26	24	22	20	18	16	14
900	180	36	36	34	32	30	28	26	24	22	20	18	16
950	190	38	38	36	34	32	30	28	26	24	22	20	18
1000	200	40	40	38	36	34	32	30	28	26	24	22	20
1050	210	42	42	40	38	36	34	32	30	28	26	24	22
1100	220	44	44	42	40	38	36	34	32	30	28	26	24
1150	230	46	46	44	42	40	38	36	34	32	30	28	26
1200	240	48	48	46	44	42	40	38	36	34	32	30	28
1250	250	50	50	48	46	44	42	40	38	36	34	32	30
1300	260	52	52	50	48	46	44	42	40	38	36	34	32
1350	270	54	54	52	50	48	46	44	42	40	38	36	34
1400	280	56	56	54	52	50	48	46	44	42	40	38	36
1450	290	58	58	56	54	52	50	48	46	44	42	40	38
1500	300	60	60	58	56	54	52	50	48	46	44	42	40
1550	310	62	62	60	58	56	54	52	50	48	46	44	42
1600	320	64	64	62	60	58	56	54	52	50	48	46	44
1650	330	66	66	64	62	60	58	56	54	52	50	48	46
1700	340	68	68	66	64	62	60	58	56	54	52	50	48
1750	350	70	70	68	66	64	62	60	58	56	54	52	50
1800	360	72	72	70	68	66	64	62	60	58	56	54	52
1850	370	74	74	72	70	68	66	64	62	60	58	56	54
1900	380	76	76	74	72	70	68	66	64	62	60	58	56
1950	390	78	78	76	74	72	70	68	66	64	62	60	58
2000	400	80	80	78	76	74	72	70	68	66	64	62	60
ACCURACY RANGE			93% - 100%		86% - 92%			78% - 85%			70% - 77%		

Directions:
Select the figure in one of the first three columns on the left that approximates the quantity of material typed in five minutes and follow across the page to the column headed by the number of errors made; there find NET WORDS PER MINUTE based on penalty of 10 words per error. The NWPM score will be found in an area that is evaluated for accuracy with letter grades. The accuracy formula used is NET WORDS divided by GROSS WORDS. (Note: Read between the lines for, say, 53 Words Per Minute, etc.)

THE PHYSICALLY CHALLENGED TRANSCRIPTIONIST

Wheelchair-bound and blind typists have done office work since the invention of the typewriter. Often they have advanced from the typing pool to secretarial positions. When transcribing equipment came into use, many new career paths developed for the blind, making it possible for them to be promoted from corresponding secretary up to and including positions in management. Typists with limited dexterity use special equipment, e.g., a stenotype machine interfaced with a word processor. Typists with one hand have been known to be as productive as those typing with both hands. With the need for good medical transcriptionists and the shortage that is always apparent in most cities, training of the physically challenged has been started in community colleges across the nation. Many medical terminology textbooks have been put into braille and onto cassettes to make learning easier and faster.

If a person has a physical impairment and needs training or assistive devices, he or she should contact the State Department of Vocational Rehabilitation. In addition to the Braille Institute, there are many other sources of help, such as the American Association for Medical Transcription, the American Heart Association, the United Way, and the Easter Seal program. See Chapter 8 for materials developed specifically for the physically challenged.

There are a number of machines available to assist the physically challenged transcriptionist. See Chapter 2 for detailed discussion of some of this equipment.

Since listening and typing are the two important skills necessary to become a top transcriptionist, a person who has an impairment of hearing or digital dexterity should seek another area of employment.

CERTIFICATION FOR MEDICAL TRANSCRIPTIONISTS

After at least three years of experience in performing medical transcription in a variety of medical and surgical specialties, a qualified medical transcriptionist may wish to take the certification examination offered by the American Association for Medical Transcription (AAMT). Those passing the examination become certified medical transcriptionists (CMTs). A CMT is recognized as a professional medical transcriptionist who participates in an ongoing program of continuing medical education to increase knowledge of medicine and improve skills in medical transcription. CMTs are required to accrue 30 Continuing Education Credits (CECs) in a three-year period after certification. AAMT also offers a specialty examination in radiology.

There are a number of other benefits of belonging to a professional association besides certification. As a student member, you will get to meet others in the field and learn how they cope with certain on-the-job problems. When attending local meetings, you receive further education from guest speakers on pertinent topics of current interest. From the professional publications you receive, you will learn about what is currently happening in the field. Sometimes part-time or full-time job opportunities are mentioned in the publications as well as at meetings, and this can lead to employment. Most importantly you will become friends with those in your chosen profession and will feel more professional by belonging to a group.

For more information regarding membership, certification, and recertification, contact

American Association for Medical Transcription
P.O. Box 576187
Modesto, California 95357
Telephone: 800-982-2182
Fax: 209-551-9317

ETHICAL AND LEGAL RESPONSIBILITIES

Before beginning work as a medical transcriptionist, it is wise to have some basic knowledge of ethical and legal responsibilities as they pertain to the medical profession and the medical transcriptionist. Ethics are not laws but are standards of conduct. The AAMT adopted a Code of Ethics in 1979 (Fig. 1–2).

This section will mention those medicolegal aspects that concern medical records and how they relate to the medical transcriptionist or typist. These standards vary from state to state, so only commonly accepted practices and procedures will be discussed. If you are employed by a health facility that has a policy manual or office procedure manual, familiarize yourself with its rules for the release of information. However, if a situation arises for which you do not have the answer, consult your supervisor regarding hospital regulations. If you are working in a private medical office, consult the local medical society or your employer's attorney if an unusual problem arises, since you fall under the jurisdiction of *respondeat superior,* or "let the master answer." This means that the physician/dictator is liable in certain cases for the wrongful acts of assistants or employees.

As we discuss the ethical and legal implications in regard to medical records, refer to the following vocabulary list to assist you in better understanding some of the difficult legal terms.

Vocabulary

breach of confidential communication: In a medical setting, this means the unauthorized release of information about the patient.

confidentiality: Treatment of the patient's medical information as private and not for publication.

custodian of records: A person put in charge of medical records.

defamation: A common tort; injury to reputation, i.e., slander or libel.

documentation: The supplying of written or printed official information that can be used for evidence.

ethics: Moral principles and standards in the ideal

AMERICAN ASSOCIATION FOR MEDICAL TRANSCRIPTION
CODE OF ETHICS

1. Be aware that it is by our standards of conduct and professionalism that the entire Association is evaluated, for the conduct of one individual can be the vertex upon which the future of the Association may depend.

2. Conduct ourselves in the practice of our profession so as to bring dignity and honor to ourselves, the profession of medical transcription, and the American Association for Medical Transcription.

3. Place the goals and purposes of the Association above greed, personal gain, and interpersonal relationships by discouraging dissension and by working for the good of the majority.

4. Refuse to participate in or conceal unethical procedures or practices in relationships with other associations or individuals.

5. Recognize the source of authority and powers delegated to us as individuals and observe the limitations and confinements of said authority and powers.

6. Discharge honorably the responsibility of any Association positions to which we are elected or appointed.

7. Preserve the confidential nature of professional judgments and determinations made by the official committees of the Association.

8. Represent truthfully and accurately all professional committees in any official transaction whether that transaction be within the Association or in the form of representation of ourselves as members of the Association.

9. Protect the privacy and confidentiality of the individual medical record to avoid disclosure of personally identifiable medical and social information and professional medical judgments.

10. Strive to increase the body of systematic knowledge and individual competence of the medical transcription professional through continued self-improvement and the constructive exchange of knowledge and concepts with others in our profession.

Revised February 1987

FIGURE 1-2. Code of Ethics of the American Association for Medical Transcription. (Revised 1987, American Association for Medical Transcription, Modesto, California.)

relationships between the physician and patient and also between physicians.

etiquette: Customs, rules of conduct, courtesy, and manners of the medical profession.

invasion of right of privacy: Unwarranted exploitation of another's personality or personal affairs with which one has no legitimate concern in such a way as to cause mental anguish or humiliation. Publication of a patient's medical record or photograph without the knowledge and authorization of the patient.

libel: Written or graphic statement to a third person that damages the reputation or subjects a patient to ridicule.

medical record: Written or computer-stored information (medical reports), tissue samples, log books, or x-ray films are considered medical records and may be used as evidence in legal issues.

medical report: Written or computer-stored information about the patient's medical history. It is part of the medical record.

medical transcription: The skill of typing medical dictation, incorporating good grammar, spelling, format, and proofreading.

nonprivileged information: The patient's authorization is not needed to disclose the information unless the record is in a specialty hospital or in a special service of a general hospital, i.e., the Psychiatric Unit. Examples: dates of treatment, dates of admission and discharge, number of times the physician attended the patient, name and address of the patient, name of relative or friend given at the time the patient was seen in the hospital or in the physician's office.

privileged communication: A confidential communication that may be disclosed only with the patient's permission.

privileged information: Information related to the treatment and progress of the patient that can be given out only on the written authorization of the patient or guardian.

release of information: Medical information given out to a third party with the written authority of the patient.

respondeat superior: "Let the master answer." A physician is liable in certain cases for the wrongful acts of his or her assistant or employees.

slander: Spoken statement in the presence of others

that damages reputation or subjects a person to ridicule.

subpoena duces tecum: "In his possession." A subpoena that requires the appearance of a witness with his or her records. Sometimes the judge permits the mailing of records and the physician is not required to appear in court.

verbatim: word for word.

Medical Reports and Records

Joint Commission on Accreditation of Healthcare Organizations

The Joint Commission on Accreditation of Healthcare Organizations (JCAHO) is a commission with a mission of improving the quality of care and services provided in organized health care settings via a voluntary accreditation process. Accreditation standards are continually updated and published in the *Accreditation Manual for Hospitals* (AMH). JCAHO conducts surveys of hospitals to measure and encourage compliance with the standards. When these standards are met, JCAHO awards accreditation to the health care facility. The Joint Commission's AMH does not address any legal aspects of the medical record as it applies to the transcriptionist. However, their chapter on "Medical Record Services" contains standards that require certain entries, information, and signatures to be entered into the medical record as determined by a prescribed format. The transcriptionist is responsible only for the accuracy of the transcribed material and seeing that it remains confidential.

A *medical report* is a permanent legal document that formally states the results of an investigation. A *medical record* is information set down in writing to authenticate evidence of facts and events and is a legal document in all cases of litigation. The three main purposes of medical records are to

1. Assist in the diagnosis and treatment of a patient by communicating with the attending physician and other medical personnel working with the patient.

2. Aid and advance the science of medicine.

3. Comply with laws and serve in support of a claim.

The Joint Commission's AMH states requirements for medical report completeness, signatures, abbreviations, deadlines, and dates of documents and details of this information are mentioned here.

Medical Report Signatures. All medical reports dictated by a physician must be signed by the physician responsible for the dictated material. In a case in which an intern does the physical examination of the patient and the attending physician dictates the history and physical, the attending physician may be the one signing the report. In regard to rubber signature stamps on medical reports, careful consideration of state regulations and statutes, system security, and system reliability must be made before such policies are adopted. Rubber signature stamps may be used by the individual whose signature the stamp represents, and there must be a signed statement placed in the hospital administration office attesting that only the physician responsible for the dictated material will use the stamp. Rubber signature stamps are not preferred to an original signature. In regard to pathology and laboratory reports, a laboratory technician must sign, initial, or stamp those reports he or she completes. A pathologist's signature is required only on work he or she performs or provides such as tissue, cytology, necropsy, and consultation reports. In regard to radiology reports, the radiologist must authenticate the examinations he or she interprets in transcribed reports. If the physician is away from the office after dictating a letter or report and the correspondence is urgent, the medical transcriptionist has two choices: he or she can either sign the physician's name with his or her own initials after it, or the medical transcriptionist can send a photocopy of the letter stating that the physician will sign and forward the original upon his or her return.

Many facilities have reports generated via computer and an electronic signature is possible. This means that an individual has computer access and uses an identification system, such as a series of letters or numbers (alpha-numeric computer key entries) or fingerprint transmissions (biometric system) to authenticate portions of the medical record. The legal requirements for electronic signature can be found in federal law, state law, and the accreditation standards of the JCAHO.

Federal law requires physician signatures in a medical record for hospital compliance with Medicare Conditions of Participation and to qualify for reimbursement under the Prospective Payment System (PPS). A handwritten signature, initials, or computer entry is allowed. However, a computer key signature system is permitted if the hospital keeps a list of computer codes and written signatures that are readily available to surveyors, adequately safeguards the codes against unauthorized access and use, and establishes sanctions for misuse. In regard to Medicare reimbursement, an electronic signature is permitted when the physician attests to the patient's diagnosis only if the fiscal intermediary has approved the system. If the attestation is transmitted by facsimile machines, the physician must keep in the files the hard copy of the original signature.

State laws vary, so it is important for you to know the legal requirements in your state so that you can comply with these laws.

The JCAHO accreditation standards for hospitals require that all entries into a medical record be authenticated and dated. A method must be established to identify the authors of entries in the medical record. This identification may be a written signature, initials, or computer key. A rubber stamp is allowed if the physician has executed a statement of exclusive possession and use of the stamp. Always consult with JCAHO before implementing any other electronic signature systems.

Abbreviations. The JCAHO requires that the medical staff of each hospital approve abbreviations and symbols that may be used in its medical records, and each abbreviation must be limited to one meaning. In regard to the diagnosis section of a report, "Diagnoses and procedures should be written in full, without the use of symbols or abbreviations." Each health care facility's list of abbreviations and symbols will vary, and it is important for the medical transcriptionist to review these before beginning work as well as refer to the approved list when necessary in performing medical transcription. Since physicians tend to dictate their own preferred abbreviations, it is the medical transcriptionist's responsibility to use only those approved by the medical institution. Abbreviations dictated by the physician and approved by the medical facility may be transcribed as abbreviations or transcribed in full, depending on the physician's preference, the medical facility's policies, or the transcriptionist's style. Abbreviations dictated by the physician but not approved by the institution must be transcribed in full. A transcriptionist may not invent abbreviations for words and phrases by the physician. Each health care facility updates the approved abbreviation and symbol list from time to time, so it is important to make sure you have the current list for reference.

Deadlines for Medical Reports. The JCAHO states the following in regard to deadlines for medical reports.

Physical Examination. "The physical assessment shall be completed within the first 24 hours of admission to inpatient services."

Discharge Summaries. "The records of discharged patients shall be completed within a period of time that will in no event exceed 30 days following discharge; the period of time shall be specified in the medical staff rules and regulations."

Operative Reports. Operative reports "should be dictated or written in the medical record immediately after surgery."

Diagnostic or Therapeutic Procedures. "Reports of pathology and clinical laboratory examinations, radiology and nuclear medicine examinations or treatment, anesthesia records, and any other diagnostic or therapeutic procedures should be completed promptly and filed in the record, within 24 hours of completion if possible."

Autopsy Reports. "When a necropsy is performed, provisional anatomic diagnoses should be recorded in the medical record within three days, and the complete protocol should be made part of the record within 60 days."

Dates of Documents. When typing the date in a letter or medical report, the date used is the day the material was dictated and *not* the day it was transcribed. A dictator might ask the typist to date a report other than the actual date of dictation to appear that the report was completed in a timely fashion. The date *should not* be changed. This is very important for a number of reasons. Comments made in the document could reflect on this date. If the document should be entered as evidence in a court proceeding, it may be discovered that the date was changed, and the physician's credibility might be questioned and accusations of concealment, tampering, fabricating, and so forth could be made.

Completeness of Medical Reports. It cannot be overemphasized that if medical records are completed promptly after the physician sees the patient, there is less chance of an omission. In a physician's office, it is the office assistant's job to ensure that an entry is made in the chart each time a patient is seen. In a hospital setting, it is the medical records personnel that alert the physician to complete a medical record.

A medical record is complete "when the required contents are assembled and authenticated, including any required clinical resume or final progress note; and when all final diagnoses and any complications are recorded, without use of symbols or abbreviations. Completeness implies the transcription of any dictated record content and its insertion into the medical record." All medical information must be entered into the record and all signatures entered within 30 days after the patient's discharge for the record to be considered complete.

Hospitals and physicians have been held liable because the handwritten notes in the charts were unclear. It is, therefore, important that the transcriptionist enter material that is accurate into the record.

Ownership

Medical records are the property of the physician, corporation, or institution, and, as such, the owner is legally and ethically obligated to protect them. The Code of Hospital Ethics adopted by the American Hospital Association and the American College of Surgeons states "It is the responsibility of the hospital and its personnel to safeguard the clinical records of the patients and to see that such records are available only to properly authorized individuals or bodies." This also applies to physicians. Information received from other hospitals and physicians regarding past history or treatment is for informational use and is not considered the property of the hospital that receives it. Correspondence or social service information, which also may be filed in the hospital medical record, is not considered part of the medical record. When a patient is referred to a radiologist for x-ray films, the films belong to the radiologist and not to the referring physician.

Corrections

Medicolegal problems might arise, so it is important to know how to correct medical reports and chart notes. If a patient's medical record is presented in court as evidence in a professional liability case and the records have been sloppily corrected, a prosecuting attorney may possibly win a case if it is proved that the records have been intentionally altered.

See Chapters 7 and 11 for detailed information on correction materials and how to make corrections. Some offices remove all regular pens from their supply and use only legal copy pens, since this eliminates alteration of records when a correction has been inserted. When self-adhesive typing strips are used, the strip should never be obliterated. Instead, place a new strip below it with the correction. If a typist in a hospital transcription pool makes so many errors on a report that it has to be sent back for retyping, insert the omitted words, correct erroneous ones, and initial each correction on the original transcript. If that produces a messy copy, retype it. Write "corrected for typing errors" on the second draft. The physician should sign both the second draft and the original and staple the two copies together. In court, the original will confirm that the report was made as soon as possible after treatment.

Right of Privacy

The invasion of the right of privacy is the "unwarranted exploitation of another's personality or personal affairs with which one has not legitimate concern—particularly, intrusions into another's affairs in such a way as to cause mental anguish or humiliation." An example of invasion of privacy is the publication of a patient's medical record without his or her knowledge or consent. Another example would be the publishing of a patient's photograph (from which the patient could be easily identified) without the consent of the patient.

Privileged Communication

Privileged communication is a confidential communication that may be disclosed only with the patient's permission. The right to the protection of the confidentiality of information in medical records belongs to the patient, not the physician. The transcriptionist should never mention the name of a patient away from the office or discuss a patient's condition within hearing distance of others. Everything he or she sees, hears, or reads about patients should remain confidential and should not leave the place of employment. Records, appointment books, charts, and ledgers should not be left where unauthorized people can see them. There are a few exceptions to the right of privacy and privileged communication. These include the records of physicians employed by insurance companies (especially for industrial cases), reports of communicable diseases, child abuse, gunshot wounds and stabbings resulting from criminal actions, and diseases and ailments of newborns and infants.

Release of Medical Records

Information in medical records falls into two classifications, nonprivileged information and privileged information. They can be defined as follows:

1. *Nonprivileged information* is unrelated to the treatment of the patient. The patient's authorization is not needed to disclose these facts to anyone unless the record is in a specialty hospital or in a special service of a general hospital, such as the Psychiatric Unit. Even so, discretion must be used at all times, and care must be taken to make certain that the inquiry is a proper one that protects the best interests of the patient. Examples of nonprivileged information are as follows:
   a. Dates of treatment.
   b. Dates of admission and discharge.

Form D-1

AUTHORIZATION FOR DISCLOSURE OF
INFORMATION BY PATIENT'S PHYSICIAN

1. I authorize Dr. _____ to disclose complete information to

_____ concerning medical findings and treatment of the undersigned from on or

about _____ 19_____ until date of conclusion of such treatment.

    2. Further, I authorize him/her to testify, without limitation, as to all of the medical findings and the treatment administered to the undersigned, in any legal action, suit, or proceedings to which I am, or may become, a party; and I waive, on behalf of myself and any persons who may have an interest in the matter, all provisions of law relating to the disclosure of confidential medical information.

Signed _____

Place _____

Date _____

Witness _____

FIGURE 1-3. Authorization for Disclosure of Information by Patient's Physician. (From Medicolegal Forms Office of the General Counsel, 1982. Copyright © 1982 American Medical Association. All rights reserved.)

    c. Number of times and dates when the physician attended the patient.
    d. Fact that the patient was ill or operated on.
    e. Complete name of the patient.
    f. Address at the time the physician saw the patient or at the time the patient was admitted to the hospital.
    g. Name of relative or friend given at the time first seen in the physician's office or at the time of admission to the hospital.

2. *Privileged information* is related to the treatment and progress of the patient and can be given out only on the written authorization of the patient or guardian (Fig. 1–3). A patient can sign an authorization to "release" only selected facts and not the entire record.

Guidelines for Release of Information

Following are guidelines for release of information.

1. The medical transcriptionist should become thoroughly familiar with state laws and with the ethics concerning release of medical information.

2. Whenever a patient fails to keep an appointment or to follow the physician's advice, a letter should be sent to the patient, since documentation is necessary in the medical record.

3. Requests from physicians concerned with patient care are honored with the written consent of the patient.

4. Requests from insurance companies, attorneys, and others concerned from a financial point of view are honored *only* with the written consent of the patient. (If the attorney cannot read the physician's handwriting, an appointment is made with the physician. The attorney should pay for the office call.) The medical transcriptionist should not attempt to interpret a medical record. Exception: See number 18.

5. When litigation is involved, information should *not* be released in the absence of a subpoena unless the patient has authorized it. Remember never to accept a subpoena or give records to anyone without the physician's prior authorization. In the case of a subpoena or interrogatories (questions directed to a physician who is being sued), the medical transcriptionist should not release records without first verifying them with the physician and having him or her correct any inaccuracies. Usually there is time to review such records, and any problems should be referred to the physician's lawyer before release.

6. Government and state agencies may have access to records pertaining to federal government–sponsored and state-sponsored programs, but these records should not be released without explicit consent of the patient.

7. Information of a psychiatric nature may present

special or delicate problems. Generally the psychiatrist or another attending physician concerned with the case should be consulted before any data are released.

8. Special care should be exercised in the release of any information to an employer, even with the consent of the patient. See number 18 for additional information regarding industrial injuries.

9. It is preferable not to allow lay persons to examine records. In this way misunderstandings of technical terms are avoided. However, according to the Privacy Act of 1974, certain patients, such as those receiving Medicare and CHAMPUS benefits, have a right to their records, since federal agencies are bound by its provisions. If the physician determines that the release may not be in the patient's best interests, most states allow for release to a representative of the patient. The only way a physician can prevent patients from gaining access to privileged information in their own medical records is by noting on the charts that he or she believes knowledge of the contents would be detrimental to the patients' best interests. This entry, however, must be made before the patient makes his or her request. Usually the courts will uphold a physician's judgment under these instances. In many states it is considered risky to allow a patient to hand-carry his or her records to a consultant, since the patient may misinterpret what has been entered in the record and may become frightened or angered. If there is a time factor involved and sending the records with the patient is the best solution to get them there on time, seal them in an envelope and send copies, not the originals. It is also a good idea to have the patient sign a receipt for any x-ray films. Consultation reports from other physicians, even those stamped "confidential," as well as billing or accounting records may also be released to the patient. Only the paper they are typed on is the physician's.

10. Care must be exercised in the release of any information for publication, since this also constitutes an invasion of the patient's right to privacy and can result in legal action against the physician or health facility releasing such information.

11. When in doubt about the release of any information, obtain the patient's authorization in writing.

12. If the signed authorization form is a photocopy, it is necessary to state that the photocopy is approved by the patient. Or write to the patient and obtain an original signed document.

13. Any transfer of records from hospital to hospital, physician to physician, or hospital to nursing home should be authorized in writing by the patient. If the patient is physically or mentally incapacitated, the next of kin or legal guardian may approve the transfer.

14. You cannot justifiably refuse to provide information to another physician just because a patient has a large outstanding bill with your office or institution.

15. If a legal photocopier comes to the office to copy the record, number the pages released or observe the record while it is copied. You may do it yourself and charge the attorney a fee for this service.

16. When working in a hospital, medical transcriptionists should check with the supervisor at all times to make sure their actions conform with hospital policy in regard to release of medical information. Whether working in a hospital or for a physician, do not hesitate to ask for clarification of matters that are unclear. If you are employed by a health facility that has a policy manual or office procedure manual, familiarize yourself with its rules regarding the release of information.

17. Oral requests can be handled in two ways. Either ask the caller to put the request in writing and include the patient's signature for release of information, or obtain the name and telephone number of the caller and relationship to the patient and have the physician return the call.

18. In an industrial injury (workers' compensation) case, the contract exists between the physician and the insurance carrier. When an insurance adjuster requests information in such a case by telephone, verify whom you are speaking to before giving out medical information. Such cases do not require a patient to have signed a release of information form on file.

19. If working in a physician's office, seek legal counsel if a patient has a positive human immunodeficiency virus (HIV) test for acquired immune deficiency syndrome (AIDS), applies for life or health insurance, and requests that the physician or hospital send medical records to the insurance company. Some state laws allow AIDS information to be given only to the patient's spouse (Table 1–1). In a hospital setting, patients infected with the HIV virus must sign an informed written consent before any medical information is released. The release of information from records of persons suffering from HIV infection or those tested for the HIV virus must be handled

TABLE 1-1. **A 1988 STATE-BY-STATE BREAKDOWN OF HIV CONFIDENTIALITY LAW***

Most states have medical confidentiality laws, usually as part of laws on communicable or sexually transmitted disease, medical records, licensure, or public health. In the past few years, however, more than two-thirds have enacted or are considering laws directly or indirectly dealing with the issue of HIV confidentiality and disclosure.

The approaches vary widely. Some states, such as California, tightly restrict disclosure of HIV data (although pending legislation and ballot initiatives would loosen those restrictions), while others, such as Georgia, permit such a wide range of disclosure that a hospital janitor could conceivably be told that a patient carries the human immunodeficiency virus.

Some states regulate whether a patient's HIV status may be shared with the medical team or entered in the medical record. Others leave that vague.

A number of states have chosen to strengthen their contagious disease laws, avoiding direct reference to AIDS.

A frank diagnosis of AIDS is reportable to public health authorities in all states.

Legislative analysts agreed that physicians should have a clear understanding with their patients on the expectations and requirements on HIV confidentiality and disclosure, and, regardless of whether it is required, put it in writing.

These states require reporting by name: Alabama, Arizona, Colorado, Idaho, Indiana, Kentucky, Minnesota, Mississippi, Missouri, Oklahoma, Oregon, South Carolina, Texas, Wisconsin, and Wyoming.

Here is a state-by-state rundown of current or pending HIV confidentiality and disclosure legislation, gleaned from state medical society legislative analysts.

ALABAMA
Mandatory reporting of AIDS and HIV-positive cases with identifiers to state Dept. of Public Health. Records are confidential; penalties for unlawful disclosure.

ALASKA
Standard notifiable disease laws.

ARIZONA
Standard notifiable disease laws.

ARKANSAS
Standard notifiable disease laws.

CALIFORNIA
Disclosure of HIV-positive status prohibited without written consent, except to spouse; penalties for unlawful disclosure. Pending legislation would allow HIV status to be shared with medical team. Pending referendum would require MDs to report names of HIV carriers and "suspected" carriers to state and would require sexual contact tracing.

COLORADO
AIDS and HIV-positive cases reportable with identifiers to local/state health departments. Strict confidentiality of Health Dept. records; penalties for unlawful disclosure. Physicians immune for good faith disclosure in compliance with law. Physicians' records not covered by confidentiality provisions.

CONNECTICUT
Standard notifiable disease laws.

DELAWARE
Oral or written informed consent required before HIV antibody test. Confidentiality provisions allow physician-to-medical-team disclosure. Penalties for unlawful disclosures.

DISTRICT OF COLUMBIA
AIDS is reportable with identifiers; HIV status is not reportable.

FLORIDA
Informed consent and counseling required for HIV antibody test. Physician-to-medical-team disclosure permitted. Penalty for unlawful disclosure.

GEORGIA
HIV is not reportable in Georgia or North Carolina. (Though Georgia law mandates HIV reporting, the state board of health has not issued rules to implement the law.) Information is confidential. Physician-to-health-care-provider disclosure permitted. Very broad definition of health care provider. Every person or entity entitled to receive such confidential information may release to another entitled to receive on a "need-to-know basis."

HAWAII
AIDS diagnosis reportable with identifiers; HIV-positive status not reportable. HIV status may be entered in medical record. Physician may share HIV status with medical team providing care. Confidentiality protections exist.

IDAHO
AIDS and HIV-positive status reportable to health department with identifiers. Confidentiality of public health records protected.

ILLINOIS
Law requiring written, informed consent before HIV antibody test was repealed; confidentiality provisions remain in place. Anonymous testing available. Disclosure allowed to state Dept. of Public Health and to medical team on need-to-know basis.

INDIANA
AIDS and HIV-positive cases reportable with identifiers. Confidentiality of HIV information protected; penalties for disclosure.

IOWA
In Iowa, reporting is required, but the name of the patient may be reported only with written authorization.
Confidentiality of records, limited access. Physician-to-medical-team disclosure permitted. Physician must inform individual that test is voluntary and may be taken anonymously. Seropositive results must be sent to state health department, but may not include name or address without written authorization.

KANSAS
AIDS reportable to state health department with identifiers. Physician-to-medical-team disclosure allowed. Anonymous testing sites provided. Penalties for unlawful disclosure.

KENTUCKY
Confidentiality of records of reported contagious diseases, including AIDS, protected.

LOUISIANA
Standard notifiable disease laws.

MAINE
Written informed consent required before HIV antibody test. Physician-to-medical-team disclosure of test results permitted. Medical record HIV information subject to patient release.

MARYLAND
Emergency medical personnel who have come in contact with an HIV-infected individual must be notified without disclosing name of patient; confidentiality of those exposed is protected as well.

MASSACHUSETTS
Written informed consent required before test. Disclosure prohibited without signed consent. Proposed legislation would allow physician-to-medical-team disclosure when necessary to protect patient's health.

MICHIGAN
Standard notifiable disease laws. Pending legislation would address confidentiality, disclosure, and physician responsibility with respect to information on AIDS and HIV status.

MINNESOTA
Mandatory reporting of AIDS and HIV-positive cases with identifiers to state health department. Reports are protected as private.

MISSISSIPPI
Communicable disease laws updated to require reporting of dangerous diseases with identifiers to state health department and notification of those exposed. Physician/patient communications are privileged.

MISSOURI
MD-to-medical-team disclosure permitted. Names of those who test seropositive must be reported to state health officials. Three anonymous test sites provided. Seropositive individuals must disclose status to health care professionals from whom they receive care. No liability for health care workers who report in good faith names of people suspected of being HIV positive. Emergency medical personnel must be notified if exposed to body fluids of infected person.

MONTANA
Reporting is required with an identifying number.

NEBRASKA
AIDS cases reportable with identifiers. Reporting without identifiers is required only by laboratories.

NEVADA
Standard notifiable disease laws.

NEW HAMPSHIRE
Informed consent required, with exceptions, before testing. MD-to-medical-team disclosure permitted. HIV records must be protected as confidential.

NEW JERSEY
Standard notifiable disease laws. Legislation pending.

NEW MEXICO
Standard notifiable disease laws.

NEW YORK
Effective February, 1989: Written informed consent required for test. Results may be disclosed only to health care workers who need to know or

TABLE 1-1. A 1988 STATE-BY-STATE BREAKDOWN OF HIV CONFIDENTIALITY LAW* (Continued)

who work with body fluids. Civil penalty of up to $5,000 for intentional violation of confidentiality. Seropositive status may not be freely shared within hospital to nontreating personnel.

NORTH CAROLINA

Physician may share HIV antibody test results with medical team. HIV-positive status must be reported with identifiers. Information not released except in exceptional circumstances, with written consent, under court order, or to protect public health.

NORTH DAKOTA

Standard notifiable disease laws.

OHIO

Standard notifiable disease laws.

OKLAHOMA

AIDS and HIV-positive cases reportable with identifiers. Exposed people must be notified. Confidentiality and disclosure procedures specified.

OREGON

AIDS and HIV-positive cases reportable to state health department with identifiers. Informed consent required for HIV test. Physician-to-medical-team disclosure allowed. HIV

data may be entered in medical record. Confidentiality protected; penalties for unlawful disclosure.

PENNSYLVANIA

Standard notifiable disease laws. Legislation pending.

RHODE ISLAND

As of Jan. 1, 1989, confidentiality of test results protected. Physician may enter results in medical record and may disclose to medical team and to third parties in close contact with seropositive individual. Written consent required before testing, with exceptions. Individual must be notified if test results were released without consent.

SOUTH CAROLINA

Sexually transmitted disease statutes updated to require mandatory reporting of AIDS and HIV-positive cases to state health department with identifiers and disclosure of sexual contacts. Confidentiality protected. Penalties for failing to report HIV-positive cases.

SOUTH DAKOTA

Standard notifiable disease laws.

TENNESSEE

Sexually transmitted disease

laws updated to required reporting of STDs to state health department. Confidentiality of records held by state or local health departments protected. STD means any disease transmitted primarily sexually as identified by the state health department.

TEXAS

Confidentiality of HIV test results protected. Physician-to-medical-team disclosure permitted. Physician permitted, but not required, to notify spouse. Civil liability for unlawful disclosure. Patient may be required to submit to HIV antibody test before medical procedure involving potential exposure to health care providers. Emergency mandatory testing allowed if justified by scientific and medical findings and imminent threat.

UTAH

Standard notifiable disease laws.

VERMONT

Standard notifiable disease laws.

VIRGINIA

Reporting of HIV-positive cases permitted with identifiers. Immunity granted for dis-

closure of HIV-positive cases to state health department.

WASHINGTON

Confidentiality of records protected with exceptions. Anonymous testing sites provided. Public health officers may require tests of people suspected of HIV infection. Legislation is still in the process of interpretation by the state Board of Health. Physician-to-medical-team disclosure prohibited without consent.

WEST VIRGINIA

Voluntary anonymous testing available. Physician may request HIV test when there is cause to believe test could be positive. Physician-to-medical-team disclosure allowed. Entry in medical chart of HIV data not a breach of confidentiality.

WISCONSIN

Informed consent required for disclosure of any HIV test result. Civil/criminal penalties for intentional disclosure; civil liability for negligent disclosure.

WYOMING

Standard notifiable disease laws.

* This table was researched in 1988 and is subject to change. (Reprinted with permission of *American Medical News*. Copyright 1988 American Medical Association, Chicago, Illinois.)

---

very carefully, especially in states with restricted access, because information about test results may appear in many sections of the health record. The use of ICD-9-CM code 795.8 reflects a positive HIV test, so this information must be considered confidential. The American Medical Record Association (AMRA) has suggested the use of a consent for release of information form (Fig. 1–4). Besides completing the blanks, it is important to list the extent or nature of the information to be released, e.g., HIV test results of diagnosis and treatment with inclusive dates of treatment. Following authorized release of patient information, the signed authorization should be retained in the health record with notation of the specific information released, the date of release, and the signature of the individual who released the information. All information released on the request of a patient with a diagnosis of HIV infection should be clearly stamped with a statement prohibiting redisclosure of the information to another party without the prior consent of the patient. The party receiving the information should

also be requested to destroy the information after the stated need is fulfilled.

Special Guidelines for Release of Hospital Information

Generally speaking, certain information is not available from the hospital medical record for release to third parties. This includes detailed psychiatric examination information, personal history of the patient or family, and information controlled by state law. If there is a question regarding the content of the medical information to be released, the attending physician should be consulted regarding its accuracy or interpretation. Hospitals prefer to release information by the use of summaries or abstracts or on standard forms recommended by the American Hospital Association or local hospital groups. Duplicating an entire record is expensive; furthermore, control of the record by the hospital would be lost, and the copy might be misused. If the attending physician wishes information from the hospital record, an abstract or a

NAME OF FACILITY

Consent for Release of Information

DATE _____

1.   I hereby authorize _____ to release the following information
                          Name of Institution
      from the health record(s) of

      _____
      Patient Name

      _____
      Address
      covering the period(s) of hospitalization from:

      Date of Admission _____

      Date of Discharge _____

      Hospital # _____ Birthdate _____

2.   Information to be released:

      ☐ Copy of (complete) health record(s)   ☐ Discharge Summary

      ☐ History and Physical   ☐ Operative Report

      ☐ Other _____

3.   Information is to be released to _____

      _____

4.   Purpose of disclosure _____

      _____

5.   I understand this consent can be revoked at any time except to the extent that disclosure made in good
      faith has already occurred in reliance on this consent.

6.   Specification of the date, event, or condition upon which this consent expires.

      _____

      _____

7.   The facility, its employees and officers and attending physician are released from legal responsibility or
      liability for the release of the above information to the extent indicated and authorized herein.

      Signed _____
                            (Patient or Representative)

             _____
                            (Relationship to Patient)

             _____
                            (Date of Signature)

FIGURE 1–4. Consent for Release of Information form. (Reprinted with permission of the American Medical Record Association (AMRA), Chicago, Illinois.)

copy can be given without the patient's written permission, as long as it is for the physician's own use.

Retention of Records

State and local laws govern the retention of records, and many states set a minimum of 7 to 10 years for keeping records in their original form. Generally, most physicians retain medical records on their patients for an indefinite period of time. In the case of minors, records should be retained three to four years beyond the age of majority.

Subpoena Duces Tecum

Subpoena duces tecum requires the witness to appear and to bring certain records to the deposition, trial, or other legal proceeding. Frequently, the records may be sent, and the physician or custodian of the records is not required to appear in court. A subpoena is a legal document signed by the clerk of the court (Fig. 1–5). In cases in which a "pretrial of evidence" or deposition is set up, the subpoena may be issued by a notary public, in which event it is called a notary subpoena. If an attorney signs it, he or she must validate it in the name of a judge, the court clerk, or other proper officer.

A *subpoena duces tecum* must be served to the prospective witness in person. If the subpoena is accepted by someone authorized to receive it, it is the equivalent to personal service. The subpoena cannot be left on a desk. It must be served with the subpoena (witness) fee and mileage fee, if requested by the witness. In some states, provision is made for substitute service by mail or through newspaper publication if all reasonable efforts to effect personal service have failed. In certain states, such as California, it is illegal for the physician to tell the custodian of the records not to release medical records when a written authorization has been signed by an adult patient.

Here are nine points to remember if a subpoena is served and you are given permission to receive it for the physician.

1. Be courteous to the deputy who is serving the subpoena. Ask for the fee when the subpoena is served because in the absence of the fee the subpoena is not legally valid and may be refused.

2. Find out from the deputy to which physician the subpoena is addressed. Get the name of the custodian of records for that particular physician if you are not the custodian. Ask to see the subpoena so that you know what action to take.

3. If the physician is on vacation, explain that you cannot accept a subpoena in the physician's absence. Suggest that the deputy contact the physician's attorney and relay this information to the attorney. Discuss the subpoena in question with one of the other physicians in the office for advice or management.

4. After receiving the witness fee and the subpoena, pull the patient's chart and place the medical record and the subpoena on the physician's desk for review. Willful disregard of a subpoena is punishable as contempt of court. After receiving a subpoena for a trial, verify with the court that the case is on the calendar. If the subpoena is for a deposition, verify the date and place to appear with the attorney.

5. You will have a prescribed time in which to produce the records. It is not necessary to show them at the time of service of the subpoena unless the court order so states. Telephone the attorney who ordered the subpoena and request permission to mail the record or a copy of the record. If the attorney agrees, send it by certified mail with return receipt requested. If the subpoena is for a trial, the witness or custodian of the records will have to appear in court unless there is permission to mail. If you do not appear, you may be in contempt of court and subject to fine or imprisonment.

6. Never give records to anyone without the physician's prior permission. When a subpoena is served, an authorization form for release of records signed by the patient is not required. Read the record to see that it is complete and that signatures and initials are identifiable.

7. Remove the records to a safe place so that they cannot be stolen or tampered with before the legal proceeding. Make photostatic copies of the records if you are in doubt about their safety. This may be expensive, but it can prevent total loss of the records and facilitate discovery of any altering while they are outside your custody. It also provides you with the record in case the patient is treated before the original is returned.

8. If you must appear in court with the records, comply with all instructions given by the court. *Do not* give up possession of the records unless instructed to do so by the judge. *Do not* permit examination of the records by anyone before their identification in court. When you leave the records in the court in the possession of the judge or jury, obtain a receipt for them.

9. If you have additional questions, call the patient's attorney or the physician's attorney.

1

Name, Address and Telephone No. of Attorney(s)	Space Below for Use of Court Clerk Only

Mitchell & Green
210 W. "A" Street
Los Angeles, California 90014
(213) 232-7461
Attorney(s) for Defendants

SUPERIOR COURT OF CALIFORNIA, COUNTY OF LOS ANGELES

		CASE NUMBER
ALBERT OTTO	Plaintiff(s) vs.	353 957
ROY M. LEDFORD, RALPH WALLACE, et al.,	Defendant(s)	**SUBPENA DUCES TECUM** (Civil)
(Abbreviated Title)		

THE PEOPLE OF THE STATE OF CALIFORNIA, to Dr. J. Brown ,

You are ordered to appear in this court, located at 111 No. Hill Street, Los Angeles, Ca. ,
(Street Address of Court and City)

on Feb. 8,199x at 9 a.m., Department 1 , to testify as a witness in this action,
(Date) (Time) (Department, Division or Room No., if any)

You must appear at that time unless you make a special agreement to appear another time, etc., with:

R. Mitchell, esq. at 232-7461
(Name of Attorney or Party Requesting This Subpena Duces Tecum) (Telephone Number)

You are also ordered to bring with you the books, papers and documents or other things in your possession or under your control, described in the attached declaration or affidavit, which is incorporated herein by reference.

Disobedience of this subpena may be punished as contempt by this court. You will also be liable for the sum of one hundred dollars and all damages to such party resulting from your failure to attend or bring the books, etc., described above.

Dated Jan. 31, 199x

Clarence E Cabell

CLARENCE E. CABELL, County Clerk and Clerk
of the Superior Court of California, County of Los
Angeles.

(To be completed when the subpena is directed to a California highway patrolman, sheriff, marshal or policeman, etc.)

This subpena is directed to a member of _____
(Name of Employing Agency)

I certify that the fees required by law are deposited with this court.

Receipt No._____ Amount Deposited $_____

CLARENCE E. CABELL, County Clerk   By _____, Deputy

NOTE: The original declaration or affidavit must be filed with the court clerk and a copy served with this subpena duces tecum.

(See reverse side for Proof of Service)

SUBPENA DUCES TECUM (Civil)   C.C.P. §§1985-1997; Evid. C. §§1560-1566; Gov. C. §§68097.1–68097.4; 35c.

FIGURE 1–5. Subpoena duces tecum (civil).

TRANSCRIPTIONIST'S NOTEBOOK OR FILE

As you prepare now for your future career as a transcriptionist, you should start by organizing an alphabetical pocket-sized notebook (Fig. 1–6). This can be a valuable tool. All new or unfamiliar material is entered in this guide. Make it an unwritten rule to add any word that you had to research because of spelling, capitalization, or usage. In this way, when you hear the word again you will be able to find it with ease. It is always easier to locate a word in your own guide, even when you know it is in the dictionary.

When working for a group of physicians, some transcriptionists prefer to indicate which physician dictated the word by placing his or her initials after the word. Where necessary when entering words, note (s) for singular, (p) for plural, (n) for noun, and (a) for adjective, e.g., mucous (a), mucus (n), vertebrae (p), vertebra (s). You might underline any capital letters in case you hurriedly make an entry and cannot tell if it is capitalized. You can also indicate (surg) for a surgical term, (ortho) for an orthopedic word, (ped) for a pediatric term, and so forth. Any other individual hints you can think of to help you may certainly be incorporated because this is your reference book. An alternative reference method is to prepare an index file of 3 × 5 inch cards with alphabetic dividers and to use them in the way mentioned previously. As your material accumulates, be sure you carefully recopy it in strict alphabetical sequence.

Now you are ready to begin Self-Study 1–2, on your way to becoming a medical transcriptionist.

B

babermycins (generic)

B̲erke ptosis forceps (Oph)

bleed (n)

bombe, iris (Dr. J.J.)

bougie (surg instr)

bruits (p)

B̲U̲S̲ (Ob–Gyn) Bartholin's, urethral, Skene's glands

FIGURE 1–6. Page B from an alphabetical pocket-sized transcriptionist notebook showing the following entries: a generic drug word, an ophthalmology term, a noun, a word dictated by Dr. John Jones, a surgical instrument, a plural word, and an obstetric and gynecologic abbreviation.

1–2: SELF-STUDY

Directions: Let's start on the right foot by beginning a pocket-sized notebook. Obtain an easy-to-handle, $\frac{1}{2}$-inch thick, three-hole ring binder with 25 sheets of lined paper and A–Z index guides. If it is difficult to locate a set of 26 alphabetical indexes, obtain the 2-letter combined alphabetical indexes. As you come to words in the text that you have difficulty spelling or that you want to be able to refer to quickly, place them under the correct alphabet letter for easy reference. Beginning with Chapter 3, look for some words to place in your notebook. For example, copy the abbreviations for the state names, as found in Chapter 4, page 91, at this time. List these on the introductory page of your notebook.

1–3: REVIEW TEST

Directions: Complete the following statements by filling in the blanks.

1. According to standards of the Joint Commission on Accreditation of Healthcare Organizations, what is the deadline for completion of a physical examination report on an inpatient?

   _____

   _____

2. Explain briefly why it is important for the transcriptionist to understand medical terminology.

   _____

   _____

   _____

3. State at least four skills a good transcriptionist should have.

   a. _____   c. _____

   b. _____   d. _____

4. In transcribing, what is even more important than speed?

   _____

5. A permanent legal document that formally states the results of an investigation is a/an _____ .

6. Written or typed information set down for the purpose of preserving memory that authenticates evidence of facts and events is a/an _____

   _____ .

7. Briefly list three main purposes of medical records.

   a. _____

   b. _____

   c. _____

8. Who owns the patient's medical records? _____

9. Confidential communication that may be disclosed only with the patient's permission is also known as _____ .

10. Name two classifications of information contained in medical records.

    a. _____

    b. _____

11. Name three places legal requirements for electronic signatures can be found.

    a. _____

    b. _____

    c. _____

12. Miss Freda Findley was in an automobile accident. Her attorney, James Burr, called and asked that a report of her condition be sent to him. What should the transcriptionist do?

    _____

    _____

13. Mr. Henry Waxman, an employer, calls your physician's office to inquire about the condition of one of his employees who had become ill while on vacation. The medical transcriptionist taking the call should do what?

    _____

    _____

    _____

14. Mrs. Jane Avers had plastic surgery done on her ears. Dr. Jeffers submitted an article to the *Medical World,* which was subsequently published, including the patient's photograph. No consent form was signed by the patient. What ethical and legal infringement would this be classified as? _____

15. The transcriptionist recognized the name of a patient as being the son of a friend of hers. The report indicated a good prognosis for the child. Since the mother had been depressed and uneasy for her child, the transcriptionist felt it was all right to telephone her and reassure her. Was this action correct? _____ Why? _____

    _____

Equipment

OBJECTIVES

After reading this chapter and working the exercises, you should be able to

1. explain the different kinds of typewriting and word processing equipment.
2. demonstrate proper typewriter and computer maintenance.
3. describe the operation of different types of transcription/dictation equipment and accessories.
4. perform the steps of transcription preparation.
5. explain how copying and fax machines are utilized in the transcription process.
6. identify equipment for physically challenged individuals.
7. define vocabulary terms related to office equipment.
8. explain the features of word processing.
9. identify ergonomic factors that affect the transcriptionist's work environment.

. . . .

INTRODUCTION

This chapter will provide you with information on computers, typewriters, transcription equipment, word processing machines, printers, fax machines, and photocopy machines, including their accessories and maintenance. Since some of the material is technical, you may come across a word that is unfamiliar. Many of these words appear in *italics*. In such cases, refer to the vocabulary list at the end of this chapter. A brief discussion of transcription equipment for the physically challenged is included, and, finally, the setting up and preparation of your materials for transcription will be explained.

THE TYPEWRITER

There are four kinds of typewriters: manual, electric, electronic or "memory," and triple-function typewriters. The electric and electronic (memory) typewriters are most often used in the physician's office and the hospital because of their efficiency and the more professional appearance of the typed material. Electric typewriters can have a movable carriage or an immovable carriage with interchangeable typing *elements.** The basic typewriter has either *pica* or *elite*

---

* Italicized words appear in the vocabulary list at the end of this chapter.

23

type, but with the advent of the typewriter with the immovable carriage, some typewriters now have both. This feature is known as *dual pitch.* One advantage of a dual-pitch typewriter is its ability to change your type size. You might prefer to do reports and letters in pica and change to elite when space is limited, as on insurance forms. With an immovable carriage, one does not need as much desk space for the equipment.

More sophisticated electric typewriters are automatic (electronic) and can be classified as text editing equipment, memory typewriters, key search, telecommunications, and other forms of electronic computer–aided machines. These help to increase the efficiency of the medical transcriptionist's output. Some specific applications in a medical practice are credit letters, personalized form letters, office procedure manuals, insurance form letters, and information gathering.

The *electronic typewriter* is a desk-top typewriter that combines the capabilities of modern electronics with single-element typewriter technology. It performs automatically many of the typing tasks a secretary must do manually with other desk-top typewriters. The memory capability built into the typewriter allows centering, phrase storage, underscoring, indenting, and automatic error correction. Other electronic features are column layout, margins and tabs, number alignment, proportional spacing, and automatic carrier return. All of these features greatly increase productivity in the medical office or hospital setting.

Triple-function typewriters operate as a self-correcting typewriter to conveniently type labels, file cards, and envelopes. The touch of a key switches the system from a personal computer to a typewriter without exiting from a document and without changing diskettes. Machines of this type have either a triple or a dual function keyboard to perform as a typewriter, word processor, or personal computer. It has standard typewriter features as well as word processing and computer features, depending on the software that is being used. Some machines have expansion capabilities and can be connected to an office's local area network or can become a terminal to a mainframe or minicomputer.

WORD PROCESSING (WP) MACHINE OR DISPLAY TEXT EDITOR

Word processing is a text editor system for electronically writing, formatting, and storing documents (letters, reports, and so forth) before printing. It is a method of producing written communication at top speed, with the greatest accuracy, least effort, and lowest possible cost, through use of proper procedures, automated business equipment, and trained personnel.

A word processing machine can be either equipped or not equipped with a video display terminal. The word processing machine can store *keyboarded* typed material *(input),* and the typist can electronically rearrange it, revise it, and then put it in a variety of final formats for "*error-free*" copy *(output* or *playback).* The machine allows the typist to rewrite or eliminate words or complete paragraphs in a fraction of the time it takes with conventional equipment.

Word processing is used in law offices, insurance companies, government agencies, hospitals, physicians' offices, clinics, and other businesses that produce a large volume of correspondence. In medical facilities, this system is used for billing and collection letters; communicating with patients and referring physicians; typing chart notes and medical reports; sending out appointment letters; repetitive typing (forms, referral letters, and so on); and developing laboratory manuals, patient information brochures, grant proposals, and other types of materials that require revisions and periodic updates.

There are several types of word processing or text editing machines available, but one of the most widely used is the *video display terminal* (VDT) with printer (Fig. 2–1). The physical components of a computer system (electrical, electronic, magnetic, and mechanical devices) are known as the *hardware,* and the programs and instructions are known as *software.*

A typing speed of at least 50 to 60 words per minute, the ability to proofread the typed material on the VDT, and the skill of machine transcription are needed for word processing.

The typist *keyboards* material to a screen called a *cathode ray tube* (CRT). It is stored temporarily in *memory,* the material is proofread from the screen, revisions and corrections are made, and it is printed as *hard copy.* If desired, it can be transferred from memory storage to magnetic media *(floppy or hard disk)* for permanent or back-up storage. In large companies, these machines can be linked to other systems, or *peripherals,* such as data processing, electronic mail, optical character readers (OCRs), and so forth. The final output may not be printed but may be sent via telecommunication satellite or telephone lines using a *modem* to be read by the receiver on a CRT screen. It can be sent to a micrographic center for production directly into microfilm or can be transmitted directly to phototypesetting equipment for in-house printing.

Some features of display *text editors* or word processing machines are as follows (Fig. 2–2):

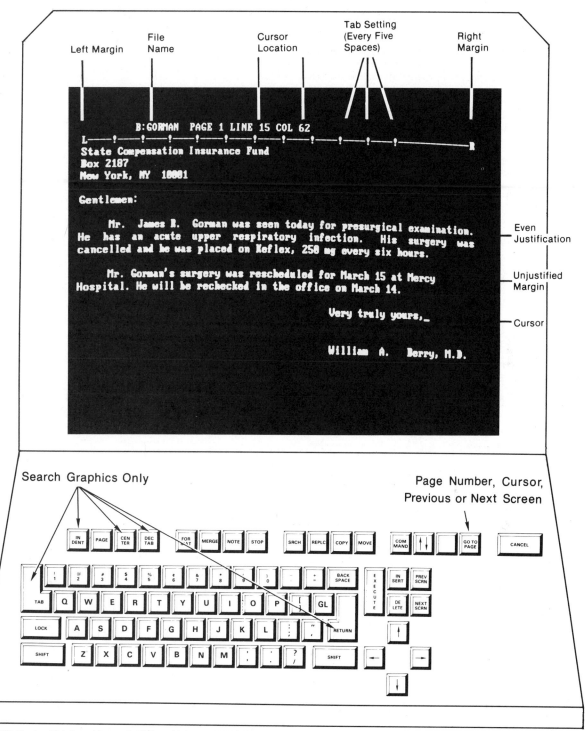

FIGURE 2-1. This is a schematic of the widely used WANG word processor. The typing keyboard is the same as a typewriter, but there are a considerable number of function keys. The position of such keys can vary considerably from machine to machine, but many of the functions are similar.

INDENT:	To indent a complete paragraph or sentence to a specific tab location. Text returns to the tab location rather than to the left-hand margin.
PAGE:	To instruct the printer where to end a page.
CENTER:	To center a line between margins.
DECIMAL TAB:	To automatically align columns of numbers or decimals on the decimal point at the tab stop.
FORMAT:	To create a new format line; also to change an existing one that is automatically created when a new document is created.
MERGE:	A document merge function that tells the printer to switch from one document to another, pick up information, and return where indicated.

Legend continued on following page

NOTE: Used as a reminder to the operator to take certain steps within a document, but does not show when printing that document.
STOP: Stops the printer at a certain spot while printing to change printwheel.
SEARCH: To search through a document and stop at any defined character sequence up to 16 characters.
REPLACE: To replace any previously typed characters with other characters.
COPY: To copy text and move to another location within that document.
MOVE: To move text to another location within that document.
GO TO
PAGE: To replace current screen with desired page of document.
CANCEL: Terminates any function or operation.
TAB: To indent the beginning of a paragraph or other text.
BACK
SPACE: Spaces back to previous character.
RETURN: To end a line of text and return the cursor to the start of next line.
EXECUTE: Tells the system that the present course of action is acceptable.
INSERT: Inserts any amount of text into an existing document.
DELETE: Deletes any amount of text out of an existing document.
NEXT SCREEN/
PREVIOUS
SCREEN: To view any screen of text in a document.
CURSOR ARROWS
UP ARROW: Moves the cursor up.
DOWN ARROW: Moves the cursor down.
LEFT ARROW: Moves the cursor left.
RIGHT ARROW: Moves the cursor right.

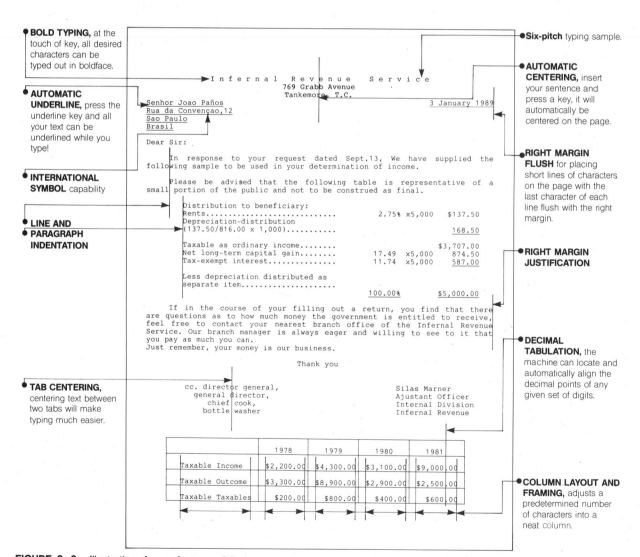

FIGURE 2-2. Illustration of some features of display text editors or word processing machines. (Reproduced by permission of Brother International Corporation, Piscataway, New Jersey.)

1. Cut and paste: extensive *editing* and revising capabilities to *insert, delete,* and move copy *(cut and paste)* easily by using *command keys* on the keyboard and moving the *cursor* to the proper location on the CRT screen.

2. Right margin justification: which justifies right margin; however, some employers prefer *ragged text,* where the right margin does not align flush.

3. Decimal tab alignment: which allows columns of figures with decimals to align automatically.

4. *Global search and replace:* which allows the operator with one instruction to search for a word or group of words everywhere in the text and automatically replace them with other words.

5. *Pagination:* which instructs the text editor to determine the ends of pages of a document and number the pages in sequence.

6. *Menus:* which aid the operator in making revisions and performing machine manipulations.

7. Automatic hyphenation: which hyphenates a word too long to fit within the right margin and moves part of the word to the next line.

8. *Word wraparound:* which moves the last word of a line to the next line if the word goes outside the predetermined right margin.

9. *Document assembly:* which allows combining prerecorded text with keyboarded text; combining selections from prerecorded text to form a new document; inserting names and addresses to create a number of nearly identical documents. Also called *merge.*

10. *Reverse index:* which allows for superscript and subscript.

11. *Scrolling:* which allows moving the text vertically and horizontally as well as flipping pages of a document on the CRT screen.

12. Indenting, underlining, centering, automatic tabulation to decimal points, and so forth: which allows these functions to be carried out.

13. Dictionary: which can be expanded and assists as a spell checker for English or medical terms in a sentence, paragraph, page, or document.

14. Thesaurus: which is a categorized index of synonyms and antonyms and assists in composition when trying to find a substitution for a word.

15. Counter: which counts words, and gives the number of words or characters per page and/or per document.

16. Grammar checker: which checks your grammar for common errors. A document can be scanned for violation of standard grammar rules.

17. Forms processing: which completes insurance claims.

18. Windows and split screens: which allow spread sheets to complete billing reports and incorporate totals into past due letters and allow graphics to be pasted into medical reports.

HIGH-SPEED TEXT ENTRY

This system uses a computer linked to electronic shorthand equipment as used in court reporting, where transcription speeds of 225 words per minute and beyond are attained. Instead of entering text by one keyboard stroke (one character at a time), one stroke (which can be one, two, or three keys hit simultaneously) is used to enter entire words, phrases, and sentences. The shorthand is keyed in and instantly converts to correctly spelled words, phrases, and sentences. By producing multiple characters with each keyboard stroke, text is entered much faster and more efficiently than possible with a one-stroke, one-character keyboard. It is possible to build extensive medical dictionaries unique to each medical specialty. The text is sent to remote systems via fax or modem so that the report does not have to be printed and delivered. Electronic signatures are used in some facilities when such high-tech systems are installed.

COMPUTERS

Computers have been developed to use software programs that can perform a multitude of functions, i.e., filing, word processing, graphics, accounting and financial management, and so forth. Many hospital facilities, medical clinics, and physician's offices have elected to install computers rather than *stand-alone word processors* to meet their needs since computers are able to perform a multitude of functions.

A computer has a keyboard that has *function keys,* which are also called *control* or *command* keys. A *program instruction* can be given by depressing certain keys and this enters a particular command into a word processing or other type of software program. *Response time,* the time it takes the system to react to a command, varies depending on how sophisticated the equipment is. Besides keyboarding in *data,* it is now possible to handwrite or speak and the data appears automatically on the VDT. It is also possible to point to a picture on a *touch-sensitive video screen* and the commands are performed. Computer accessories, such as a *mouse* or a *light pen,* enable the operator to

2

draw images, mark choices, or add and delete text on the VDT. Light pens are used in some facilities to scan the patient's admitting information so that the operator does not have to keyboard in the patient's name and other identifying data.

An *on-line processing* system is one composed of a central processing unit (CPU), a communications linkage, a terminal, and a user that interact to carry out a task. The CPU is where data is added, subtracted, multiplied, divided, and sorted. The software programs that give the computer the electronic instructions to do the work are executed in the CPU. When entering data, a zero (0) is the smallest unit of information a computer can understand and is called a *bit.* The word stands for *b*inary dig*it.* Computers use binary logic to process information. A group of 8 bits is called a *byte.* One byte is equal to one alphanumeric *character.* Computers have random access memory (RAM) and read-only memory (ROM). RAM is used to describe machine memory that can be stored in any order, accessed immediately, and modified. ROM refers to computer memory that can be addressed but not modified. Refer to the section in this chapter on word processing because most of the features in *stand-alone word processors* are found in word processing computer software programs. Computers can be hooked up to the telephone line to assist in transmitting and receiving fax or *electronic mail.* A microcomputer or minicomputer has one or more *disk drives,* and the drive functions to hold a software or data disk so that information can be saved and retrieved from the disk.

Data Storage

Magnetic media is used for word processors and microcomputers (personal computers). The following methods will be discussed: diskettes, digital cassettes, Winchester disks, and optical disks.

Diskettes

A *diskette* is a thin, circular piece of magnetically coated plastic that is contained in a protective envelope to shield its surface from contamination by dust and fingerprints. A standard (8″) diskette can store 40 to 350 K *(kilobyte)* characters, or about 100 pages of text per side. A minidiskette (5¼″) storage capacity is determined by whether the diskette is single-sided or dual-sided, single-tracked or double-tracked. A microdiskette (3½″, 3¼″, 2½″) has many of the same functions as the 5¼″ version but at about 25% the size and half the weight.

Computer software is sold on diskettes, so it is always wise to make a *backup* of expensive software

programs after you purchase the software. If a *crash* or any problem develops with the backup/working diskette, you always have the original to fall back on. If your system does not automatically back up the data that you input, you should make backup copies of your data onto floppy disks on a daily basis.

Digital Magnetic Tape Cassettes

A digital cassette consists of a cartridge-enclosed, magnetically coated tape. The data on the cassette is accessed serially. They have instant start-stop times and higher read-write speeds. Cassettes are part of electronic typewriters as a form of extended memory.

Winchester Disks

A Winchester disk drive is used for huge on-line storage requirements or for multiple, related documents of over 200 pages. The Winchester disk is enclosed in a hermetically sealed diskhead assembly (HDA) in which the air is continuously circulated and filtered. This eliminates contamination problems and requires little preventive maintenance. Storage capacity is measured in megabytes (MB) ranging from 20 to 600 MB.

Optical Disks

The optical disk can store digital and analog data as well as halftones, graphs, and drawings. Some optical disks are recorded on so that the data cannot be charged or written over, and other optical disks are erasable.

COMPUTER PRINTER

Typewriters and word processors that are not equipped with a VDT combine keyboarding and printing in the same unit. However, display word processors and microcomputers have a printer as a separate component. There are two categories of printers: impact *(daisy wheel, thimble, dot matrix)* and nonimpact (ink jet, thermal transfer, laser). Printers are designed so that a tractor guides *continuous form stationery* on sprockets, or individual sheets can be fed in manually or automatically by a sheet feeder. While keyboarding in data at a computer, the program instructions (commands or functions) signal the printer. For example, a *stop code* embedded in a document signals the printer to stop. There is a wide range of printing quality and speed. Output from the printer is called *hard copy.*

TYPEWRITER ACCESSORIES

Typewriter ribbons come in a variety of materials, such as cotton, silk, nylon and carbon film. The cotton, silk, and nylon are heavy, medium, or lightly inked, the choice depending on the touch of the typist and the size of the type. For clean, sharp copy, the carbon film ribbon gives the best appearance. Remember that it is not economical to purchase a cheap ribbon because it dirties the keys and typewriter and wears out quickly. There are also various types of correcting ribbons. Some of these are inked with white ink so that the typist can white-over a typed character. Others are coordinated with a specific carbon film ribbon. The correction portion chemically lifts off the incorrectly typed letter so that an error is impossible to identify after a correction has been accomplished. A convenient type of ribbon is the snap in/snap out cartridge, which keeps the hands clean.

TYPEWRITER/WORD PROCESSOR/COMPUTER ERGONOMICS

Real problems exist for medical transcriptionists because they work in one position hour after hour and perform repetitive movements. These are known as cumulative trauma disorders (CTDs) or repetitive stress injuries (RSIs). Other factors that can contribute to on-the-job injuries are indoor air pollution, electromagnetic radiation, and stress. Therefore, steps must be taken to avoid these disorders or injuries. The height of the surface on which the typewriter, word processor, or computer sits is very important. Improper height can cause early fatigue and will reduce productivity. The chair is equally important and should be adjusted to the individual's height and build. A well-adjusted and properly designed chair can reduce fatigue and tension. Sometimes a small footstool will help the short typist to avoid back problems. To prevent fatigue, neck aches, backaches, eyestrain, or duplicating or leaving out a sentence, use an electronic copyholder with a foot pedal control and magnifying cursor so that proper posture can be maintained and material can be easily read when retyping. To prevent frozen shoulders and carpal tunnel wrist syndrome, a computer keyboard should be placed low enough so the arms are relaxing comfortably in a neutral or downward position on the keyboard. Hand and wrist supports and placement may be of some help. The computer monitor screen should be in place and the typist should take frequent breaks and periodically do body and wrist stretches and focus the eyes on distant objects to eliminate eyestrain and static, low-frequency radiation, sharpen images, and prevent glare and light reflection. If you begin to feel pain, apply ice to the area after work and on break to prevent inflammation.

TYPEWRITER MAINTENANCE

Because you want to have professional-looking reports and letters, it is essential that your equipment be maintained in good working condition. Your machine should always be covered when you leave the office at the end of a work day. The keys and body should be kept dust-free and cleaned by using a slightly dampened cloth. Avoid using abrasive cleaners on any parts of your equipment. The typing characters should be cleaned periodically with a brush and typecleaning fluid, since ink and carbon from the ribbon can accumulate with use, diminishing the sharpness of the characters. If typing on lightweight paper, use a backing sheet to protect the platen. Above all, become familiar with the equipment manual and know who to call to make repairs. If the typewriter is producing erratic functions, turn off the equipment, locate the section in the equipment manual on troubleshooting, and follow the instructions. If your machine is under *warranty* on an *equipment service contract,* it will receive periodic cleaning. Have a repairperson check any irregularities, and keep a list of problems for him or her. Save any typed material that demonstrates the problem so it can be easily corrected.

Before you make a service repair call, be sure that you are not making an "idiot" call, which can be quite costly. Run over these checklists.

Typewriter or word processor checklist:

1. Is the equipment plugged in?

2. Is the outlet in working order?

3. Is the equipment turned on?

4. Is the paper release lever that puts pressure on the typewriter platen pushed all the way back?

5. Is the multiple copy control lever pulled all the way forward?

6. Do you have ribbon?

7. Is the typewriter ribbon on stencil? Or has the carbon ribbon gone to the end? Or has the correction ribbon run out?

8. Do you still have typewriter ribbon that is inked?

9. Do you still have correction ribbon that is inked?

Transcriber checklist:

1. Is the equipment plugged in?

2

2. Is the outlet in working order?

3. Is the equipment turned on?

4. Is the "play" button pushed down preventing you from hearing through the headset?

5. Is the foot pedal attached to the machine?

If you have decided that your equipment needs repairs, type a note explaining the problems your machine is giving you, then tape the note to the side of your machine. This way the repairperson will know what to look for even if you are not present. This also should be done in a classroom setting.

COMPUTER SOFTWARE

Computers have a *disk operating system* (DOS), which controls the loading and storage of files from and to a computer's memory and to a magnetic disk. There is no standard operating system in the personal computer environment. Some systems are CP/M (control program/microprocessor), MS/DOS (MicroSoft/Disk Operating System), PC-DOS (the IBM PC operating system), and the UNIX system developed by Bell Laboratories. If you are working on a word processor (stand-alone or text editing) or are using a microcomputer, sophisticated word processing software is available as well as English, medical, and pharmaceutical dictionaries. Some word processing packages have macro capabilities, or you can purchase software with a modified keyboard to allow macro or "chording," the simultaneous depression of multiple keys. This feature is for frequently used words and phrases. For example, keying in "PE" would appear as "physical examination" on the computer screen. Integrated software packages have *windows* that let you see various functions simultaneously. There are also computer programs that can be activated by voice instead of keyboarding command keys. *Utility programs* are general-purpose software programs that perform activities which are not specific to an application, i.e., spell checkers, line count, macro makers, install *fonts* (the size and style of type), *initialize* a disk (to prepare the magnetic surface of a blank diskette so it can accept data), and so forth. Sometimes a word processing software program will have these utility features incorporated in it. If data is to be stored, a blank disk is initialized and the data is given a file name so it can be *retrieved* from the *file.*

COMPUTER RIBBONS

Cartridge ribbons for printers may look identical, but they can vary considerably in their construction, ink,

fabric specifications, print quality, and print durability. The price of the ribbon is not always a good measure of product quality. Generic-brand ribbons are less expensive but may be acceptable, or of poor quality and could cause printer damage. Brand-named ribbons are usually of high quality but also the most expensive. Some features to look for in a good quality ribbon are

1. crisp characters that will not smudge or smear.

2. print quality that is consistent for the life of the ribbon.

3. durable cartridge and ribbon materials.

4. correct and durable packaging to avoid drying out of the ribbon.

5. written guarantee by the dealer to replace or credit defective ribbons.

COMPUTER DISKS

Because you will have important information stored on computer floppy disks, it is wise to take care of them. The information is magnetically recorded. Therefore, any magnetic or electromagnetic field can scramble or destroy data recorded onto a disk. Your telephone, printer, or video terminal contain magnetic fields, so do not place a disk on top of this equipment. Each disk should be properly stored in a protective envelope. If two disks are stored in one envelope, information on one disk can be "imprinted" or transferred onto another. All the disks should be put into a box. The container should be kept away from extreme heat (100°F or above) and out of direct sunlight, since valuable information could be destroyed or the disk could melt. Never attach rubberbands or paper clips to disks because these could bend or damage them.

When labeling a disk, use felt-tip pens when writing on the label if it is affixed to a disk. It is better to fill out the label before adhering it to the disk. Do not stack labels on a disk because this can cause an imbalance in the weight of its surface.

Above all, keep the disks clean and out of the way of possible spills or stains. Therefore, never eat or smoke around the computer area. If a disk must be cleaned, use only tap water.

COMPUTER MODEM

The word *modem* is an acronym for MOdulator DEModulator unit and is a device that converts data into signals for telephone transmission and then (at the receiving end) back again into data. Some transcription services offer this type of telecommunication by hooking their word processing or computer equipment into the telephone lines. Then they can transmit correspondence or reports to an office, clinic, or hospital facility many miles away. Documents transmitted in this way can be revised and edited by the receiving office before they are printed out into a hard copy.

TRANSCRIPTION EQUIPMENT

Dictation and transcription equipment has advanced considerably since the development of electronic and high-*fidelity* recordings. Shorthand has become almost passé because of improved dictating equipment, and the medical transcriptionist can now do other tasks while the physician is dictating reports. There are a variety of models that the physician may use in the office, home, or hospital or while attending conferences. They are as follows:

1. *Digital dictation.* The dictated voice is digitized (converted to a string of O's and I's representing the audio waveform) and stored as data on a computer disk with identifying data (patient and dictator identification and worktype). The data is instantly and selectively accessible before, during, or after transcription. When accessed (from a dictation/transcription station or telephone), the binary

digits are converted back to analog waveform to sound just as the original dictation. This type of system features better sound quality, thereby enhancing the dictator's ability to insert or delete for *error-free* dictation. Digital dictation is making analog tape dictation obsolete in the same way that word processors are replacing typewriters.

2. *Voice recognition.* This is transcriptionless dictation and is composed of a computer system equipped with sound sensors. The physician trains the system to understand his or her speech patterns, and the system translates the tones of the human voice into computer commands and text on the screen. The report must be proofread and edited for grammar and punctuation before it is printed and ready for signature.

3. *Telecommunications.* The physician dictates by telephoning from home to the office or the hospital. He or she dials a special number that seizes the transcribing equipment. Physicians may find that they are able to think more quickly and clearly while talking into a telephone-like device rather than into traditional microphone equipment. Phone-in adaptors can be set up to work with a variety of transcribing equipment.

4. *Tank-type machines.* The transcribing unit is located in a remote area with direct input from one or more dictating stations in a building that utilizes telephone-type services (Fig. 2–3). This equip-

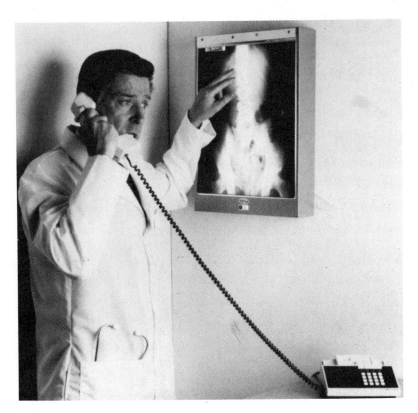

FIGURE 2-3. The doctor is talking into a telephone-like device to the hospital or office, and it is recording onto a Dictaphone transcribing machine. (Courtesy of Dictaphone Corporation.)

ment is popular in the hospital word processing department and uses an *endless loop* system. The transcriptionist does not have to be concerned with the physical transfer of recorded medium from the machine, and only the foot pedal and manual controls on the transcribing units are used. This eliminates the problem of lost reports.

5. *Cassette-changer central recorder.* This holds 15 to 25 cassettes, which can be programmed to change automatically, either by the number of dictators having access to the recorders or by the percentage of tape used. It can also be set up so that each person dictating can be on a separate cassette. Dictators can access the equipment from any telephone, at work or at home.

6. *Desk-top machines* (Fig. 2–4). This is used by the physician and medical transcriptionist in the office. The most common units available include the following:
   a. *A dictation unit,* for dictating purposes only.
   b. *A transcription unit,* designed for the transcriptionist who will transcribe the dictation.
   c. *A combination unit,* which can be used for both dictation and transcription.

7. *Portable dictating machine.* The physician may hand-carry this to a meeting or use it in a car to dictate whenever he or she wishes (Fig. 2–5). It can be wall plug or battery operated. Portable cassette recorders are popular because they can be used at conventions and conferences. Minicassettes or picocassettes can be played back at the office if the physician has purchased a transcribing unit that

features the minicassette adaptor or minicassette or picocassette transcriber.

MEDIA

The media used in dictating machines are of a variety of types. They may be in the form of magnetic tapes; wax coated, plastic, or magnetic belts; plastic or magnetic disks; and minicassette, microcassettes, and pico- or standard cassettes (Fig. 2–6). It makes little

FIGURE 2–5. A physician using portable dictating machine equipment.

2

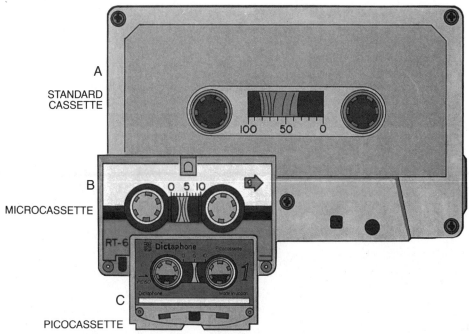

FIGURE 2-6. Media for various dictation/transcription equipment. *A*, Standard-size magnetic tape cassette; *B*, microcassette; *C*, picocassette. (Reprinted from the July issue of *Modern Office Technology*, and copyrighted 1985 by Penton Publishing, subsidiary of Pittway Corporation, Cleveland, Ohio.)

difference what medium you use, since the transcribing process is the same; however, fidelity does vary considerably. Some instruments actually enhance the speaker's voice. Be sure to check carefully for good voice fidelity when purchasing new equipment.

An embossing medium records sound in grooves pressed by a stylus on the surface. Because embossing is permanent, these can be used only once, but they are inexpensive. In some instances, they are filed for later reference as a permanent record. Errors dictated cannot be erased, so the dictator must indicate on the index or indicator strip the point at which an error was dictated and the corrected version.

Magnetic tapes, disks, or cassettes allow the dictator to correct his or her own errors so that the medical transcriptionist does not have to look ahead for corrections. Minicassettes, microcassettes, and pico- and standard cassettes are most popular and can record from 15 to 90 minutes on each side. They can be easily erased and reused. Some machines have a minicassette adaptor, so that you can use both standard cassettes and smaller sizes (see Fig. 2-4). Olympus Optical Company, Ltd., has a micro/mini transcriber.

Most machines emit a warning tone when ap-

proaching the end of a tape, and some machines will warn you if the tape is broken.

INDEX COUNTER

An index counter, also known as a digital counter, is available on some machines and is used to locate material with speed or to establish the length of a letter or report. When beginning to transcribe a new tape, the counter is brought back to zero. If you complete only part of a tape in class, look at the counter, record the number shown, rewind the tape to its beginning, and remove the tape for filing for use by other students. On returning to class, run the tape to the recorded number to complete your transaction.

INDICATOR STRIPS

Many dictating and transcribing machines have paper indicator strips inserted into the machine that enable the dictator to mark where a report begins, ends, or needs corrections. The dictator attaches the strip to the media for the transcriptionist's reference.

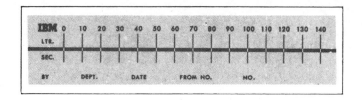

Some machines use *cue-tone indexing,* which allows the dictator to insert this information magnetically onto the medium while dictating. One such machine is the Dictaphone (Fig. 2–7). Another method of indication involves display windows that electronically show you the number of documents on the tape, how many special instructions within each document,

how much time is left as you are typing the dictated material, which document you are on, and how many pieces of work you have completed.

Indication features help you plan your day more efficiently, since you can judge the length of a document before transcribing it and can scan for special instructions.

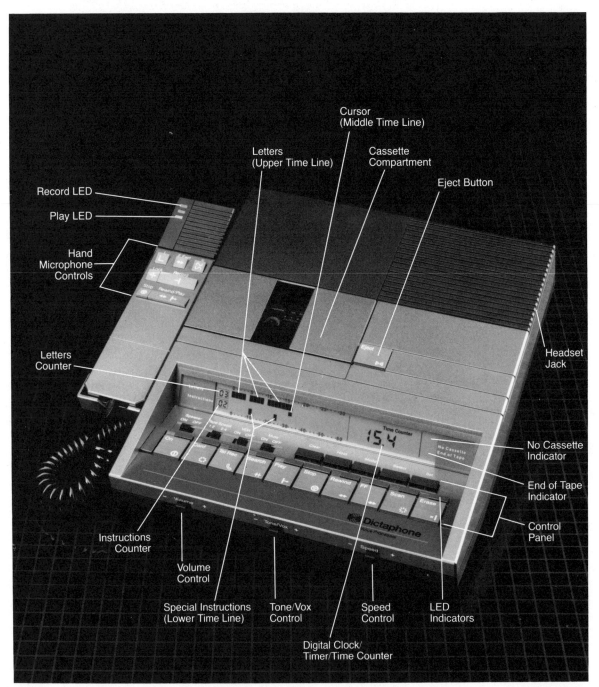

FIGURE 2-7. Dictaphone's ExecTalk Plus voice processing system, a compact desktop system, features advanced dictation and transcription capabilities. Multicolor indicator light display, light emitting diode (LED), shows various functions on the control panel for recording or transcribing a document.

HAND/FOOT CONTROL

Transcription machines have a foot pedal that will start the machine. Pressure on the pedal causes the machine to play; as soon as you release the pedal, the machine stops. You have complete control over how much of the dictation you hear. The control is so sensitive that you can stop and restart in the middle of a word. The machine also has a backup pedal that permits you to relisten to a few words or as much as you need to hear again before you transcribe. Some machines can be adjusted to replay a phrase or a word automatically every time you restart. This is also called auto rewind. In addition, the control may have a *fast forward* feature.

Initially, you will listen to as much of a sentence as you can retain by memory, and you will type it before listening to the next phrase. Eventually, you will learn to type as you listen, ceasing to listen only long enough to catch up to the dictation; then, just before you type the last of what you heard, start to listen

again so that there is as little time as possible during which you are not typing at all. If the foot pedal of the transcription machine constantly or frequently slips out of reach, glue two strips of the looped side of some Velcro tape to the bottom of the pedal. Velcro sticks to a carpeted floor just as it would to the soft-side Velcro. If the floor is not carpeted, glue two matching strips of soft-side Velcro to the floor at the place where the pedal is most comfortable.

Dictation equipment has a speed control that should be adjusted to a natural voice sound, neither too fast or too slow. The voice should not sound distorted. If the transcriptionist has difficulty understanding a word or phrase, the speed control can be adjusted to slow down the voice to see if this makes it audible or clear. However, the speed control should not be left in the slow mode but should always be adjusted to a natural-sounding voice quality.

Some manufacturers make a hand control available to the physically challenged as an alternate accessory. The operation of the control plays a vital role in

TABLE 2–1. **GENERAL FEATURES OF THE TRANSCRIBER**

PART NAME		WHAT THEY DO, DON'T DO, AND HANDY HINTS TO REMEMBER
Audio speaker control	*Does:*	clarify words
		disrupt room environment
		maintain confidentiality when not in use
		Remember: Operate briefly when using
Cassette media	*Does:*	have adaptors available on standard-size cassette
		transcriber for smaller size cassettes
	Does not:	allow for prolonged use of media since this results in worn tape and poor sound reproduction
Foot pedal	*Does:*	allow hands to remain on keyboard
		have a setting adjustment to your need so words are not backspace missed. This adjustment should be changed as the transcriptionist becomes more experienced. A zero adjustment (slight rewind of tape when stopped and then restarted) should be aimed for before obtaining a job
	Does not:	have standardized pedal parts on machines, and location of function features can be easily confused
Erase button	*Does:*	allow for clean erasure of tape
	Does not:	have a safety feature so accidental erasures can occur
Headset	*Does:*	enhance sound quality biaurally
		shut out office sounds
		preserves confidentiality
	Does not:	have loan out properties since earpiece fits inside ear canal, and infections can be transmitted unless the earpiece is thoroughly cleaned. Note: Clean earpieces from time to time
Indicator strip	*Does:*	locate special instructions or comments
		indicate length of documents
	Does not:	consistently line up accurately with the beginning of each report
Insert control	*Does:*	allow insertion of dictation without rerecording or erasing dictation
Scanning	*Does:*	allow for quick location and identification of all dictation on tape
Sensor for voice-activation	*Does not:*	require the dictator to hold the microphone
	Does:	provide gag-free dictation
Speed control	*Does:*	distort speech when speed is decreased too much
		slow down the fast dictator
		increase a naturally slow dictator
		match dictation speed with transcription speed
Tone control	*Does:*	mute consonants when too much bass is used
		accentuate consonants and clarify dictation when put in treble pitch
		cause static when too much treble pitch is used
Volume control	*Does:*	distort sound when the volume is too high. It is important to adjust the volume for each transcription

2

developing the essential skill of typing steadily and quickly.

Table 2–1 will assist you with avoiding some of the pitfalls and taking advantage of some of the benefits when operating a transcriber.

DICTATION

Dictating is a communications skill, and there are good and poor dictators. Transcribing is definitely improved by good dictation. Sometimes the transcriptionist can aid his or her employer by talking about the problems encountered to see if there is some solution. If that does not work, try watching the dictator dictate. You might find the following problem-causing areas: eating while dictating, speaking directly into the mike and not across the mike as one should, having an "intimate conversation" with the mike (resulting in a low-pitched, quiet, sultry, and inaudible voice), stretching arms out with microphone in one of them (resulting in fade-in and fade-out). A little lecture from the salesperson who gave the original presentation on the equipment is often very helpful. There might be some features of the equipment that the dictator has forgotten existed or has never used or perhaps didn't know were there in the first place. Many dictators neglect to use the indicator strip, and the transcriptionist should explain how important this is and why. Some dictators do not understand how to dictate and think they have to keep up with the machine or leave it on while thinking of what to say. This results in poor copy. Some dictators mislead the transcriptionist by dropping their voices as if they were finished and then going on with an "and" or a "but." You may help the dictator by tactfully letting him or her know about such problems. In a hospital setting where one does not have an opportunity to interact with the dictator, the supervisor and medical transcriptionists might prepare a check sheet for the dictator or an orientation packet for the new dictator giving hints, suggestions, policies, procedures, and so forth.

The transcriptionist should be sure that the dictator's equipment is always prepared for use. It should be plugged in, and the medium, such as tape, belt, disk, or cassette, should be properly installed. One should remove the medium as soon as the dictator completes recording and install a new indicator strip and medium immediately, so the dictator can work if he or she wishes. To avoid misplaced patient's charts and to make dictating easier, a flow sheet can be designed for the physician's specialty. After a patient is seen, the sheet is removed from the patient's chart and placed inside a plastic sleeve. At the end of the day, place the accumulated pile of sheets into the physi-

cian's briefcase along with the portable dictation equipment. Thus, the physician can dictate at the hospital, at home, or wherever he or she may be and will not have to remove the patient's chart from the office. Another problem is the confusion of dictated tapes with transcribed tapes, which often results in tapes being transcribed again. The physician can be asked to apply a small, removable colored dot to the media that is ready for transcription. After the tape has been transcribed, the transcriptionist removes the dot. Thus, it becomes easy to distinguish the media that have been transcribed from those that have not.

Let your employer know if the dictation is good. Don't just scold—praise good dictation and show that you appreciate the punctuation, the clearly enunciated words, the nicely modulated voice, the paragraph indications, and so forth.

The following are some hints to aid the person dictating:

1. Indicate what is being transcribed (such as a letter, memo, report, rough draft, or form letter) and on what kind of paper it should be typed (letterhead, personal stationery, or colored paper).

2. Indicate the number of copies needed.

3. Give the names of the patient and the person for whom the item is intended, and spell out the names if they are difficult to ascertain.

4. Dictate the street address, city, state, and zip code to which the correspondence is being sent when this is not readily available to the transcriptionist.

5. Separate the ideas into paragraphs. Spell a word that you think the typist might have difficulty understanding.

6. Call the paragraphs by stating after the first paragraph "period paragraph."

7. Remember to say *comma* specifically where you want the reader to pause.

8. Indicate when a word is a plural, needs quotes, parentheses ("paren open and paren closed"), indentations, columns, or subparagraphs.

9. If dictating a form, keep a blank copy of the form in front of you while dictating.

10. Eliminate extraneous sounds such as "ugh," "um," "eh," "and," "that." Remember to speak slowly and clearly. Don't slur word endings. Add a personal touch to the end of the tape by saying "thank you" to the transcriptionist. This will certainly make the transcriptionist feel he or she is a valuable part of the team.

Table 2–2 will assist you in solving problem dictation.

TABLE 2-2. DICTATION PROBLEM SOLVING

PROBLEM	SOLUTION
Fast dictation	Decrease the speed of the dictation if words and phrases are running together
	Write out slurred phrases phonetically and separate the syllables to try to form words
Foreign accent	Get a copy of a report by the same physician dictated and transcribed previously and compare words and phrases
	Distinguish the accent and substitute the correct sound to identify the word
Garbled word	Increase or decrease dictation speed and relisten
	Relisten on audio speaker
	Ask someone else to listen
	Leave a blank, continue transcribing, and listen for the word to be dictated again within the transcript
Mumbled dictation	Increase the tone control
	Clean the recording head with a cleaning cassette tape
Static obscures dictaton	Decrease the tone control
Unfamiliar word	Look up the word in a medical or English dictonary
	Use the Sound and Word Finder Table in Appendix B

TRANSCRIPTION PREPARATION

Here are some suggestions to help you organize and plan your work before you begin to transcribe and to help you increase your efficiency and production.

1. Gather all necessary information and materials at your desk.

2. Make sure the headset, earphones (or amplifier), and foot control are attached to the unit and comfortably positioned.

3. Verify that the unit is operating properly, plugged in, and turned on.

4. Insert the medium. Priority (STAT) reports are transcribed immediately. Then the oldest dictation is transcribed and the most recent dictation typed last.

5. Insert the indicator strip and estimate the length of the report or letter and listen for special instructions or comments.

6. Listen to the instructions or cue in to see if there are corrections by scanning the media.

7. Adjust the volume, *tone,* and speed controls to your taste. Remember too slow a speed will only distort the sound.

8. Adjust the typewriter margins and tabulator stops.

9. Select the paper and note how many copies are necessary.

Remember: Listen to *all* instructions *before* beginning to transcribe, since failure to do so may result in redoing the work. Punctuate as you go and leave a blank space for words that you do not understand. Attach notes to your transcript for any unclear phrases or sentences. See Chapter 7, for help in flagging unfamiliar copy. The more you transcribe, the more you will retain in memory when coordinating listening and typing. Save the dictation until after the physician reads and signs the report in case a problem or question arises.

EQUIPMENT FOR THE PHYSICALLY CHALLENGED

Several methods have been developed to make it easier for the blind or visually handicapped medical secretary. One of the simplest solutions enables the secretary to "read" where he or she is on the margin scale and to set tab stops. A strip of plastic tape with dots on it is used to replace the margin scale. The dots on this strip are equivalent to the braille ruler and are easily recognized by the blind typist. By feeling where the point is against the dots, the typist is able to set margins and tabulator stops.

A blind person wishing to take notes may use a mechanical brailler known as the Perkins' Brailler. This employs six keys to emboss the proper configuration of the six dots in the braille cell (raised dot) system. A correction is made by rubbing out the incorrect cell dots.

A partially sighted typist can produce perfect letters and reports by using a video magnifier. This system comes in two parts: a movable stand with a high-powered lens focused on it and a small-to-medium-sized closed circuit television (CCTV) screen where the material on the stand is magnified and enlarged. By adjusting the primary lens, the typist can enlarge the copy on the stand to any size suitable to his or her visual needs. The screen can be switched from a black background with white letters to the reverse. There are also brightness, color contrast, and zoom features. A split-screen facility allows simultaneous viewing on the screen of both the copy and the typewritten version. Some systems have models that work effectively with word processing machines that have CRTs. The video magnifier transmits what appears on the CRT screen to the magnifier's screen. Working with either of these machines, the typist with poor vision can type rough-draft copy, correct it, and complete the job in a normal time period.

The Optacon, or OPtical to TActile CONverter, is a device that allows a blind person to read any printed

2

material. It consists of a small portable case with a removable electronic eye. The case is designed to allow a person's hand to be inside, with the index finger resting on a transmitter plate so that the person can feel the images. With experience, a typist can read an $8\frac{1}{2} \times 11$ inch page of single-spaced copy in a matter of minutes. A cross-bar attachment can be placed on a typewriter so that another Optacon model can rest on top of it. This allows a blind typist to read and correct while the paper is still in the typewriter and to produce final copy. Optacon has a model for those who work with a word processor and a CRT that enables the blind typist to read the luminous display of a CRT. Future developments are a portable module that can be added to an Optacon to convert the output into natural-sounding synthetic speech and an automatic scanning system with voice output. The portable module voice accessory is available in both hand-scanning and automatic-scanning versions.

To eliminate the need to have other employees proofread text produced by a blind typist on a word processor, *voice synthesizers* have been developed. A blind terminal user can hear the information that is displayed on the screen and can learn how to operate the machine by listening to cassette-recorded instructions or by braille writing. Usually, the audio output formats available on such systems include the following:

1. *Pronounce* format. The contents of the screen are read in the same way as you would read a book, with each word pronounced separately but without incorporating punctuation. Numbers are announced individually, so that one-hundred and thirty-two would be announced "one, three, two."

2. *Punctuate* format. This is similar to the pronounce format. In addition, single or double spaces are identified by a sound (the number of spaces are given if more than two), and punctuation marks are also announced.

3. *Spell* format. All words are spelled out, spaces and capital letters are identified, number of spaces or repeated characters are given, and punctuation marks are announced. In cases of similar-sounding letters, the operator can select spelling using the international alphabet, such as L for Lima, I for India, and so forth.

Speech can be slowed to aid transcription or sped up for casual scanning of data. Words can be spoken in monotone or with intonation on some systems. Some machines use a keypad to control the audio output, or when the operator's hands are busy, an external foot switch can be used. The cursor is positioned on the screen, and then the machine reads out the row number and column number. It will read the word at, before, or after the cursor; it can read the entire row on which the cursor is located, the row before it, or the row after it; or the complete screen can be read out. It is easy to go back and verify something not understood by backspacing and then changing the output format from *pronounce* to *punctuate* or *spell*.

Braille-Edit is a sophisticated word processing program that enables blind and sighted people to work together in using the power of microcomputers. This program is used by a number of medical transcriptionists and works with voice or braille devices. A user can hear material entered by letter, word, phrase, or section, and material can be entered on a braille device, such as the VersaBraille (a paperless brailler). This program provides a broad range of translation, formating, and printing operations. It can set up "transformation chapters" in which certain characters can be removed and replaced by other characters. For example, "qqra" could be replaced by a long medical phrase. The "transformation chapters" can be prestored and invoked by name. Thus, you can enter some medical phrases using a personal abbreviation and obtain a printout of regular text. Braille-Edit has many additional features for blind, partially sighted, or sighted persons too numerous to mention here.

Another aid for medical transcriptionists who are blind or visually impaired is the series of ridges located in the upper right corner when side one of a Norelco minicassette or "ultra" minicassette is facing the user. This allows quick determination of the cassette side being used.

Photocopy equipment has also been developed to produce raised copy images, such as raised-relief maps, drawings, and braille writing. Illustrations enhance the learning process, and such equipment decreases the cost and time involved in producing documents for the vision-impaired.

For further reference information, refer to Appendix C.

FAX MACHINES

Facsimile (Fax) machines are used by clinics and physician's offices to send and/or obtain charts, electrocardiogram (ECG) tracings, laboratory reports, letters, medical reports, and insurance claims; for ordering supplies; and so forth. Hospitals use them to transmit within the facility, such as medical records, laboratory and pathology reports, prescriptions to the hospital pharmacy, surgical scheduling, patient admissions, patient room scheduling, ECGs, face sheets, medical staff committee meetings, and so forth. Pharmacies send physicians requests and confirm orders, and physicians send prescription orders. Information can also be sent and/or received from medical libraries, attorneys, accountants, financial advisors, or vendors of medical and office supplies. Transcription services offer fax as a benefit for fast turnaround of medical reports since documents can be faxed from the service to different floors within a hospital facility, from physician's office to the hospital across town, or around the world within a few minutes.

A fax machine is connected to a telephone line. A document is scanned, and this converts the image to electronic impulses for transmitting over telephone lines. The receiving fax machine converts the impulses back to an identical hard copy of the original, and a printed copy is generated. Fax machines print on plain paper or thermally treated paper, but because thermal paper fades on exposure to sunlight, it is wise to photocopy important documents using bond paper. Thermal paper also has a tendency to curl at the edges, so if the appearance of a document is crucial, you may prefer to use an overnight-delivery service instead of fax. Many fax machines generate open document communications, so someone must be assigned to secure incoming documents to provide for confidentiality. Some personal computer–based fax boards solve the security problem for sending and receiving documents because these boards give personal computers the ability to function like stand-alone fax machines. Thus, the documents are printed on quality bond paper and have very good image quality.

Many features are available for fax machines, the most useful being user and receiver confidentiality, automatic dialer, automatic document cutter, document feeder, 9,600 baud or bits per second (bps) transmission speed, half-tone or gray-scale mode, full-size (328′) paper roll, plain paper printing, auto-dialers, and delayed broadcasting for sending documents when phone tolls are low.

When sending confidential material such as medical or legal records, telephone the recipient before faxing the information so that he or she can stand by. Incoming documents may be available for inspection by anyone at the receiving end and the fax may be unmanned. Begin every transmission with a cover sheet (a half-sheet size is sufficient) detailing the sender (name, phone number, and fax number), the number of pages being sent, who is to receive the transmission (name and address), and any other information that will help get the fax to the proper person. Include a telephone number to call in case there is a problem with the transmission, such as a lost page or dropped line. A handy hint is to make up a standard cover sheet letter on the employer's stationery and enclose it in a clear plastic sleeve (one that will allow you to fax a cover sheet within it). Fill in the information on the plastic sleeve with a dry erasable marker, using the cover sheet in between it as your

guide. After completing it, check to make sure the markings are dry, then fax. When the fax is complete, erase the cover information from the plastic sleeve with a blackboard eraser and put it aside for the next fax transmission. If you are concerned about clarity, test your material by making a copy on your fax machine before you send that important document. Perhaps you may have to make a photocopy of the document or enlarge the document on your copy machine and transmit the copied page. If the document contains numbers, type the numbers using words to avoid misinterpretation. Do not use color on fax documents without making a test copy. Dark colors can block copy and sometimes slow transmission. Do not use correction tape or fluid on documents to be faxed. Always remove paper clips and staples to prevent damaging the fax machine. If the original document has copy near the left or right edges of the page, position the paper in such a way so the entire image will reproduce. Learn your fax's error messages and how to correct the problems that caused them. Noise or interference from telephone lines can garble your message requiring you to resend or slow down the transmission rate. Be sure the transmission has been completed before you leave the fax machine.

PHOTOCOPYING MACHINES

Every office should have some type of copying equipment. There is a great variety of equipment that may use dry heat, fluid, special paper, or plain bond paper. Some machines copy only single sheets, whereas others copy pages from magazines or books as well as single sheets. It is important to make sure you invest wisely and purchase the equipment that will fit your particular needs. The copies are representative of you and your office, and a machine should be selected that produces the copies that most closely look like your original. Since some copiers take special paper, which can be expensive, it is important to investigate those that can take any type of paper. Speed of copying may be another essential factor to consider. Before purchasing new equipment, you should discuss upkeep, ease of operation, and rate of breakdown with other owners. Special opaquing fluid specifically formulated for correcting copies can be obtained from your local stationers.

VOCABULARY

Audio device: Any computer device that produces sound. See *Voice synthesizer*.

Backup: A copy of a file that is kept in case the original file is destroyed.

2

Bit (binary digit): The smallest unit of information recognized by a computer.

Byte: A given number of bits considered as a unit of computer storage. (A byte is to a bit what a word is to a single letter.)

Cassette: A magnetic tape wound on two reels encased in a plastic or metal container that can be mounted on or inserted in a tape recording or playback device.

Cathode ray tube (CRT): A television screen attached to word processing equipment. See *Video display terminal (VDT).*

Character: Usually synonymous with byte. Also, a letter, symbol, or number contained in a text.

Command key: A key that enters a particular command into a word processing system. Also called control or function key.

Continuous form stationery: Forms, letterhead, or envelopes joined in a series of accordion-pleated folds and used in printers.

Copy: Text material in typed or printed form.

Crash: Sudden and complete failure of all or a substantial part of a system. See also *Head crash.*

Cue tone indexing: Inserting information magnetically onto a medium for the purpose of making corrections, deletions, or pertinent notes.

Cursor: A lighted indicator on a CRT screen that shows the place for entering new text or making editing changes.

Cut and paste: A term that means moving a segment of one document into another. The Wang system refers to this as Supercopy.

Daisy printwheel: A printwheel resembling a flat disk with the keyboard characters around the circumference.

Data: Information that can be processed or produced by a computer.

Delete: A command in word processing that removes a specific section of text from the recording medium.

Digital dictation: The process whereby the dictated voice is digitized (converted to a string of O's and I's representing the audio waveform) and stored as data on a computer disk. When instantly and selectively assessed from a dictation/transcription station or telephone, the binary digits are converted back to analog waveform sound.

Disk: A magnetic storage device made of rigid material (hard disk) or flexible plastic (floppy disk).

Disk drive: A device that holds the disk, retrieves information from it, and saves information on it.

Disk operating system (DOS): A program that controls the loading and storage of files from and to a computer's memory and to a magnetic disk.

Display: 1. Text appearing on a CRT screen. 2. The act of commanding a CRT-equipped word processing system to produce specified text on its screen.

Document assembly: Device that allows combining of prerecorded text with keyboarded text, combining of selections from prerecorded text to form a new document, and inserting of names and addresses to create a number of nearly identical documents.

Dot matrix printer: An impact printer that prints characters composed of many dots.

Dual pitch: A typewriter that can convert to pica or elite type spacing.

Editing: To revise and correct text (read back, scan, delete, insert, reformat) before final document printout.

Electronic mail system (EMS): Transmission of letters and reports from one computer to another via telephone lines.

Electronic typewriter: An electric typewriter featuring memory, programmable formating, correction capabilities, letter-quality printing, external storage, and so forth.

Element: The spherical component, resembling a golf ball, used on certain electric typewriters to print the keyboard characters.

Elite: A size of type for typewriters, measuring 12 characters to the linear inch.

Endless loop: A system in which the first tape head records, spilling tape into a storage channel until the transcriptionist activates the second head, which draws the recorded tape from the channel and passes it through and around the loop for reuse by the same or a different dictator

Equipment service contract: Routine maintenance and emergency repair services provided for a set fee per year.

Ergonomics: The science of adapting working environment, conditions, and equipment to suit workers.

Error-free: A characteristic of recording on magnetic media that allows correction of errors by recording over unwanted material.

Facsimile machine: A machine connected to a telephone line and electrical wall outlet that scans a document's image, transmits and/or receives and prints an exact facsimile. Also called Fax.

Fast forward: A tape recorder feature that permits the tape to be run rapidly in normal-play direction for search purposes.

Fidelity: The degree of accuracy with which sound is reproduced.

File: A single, stored unit of information that is given a file name so it can be accessed.

Floppy disk: See *Disk.*

Font: The size and style of type.

Global search and replace: The ability of a word processing system to change a word or other text element everywhere it appears in a document, with one instruction. Also called *global change.*

Hard copy: Written, typed, or printed matter; a document.

Hardware: The physical components (electrical, electronic, magnetic, and mechanical devices) of a computer system, which, combined with software (programs, instruction, and so forth), create a system.

Head crash: When the read/write head of a disk drive flies above the disk and strikes the surface, severely damaging it. See *Crash.*

Index counter: A fast forward feature with numerical display on the tape recorder or transcription machine that is used for search purposes; digital counter.

Initialize: To prepare the magnetic surface of a blank diskette so that it can accept data. This is sometimes referred to as formating the disk.

Input: Information entered into a system to be processed.

Insert: A word processing function allowing introduction of new material within previously recorded text.

Justification: The adjustment of spacing in a line of type to produce a right margin that is flush to a specific measurement.

K (kilobyte): A symbol that refers to 1024 bytes or units of memory, i.e., 64 K means 64 times 1024 bytes or 65,536 bytes, not 64,000.

Keyboarding: Like typing, but including the extra instruction keys of a word processing machine.

Light pen: A computer input device that looks like a pen on a string. It allows an operator to "draw" images on the screen of a VDT, mark choices on a displayed menu, add/delete displayed text, and so forth.

Medium (plural: Media): Material on which information can be recorded.

Memory: The section of the computer where instructions, data, and information are stored; also called *storage* and *internal* or *main memory.*

Memory typewriter: A device into which data can be entered, held, and retrieved at a later time.

Menu: In word processing, a list of items displayed on a CRT from which the typist can choose the

word processing function to be performed. Also known as *prompt.*

Merge: Document assembly, such as combining prerecorded text with keyboarded text, combining selections from prerecorded text to form a new document, and inserting names and addresses to create a number of nearly identical documents.

Modem: Acronym for MOdulator DEModulator unit. A modem is a device that converts data into signals for telephone transmission and then (at the receiving end) back again into data.

Mouse: A hand-held computer input device, separate from a keyboard, used to control cursor position on a VDT.

Network dictation: See *Endless loop.*

On-line processing: A system composed of a CPU, a communications linkage, a terminal, and a user that interact to carry out a task.

Output: The final results after recorded information is processed, revised, and printed out.

Pagination: The automatic renumbering of pages in a document.

Patching: A method of transferring recorded material from one tape or card to another.

Peripheral: Any input, output, or storage device (hardware) connected to the computer, such as disks, CRT terminals, or printers.

Pica: A size of type, 10 point, which is larger than elite type, measuring 10 characters to the linear inch.

Platen: The roller against which the keys strike.

Playback: 1. Listening to recorded dictation. 2. Automatic typing out of recorded text from a word processing machine.

Power typing: A system that allows the typist to type at maximum or "rough draft" speed without concern for errors. These are corrected by backspacing and typing over to produce a perfect recording from which an error-free document is automatically printed out.

Printwheel: A typing element, daisy printwheel, or thimble used on word processing printer units.

Program: See *Software.*

Program instruction: A code or command keyboarded into a word processing typewriter causing the equipment to respond as desired.

Programmed search: A word processing feature that automatically puts together parts from separate recorded material. Also called *random assembly.*

Ragged text: Text that does not align flush with the left and/or right margin of the page.

RAM: Random access memory. Memory that can be

2

stored in any order and can be accessed immediately.

Random assembly: See *Programed search.*

Response time: The time a word processing system takes to react to a given input.

Retrieve: Finding stored information from the archive diskette to the word processing diskette.

ROM: Read-only memory. Memory that can be accessed but not modified.

Reverse index: A word processing feature that allows for superscript or subscript.

Scanner: A machine or hand-held device that converts text or a printed image into a format readable by the computer and printer. Also referred to as optical character reader (OCR).

Scanning: To locate quickly, listening to a specific part of a recorded dictation by moving the sound head across a magnetic belt.

Scrolling: The ability to move the text vertically and horizontally and to flip pages of a document on a CRT screen.

Search: The function of a text-editing typewriter in which referenced material is located on a magnetic tape.

Software: This refers to programs or instructions used to support a piece of equipment, as opposed to the equipment itself or hardware.

Stand-alone word processor: Equipment that can operate independently, i.e., outside of the control of a CPU.

Stop code: To embed a code in a document that signals the printer to stop.

Telecommunications: The transmission of information between widely separated locations by means of electric or electromagnetic systems such as telephone or telegraph.

Terminal: In word processing, often a reference to a communicating typewriter.

Text editing: A type of equipment in which the typist keyboards only new material and instructs the machine to skip unwanted text already recorded. The revised document is then printed out automatically from the stored material.

Thimble: A cylindrical typing element used on certain word processing printer units.

Tone control: A feature on transcribing equipment used to vary treble and bass response during playback.

Touch-sensitive video screen: The user gives instructions to a computer by pointing to a picture on the screen instead of keyboarding.

Transcription: Conversion by a secretary of recorded dictation to hard copy.

Tuning: Alignment of a sound head with the track on the recording medium.

Utility program: A general-purpose software program that performs activities (i.e., initializing a disk) which are not specific to an application.

Video display terminal (VDT): See *Cathode ray tube (CRT).*

Voice activation: Ability of a machine to recognize and respond to spoken words.

Voice recognition: The ability of a computer system (equipped with sound sensors) to translate the tones of the human voice into computer commands.

Voice synthesizer: A device that allows the computer to respond orally. It is used by the visually impaired medical transcriptionist. Also called *Audio device.*

Warranty: A written statement from the manufacturer regarding responsibility for replacement and repair of a piece of equipment over a specified period of time.

Window: An area on a VDT screen in use that gives a view of additional files or portions of files other than those currently being edited on-screen.

Word processing (WP): A combination of people, procedures, and equipment that transforms ideas into printed communications and helps facilitate the flow of related office work.

Word Processing Center: The room with equipment and personnel for processing written communications.

Word wraparound: A feature in which a word processor can automatically carry a word that has more characters than will fit at the end of a line over to the beginning of the next line on the display screen. Thus, the operator does not have to enter a return command at the end of each line.

 2–1: REVIEW TEST

Directions: Complete the following statements by filling in the blanks.

1. Name two out of four kinds of typewriters.

    a. _____

2

b. _____

2. Name seven working characteristics to reduce typewriter, word processor, or computer fatigue and tension and increase productivity.

a. _____

b. _____

c. _____

d. _____

e. _____

f. _____

g. _____

3. Name two of the seven types of dictation/transcription equipment available.

a. _____

b. _____

4. In regard to transcription preparation, what is the most important thing to do to prevent retyping a report or letter? _____

_____

5. Match the definitions in the first column with their correct terms in the second column. Place letters on blanks.

_____	Refers to 1024 bytes or units of memory.	a. fidelity
_____	Printout of material recorded from a word processing machine.	b. warranty
_____	Alignment of the sound head with the track on the recording medium.	c. elite
_____	Information entered into a system to be processed.	d. playback
_____	Adjustment of spacing in a line of type to produce a right margin flush to a specific measurement.	e. media
_____	The degree of accuracy with which sound is reproduced.	f. kilobyte (K)
_____	Materials on which information can be recorded.	g. cassette
_____	A size of type for typewriters measuring 12 characters to the linear inch.	h. tuning
_____	A reel of magnetic tape in a container that feeds the tape into an automatic typewriter.	i. input
_____	Written statement from manufacturer stating responsibility for equipment replacement and repair.	j. justification
_____	Magnetic tape, wound on 2 reels and encased, which is inserted in a dictation and/or transcription device.	k. output
_____	Final results after recorded information is processed, revised, or printed out.	

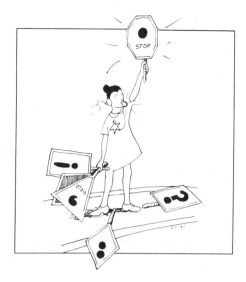

Punctuation

OBJECTIVES

After reading this chapter and working the exercises, you should be able to

1. demonstrate the ability to use reference materials to select the proper punctuation needed in unfamiliar copy.
2. list, in your own words, the reasons for the accurate use of punctuation marks.
3. state the grammatical terms for different parts of speech and for the various parts of a sentence; match these terms with a written example.
4. use the vocabulary of punctuation by writing the rule, using your own words and the proper terms, while working with an illustration of the rule in use.
5. demonstrate the ability to use proper punctuation marks accurately, by inserting punctuation into unpunctuated copy.

INTRODUCTION

Transcriptionists have more trouble with punctuation than with any other aspect of document preparation. To add to the confusion, many authoritative reference books disagree with one another and with common usage. Thus the following rules and exercises adhere to not only traditional guidelines but also popular contemporary lay magazines and medical journals.

Since proper punctuation is vital to business writing and document preparation, this summary is included to help you establish the rules in your mind so that you will acquire good punctuation habits. Proper punctuation helps the reader understand which items belong together, when to pause, or what is being emphasized. Some of us never learned to punctuate correctly, and many keyboard operators add a comma when it seems time for the reader to take a breath!

Without proper punctuation, communication simply breaks down, meaning can be lost or distorted, or the flow of ideas is interrupted. For example, the comma is used to clarify the meaning for the reader; therefore, comma misuse may either mislead the reader or delay his or her comprehension. Undoubtedly you have seen sentences whose meaning changes when a comma is moved.

In reviewing, remember that punctuation is often simple; but also keep in mind that it is not always subject to precise and unchanging rules. Certain punctuation marks are simply common practice, so if you rely on *common sense* you may not always be right.

Finally, because this chapter is not, and cannot be, a guide to proper punctuation under all circumstances, a professional writer, typist, or transcriptionist should have a comprehensive guide book in his or her desk library. (A list of suggested references appears in Appendix C.)

VOCABULARY

The following terms will be used freely and without further definition in the rules that follow, so you should be quite comfortable with them.

Subject: That part of a sentence about which something is being said. This part is properly called the *complete subject,* but within the complete subject there is always a word or group of words that is the principal word within the complete subject and is called the *simple subject.* The subject is usually a noun or pronoun.

Noun/pronoun: The name of a person, place or thing.

> **Example:** My *goal* is to become a certified medical transcriptionist.
> **Example:** A year after she started working, *Janet* was promoted. (Because the subject may appear at almost any point in a sentence, it is usually easier to locate it if you pick out the verb first.)

Verb: A word or group of words that express action or otherwise help to make a statement.

> **Example:** Instructors *may be* critical of students' work.
> **Example:** The patient *was admitted* at 6 a.m.

Clause: A group of words containing a subject and a verb.

> **Example:** Everyone *who is learning to transcribe* should study punctuation.
> **Example:** Routine laboratory studies *which we carried out on admission* disclosed a white count of 19,200.

> NOTE: *Routine laboratory studies* is the complete subject of the sentence, and *disclosed* is the verb.

Independent Clause: A group of words containing a subject and a verb, making a complete statement, and able to stand alone as a complete sentence.

> **Example:** *There was a small area of fibrotic scarring* involving the right uterosacral ligament.

> NOTE: In this example *there* is the subject, and *was* is the verb.

Sentence: A group of words containing a subject and a verb, making a complete statement, and able to stand alone. The subject need not always be expressed but may be understood.

> **Example:** Get this to the lab stat. (The subject "you" is understood.)

Compound Sentence: Two or more independent clauses together make up a compound sentence.

> **Example:** *I understand that you will complete the history and physical for the admission,* and *I will order the preoperative evaluation.*
> **Example:** *Good English skills are essential to the secretary,* and *she will study hard to ensure her success.*

Dependent Clause: A group of words containing a subject and a verb that depends on some other word or words in the sentence for completeness of meaning.

> **Example:** He is a patient *who must have general anesthesia* because he does not respond normally to routine dental care.
> **Example:** Many students find transcribing easy *because they have prepared themselves well for it.*

> NOTE: In this example, *Many students find transcribing easy* is the independent clause, and *because they have prepared themselves well for it* is the dependent clause. This is one of the common ways that sentences are formed. Notice how the dependent clause *depends* on other words for completeness of meaning.

Introductory Phrase: A group of words that occurs at the beginning of a sentence. This phrase can be thought of as being out of order or transposed in the sentence.

> **Example:** *By now,* you should have decided what courses you will need for graduation.

> NOTE: The simple order of the sentence would be *You should have decided what courses you will need for graduation by now.*

> **Example:** *In view of the continuing excessive tone in the plantar flexor muscles,* it will be necessary to continue with orthotic control.

Essential: A word, phrase, or clause that is vital to the meaning of the sentence. Sometimes these are called "restrictive."

> **Example:** Everyone *employed in the Medical Records Department* received a commendation from the administrator.
> **Example:** The patient *who was born with a meningomyelocele* underwent closure of his spinal dysrhaphia in the newborn period.

Nonessential: A word, phrase, or clause that is not vital to the meaning of the sentence and simply provides explanatory material. Sometimes these are called "nonrestrictive."

3

Example: Marlene Bruno, *who took medical terminology with me last semester,* is on the Dean's List.

NOTE: It is interesting that Marlene Bruno took *medical terminology* with the writer, but it is not essential or vital to the meaning of the sentence.

Example: The patient's weight was 83.5 kg, *up presumably as a result of inactivity,* and his height was 166 cm.

Parenthetical Expression: An interrupting group of words that does not change or contribute to the meaning of a sentence. It may appear at the beginning, middle, or end of the sentence. It is always nonessential.

Example: It is important, *as you know,* for medical records to be typed accurately.

Example: I do not question the diagnosis; *however,* review of his urinalysis and culture is negative.

NOTE: Some very common parenthetical expressions are *therefore, however, furthermore, in my opinion, strictly speaking, for example, in the first place, on the other hand.*

Appositive: A noun or pronoun that closely follows another noun or pronoun to restate, rename, explain, or clarify it. It may be essential or nonessential. An appositive must always consist of a word or words that can be directly substituted for the noun or pronoun it follows.

Example: Dr. Pappin, *my employer,* prefers to dictate all chart notes.

Example: This one-month-old male child, *a Hmong Laotian,* was admitted via the Emergency Room with a cough, fever, and congestion.

Conjunction: A word that connects other words, phrases, or clauses.

Examples: *and, or, for, nor, so, but, yet*

Sometimes parenthetical expressions are used as conjunctions also.

Examples: *however, furthermore, therefore.*

 3–1: SELF-STUDY

Directions: Examine the sentences or parts of sentences that follow and write the part of the sentence or phrase that is requested on the line provided. The first exercise is completed for you.

1. Furthermore, I feel that a well-trained medical transcriptionist should be very well paid.

    Subject of the sentence   I

    Parenthetical expression   furthermore

    Independent clause   I feel that a well-trained medical transcriptionist should be very well paid.

    Appositive   none in this sentence

2. I appreciate my understanding of medical terminology.

    Subject of the sentence _____

    Independent clause _____

3. Please return this to Medical Records as soon as possible.

    Subject of the sentence _____

    Independent clause _____

4. After spending five hours in the operating room, the patient was sent to the recovery room.

    Introductory phrase _____

    Subject of the sentence _____

    Independent clause _____

3

5. The patient is a well-developed, well-nourished black female and reported that she has been well until this time.

Subject of the sentence _____

Independent clause _____

Dependent clause _____

Appositive _____

Conjunction _____

6. Joan, the medical secretary, and Beth, the file clerk, are taking an evening college course in medical ethics.

Subject _____

Independent clause _____

_____

Appositive 1 _____

Appositive 2 _____

Parenthetical expression _____

7. The reception room is well lighted and stocked with current literature, so the patients do not mind their wait to see Dr. Jordan, who never seems to arrive on time.

First subject _____

Independent clause _____

_____

Second subject _____

Independent clause _____

_____

Conjunction joining independent clauses _____

Appositive _____

Nonessential clause _____

8. There is overwhelming evidence, however, to prove that the ability to spell is vital to success in this field.

Independent clause _____

Parenthetical expression _____

Appositive _____

9. The American Association for Medical Transcription, the national organization for medical transcriptionists, has a business and educational meeting every month.

Subject _____

Independent clause _____

_____

Appositive _____

Parenthetical expression _____

Conjunction joining two independent clauses _____

3

10. Perfection, not speed, is the key word in medical transcription skills.

Subject _____

Verb _____

Independent clause _____

Appositive _____

Parenthetical expression _____

Nonessential phrase _____

11. Hospital transcriptionists often need to.

Subject _____

Independent clause _____

12. When you telephone the hospital, please have the patient's complete name, address, and telephone number and the admitting diagnosis.

Subject _____

Verb _____

Independent clause _____

_____

Nonessential phrase _____

Introductory clause _____

Conjunction joining words in a series _____

13. Appointment scheduling, contrary to what you might think, requires skill; it should be, and can be, a real art.

Independent clause _____

_____

Nonessential clause or phrase _____

Parenthetical expression _____

14. A perfectly typed resume, well-planned and prepared, should accompany your letter of application.

Independent clause _____

_____

Introductory phrase _____

Nonessential phrase _____

15. He walks with his heel down with a varus tendency in the ankle but with no severe problem.

Independent clause _____

Dependent clause _____

Conjunction joining two independent clauses _____

16. To minimize the chance of overlooking a recurrence of the infection, a CBC and sed rate were carried out today.

Subject _____

Independent clause _____

Introductory phrase _____

Nonessential phrase _____

NOTE: After you have completed the entire exercise, check your answers to the problems with those on page 76 of this chapter. Review the vocabulary if you have made any errors.

PUNCTUATION

The Comma

The comma is the most used mark of punctuation and often causes the most problems for writers. At the same time, it is a very important aid in clarifying the meaning for the reader. Commas should be used appropriately and sparingly. Therefore it is important to learn the rules for proper placement. Once the basic rules have been learned, the rest of the punctuation marks should cause little problem.

RULE 3.1   Use a comma, or pair of commas, to set off nonessential words, phrases, or clauses from the rest of the sentence.

These may also be called *parenthetical expressions* or *nonrestrictive phrases*. We need to take some time and examine them carefully.

> **Example:** Nonessential clause
> Paul Otis, *who had a coronary last year,* came in for an examination today.

You may test yourself to be sure this is nonessential by asking the question: "Do I need to know which Paul Otis?" Unless we have several or even two patients with this name, we can say that the clause is nonessential to the meaning of the sentence. When you are in doubt, ask yourself if you need to know *which one.*

> **Example:** *Nonessential phrase*
> Please notice, *for example,* the depth of the incision.

> **Example:** *Nonessential word*
> Type this, *please,* before you leave this afternoon.

> **Example:** *Parenthetical expression*
> She should have, *in my opinion,* immediate surgery.

NOTE: Nonessential or nonrestrictive descriptive phrases or clauses add information that is *not* essential to the meaning of the sentence. However, do not enclose essential material within commas. (This essential material will indicate who, what, why, when, or where.)

Example
I want to examine all of the children, *when they have been prepared.* (incorrect)
I want to examine all of the children when they have been prepared. (correct)
Medical staff members, *who fail to attend the meeting,* will lose their consulting privileges. (incorrect)
Medical staff members who fail to attend the meeting will lose their consulting privileges. (correct)

Do not create a comma fault by leaving out one of the commas when a pair is required.
> Her temperature, *which has been high* fell suddenly. (incorrect)
> Her temperature, *which has been high,* fell suddenly. (correct)

NOTE: Many people often have difficulty with correct usage of *who/whom/whose, that,* and *which* as function words in essential and nonessential clauses.
Who/Whom/Whose is used in both essential and nonessential clauses.
That is used in essential clauses.
Which is generally used in nonessential clauses.

Example
This is a 26-year-old male *who* cut his left index finger on a pocket knife.
The patients *whose* Pap smears are Class II must be notified.
She twisted her left knee, *which* has an artificial prosthesis in it.
The recommendation *that* she undergo radiation therapy was rejected by the family.

RULE 3.1a   Nonessential appositives are separated from the rest of the sentence by commas.

> **Example:** *Appositive*
> John Munor, *your patient,* was admitted to Center City Hospital today.
> Laralyn Abbott, *the head nurse,* summoned me to the phone.

As with phrases and clauses, these may be essential to the complete meaning of the sentence, and then they must not be separated from the rest of the sentence by commas. Remember to ask yourself if you need to know *which one.*

Example: *Essential appositive*
Your patient Ralph Swansdown died at 3:45 a.m.

Notice that if *Ralph Swansdown* is separated from the rest of the sentence with a pair of commas, it appears that the person being addressed by this remark had only one patient, the lately deceased, Mr. Swansdown. It *is essential* to know *which* patient. Likewise, one-word appositives do not require commas.

Example
I *myself* will stay late and finish the report.

Example
My cousin *Pat* just became a certified medical transcriptionist.

RULE 3.1b   Use a comma, or pair of commas, to set off a short parenthetical expression from the rest of the sentence.

These expressions may begin, interrupt, or end a sentence and are always nonessential.

Example
However, I want this report typed.
I want this report typed, *however.*

These comma pairs can also be used to draw emphasis to a nonessential expression. The rule is not superseded in this case, of course.

Example
He is an excellent surgeon, *whether or not you care for my opinion,* and I feel that you must trust his judgment.

To restate these three similar rules: Set off nonessential words from the main body of thought. Commas must be placed before and after such words, phrases, or clauses. If they occur at the beginning of a sentence a single comma follows the expression. Your ability to recognize the difference between essential words, phrases, or clauses and those that are nonessential is important. Remember that an essential or restrictive element identifies or further defines the meaning of the sentence and must *not* be separated from the sentence; a nonessential element is separated.

3–2: Self-Study

Directions: Using Rule 3–1 and its subtopics A and B, add a comma or comma pair to the following sentences where required. Be careful not to enclose essential sentence parts. In the space provided, briefly state why you did or did not punctuate the sentence. A simple test for a nonessential element is to read the sentence without it. If the missing element does not change the basic meaning of the sentence, it should be set off by commas.

Example: She said *if my memory serves me right* that she had graduated from medical school in 1975.

"if my memory serves me right" is nonessential. It is also a parenthetical expression.

1. John Munro your patient was admitted to Center City Hospital today.

   _____

2. He is an excellent surgeon whether or not you care for my opinion and I feel that you must trust his judgment.

   _____

3. She required trifocal not bifocal lenses at this time.

   _____

4. Dr. Mitchell having been in surgery since two this morning collapsed on the day bed.

   _____

5. The wound was closed with #3–0 silk sutures.

   _____

The answers to these self-study questions will be found at the end of this chapter on page 78. Please check your answers before you continue.

3-3: PRACTICE TEST

Directions: Using the directions found with Self-Study 3-2, complete the following problems.

1. Please telephone my nurse *if you are agreeable to postponing the surgery.*

   _____

2. He has done well following the transurethral resection of his prostate *with the exception of one episode of postsurgical hemorrhage.*

   _____

3. Our daughter Pat *who is a senior this year* is studying for a degree in rehabilitation therapy.

   _____

4. I want to examine all of the children *who have been exposed.*

   _____

5. Bill Birch's father *Ralph Birch* is Chief-of-Staff at Beech Hospital now.

   _____

6. His decision *not to operate* was a bit hasty if you ask me.

   _____

7. Only the second copy which is a carbon should be mailed to the referring physician.

   _____

8. I will contact the anesthesiologist *as soon as the operating room is free.*

   _____

9. *Essentials of Medical History* my textbook is excellent.

   _____

10. Nephritis *Bright's disease* will be the topic of his presentation at our meeting.

    _____

11. I had lunch with Alex St. Charles the new resident.

    _____

12. I would like to thank all of those patients *who donated blood.*

    _____

13. All patients wearing pacemakers should be told the good news.

    _____

14. Medical staff members *who fail to attend the meeting* will lose their consulting privileges however.

    _____

15. The secretary not the receptionist was promoted to office manager.

    _____

16. Furthermore she is to be prepped before Dr. Summers arrives.

    _____

3

17. Your patient Ethel Clifford saw me in consultation.

_____

18. Ethel Clifford your patient saw me in consultation.

_____

See Appendix E, page 414, for the answers to Practice Test 3–3.

RULE 3.2a Use a comma to set off an introductory dependent phrase or clause.

Example

After you have an x-ray, I will examine you.
(simple introductory clause)

Dr. Chriswell was having difficulty dictating; however, *after the equipment was adjusted,* she was able to finish her reports.
(part of the second independent clause)

Fully aware of his budget restrictions and with concern for the high cost of the equipment, Dr. Jellison approved the purchase of the word processor.
(compound introductory phrase)

To transcribe this accurately the first time is the main goal.
(This introductory phrase serves as the subject of the sentence and must not be separated from the rest of the sentence by a comma.)

You will recall that this introductory element can be thought of as being "out of place" in the sentence. Many of these introductory dependent phrases or clauses begin with words such as *since, because, after, about, during, by, if, when, while, although, unless, between, so, until, whenever, as,* and *before,* and verb forms such as *hoping, believing, allowing, helping,* and *working.*

RULE 3.2b Do *not* use a comma when the essential clause appears in natural order: at the end of the sentence or at the end of the independent clause.

Essential clauses limit the meaning of the main clause.

Example

I will examine you *after* you have an x-ray.
(Tells *when* the patient will be examined.)

Example

She was able to finish her report *after* the equipment was adjusted.

Example of introductory

During the course of the procedure, a power failure occurred.

Example of natural order

A power failure occurred *during* the course of the procedure.

OPTIONAL: The comma may be omitted after a very brief introductory element if clarity is not sacrificed.

Example

If possible schedule the thoracotomy to follow the bronchoscopy.

3–4: Self-Study

Directions: Using the rules you have just learned, add a comma or comma pair where required. Be wary of separating the subject from the verb with a comma, which you might attempt to do when the subject is lengthy. Always check to be sure there is an intact independent clause. Please insert and circle optional commas.

Example: After the surgery was completed, he dictated the operative report. (Note the comma after the introductory phrase.)

1. That you have lost your secretarial position is not my concern.

2. Although she had been in pain for some time she failed to seek medical attention.

3. If you are not feeling better by tomorrow take two aspirin and call Dr. Meadows.

4. When initially seen the patient was in restraints lying in bed.

5. To transcribe and complete the insurance billing is her responsibility.

6. Our receptionist whom I hired yesterday failed to come in today.

The answers to Self-Study 3–4 will be found at the end of this chapter on page 78. Please check your answers before you continue.

3–5: PRACTICE TEST

Directions: Using the directions found with Self-Study 3–4, complete the following problems.

1. She will go immediately into the operating room as soon as it is free.

2. Whatever he said to her was misunderstood.

3. Dr. Johnston the pathologist deserves the credit for that diagnosis.

4. The delivery of the baby a girl was uneventful.

5. Furthermore I will not be here to interview the new medical transcriptionist.

6. When you have the opportunity please dictate the operative note.

7. To be sure she was safe the nurse took her to the car in a wheelchair.

8. After lunch he must rest quietly.

9. Thinking he was at home the patient attempted to get out of bed.

10. Helping the blind transcriptionist research a word is Janet's responsibility.

The answers to Practice Text 3–5 are found in Appendix E at the end of the book, page 414.

RULE 3.3 Use a comma to set off a year date that is used to explain a preceding date of the month.

Example
He was born on March 3, 1933, in Reading, Pennsylvania.
Make her an appointment for Wednesday, July 6, 199X.

Omit commas when the complete date is not given.

Example
We will see the patient again on May 6.
He had surgery in April 1989 in Arizona.

Omit the comma with the military date sequence.

Example
11 November 1990

RULE 3.4 Use a comma to set off the name of the state when the city precedes it.

Example
The pacemaker was shipped to you from Syracuse, New York, by air express.

Use commas to separate all the elements of a complete address.

Example
Please mail this to my home address: 132 Winston Street, Park Village, IL 60612.

NOTE: Do not place a comma between the state name and the ZIP code. The ZIP code is considered part of the state name.

RULE 3.5 Do not use a comma to set off ''Inc.'' and ''Ltd.'' following the name of a company unless the company prefers the usage.

Example
I was employed by Thoracic Surgery Medical Group Inc., in Encino, California, for five years.
Headquarters for the American Association of Medical Assistants Inc. is Chicago, Illinois.

RULE 3.6 Use a comma or pair of commas to set off titles and degrees following a person's name.

Example

John A. Meadows, M.D., saw the patient in consultation.

Example

Ms. Nancy Bishop, administrator, gave him ten days to bring his incomplete charts up to date.

Example

Nancy Casales, CMT, is the new president of AAMT, Mountain Meadows Chapter.

NOTE: There is a trend to eliminate commas, particularly when meaning is not sacrificed. Some writers are not using commas to separate degrees and titles following a person's name. As always, follow the wishes of the bearer of the name.

Do not place a comma before roman numbers indicating first, second, third, etc. or Jr. or Sr. following a name unless the bearer of the name prefers that usage.

Example

Howard J. Matlock III
Carl A. Nichols Jr. was admitted to Ward B.
A Billroth I anastomosis was performed.

RULE 3.7 Use a comma after each element or each pair of elements in a series of coordinate nouns, adjectives, verbs, or adverbs.

Example

Please copy the patient's operative report, pathology report, and consultation report for Dr. Gifford.

Example

The various hospital departments were decorated in green and yellow, blue and brown, and green and white.

Example

There were papers to be filed, charts to be sorted, ledgers to be posted.

Do not use a comma between the last adjective and the word series it modifies.

Example

The patient is a well-developed, well-nourished, elderly, white female telephone operator.

OPTIONAL: You *may* omit the comma before the conjunction if clarity is not sacrificed. However, most publishers do not take this option.

Furthermore, no comma is used before the ampersand (&).

Example

The law firm is listed as Claborne, Franklin & Bowers.

NOTE: "Etc." in a series has a comma both before and after it unless it occurs at the end of a sentence; then its period ends the sentence.

RULE 3.8 Use a comma to separate two or more independent clauses when they are joined by the conjunctions *and, or, nor, but, for, yet,* or *so.*

NOTE: The comma is placed in front of the conjunction.

Example

Your appendix appears to be inflamed, but I do not believe that you need surgery at this time.

BUT: Your appendix appears to be inflamed but not acutely. (*not two independent clauses*)

Example

The diagnosis of urinary tract infection was made, and he was treated with Septra.

BUT: The child weighed 7 pounds at birth and was the result of an uncomplicated pregnancy and delivery. (*not two independent clauses*)

Two of these examples do not contain two independent clauses, and it would be incorrect and misleading if you placed commas in front of the conjunctions. Be careful not to make this error. Check the sentence to see if the clauses are independent by testing each clause to see if it expresses a complete thought and could stand alone as a sentence, omitting the conjunction. When the second (or third) clause is *dependent,* the subject is usually missing. There must be a subject in the second clause to make it independent. Don't make the mistake of using a comma just because there is a conjunction present. Know why you are punctuating, and when in doubt, leave it out!

OPTIONAL: You *may* omit a comma between two short, closely related independent clauses if there is no chance of the meaning being confused.

Example

She came in just after noon so we invited her to lunch.

BUT: I kicked the ball, and John accidentally slipped reaching for it.

If you omit the comma after "ball" it appears, at first glance, as if you also kicked John accidentally.

3–6: SELF-STUDY

Directions: Using Rules 3.3 through 3.8, add a comma or commas where required. Briefly state why you inserted the comma or commas.

1. The patient was first seen in my office on Wednesday July 14 199X.

2. Please send this to Natalie Jayne RN Chief of Nurses Glorietta Bay Hospital.

3. Carl A. Nichols Jr. was admitted to Ward B.

4. The blood test included a white blood count red blood count hematocrit and differential.

5. There is a story of a mild head injury at age ten and she was in a moderately severe motorcycle accident about fifteen years ago.

6. The condition is now stationary and permanent and he should be able to resume his normal work load.

7. She was fully dilated at 2:30 a.m. but did not deliver the second twin until 2:55 a.m.

Please see pages 78 and 79 at the end of the chapter for the answers to this Self-Study.

3–7: PRACTICE TEST

Directions: In the following sentences, fill in the missing punctuation, and in the space after each sentence, fill in the letter or letters of the rule or rules you used from the list given after **Rule Review.** Each rule may be used more than once, and it is not necessary to refer back to the point in the chapter where the rule was introduced. Make a circle around any optional commas.

RULE REVIEW

Use a comma or pair of commas to

   a. set off nonessential words from the rest of the sentence

   b. set off nonessential appositives

   c. set off a parenthetical expression

   d. set off an introductory phrase or clause

   e. set off the parts of a date

   f. set off "Inc." or "Ltd." in a company name only if the firm prefers

   g. set off titles and degrees following a person's name

   h. separate words in a series

i. separate two independent clauses

j. separate the name of the state from the name of the city

Example

On auscultation, there are diffuse rhonchi and occasional rales heard.

Rule ___d___

1. He will be able to return to light work at any time but he should not be allowed to operate a jackhammer.

    Rule _____

2. His wounds are all healing well and he has had no further pain.

    Rule _____

3. In the preceding week he had had an automobile accident and was under the care of Dr. Finish.

    Rule _____

4. The patient continued her labor and was closely monitored for fetal heart tones.

    Rule _____

5. I have consulted with the Radiation Therapy Department at University Hospital and they have suggested that radiation therapy would be the best approach to this problem.

    Rule _____

6. It is my understanding that you will do the history and physical for the hospital but not the consultation.

    Rule _____

7. Please contact Charles Rick M.D. in Nogales Arizona as soon as possible.

    Rule _____

8. He had surgery July 14 1989 for carcinoma of the prostate but is now free of disease.

    Rule _____

9. Dr. Phillip is the newest member of St. Peter's Medical and Surgical Group Inc.

    Rule _____

10. On physical examination I found a well-developed well-nourished white woman in no acute distress.

    Rule _____

11. He noticed increasing dyspnea with effort extreme shortness of breath and night sweats.

    Rule _____

12. She is to be admitted with your concurrence on Wednesday July 1 199X at 2 P.M.

    Rule _____

13. Before you call surgery to schedule this and before you telephone Mrs. Jones will you report to me?

    Rule _____

14. As you know John Briggs M.D. my partner is retiring on July 31 this year.

    Rule _____

3

15. On March 26 199X she had a left lower lobectomy and postoperatively had broncho-pneumonia which required intravenous antibiotics.

   Rule _____

See Appendix E at the end of the book for a list of the rule or rules used in this exercise. After you have completed the assignment, you may consult this list to check yourself. If you chose the wrong rule, perhaps you have misplaced the comma!

RULE 3.9   When the name of a person is used in direct address, it is enclosed in commas.

Example
My thanks, Paul, for sending Mr. Byron in for a consultation.

RULE 3.10   If two or more words independently modify the same noun, separate them with a comma if a mental "and" can be placed between them or if the order in which they are used can be reversed.

Example
She is a tall, slender woman.
It was a wide, deep wound.

BUT: She is an efficient medical secretary.

RULE 3.11   Use a comma or a pair of commas to avoid misleading or confusing the reader.

Example
In 1984, 461 babies were delivered in our new obstetrics wing.

Example
Soon after, he got up and discharged himself from the hospital.
He spells out difficult terms, for example radioactive isotopes.

RULE 3.12   Use a comma after the complimentary close when using "mixed punctuation" in a letter.

Example
Sincerely yours,

RULE 3.13   Use commas to group numbers in units of three.

Example
platelets 250,000; WBC 15,000

NOTE: Addresses, year dates, ZIP codes, four-digit numbers, and some ID and technical numbers are traditionally not separated by commas, nor are commas used with decimals or the metric system.

Example
1000 ml (correct) 1,000 ml (incorrect)
My bill to Medicare was $1250.

RULE 3.14   Use a comma to separate the parts of a date in the date line of a letter.

Example
November 11, 1991

BUT: 11 November 1991

 3–8: PRACTICE TEST

Directions: Using your text and any other reference materials, properly punctuate the following letter. There are 18 commas missing. (Other punctuation marks, including two commas, are provided for you, so your completed letter will contain 20 commas.) In the margin, number each comma you insert and, on a separate sheet of paper, give your reason for using each comma.

   This letter should be retyped and punctuated, but it may be punctuated as is if there is a time problem or if typewriters are not available in the teaching lab. The correct version is in Appendix E.

September 16 199x

Tellememer Insurance Company
25 Main Street, Suite R
Albuquerque NM 87122

Gentlemen:

RE: Ron Emerson

I understand from Mr. Emerson that the insurance company feels
that the charges for my services on June 30 199X are excessive.

Mr. Emerson was seen on an early Sunday morning with a stab
wound in his chest, which had penetrated his lung producing
an air leak into his chest wall. In addition he had a laceration
of his lung.

After consultation and review of his x-rays his laceration was
repaired. He was observed in the hospital for two days to be
sure that he did not have continuing hemorrhage or collapse
of his lung.

I feel that the bill given to Mr. Emerson is a fair one. We
received on July 31 199X a Tellememer Insurance Company check
for $40 and I feel that your payment of $40 is unreasonable.
It is doubtful that one could get a plumber to come out early
Sunday morning to fix a leaky pipe for $40 and Mr. Emerson's
situation in my opinion was much more serious than would be
encountered by a plumber.

We will bill Mr. Emerson for the remainder of the $200 balance
on his account but I want you to know that we feel that your
payment is insufficient. If he feels that the bill is excessive
we would be glad to submit to arbitration through the County
Medical Society Fee Committee. If this fails I suggest we
seek help through the New Mexico Insurance Commission.

Sincerely yours

William A. Berry M.D.

rl

Enclosed: X-ray report; history and physical report

Copy: Mr. Ron Emerson

3-9: REVIEW TEST

Directions: Place a comma or commas where needed in the sentences that follow. Please circle optional commas.

1. In the meantime he was discharged to his home.
2. She is scheduled to be seen again on February 3 at 10:30 a.m.
3. Laralyn Abbott the trauma team nurse issued a code blue.
4. Your patient Kay Hai Wong was readmitted to the Veterans Administration Hospital with a diagnosis of cholecystitis pancreatitis and mild gastritis.
5. As demonstrated earlier chemotherapy had little effect on the rate of tumor growth.
6. In 1995 461 cases were reviewed by the Tumor Board.
7. Soon after he got up and discharged himself from the hospital.
8. Dr. Powell not Dr. Franklyn delivered the infant.
9. After three surgeries are not scheduled.
10. I would like her to be and she probably will be a candidate for heart surgery.
11. She is a spastic retarded child.
12. He had crystal clear urine.
13. It has been a pleasure Winton to help you take care of Mr. Ibarra.
14. She required trifocal not bifocal lenses at this time.
15. Dr. Chriswell was having difficulty dictating; however, after the equipment was adjusted she was able to finish her reports.
16. He was indeed concerned about her progress.
17. Even though he was experiencing difficulty breathing we decided not to perform a tracheotomy.
18. Gastric lavage was carried out and the patient was placed in four-point restraints.
19. The surgery was completed in 2 hours 40 minutes.
20. There were normal reflexes of suck root and startle.

The voice of the speaker usually gives us clues to understanding the meaning of what is being said because of voice inflection, pauses, tone, and word emphasis. To convey this to the person to whom the dictator is communicating, the vocal clues must be translated into written clues.

You have just completed your study of the most used written clue: the comma; and now we will tackle the rest of the basic aids to understanding the written word. Again, special emphasis has been placed on the punctuation rules you will use most often in medical typing.

The Period and Decimal

NOTE: Some dictators will indicate the end of a sentence by saying "period" or "full stop." Others drop their voice to indicate closure. You will need to learn the individual styles of your dictators.

RULE 3.15   Place a period at the end of a sentence and at the end of a request for action that is phrased as a question out of politeness.

Example

His chest was clear to percussion and auscultation.
You must be seen by a surgeon at once.
Will you please send a copy of the operative report to Dr. Blanche.

RULE 3.16   Place a period with the following:

---

1. single capitalized words and single letter abbreviations.

Mr. Jr. Dr. Inc. Ltd. Joseph P. Myers E. coli

2. academic degrees and religious orders

    M.D. Ph.D. D.D.S. B.V.E. M.S. S.J.

3. lower case Latin abbreviations

    a.m. p.m. e.g. t.i.d. p.o. q.4 h.

The following are *not* punctuated:

1. metric and English units of measurements

    wpm mph ft oz sq in mg mL L cm km

2. certification, registration, and licensure abbreviations

    CMA-A CMT RN RRA ART LPN

3. acronyms

    CARE Project HOPE AIDS MAST

4. most abbreviations typed in capital letters

    UCLA PKU BUN CBC COPD D&C
    T&A I&D PERRLA

5. scientific abbreviations typed in a combination of capital and lower case letters

    Rx Dx ACh Hb IgG mEq mOsm Rh
    Na K pH

6. abbreviations that are brief forms of words

    exam phenobarb sed rate flu Pap smear

RULE 3.17 A period (decimal point) is used to separate a decimal fraction from whole numbers.

Example
His temperature on admission was 99.8°F.
The new surgical instrument cost $64.85.

The Semicolon

The semicolon is always used as a mark of separation. It is frequently equivalent to a period, and then both sides of the semicolon must be independent clauses. Sometimes the semicolon replaces a comma and tells the reader, "Keep reading, the second part is related."

RULE 3.18 Use a semicolon to separate two or more closely related independent clauses when there is no conjunction used.

Example
You have requested our cooperation; we have complied.
The nose is remarkable for loud congestive breathing; there is no discharge visible.

RULE 3.19 Use a semicolon to separate independent clauses if either one or both have already been punctuated with two or more commas.

Example
Around the first of July, he developed pain in his chest, which he ignored for several days; and, finally, he saw me, at the request of his family doctor, on July 16.

RULE 3.20 Use a semicolon before a parenthetical expression when it is used as a conjunction between two independent clauses. (A comma is placed after the expression.)

Example
I attempted a labor induction with Pitocin, and contractions occurred; however, the patient failed to develop an effective labor pattern, and I discharged her after eight hours.

NOTE: Some of the most common parenthetical (transitional) expressions used as conjunctions are as follows: *however, furthermore, therefore, consequently, nevertheless,* and *accordingly.*

RULE 3.21 Use a semicolon between a series of phrases or clauses if any item in the series has internal commas.

Example
Among those present at the Utilization Committee Meeting were Dr. Frank Byron, chief-of-staff; Mrs. Joan Armath, administrator; Ms. Nancy Speeth, medical records technician; and Mr. Ralph Johnson, director of nurses.

The Colon

Think of the colon as a pointer, drawing your attention to an important and concluding part. It is a mark of *anticipation.* It helps to couple separate elements that must be tied together but emphasized individually. Often the material to the right of the colon means the same as the material to the left of the colon.

3

RULE 3.22 Use a colon followed by a double space to introduce a *list* preceded by *a complete sentence.* These lists are often introduced by the following expressed or implied words: *as follows, such as, namely, the following.*

Example

Please bring the following items with you to the hospital: robe, slippers, toilet articles, and two pairs of pajamas.

INCORRECT: The patient had: a history of chronic obstructive lung disease and congestive heart failure.

CORRECT: The patient had a history of chronic obstructive lung disease and congestive heart failure.

RULE 3.23 Place a colon after the salutation in a business letter when "mixed" punctuation is used.

OPTIONAL: When the salutation is informal and the person is addressed by his first name, you *may* use a comma.

Example

Gentlemen:
Dear Dr. Berry:
Dear Bill: (or) Dear Bill,
To Whom It May Concern:
Dear Sir or Madam:

RULE 3.24 Place a colon between the hours and minutes indicating the time in figures.

Example

Her appointment is for 10:30 A.M.

NOTE: The colon is not used in expressions of military time

Example

The patient was seen at 1430.

NOTE: The colon and double zeros are not used with the even time of day.

Example:

10 a.m.

RULE 3.25 Place a colon after the introductory word or words in preparing a written history and physical, introducing a reference line, listing the patient's vital signs, or with the introductory words in an outline.

Example

Chief Complaint: Hyperemesis.
Past History: Usual childhood diseases; no sequelae.
Allergy: Patient denies any drug or food sensitivity.

Example

Re: Mrs. Blanche Mitchell.
Reference: #306-A.
Subject: Stress test.

Example

Vital Signs:
 Temperature: 101°.
 Pulse: 58.
 BP: 130/90.
 Respirations: 18.

Example

Diagnoses: 1. Gastritis.
 2. Pancreatitis.
 3. Rule out cholecystitis.

NOTE: Close your listed items with a period.

RULE 3.26 Use a colon to introduce an example or clarification of an idea.

Example

I see only one alternative: chemotherapy.
You have only one goal here: accuracy.

NOTE: These examples are often introduced by the expressions "thus" or "that is"; or the expression could be supplied mentally.

 3-10: SELF-STUDY

Directions: Using Rules 3.15 through 3.26, add a semicolon, colon, or period where required.

1. Mr Clark E Rosamunde is scheduled to arrive at 4 30 pm

2. Josephine Tu, MD, will present six cases to the Oncology Review Board Dr Richland will be unable to attend.

3. Would you please send this on to Ralph Desmond Jr

4. Please place the following warning on the door to Room 16 "Caution Radioactive materials in use."

5. The ambulance arrived at precisely 2110

6. The patient was treated for the following problems insomnia, malaise, depression.

7. The consultation fee of $85 was not covered by insurance

Please turn to the end of the chapter, page 79, for the answers to these problems.

3

3–11: PRACTICE TEST

Directions: In the following exercises, fill in the missing punctuation, and in the space after each exercise, fill in the letter of the rule you used from the list given after **Rule Review.** Each rule may be used more than once, and it is not necessary to refer back to the point in the chapter where the rule was introduced.

RULE REVIEW

Use a period:	a. with single capitalized word abbreviations.
	b. to separate decimal fractions.
Use a semicolon:	c. between two independent clauses that have internal punctuation.
	d. between two independent clauses with a parenthetical expression acting as a conjunction.
	e. between two independent clauses with no conjunction.
	f. to simplify reading the sentence because of other punctuation marks.
Use a colon:	g. to introduce a series of items.
	h. to clarify an idea.
	i. with introductory words in an outline.
	j. with a reference notation.

Example
The child had a full-term gestation; his birth weight was 9 lb 4 oz.

Rule ___e___

1. She hasn't quite returned to full physical activity yet therefore, I will want to see her again in a month to re-evaluate her status.

   Rule _____

2. As you recall, Mr Scout is a 41-year-old man with severe angina, myocardial ischemia, and triple artery disease but he does have a well-functioning ventricle.

   Rule _____

3. The procedures performed were as follows bronchoscopy, bronchography, scalene node biopsy, right pneumonectomy. The insurance reimbursement (welcome as it was) amounted to only $65075. *(Six hundred fifty dollars and seventy five cents.)*

   Rule _____

4. The panel members included the following staff Dr Mary A Jamison, chief resident Dr Peter R Douglas, Jr, surgical director Mrs Nancy Culpepper, operating room supervisor and Jane Morris, RN, ICU supervisor.

   Rule _____

3

5. One fact stands out in all this discussion about this young man he has a great element of fear about being anesthetized.

Rule ——————

6. The patient was admitted with a temperature of 1012°, *(one hundred and one point two degrees)* chills, and nausea she also complained of low back pain and cervical pain.

Rule ——————

7. The operative site was injected with 05% *(point five per cent)* Xylocaine and epinephrine.

Rule ——————

8. Her neurologic examination now, as in the past, has been completely normal and there has never been any evidence of cerebral injury as a result of the gunshot wound.

Rule ——————

9. Her neurologic examination is normal she has full rotation of her neck, with flexion and extension unlimited.

Rule ——————

10. Final clinical diagnosis Acute cervical sprain, resolved. Condition on discharge Improved.

Rule ——————

Answers are given in Appendix E at the end of the book.

The Hyphen

RULE 3.27 Use a hyphen when two or more words have the force of a single modifier before a noun.

Example
figure-of-eight sutures
self-addressed envelope
end-to-end anastomosis
self-inflicted knife wound
well-known speaker
ill-defined tumor mass
large-for-dates fetus
non-English-speaking patient
He was seen today in follow-up examination.
The resident consulted the alcoholism counselors on his two MAST-positive patients.

NOTE: Omit the hyphen when the compound follows the noun.

Example
The patient is a well-developed, well-nourished black male.
HOWEVER: The patient is well developed.

This is a very up-to-date reference for drug names.
HOWEVER: This reference needs to be brought up to date.

This 19-year-old Mayview College student was injured in the accident.
HOWEVER: This Mayview College student is 19 years old.

During her pregnancy she experienced a 45-pound weight gain.
HOWEVER: She gained 45 pounds during her pregnancy.

NOTE: An adverb ending in "ly" is not hyphenated before the adjective and noun.

Example
She is a moderately obese waitress.
That was a poorly dictated report.

NOTE: *Common* compound expressions as well as essential parts of disease descriptions are not hyphenated.

Example
low cervical incision
normal sinus rhythm
pelvic inflammatory disease
congestive heart failure
right upper quadrant
chronic obstructive pulmonary disease
central nervous system
intensive care unit

rapid frozen section
atrial septal defect
low back pain

RULE 3.28   Use a hyphen between coordinate expressions after the verb.

Example

The waiting room was painted a sort of yellow-orange.
That remark was well-taken.
The patient's expression was happy-sad.

RULE 3.29   Use a suspending hyphen in a series of compound modifiers.

Example

There were small- and large-sized cysts scattered throughout the parenchyma.
He has a two- or three-month convalescence ahead of him.

RULE 3.30   Use a hyphen when numbers are compounded with words and they have the force of a single modifier.

Example

He is a 56-year-old janitor in no acute distress.
We work a 35-hour week.
Four-vessel angiography showed a narrowing of the left carotid artery.

RULE 3.31   Hyphenate compound numbers 21 to 99 when they are written out.

Example

Fifty-five medical transcriptionists attended the meeting last night.
Ninety-nine percent of the time I am confident of the diagnosis.

RULE 3.32   Use a hyphen when there is a prefix before a proper noun.

Example

anti-American pseudo-Christian
The estimated date of confinement is mid-May.

RULE 3.33   Use a hyphen after the prefixes *ex, self,* and *vice* and after other prefixes to avoid an awkward combination of letters, such as two or three identical vowels in a sequence.

Example

salpingo-oophorectomy   anti-immune
self-inflicted   vice-president
ex-patient   co-op

BUT: preeclampsia
     intraarterial

RULE 3.34   Use a hyphen after a prefix when the unhyphenated word would have a different meaning.

Example

re-infuse (infuse again)
re-treat (treat again)
re-creation (create again)

RULE 3.35   Do not use a hyphen with the prefixes *bi, tri, uni, co, extra, infra, inter, intra, mid, mini, multi, pseudo, sub, super, supra, ultra, out, over, ante, anti, semi, un, non, pre, post, pro, trans,* and *re* unless there are identical letters in a sequence.

Example

preoperative   postoperative
pre-evaluation post-traumatic
antenatal   antidepressant
semiprone   nondrinker

BUT: non-Hodgkin's (see Rule 3.32)
     transsacral
     preeclampsia
     reexamine
     reemploy

NOTE: Since hyphens are not generally used with prefixes, it is easiest to remember those few that are hyphenated: *ex, self,* and *vice.*

RULE 3.36   Use a hyphen with the letters or words describing chemical elements except with sub- or superscripts.

Example

I-131 or 131-I
Uranium-235

BUT: I^{131}
     U^{235}

3

RULE 3.37 Use the hyphen to take the place of the words "to" and "through" to identify numeric and alphabetic ranges.

Example
Rounds were made in Wards 1-4.
Check V2-V6 again.
Take 100 mg Tylenol, 1-2 h.s.

RULE 3.38 Use a hyphen following a single letter joined to a word forming a coined word.

Example
x-ray   Z-plasty   S-shaped
T-cell   U-bag   X-Acto

RULE 3.39 Place a hyphen between compound nouns and compound surnames.

Example
A Davis-Crowe mouth gag was used.
Mary Smyth-Reynolds was in today for her yearly Pap smear.
Antonia is the secretary-treasurer for our local chapter of the American Association for Medical Transcription.

Please refer to Chapter 8, Rules 8–1 through 8–22, for further discussion on use of the hyphen.

The Dash

A dash is made on the keyboard with two hyphens. There is no space before, between, or after the two hyphens. The dash indicates a sudden shift in thought and should be used very sparingly.

RULE 3.40 Use the dash for a forceful break for emphasis.

Example
I want you to--no, I insist that you--consult a surgeon about the growth in your breast.

RULE 3.41 Use the dash for summary.

Example
Red, white, and blue--these are my favorite colors.

The Apostrophe

RULE 3.42 Use an apostrophe to show singular or plural possession of nouns, relative pronouns, and abbreviations.

Example: (singular possessive).
the typist's responsibility (one typist)
Bob's doctor
Dr. Farnsworth's office

Example: (singular nouns that end in an *s* or in a strong *s* sound are made singular possessive by adding an apostrophe).
the waitress' table (multiple syllable noun)
for appearance's sake (multiple syllable noun)
Mr. Gomez' surgery (multiple syllable noun)
James Rose's appointment (single syllable noun)
Mr. Jones's medical record (single syllable noun)

NOTE: Concerning Mr. Walters:
Mr. Walter's point of view (incorrect)
Mr. Walters' point of view (correct)

Example: (plural forms of nouns).

Singular	*Plural*
woman's watch	women's watches
child's toy	children's toys
man's shoe	men's shoes

Example: (plural nouns ending in *s* are formed by adding an apostrophe).
typists' responsibility (more than one typist)
the Joneses' medical records (more than one Jones)
the employees' records

Example: (pronouns).
nobody's fault
anyone's guess
somebody else's responsibility

Example: (understood noun).
The stethoscope is Dr Green's. (stethoscope)
I consulted Dorland's. (dictionary)

Example: (abbreviation).
Proofreading is the CMT's responsibility.

Personal pronouns such as *its,** hers, yours, his, theirs, ours, whose,** or *yours* do not require an apostrophe.

---

* Notice these contractions, however:
It's time for your next appointment. (*It's* is a contraction for *it is.*)
Who's going to clean the operatory? (*Who's* is a contraction for *who is.*)

Example

The next appointment is hers.
The dog injured its foot.
You're coat is soiled. (incorrect)
Your coat is soiled. (correct)

NOTE: Probably one of the most common errors made concerns the misuse of the apostrophe with *it*. Because *its* and *it's* are both correct when used in the proper context, writers often make an improper choice. Remember that *it's* means *it is*.

There are many eponyms (adjective derived from a proper noun) used in medical typing. When these are used to describe surgical instruments, they *do not* take the possessive. However, when they are used to describe parts of the anatomy, diseases, signs, or syndromes they may show possession. Refer to Chapter 10 for further discussion on eponyms.

Examples: (Eponyms).

*Surgical
Instruments:*
Mayo scissors
Richard retractors
Foley catheter
Liston-Stille forceps

Signs and Tests:
Romberg's sign
Hoffmann's reflex
Babinski's sign
Ayer's test

Anatomy:
Bartholin's glands
Beale's ganglion
Mauthner's
    membrane

*Diseases and
Syndromes:*
Fallot's tetralogy
Tietze's syndrome
Hirschsprung's
    disease

RULE 3.43 Use an apostrophe in contractions of words or figures.

Example

'84, won't, can't, she'll, o'clock, doesn't, couldn't

NOTE: *Avoid* the use of contractions of words or figures except for "o'clock" in all medical reports and formal business letters.

Example

You hear:	*You type:*
'84	1984
won't	will not
she'll	she will
doesn't	does not
couldn't	could not
nine o'clock	nine o'clock

RULE 3.44 Use an apostrophe in possessive expressions of time, distance, and value.

Example

He should be able to return to work in a month's time.
You should have full range of motion in your elbow in two months' time.
The bullet came within a hair's breadth of the thoracic aorta.
I want the patient to feel that she got her money's worth.

RULE 3.45 Use an apostrophe to form the plural of the capital letters *A, I, O, M,* and *U,* all lower case letters, and after a lower case letter in an abbreviation.

NOTE: The reason for this rule is to avoid making what might appear to be a word with the combination of some letters and "s." For example *Is, Ms, Us, is, as.* It is not necessary to use the apostrophe to form the plural of numbers or capital letter abbreviations.

Example

When you make an entry in a chart, be careful that your 2s don't look like z's.
You used four I's in that first paragraph.
He has a note for three Rx's on his desk.
The TMs were intact.

Quotation Marks

RULE 3.46 Use quotation marks to enclose the exact words of a speaker.

Example

The patient said, "There has been hurting in the pelvic bones."

BUT: The patient said there has been some pain in the pelvic bones.

RULE 3.47 The titles of minor literary works are placed within quotation marks.

Example

His photographic entry "The Country Doctor" won first place in the contest.

NOTE: Underline the titles of published books, magazines, and articles. Place in quotation marks the titles of chapters, papers, sections, and subdivisions of published work.

Example

Your homework assignment is to read "Capitalization" in <u>Medical Typing and Transcribing: Techniques and Procedures.</u>

RULE 3.48 Use quotation marks to single out words or phrases for special attention.

Example

I can see no need for "temper tantrums" in the operating suite.

RULE 3.49 Use quotation marks to set off slang, coined, awkward, whimsical, or humorous words that might show ignorance on the part of the author if it is not known that the writer is aware of them.

Example

See if you can schedule a few "well" patients for a change.

NOTE: Punctuation with quotation marks is as follows: periods and commas go *inside* the quotation mark; semicolons and colons go *outside* the quotation mark. Question marks and exclamation marks belong inside the quotation marks when they are part of the quoted material; they are placed outside the final quotation marks when they are part of the entire sentence.

Example

The third chapter, "Punctuation," is the most difficult for me.

The patient related that she spoke with her hands "like an Italian."

The medical report answers my original question, "What is the secondary diagnosis?"

Parentheses

Introduction. Parentheses, commas, and dashes are all used to set off incidental or nonessential elements in text. Which you choose will be determined either by the dictator/writer of the material or by the closeness of the relationship between the material enclosed and the rest of the sentence. In general, commas are used to set apart closely related material slightly; parentheses are used when commas have already been used

within the nonessential element or the material itself is neither grammatically nor logically essential to the main thought. The dash is a more forceful and abrupt division and draws attention to a statement; parentheses de-emphasize. Enclosed material can range from a single punctuation mark (!) to several sentences.

RULE 3.50 Use parentheses to set off words or phrases that are clearly nonessential to the sentence. These are often definitions, comments, or explanations.

Example

She felt that she had inhaled some sort of ornamental dust (gold, silver, bronze, etc.) while working in her flower shop.

The administrative medical assistant (receptionist, secretary, bookkeeper, insurance clerk, transcriptionist, file clerk) requires the same length of training as the clinical medical assistant.

RULE 3.51 Use parentheses around figures or letters indicating divisions.

NOTE: You may elect to use a period after figures or letters indicating divisions as long as they do not occur within a sentence.

Example

(1) Sterile field	*or*	1. Sterile field
(2) Suture materials		2. Suture materials
(3) 4 × 4 sponges		3. 4 × 4 sponges

However, only the parentheses are acceptable in the following illustration:

Example

It is my impression that she has (1) progressive dysmenorrhea, (2) uterine leiomyoma, (3) weakness of the right inguinal ring.

The Slash (also called the bar or diagonal)

RULE 3.52 Use the slash in writing certain technical terms. The slash sometimes substitutes for the words "per," "to," or "over."

Example

She has 20/20 vision. *(Indication of visual acuity)*
His blood pressure is 120/80. (120 *over* 80)
The dosage is 50 mg/day. (milligrams *per* day)

3

RULE 3.53   Use the slash to offer word choice.

Example
and/or
Mr./Mrs./Miss/Ms.

RULE 3.54   Use the slash to write fractions.

Example
⅔ 1½

Spacing with Punctuation

RULE 3.55   NO SPACE
following a period within an abbreviation
following a period used as a decimal point
between quotation marks and the quoted material
before or after a hyphen
before or after a slash
before or after a dash (two hyphens)
between parentheses and the enclosed material
between any word and the punctuation following it
between the number and the colon in a dilute solution

on either side of the colon when expressing the time of day
after the closing parenthesis if another mark of punctuation follows

Example
If Mrs. Ross is promoted (to lead transcriptionist), she will leave this department.

RULE 3.56   ONE SPACE
after a comma
after a semicolon
after a period following an initial
after the closing parenthesis

RULE 3.57   TWO SPACES
after a period, question mark, or exclamation point at the end of a sentence
after a quotation mark at the end of a sentence
after a colon (except when used with the time of day or when expressing a dilute solution)

Please do not be intimidated by the large number of rules. You must already be comfortable with a great many of them, so some of this instruction is just a review for you. Take a little time to re-examine those rules that cause you problems.

 3–12: SELF-STUDY

Directions: Using Rules 3–27 through 3–54, add a hyphen, apostrophe, quotes, parentheses, or slash where required.

1. Her favorite response is that weve always done it this way.

2. It was an ill defined tumor mass.

3. The diagnosis is grim I feel helpless.

4. Her temperature peaked at 106.5 degrees we were relieved when this occurred and the seizures subsided.

5. There were no 4 × 4s left in the box.

6. Because of his condition emphysema and age 88, he is a poor risk for anesthesia at this time.

7. Eighty five of the patients are seen first in the Outpatient Department.

8. The patient with the self inflicted gun shot wound had a poorly applied bandage.

9. The blood pressure ranged from 120 to 140 over 80.

10. This is a very up to date drug reference.

Please turn to the end of the chapter, page 79, for the answers to these problems.

3-13: PRACTICE TEST

Directions: In the following exercises, fill in the missing punctuation and indicate which of the rules you used. (Refer to the brief rule review.) In the space following the sentence, write the letter of the rule or rules used. Each rule is used more than once. Note, the rules are listed as an aid. If you want to fill in the punctuation and not list the rule, it will be acceptable.

RULE REVIEW

Use a hyphen:
  a. when two or more words have the force of a single modifier.
  b. when figures or letters are mixed with a word.
  c. between compound names or words.
  d. between coordinate expressions.

Use an apostrophe:
  e. to show possession.
  f. to show letters are missing.
  g. to form the plurals of lower case letters.

Use quotes:
  h. to show slang or awkward wording.
Use parentheses:
  i. to set off a strongly nonessential phrase.
Use a slash:
  j. to divide certain technical terms.
  k. to write fractions.

Example

"Accommodation" is spelled with two c's, two m's, and three o's.

Rule _____g_____

1. Mrs. Gail R. Smith Edwards was hospitalized this morning. She is the 47 year old woman Dr. Blank admitted with a self inflicted knife wound. Her blood pressure was 60 40. *(sixty over forty)*

   Rule _____

2. Barbara Ness happy go lucky personality was missed when she was transferred from Medical Records.

   Rule _____

3. Glen Mathews, the well known trial lawyer, and the hospitals Chief of Staff, Dr. Carlton Edwards, will appear together if you can believe that on TVs latest talk show tonight. Its the only subject on the hospitals gabfest.

   Rule _____

4. I want a stamped, self addressed envelope enclosed with this letter and sent out with todays mail.

   Rule _____

5. Dr. Davis said his promotion was a good example of being kicked upstairs. He obviously didnt want to leave his job in the X ray Department.

   Rule _____

6. Havent you ever seen a Z fixation? Bobbi Jo will be happy to explain it to you.

   Rule _____

7. Were all going to the CCU at 4 oclock for instructions on mouth to mouth resuscitation.

   Rule _____

8. Right eye vision: 20 20
   Left eye vision: 10 400
   Right retinal examination: Normal
   Left retinal examination: Inferior retinal detachment

   Rule _____

9. You were seen on September 24 at which time you were having some stiffness at the shoulders which I felt was due to a periarthritis a stiffness of the shoulder capsule; however, xray of the shoulder was negative.

   Rule _____

10. After he completed the end to end anastomosis, he closed with #1 silk through and through, figure of eight sutures.

    Rule _____

11. Dr. Chriswells diagnosis bears out the assumption that the red green blindness is the result of an X chromosome defect.

    Rule _____

12. After his myocardial infarction MI, his blood test showed high level C reactive protein.

    Rule _____

Please refer to Appendix E at the back of the book for the answers to this exercise.

3–14: SELF-STUDY

Directions: In the following exercises, the marks of punctuation are missing; but the number of marks that are needed has been provided. This number includes any optional marks and the periods needed at the end of a sentence. Some periods are indicated for you with an asterisk (*). Parentheses and quotes will count as 2. You may not use your text or reference materials. The exercise is to be retyped for proper placement.

1. Dr Younger couldnt find the curved on flat scissors therefore all heck broke loose* (Needs 9 marks)

2. The patients admission time is 330 *(three thirty)* pm* When he comes in please call me for a face to face confrontation with him about his visitors* (Needs 8 marks)

3. This 68 year old right handed Caucasian retired female telephone operator was well until mid February* While sitting in a chair after dinner she had the following symptoms paralysis of her left arm and left leg paresthesia in the same distribution bilateral visual blurring and some facial numbness* (Needs 14 marks)

4. The patient was admitted to the Ward at one oclock in the morning screaming Alls fair in love and lust the attending physician sedated him with Thorazine 600 mg day* *(600 mg per day)* (Needs 7 marks)

5. The following describes a well prepared business letter neat accurate well placed correctly punctuated and mechanically perfect* The dictator expects to see an attractive letter with no obvious corrections smudges or unevenly inked letters* It is an insult in my opinion to place a letter that appears other than described on your employers desk for signature* (Needs 15 marks)

Please look at the end of this chapter for the answers to this Self-Study.

3–15: PRACTICE TEST

Directions: Follow the directions given in Self-Study 3–14 and type the following exercises.

1. She inadvertently sterilized the Smith Petersen nail instead of the V medullary* (Needs 3 marks)

2. She has had no further spells but she did have two episodes prior to this one several years ago* (Needs 4 marks)

3. The patient presents as a well developed asthenic elderly extremely bright and oriented Caucasian female* She is fully alert and able to give an entirely reliable history however she is somewhat anxious and concerned over her present condition* (Needs 9 marks)

4. The patient has just moved to this community from Anchorage Alaska where he was engaged in the lumber industry* He had an emergency appendectomy performed at some remote outpost in January 1986* According to the patient he has always felt like somethings hung up in there* Roentgenograms taken July 17 199X failed to reveal anything unusual* (Needs 12 marks)

5. He is a 35 year old well developed well nourished black truck driver oriented to time place and person* (Needs 10 marks)

6. The X chromosome defect resulted in her ovarian aplasia undeveloped mandible webbed neck and small stature Morgagni Turner syndrome* (Needs 7 marks)

7. Vital signs Blood pressure 194 97 pulse 127 respirations 32 regular and gasping* General Healthy appearing male looking his stated age in moderately severe respiratory distress with slightly dusky colored lips* (Needs 17 marks)

Please turn to Appendix E at the end of the book for the answers to this Practice Test.

3–16: REVIEW TEST

Directions: Please follow the directions given in Self-Study 3–14 and complete the following exercises.

1. His heart is in regular sinus rhythm without murmurs or thrills the distal pulses are all palpable and Phalens maneuver is negative* (Needs 5 marks)

2. I want to raise the charge for office calls to $15 this is long overdue and hospital calls to $25* Please explain this to all the patients including the new ones when they call for an appointment* (Needs 6 marks)

3. I took the samples of the powder to Dr Peterson White pathologist and he has not as yet made any report* As you can see from the initial report there is no evidence of powder in the biopsy specimen* (Needs 9 marks)

4. Really the prognosis is not too good but well hope that maybe shell defy the usual course of events* (Needs 5 marks)

5. I will restate the situation Mr Goodman has a right superior mediastinal widening which has proven to be secondary to some dilatation and lateral displacement of the superior vena cava* (Needs 3 marks)

6. It is anticipated that following completion of this radiation therapy and your recovery from it in a period of 4 to 6 weeks you should be able to return to your former employment without difficulty* (Needs 3 marks)

7. Dr Lopez advice was to transfer the patient* Please see that his x rays are sent with him to the Veterans Administration Hospital* (Needs 5 marks)

8. She is a spastic retarded child with bilateral hip bowing greater on the right than on the left whose mother is very very anxious for non invasive correction* (6 marks)

9. Notice please There will be no further parking allowed in the staff lot without an up to date sticker violators will be towed away at the owners expense* (6 marks)

10. According to the pathology report see enclosed there is no evidence of Mr Neibauer my patient having active pulmonary tuberculosis at this time* The debate concerning the approval of his attending the Contagious Disease Conference became heated we had to recess several times once for 40 minutes and we finally adjourned with no definite policy established* Ann Reynolds my administrative assistant will get in touch with Mr Neibauer to let him know* (16 marks)

3–17: PRACTICE TEST

Directions: Using your text and reference materials, punctuate the letter on page 74. Use mixed punctuation for the salutation and complimentary close. The letter is to be retyped, but you may proofread it by marking your text before you copy the letter.

See Appendix E at the end of the text to see this letter punctuated correctly. Optional commas have been circled.

Let's Have a Bit of Fun

1. In which sentence is Miss Hamlyn in trouble?
   a. Miss Hamlyn, the medical assistant failed to report for work.
   b. Miss Hamlyn, the medical assistant, failed to report for work.

2. Which shows a breach of ethics?
   a. Five nurses knew the diagnosis, all told.
   b. Five nurses knew the diagnosis; all told.

3. Which shows compassion?
   a. I left him, feeling he'd rather be alone.
   b. I left him feeling he'd rather be alone.

4. Which is harder for the interns?
   a. Down the hall came four interns carrying equipment and several doctors with their patients.
   b. Down the hall came four interns, carrying equipment, and several doctors with their patients.

5. Which is unflattering to the hostess?
   a. The party ended, happily.
   b. The party ended happily.

6. In which does the writer know about the private lives of her fellow workers?
   a. Every secretary, I know, has a secret ambition.
   b. Every secretary I know has a secret ambition.

7. Where would you prefer to work?
   a. The hospital employs a hundred odd men and women.
   b. The hospital employs a hundred-odd men and women.

8. Who's late?
   a. The receptionist said the nurse is late.
   b. The receptionist, said the nurse, is late.

9. Which is the worse problem?
   a. All my money, which was in my billfold, was stolen.
   b. All my money which was in my billfold was stolen.

10. Who filled up the emergency ward?
    a. All of the students who ate in the snack bar got food poisoning.
    b. All of the students, who ate in the snack bar, got food poisoning.

11. Who is the best leader?
    a. I intend to serve you fairly energetically and enthusiastically.
    b. I intend to serve you fairly, energetically, and enthusiastically.

The answers are in Appendix E.

William A. Berry, M.D.

3933 Navajo Road

San Diego, California 92119

463-0000

August 13   199x

John D Mench   M D
455 Main Street
Bethesda MD 20034

Dear Dr Mench

Re   Debra Walters

This letter is to bring you up to date on Mrs Walters who was first seen in my office on March 2 199x at which time she stated that her last menstrual period had started August 29   199x . Examination revealed the uterus to be enlarged to a size consistent with an estimated date of confinement of June 5 199x .

The pregnancy continued uneventfully until May 19 at which time the blood pressure was 130 90. Hygroton was prescribed and the patient was seen in one week. The blood pressure at the next visit was 150 100 and additional therapy in the form of Ser-Ap-Es was prescribed in addition to other antitoxemic routines. The blood pressure stabilized between 130 and 140 90.

The patient was admitted to the hospital on June 11 199X with ruptured membranes mild preeclampsia and a few contractions of poor quality. Intravenous oxytocics were started and after two hours of stimulation there was no change in the cervix with that structure continuing to be long closed and posterior. The presenting part was at a -2 to a -3 station and the amniotic fluid had become brownish-green in color suggesting some degree of fetal distress.

Consultation was obtained and it was recommended that a low cervical cesarean section be performed. A female infant was delivered by cesarean section. It was noted at the time of delivery that the cord was snugly wrapped around the neck of the baby three times and this might have contributed to the evidence of fetal distress as evidenced by the color of the amniotic fluid.

The patients postoperative course was uneventful and she and the baby were discharged home on the fifth postpartum day.

Sincerely yours

William A Berry M D

mlo

Punctuation Rule Synopsis

Use a Comma or Pair of Commas:

to set off a nonessential word or words from the rest of the sentence
Rule 3.1, page 50
to set off nonessential appositives
Rule 3.1a, page 50
to set off a parenthetical expression
Rule 3.1b, page 51
to set off an introductory phrase or clause
Rule 3.2a, page 53
(See also Rule 3.2b, page 53)
to set off the year in a complete date
Rule 3.3, page 54
to set off the name of the state when the city precedes it
Rule 3.4, page 54
to set off "Inc." or "Ltd." in a company name
Rule 3.5, page 54
to set off titles and degrees following a person's name
Rule 3.6, page 55
to separate words in a series
Rule 3.7, page 55
to separate two independent clauses
Rule 3.8, page 55
to set off the name of a person in a direct address
Rule 3.9, page 58
to separate certain modifiers
Rule 3.10, page 58
to avoid confusion
Rule 3.11, page 58
after the complimentary close
Rule 3.12, page 58
in certain long numbers
Rule 3.13, page 58
to separate the parts of a date in the date line of a letter
Rule 3.14, page 58

Use a Period:

at the end of a sentence
Rule 3.15, pages 60 and 61
with single capitalized word abbreviations
Rule 3.16, pages 60 and 61
with academic degrees
Rule 3.16, pages 60 and 61
in certain lower case abbreviations
Rule 3.16, pages 60 and 61
to separate a decimal fraction from whole numbers
Rule 3.17, page 61

Use a Semicolon:

between two independent clauses when there is no conjunction
Rule 3.18, page 61

between independent clauses if either or both are already punctuated
Rule 3.19, page 61
before a parenthetical expression when it is used as a conjunction
Rule 3.20, page 61
between a series of phrases or clauses when any item in the series has internal commas
Rule 3.21, page 61

Use a Colon:

to introduce a list or series of items
Rule 3.22, page 62
after the salutation in a business letter when using "mixed" punctuation
Rule 3.23, page 62
between the hours and minutes indicating the time in figures
Rule 3.24, page 62
after the introductory word or words in a history and physical report
Rule 3.25, page 62
with the introductory words in an outline
Rule 3.25, page 62
to introduce an example or clarify an idea
Rule 3.26, page 62

Use a Hyphen:

when two or more words have the force of a single modifier
Rule 3.27, page 64
between coordinate expressions
Rule 3.28, page 65
in a series of modifiers
Rule 3.29, page 65
when numbers are compounded with words
Rule 3.30, page 65
in certain chemical expressions
Rule 3.36, page 65
within compound numbers 21 to 99 when they are written out
Rule 3.31, page 65
between a prefix and a proper noun
Rule 3.32, page 65
after prefixes *ex, self,* and *vice,* to avoid awkward combinations of letters
Rule 3.33, page 65
after a prefix when the unhyphenated word would have a different meaning
Rule 3.34, page 65
exceptions, see Rule 3.35, page 65
to take the place of the words "to" and "through"
Rule 3.37, page 66
following a single letter joined to a word, forming a coined word

between compound nouns and compound surnames
    Rule 3.39, page 66

Use a Dash:

for a forceful break
    Rule 3.40, page 66
for summary
    Rule 3.41, page 66

Use an Apostrophe:

to show singular or plural possession
    Rule 3.42, page 66
in contractions
    Rule 3.43, page 67
in possessive expressions of time, distance, and value
    Rule 3.44, page 67
to form the plural of some letters
    Rule 3.45, page 67

Use Quotation Marks to:

enclose the exact words of a speaker
    Rule 3.46, page 67
enclose the titles of minor literary works
    Rule 3.47, page 67
single out words or phrases
    Rule 3.48, page 68

set off slang, coined, awkward, whimsical words
    Rule 3.49, page 68

Use Parentheses:

to set off clearly nonessential words or phrases
    Rule 3.50, page 68
around figures or letters indicating divisions
    Rule 3.51, page 68

Use a Slash:

in certain technical terms
    Rule 3.52, page 68
to offer a word choice
    Rule 3.53, page 69
to write fractions
    Rule 3.54, page 69

Spacing With Punctuation Marks:

no space
    Rule 3.55, page 69
one space
    Rule 3.56, page 69
two spaces
    Rule 3.57, page 69

▣ Answers to 3 – 1: Self-Study

NOTE: Material in parentheses may be included in your answers.

2. *Subject*   I

   Independent clause   I appreciate my understanding of medical terminology.

3. *Subject*   You (this is "understood")

   Independent clause   Please return this to Medical Records (as soon as possible)

4. *Introductory phrase*   After spending five hours in the operating room

   Subject   (the) patient

   Independent clause   the patient was sent to the recovery room

5. *Subject*   (the) patient

   Independent clause   The patient is a well-developed, well-nourished black female

   Dependent clause   reported that she has been well until this time.

   Appositive   none

   Conjunction   and

6. *Subject*   Joan (and) Beth

   Independent clause   Joan and Beth are taking an evening college course in medical ethics

Appositive 1 __the medical secretary__

Appositive 2 __the file clerk__

Parenthetical expression __(none)__

7. *First subject* __(the) reception room__

Independent clause __the reception room is well lighted and stocked with current literature__

Second subject __(the) patients__

Independent clause __the patients do not mind their wait to see Dr. Jordan__

Conjunction joining independent clauses __so__

Appositive __(none)__

Nonessential clause __who never seems to arrive on time__

8. *Independent clause* __There is overwhelming evidence to prove that the ability to spell is vital to success in this field__

Parenthetical expression __however__

Appositive __(none)__

9. *Subject* __American Association for Medical Transcription__

Independent clause __The American Association for Medical Transcription has a business and educational meeting every month.__

Appositive __the national organization for medical transcriptionists__

Parenthetical expression __(none)__

Conjunction joining two independent clauses __(none)__

10. *Subject* __Perfection__

Verb __is__

Independent clause __Perfection is the key word in medical transcription skills.__

Appositive __(none)__

Parenthetical expression __(none)__

Nonessential phrase __not speed__

11. *Subject* __(hospital) transcriptionists__

Independent clause __(none) This is not a complete sentence; there is no verb.__

12. *Subject* __the second "you," which is understood as occurring just before "please"__

Verb __have__

Independent clause __please have the patient's complete name, address, and telephone number and the admitting diagnosis__

Nonessential phrase __(none)__

Introductory clause __When you telephone the hospital__

Conjunction joining words in a series __and__

13. *Independent clause* __Appointment scheduling requires skill/it should be a real art__

Nonessential clause or phrase __and can be/contrary to what you might think__

3

Parenthetical expression   contrary to what you might think

14. *Independent phrase*   A perfectly typed resume should accompany your letter of application

Introductory phrase   (none)

Nonessential phrase   well-planned and prepared

15. *Independent clause*   he walks with his heel down (with a varus tendency in the ankle)

Dependent clause   with no severe problem

   also with a varus tendency in the ankle

Conjunction joining two independent clauses   (none)

16. *Subject*   a CBC and sed rate

Independent clause   a CBC and sed rate were carried out today

Introductory phrase   To minimize the chance of overlooking a recurrence of infection

Nonessential phrase   (none)

■ Answers to 3 – 2: Self-Study

1. commas around "your patient." It is a nonessential appositive.

2. comma after surgeon and after opinion. "Whether or not you care for my opinion" is a parenthetical expression.

3. comma after "trifocal" and after "bifocal" to enclose a nonessential expression.

4. comma after "Mitchell" and "morning" to enclose a nonessential expression.

5. no commas in this sentence.

■ Answers to 3 – 4: Self Study

1. No comma. Be careful not to separate the subject from the verb by placing a comma after *position.*

2. Place a comma after *time.* This is an introductory phrase.

3. Place a comma after *tomorrow.* This is an introductory phrase.

4. Place a comma after *seen.* This is an introductory phrase.

5. No comma. Be careful not to separate the subject from the verb by placing a comma after *billing.*

6. Enclose *whom I hired yesterday* in commas. This is nonessential.

■ Answers to 3 – 6: Self-Study

1. The patient was first seen in my office on Wednesday, July 14, 199X. *Separate all parts of a complete date.*

2. Please send this to Natalie Jayne, RN, Chief of Nurses, Glorietta Bay Hospital. *Separate degrees and titles following a person's name.*

3. Carl A. Nichols Jr. was admitted to Ward B. *No comma is used before Jr. or Sr. unless the user prefers it.*

4. The blood test included a white blood count, red blood count, hematocrit, and differential. *Separate words in a series. The comma after "hematocrit" is optional.*

5. There is a story of a mild head injury at age ten, and she was in a moderately severe motorcycle accident about fifteen years ago. *Separate two independent clauses with a comma before the conjunction.*

6. The condition is now stationary and permanent, and he should be able to resume his normal work load. *Separate two independent clauses with a comma before the conjunction.*

7. She was fully dilated at 2:30 a.m. but did not deliver the second twin until 2:55 a.m. *No comma because the second clause is dependent.*

▣ Answers to 3 – 10: Self-Study

1. Insert period after "Mr.," the "E.," the "p.," and "m" at the end of the sentence. Place a colon between the four and the thirty.

2. Insert a period between the "M" and "D" and after "Dr.," and a semicolon after "Board."

3. A period serves both to close the sentence and to punctuate the abbreviation. This is a polite question so no question mark is required.

4. A colon is placed after 16 and after "caution."

5. A period closes the sentence. No punctuation mark used with military time of day.

6. A colon is placed after "problems."

7. A period closes the sentence. No decimal point needed with the $85.

▣ Answers to 3 – 12: Self-Study

1. Insert an apostrophe in the contraction "we've." Enclose *we've always done it this way* in quotes.

2. Place a hyphen between *ill* and *defined.*

3. Insert a dash between *grim* and *I.*

4. Place parentheses around *we were relieved when this occurred.*

5. No marks placed in this one.

6. Place parentheses around *emphysema* and *88.*

7. Place a hyphen after *eighty.*

8. Place a hyphen after *self.* There is no hyphen after poorly.

9. Place a slash between 140 and 80, e.g. 140/80.

10. Place a hyphen after *up* and after *to.*

◧ Answers to 3 – 14: Self-Study

1. Dr. Younger couldn't find the curved-on-flat scissors; therefore, "all heck broke loose." *(It would also be correct to just place "heck" in quotes.)*

2. The patient's admission time is 3:30 p.m. When he comes in, please call me for a face-to-face confrontation with him about his visitors.

3. This 68-year-old, right-handed, Caucasian, retired female telephone operator was well until mid-February. While sitting in a chair after dinner, she had the following symptoms: paralysis of her left arm and left leg, paresthesia in the same distribution, bilateral visual blurring, and some facial numbness.

4. The patient was admitted to the Ward at one o'clock in the morning screaming "All's fair in love and lust"; the attending physician sedated him with Thorazine 600 mg/day.

5. The following describes a well-prepared business letter: neat, accurate, well-placed, correctly punctuated, and mechanically perfect. The dictator expects to see an attractive letter with no obvious corrections, smudges, or unevenly inked letters. It is an insult, in my opinion, to place a letter that appears other than described on your employer's desk for signature.

4

Capitalization

OBJECTIVES

After reading this chapter and working the exercises, you should be able to

1. demonstrate the ability to capitalize words accurately from copy prepared in lower case letters.
2. explain the special uses of capital letters in the preparation of medical reports and correspondence.
3. use the reference materials to check unfamiliar medical and business terms.

· ·

INTRODUCTION

This review of capitalization rules should be a pleasant interlude after your study of punctuation. Only a few capitalization rules cause problems for transcriptionists, so we will review those and emphasize where they most commonly occur in medical and business transcription.

The purpose of capitalizing a word is to give it emphasis or distinction. As with rules regarding punctuation, authorities disagree somewhat. The current trend is toward less, rather than more, capitalization. Consequently, as with a punctuation mark, be sure you have a reason for using a capital letter, and, when in doubt, learn to check your references.

VOCABULARY

Capital letter: upper case letter, also called "Caps."
Small letter: lower case letter, noncapital letter.
Eponym: an adjective derived from a proper noun.

Examples
Bright's disease
Skene's glands

Acronym: a word formed from the initial letters of other words.

Examples
NOW (National Organization for Women)
HOPE (Health Opportunities for People Everywhere)

WHO (World Health Organization)
CARE (Cooperative for American Remittances to Everywhere)

Lower case letters are used when the acronym passes into the language.

Examples
laser, radar, scuba

Proper noun: the name of a specific person, place, or thing.

Some *common nouns* may be used to name a specific person, place, or thing but are often modified by *my, your, his, our, their, these, the, this, that,* or *those.*

Examples of common nouns: my mother, the doctor, your patient, our president.

NOTE: They refer to specific persons, yet they are not proper nouns.

Examples of proper nouns: Secretary Lewis, Dr. Smith, Mary Tunnell, President Lincoln, the Brooklyn Bridge.

RULES

The following five rules pertain to typing business letters:

RULE 4.1 Capitalize the first word of the salutation and the complimentary close.

Examples
Dear Dr. Reynolds:
Sincerely yours,
Yours very truly,

RULE 4.2 Capitalize boulevard, street, avenue, drive, way, and so on, when used with a proper noun.

Examples
321 Westvillage *Drive*
One of the most attractive *streets* in La Mesa is Palm *Avenue.*

RULE 4.3 Capitalize a person's title in business correspondence when it appears in the inside address, typed signature line, or envelope address.

Examples
Sincerely yours,
Ms. Marilyn Alan, *President*
W. Peter Deal, M.D., *Director*

ATTENTION Ralph Cavanaugh, *Buyer*
Gene Ham, *Instructor*

RULE 4.4 Capitalize the first letter or all of the letters in the word *Attention* when it is part of an address; capitalize the first letter of each word or all the letters in the title *To Whom It May Concern.*

Examples
ATTENTION Reservation Clerk
(or)
Attention Paul Glenn, M.D., Director

TO WHOM IT MAY CONCERN:
(or)
To Whom It May Concern:

RULE 4.5 Capitalize both letters of the state abbreviation in the inside address and the envelope address.

Examples
District Heights, *MD* 20028
San Diego, *CA* 92119

See page 91, Figure 4–1, for a complete list of the Postal Service abbreviations for state names.

The next eight rules will be used often in transcribing medical letters and reports.

RULE 4.6 Capitalize professional titles, political titles, family titles, and military ranks when they immediately *precede* the name.

Examples

Military and Professional Titles
Capt. Max Draper, U.S.N. Medical Corps, will be the guest speaker at the annual meeting of the AMA. *Dr.* Smith, the *president,* plans to meet his plane. The *doctor* will leave for the airport at four o'clock. We will meet with *President* Austin at the university this evening. *Dean* Caldwell may not be able to join us, however.

Examples

Professional and Political Titles
Dr. Randolph, the *president* of the medical society, was invited to speak at the joint meeting with the local bar association. *Rev.* John Hughes will give the invocation.
The *attorney* will be here at 9:30 a.m. to meet with the *doctor* about his testimony.

DO NOT: capitalize the names of medical or surgical specialties or the names of the specialists.

NOTE: Only titles of high distinction are capitalized *following* a person's name except in the address and typed signature line. "High distinction" can be very subjective, depending on who is doing the writing. "High distinction" often refers to the persons of rank in one's own firm and to high government officials.

Examples
The internist referred him to a thoracic surgeon.
He is studying to be an emergency room specialist.
We asked for a second opinion from the cardiologist.

Example
Parkland Community College
3261 Parkview Drive
Boise, ID 83702
ATTENTION Ms. P. Lombardo, *Administrator*

Examples

Family Titles
My *father* is bringing *Aunt* Mary here this afternoon for her flu shot.
The patient's *mother* died of carcinoma of the breast at age 56, and his *father* is living and well.

EXCEPTION: A title is not capitalized when followed by an appositive.

Example
My *uncle,* William Peters, moved here recently from Cleveland.

RULE 4.7 Capitalize proper nouns, well-known nicknames for proper nouns, and eponyms.

Example
Josephine Holman just moved here from the *Rockies* and is looking for a job as a medical assistant.

Examples
We need a #15 *Foley* catheter. (eponym)
We learned that *valley fever* is endemic to *Imperial Valley, San Joaquin Valley,* and the *Sonoran* deserts.
I am afraid that the diagnosis is *Hodgkin's* disease.

EXCEPTION: Use lower case letters for the following eponyms, which have acquired independent common meaning. (When you are in doubt, remember to check your dictionary.) Refer to Chapter 10 for further discussion on eponyms.

Examples
arabic numbers	manila folder
braille symbol	mendelian genetics
cesarean section	paris green
chinese blue	parkinsonism*
curie unit	pasteurized milk
cushingoid signs	petri dish
epsom salt	plaster of paris
eustachian tube	portland cement
fallopian tube	roentgen unit
french fries	roman numeral
india ink	siamese twins
kleig light	

NOTE: Words derived from eponyms are not capitalized. *Parkinson's* disease but *parkinsonism.*

Examples
Cushing but *cushingoid* facies.
Gram stain but *gram*-positive.

RULE 4.8 Capitalize the names of races, people, religions, and languages.

Example
He is a well-developed, well-nourished, *Oriental* businessman in no acute distress.

Example
She is a *Catholic,* but they decided to be married in the *Jewish* temple.

Example
We are taking an evening course in medical *Spanish* because we have many *Hispanic* patients who do not speak *English.*

NOTE: Designations based on skin color are not capitalized.

Examples
She is a well-developed, well-nourished *black* female student.
This 43-year-old *Caucasian* farm worker fell from the back of a truck at 3:55 a.m.

RULE 4.9 Capitalize the name of the genus but not the name of the species that follows it.

Example
The patient was admitted by the ophthalmologist with *Onchocerca* volvulus.

Example
Ralph saw the doctor because he had a bad reaction to *Cannabis* sativa.

NOTE: The genus may be referred to by its first initial only; this is capitalized with a period and followed by the species name.

Examples

E. coli (Escherichia coli)
M. tuberculosis (Mycobacterium tuberculosis)
H. influenzae (Hemophilus influenzae)

DO NOT: capitalize the plural or adjective form of a genus name.

Examples

Diplococcus but *diplococci* and *diplococcal*
Streptococcus but *streptococci* and *streptococcal*

RULE 4.10 Capitalize trade names and brand names of drugs and other trademarked materials.

NOTE: It is often difficult for the beginning medical transcriptionist to recognize a brand name (capitalized) in contrast to a generic name (lower case). Until you become familiar with these and various suture materials and instruments, it will be necessary to use reference books. Please see Appendix C for a list of such reference materials. You will study one of these drug references in Chapter 8.

Examples

Generic Names of Drugs and Suture Materials

nitroglycerin, analgesic, hydrocortisone, potassium iodide, alcohol, ether, silk, catgut, cotton.

Examples

Trade Names of Drugs and Suture Materials

Nitora, Darvon, Cortisporin, Theokin, pHisoHex, Gelfoam, Surgicel, Dermalon, Ser-Ap-Es, HydroDiuril.

NOTE: See Rule 4.22.

RULE 4.11 Capitalize the names of *specific* departments or sections in the hospital.

Examples

Admitting Office
Medical Records Department
Intensive Care Unit
Pathology Department
The *Pathology Department* received the specimen.
All *pathology departments* should have this notice posted.

NOTE: If the treatment room and emergency room are areas within an Emergency Department, they are not capitalized. However, if the specific name of the department is "Emergency Room," it is capitalized.

RULE 4.12 Capitalize nouns that are closely associated with and that immediately precede numbers.

Examples

We ordered a *Model* 14 Medtronic pacemaker.
Siegfried Hinz, your patient from Germany, has a *Grade* II systolic murmur.
You have a reservation on *Flight* 707.

EXCEPTIONS: page number, paragraph, line, sentence, note, size.

Example

There is an error in your copy on page 27, *paragraph* 2, *line* 3.

RULE 4.13 Capitalize the first word of each line in an outline.

Examples

Diagnoses:
(1) *Stress* incontinence of urine.
(2) *Monilial* vaginitis.

Examples

HEENT:

HEAD: Normal.
EYES: Pupils round and equal, react to L & A.
EARS: Hearing normal, TMs intact, canals patent.

The next eight rules are used in all kinds of writing.

RULE 4.14 Capitalize the first word of the sentence, the first word of a complete direct quotation, and the first word after a colon if that word begins a complete thought.

Example

The instructor said, "*Strive* for mailable copy even when you are practice-typing."

Example

These are your directions: *Begin* typing as soon as you hear the signal and stop when the timer rings.

RULE 4.15 Capitalize the first and last words and all other words in the titles of articles, books, and periodicals with the exception of conjunctions, prepositions, or articles.

NOTE: Remember, book titles are also underlined.

Example

Do you use the reference <u>The Medical Word Book</u> by Sheila Sloane?

RULE 4.16   Capitalize the names of the days of the week, months of the year, holidays, historic events, and religious festivals.

Example

There will be no class on *Friday, November* 11, because it is *Veterans'* Day.

Example

Do we get an *Easter* holiday or *Passover* vacation? Neither, it's called "*Spring Vacation.*"

BUT: I am taking an advanced transcription class in the *spring* semester; I wish I had taken it this *fall.*

RULE 4.17   Capitalize both the noun and the adjective when they make reference to a specific geographic location.

Example

The patient was born and raised in the *Southwest;* he has lived in the *Deep South* only a short while.

Example

We plan to stay at a resort by the *Atlantic Ocean* when we go *east* for the medical meeting this fall.

Examples

the Great Lakes
Cape of Good Hope
Apache Reservation
Statue of Liberty

EXCEPTION: The names of places are not capitalized when they appear before the names of a specific place or are general directions.

Example

New York State
(but)
the state of New York

RULE 4.18   Capitalize abbreviations when the words they represent are capitalized. Capitalize most abbreviations of English words; capitalize each letter in an acronym.

Examples

ECG and EKG are both abbreviations for "electrocardiogram."

James A. Smith, M.D., graduated from UCSD.
Dr. Bowman is working with Project HOPE and UNICEF.

NOTE: Metric and English forms of measurement or Latin abbreviations are not capitalized.

Examples

e.g. t.i.d. ft cm oz mph ml p.o. q.4h.

RULE 4.19   Capitalize (and punctuate) the abbreviation of academic degrees and religious orders.

Examples

M.D. Ph.D. D.D.S. M.S. S.J.

NOTE: Please refer to Chapter 5 for a complete review of the use of abbreviations.

RULE 4.20   Capitalize the names of all organizations and the titles of officers in the organizations' minutes, bylaws, or rules.

NOTE: The word "the" is not capitalized when it immediately precedes the name of the organization unless it is an official part of the name.

Examples

The *Secretary* read the minutes, and they were approved as read.
Dr. Sanderson has recently retired from *the Navy.*
International Clinical Congress
American College of Internal Medicine
American Cancer Society
Knights of Columbus
Toastmasters, Inc.
Eastridge *Clinic*

BUT: She went to the *clinic* for her annual physical.

RULE 4.21   Capitalize the names of specific academic courses.

BUT: Academic subject areas are not capitalized unless they contain a proper noun.

Example

I am enrolled in *Medical Assisting* 103; I am also taking *typing* and *business English.*
These last three rules are frequently used in medical writing.

RULE 4.22   Capitalize each letter in the name of a drug when reporting drug allergies in a chart note or patient's history.

Example

Allergies: Patient is allergic to PHENOBARBITAL and CODEINE.

OPTIONAL: Underline or highlight the capitalized drug name as well.

Allergies: The patient reports a sensitivity to SULFA.

There has been an increase in *Chlamydia* infections in this age group. (genus)

We have had the usual problems with *rubella, rubeola,* and *chicken pox* in the kindergarten population. (common diseases)

We do not know if he should be designated as showing signs of early senility or *Alzheimer's* disease. (eponym)

RULE 4.23 Capitalize the names of diseases that contain proper nouns, eponyms, or genus names. The common names of diseases and viruses are not capitalized.

Examples

The patient tested positive for *Rocky Mountain* spotted fever. (proper noun)

She was given the final series of *diphtheria, pertussis,* and *tetanus.* (common diseases)

She is now suffering from *postpoliomyelitis syndrome* and is unable to breathe without the use of her respirator. (virus name)

RULE 4.24 Capitalize cardiologic symbols and abbreviations that are used to express electrocardiographic results.

Examples

The P waves are slightly prominent in V_1 to V_3. (or $V_1 - V_3$) (or V1 – V3)

It is not clear whether it contains a U-wave.

The QRS complexes are normal, as are the ST segments.

There are T-wave inversions in LI, aVL, and V1 – 4.

---

 4 – 1: SELF-STUDY

Directions: Draw a single line under each letter that should be capitalized. You may refer to your reference materials.

1. after i finish medical transcription 214, i will take a class in medical insurance billing. i want to get a job with goodwin-macy medical group.

2. all the patients were reminded that the office will be closed on labor day, monday, september 7.

3. dr. albert k. shaw's address is one west seventh avenue, detroit, michigan.

4. two of the common sexually transmitted pathogens are chlamydia trachomatis and neisseria gonorrhoeae.

5. it was mr. geoffry r. leslie, vice-president of medical products, inc., who returned your call.

6. dr. johnson exclaimed "it is necessary for me to leave for the coronary care unit at once!"

7. patsy, who works in the valley view medical center, is studying to become a certified medical transcriptionist.

8. the dorcus travel bureau arranged dr. berry's itinerary through new england last fall.

9. keep this in mind: accuracy is more important than speed.

10. the following are my recommendations:
    (1) continuing treatment through the spinal defects clinic.
    (2) evaluations at 2-month intervals during the first year of life.
    (3) physical therapy re-evaluation at six months of age.

11. the patient has four siblings, all living and well; his mother died of heart disease at age 45 and his father of an automobile accident when he was 24; there is no history of familial disease.

12. we expect judge willard frick to arrive from his home on the pacific coast for the memorial day weekend.

13. i find current medical terminology by vera pyle, cmt, to be an excellent reference book for the x-ray department transcribing station.

14. my uncle, sam, is a thoracic surgeon in houston.

15. mr. billingsgate wrote to say that he had moved to 138 old highway eight, space 14.

Please turn to page 92 for the answers to these problems.

4–2: PRACTICE TEST

4

Directions: Draw a single line under the letters that should be capitalized in the sentences below.

1. the right rev. michael t. squires led the invocation at the graduation ceremony for greenlee county's first paramedic class.

2. nanci holloway, a 38-year-old caucasian female, is scheduled for a cesarean section tomorrow.

3. the internist wanted him to have meprobamate, so he wrote a prescription for miltown.

4. johnny temple had chickenpox, red measles, and german measles his first year in school.

5. unfortunately, the patient in icu whom dr. berry saw this morning has hodgkin's disease.

6. the pathology report showed a class IV malignancy on the pap smear.

7. some patients have been very sick with kaposi's sarcoma, the rare and usually mild skin cancer that seems to turn fierce with aids victims.

8. the mustard procedure is often used to reroute venous return in the atria.

9. the young man was an alert, asthenic, indochinese male who was well-oriented to time and place.

10. the gynecologist wrote a prescription for flagyl for the patient with trichomonas vaginalis.

11. please note on mrs. stefandatter's chart that she is allergic to phenobarbital.

12. dr. collier recommended a combination of penicillin G (2,000,000 to 5,000,000 units, t.i.d.) and an aminoglycoside, such as gentamicin (3–5 mg/kg/day), for our patient with endocarditis.

13. barbara, our lpn, is the new membership chairman for the local now chapter; she asked me to join.

14. the od victim was brought to the er by his roommate.

15. rhonda keller, mr. zimmer's executive secretary, spoke to the aama about good telephone manners.

The answers to these will be found in Appendix E at the back of your text. Do not be concerned with your progress if you had trouble with some of the abbreviations. An in-depth study will be taken up in the next chapter.

4–3: SELF-STUDY

Directions: Retype the following letter, inserting capital letters where necessary. You may use your reference materials. Use the Postal Service abbreviations for the state name in the address. After you have retyped the letter, turn to page 94 at the end of the chapter.

4

William A. Berry, M.D.

3933 Navajo Road
San Diego, California 92119

463-0000

1   may 17, 199X

2   barbara h. baker, m.d.
3   624 south polk drive
4   boothbay harbor, maine   04538

5   dear dr. baker:

6   at the request of dr. thomas brothwell, i saw mrs. brenda woodman
7   in the office today. he, apparently, felt that her thyroid was
8   enlarged.

9   mrs. woodman stated that she is on tedral, ½ tablet q.i.d.; sski
10   drops, 10 t.i.d.; choledyl b.i.d.; and prednisone. she has had
11   asthma for twelve years and, other than a t & a in childhood, has
12   never been hospitalized.

13   on physical examination her thyroid was 2+ enlarged, especially
14   in the lower lobes, and smooth. the heart was in regular sinus
15   rhythm of 110, and she had findings of moderate bronchial asthma
16   at this time. on pelvic examination, she had a virginal introitus
17   and a moderate senile vaginitis. she had heberden's nodes on the
18   fingers and vibration sense was decreased by about 25 seconds.

19   the laboratory tests, a copy of which is enclosed, showed a normal
20   thyroid function. the urinalysis was negative; and the electrocardio-
21   gram, a copy of which is enclosed also, showed some nonspecific st
22   and t-wave changes and some positional changes suggestive of pul-
23   monary disease.

24   in summary, i do not feel that the lady has hyperthyroidism but
25   simply an enlarged thyroid due to the prolonged iodide intake.

26   it was my pleasure to see your sister in the office and i hope
27   that the above findings will reassure her family in the northeast.

28   sincerely,

29   william a. berry, m.d.

30   jr

31   enclosures

32   cc: thomas b. brothwell, m.d.

4–4: PRACTICE TEST

Directions: Retype the following two letters, inserting capital letters where necessary. Use the correct Postal Service abbreviations (Fig. 4–1) for the state name in the address.

See Appendix E for the correct version of these letters.

William A. Berry, M.D.

3933 Navajo Road

San Diego, California 92119

463-0000

may 6, 199X

mrs. adrianne l. shannon
316 rowan road
clearwater, florida 33516

dear mrs. shannon:

dr. berry asked me to write to you and cancel your appointment for friday, may 15. we hope this will not inconvenience you, but dr. berry has made plans to attend the american college of chest physicians meeting in kansas city at that time. i have tentatively re-scheduled your appointment for monday, may 18, at 10:15 a.m.

by the way, you might be interested to know that dr. berry has been asked to read the paper that he wrote, entitled "the ins and outs of emphysema." i believe that you asked him for a copy of this article the last time you were in the office.

sincerely yours,

(ms.) laverne shay
secretary

William A. Berry, M.D.

3933 Navajo Road
San Diego, California 92119

———————

463-0000

march 3, 199X

state compensation insurance fund
p. o. box 2970
winnetka, illinois 60140

attention ralph byron, inspector

gentlemen

re: james r. gorman

the above-referenced patient was seen today for pre-
surgical examination in the office. he has an acute
upper respiratory infection with a red left ear and
inflamed tonsils.   therefore, his surgery was can-
celled, and he was placed on keflex, 250 mg every
six hours.

mr. gorman's surgery was rescheduled for march 15 at
mercy hospital. he will be rechecked in the office
on march 14.

very truly yours

william a. berry, m. d.

ref

Two-letter State Abbreviations for the United States and its Dependencies.

Alabama	AL	Kentucky	KY	Oklahoma	OK
Alaska	AK	Louisiana	LA	Oregon	OR
Arizona	AZ	Maine	ME	Pennsylvania	PA
Arkansas	AR	Maryland	MD	Puerto Rico	PR
California	CA	Massachusetts	MA	Rhode Island	RI
Canal Zone	CZ	Michigan	MI	South Carolina	SC
Colorado	CO	Minnesota	MN	South Dakota	SD
Connecticut	CT	Mississippi	MS	Tennessee	TN
Delaware	DE	Missouri	MO	Texas	TX
District of Columbia	DC	Montana	MT	Utah	UT
Florida	FL	Nebraska	NE	Vermont	VT
Georgia	GA	Nevada	NV	Virginia	VA
Guam	GU	New Hampshire	NH	Virgin Islands	VI
Hawaii	HI	New Jersey	NJ	Washington	WA
Idaho	ID	New Mexico	NM	West Virginia	WV
Illinois	IL	New York	NY	Wisconsin	WI
Indiana	IN	North Carolina	NC	Wyoming	WY
Iowa	IA	North Dakota	ND		
Kansas	KS	Ohio	OH		

Two-letter Abbreviations for Canadian Provinces and Territories.

Alberta	AB	Newfoundland	NF	Quebec	PQ
British Columbia	BC	Northwest Territories	NT	Saskatchewan	SK
Labrador	LB	Nova Scotia	NS	Yukon Territory	YT
Manitoba	MB	Ontario	ON		
New Brunswick	NB	Prince Edward Island	PE		

FIGURE 4–1. *Note to student:* Copy the above list for your personal notebook. Copy it all on one page, filed under "S" for state abbreviations, or place this at the front of your notebook.

CAPITALIZATION RULE SYNOPSIS

Capitalize:

1. The first word of the salutation and complimentary close.

2. Boulevard, street, avenue, and so on when used with a proper noun.

3. Titles in the address and typed signature line.

4. The word "Attention" or each letter, when used in an address.

5. "To Whom It May Concern" or each letter of this expression.

6. State abbreviations in the address.

7. Titles when they immediately precede the name.

8. Proper nouns and nicknames for proper nouns.

9. Eponyms.

10. The names of races, peoples, religions, and languages.

11. The name of the genus (but not the name of the species).

12. Trade names and brand names for drugs and other products.

13. The names of specific departments in the hospital.

14. Certain nouns that precede numbers or letters.

15. The first word in an outline and the first word in a sentence.

16. The first word in a complete direct quote.

17. Certain words in the titles of articles, books, and periodicals.

18. Names of the days of the week, months of the year, and holidays.

19. Historic events and religious festivals.

20. Specific geographic locations.

21. Each letter in an acronym.

22. Most nontechnical abbreviations.

23. Names of organizations.

24. Titles of officers in the organization's minutes, bylaws, or rules.

25. Specific academic courses.

26. Academic degree abbreviations.

27. Drugs when the patient has an allergic reaction to them.

28. Cardiologic symbols and abbreviations.

▣ Answers to 4–1: Self-Study

1. After I finish Medical Transcription 214, I will take a class in medical insurance billing. I want to get a job with Goodwin-Macy Medical Group.

2. All the patients were reminded that the office will be closed on Labor Day, Monday, September 7.

3. Dr. Albert K. Shaw's address is One West Seventh Avenue, Detroit, Michigan.

4. Two of the common sexually transmitted pathogens are Chlamydia trachomatis and Neisseria gonorrhoeae.

5. It was Mr. Geoffry R. Leslie, vice-president of Medical Products, Inc., who returned your call.

6. Dr. Johnson exclaimed "It is necessary for me to leave for the Coronary Care Unit at once!"

7. Patsy, who works in the Valley View Medical Center, is studying to become a certified medical transcriptionist.

8. The Dorcus Travel Bureau arranged Dr. Berry's itinerary through New England last fall.

9. Keep this in mind: Accuracy is more important than speed.

10. The following are my recommendations:

    (1) Continuing treatment through the Spinal Defects Clinic.

(2) Evaluations at 2-month intervals during the first year of life.

(3) Physical therapy re-evaluation at six months of age.

11. The patient has four siblings, all living and well; his mother died of heart disease at age 45 and his father of an automobile accident when he was 24; there is no history of familial disease.

12. We expect Judge Willard Frick to arrive from his home on the Pacific Coast for the Memorial Day weekend.

13. I find *Current Medical Terminology* by Vera Pyle, CMT to be an excellent reference book for the X-ray Department transcribing station.

14. My uncle, Sam, is a thoracic surgeon in Houston.

15. Mr. Billingsgate wrote to say that he had moved to 138 Old Highway Eight, Space 14.

4

4

William A. Berry, M.D.

3933 Navajo Road

San Diego, California 92119

463-0000

1   may 17, 199X

2   barbara h. baker, m.d.
3   624 south polk drive
4   boothbay harbor, ~~maine~~ 04538 — ME *substituted*

5   dear dr. baker:

6   at the request of dr. thomas brothwell, i saw mrs. brenda woodman
7   in the office today. he, apparently, felt that her thyroid was
8   enlarged.

9   mrs. woodman stated that she is on tedral, ½ tablet q.i.d.; sski
10 drops, 10 t.i.d.; choledyl b.i.d.; and prednisone. she has had
11 asthma for twelve years and, other than a t & a in childhood, has
12 never been hospitalized.

13 on physical examination her thyroid was 2+ enlarged, especially
14 in the lower lobes, and smooth. the heart was in regular sinus
15 rhythm of 110, and she had findings of moderate bronchial asthma
16 at this time. on pelvic examination, she had a virginal introitus
17 and a moderate senile vaginitis. she had heberden's nodes on the
18 fingers and vibration sense was decreased by about 25 seconds.

19 the laboratory tests, a copy of which is enclosed, showed a normal
20 thyroid function. the urinalysis was negative; and the electrocardio-
21 gram, a copy of which is enclosed also, showed some nonspecific st
22 and t-wave changes and some positional changes suggestive of pul-
23 monary disease.

24 in summary, i do not feel that the lady has hyperthyroidism but
25 simply an enlarged thyroid due to the prolonged iodide intake.

26 it was my pleasure to see your sister in the office and i hope
27 that the above findings will reassure her family in the northeast.

28 sincerely,

29 william a. berry, m.d.

30 jr

31 enclosures

32 cc: thomas b. brothwell, m.d.

Note: The letters that you see underlined should be capitalized.

Transcribing Numbers, Figures, and Abbreviations

OBJECTIVES

After reading this chapter and working the exercises, you should be able to

1. explain when a number should be typed as a figure, typed in spelled-out form, or typed as a roman numeral.
2. type medical and business symbols and abbreviations when appropriate.
3. demonstrate your ability to prepare accurately typed material containing numbers, symbols, and abbreviations commonly found in medical writing.

• •

INTRODUCTION

This chapter is a discussion of the various typing techniques peculiar to medical and scientific reports. We are going to be working with rules, and they, like those we have been studying previously, are not sacred; however, they are sound and practical. When you master the techniques presented in this chapter, you will have the mechanical skill necessary to type medical and scientific papers with confidence.

One of the most difficult tasks in studying machine transcription is learning the technical and mechanical manner of writing used by those individuals already working in the field. Therefore, even a mastery of medical terminology may not give you the confidence that what you are typing is being done exactly the way it should be.

Furthermore, absence of basic mechanical skill results in copy that lacks refinement or accuracy. Unfortunately, errors can occur because the transcriptionist "thought" he or she heard a certain word and then typed a senseless remark or a fragment of material. A more thorough understanding of the topic helps to prevent such an error. It is important for the transcriptionist to be both grammatically and technically proficient.

If you want to be able to avoid mistakes in your work, you should learn correct terms and practices, and, at the same time, keep "current" by reading medical reports, papers, and journals. You do not have to understand the complete technical content of an article, but you must read to become familiar with how the copy is prepared.

You will find that there may be several ways of doing something—not several ways of doing something "right," just several ways of doing something. One of the ways is the preferred way, although other methods might be acceptable. The extra trouble that you take to learn the "best" way will make the extra difference in your work—that touch of polish. You

95

may hear a veteran transcriptionist say "I have always done it this way" with a tone of voice indicating that it therefore makes it correct. This may not always be so. Many people learn by copying other people's work whom they trust and admire. Those persons may just have "invented" a format, setup, or method of transcription. Years of doing something incorrectly does not make it correct. Learn now which references and role models are trustworthy. Learn to question practices that do not look or sound exactly right.

TYPING NUMBERS

The first set of rules has to do with typing numbers. We have already discussed punctuating numbers and even capitalizing words that appear with them. Now the spotlight is on the numbers themselves. Numbers can be expressed in a variety of ways: We have the terms *numeral, Arabic numeral, figure, numeric term, roman numeral, cardinal number,* and *ordinal number.* Each one describes a different way that numbers themselves are expressed or written. Numbers can be spelled out, written as figures, or written in a combination of a figure and a part of a word (e.g., 3rd).

Numeral and *Arabic numeral* mean the *figures* and combination of the figures 0, 1, 2, 3, 4, 5, 6, 7, 8, 9.

Numeric term refers to written-out numbers.

Roman numerals refer to the use of certain letters of the alphabet, most frequently the capital letters and combination of the letters I, V, X.

Cardinal numbers refer to the quantity of objects in the same class. It may be a whole number, a fraction, or a combination, e.g., 3 days, $15, and so forth.

Ordinal numbers express position, sequence, or order of items in the same class. They can be spelled out or written as a figure plus a word part, e.g., first, 1st, third, eleventh, 14th, and so forth. The following rules will be separated into these different groups, with some numbers being expressed in more than one way.

Ordinal Numbers (first, second, third, and so on)

RULE 5.1 Spell out ordinals *except* when used as a date appearing *before* the month or in street numbers above ten.

Examples
The *fourth, fifth,* and *sixth* ribs were fractured.
The patient was discharged to his home on the *tenth* postoperative day.

Give the patient an appointment for the *6th* of August.
The office address is 1335 *11th* Street.

Numbers Spelled Out (Written as Words) (one, two, three)

RULE 5.2 Spell out numbers at the beginning of a sentence.

Example
Fourteen patients were studied at the request of the staff, *four* were studied at the request of their physicians, and *eleven* were studied as interesting problems for discussion.

NOTE: When several related numbers are used in a sentence, be consistent; type all numbers in figures or write them all out. Normally, it is easier to type all of them in figures. If the number beginning the sentence is large (over two words), it may be necessary to rewrite the sentence so that the number may be used as a figure within the sentence. *However, if you must begin a sentence with a numeric term, you are not bound to write out the other large numbers in the sentence.*

Example: *Seventy-one* percent responded to the questionnaire; *33%* were positive, *21%* were negative, and *17%* gave a "no opinion" response.

NOTE: Be sure to spell out an abbreviation or symbol used with a number if the number has to be spelled out for some reason, e.g., the word "percent" in the previous example.

RULE 5.3 Spell out all whole numbers *one* through and including *ten* when they do not refer to technical terms.

Examples
She had pulmonary tuberculosis *three* years ago and spent *seven* months in a sanitorium.
The EEG was run for *three* minutes with no activity.

BUT: The EEG was run for *20* minutes with no activity.

ALSO: The EEG was run for *5½* minutes with no activity.
The address for the American Association of Medical Assistants is *One* East Wacker Drive, Chicago, IL 60601.
He will have to convalesce for *five* to *six* weeks before returning to work.

RULE 5.4   Spell out numbers that are used for indefinite expressions.

Examples

I received *thirty-odd* applications.
He had diphtheria in his *mid-forties.*
Hundreds thronged to see my "celebrity" patient.

RULE 5.5   Spell out fractions when they appear without a whole number.

Examples

He smoked a *half*-pack of cigarettes a day.
He smoked *one-half* pack of cigarettes a day.

BUT: He smoked $1\frac{1}{2}$ packs of cigarettes a day.

RULE 5.6   Spell out the first number and use a figure for the second number when two numbers are used together to modify the same noun.

Examples

two 1-liter solutions
six 3-bed wards

NOTE: Remember Rule 3.30, page 65, and use the hyphen when words are compounded with figures.

RULE 5.7   Spell out the *even time of day* when written with or without o'clock or without a.m. or p.m.

Examples

The staff meeting is scheduled to begin at *three.*
He is due at *nine* this evening.
Give her an appointment for *two* o'clock.

NOTE: Figures are used for all other expressions of time. See Rule 5.9. The phrases *in the morning, in the afternoon,* and *at night* are written with "o'clock" and not with a.m. or p.m.

Example

I met her in the Emergency Room at *three* o'clock in the morning.

NOTE: Don't use the expression "o'clock" with a.m. or p.m. or when both hour and minutes are expressed.

Examples

She is expected at *3* o'clock p.m. (incorrect)
She is expected at *three* o'clock. (correct)
She is expected at *3:30* o'clock. (incorrect)
She is expected at *3:30* p.m. (correct)

RULE 5.8   Spell out large round numbers that do not refer to technical quantities.

Example

There were *eighteen hundred* physicians present at the symposium.

NOT: There were one thousand, eight hundred present.

HOWEVER: He was given *600,000* units of penicillin. (technical)

In general, figures are easier for us to understand than numbers in written-out form. Since medical typing is technical, numbers in figures are preferred because they stand out clearly, are emphatic, and are easier to read.

Numbers as Figures (Also Called Cardinal Figures or Arabic Figures — 1, 2, 3, 4, and so on)

RULE 5.9   Use figures to express the time of day with a.m. or p.m. and the time of day when *both* hours and minutes are expressed alone.

Examples

He arrived promptly at 2:30.
Office hours are from 10:00 a.m. to noon. (incorrect)
Office hours are from 10 a.m. to noon. (correct)

NOTE: Don't use *a.m.* or *p.m.* with 12. You may use the figure 12 with the word *noon* or *midnight* or use the words alone without the figure 12.

Examples

We close the office at 12 noon.
My shift is over at midnight.

RULE 5.10   Use figures to write numbers larger than ten.

RULE 5.11   Use figures to write numbers under ten when they occur with a larger number on the same subject.

Example

There are *3* beds available on the maternity wing, *14* on the surgery wing, and *12* on the medical floor.

RULE 5.12   Use figures to write numbers with the expression "o'clock" when used to designate areas on a circular surface.

Examples

The sclera was incised at about the 3 o'clock area.
The cyst was in the left breast, just below the nipple at the 5 o'clock position.

RULE 5.13   Use figures to write dollar amounts.

Example

The initial consultation is $85.

NOTE: Not $85.*00* (no period and zeros)

RULE 5.14   Use figures in writing vital statistics such as age, weight, height, blood pressure, pulse, respiration, dosage, size, temperature, and so forth.

You Hear: he is a sixteen year old well developed well nourished white male height is seventy two inches weight is one hundred forty five pounds blood pressure is one hundred twenty over eighty pulse is seventy two and respirations are eighteen.
You Type: He is a 16-year-old, well-developed, well-nourished, white male. Height: 72″. Weight: 145 lb. Blood Pressure: 120/80. Pulse: 72. Respirations: 18.

NOTE: In the above example, the transcriptionist eliminated the verbs "is/are" and substituted the colon when the vital statistics were given. Each set of "vitals" is closed off with a period (a semicolon would also be correct).

Example

Height: 72″. (correct)
Height: is 72″. (incorrect)

You Hear: this is a three day old black female infant with a rectal temperature of one hundred two degrees weighing seven pounds and nine ounces and measuring twenty one inches in length.
You Type: This is a 3-day-old black female infant with a rectal temperature of 102°, weighing 7 lb 9 oz, and measuring 21 in. in length.

You Hear: he is to take tofranil seventy five milligrams per day for three days to be increased to one hundred to one hundred fifty milligrams per day if there is no response.
You Type: He is to take Tofranil, 75 mg/day for three days to be increased to 100–150 mg/day if there is no response.

You Hear: the patient has twenty forty vision in the right eye and twenty one hundred in the left eye.
You Type: The patient has 20/40 vision in the right eye and 20/100 in the left eye.

RULE 5.15   Use figures when numbers are used *directly* with symbols, words, or abbreviations.

You Hear:	*You Type:*
one plus protein	1+ protein
fifteen millimeters of mercury	15 mmHg (also 15 mm Hg)
two percent	2%
seventy five milliliters per kilogram per twenty four hours	75 ml/kg/24 hours
one "cue aye dee"	1 q.i.d.
ten milligrams "tee aye dee"	10 mg t.i.d.
the "bee you en" is forty five milligrams percent	the BUN is 45 mg%
ninety nine degrees fahrenheit	99° F *or* 99 degrees Fahrenheit
a ten day history	a 10-day history
ten dollars	$10 *not* $10.00
sixty three cents	63 cents *not* 63¢ *or* $.63
number fourteen foley	#14 Foley *or* No. 14 Foley
thirty to thirty five milliequivalents	30–35 mEq (also 30 to 35 mEq)
four hundred milliosmol of solute	400 mOsm of solute
oh-ess equals plus two point five oh plus oh point seven five	O.S. = +2.50 + 0.75

RULE 5.16   Use figures for the day of the month and the year; write out the month.

Example

November 23, 1984
23 November 1984 *(military and foreign style)*

RULE 5.17   Use figures when writing the military time of day.

You Hear:	*You Type:*
zero three fifteen *(3:15 a.m.)*	0315
twelve hundred hours *(noon)*	1200
fourteen hundred hours *(2 p.m.)*	1400
sixteen thirty *(4:30 p.m.)*	1630

Example

Your appointment is set for 16:30. (incorrect)
Your appointment is set for 1630 p.m. (incorrect)
Your appointment is set for 1630. (correct)

NOTE: Military time is not used with a.m., p.m., or o'clock.

RULE 5.18   Use figures in writing suture materials.

NOTE: When the dictator says "three oh" or "triple oh" in referring to suture materials, you may type 000 or 3-0. For reading ease, use only the number, hyphen, and the zero when the number is larger than three, that is, from 4-0 through 11-0.

Examples

The incision was closed with #6-0 fine silk sutures. (correct)

The incision was closed with #000000 fine silk sutures. (incorrect)

The incision was closed with #60 fine silk sutures. (incorrect)

She used 000 chromic catgut for suture material. (correct)

She used 3-0 chromic catgut for suture material. (correct)

She used #3-0 chromic catgut for suture material. (correct)

RULE 5.19   Use figures and symbols when writing dimensions.

You Hear:
eight point five by five by four

You Type:
$8.5 \times 5.0 \times 4.0$ (correct)
$8.5 \times 5 \times 4$ (incorrect)

NOTE: Add a zero after the decimal point and whole numbers for consistency in the *set* of numbers. Leave a space on each side of the "X."

Subscript and Superscript

At one time, many numbers were typed in subscript or superscript (slightly below or above the line). With the advent of word processing equipment, this technique has become easier to employ without stopping twice to turn the platen up and down.

Examples

H_2O *(the symbol for water)*

A_2 is greater than P_2 *(the aortic second sound is greater than the pulmonic second sound)*

The L_4 area was bruised *(reference to the fourth lumbar vertebra)*

^{131}I was given *(reference to radioactive iodine)*

You might like to learn this technique and it will be shown in the examples, along with numbers typed on the line. It is not a necessary practice, and the same symbols are usually just as correct when typed properly on the line. It is often easier and quicker to type the numbers directly on the line, and many numbers are more easily read when typed this way, since most reports are single-spaced. An exception to the general rule of avoiding subscripts and superscripts is in the case of numbers given to the power of 10, e.g., *"urine culture grew out 10^5 colonies of E. coli."* It is obvious that in this case, to write the superscript on the same line would change the value of the number.

RULE 5.20   Use figures with capital letters to refer to the vertebral (spinal) column.

NOTE: C is used for the cervical vertebrae 1-7
T (or D) is used for the thoracic (or dorsal) vertebrae 1-12
L is used for the lumbar vertebrae 1-5
S is used for the sacral vertebrae 1-5

Normally the physician would not say "thoracic six" but "tee six."
You Type: T-6 or T_6

You Hear: he has a herniated disk at el four five.
You Type: He has a herniated disk at L4-5 (*or* L_{4-5}).

You Hear: there was an injury to the spine between see seven and tee one.
You Type: There was an injury to the spine between C-7 and T-1.
or
There was an injury to the spine between C7 and T1 (or C_7 and T_1).

NOTE: The reference to the spinal nerves is made in the same manner.

RULE 5.21   Use figures when writing electrocardiographic *chest* leads. These leads are V_1 through V_6 and aV_L, aV_R, and aV_F.

You Hear: there is es tee elevation in leads vee two and vee six.
You Type: There is ST elevation in leads V-2 and V-6 (*or* V_2 and V_6 *or* V2 and V6).

You Hear: the leads one, two, "a vee el," and "a vee ef" are missing in this sequence.
You Type: The leads I, II, aV_L (aVL also correct), and aV_F (aVF also correct) are missing in this sequence.

NOTE: Roman numerals are used with *limb* leads. See page 102.

5

RULE 5.22 Use figures in writing ratios.

You Hear: the solution was diluted one to one hundred.
You Type: The solution was diluted 1 : 100.

You Hear: there is a fifty-fifty chance of recovery.
You Type: There is a 50-50 chance of recovery.

NOTE: A *ratio* expresses the elements of a proportion and expresses the number of times the first contains the second.* A *range* is the linking of a sequence of values or numbered items by expressing only the first and last item in the sequence or the difference between the smallest and the largest varieties in a statistical distribution.

Ratios made up of words are expressed by a slash, a hyphen, or the word "to."

Examples
The odds are ten to one.
the female/male ratio or female-male ratio

Numerical ratios are expressed using a colon.

Examples
The odds are 10 : 1.
The solution was diluted 1 : 100,000.

Symbolic ratios are written with a slash.

Example: The a/b ratio

The word "to" or a dash may be used in expressions of range.

Examples
The projected salary increases are $2.75 to $3.00 per hour.
The projected salary increases are $2.75-$3.00 per hour.
We released all the medical records from 1980-1985 to microfilm storage.
There is a 3-6 month waiting period.

NOTE: Avoid using the dash when the range includes a plus and/or minus sign.

Examples
There was a weight change expected of anywhere from −6.5 to +10.5 kg.
The presenting part was at a −2 to a −3 station.

RULE 5.23 Use figures and symbols when writing plus or minus with a number.

You Hear:
one to two plus

You Type:
1-2+
1 to 2+

You Hear: pulses were two plus
You Type: pulses were 2+

You Hear: the presenting part was at a minus two station
You Type: The presenting part was at a −2 station.

You Hear: visual acuity with correction was increased to twenty two hundred by plus eight point fifty lens
You Type: Visual acuity with correction was increased to 20/200 by +8.50 lens.

Mixed Numbers

RULE 5.24 Use figures to write both technical and nontechnical mixed numbers (whole numbers with a fraction).

NOTE: Fractions are not used with the metric system nor with the percent (%) sign. Decimals are used with the metric system to describe portions of whole numbers.

Example
You Hear: three-fourths percent
You Type: 0.75% (not 3/4%)

Example: The patient moved to this community $2\frac{1}{2}$ years ago. (mixed number)

BUT: The patient moved to this community two years ago. (whole number less than ten)

You Hear: one and one half years ago
You Type: $1\frac{1}{2}$ or 1 1/2 years ago

You Hear: one and a half centimeters
You Type: 1.5 cm (not $1\frac{1}{2}$ cm)

NOTE: To type fractions, type the numerator, the slash, and the denominator when you do not have the fraction represented on your keyboard. Leave a space between the whole number and the numerator of the fraction: 2 1/4. It is not necessary to leave a space between the number and the fraction when the fraction is represented on your keyboard: $2\frac{1}{4}$.

RULE 5.25 Use figures in writing numbers containing decimal fractions.

---

*An example in making lemonade might be the following: Water : lemon juice : sugar ratio : 10 : 1 : 2 tablespoons.

Example

The incision site was injected with *0.5%* Xylocaine. (not ½%)

NOTE: A zero is placed before a decimal that does not contain a whole number to avoid its being read as a whole number. Be very careful with the placement of the zero and decimal. Incorrect placement could result in a 10-fold or 100-fold error.

EXCEPTION: By tradition and custom, no zero is used when expressing the caliber sizes of weapons.

Example: He used a .22-caliber rifle.

Unrelated Numbers and Other Combinations

RULE 5.26 Unrelated numbers in the same sentence follow the rules governing the use of each one.

Example: He has *three* offices and employs *21* medical assistants, including *2* transcriptionists. (Rule 5.3 and Rule 5.11)

RULE 5.27 Round numbers in millions and billions are expressed in a combination of figures and words.

Example: Do you know that Keane Insurance sold over *$3½ billion* of medical insurance last year?

Spacing

Notice that the symbols +, −, %, #, $, °, ', ", / are typed directly in front of or directly following the number they refer to with no spacing.

5–1: SELF-STUDY

Directions: Imagine that you hear the following "phonetic" phrases or sentences. On a separate sheet of paper, retype the phrases properly. Do not copy the quote marks that are placed around the "phonetic" phrase. Watch for the proper use of capitalization and punctuation. There is a synopsis of rules on page 112 to help you locate the rules quickly.

Example

the patient was seen in the emergency room at twenty hundred hours on eleven august nineteen ninety

The patient was seen in the Emergency Room at 2000 hours on August 11, 1990.

1. the wound was closed in layers with "two oh" and "three oh" black silk sutures

2. the three month premature infant was delivered by cesarean section

3. he is a twenty four year old black male with an admitting blood pressure of one hundred eighty over one hundred

4. paresis is noted in four fifths of the left leg

5. it was then suture ligated with chromic number one catgut sutures

6. there were multiple subserous fibroids ranging in size from point five to two point five centimeters in diameter

7. there are a thousand reasons why i wanted to be a doctor but at three "ay em" after i have been awakened from a deep sleep it is hard to think of any

8. my charge for the procedure is seven hundred and fifty dollars and the median fee in the community is eight hundred dollars

9. the patient received four units of blood

10. the bullet traveled through the pelvic plexus into the spinal cord shattering "es" two "es" three and "es" four

After you have typed this exercise, check the end of the chapter on page 113 to see if you completed it properly. *Retype* any problems that you missed so that you get the "feel" of producing them correctly and another chance to see them written accurately.

5–2: PRACTICE TEST

Directions: Follow the directions given in Self-Study 5–1.

1. on september twenty six nineteen ninety she had a left lower lobectomy

2. two sutures of triple oh cotton were placed so as to obliterate the posterior cul de sac

3. he smoked one and one half packs of cigarettes a day

4. there was a tear in the iris at about six oh clock

5. the resting blood pressure is seventy six over forty

6. please mail this to doctor ralph lavton at ten dublin street bowling green ohio four three four oh two

7. we had seven admissions saturday twenty four sunday and three this ay-em

8. In the accident the spine was severed between see four and five

9. the child was first seen by me in the x ray department on the evening of eleven may nineteen ninety

10. i recommend a course of cobalt sixty radiation therapy

The answers to these problems are in Appendix E at the back of the book. Retype any that you missed so that you have the opportunity of producing them correctly.

Roman Numerals

Roman numerals are generally used as noncounting numbers. There are many medical phrases *traditionally* expressed with capital roman numerals. These are made on the typewriter with the capital letters I, V, and X. Lower case roman numerals are used in the preparation of prescriptions and are made with the lower case i, v, and x; however, they are seldom required in typing. Generally capitalize the noun occurring with the roman numeral because it looks better with the capital letter used to make the numeral. Of course, proper names or words at the beginning of the sentence are always capitalized with the numeral.

RULE 5.28 Type numbers with the following expressions using roman numerals.

Expressions	*Examples*
Type	Type I hyperlipoproteinemia
Factor (blood clotting)	missing Factor VII (I to XIII)
Stage	Stage II carcinoma
	Stage I coma
	lues II (secondary syphilis) (I to III)
	Billroth I (first stage of an operative procedure)

Expressions	*Examples*
Phase	Phase II clinical trials
Class	Class II malignancy cardiac status: Class IV
Grade	Grade II systolic murmur
pregnancy and delivery	Gravida II Para II

NOTE: Considered as a set so no comma required.

cranial nerves	cranial nerves II-XII are intact (I to XII)
cranial leads (EEG)	lead I reading
limb lead (ECG)	lead II reading (I to III)
technique	Coffey technique III
with Greek alphabet	alpha II*

NOTE: Since the use of roman numerals is based only on tradition, some professionals prefer the use of arabic numbers. Always follow the desires or customs of your employer.

Examples

There was a grade 2 systolic murmur.
GYN: Gravida 2 Para 2.

---

* The symbols for the Greek alphabet cannot be made on the standard typewriter, so the names are written out. The most common letters used are the lower case alpha, beta, gamma, delta, lambda, and theta.

5–3: Self-Study

Directions: Imagine that you hear the following phonetic words, phrases, or sentences. On a separate sheet of paper, retype the sentences properly. Watch for the proper use of capitalization and punctuation.

1. there is a loud grade three musical bruit over the bifurcation of the left carotid artery. there is a soft grade one to two over the right internal carotid artery

2. bleeding was controlled with two oh ties

3. she is a gravida four para zero

4. the doctor's callback time is every day at four oh clock

5. i was called to the "ee" "are" at three in the morning where i performed an emergency tracheotomy on a four day old male infant. i remained in attendance for two hours to be sure he was out of danger

6. he came in for a class three flight physical

7. he has passed the five year mark without any evidence of a recurrence

8. he has a grade two beta strep infection

9. send my mail to post office box six not my home address

10. this is her fourth admittance this year

After you have typed this exercise, check the end of the chapter on page 113 to see if you completed the sentences properly. Retype any that you missed so that you will get a chance to produce them correctly.

5–4: PRACTICE TEST

Directions: Follow the directions given in Self-Study 5–3 above.

1. he has a grade one arteriosclerotic retinopathy and a grade four hypertensive retinopathy

2. she was gravida five para one abortus four and denied venereal disease but gave a history of vaginal discharge

3. i can see only fifteen to twenty patients a day

4. please order twelve two gauge needles

5. use only one eighth teaspoonful

6. the dorsalis pedis pulses were two plus and equal bilaterally

7. the ear was injected with two percent xylocaine and one to six thousand adrenalin

8. please check the reading in "vee four" again

9. this is her third "see" section

10. she quickly advanced from a stage two to a stage four lymphosarcoma

After you have checked your answers in Appendix E, retype any that you missed so that you will have the opportunity of producing them correctly.

USE OF SYMBOLS

You will notice many symbols printed in medical journals and texts, but the only symbols we are going to consider here are those that can be typed since not all students have access to word processing or computer-type fonts.

Symbol	Means	Explanation
&	and	symbol is called an "ampersand"
°C	degree Celsius	degree symbol is made by turning the carriage down a half space and typing an "o" off line.*
°F	degree Fahrenheit	
=	equals	the symbol is on the typewriter
′	feet	made with the apostrophe
″	inches	made with quotation marks
—	minus *or* to	made with the hyphen
#	number	the symbol is on the typewriter
/	per *or* over	made with the slash
:	ratio	made with the colon
%	percent	the symbol is on the typewriter
+	plus	if the symbol is not on the keyboard, it is made with the dash superimposed on the slash (∓)
×	times *or* by	the lower case x

RULE 5.29   Use symbols *only* when they occur in immediate association with a number.

Examples

You hear:	You type:
eight by three	8 × 3
four to five	4-5 *or* 4 to 5
number three oh	#3-0
pulses are two plus	pulses are 2+
vision is twenty twenty	vision is 20/20

---

* Some typists will avoid using the degree sign when it is not represented on their typewriter because it means rolling the typewriter carriage down to place it properly. This slows down the transcription process and it is difficult to correct if done wrong. If the dictator does not say "degree" then you do not have to type it or the symbol.

You hear:	You type:
six per day	6/day *or* 6 per day
diluted one to ten	diluted 1:10
at a minus two	at a −2
sixty over forty	60/40
grade four over five	Grade IV/V
patient had nocturia times two	patient had nocturia × 2
performed a tee and a	performed a T&A
25 millimeters per hour	25 mm/hr *or* 25 mm per hour
extension limited by 45 percent	extension limited by 45%
thirty degrees celsius	30°C *or* 30 degrees C
lost a few see sees	lost a few cubic centimeters

Be consistent when you have a choice.

Further illustration of symbol usage will be combined with the discussion of abbreviations.

USE OF ABBREVIATIONS

There are some abbreviations and symbols that we use so often that we no longer think of them as abbreviations but as complete words in themselves. We hear "percent" and we see %. "Mister" and "Doctor" look a bit out of place because Mr. and Dr. are such familiar titles. Medicine, like other technical fields, uses many abbreviations and symbols particularly familiar to the medical writer and reader; this section is a guide to their proper use.

It is difficult for the beginning transcriptionist to know exactly how abbreviations should be typed. To cause more of a dilemma, some abbreviations are typed in full capital letters, some in lower case, and some in a combination of both. They are written with or without periods. Chapter 3 introduced a punctuation rule using periods with abbreviations, and that rule will be repeated for you in this chapter so you need not turn back for review.

Symbols and abbreviations can save time, space, and energy and can prevent the needless duplication of repetitious words. The overuse of abbreviations is to be avoided, however, with only standard abbreviations appearing in the patient's record where permitted. Office and hospital "shortcuts" and hieroglyphics should be confined to memos and telephone messages. Furthermore, abbreviations of any type should never be used when there is a chance of misinterpretation. When in doubt (and you know the meaning of the abbreviation), spell it out.

The medical transcriptionist in the medical office is permitted far greater latitude in using abbreviations than either the hospital transcriptionist or those employed by trasncription services. The Joint Commission on Accreditation of Healthcare Organizations governs the documents prepared in the hospital, and their guidelines will be incorporated into the rules that follow.

To add further to the problem, many reference books disagree on both the capitalization and the punctuation of abbreviations.

RULE 5.30 Do not use abbreviations in the following parts of the patient's medical record: admission and discharge diagnoses, preoperative and postoperative diagnoses, and the names of surgical procedures.

Examples

Incorrect
Discharge diagnosis: PID

Correct
Discharge diagnosis: Pelvic inflammatory disease

Incorrect
Postoperative diagnosis: OMChS

Correct
Postoperative diagnosis: Otitis media, chronic, suppurating

Incorrect
Operation performed: T&A

Correct
Operation performed: Tonsillectomy and adenoidectomy

RULE 5.31 Use symbols and abbreviations in the medical record only when they have been approved by the medical staff and there is an explanatory legend available to those authorized to make entries in the medical record and to those who must interpret them.

NOTE: These lists will vary, of course, among institutions. Obtain lists from the institutions for which you work and refer to them carefully.

RULE 5.32 Spell out an abbreviation when you realize there could be a misunderstanding in the interpretation of the definition. You must be positive, of course, that *your* interpretation is correct; otherwise leave it alone or flag the transcript for the dictator to interpret.

Examples

"The patient had a history of CVRD."
cardiovascular renal disease?
cardiovascular respiratory disease?

RULE 5.33 Use an abbreviation to refer to a test, committee, drug, diagnosis, and so on in a report or paper *after* it has been used once in its completely spelled-out form.

Example: "All newborns are routinely tested for phenylketonuria (PKU). As a result, the incidence of PKU as a cause of infant . . . "

RULE 5.34 Check any unfamiliar abbreviations or those that seem inappropriate with your reference lists. Individual letters in spoken form can sound alike.

Example: "I performed an IND . . . " (or I & D or IMD or IMB or IMP or IME) (This could go on and on.)

Appendix C has a list of excellent medical abbreviation reference books. You should have one of them in addition to your hospital-approved list.

RULE 5.35 Type familiar, common abbreviations and words usually seen as abbreviations, as abbreviations.

Examples

Mr. Dr. Mrs. oz a.m. p.m. CBC C-section DNA ER pH Rh

NOTE: Further on in this chapter is a very brief list of many common abbreviations, with their capitalization and punctuation. These should be in your personal dictionary.

RULE 5.36 Use abbreviations for all metric measurements used *with* numbers.

Examples

You hear:	*You type:*
one millimeter	1 mm
five millimeters	5 mm
ten centimeters	10 cm
point five millimeters	0.5 mm*
six cubic centimeters	6 cc
seven milliliters	7 mL *or* ml
twenty kilograms	20 kg (not kilos)
thirty seven degrees celsius	37°C or 37 degrees C
BUT: there was only *a centimeter* difference between the two.	(no abbreviation)

* Please notice the zero (0) in front of the decimal point. Refer to Rule 5–25. You will also notice that metric abbreviations are always written in lower case letters, are typed one space after the number, and are not made plural. An exception is the capital C for *Celsius* and capital L for *liter*. In addition, some physicians use the word *centigrade* rather than *Celsius*. Use the capital C as the abbreviation for both.

5

RULE 5.37 Periods are used with single capitalized words and single letter abbreviations:

Mr.   Jr.   Dr.   Inc.   Ltd.   Joseph P. Myers   E. coli

- academic degrees and religious orders:
  M.D.   Ph.D.   D.D.S.   B.V.E.   M.S.   S.J.

- lower case abbreviations made up of single letters:
  a.m.   p.m.   e.g.   t.i.d.

NOTE: • Units of measurement are *not* punctuated.
  wpm   mph   ft   oz   sq in

  • Certification, registration, and licensure abbreviations are *not* punctuated.
  CMA-A   CMT   RN   RRA   ART   LVN

  • Acronyms and metric abbreviations are *not* punctuated.
  CARE   Project HOPE   AIDS   mg   mL   L   cm   km

  • Most abbreviations typed in full capital letters are *not* punctuated
  UCLA   PKU   BUN   CBC   WBC   COPD   D&C   T&A   I&D   P&A   NBC   FICA   KEZL   TV   FM

  • Scientific abbreviations written in a combination of capital and lower case letters are *not* punctuated.
  Rx   Dx   ACh   Ba   Hb   IgG   mEq   mOsm   Rh

(This is also Rule 3.16.)

RULE 5.38 Chemical and mathematical abbreviations are written in a combination of both upper and lower case letters without periods.

Examples

cc	*(cubic centimeter)*
CO_2 (CO2)	*(carbon dioxide)*
Hb	*(hemoglobin)*
Hg	*(mercury)*
Na	*(sodium)*
T_4 (T4)	*(thyroxine)*
O_2 (O2)	*(oxygen)*
Ca^{++}	*(calcium ion)*
NaCl	*(sodium chloride)*
pH	*(hydrogen ion concentration)*
DNA	*(deoxyribonucleic acid)*
HCl	*(hydrochloric acid)*
10^4	*(ten to the fourth)*
K	*(potassium)*

Dictated: the patient had a pee h of five point two.
Transcribed: The patient had a pH of 5.2. (not hydrogen ion concentration)

Dictated: The dee en a is unavailable for further study.
Transcribed: The DNA is unavailable for further study.

Dictated: stat report shows sodium one hundred thirty eight milliequivalents per liter potassium three point three milliequivalents per liter chloride ninety seven milliequivalents per liter and a total see oh two of five milliequivalents per liter blood glucose is seven hundred milligrams percent.
Transcribed: STAT report shows sodium (or NA) 138 mEq/L; potassium (or K) 3.3 mEq/L, chloride (or Cl) 97 mEq/L and a total carbon dioxide (CO_2 or CO2 correct) of 5 mEq/L. Blood glucose is 700 mg% (not mg percent or milligrams percent).

RULE 5.39 Latin abbreviations are typed in lower case letters, with periods.

Examples

i.e. (that is)	etc. (and so forth)
et al. (and other people)	e.g. (for example)
op cit. (in the work cited)	a.m. (ante meridian)
b.i.d. (twice a day)	p.m. (post meridian)
t.i.d. (three times a day)	p.c. (after meals)
q.i.d. (four times a day)	a.c. (before meals)

EXCEPTION: A.D. (in the year of Our Lord)

NOTE: It has become acceptable to write "a.m." and "p.m." in capital letters. This form is not punctuated: AM and PM.

RULE 5.40 Do not abbreviate names unless the name is abbreviated in the correspondent's own letterhead. Shortened forms of a person's name, such as a nickname, are allowed in the salutation.

Example: Steven J. Clayborn *and* Dear Steve:

NOT: "Geo." "Chas." used with a last name unless thus abbreviated in the letterhead.

NOTE: Some "nicknames" might not be a shortened form but the entire name.

Examples: Ray, Gene, Will, Al, Alex, Ben, Ed, Fred, Sam, Pat, Beth, Hugh, Betty.

> Do not abbreviate in some other cases:

1. Titles other than Dr., Mr., Mrs., Ms., unless a first name or initial accompanies the last name.

   Examples
   Maj. Ralph Emery *but* Major Emery
   Hon. John Wilson *but* Honorable Wilson
   Rt. Rev. Donald Turnbridge *but* Right Reverend Turnbridge.

2. The words *street, road, avenue, boulevard, north, south, east,* and *west* in an inside address. However, *Southwest (SW), Northwest (NW),* and so on are abbreviated *after* the street name.

   Examples
   936 North Branch Street
   1876 Washington Boulevard, NW

3. Days of the week and months of the year. To avoid confusion, numbers should not be substituted for the names of the months in correspondence; however, they are acceptable in some records and reports.

   Example
   January 11, 1991 (narrative copy)
   NOT: Jan 11, 1991, *or* 1-11-91 *or* 1/11/91 *or* 01-11-91

ABBREVIATION REFERENCE

The following list of abbreviations is brief and not intended as a complete reference but will serve as a reference for your exercises and also serve to illustrate the variety of ways that many common abbreviations are typed: full caps, combination of capitalized letter and lower case letters, and lower case letters. The italics will indicate how the abbreviation is generally said, when it is not said as the individual letters of the abbreviation itself. Meanings are not given because we are concerned now with typing format and not terminology. Furthermore, you should know that abbreviations, symbols, and contractions are used far more freely in chart notes (progress notes) and history and physical reports than they would be in a discharge summary, operative report, legal report, or formal correspondence. For example, you would type "The GU tract was clear" in the patient's medical office record but would type "The genitourinary tract was clear" in a report to an insurance examiner. The medical office record might note that "the *pt* had an *appy* on *7-1-9X*" and "*she's* waiting for the results of a *cysto.*" The letter to another physician reports that "the *patient* had an *appendectomy* on *July 1, 199X*"; likewise, "*she is* waiting for the results of a *cystoscopy.*"

Please examine your list carefully and say aloud each abbreviation so you will know how it sounds.

A_2
A, B, AB, O
These are blood types and can also be dictated with subscript numbers, e.g., A_1, O_2, and so on.

A/B *ay-bee ratio*	D_5W; also D5W
a.c.	Dx *diagnosis*
ACh *acetylcholine*	Dr. *doctor*
AD or a.d. *right ear*	ECG
A.D.	EEG
A&D *ay-en-dee*	EENT
AIDS *aids*	e.g. *example given* or *e-gee*
a.m. or AM	E/I ratio *e-eye ratio*
AP	EKG
ART	Eq *equivalent*
AS or a.s. *left ear*	ER
aV_F or aVF	Esq. *esquire*
aV_L or aVL	ESR
aV_R or aVR	et al. *et-all*
Ba *barium*	fl oz *fluid ounce*
b.i.d.	ft *feet*
BP	Fx *fracture*
BUN	GI
B.V.E.	gm *gram*
Ca^{++} *calcium ion*	G neg *gram negative*
CA or Ca	G pos *gram positive*
CARE *care*	gr *grain*
CBC	gtt *drop(s)*
cc *see-see* or *cubic centimeter*	GU
	GYN
CC *chief complaint*	H^+ *hydrogen ion*
CCU	Hb *hemoglobin*
cm *centimeter*	HCl *hydrochloric acid*
CMA-A	Hct *hematocrit*
CMT	HEENT
CNS	H_2O *h-two-oh* or *water*
COPD	HOPE *hope* (Ship and Project)
CPX	
CR	H&P *h-en-pee*
X match *crossmatch*	h.s.
C-section *see section*	Hz *Hertz*
CVA	^{131}I *one thirty one eye;* also *I-131*
D&C *dee-en-see*	
D.D.	ICU
D.D.S.	I&D *eye-en-dee*
°C *degrees Celsius* or *centigrade*	i.e., *eye-e* or *that is*
	IgA *immunoglobulin a* or *eye-gee-ay*
°F *degrees Fahrenheit*	
DNA	IgG *immunoglobulin gee* or *eye-gee-gee* or *gamma immunoglobulin*
D.O.	
D.P.M.	
DTR	

IgM *eye-gee-em*
in. *inch*
Inc. *ink* or *incorporated*
IPPB
Jr. *junior*
K *potassium*
kg *kilogram*
km *kilometer*
a.s. *left ear*
o.s. *left eye*
L *liter*
LLQ
LMP
LPN
Ltd. *limited*
LUQ
LVN
L&W *el-en-double you*
MAST *mast*
M.D.
Hg *mercury*
mEq *milliequivalent*
mg *milligram*
ml or mL *milliliter*
mg% *milligrams percent*
mm *millimeter*
mmHg or mm Hg
    millimeters of mercury
mOsm *milliosmol*
mph
Mr. *mister*
mr *milliroentgen*

M.S. (means master's
    degree in science)
MS (means multiple
    sclerosis)
NM
O$_2$ *oxygen*
OBG
Ob-Gyn *oh-bee-gee-
    why-en*
OCG
OD or o.d. *oh-dee* or
    right eye
op. cit. *in the work quoted*
OR
OS or o.s. *left eye*
oz *ounce*
P$_2$
PA
P&A *pee-en-a*
Pap *pap* (smear, test,
    exam)
p.c.
pCO$_2$ *pee-see-oh two* or
    *pressure of carbon
    dioxide*
PE *physical exam*
PERRLA *purr-lah*
pH
Ph.D.
PKU
pO$_2$ *pee-oh-two* or
    pressure of oxygen

p.m. or PM
PO (means postopera-
    tive)
p.o. (means "by mouth")
PR interval
PRN
Pt *patient*
PX *physical exam*
K *potassium*
Px *prognosis*
P, Q, R, S, T, U (use the
    letter and hyphen for
    wave) P-wave
q2h *every two hours*
q3h *every three hours*
q4h *every four hours*
q.i.d.
QRS complex
rbc *red blood cells*
RBC *red blood count*
Rh *are-h* or *Rhesus
    factor*
RhoGAM *row-gam*
RN
RLQ
R/O *rule out*
RUQ
Rx *prescription*
S$_1$ (through S$_4$)
SMAC *smack*
SOAP *soap*
SOB

Na *sodium*
NaCl *sodium chloride*
Sr. *senior*
STAT *stat*
STD
ST segment
ST-T interval
T&A *tee-en-ay*
T$_3$
T$_4$
10^4 *ten to the fourth* or
    *ten to the power of
    four;* this can be used
    with any number
i.e. *that is*
t.i.d.
TM
UA
UCLA
UNICEF *uni-sef*
URI
V$_1$ (through V$_6$)
VD
VDRL
H$_2$O *water* or *h-two-oh*
wbc (means white blood
    cell)
WBC (means white
    blood count)
wpm
X match *crossmatch*
x-ray *ex-ray*

 5–5: SELF-STUDY

Directions: Please study the *Abbreviation Reference* and type the answers to the questions on a separate sheet of paper.

1. You hear: eye gee gee
   You type: _____

2. You hear: fifteen millimeters of mercury
   You type: _____

3. You hear: ten to the fourth
   You type: _____

4. You hear: are-h negative
   You type: _____

5. You hear: clear to pee-en a
   You type: _____

6. You hear: h double e en tee
   You type: _____

7. You hear: take one bee eye de pee are en for pain
   You type: _____

8. You hear: h en pee
   You type: _____

9. You hear: pee oh two
   You type: _____

10. You hear: acetylcholine
    You type: _____

After you have typed this exercise, refer to the end of this chapter, page 114, to check your answers.

 5–6: SELF-STUDY

Directions: Imagine that you hear the following phonetic phrases or sentences. On a separate sheet of paper, retype the sentences and phrases properly. Watch for proper use of symbols, numbers, abbreviations, punctuation, and capitalization.

Example
the "pee-h" was seven: neutrality; just between alkalinity and acidity
The pH was 7: neutrality; just between alkalinity and acidity.

1. flexion was limited to fifteen degrees, extension to ten degrees, adduction to ten degrees and abduction to twenty degrees

2. by use of a half inch osteotome one centimeter of the proximal end of the proximal phalanx was removed

3. "dee tee ares" are one to two plus

4. range of motion of the neck is limited to approximately seventy percent of normal

5. the date on the cholecystogram was nine one ninety one

6. estimated blood loss was one hundred "see-sees" none was replaced

7. at two "ay-em" the patients temperature was thirty eight point nine degrees celsius

8. the "pee-ay" and right lateral roentgenograms show a fracture of the right third and fourth ribs

9. lenses were prescribed resulting in improvement of his visual acuity to twenty thirty in the right eye and twenty forty five in the left eye. the visual field examination was normal and the tension is seventeen millimeters of mercury of schiotz with a five point five gram weight

10. the number twenty two foley with a thirty "see-see" bag was then inserted

11. i removed six hundred milliliters of serosanguineous fluid from the abdomen

After you have typed this exercise, check the end of the chapter on page 114 to see if you completed it properly. Retype any portions that you missed so that you get the "feel" of producing them correctly and another chance to see them written accurately.

 5–7: PRACTICE TEST

Directions: Follow the instructions given in Self-Study 5–6.

1. hemoglobin on seven twenty seven was eleven point two grams hematocrit was thirty seven

2. did you know that the postal rates were twenty five cents for the first ounce and twenty cents for each additional ounce to mail something first class in nineteen eighty nine

3. the protein was sixty five milligrams percent

4. electromyography shows a three plus sparsity in the orbicularis oris

5. an estimated point two cubic centimeters of viscid fluid was removed from the middle ear cavity

6. he entered the "e-are" at four "ay-em" with a temperature of ninety nine degrees fahrenheit

7. there was a reduction of the angle to within a two degree difference

8. take fifty milligrams per day

9. i then placed two four by four sponges over the wound

10. the "tee-bee" skin test was diluted one to one hundred

11. drainage amounts to several "see-sees" a day

After you have checked your answers with Appendix E, retype any that you missed so that you will have the opportunity of producing them correctly.

5-8: SELF-STUDY

Directions: Follow the instructions given in Self-Study 5–6.

1. the urine was negative for sugar, "pee-h" was seven and specific gravity was one point zero one two

2. the "bee-you-en" is forty five milligrams percent, one plus protein

3. i excised a small well circumscribed tumor two millimeters in diameter

4. use a three "em" vi-drape to cover the operative site

5. she received her second dose of "five-ef-you"

6. the culture grew one hundred thousand colonies of e coli per cubic centimeter

7. the surgeon asked for a number seven jackson bronchoscope

8. there were high serum titers of "gee" immunoglobulin antibodies

9. the phenotype "a-two-b" was found consistently in the family blood history

10. respirations sixteen per minute

After you have typed this exercise, check the end of the chapter on page 115 to see if you completed it properly. Retype any portions that you missed before you go on to your final exercise.

 ## 5-9: REVIEW TEST

Directions: Follow the instructions given in Self-Study 5–6.

1. the patient has a "pee-h" of six point ninety six "pee oh two" of twelve and "pee see oh two" of fifty four

2. there is a one by point five centimeter area of avulsed tissue and a three centimeter gaping deep laceration of the chin

3. lungs: clear to "pee and a." heart: not enlarged, "ay-to" is greater than "pee-to" there was a grade one to two over six decrescendo early diastolic high frequency murmur

4. cycloplegic refraction: "oh-dee" equal plus three point two five plus oh point seven five times one hundred twenty five equals twenty thirty minus one

5. the patient received a six thousand gamma roentgen dose

6. iodipamide sodium i one hundred thirty one was used

7. we used a concentration of five times ten to the fifth per milliliter

8. a dilute solution of one to one was used

9. he was scheduled for a "tee three" uptake

10. aqueous procaine penicillin "gee," four point eight million units intramuscularly with one gram of probenecid orally, is still recommended for uncomplicated gonorrhea

11. she returned today for her vitamin "bee-twelve"

12. my plan was to give her six hundred thousand units of penicillin on the first day and give her half that on the second

13. he denied symptoms of dysuria hematuria and urgency but did report nocturia times two

14. she is to take her medication "cue-four-h" with an additional one half dose "a-see"

15. i have an appointment for the eleventh of june and i need to change it to the first of july

16. six case histories were presented at the tumor board meeting today for a total of ninety seven this year

17. we expect that thousands of students will be able to participate in this surgery through the use of closed circuit "tee vee"

18. he has been a two pack a day cigarette smoker for the last forty years

19. please order six twenty gauge catheters

20. plan the surgery to begin at seven "ay em" sharp

21. i feel that my fee of twelve hundred dollars is fair

22. the jury awarded one point two million dollars in damages to the parents of the child

23. i removed a forty five slug from the left lower liver margin

24. how many centimeters long was that tear in her thumb

25. the hemoglobin was eight point eight, hematocrit twenty six point five white blood cells eight thousand one hundred with eighty segs and eighteen lymphs

26. you will notice that the standard leads one, two, "a vee el" and "a vee ef" are missing in the "ee-see-gee" lead-sequencing formats

27. then five to ten milliliters of one percent lidocaine was injected into the right breast at the four oclock and eight oclock areas

28. call back all "are-h" negative women with no demonstrable antibody titer for an injection of "row-gam"

5

POSTSCRIPT

Some of the phrases and expressions discussed in this chapter occur frequently in dictation and are worthy of mention one more time. Be sure that you are able to use them correctly.

You Hear	*Properly Transcribed*
it was her fifth admission	it was her fifth admission.
will be admitted at four pee em	will be admitted at 4 p.m. (PM)
came to see me at four oclock	came to see me at four o'clock
ay two is greater than pee two	A-2 is greater than P-2 (or A_2, P_2)
vision is twenty twenty	vision is 20/20
a twenty nine year old	a 29-year-old
weight is six pounds five ounces	weight is 6 lb 5 oz
taken tee i dee for three days	taken t.i.d. for three days
ninety nine degrees	99° (99 degrees)
diluted one to ten	diluted 1:10
sixty-five milligrams percent	65 mg%
bee pee is one hundred over eighty	BP is 100/80
sutured with three oh chromic	sutured with 3-0 (or 000) chromic
injected with point five percent	injected with 0.5%
used three four by fours	used three 4 × 4s
nocturia times two	nocturia × 2
one plus protein	1+ protein
drink seven hundred fifty milliliters per twelve hour period	drink 750 mL/12-hour period
herniated disk at tee three four	herniated disk at T3-4 or $T_{3\text{-}4}$
dorsalis pedis pulses were two plus	dorsalis pedis pulses were 2+
class two infection	Class II infection
cranial nerves two through twelve	cranial nerves II-XII
cut was ten centimeters long	cut was 10 cm long
fifteen millimeters of mercury	15 mmHg (or mm Hg)
the pee h was seven point oh	the pH was 7.0
he takes two pee see	he takes two p.c. or 2 p.c.
seen on four twenty-one	seen on April 21

RULE SYNOPSIS

	RULE	PAGE NO.
General		
Abbreviations and numbers	5.15	98
Date	5.1, 5.16	96, 98
Decimals	5.24, 5.25	100
Dimensions	5.19	99
Fractions	5.5, 5.24	97, 100
Indefinite expressions	5.4	97
Large numbers	5.8, 5.10, 5.27	97, 100, 101
Money	5.13	98
Multiple use of numbers	5.2, 5.6, 5.11, 5.24, 5.26	96, 97, 100, 101
Numbers in the address	5.1	96
Ordinal numbers (first, second)	5.1	96
Spelling out numbers	5.2 to 5.8	96 to 97
Time of day	5.7, 5.9, 5.17	97, 98
Unrelated numbers	5.26	101
Written-out numbers	5.2 to 5.8	96 to 97
Technical		
Abbreviations	5.30 to 5.40	105 to 106
Capitalization of abbreviations	5.37	106
Chemical abbreviations	5.38	106
Dilute solutions	5.22	100
Electrocardiographic leads	5.21, 5.28	99, 102
Figures with plus or minus	5.23	100
Foreign abbreviations	5.39	106
Greek letters	5.28	104
Metric abbreviations	5.36	105
Military time	5.17	98
Miscellaneous abbreviations		107
O'clock area	5.12	98
Punctuation with abbreviations	5.37	106
Ranges	5.22	100
Ratios	5.22	100
Roman numerals	5.28	102
Spacing with symbols		101
Spinal column and nerves	5.20	99
Subscript and superscript		99
Suture materials	5.18	99
Symbols	5.15, 5.29	98, 104
Units of measurement	5.14, 5.19, 5.22	98, 100
Vital statistics	5.14	98
When not to abbreviate	5.30 to 5.32, 5.40	105, 106

🖪 Answers to 5 – 1: Self-Study

1. The wound was closed in layers with 2-0 and 3-0 black silk sutures. (00 and 000 also correct.)

2. The 3-month-premature infant was delivered by cesarean section. (note hyphens)

3. He is a 24-year-old black male with an admitting blood pressure of 180/100. (note hyphens and slash)

4. Paresis is noted in four-fifths of the left leg. (note hyphen)

5. It was then suture ligated with chromic #1 catgut sutures. (No. 1 also correct)

6. There were multiple subserous fibroids ranging in size from 0.5 to 2.5 cm in diameter.

7. There are a thousand reasons why I wanted to be a doctor; but at 3 a.m., after I have been awakened from a deep sleep, it is hard to think of any. (check your commas and semicolon too; capital AM also correct)

8. My charge for the procedure is $750, and the median fee in the community is $800. (not $750.00 and $800.00; nor is 750 dollars correct)

9. The patient received 4 units of blood.

10. The bullet traveled through the pelvic plexus into the spinal cord shattering S_2, S_3, and S_4. (S-2, S-3, and S-4 also correct) (S2, S3, and S4 also correct)

🖪 Answers to 5 – 3: Self-Study

1. There is a loud Grade III musical bruit over the bifurcation of the left carotid artery. There is a soft Grade I-II over the right internal carotid artery. (Grade I to II also correct)

2. Bleeding was controlled with 2-0 ties. (00 also correct)

3. She is a Gravida IV Para 0. (gravida and para also correct)

4. The doctor's callback time is every day at four o'clock.

5. I was called to the ER at three in the morning where I performed an emergency tracheotomy on a 4-day-old male infant. I remained in attendance for two hours to be sure he was out of danger.

6. He came in for a Class III flight physical.

7. He has passed the five-year mark without any evidence of a recurrence.

8. He has a Grade II beta strep infection.

9. Send my mail to Post Office Box Six, not my home address. (PO Box 6 also correct)

10. This is her fourth admittance this year.

5

▣ Answers to 5–5: Self-Study

1. IgG

2. 15 mmHg or 15 mm Hg

3. 10^4

4. Rh−

5. clear to P&A

6. HEENT

7. take 1 b.i.d., p.r.n. pain (PRN is also correct)

8. H&P

9. pO2 or pO_2

10. acetylcholine

▣ Answers to 5–6: Self-Study

1. Flexion was limited to 15°, extension to 10°, adduction to 10°, and abduction to 20°. (degrees can also be written out, e.g., 15 degrees)

2. By use of a half-inch osteotome, 1 cm of the proximal end of the proximal phalanx was removed.

3. DTRs are 1-2+. (also 1 to 2+)

4. Range of motion of the neck is limited to approximately 70% of normal. (70 percent also correct)

5. The date on the cholecystogram was September 1, 1991.

6. Estimated blood loss was 100 cc; none was replaced. (note semicolon)

7. At 2 a.m., the patient's temperature was 38.9°C. (also 38.9 degrees Celsius; also capital AM)

8. The PA and right lateral roentgenograms show a fracture of the right third and fourth ribs.

9. Lenses were prescribed resulting in improvement of his visual acuity to 20/30 in the right eye and 20/45 in the left eye. The visual field examination was normal and the tension is 17 mmHg of Schiotz with a 5.5 gm weight. (also 17 mm Hg) *Note:* The medical office record could use the right eye and left eye abbreviations in that sentence so the phrase would appear as follows: 20/30 o.d. and 20/45 o.s.

10. The #22 Foley with a 30 cc bag was then inserted. (No. 22 also correct)

11. I removed 600 mL of serosanguineous fluid from the abdomen (ml also correct)

Answers to 5–8: Self-Study

1. The urine was negative for sugar, pH was 7, and specific gravity was 1.012.

2. The BUN is 45 mg%, 1+ protein.

3. I excised a small, well-circumscribed tumor, 2 mm in diameter.

4. Use a 3M Vi-Drape to cover the operative site. (3-M might be how you typed it, but this company does not print it that way. Vi-Drape is a brand name that you now know. Always expect that words of this sort that are not in the dictionary are brand names. The letter after the hyphen in a brand name is generally capitalized.)

5. She received her second dose of 5-FU.

6. The culture grew 100,000 colonies of E. coli/cc. (E. coli per cubic centimeter is also correct. In the first example, the abbreviation is used correctly with a symbol (/), and in the second example, the word is written out following the word "per." Consistency is important.)

7. The surgeon asked for a #7 Jackson bronchoscope. (also No. 7)

8. There were high serum titers of IgG antibodies.

9. The phenotype A_2B was found consistently in the family blood history.

10. Respirations: 16/min (16 per minute also correct). (Don't forget to check your punctuation.)

ARE WE COMING TO THIS?

Patient Name: N/A
Identifying number: 786-65-98765-430-A_1

GENERAL:	Pt is a w-d, w-n, 50Y/O, W/M, in NAD, O. to time, place, person.
EYES:	PERRLA. EOMs intact, fundi benign.
EARS:	TM intact, canals patent.
MOUTH:	Edentulous.
NECK:	No JVD.
CHEST:	Narrow AP diameter; clear to P&A.
HEART:	PMI in 5th IC space. A_2 greater than P_2.
PAST HISTORY:	Pt had U&C childhood diseases and has history of ASCVHD, NYHA classification II/VI. Also had HNP, BPH, and PIP dysfunction, left ring finger.
FAMILY:	M&F, L&W.
SURGICAL:	T & A as child; laminectomy at L_{4-5}, S_1; TURP in 1987. Had MCP repair of PIP joint, left ring finger.

Letter Transcription

OBJECTIVES

After reading this chapter and working the exercises, you should be able to

1. appraise the value of an attractive letter to a business.
2. assess how the business letter reflects the public image of a medical practice.
3. describe the specific qualities that make a letter mailable.
4. demonstrate the three basic mechanical formats of letter preparation.
5. demonstrate the ability to paragraph properly and to place a letter attractively on a page.
6. use a specific letter format in preparation of a letter from copy typed as a single paragraph.
7. prepare envelopes using the recommended U.S. Postal Service procedure.
8. prepare a two-page letter following the rules for multiple-page letters.

. . . .

INTRODUCTION

You are the key factor in turning out a product: the letter.

The letter is the personal representative of the writer and expresses his or her professional standing by its contents as well as its appearance. You control its appearance, and you may partially control how it reads; thus it represents you, also.

It is important that the letter be perfect in every way, beginning with "eye appeal" and with absolute attention to such details as format, punctuation, para-graphing, spelling, and grammar. Your success depends on your ability to produce a mailable letter. Therefore, in learning to identify the specific qualities that make a letter mailable, you should also be able to recognize errors in form, grammar, punctuation, typing, and spelling.

VOCABULARY

Open punctuation: Style of letter punctuation in which no punctuation mark is used after the saluta-

117

tion or complimentary close. (See Fig. 6 – 1*B*, page 120.)

Mixed punctuation: Style of letter punctuation in which a colon or a comma is used after the salutation and a comma is used after the complimentary close. (See Fig. 6 – 1*A*, page 119.)

Letter format: The mechanical set-up of a letter, which dictates placement of the various letter parts. (See Fig. 6 – 2, page 124.)

Continuation sheets: The sheets of paper used to type a second and subsequent pages of a letter. These are often called second sheets.

Full block: The name of a particular letter format. (See Fig. 6 – 1*A*, page 119.)

Modified block: The name of a particular letter format. (See Fig. 6 – 1*B*, page 120.)

Qualities of a Mailable Letter

1. *Placement.* The letter should:
   a. be attractively placed on the page with the right margin fairly even (no more than five figures in variation).
   b. have "eye appeal," with the letterhead taken into consideration when format is chosen.
   c. have picture-frame symmetry as an achievable ideal.

2. *Form.* The following should be taken into consideration:
   a. correct format (such as full block or modified block).
   b. double spacing between paragraphs.
   c. consistent punctuation (open or mixed).
   d. correct usage of enclosure and copy notations.

3. *Typing techniques.* There should be no typing errors such as strikeovers, letters touching, letters too light to read, incorrect spacing, transposition of words, typographic errors, messy erasures, material omitted, or words divided incorrectly at the end of a line.

4. *Proper mechanics.* You should show proper knowledge of technical writing techniques, e.g., abbreviations, numbers, and symbols. (See Chapter 5.)

5. *Grammar usage.* The words in the letter should be used correctly in accordance with their meaning, e.g., all ready/already.
   Homonyms should be used correctly, e.g., their/there, site/sight/cite.
   Contractions should be avoided whenever possible.

6. *Spelling.* There must be no doubt about the correct

spelling of a word, and a dictionary must be consulted without hesitation. (See Chapter 8).

7. *Overall appearance.* Be sure to check the following:
   a. clean type.
   b. well-inked ribbon.
   c. no smears or smudges.

8. *Content.* Be sure of the following:
   a. accurate as dictated.
   b. no material omitted.
   c. no material changed that alters the meaning of the letter.

Letter Formats

Secretarial manuals illustrate and name many different formats in which letters may be prepared. There are variations in the names given to these arrangements, but the formats are standard.

The following formats have been named to match closely those names you might already have learned and, at the same time, to describe as nearly as possible the appearance of the letter:

Full Block (Fig. 6 – 1*A*). This is the most frequently used format. Notice that the date line, address, salutation, all lines of the body of the letter, complimentary close, and typed signature line are flush with the left margin. This is a popular format because no tab stops are needed. As long as it is compatible with the letterhead and the wishes of the dictator, you may use it.

Modified Block (Fig. 6 – 1*B*). The date line, complimentary close, and typed signature line are typed to begin just to the right of the middle of the page. This format has a little more "personality" and is compatible with most letterheads. Most dictators are comfortable with the signature area.

At this point, please notice that placement of the date line sets your format. If you place the date at the left margin, you must continue with Full Block format. If you place your date at the center point you must follow through with this format, making sure that the complimentary close and typed signature line are lined up with it.

Modified Block with Indented Paragraphs (Fig. 6 – 1*C*). The third and final format is not as popular as the first two because of the tab stop necessary at each paragraph. It is a traditional format and might be preferred by the dictator. Additional formats you may have learned in business typing classes are not used for medical letters owing to their informality.

Many general business offices have one letter for-

(Text continued on page 123)

FAX: College Park Hospital and Medical Center
212-555-1247   555 Lake View Drive   216-555-1234
                                  Bay Village, OH 44140

full block format

February 7, 199X

Herbert A. Rothschild, M.D.
1721 Cedar Street, Suite B
Bay Village, OH 44140

Dear Herb, ◄——— mixed punctuation

RE: William Santee ◄——— reference line

Young Bill Santee came in to see me today.

As you know, his problem is one of a very mild pectus excavatum
with some tenderness in the area. It is my feeling that this
child's pectus problem was brought to his attention when he
strained his pectoral muscles lifting weights about six weeks
ago. This was then accentuated when his older brother gave him
a "bear hug." Following that, he did a little introspection
and found that he actually had a pectus excavatum, but both he
and the brother thought this had occurred during the "bear hug"
episode.

In any event, there is not one thing you or I can, or should, do.

Both of the parents and the boy were reassured that he had a
mild congenital anomaly that would not in any way disable
him, and there was nothing more to do about it. I think my
explanation was well accepted by the parents and the child.

Thank you very much for sending this nice family to see me.

Sincerely yours, ◄——— mixed punctuation

full block format

Patrick D. Quinn, M.D.

aoa

cc: Mr. and Mrs. H. James Santee

FIGURE 6-1. Letters illustrating varying styles and punctuation. *A*, Full-block style and mixed punctuation.

FAX:
212-555-1247

College Park Hospital and Medical Center
555 Lake View Drive
Bay Village, OH 44140

216-555-1234

February 7, 199X ← modified block

Herbert A. Rothschild, M.D.
1721 Cedar Street, Suite B
Bay Village, OH 44140

RE: William Santee ← reference line

Dear Herb ← open punctuation

(breaking the placement rule)

Young Bill Santee came in to see me today.

As you know, his problem is one of a very mild pectus excavatum with some tenderness in the area. It is my feeling that this child's pectus problem was brought to his attention when he strained his pectoral muscles lifting weights about six weeks ago. This was then accentuated when his older brother gave him a "bear hug." Following that, he did a little introspection and found that he actually had a pectus excavatum, but both he and the brother thought this had occurred during the "bear hug" episode.

In any event, there is not one thing you or I can, or should, do.

Both of the parents and the boy were reassured that he had a mild congenital anomaly that would not in any way disable him, and there was nothing more to do about it. I think my explanation was well accepted by the parents and the child.

Thank you very much for sending this nice family to see me. ← open punctuation

Sincerely yours ← modified block

Patrick D. Quinn, M.D.

aoa

cc: Mr. and Mrs. H. James Santee

FIGURE 6-1 *Continued*. *B,* Modified-block style and open punctuation. Illustrates reference line that breaks the placement rule.

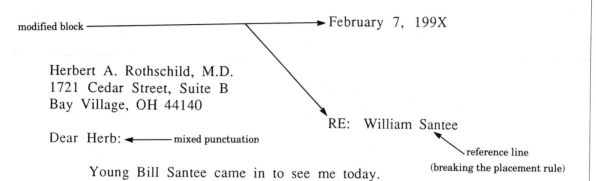

FAX:
212-555-1247

College Park Hospital and Medical Center
555 Lake View Drive
Bay Village, OH 44140

216-555-1234

modified block ——————————→ February 7, 199X

Herbert A. Rothschild, M.D.
1721 Cedar Street, Suite B
Bay Village, OH 44140

RE: William Santee

Dear Herb: ←——— mixed punctuation

reference line
(breaking the placement rule)

6

Young Bill Santee came in to see me today.

As you know, his problem is one of a very mild pectus excavatum with some tenderness in the area. It is my feeling that this child's pectus problem was brought to his attention when he strained his pectoral muscles lifting weights about six weeks ago. This was then accentuated when his older brother gave him a "bear hug." Following that, he did a little introspection and found that he actually had a pectus excavatum, but both he and the brother thought this had occurred during the "bear hug" episode.

In any event, there is not one thing you or I can, or should, do.

Both of the parents and the boy were reassured that he had a mild congenital anomaly that would not in any way disable him, and there was nothing more to do about it. I think my explanation was well accepted by the parents and the child.

Thank you very much for sending this nice family to see me.

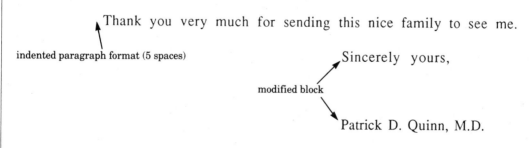

indented paragraph format (5 spaces)

Sincerely yours,

modified block

Patrick D. Quinn, M.D.

aoa

cc: Mr. and Mrs. H. James Santee

FIGURE 6-1 *Continued.* *C,* Modified-block style with indented paragraphs and mixed punctuation.

PERFECT PUNCTUATION COMPANY
2526 LA MAL AVENUE
SAN VALLEY, CA 92014
(714) 555-7185

July 16, 199X

Ms. Amy L. Wing
1234 College Avenue
Columbus, OH 43201

Dear Ms. Wing:

1

Sincerely yours,

Robert T. Bowhay, President
mlo
cc: Eric T. Myhre

PERFECT PUNCTUATION COMPANY
2526 LA MAL AVENUE
SAN VALLEY, CA 92014
(714) 555-7185

May 29, 199X

Ms. Amy L. Wing
1234 College Avenue
Columbus, OH 43201

Dear Ms. Wing

2

Sincerely

(Mrs.) Nora George
Secretary

Enclosure

PERFECT PUNCTUATION COMPANY
2526 LA MAL AVENUE
SAN VALLEY, CA 92014
(714) 555-7185

June 4, 199X

Miss Amy R. Wing
12345 College Avenue
Columbus, OH 42301

Dear Miss Wing:

3

Sincerely,

(Miss) Nanci Thomas
Supervisor

rlr

FIGURE 6-1 *Continued.* *D*–1, Full-block style and mixed punctuation. *D*–2, Modified-block style and open punctuation. *D*–3, Modified-block style with indented paragraphs and mixed punctuation.

mat that is used by all the secretaries in the company. However, you may find few formal rules about letter styles in a hospital or medical office.

Each of the following items refers to the corresponding number in Figure 6–2. Please refer to this figure as we examine a business letter and discuss its components.

Item 1 — Paper

Standard $8\frac{1}{2} \times 11$ inch, 25 percent cotton content bond paper is most often used. Paper is usually white, although off-white or eggshell may be preferred.

Item 2 — Letterhead

The letterhead must be appropriate and current. The physician will use stationery with his or her name (or the corporate name) and address printed on it. Other information, such as the telephone number, medical specialty, or board membership, is often included. The letterhead should be confined to the top two inches of the page. Avoid a letterhead that is continued to the bottom of the page because it makes placement difficult, and the style is unnecessary. Printed borders on the paper are equally distracting.

Many physicians choose to have steel die engraved letterheads. Engraving makes the finest quality letterhead; it looks very professional and will further enhance the appearance of the correspondence. Thermographing (raised printing) is also popular.

Embossing and color art, which are very popular on business letters, were seldom seen on physicians' letterheads until recently. However, these are gaining in popularity. Be sure to obtain the approval of your employer before you change the letterhead, the type of printing, or the quality of the paper you have been using.

Continuation sheets do not have a letterhead but are of the same color and quality as the first sheet. When using continuation sheets, be careful to type on the face of the paper. You can tell the face from the back by holding the paper to the light. The watermark (a faint symbol that is part of the paper itself) will be visible and can be read from the front. If you type on the back, the paper may appear to be of a different color and texture and will not match your letterhead paper.

Number 10 ($4\frac{1}{8} \times 9\frac{1}{2}$ inch) envelopes should match the paper in color and quality. The return address is engraved or printed to match the letterhead. Since the envelope is the first impression one makes on a correspondent, deliberate care must be taken in its preparation.

A variety of typefaces and set-up styles are available (Fig. 6–3). The secretary may be asked to set up an appropriate letterhead when a change is made in what is currently being used. A reputable printer will provide you with a list of available typefaces and will help you design an attractive letterhead.

Item 3 — Date

The date is in keeping with the format of the letter and is placed in line with the complimentary close and typed signature line. It is typed approximately three lines below the letterhead (no closer but you may drop it farther down for a brief letter). The date used is the day the material was dictated and *not* the day it was transcribed. This is very important since comments made in the document could reflect on this date. Spell out the date in full in either the traditional or the military style. Note the use of the comma in the example of the traditional style below.

Examples
December 22, 1991 (traditional style)
22 December 1991 (British and military style)

Item 4 — Inside Address

The inside address is typed flush with the left margin and is begun on approximately the fifth line below the date (it may be moved up or down a line or two depending on the length of the letter). The name of the person or firm is copied exactly as printed on their letterhead or as printed in the medical society directory or as printed in the phone book. A courtesy title is added to a name. If you do not know if the person is a man or woman, use the title "Mr." The title "Ms." is used when you do not have a title for a woman. Today it may also be used as a substitute for "Miss" or "Mrs.," since many women prefer this usage. The degree is preferred over a title in the case of a physician, and in no case should a title and a degree be used together. Use the middle initial when it is known.

Examples
Ms. Mary T. Jordan
Professor Otis R. Laban
Drs. Reilly, Lombardo, and Ham
Dora F. Hodge, M.D.
Captain Denis K. Night
Glenn M. Stempien, D.D.S. *or* Dr. Glenn M. Stempien
Neal J. Kaufman, M.D., FACCP
Rabbi Bernice Gold

NOT: Dr. Clifford F. Adolph, M.D.
      Dr. Bertrum L. Storey, Ph.D.

If a business title accompanies the name, it may follow the name on the same line, or, if lengthy, it may appear on the next line. (Please notice the punctuation in the examples.)

6

Item 1—Paper

KARL ROBRECHT, M. D.
INTERNAL MEDICINE

ROBERT T. SACHS, M. D.
PHYSICIAN AND SURGEON

Gulf Medical Group
A PROFESSIONAL CORPORATION
800 GULF SHORE BOULEVARD
NAPLES, FLORIDA 33940
TELEPHONE 262-9976

2—Letterhead

Approximately 3
blank lines
below letterhead

_____   3—Dateline

Fifth line below
date line

_____   4
_____   5—Inside address
_____   6
                 _____   Reference
double space after
last line of address

_____ :   7—Salutation

_____
_____
_____
_____ .   8—Body

single spaced with
double space
between paragraphs

_____
_____
_____
_____ .

double space after
last line typed

_____ ,   9—Complimentary
                        close

                        Signature area

3 blank lines

_____   10—Typed
_____   signature line
                        Title

double space   ____   11—Reference
                            initials

double space   ____   12—Enclosure
                            notation

double space   ____   13—Distribution

FIGURE 6-2. Business letter set up mechanics showing modified block format and mixed punctuation. (See text for a description of each item illustrated.)

College Park Hospital and Medical Center
555 Lake View Drive
Bay Village, OH 44140

Patrick D. Quinn, Administrator
(216) 871-9486
FAX (216) 555-9486

THORACIC SURGERY MEDICAL GROUP, INC.
ROBERT T. STEINWAY, M.D.
STEPHEN R. CLAWSON, M.D.
CHRISTIAN M. LOW, M.D.
MARY SUE LOW, M.D.

504 WARFORD DRIVE
SYRACUSE, NEW YORK 13224
TELEPHONE 466-4307

19098 CHATHAM ROAD
SYRACUSE, NEW YORK 13203
TELEPHONE 279-2345

Kwei-Hay Wong, M.D.
1654 PIIKEA STREET
HONOLULU, HAWAII 96818
TELEPHONE 534-0922

DIPLOMATE, AMERICAN BOARD
OF OTOLARYNGOLOGY

EAR, NOSE, THROAT,
HEAD AND NECK SURGERY

KARL ROBRECHT, M.D.
INTERNAL MEDICINE

ROBERT T. SACHS, M.D.
PHYSICIAN AND SURGEON

Gulf Medical Group
A PROFESSIONAL CORPORATION
800 GULF SHORE BOULEVARD
NAPLES, FLORIDA 33940
TELEPHONE 262-9976

FIGURE 6-3. Letterhead styles and type faces. These typesetting and reproduction proofs were provided by Medical Printing Company, Inc., 9108 Olive Drive, Spring Valley, California 92077

Examples

F. E. Stru, M.D., Medical Director

Ms. Sheila O. Wendall
Purchasing Agent

Adrian N. Abott, M.D.
Chief-of-Staff
Sinai-Lebanon Hospital

Item 5 — Street Address

Following the name of the person or firm is the street or post office box address. (If both are given, use the post office box address. The street address has been provided for those visiting the firm. They may not even have the facilities for receiving mail there. At any rate, they have indicated that they prefer post office box delivery.) Abbreviations are permitted *after* the street name only. They include NW, NE, SW, and so on. Do not abbreviate North, South, East, West, Road, Street, Avenue, or Boulevard. "Apartment" is abbreviated only if the line is unusually long. The apartment, suite, or space number is typed on the same line with the street address, separated by a comma.

Examples

321 Madison Avenue
1731 North Branch Road, Suite B
845 Medford Circle, Apartment 54
8895 Business Park NW
P.O. Box 966
P.O. Box 17433, Foy Station

Item 6 — City and State

The name of the city is spelled out and separated from the state name with a comma. The state name may be spelled out or abbreviated and is separated from the ZIP code by one to three spaces and no punctuation. The U.S. Postal abbreviations are not used without the ZIP code. (See Abbreviations, page 91, Fig. 4–1.)

Example

Honolulu, Hawaii 96918 *or* Honolulu, HI 96918

NOT: Honolulu, HI

Item 7 — Salutation

The salutation is typed a double space after the last line of the address as follows:

1. Open punctuation format: no mark of punctuation used.

2. Mixed punctuation format (formal): followed by a colon.

3. Mixed punctuation format (informal — first name used): followed by a comma or a colon.

Examples

Open: Dear Mr. Walsh
Mixed (formal): Dear Mr. Walsh:
Mixed (informal): Dear Don: or Dear Don,

Please see Figures 6–1*A* and 6–1*C* for examples of mixed punctuation and Figure 6–1*B* for an example of open punctuation.

Examples of Salutations Used for Men, Showing Mixed Punctuation

Gentlemen:
Dear Mr. Sutherland:
Dear Dr. Hon:
Dear Drs. Blake and Fortuna:
Dear Dr. Blake and Dr. Fortuna:
Dear Rabbi Ruderman:

William A. Berry, M.D.

3933 Navajo Road
San Diego, California 92119

463-0000

March 27, 199x

Mrs. Lila Hadley
1951 52nd Street, Apartment 21
Tucson, AZ 85718

Dear Mrs. Hadley:

This is in reply to your letter concerning the results of your tests that were done here and by Dr. Galloway.

    1) Intestinal symptoms, secondary to a lactase deficiency.

    2) Generalized arteriosclerosis.

    3) Mitral stenosis and insufficiency.

    4) History of venous aneurysm.

You were seen on February 2, at which time you were having some stiffness at the shoulders which I felt was likely to be due to a periarthritis. This is a stiffness of the shoulder capsule.

FIGURE 6–4. Letters illustrating use of tabulated copy.

(likewise Father, Bishop, Reverend, Monsignor, Cardinal, Brother, Deacon, Chaplain, Dean, and so on)
Dear Mr. Tony Lamb and Mr. Peter Lamb:

Examples of Salutations Used for Women, Showing Mixed Punctuation
Ladies:
Mesdames:
Dear Dr. Martin:
Dear Mrs. Clayborne:
Dear Ms. Robinson:
Dear Judge Peterson:
(likewise Reverend, Rabbi, Chaplain, Dean, Deacon, Bishop, Captain, Professor, and so on)
Dear Sister Rose Anthony:
Dear Miss Thomas and Mrs. Farintino:

Examples of Salutations Used for Addressing Men and Women Together
Dear Sir or Madam:
Ladies and Gentlemen:
Dear Doctors:

Dear Mr. and Mrs. Knight:
Dear Dr. and Mrs. Wong:
Dear Professor Holloway and Mr. Blake:
Dear Drs. Candelaria or Dear Dr. Lois Candelaria and Dr. Fred Candelaria:
Dear Mr. Claborne and Mrs. Steen-Claborne:
Dear Dr. Petroski and Mr. Petroski:
Dear Captain and Mrs. Philips:
Dear Dr. Mitchelson et al.: (Used for addressing large groups of men and/or women)

Item 8 — Body

The body of the letter is begun a double space from the salutation and is single-spaced. The first and subsequent lines are flush with the left margin unless indented paragraphs are used, in which case the first line of each paragraph is indented five spaces. There is always a double space between paragraphs.

Make use of tabulated copy when it is appropriate. This will add emphasis to the material, make the letter

---

William A. Berry, M.D.

3933 Navajo Road
San Diego, California 92119

463-0000

March 27, 199x

Roy V. Zimmer, M.D.
6280 Jackson Drive
San Antonio, TX 78288

Re: Mrs. Florida Sanchez

Dear Roy:

Thank you for referring Mrs. Florida Sanchez to my office. She was first seen on February 17, 199x.

Her past history is of no great significance and will not be reiterated at this time.

Physical examination revealed the following:

    Thyroid: Normal to palpation, with no cervical adenopathy.

    Breasts: No masses, tenderness or axillary adenopathy.

    Abdomen: Flat. Liver, kidneys, and spleen not felt. There is a well-healed McBurney scar present. No masses, tenderness, or

FIGURE 6-4. *Continued.*

easier to read, and add visual interest. This part of the letter is indented at least five spaces from *each* margin. Figure 6–4 illustrates two examples of appropriate use of tabulated copy.

Item 9 — Complimentary Close

The complimentary close is lined up with the date and is typed a double space below the last typed line. Only the first word is capitalized. A comma is used after the close if a colon appears with the salutation (mixed punctuation). No punctuation mark is used with "open" format.

Examples of Mixed Punctuation
Sincerely,
Yours very truly,

Examples of Open Punctuation
Sincerely
Yours very truly

See Figure 6–1 for mixed and open punctuation.

Item 10 — Typed Signature Line

The dictator's or writer's name is typed exactly as it appears in the letterhead, leaving three blank lines after the complimentary close. Hit the return key four times after you type the complimentary close. Then type the name lined up with the complimentary close. If an official title accompanies the name, it may appear on the same line, preceded by a comma, or it may be typed on the line directly below the signature without a comma.

Example
Sincerely,

Samuel R. Wong, M.D.
Chief-of-Staff

Example
Yours very truly,

Carla B. Black, M.D., Medical Director

(note the punctuation)

NOTE: An office employee using the letterhead stationery will always identify his or her position in the firm and provide a courtesy title. The title enables the correspondent to have a title to use in writing or telephoning. The title is enclosed in parentheses.

Examples
(Ms.) Lynmarie Myhre, CMT, Secretary

(Mrs.) Elvira E. Gonsalves
Receptionist

(Miss) Paula de la Vera, CMA-A
Office Manager

Item 11 — Reference Initials

The transcriptionist's initials are typed a double space below the typed signature, flush with the left margin. Only two or three of the transcriptionist's initials are used, and humorous or confusing combinations are avoided. You do not type your initials when you type a letter for your own signature.

Examples
crc (rather than cc)
db (rather than dmb)
dg (rather than dog)

Note: If the dictator wants his or her initials used, they will precede the initials of the typist, or if the dictator differs from the person who signs the document, the dictator's, the signer's, and the typist's initials are used.

Examples
lrc/wpd *or* lrc:wpd
RF:BJT:wpd

Item 12 — Enclosure Notation

If the dictator is enclosing one or more items with the letter, attention is called to the item or items with a notation. The notation is typed flush with the left margin, and the number of enclosures should be noted if there are more than one. A wide variety of styles is acceptable. We have underlined the example most commonly used.

Examples
Enc.   Enclosure   Check enclosed
Enc. 2   2 Enc.   2 enclosures
Enclosures
Enclosures: 2
Enclosed: (1) Operative report
         (2) Pathology report
         (3) History and physical

NOTE: This last notation is helpful to you so that you make sure to enclose all items before the letter is sealed. The recipient's secretary should also check the enclosure line when the letter is opened to ascertain that he or she has all the items before the envelope is discarded.

Item 13—Distribution Notation

It is understood that a file copy is made of every item prepared by the secretary/transcriptionist. If a copy of the correspondence is sent *to someone else,* this is noted on the original copy. The notation is typed flush with the left margin a double space below the reference initials or last notation made. A variety of styles are used, and all are followed by the complete name of the recipient. A colon may be used with the notation. Even though most copies mailed out today are photocopies, rather than carbon copies of the original, the abbreviation "cc" still remains correct and popular. It used to mean "carbon copy" and now means "courtesy copy."

Examples
cc: Frank L. Naruse, M.D.
c: Ruth Chriswell, Business Manager
CC Hodge W. Lloyd
Copy: Carla P. Ralph, Buyer
Copies: Kristen A. Temple
   Anthony R. McClintock

Since most copies mailed out today are photocopies, some people prefer to use the abbreviation "pc."

Example: pc: John Smith

NOTE: You *never* type a copy notation without a name following it.

Other Letter Mechanics

Blind Carbon Copy

If the sender wishes a copy of the correspondence to be sent to a third party and does not wish the recipient of the original copy to know that this was done, he will direct that a "blind copy" be mailed. Do *not* make a copy notation on the original but do make a notation on the file copy with the name of the recipient following the notation. Use of a removable adhesive note on the original letter will show the "bcc" notation on your filed photocopy.

Example
(typed on *file copy only*)
bcc Ms. Penelope R. Taylor

Postscript

The postscript is typed one double space below the last reference notation and is flush with the left margin. The abbreviation "P.S." usually introduces the item. You may use P.S.: or PS:

NOTE: The P.S. can be an afterthought or a statement deliberately withheld from the body of the letter for emphasis or a restatement of an important thought, e.g., a phone number in a letter of application. A handwritten afterthought, added by the dictator, does not need to be introduced with "P.S."

Example
(afterthought)
P.S. By the way, I saw Flo Douglas in the elevator in St. Michael's Hospital the other day. She has certainly recovered nicely from her surgery.

Example
(emphasis)
P.S. Please do not hesitate to call on me if I can help you in any way.

If the postscript is longer than one line, indent any subsequent lines to align with the first word of the message.

If the transcriptionist has made a rough copy of the letter, he or she may insert an "afterthought P.S." in the appropriate place in the final copy. If the original P.S. reads "By the way, I will return the x-rays to your office after I see Mrs. Theobald next week," you insert the same statement in the body of the letter where the x-rays were last mentioned and then eliminate the P.S.

Attention Line

The attention line is typed two spaces below the last line of the address. "Attention" may be spelled out in full caps or with only the first letter capitalized. It is not abbreviated, nor is any punctuation used with it. The attention line is used so that the letter will receive attention by a specific person if he or she is available; if not, another member of the firm will take care of the matter. The appropriate salutation with an attention line is "Gentlemen" or "Dear Sir or Madam," because the letter is addressed to the firm. The salutation should agree with the first line of the address.

Example

PERFECT PUNCTUATION COMPANY
2526 LA MAL AVENUE
SAN VALLEY, CA 92014
(714) 555-7185

                                        August 18, 199x

Engraved Letterhead Company
2171 Lincoln Boulevard
Philadelphia, PA 19105

ATTENTION Mr. Charles P. Trask, Buyer

Gentlemen:

To Whom It May Concern

This line is used when you have no person or place to send a document. It is typed in full caps or the first letter of each word is capitalized. It may be typed flush with the left margin or centered on the page. Open or mixed punctuation is used with it. Generally the complimentary close is not used with this format.

Reference Line

A reference line is used to save time and delay by giving the addressee a specific named reference. It also assists when filing the document. A reference line is used very often in medical correspondence and in medicolegal reports. Its placement is determined by the letter format chosen. In full block format it is

Example

W. B. SAUNDERS COMPANY
Harcourt Brace Jovanovich, Inc.

                                        November 11, 199X

To Whom It May Concern:

The Curtis Center
Independence Square West, Philadelphia, PA 19106-3399
215-238-7800
FAX 215-238-7883   TELEX 173146

Example
(For use with any format)

```
                    THORACIC  SURGERY  MEDICAL  GROUP,  INC.
                          ROBERT T. STEINWAY, M.D.
                          STEPHEN R. CLAWSON, M.D.
                          CHRISTIAN M. LOW, M.D.
                          MARY SUE LOW, M.D.

    504 WARFORD DRIVE                              19098 CHATHAM ROAD
 SYRACUSE, NEW YORK 13224                       SYRACUSE, NEW YORK 13203
   TELEPHONE 466-4307                             TELEPHONE 279-2345


                              October 3, 199x


 Matthew R. Bates, M.D.
 7832 Johnson Avenue
 Denver, CO  80241

 Dear Dr. Bates:

 RE:  Leah Hamlyn
```

always placed at the left margin. It is typed a double space *below* the salutation because it is considered part of the body of the letter. In modified block format one has two choices: (1) Flush with the left margin a double space *below* the salutation. (This is best used when the line is lengthy.) (2) Lined up with the date line of the letter on *the next line* after the city, state, and ZIP code of the address. This final style is called "breaking the format rule" and is popular because it saves two lines of space. It is technically out of place since it appears above the salutation. (See Fig. 6–1*B, C*.)

A colon is typed after the RE (or Re), which is used to introduce the reference. After typing the reference line, *single space down one line* and type the salutation.

Dictators, not concerned with style or format, frequently dictate the reference line right after they indicate to whom the letter is addressed. This causes many transcriptionists to place it incorrectly, so study the placement and spacing in the examples of the two different styles.

See Figures 6–1 *A*, *B*, and *C* for examples of reference line placement.

Example
(For use with modified block format only)

```
                    PERFECT PUNCTUATION COMPANY
                        2526 LA MAL AVENUE
                       SAN VALLEY, CA 92014
                          (714) 555-7185


                              October 3, 199x


 Matthew R. Bates, M.D.
 7832 Johnson Avenue
 Denver, CO 80241
                              Re:  Leah Hamlyn

 Dear Dr. Bates:
```

Two Page Letters

If a letter is too long for one page, it must be appropriately continued on a second page. The following rules apply:

1. Continue to the second page at the end of a paragraph whenever possible.

2. Carry at least two lines of the paragraph to the second page.

3. Leave at least two lines of a paragraph on the first page.

4. Type no closer than one inch from the bottom of the page.

5. Do not divide the last word on the page.

6. Place headings one inch from the top of the page.

7. Leave two blank lines between the last line of the heading and the first line of the continuation of the letter. To do this use the return key three times at the end of the typed data in the heading.

The second sheet or continuation sheet is plain paper that is identical to the letterhead paper. Headings are placed on the second sheet to identify it as belonging to the first sheet. There are two styles for page headings.

Example: (for horizontal form)

RE: Leah Hamlyn   2   October 3, 199X
(patient's name)   *(page number)*   *(date)*

Example: (for vertical form)

RE: Leah Hamlyn
Page 2
October 3, 199X

NOTE: The page number is centered in the horizontal form. In a nonmedical letter, the name of the correspondent is listed in place of the patient's name.

Copies

The transcriptionist makes a copy of every item he or she types. One needs to ensure with great care that a copy is made of every corrected original before it is sent from the office. A document may need to be rushed to the mail after signature, so make it a habit to photocopy the letter *before* it is signed. If there are corrections or additions, make another copy and discard the first photocopy. Be sure that good quality paper is used for copies that are mailed out of the office. The office copy becomes part of the patient's permanent record and is filed in his or her chart.

Placement

Placement should have picture-frame symmetry and balance of the three blank margins and the letterhead. A good rule to follow for margins is to use 2-inch margins with short letters (fewer than 100 words), $1\frac{1}{2}$-inch margins with medium-length letters (100 to 200 words), and 1-inch margins with long (200+ words) letters.

To achieve symmetry and to squeeze a letter onto one page, you may adjust the spacing at the end of the letter (beginning with the typed signature line). Leave two, rather than three, spaces for the signature and single space between the typed signature line, the reference initials, and other notations. If you are using the modified block format, you may type the reference initials on the same line as the typed signature line to save more space. If you still find that you cannot fit the letter on one page, retype the letter, widen the margins, and type the final paragraph on a second page. Of course, if you are using a word processor, it is very easy to simply reformat the document.

The visual appeal of the letter is very important. Try to keep the right margin as even as possible and try not to vary the line length by more than five characters.

Using an $8\frac{1}{2} \times 11$ inch sheet of plain paper, copy the letter placement guide in Figure 6–5. Make the heavy dark lines with a felt tip marking pen so they will show through your typing paper. The outer lines are 1 inch from the edge of the paper, the middle line is $1\frac{1}{2}$ inches from the edge of the paper, and the inner line is 2 inches from the edge of the paper. Type numbers on the lower right-hand edge of the paper to indicate how many lines are remaining at the bottom of the page. You will type "1" on the last line of the page, close to the right edge of the paper. Come up a line and type the number "2" and so on up the page for about 2 to 3 inches and 24 lines marked. When this guide is placed behind your typing paper, it will help you achieve good placement.

Please see Figure 6–6, which is a complete letter typed in modified block format with mixed punctuation, and illustrates proper spacing and margin width. Notice the placement of the reference line in particular since it was typed using the "break the placement" rule. (Note: the bottom of the page was cut off to fit the figure size, so it does not properly reflect bottom spacing.)

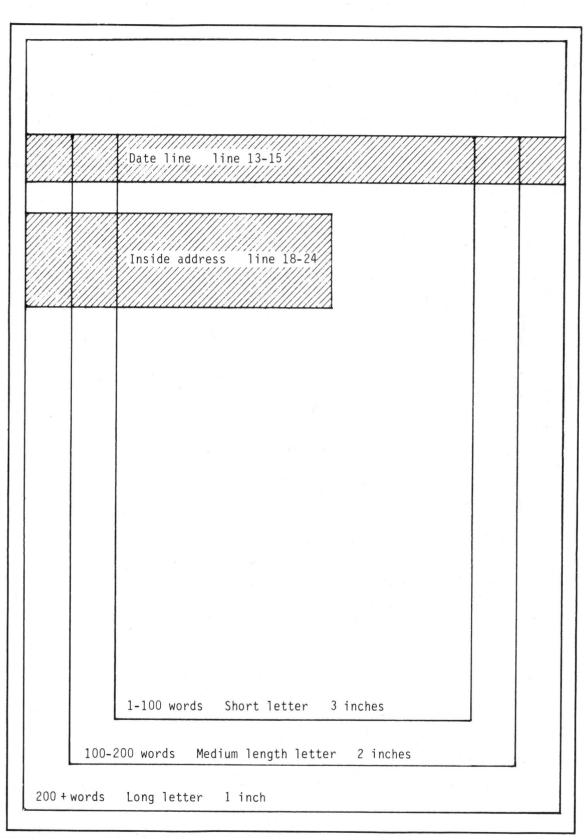

FIGURE 6-5. Placement guide for letters of various lengths.

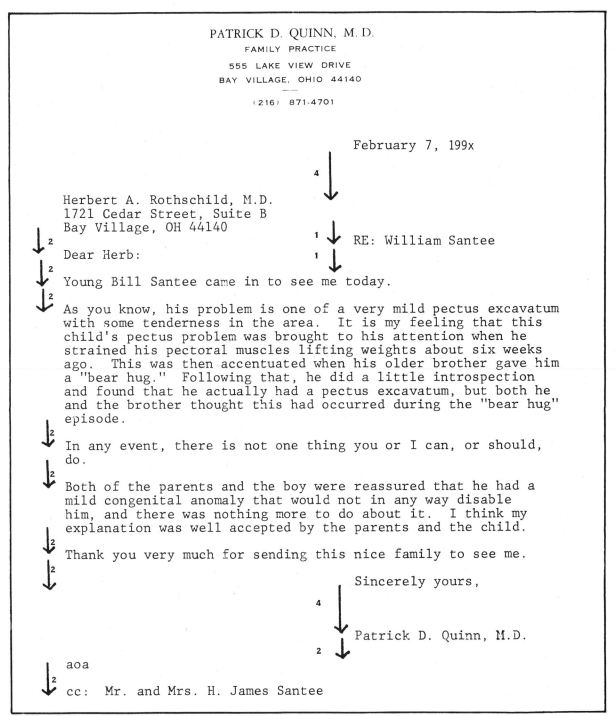

FIGURE 6-6. Letter typed in modified block format and mixed punctuation to illustrate proper spacing and margin width. The illustration is smaller than the standard 8½ × 11″ paper.

6-1: TYPING ASSIGNMENT

Directions: Retype the following material into letter form. Make letterhead paper to match the name of the dictator, inventing an appropriate address. Or you may use any prepared letterhead paper as your instructor directs. Use full block format, open punctuation, a reference line, and the current date. Refer to the vocabulary list at the beginning of the chapter if necessary. Pay close attention to placement and mechanics. Remember to use the proper state abbreviations you learned in Chapter 4. (See Figure 4-1, page 91.)

To help you with placement, notice the length of the material (164 words equals medium length) and place your margins accordingly. Paragraph beginnings are indicated by the symbol ¶. Save this letter after your instructor has checked it because you will need it for Self-Study 6–3.

The letter is from Laurel R. Denison, M.D., and is to Gregory O. Theopolis, M.D., 4509 Roessler Road, Detroit Michigan 48224, and is in reference to Bobby West.

Dear Dr. Theopolis ¶ This one-month-old baby was seen in my office yesterday for evaluation of difficulty with the right foot. ¶ The mother reports that this is the third sibling in the family. The older two siblings have no difficulty with the feet. When this baby was born, there was obvious deformity of the right foot which has not corrected itself. ¶ Physical examination reveals that the hips are normal. There is internal tibial torsion. There is pes equinus; there is hindfoot supination and forefoot adduction. It is obvious that this baby has a congenital talipes equinovarus in the right foot. ¶ He was casted in the office yesterday. ¶ We do not know the prognosis yet since this is the first experience with the child. Prognosis depends on the congenital factors that caused the deformity, in the first place, and the elasticity of the tissues, in the second place. We will follow the child at weekly intervals. ¶ Thank you for the opportunity of seeing this baby. Sincerely

6–2: TYPING ASSIGNMENT

Directions: Retype the following material into letter form. Use letterhead paper as your instructor directs. Use modified block format, mixed punctuation, and a reference line that "breaks the placement rule." See pages 130 and 131. Use the current date and the state abbreviation. Pay close attention to placement and mechanics. Notice that the letter contains _____ words, which equals a _____ size letter requiring _____ inch margins. Paragraph beginnings are indicated by the symbol ¶. Remember, we are not making office copies of our documents, but one would *always* do this in the workplace.

This letter is from Emery R. Stuart, M.D., to Walter W. von der Meyer, M.D., 6754 Sunrise Circle, Ft. Lauderdale, Florida 33312. Copies should be sent to Dr. Barney P. Haber and Dr. Herbert W. Delft. (It is not necessary to make these copies, just the notation.) The patient is Mrs. Nora George.

Dear Walter. ¶ This is a final follow-up letter on Nora George who you will recall was admitted to Sunrise View Hospital in February, 199X, for aortic valve replacement with a diagnosis of aortic stenosis. ¶ Nora has done well; she is in normal sinus rhythm, and she is well controlled on her Coumadin. She, at times, has some swelling of her hands and feet and has gained considerable weight since surgery. She needs continued close medical observation of her prothrombin level, which should be maintained at about 20% of normal, indefinitely. She should also be maintained on Lanoxin and may possibly require diuretics intermittently. ¶ We will not follow Nora any further for her heart disease. She has had an uneventful postoperative course and can continue her medical follow-up through your office or that of Dr. Herbert Delft, whichever you decide. ¶ Thank you very much for letting us see this patient with you and perform her surgery. We will be glad to see her at any time if there are any questions regarding her valve function or clinical course. Sincerely yours.

Save this letter after your instructor has checked it.

Paragraphing

Paragraphs give the letter shape. The subject is divided into topics, and these topics are paragraphs, which aid the reader by signaling a *new* idea with each division.

The paragraphing will contribute to the visual appeal of the letter and should be well balanced. Therefore, the first and last paragraphs are usually brief, and the middle paragraphs are longer. Nevertheless, a paragraph may be of any length, and you should not hesitate to make one sentence a paragraph when it is appropriate. A series of brief paragraphs in a row, however, can be distracting to the reader. On the other hand, with a brief letter a long paragraph may appear uninviting, and you may have to break it up to provide visual appeal.

Many dictators will not directly indicate the beginning (or end) of a paragraph. But they may give indirect clues with voice inflections or other subtle voice changes. Each new paragraph is begun with a sentence that suggests the topic or further explains it in a different way.

Correct paragraphing is not difficult with most medical letters, since the letters generally follow a well-established pattern. The knowledge of this pattern will help you determine the paragraph breaks with or without vocal hints.

The physician's letters dealing with patient care are usually narrative reports to workers' compensation carriers, consultation reports, follow-up notes, or discharge summaries.

The first paragraph is normally a brief introduction or explanation for the letter. In patient-related letters, the patient and his or her chief complaint are introduced in the initial brief paragraph. The next paragraph may contain the history of the complaint, along with a general description of any contributing problems in the patient's past history. This is followed in the third or fourth paragraph with the findings on examination of the patient. (At times, these remarks may be so brief that they constitute only one sentence.)

The next to last paragraph is confined to a medical opinion, prognosis, diagnosis, recommendation, report of tests, results of surgical procedures, detailed outlines for proposed care or treatment, evaluation of return-to-normal status, or summary. Then the subject is closed in the final paragraph. At this time, the dictator may thank a referring physician, may indicate what will take place next with the patient, or request some action on the patient's behalf.

6–3: SELF-STUDY

Directions: Obtain your copy of Typing Assignment 6–1. Notice the paragraph breaks. Answer the following questions. Answer here or on a separate sheet of paper as your instructor directs.

1. Notice that the first paragraph is only one sentence long. What does the dictator do with this sentence? _____

2. Notice that the second paragraph is three sentences long. Could the first of these sentences have been placed in the first paragraph? _____ Why or why not? _____

3. What is the dictator *doing* in this second paragraph? _____

4. Could any part of the third paragraph logically be part of the second or fourth paragraph? _____ Why or why not? _____

_____

5. What is the dictator *doing* in the third paragraph? _____

_____

6. Again, we have a one-sentence paragraph in number four. Could the typist have joined this sentence to paragraph three? _____ What did the dictator *do* in this paragraph?

_____

7. What is the subject of paragraph five? _____

Could this paragraph be joined to paragraph four? _____ Why or why not?

_____

8. Notice the last line of paragraph 5. Could this have been a paragraph on its own? _____ Why or why not? _____ Could you make it a part of the last paragraph? _____ Why or why not? _____

_____

9. What is the dictator doing in the final paragraph, number 6? _____ Do you think it is appropriate to have this single sentence standing as an entire paragraph? _____ Why or why not? _____

Turn to the end of the chapter for answers to these questions.

6–4: SELF-STUDY

Directions: Obtain your copy of Typing Assignment 6–2. Notice the paragraph breaks. Answer the following questions. Answer here or on a separate sheet of paper as your instructor directs.

1. Paragraph 1 tells us the type of document this is. What is it? _____

2. Paragraph 1: What is the subject(s) of this paragraph? _____

3. Paragraph 2. What is the dictator *doing* in this paragraph? _____

Could the last two sentences of this paragraph be used to form a new paragraph?

_____

Why or why not? _____

_____

4. Paragraph 3. What is the dictator saying in this paragraph?

_____

Could this one have been combined with the last two sentences of paragraph two? _____ Why or why not? _____

_____

5. Paragraph 4. Subject of this paragraph? _____

Should this be arranged as two short paragraphs? _____

Please see the end of the chapter for the answers.

6–5: TYPING ASSIGNMENT

Directions: Retype the following material into letter form using full block format, mixed punctuation, and the current date. Watch for proper paragraphing, placement and mechanics. Use letterhead paper. Carefully mark your book where you think the paragraph breaks should be. Ask yourself if they follow the pattern you have just learned. If not, consider some different breaks. Remember that there is sometimes more than one choice for a new paragraph break. On your final draft, print a number by each paragraph break. On a separate sheet of paper, type an explanation for that paragraph break and turn it in with your letter.

The letter is from Steven A. Flores, M.D. and is to another physician, Willard R. Beets at 7895 West Sherman Street, San Diego, California 92111. Dear Dr. Beets. I saw Mr. Tim Molton, your patient, in my office yesterday afternoon. As you will recall, Mr. Molton is a 49-year-old professional gardener who came to see you with a chronic cough and a history of expectoration of a whitish material. He brought the x-rays from your office with him, and I noted a fossa on the superficial surface of his lung. He was afebrile today and stated that he had been so since the onset of his symptoms. He did not complain of pain but did experience some dyspnea on exertion and some shortness of breath. I did not carry out a physical examination, but I did skin test him for both tuberculosis and coccidioidomycosis. I did not give him a prescription for any medication and will wait until we get the results of his skin tests. It seems to me that your diagnosis of his problem is correct, so we will proceed with that in mind. As you probably know, valley fever is endemic to San Diego; and since Mr. Molton was born and raised in New York State, he could be very susceptible. You may tell his employer that if he does have valley fever, he will have to convalesce for a month to six weeks, after which time he should be fully able to return to his normal duties. I will keep you posted on the results of his tests. Thank you very much for letting me help you with Mr. Molton's problem. Sincerely.

6-6: TYPING PRACTICE TEST

Directions: Retype this material in letter form. Use modified block format with indented paragraphs, mixed punctuation, and a reference line. Use letterhead paper. You will have to supply proper punctuation, capitalization, paragraphing, and mechanics. Good luck!

may 1 199X ian r wing m d 2261 arizona avenue suite b milwaukee wisconsin 53207 dear dr wing i saw your patient mrs elvira martinez in consultation in my office today. she brought the x-rays from your office with her. she was afebrile today but on questioning admitted a low grade fever over the past few days i removed the fluid as seen on your film of april 30 from the right lower lung field and she felt considerably more comfortable. on thoracentesis there was 50 cc of straw colored fluid her history is well known to you so i will not repeat it. on physical examination i found a well developed well nourished white female with minimal dyspnea there was no lymphadenopathy breath sounds were diminished somewhat on the right there was dullness at the right base the left lung was clear to percussion and auscultation. the remainder of the examination was negative. because of her history of chronic asthma i suggested she might consider bronchoscopy if this fluid reaccumulates. because she is a heavy smoker i insisted she stop smoking completely. if she does not she will not enjoy continuing good health although i have no idea of the actual prognosis. mrs martinez has been returned to you for her continuing care i will be glad to see her again at any time you think it necessary thank you for letting me see this pleasant lady with you sincerely yours jon l mikosan m d ps i am enclosing a copy of the pathology report on the fluid as you can see it is negative

This letter, prepared properly, is in Appendix E.

Envelope Preparation

A Number 10 ($4\frac{1}{8} \times 9\frac{1}{2}$ inch) envelope, printed to match your letterhead stationery, is always used with your $8\frac{1}{2} \times 11$ inch paper.

The U.S. Postal Service can process mail using an Optical Character Reader (OCR) to read, code, and sort the mail mechanically. However, mail must be prepared properly in a format that the OCR can "read." Nothing other than the address must appear in the "read zone" or it will confuse the scanner. Furthermore, proportional spacing and script type styles should not be used because they do not "read" well.

Here are the guidelines for typing the envelope properly:

1. Type all envelopes in the *block format,* single-spaced, 2 inches from the top (12 lines down) and aligned 4 inches from the left edge (Fig. 6–7).

2. Capitalize *everything.*

3. Eliminate *all* punctuation (periods, commas).

4. Use the standard two-letter state code and the ZIP code.

5. The last line of the address must contain the name of the city, state code, and ZIP code.

6. The address should end at least $\frac{5}{8}$ inch from the bottom, parallel with the bottom edge of the envelope (not slanted), and it must end within at least 1 inch from the right edge of the envelope; a near-center location is best. No printing can appear to the left, right, or below the address.

Practice with a No. 10 envelope: Fold it in quarters. Unfold it and place it in the typewriter. Type your name and address beginning your first line five spaces to the left of your midline crease and directly under your horizontal crease. Type each line beneath the one before. Remove it from the typewriter and examine your placement.

The OCR "reads" only the last two lines of the address and can read only the city, state, and ZIP code as the last line. Therefore, the last line of the address must contain only these items spelled accurately, and nothing must be typed below the last line. The next-to-the-last line must contain the address & street

name only. An *"Attention"* line, when necessary, must be placed as the second line of the address, out of the "read zone." Special notations, such as *"Special Delivery"* or *"Certified Mail,"* should be typed two lines below the postage area. *"Personal"* or *"Confidential"* may be typed two lines below the return address.

The only abbreviations permitted are those found in the Abbreviations section of the National ZIP Code Directory. It is unacceptable to abbreviate any city name containing 13 or fewer letters because the OCR will not be able to read a nonstandard abbreviation. The National ZIP Code Directory will give standard abbreviations for the city names containing more than 13 digits.

Mail addressed to occupants of multiunit buildings should include the number of the apartment, room suite, or other unit. The unit number should appear immediately after the street address on the same line and never before, below, or in front of the street address.

Notice these envelope addresses. Which ones appear neater and will speed their way through the postal service routing machines?

DEMOREST, SEDWICH, AND TRALL
   224 East Van Buren Street
  Room 22B
FT. WAYNE, INDIANA 46818
ATTN: JOHN DEMOREST, ATTORNEY-AT-
  LAW

or

JOHN DEMOREST
DEMOREST SEDWICH AND TRALL
224 E VAN BUREN ST ROOM 22 B
FT WAYNE IN 46818

or

DEMOREST SEDWICH AND TRALL
ATTN JOHN DEMOREST
224 E VAN BUREN ST ROOM 22 B
FT WAYNE IN 46818

We do not have to place the "attorney-at-law" title on the envelope; we may place ESQ after Mr. Demorest's name if we so wish, however.

6

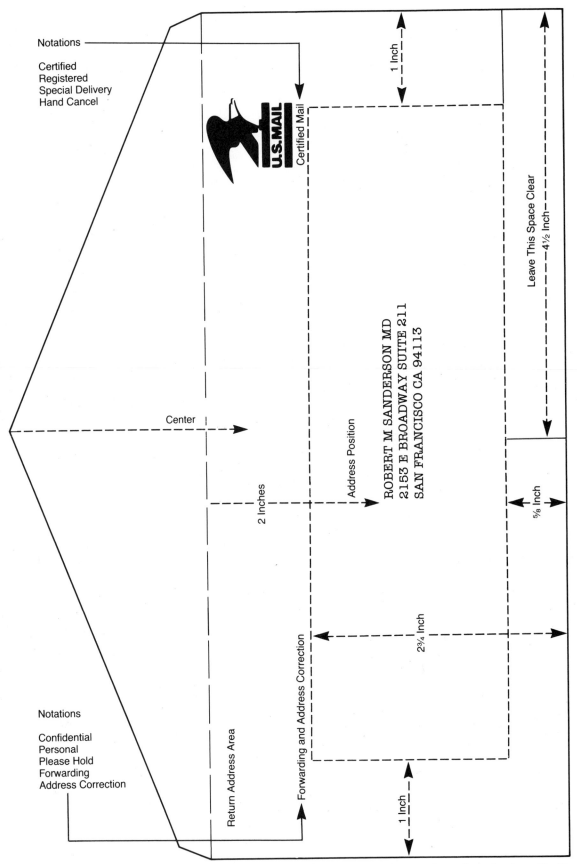

FIGURE 6-7. Address placement on a No. 10 envelope, showing location for notations. This illustration is smaller in size than a No. 10 envelope, which is $4\frac{1}{8} \times 9\frac{1}{2}''$.

Examples

Traditional Style

Mrs. Anne Potts
Post Office Box 7893
Littleton, Colorado 80120

Frank W. Paulson, M.D.
1335 11th Street
Tucson, Arizona 85715

Mrs. Sheila Meadows
8765 Broadway, Suite 16
Los Angeles, CA 90057

National Paper Company
1492 Columbus Avenue, North
Syracuse, NY 13224
Attention: Frank Honeywell

Recommended Style

MRS ANNE POTTS
PO BOX 7893
LITTLETON CO 80120

FRANK W PAULSON MD
1135 11 ST
TUCSON AZ 85715

MRS SHEILA MEADOWS
8765 BROADWAY SUITE 16
LOS ANGELES CA 90057

ATTN FRANK HONEYWELL
NATIONAL PAPER CO
1492 COLUMBUS AVE N
SYRACUSE NY 13224

Mail addressed to a foreign country should have the name of that country as the last line of the address block, a double space below the city, state, and ZIP code line. Coding will vary from country to country.

Example

PROF WOLFGANG HINZ
ART DIRECTR RHINELAND INST
SCHULSTRASSE 21
SIEGELBACH
PFALZ 6751

GERMANY

Here is a list of common address abbreviations approved by the U.S. Postal Service that you will want to place in your reference notebook:

Apartment, APT	Plaza, PLZ
Association, ASSN	Post Office, PO
Attention, ATTN	President, PRES
Avenue, AVE	Ridge, RDG
Boulevard, BLVD	River, RIV
Circle, CIR	Road, RD
Department, DEPT	Room, RM
East, E	Route, RT
Expressway, EXPY	Rural, R
Freeway, FWY	Rural Route, RR
Heights, HTS	Secretary, SECY
Highway, HWY	Shore, SH
Hospital, HOSP	South, S
Institute, INST	Southeast, SE
Junction, JCT	Southwest, SW
Lake, LK	Square, SQ
Lakes, LKS	Station, STA
Lane, LN	Street, ST
Manager, MGR	Terrace, TER
Meadows, MDWS	Treasurer, TREAS
North, N	Turnpike, TPKE
Northeast, NE	Union, UN
Northwest, NW	Vice President, VP
Palms, PLMS	View, VW
Park, PK	Village, VLG
Parkway, PKY	West, W
Place, PL	

6

6-7: PRACTICE TYPING TEST

Directions: Using the following names and addresses, prepare four No. 10 envelopes using the method recommended by the U.S. Postal Service for OCR processing. Pay close attention to placement, and consult the list of common address abbreviations above. Don't forget to practice with the folded envelope and your own name and address first.

1. Noam L. Flickenger, M.D.
   435 North Michigan Avenue
   Chicago, Illinois 60611

   Special Delivery

2. Mr. Steven R. Madruga
   Post Office Box 9982
   Philadelphia, Pennsylvania 19101

3. Occidental Life Insurance Company
   1150 South Olive, Suite 16
   Los Angeles, California 90015

   ATTENTION Mrs. Sylvia Farquar

4. Ms. Marijane N. Woods
   Manager, Desert Realty
   2036 East Camelback Road
   Phoenix, Arizona 85018

   Confidential

Answers are on page 425, Appendix E.

Signing and Mailing

When the letter is ready for signature, use a paper clip to attach the envelope (and any enclosures) to the top of the letter, with the flap over the letterhead. Until you present the letter for signature, keep it in a folder protected from soiling and the curiosity of any passer-by. After the letter is signed and before you place it in its envelope, make sure that there are no smudges and all enclosures are attached.

Fold the letter by bringing the bottom of the page one third up the page and then creasing. Next, fold the upper third down to within $\frac{1}{2}$ inch of the first crease and make the second crease. Insert the letter into the envelope so that when it is removed it will open right side up. Bundle your OCR mail separately and label it "OCR."

On occasion, the dictator will be unavailable to sign the mail after dictation but will request that it be sent out rather than delayed for his or her signature. You should handle this as directed, by signing his or her name followed by your initials, by typing below the signature area "Dictated but not signed" followed by your initials, or by simply signing his or her name. Be particularly careful that the letter is completely error free in every way. Keep the copy available for the dictator's return rather than filing it immediately.

A Final Note

Letterhead stationery in addition to the standard $8\frac{1}{2} \times 11$ inch type is often kept in the office for brief

---

No. 10 Envelope (9-1/2 x 4-1/8 Inches)

DO   bring up the bottom third of the sheet, and crease. Fold down the upper third of the sheet so the top edge is a one-inch from the first fold, and crease. Insert the last creased edge into the envelope first.

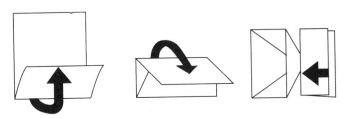

Window Envelope

DO   bring up the bottom third of the sheet and fold. Fold the top of the sheet *back* to the first fold so that the inside address is on the outside, and crease. Insert the sheet so the address appears in the window.

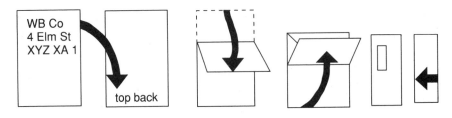

letters or secretarial correspondence. There are two standard sizes, Monarch ($7\frac{1}{2} \times 10\frac{1}{2}$ inches) and Baronial ($5\frac{1}{2} \times 8\frac{1}{2}$ inches). Envelopes are printed to match these two sizes, and papers and envelopes should *not* be mixed. Follow the same general guidelines in preparing the envelopes except begin the address $2\frac{1}{2}$ inches from the left edge of the envelope rather than 4 inches.

6–8: TYPING REVIEW TEST

Directions: Instruction sheet for retyping the following material into letter form.

1. Paper: use letterhead, size $8\frac{1}{2} \times 11$

2. Envelope: use number 10

3. Copies: single

4. Equipment: typewriter, word processor, computer

5. Format: Modified block, open punctuation

6. Date: May 16 + current year

7. Mechanical needs: proper paragraphing, placement on page, *some* internal punctuation, other mechanics as may be required

8. Placement on page: proper alignment for attractiveness and "eye appeal."

9. Patient's name: LeeAnn Jensen

10. Dictator: Dr. Randolph R. Bever

11. Addressed to: Dr. Norman C. Kisbey Jr, at Post Office Box 1734, Washington, DC 20034

Dear Dr. Kisbey. Today I have seen your patient Mrs. LeeAnn Jensen in neurosurgical consultation at your request. As you know, she is a very pleasant 40-year-old, right-handed lady who comes in with a history of seizure-like episodes beginning in January of 199X. These seizures consist of a sense of unreality and a feeling as though she were observing herself as an actress on a stage. Prior to the onset of, or associated with, these seizure-like episodes, she has noted a smell of heavy fragrant flowers. She describes the smell of the flowers as slightly unpleasant, almost funereal. Each of these so-called seizure states lasts only a few seconds and is followed by a tremendous feeling of unreality. This is also associated with a great fear that she won't be able to move and she always gets up and walks around afterward to make sure she is not paralyzed. During the episode there is no loss of cognitive ability and she is able to converse with her husband and she has virtually total recall for the entire episode. She had episodes, as described, in January and February of 199X, four in March and five in April. There is no family history of seizures. There is a story of a mild head injury at age ten and apparently she was in a moderately severe motorcycle accident about fifteen years ago which resulted in a broken mandible. The neurological examination at this time is essentially normal. The extraocular movements and fundi show no abnormalities. The visual fields and confrontation testing are intact. There is no Babinski sign. The only abnormality that I could detect in the entire examination was a stiffened right shoulder which she tells me came on after a lengthy game of tennis. I could palpate no masses over the head and there were no audible bruits over the head or over either carotid bifurcation. She had been on a dose of phenobarbital, gr 1, b.i.d. and did not care to add any Dilantin. The phenobarbital keeps her in a drowsy state consequently she is not able to think creatively or participate in sports activities. She brought with her the skull x-rays and brain scan taken at University Hospital and I have reviewed them. In my opinion, they are within normal limits. In addition, she brought with her several EEG records which I have gone over. The neurologist's summary is enclosed. I thought there was a slight abnormality present in the right temporal area. At this time, I do not believe there is evidence of intracranial mass lesion or of focal neurologic deficit. A number of features argue against interpreting her spells as true psychomotor seizures: Firstly, the fact that the aura is unusual, and secondly the fact that she has total recall for the entire episodes. Thirdly, there is the fact that she has no postictal abnormality. My tendency at this time would be to gradually switch her over to Dilantin gr $1\frac{1}{2}$ t.i.d. and, in addition, place her on Diamox, 25 mg each morning. I suggest the Diamox because she tells me that the "seizure" episodes tend to come on within a few days of her menstrual periods. We have agreed that if she is not markedly improved within a period of one month on this regimen she would come into the hospital for 4-vessel angiography. Thank you for the privilege of seeing this interesting patient and for thinking of me in connection with her problems. Your sincerely. Randolph R. Bever, M.D. Professor of Neurosurgery, Weeks Medical School.

Food for Thought

Directions: Imagine for a few minutes that you have just received the letter on page 145 in the mail. Try to read it with the assumption that it is to YOU personally. What is your reaction to the letter? How many errors can you find?

If nothing else, you formed a definite opinion about this company based entirely on their written representation of themselves. It is doubtful that you would consider asking them for any information about their tours. Nor would you give them further thought other than to wonder how they stay in business. Certainly, you would not feel they could be trusted to handle a tour, since they are unable to handle their correspondence.

The recipients of your office correspondence will be equally affected by the preparation and thought that go into the letters they receive from your office. It is inconsistent to ignore the fact that careless preparation could affect their opinion of *your* employer.

BLOTCHETT TOURS

8888 Malarky Drive

Fun Valley, UT 99999

1   4/1/9x

2   Ms.. Glendora Kirsch
3   211 Elm Ave. Apt a
4   Losangeles, Cal. 99999

5   Dear Miss Kirsch,

6   It seems that each year about this time we sended
7   you a letter inquiring about your plans for this
8   sumer. Each year for the passed three years now
9   we have had no answer.

10   According to our records, you wrote Blotchett Tours
11   inquiring about some information concerning different tours.
12   We sent you our price lists, departure date list, special
13   off season excursions, etc. Wouldn't it be nice
14   if you could plan to travel this summer. Why not
15   reserve a place for yourself in one of our package
16   deals.

17   Enclosed herewith please find an application blank
18   for you to fill out. Just return it in the business reply
19   envelope with your small check for only $35 and your place will
20   be assured. Naturally your deposit will aply toward the fu-
21   ll purchase of your tour. We are guaranteed and bonded.

22   We will be looking for your response soon.

23   Very Truly Yours,

24   Hank Behn, Sales rep.

◨ Answers to 6–3: Self-Study

1. Notice that the first paragraph is only one sentence long. What does the dictator do with this sentence? *She introduces the patient with his age, problem, and date first seen.* (Notice that the reference line is the only place that the patient's name is mentioned.)

2. Notice that the second paragraph is three sentences long. Could the first of these sentences have been placed in the first paragraph? *Yes.* Why or why not? *The other sentences would need to go along with it, however, since they are part of the past history of the patient. It is better as it stands.* (By this final statement, one sees that "no" is the better answer.)

3. What is the dictator doing in this second paragraph? *Giving a brief past history.*

4. Could any part of the third paragraph logically be part of the second or fourth paragraph? *No.* Why or why not? *This is a definite change from past to present.*

5. What is the dictator doing in the third paragraph? *Giving the physical evidence of the patient's problem.*

6. Again, we have a one-sentence paragraph in number four. Could the typist have joined this sentence to paragraph three? *Yes, but why? Is the typist afraid of one-line paragraphs?* What did the dictator do in this paragraph? *She told how she handled the patient's problem.*

7. What is the subject of paragraph five? *The prognosis.* (What the expected outcome will be.) Could this paragraph be joined to paragraph four? *No.* Why or why not? *Because there is a definite shift from "treatment" to "prognosis." It would weaken the impact of each paragraph.*

8. Notice the last line of paragraph 5. Could this have been a paragraph on its own? *Yes.* Why or why not? *It could have stood alone since it is the "plan" to be followed in the treatment program; however, since there are so many brief paragraphs it is fine where it is.* Could you make it a part of the last paragraph? *Yes.* Why or why not? *It could be done, but there is no reason for it. Actually it would serve to weaken the final paragraph. No.* Why or why not? *It will weaken the final paragraph. Leave it alone.*

9. What is the dictator doing in the final paragraph, number 6? *Saying "Thank you," which is standard protocol and acknowledges that the recipient of the letter is the patient's primary physician.* Do you think it is appropriate to have this single sentence standing as an entire paragraph? *Yes.* Why or why not? *It gives impact.*

Note: Your words do not have to match the answers exactly, but the ideas expressed should be the same or similar.

▣ Answers to 6–4: Self-Study

1. Paragraph 1 tells us the type of document this is. What is it? *A final follow-up letter.*

2. Paragraph 1: What is the subject(s) of this paragraph? *an introduction of the patient about whom the letter is written and a reminder about what has transpired with her. We could call this her "immediate past history."*

3. Paragraph 2: What is the dictator *doing* in this paragraph? *Stating the patient's present status and proposed plan of treatment.* Could the last two sentences of this paragraph be used to form a new paragraph? *Yes.* Why or why not? *Because it indicates a new subject: the proposed plan. However, that would make three very short paragraphs in a row, which is somewhat unattractive. One must think of appearance as well as content when it is possible to do so. (Therefore, "no" would be the better answer.)*

4. Paragraph 3. What is the dictator saying in this paragraph? *What his involvement with the patient is now.* Could this one have been combined with the last two sentences of paragraph two? *Yes.* Why or why not? *This would be appropriate because it all pertains to plans for the patient's future care. (Note that the typist's choice here is probably best as a result of the strong opening of paragraph 3: "we will NOT follow Nora. . . . "*

5. Paragraph 4. Subject of this paragraph? *A brief thank you and close.* Should this be arranged as two short paragraphs? *No. That would not be appropriate.*

Proofreading and Making Corrections

OBJECTIVES

After reading this chapter and working the exercises, you should be able to

1. explain where errors may occur in your work.
2. illustrate how important it is to check your copy very carefully for possible errors.
3. demonstrate the ability to use and recognize formal proofreader's symbols.
4. demonstrate the ability to proofread and mark your own work for revision.
5. retype a document that has been corrected and marked.
6. prepare a document for retyping, using the revision marks.
7. explain the variety of methods for correcting different types of errors.
8. identify and correct errors after editing sentences.

● ●

INTRODUCTION

Now that you are beginning to learn to produce good medical typing, it is important that you also learn sound proofreading skills. The largest medical vocabulary, the fastest fingers, and the latest equipment all mean nothing if the final document does not reflect the professional quality for which you are striving. Proper proofreading skills can give you this quality, and lack of it can cause embarrassment and poor self-image. You need these skills right now because you will have to check your work carefully to earn high marks on the copy you submit for grading. Later on, you will want to have excellent skills when you begin your career as a transcriptionist. Since accurate written communication is so important today, the abili-

ties to proofread your own work and to work without supervision will give you an advantage: you may well be promoted on these bases to supervisory capacity.

A great deal of self-discipline is required of the transcriptionist who wishes to turn out perfect copy. No matter how accurate a speller you are and no matter how highly trained your punctuation, capitalization, and mechanical skills, errors can and do occur, and it is necessary to approach every document you type with the attitude that errors may be present. A systematic search for errors is then begun. Over half the mistakes made are due not to ignorance or to carelessness, but to the inability to "see" the mistake or recognize it when we become too familiar with the material.

Because you have progressed this far, you know

where many mistakes can be found. It is unlikely you will make errors in format; if you learned your punctuation, capitalization, and mechanical rules well, these areas should not bother you. If you are careful to stop and check spelling each time you have a doubt about accuracy, where will you look for errors?

Let's find out.

WHERE ERRORS OCCUR

There are differences of opinion among teachers, students, and your prospective employers as to what an error is and how important different errors are. For example, transposed letters in the name of a drug could be very serious, whereas a capital letter typed off line, although upsetting to a fastidious instructor, would hardly be grounds for dismay on the part of an employer.

In fact, how far off line does a "galloping" capital letter have to be before it is an error? When does improper spacing between letters become an error, and what is the difference between a sloppy correction and a good one? There are many kinds of errors that are value judgments on the part of the student, teacher, or employer checking the paper. Finally, the quality of the paper used will also contribute to the ease with which errors are repaired.

There are, in fact, some kinds of errors that are "permissible" and the copy is still mailable; other errors are easily corrected; and, finally, some errors can be eliminated only by redoing the material.

On the other hand, you do not want to type so slowly to avoid making errors that your production drops or you become nervous about the errors you "might" be making. Instead, try to keep your errors to a minimum, learn to find those you do make, and learn to correct them quickly and easily.

When transcribing from equipment (in contrast to copy typing or transcribing from notes), you can look at your work while typing; therefore, you can see any mistakes you make and correct them as they occur. You will gain skill with this in time, and it is easier and less time-consuming than redoing your work. Later, in rereading, you may discover an error that requires retyping because it went unnoticed as you worked. Listen ahead to avoid grammar problems in particular.

ACCURACY

Medical records must be as accurate as you can possibly type them. This requires accuracy on the part of *both* dictator and transcriptionist. The problem with accuracy sometimes is the meaning of the word "ac-

curacy." Who determines what is accurate? For instance, you have just learned some basic letter formats, yet the dictator asks that the reference line be placed at the top right edge of the page, canceling the professional appearance of the letter. You know this is incorrect, and you know that those who receive the document will also question your skills, yet you must do as the dictator directs. To him or her, that is accuracy.

Likewise, you have just had a thorough study of punctuation, capitalization, and abbreviations. An employer may insist that all drug names be typed in full caps, all abbreviations be punctuated, or inappropriate dashes be used in every other sentence. When you comply with these directions, you are being accurate. In certain circumstances, you might consider discussing these and any similar problems with the dictator, always remembering that we must comply with our employers' version of accuracy.

Finally, you may have the problem of rules set up by a governing body, either the hospital itself or its governing body. The physician may dictate an abbreviation in the final diagnosis that you know is incorrect according to the rules of the Joint Commission on Accreditation of Healthcare Organizations. Both you and the dictator must comply with these rules; therefore, accuracy demands that you spell these abbreviations out, and it also demands that you check with the dictator to be sure you have the correct words if you have any doubts.

The transcriptionist needs to develop a trust relationship with the dictator, and when he or she becomes aware of inappropriate, incomplete, or inconsistent use of grammar, abbreviations, and so on, the transcriptionist needs to inform the dictator and discuss this with him or her. If possible, discuss these possible problem areas when you are hired so that you will know exactly how they are to be transcribed.

TYPES OF ERRORS

Misspelling. Whether a word is misspelled or just mistyped, it results in the same thing: a spelling error that can mislead or distract the reader. A misspelling can be the result of a dropped letter, an added letter, transposed letters, wrong letters, substituted letters, or a homonym used in place of the word dictated. For simplicity's sake, we will just call the word "misspelled," and you might want to analyze on a personal basis the "why" and "how" of your spelling errors.

Many pieces of equipment today have the ability to electronically check the spelling of our documents. Both English and medical dictionaries may be available on the system. Make good use of this when it is available but be careful not to rely on it entirely.

Homonyms, of course, are not recognized as misspelled words, and of course the spelling checker will not recognize a wrong word substitute or other grammatical errors.

Some dictators will carefully spell drug names or medical words they feel you could have trouble locating. It is important to double check these words, just as you would check your own spelling, if you have any doubt about their accuracy.

RULE Always consult a dictionary whenever you have the slightest doubt about spelling.

Word Division. Words may be divided only between syllables or word parts. There are preferred places to divide a word, and every effort must be made to divide at this point. Some words may not be divided. (See Chapter 8, page 174.) Professional typists avoid dividing words because it slows down production and usually requires checking with reference materials.

RULE If you must divide a word, divide it only at the proper point.

Spacing. Normally, this is not much of a problem. With electric typewriters to do part of the work, letters seldom touch unless you attempt to crowd a large word into a small space. Rules concerning the spacing after certain punctuation marks, abbreviations, and symbols should be carefully followed; however, the spacing error that frequently slips past us may be made by hitting the space bar at the wrong time. Notice what can occur with this spacing error.

Example: The patient was prepped andd raped in the usual manner.

Spacing problems often occur with word processing and computer printouts that automatically take material to another line (or page) when we did not intend to do so.

RULE Always check printouts to be sure they conform to proper placement protocol.

When you type or make changes to something you have entered into the word processor, it is possible to create a new error in the process. Double check your correction! One common "newly created" error is to repeat a word on the line following the word, such as "and and."

Punctuation. Placing punctuation marks where they do not belong and omitting others that should be included are the obvious problems here. A comma fault (one comma missing from a comma pair, a comma separating a dependent clause, or commas enclosing essential elements) is a common error to check for. The improper use and substitution of marks (e.g., a colon for a semicolon or a comma for a semicolon) are examples of other errors. Punctuation errors are often made because the transcriptionist has not listened far enough ahead in the material to grasp the sense of the sentence.

RULE Always know *why* you are placing a punctuation mark.

Capitalization. Most capitalization errors are caused by a failure to capitalize; however, you should be careful not to capitalize unless there is a reason for the capital letter. In medical typing, the two areas where capitalization problems most often occur are with drug names (see Chapter 8, page 191) and abbreviations (see Chapter 5, page 106).

RULE Always know why you are using a capital letter.

Figures and Symbols. Errors with figures and symbols are usually caused by writing numbers out rather than using figures. Remember to express age, drug dosage, time of day, and other technical terms in figures (see Chapter 5). Omission of a symbol is certainly a minor error and usually occurs because the typist is unaware of the symbol or abbreviation.

RULE Know the technical symbols for your specialty area.

Accuracy. Errors occur when figures, dates, times, names, positions, and types and kinds of procedures and treatments are changed slightly or transposed with other similar material. Drug names can be particularly confusing because of the wide variation in pronunciation.

RULE Recheck any vital materials you transcribe.

Typographical. As you correct your work, watch to see if your typographical errors form a pattern. When you can recognize the types of errors you make (e.g., transposing the last two letters of a four-letter word), pay particular attention to overcoming the problem.

7

RULE Proofread carefully and correct all typographical errors.

Electronic. Many pieces of equipment today have the ability to convert certain codes or symbols that are typed within the text to complete words, phrases, sentences, or paragraphs. Codes are also used by some programs to indicate a certain style, set-up, or format. The inadvertent use of these symbols or mistyping them will result in a printout containing an incorrect format (e.g., set-up, underlining, spacing, centering, indenting, and so forth) or an inappropriate word, phrase, or even an entire paragraph or two.

RULE Use all electronic shortcuts slowly and carefully. Check the final printout carefully.

Example:
Conclusion:
Relatively
severe
L4-5
spinal
stenosis.
(somehow a code was given to the computer to print this format)

EDITING

The area we have been examining in your transcript has been material you have produced. Now we must look at the words themselves and see what, if any, control you have over the "sound" of the transcript. To a certain extent, the medical transcriptionist must edit the transcription. The term "edit" means making minor corrections in certain areas of the transcript *yet preserving the exact meaning* of the author or dictator. We will now examine where these problems lie.

Grammar

Change improper grammar.

RULE Make sure that the verb and noun match in number.

Example: There *was* fifteen members present. (were)

RULE Use proper parts of speech.

Example: The patient was found *laying* on the floor. (lying)

RULE Use proper words.

Example: There was no *reoccurrence* of his tumor. (recurrence)

RULE Use nouns and adjectives correctly.

Example: He was scheduled for replacement of his *aorta* valve. (aortic)

RULE Use proper singular or plural nouns.

Example: The *conjunctiva* were bilaterally inflamed. (conjunctivae)

RULE Position the modifiers correctly.

Example:
The patient had a hysterectomy leaving one tube and ovary in Jacksonville. (incorrect)
The patient had a hysterectomy in Jacksonville, leaving one tube and ovary. (correct)

RULE Use the proper tense:
Past tense is used: in the *past history* portion of a report
in discharge summaries
to discuss an expired patient.
Present tense is used: in the current illness or disease
in the history and physical.

Example: The patient *has had* left sciatica for the past two years; this *is* now exacerbated.

Inconsistencies, Redundancies, and Technical Errors

RULE Adjust or rephrase inconsistencies.

Example:
The patient drinks several beers per day, occasional cigars and cigarettes. (incorrect)
The patient drinks several beers per day and occasionally smokes cigars and cigarettes. (correct)

===

RULE   Delete redundancies.

Example:
The patient has no sisters and no siblings. (incorrect)
The patient has no siblings. (correct)

When you become more proficient at transcription, you will be able to recognize that there are other medical inconsistencies that you have the ability to correct. At this point, you will recognize them, but you might not know what to do with them. You do have the obligation to ask when in doubt.

RULE   Correct technical errors.

Example:
The *suture* was closed with #6-0 silk sutures. (incorrect)
The *wound* was closed with #6-0 silk sutures. (correct)

NOTE: When you are working, and errors such as this one occur, you will have to ask your supervisor or the dictator for the correct word unless you are *positive* you know what word was intended but not dictated.

Example: The tonsils were removed by blunt and sharp *diagnosis.* (dissection)

Most physicians depend on the medical transcriptionist to discover dictation errors, and they appreciate being alerted to possible errors or inconsistencies so they can make appropriate corrections if necessary. Consider these sentences:

"This 33-year-old woman had her gallbladder removed in 1950."

"The patient presented with diffuse infiltrate in the left lower lung fields and bronchography confirmed her lower lobe bronchiectasis; therefore, a right thoracotomy and right lower lobectomy were performed the following day."

You may have access to the patient's medical record and be able to determine the correct age of the woman or the date of her cholecystectomy. Examination of the actual x-ray films or the medical record should help you clarify the right/left problem in the second sentence. If not, you must check these with the dictator. Sometimes the dictator makes "he/she" substitutions or substitutes the referring physician's name for the patient's name.

Misunderstandings

One problem that even the most experienced medical transcriptionist confronts is that of not quite hearing, or not being able to understand, a word or phrase dictated. Because we can back up the tape over and over again, the word or words may eventually "come to us." Sometimes it helps to listen ahead; the word may be used again and said more clearly, or the meaning of the word may become obvious because of other words or other parts of the document itself. Many transcribing units have controls that permit the operator to increase and decrease the speed of play back. The use of this may facilitate the understanding of a word. Here are some simple examples of these words or phrases:

Examples:
The labwithdrawn on June 1, 199X . . .
The lab work drawn . . .
or   Lot sa snow how can I help you in the future
Let us know . . .
or   The middlehear was hair containin'
The middle ear was air containing

Such problems become increasingly more difficult as the words themselves or the phrases become more complex.

Foreign dictators, speaking according to the grammatical rules governing their own language, know what they want to say but may make odd English word choices. These expressions indicate a language barrier, not poor patient care. It is your responsibility to determine what the dictator intended to say and type it that way, again taking care to preserve the integrity of the meaning of the sentence.

Examples:
The incision was prolonged. (extended)
The patient's painful feets had disappeared. (foot pain had disappeared)

This is easier to accomplish if you are working in an office, having regular conversation with a dictator whose first language is not English. Then you become used to the nuances of his or her English translation problems. Each language is structured in a particular way; when we know or understand that structure, it is easier for us to work with such problems as omitting the past tense particle, making all words plural by adding an "s" to the singular, transposing, or choosing the incorrect synonym. Many foreign-born physicians have extensive English vocabularies and speak perfect English as well; however, heavy accents or inability to pronounce certain letters in our language makes it difficult to understand them until we have "tuned in our ears." You have the obligation to assist the dictator and make him or her sound good. Actually the dictator trusts that you will make his or her dictation appear as correct and professional as possible.

Flagging

We can "get away with" many bad habits in our spoken language that are not correct in written form. Avoid using contractions. Do not type material that does not make sense to you. If you cannot understand a word and the dictator is unavailable, ask your supervisor or another transcriptionist for help. If they cannot help, leave a blank space in your material that is long enough to allow you to insert the correct word later and attach a flag sheet to the material. This flagging (also called carding, tagging, or marking) can best be done by using the repositionable adhesive notes.

They have just enough adhesive on the back to hold them firmly in place until removed. You can also staple or paperclip your card or flag. The flag should include the patient's name, the page number, the paragraph, and the line of the missing word. If you are in a large organization, add your name. It will help the dictator if you put the missing word in context, that is, include a few words that come before and after it.

Example: Williams, Maribeth #18-74-78. Under PX, Respiratory (page 2, line 8) "???respirations present." Sounds like "chain smokes." Judy, 5-17-91

The reply to this will read "*Cheyne-Stokes* respirations present." Students, remember to follow this format as well on your practice transcripts. See Fig. 7–1 below for a preprinted note that can be attached to your transcript.

```
Dear Doctor _____ :

    RE:   Patient name   _____

          Report name    _____

          Date dictated  _____

☐ Please see blank on page ___ , paragraph _____ of this
     report. It sounded like _____

☐ Dictate more slowly and distinctly.

☐ Spell proper names.

☐ Spell unusual words in address.

☐ Spell patient names.

☐ Spell new and unusual surgical instruments.

☐ Spell new drug names.

☐ Spell new laboratory tests.

☐ Indicate unusual punctuation.

☐ Indicate closing salutation.

☐ Indicate your title.

☐ Indicate end of letter.

☐ Give dates of reports.

☐ Speak louder.

☐ Give patient's hospital number.

☐ Please read the area of this report indicated by the penciled
     checkmark for accuracy.

☐ Your dictation was cut off. Please fill in the rest of the report
     or redictate.

Thank you. Please return this note with corrections via hospital
mail to:
Transcriptionist _____

Telephone No. _____ Date _____
```

FIGURE 7–1. Example of a flagging or tagging note to be appended to a medical manuscript for solving problem dictation. This form may be printed on colored paper. (From Fordney, M. T., and Diehl, M. O.: *Medical Transcription Guide. Do's and Don'ts.* W. B. Saunders Company, Philadelphia, 1990.)

Slang and Vulgar and Inflammatory Remarks

When you are employed in the word processing department of a large clinic or hospital, your supervisor will be able to assist you in the handling of questionable material. Those transcribing for a service whose policy demands verbatim transcription will likewise have a supervisor or director for help. In a private medical office you may, of course, approach the dictator directly. Very few physicians make derogatory or inflammatory remarks, and they may speak in this manner owing to frustrations with their care of the patient. A surgeon may have just lost his or her patient to cancer and tears through the hospital, leaving a path of destruction behind. The "stupid physician" referred to in the dictation he or she leaves behind in your department reflects the frustration in not having a cure. That remark, obviously, is not meant to appear in black and white.

Questionable remarks can reflect on you and your judgment, the physician, the hospital, and the patient. The dictator may refer to patients, patients' families, or other members of the health care team as *stupid, crocks, dumb, lousy surgeons, quacks, "too dumb to know any better,"* and so on. The dictator will usually have forgotten the irritation that precipitated the problem in the first place by the time you transcribe it. Do you transcribe it? Consider these alternatives:

1. Check with your supervisor before transcribing it.

2. Contact the dictator and diplomatically and tactfully ask about it.

3. Make two transcripts, flag the problem, and ask the dictator to make a choice, destroying the original and copies of the rejected transcript (very costly and time-consuming).

4. Leave a blank with a flag that says "I'm sorry but I couldn't quite make out the first three words in paragraph two."

It is better to leave a blank than to type a questionable remark. How you handle the problem will depend on your work situation and your personal contact with the dictator.

Consider this example:

"This patient's condition would never have deteriorated to this extent if the nitwit charge nurse on four had brought it to my attention instead of taking it upon herself to practice medicine without a license."

Inflammatory remarks have no place in a medical record and could place innocent people in jeopardy. You were not there when the incident occurred and you have no idea what precipitated this remark, so it would not be your responsibility to edit or delete it. Your responsibility *is* to bring it to the attention of the dictator or supervisor *before* it becomes a permanent part of the patient's medical record.

Your ability to analyze and polish and to proofread effectively and accurately will reflect your professional development. Remember: Follow the protocol available, master the intricacies of English, and become familiar with reference materials and how to use them.

One must remember that medical records are legal documents and while they are vital in the care of the patient, they are also vital historically and could be the major protection for the physician in the case of a misunderstanding or a professional liability lawsuit. It is imperative that they be current, accurate, legible, unaltered, and clear.

---

 7 – 1: SELF-STUDY

Directions: In the following sentences, locate and underline any error and then write the correct word or words in the blank provided. If the sentence is correct, write "C" after it. It may be necessary to rewrite an entire sentence to correct some errors.

Example: The nurse said the count of the instruments *were* correct. *was*

1. The patient was all ready anesthetized when the resident arrived.

_____

2. Congradulations. You have just been promoted. _____

3. Dr. Thomas, a Thoracic Surgeon, has been setting in the reception room for over 1 hour waiting. _____

_____

4. He was transported by the Paramedics to Brookview hospital.

_____

5. Three students passed the transcriptionist's test with no mistakes.

_____

6. The patient was first seen in November of last year.

_____

7. The patients hobbies are knitting, painting, and to read in her spare time.

_____

8. Closing the wound, the bladder was nicked. _____

_____

9. *Dorland's Dictionary,* along with three other medical references, are sitting on my desk. _____

10. The number of surgeries we can accomodate because of the new surgery wing are increased. _____

11. The patient was mad as hell because of the delay in being seen.

_____

12. She has the option, does she not, of still going ahead with the surgery?

_____

13. Send copies of the operative report to Dr. Stuart Jamison, Dr. Claude Weiss and myself. _____

14. Neither the patient nor his wife have discussed the prognosis with me.

_____

15. Neither the surgeon or the referring doctor have been notified.

_____

16. The diagnosis of three of our staff members are listed on the report.

_____

17. Each of the instruments have been tested. _____

18. The raise policy has certainly boosted the morale of all who work here.

_____

19. She experienced numb and swollen in her left leg.

_____

20. The sputum grew out H. flu.

_____

21. The adnexa was negative. _____

_____

22. Patient has chest pain if she lies on her left side for over a year.

_____

23. The patient is edentulous and the teeth are in poor repair.

_____

24. He was seen by whomever was on duty in the Emergency Department.

_____

25. A intravenous pyelogram demonstrated functioning lower tracts.

_____

26. He was seen on November 7 and is doing quite well.

_____

27. 4-0 plain chromic catgut was used to secure and reapproximate the skin edges of both incisions. _____

28. He had two episodes of basilar pneumonia in 1980.

_____

29. The specimen was removed and sent to pathology in total.

_____

30. When three weeks old, his mother first noticed he was not responding to loud noises.

_____

Please turn to the end of this chapter for the answers to some of these problems and suggestions for some of the others.

HOW TO PROOFREAD

Establish good proofreading habits now and follow these general rules:

1. Always proofread as you go along. This is easy to do, unlike in copy typing, because you are able to look at your work as you transcribe. Production typists do not have time for complex editing. Some sophisticated equipment, however, makes error correction very easy, and little thought is given to errors until final hard copy is ready to be printed out.

2. Don't proofread too fast. Read aloud, if you can, because this will keep you from skimming over material.

3. Read everything before you remove it from the typewriter. Print out a fast, low-quality copy on machines with this feature. Check for typographical errors, mechanical errors, style, spelling, grammar, and meaning. If possible, do not look for everything at once. In one reading, look for the typographical errors and mechanical errors. Then, in a second reading, check for style, grammar, and meaning.

4. Read everything again after removal or final printout. Check carefully for placement, appearance, and format.

5. After a "cooling off" period, when you are not as familiar with the material, read it once again. "Cold" errors are easier to spot.

6. On long, complicated material, have someone read your work back to you, spelling out difficult words as you check the copy, or replay the tape and check your work as you listen again.

7. To check for spelling alone, try reading each line backwards, a word at a time.

When you proofread your material, you will not mark it unless it is a rough draft. Rough draft material is double spaced, leaving room for corrections and comments. Some "final draft" material becomes single-spaced "rough draft" because you have to make changes or corrections. You will make the corrections, if you can, as you find them. Only if you find you must redo the material do you mark the copy.

Most typists have their own set of marks indicating their revisions. When your employer asks you to prepare a rough draft so that he or she can revise it and

7

mark it before it is typed in final form, informal marks and symbols are generally used. If, however, your employer is writing for publication, it will be necessary for you to recognize and use the more formal symbols. We will consider this particular problem in Chapter 16.

Proofreading Marks

When copy is prepared for printing, it is corrected and marked, with correction symbols placed either in the margin or between the lines to indicate the changes to be made. If more than one marginal note is necessary, a slash mark (/) divides the notes. Either or both margins are used.

In proofreading your own copy, you may be more informal, using marginal notes only when there is no room on the single-spaced copy to indicate the change.

While you are a student, your instructor will proofread your work and may mark the copy and use marginal notes in a variety of ways. Therefore, let us examine the proofreading marks as they are used formally and see how we may modify them for our own use. Your instructor may wish to add his or her marking symbols as well.

The following examples will introduce you to the formal proofreader's marks (Fig. 7–2) and will show you how the copy is marked, as well as illustrating how the correction is highlighted with margin symbols. In addition, we will show you how you might use some of the symbols in a less formal way to mark your own copy.

The following abbreviations will be used to indicate each example.

1.   E = Error or incorrect copy

2. FM = Formal markings with the correction indicated

3. IM = Informal markings such as you, your employer, or instructor might use. These should probably be done with a contrasting color (teachers love red!)

4.   C = Copy as it appears when corrected

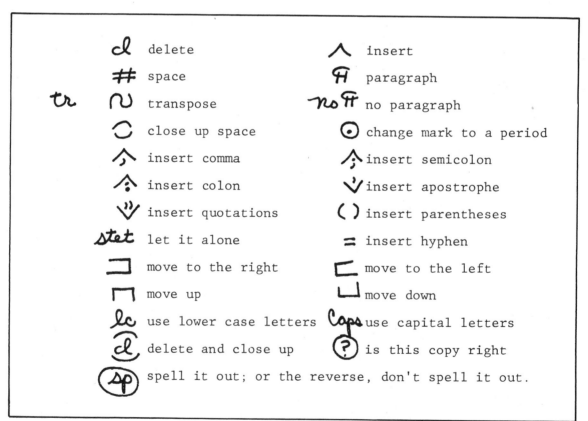

FIGURE 7–2. Formal proofreaders' marks.

Spacing. The proofreader's margin symbol # indicates that spacing is to be increased. A slash (/) is made on the copy to indicate where this correction is to be made. The mark ⌒ indicates that there is too much space and that the copy should be closed up.

```
E         John Jonesis scheduled.

FM   #    John Jones/is scheduled.

IM        John Jones/is scheduled.

C         John Jones is scheduled.


E         Look at this.See how it is typed.

FM   #    Look at this./See how it is typed.

IM        Look at this./See how it is typed.

C         Look at this.  See how it is typed.


E         Too much spa ce here.

FM   ⌒    Too much spa⌒ce here.

IM        Too much spa⌒ce here.

C         Too much space here.
```

Delete. The margin symbol to take out a word, a line, or a punctuation mark looks something like this ℓ. A line is drawn through the copy to be deleted and a "tail" is added to the top of the line.

```
E         There are too many patients waiting.

FM   ℓ    There are ᵗᵒᵒ̶ many patients waiting.

IM        There are ᵗᵒᵒ̶ʳ many patients waiting.

C         There are many patients waiting.


E         I will dictate the summary, but not the formal report.

FM   ℓ    I will dictate the summary/ but not the formal report.

IM        I will dictate the summary/ but not the formal report.

C         I will dictate the summary but not the formal report.
```

Insert Bottom Punctuation. The symbol ∧ is drawn in the margin with the correct punctuation mark to be inserted within it.

Comma: ⋏   Colon: ⩘   Semicolon: ⋏

NOTE: Often one punctuation mark is deleted and another is added. When two or more margin notes are used they are separated by a slash (/).

E   Jean Bradley your patient, came in

FM ⋏   Jean Bradley‸your patient, came in

IM   Jean Bradley‚ your patient, came in

C   Jean Bradley, your patient, came in

E   He agreed to the surgery I scheduled it.

FM ⋏   He agreed to the surgery‸I scheduled it.

IM   He agreed to the surgery; I scheduled it.

C   He agreed to the surgery; I scheduled it.

E   I wanted to remove the tumor, however, he refused.

FM ↺/⋏ I wanted to remove the tumor‸however, he refused.

IM   I wanted to remove the tumor; however, he refused.

C   I wanted to remove the tumor; however, he refused.

E   Gentlemen;

FM ↺/⩘ Gentlemen‸

IM   Gentlemen:

C   Gentlemen:

E   Diagnosis Bronchogenic carcinoma.

FM ⩘/# Diagnosis‸Bronchogenic carcinoma.

IM   Diagnosis: Bronchogenic carcinoma.

C   Diagnosis: Bronchogenic carcinoma.

Insert Top Punctuation. The symbol ∨ is drawn in the margin with the correct punctuation mark to be inserted within it. Notice how this symbol for the margin differs from the three we just examined.

Apostrophe: ∨   Quotation marks: ∨

E   The patients incision has healed quickly.

FM ∨   The patients incision has healed quickly.

IM   The patient's incision has healed quickly.

C   The patient's incision has healed quickly.

E   She had these seizures frequently.

FM ∨   She had these seizures frequently.

IM   She had these "seizures" frequently.

C   She had these "seizures" frequently.

Insert a Period. A circle is drawn around a period in the margin and is drawn around the punctuation mark in the copy that is to be changed to a period.

E   Joaquin R, Navarro, M.D.

FM ⊙   Joaquin R, Navarro, M.D.

IM   Joaquin R. Navarro, M.D.

C   Joaquin R. Navarro, M.D.

Insert a Hyphen. The symbol = in the margin indicates a hyphen is to be inserted in the copy.

E   She is a well developed, well nourished

FM =/=   She is a well developed, well nourished

I   She is a well-developed, well-nourished

C   She is a well-developed, well-nourished

Insert a Word. When you wish to indicate that a word is missing from a single-spaced copy, the missing word is written in the margin and a line is drawn to the place where it is to be inserted. When the copy is double spaced, it is fairly easy to insert the word above the copy with the ∧ symbol showing where it belongs.

E	The blood pressure was 160/90.
FM	The blood pressure ∧was 160/90. *on admission*
IM	The blood pressure ∨was 160/90 — *on admission*
C	The blood pressure on admission was 160/90.

Transpose. This symbol ∩ is placed around the letters, words, or other marks to be transposed and "tr" is written in the margin.

E		He was credited with savign
FM	*tr*	He was credited with savi(gn)
IM		He was credited with savi(gn)
C		He was credited with saving
E		A new medication was prescribed and, she seemed
FM	*tr*	A new medication was prescribed (and,) she seemed
IM		A new medication was prescribed (and,) she seemed
C		A new medication was prescribed, and she seemed
E		She was, however, seen as an outpatient.
FM	*tr/d*	She was, (however,) seen as an outpatient.
IM		She was / however / seen as an outpatient, *however.*
C		She was seen as an outpatient, however.

Let It Alone. Occasionally, after a correction is made the proofreader will change his or her mind. The formal marking is to place dots under the material that was originally marked and to write the word *stet* (let it stand) in the margin.

E		He should have cobalt-65 radiation therapy.
FM	*stet*	He should have cobalt-/65/ radiation therapy.
IM		He should have cobalt-/65/ radiation therapy.
C		He should have cobalt-65 radiation therapy.

Use Capital Letters. Three lines are drawn under the lower case letters that should be capitalized and the word *Caps* is written in the margin.

```
    E           I called the Admitting department

    FM  Caps    I called the Admitting department
                                        ‗‗‗

    IM          I called the Admitting Department

    C           I called the Admitting Department
```

Use Small (Lower Case) Letters. A slash (/) is drawn through the capital letter and the letters "lc" are written in the margin.

```
    E           The patient's Mother died of heart disease.

    FM  lc      The patient's /Mother died of heart disease.

    IM          The patient's /Mother died of heart disease.

    C           The patient's mother died of heart disease.
```

Spelling. Misspelled words, symbols that should be expressed as words, words that should be expressed as symbols, numbers that should be spelled out, and spelled-out numbers that should have been written as figures are circled. The margin notation is "sp." If the editor is not sure what the writer meant with the circled word in question, a question mark appears in the margin.

```
    E           The patient's temperature was ninty-nine degrees.

    FM  sp      The patient's temperature was (ninty-nine degrees).

    IM          The patient's temperature was (ninty-nine degrees).

    C           The patient's temperature was 99°.

    E           3 of the most serious problems

    FM  sp      (3)of the most serious problems

    IM          (3)of the most serious problems

    C           Three of the most serious problems

    E           Move her to the ICU immediately.

    FM  sp      Move her to the (ICU) immediately.

    IM          Move her to the (ICU) immediately.

    C           Move her to the Intensive Care Unit immediately.
```

Paragraphing. The symbol ¶ is used in the margin and the copy is also marked to indicate where a new paragraph should begin. If the paragraph beginning is incorrect, the symbol 𝓝𝓸 ¶ is used at the beginning of the paragraph to indicate it should be a continuation of the preceding paragraph.

E   Her history is well known to you, so I will not repeat it. On physical examination, I found

FM   ¶   Her history is well known to you, so I will not repeat it.∧On physical examination, I found

IM   Her history is well known to you, so I will not repeat it.¶ On physical examination, I found

C   Her history is well known to you, so I will not repeat it.

On physical examination, I found

Move the Copy. The following symbols indicate that copy is to be moved to the right ⌐, to the left ⌐, up ⌐, or down ⌐.

E   On physical examination, I found

FM   **5**⌐ On physical examination, I found

IM   **5**⌐ On physical examination, I found

C   On physical examination, I found

FINAL EXAMPLE:

sp/=/=/⌃ This (sixty-five) year∧old∧white∧widowed female was bei(ng) admitted ∧/tr
sp/sp/⌃ for the (1st) time. Her blood pressure was 120 (over) 80∧supine.
lc/cl/∧ She ᵂeighed 98 lb⌿. Height⌃(fifty seven)(inches⌿) she was sp/cl/⊙/caps
?/lc taking (quinadine) t././ɖ.

This 65-year-old, white, widowed female was being admitted
for the first time. Her blood pressure was 120/80, supine.
She weighed 98 lb. Height: 57". She was taking quinidine t.i.d.

7 – 2: SELF-STUDY

Directions: Now try to interpret these symbols yourself. All formal marks are used with marks in the margin. Retype this paragraph on a separate piece of paper and use single spacing. After you have retyped your paper, compare it with the key at the end of the chapter.

At cystoscopy, their were multiple urethral polyps, small in calibre, and an irritated bladder neck; the ureteral orifices were normal, & the remainder of the bladder wall was no remarkable. I will have to presume that the bleeding is coming from the urethral polyp/s. I don't think this accounts for all this womans symptoms, however. I am returning her to your care/ and will follow her along for a while to see what we can do about the hematuria.

 7 – 3: SELF-STUDY

Directions: Retype the letter on page 164 correctly following the proofreader's symbols. You will notice that the symbols used are a combination of formal and informal markings, just as your instructor or employer might use. Use letterhead paper and your own initials but please be careful not to create any new mistakes! Check the end of the chapter to see the corrected copy and compare it with your work.

7

PATRICK D. QUINN, M. D.
FAMILY PRACTICE
555 LAKE VIEW DRIVE
BAY VILLAGE, OHIO 44140

(216) 871-4701

July 17, 199x

Northern Ohio Gas & Electric Co.
Post Office Box 1831
Bay Village, Oh 44140

Attention T. J. Thompson Insurance Analyst

RE: Richard Wright

Gentlemen

Mr. Richard Right was seen in my office on July 9 199x . He was still having considerable pain in the right shoulder area but there was full range of passive motion and he felt like he was gradually improving, although he was not nearly as pain free as before the recent surgery. The surgical wound was well healed on inspection. Their continued to be considerable tenderness to palpation in the depths of the surgical incision sight. There was not swelling or increased heat or readness and as noted above, there was a full range of passive motion of the right shoulder.

Because of the continuing rather excessive pain symptons, xrays were reexposed and felt to be completely within normal limits.

I continue to have no real good explanation for the patients' continuing right shoulder symptom, particularly in there present degree of severity. It would seem to me that he would be much improved what he was prior too his recent surgery.

over

I have asked him to use the part as much as possible and to return in 2 weeks. Hopefully at that time some consideration can be given to a return to work date. Further reports will be forwarded as indicated. Thank you for the plresure of careing for this patient.

Very Truly Yours,

Patrick D. Quinn, m.d.

right margin
too uneven
and narrow

ref

7-4: PRACTICE TEST

Directions: Identify all errors in the letter on page 166 by marking them in red, using the informal proofreader's marks. (You do not have to make margin markings.) The letter should have been typed in modified block format, using a reference line and using mixed punctuation. After you have proofread it, retype it properly. See the corrected version in Appendix E. *Clue:* There are 45 corrections to make, including errors of style, spelling, and punctuation.

Certainly, your letters will not look like those in the previous exercises, and you will be able to correct any errors while your copy is still in the typewriter or word processor. You will mark your copy only when it has to be retyped.

In the beginning, you will want to transcribe letters and other documents in rough form. However, even in the beginning, try to make your rough copy look as much as possible like the finished product as far as placement and spacing go. It is much easier to work with double-spaced material, but you lose your placement advantage when you type a letter this way. Also, if you are trying to save paper and begin to type on the first inch of paper, another opportunity to achieve proper placement is lost. As you prepare your copy, use letterhead paper, place the date, space properly, and work from there.

However, when the dictator or writer asks for a rough draft, double space so that there will be plenty of room for editing.

An accomplished medical transcriptionist learns to make rough drafts "in his or her head" by learning how far ahead to listen. One day you will find that what started out as a rough copy was actually polished as you typed. However, do not be dismayed if you never accomplish this. There are some dictators whose dictation is so disjointed that it is always necessary to type it first in rough and then to revise and edit. The use of a word processor makes the job of revision an easy task.

Correction Tools for the Typewriter

Try to correct errors neatly so that your copy will not have to be retyped. It is necessary to have good correction tools.

Eraser. Use a clean ink eraser. You can keep it clean by removing any residual ink with an emery board.

Soft Brush. This is useful for whisking crumbs from your paper.

Correction Paper. There are several brands of correction paper on the market. These are packaged in a variety of ways: rolls, large sheets, little tablets, and small individual sheets. This paper is actually white carbon paper (it also comes in off-white and pastel colors to match your paper). You place the correction paper over the error you typed and retype the *error.* The typewriter key forces the white carbon over the ink and into the impression. If you find that when you strike over an error with correction paper the correction substance does not completely cover the typed character, try placing a piece of transparent film over the correction paper. The added layer should cause a thicker, denser correction strikeover.

Correction Fluid. This is very useful for removing small errors and is particularly helpful in covering up unwanted punctuation marks. Use it very sparingly and carefully or it will be noticeable. The manufacturers of these products produce fluid in shades of white and pastel, since the fluid must match the paper. You may use greater amounts of correction fluid *only* if the original is going to be used as a master and then photocopied. This process is never used to obliterate an error found in a medical record.

Correction Tape. This is produced in roll form about the width of a typed line and is lightly attached to a waxy paper backing. You cut off the amount needed to hide your error and place it on your paper and type over it. This is used *only* when you are making a master to be copied and is never used to obliterate an error found in a medical record.

Erasable Paper. When you use erasable paper, a regular pencil eraser or soft typing eraser will suffice. However, punctuation marks are difficult to remove from this paper, and you may want to use fluid for this type of error. Be careful when handling erasable paper because ink does not dry quickly on its special finish. While you are waiting for it to dry, it can be smudged by improper handling or by presenting it too quickly for signature.

Razor Blade. Some typists become expert at picking small inked errors off the page with the corner of a

7

Kwei-Hay Wong, M.D.
1654 PIIKEA STREET
HONOLULU, HAWAII 96818
TELEPHONE 534-0922

DIPLOMATE, AMERICAN BOARD
   OF OTOLARYNGOLOGY

EAR, NOSE, THROAT,
HEAD AND NECK SURGERY

1 Sept. 15 199x

2 Dr. Carroll W. Noyes M.D.
3 2113 4th Ave.
4 Suite 171
5 Houston, Tex.   77408

6 Dear Dr. Noyes;

7 I first saw Erma Hanlyn your patient on July 18 199x with a
8 history of a thyorid nodule since March of this year. This
9 thirty five year old woman had it diagnosed at Alvarado
10 Hospital where they urged her to have surgery I guess.

11 She gave a history that the nodule was quite tender when she
12 was seen there and that she was on thyroid when they took her
13 scan. However when I saw her the tenderness was gone. I
14 couldnt feel any nodule.

15   We have had her stay off of the thyroid so that we could
16 get an accurate reading and on Sept 8 199x we had another
17 scintigram done at Piikea General hospital which revealed a
18 symmetrical thyroid it was free of any demonstrable nodules.

19 All of the tenderness is gone and she feels well. She is
20 elated over the fact that she has avoided surgery

21 In my opinion Mrs. Hannlynn probably had a thyroiditis when
22 she was seen at Alvarado and the radioactive iodine that she
23 was given for the test is responsible for the cure.

24 Thank you very much for letting me see her with you and I will
25 will be happy to see her again at any time you or she feel
26 its necessary.

27   Sincerely

28   Kwei-Hay Wong, MD

29 lmp

30 cc

31

razor or the end of a scalpel blade. These tools are useful for punctuation errors but become too tedious for anything much larger.

Lift-Off Tape. Special typewriter ribbon is available for certain brands of typewriters and is sold with a special "lift-off" paper. This paper works somewhat like the correction paper except that the ink is actually removed from your paper. Excellent correction results can be obtained, but the special ribbon and tape will only work together. Check with your stationery supply store to see if these ribbons are available for your typewriter.

Correctable Film Ribbon. This special typewriter ribbon is made for correcting typewriters, and the ink is also easily erased from most papers with a regular pencil eraser.

Chalk. A small piece of chalk can be used to fill in erasures of punctuation marks.

Techniques for Erasing

Begin by removing the paper from the typewriter. Using a clean eraser, apply several strokes with the grain of the paper. Use care to remove only the errors when you erase and not parts of the surrounding letters. Only a complete, neat erasure, is acceptable. Carefully brush all the erasure crumbs away. Roll the paper back into place, and make your correction. You may be concerned about obtaining proper alignment after replacing the paper in the typewriter, and getting to "know" your typewriter helps; however, if you are in doubt about exact placement, keep a small piece of very thin paper at your desk. Place it over the area where your correction must go. The transparent portion of a window envelope is excellent for this purpose. Place the window where the keys will strike the paper. Then type your correction on this paper and see if it fits on the line. If not, reposition your paper by using the paper release, and try again. If the correction fits, remove your transparent sheet and type on the original sheet.

◨ Answers to 7 – 1: Self-Study

1. already

2. Congratulations!

3. thoracic surgeon / sitting / one

4. paramedics / Hospital

It is important to "know your typewriter," and you can learn to do this by practicing with it and noting where the bottoms and sides of the letters are in relation to the lines on the paper guide.

Whenever possible, try to make all corrections in the typewriter with correction paper, lift-off tape, or the correction key because it is much easier and faster than the erasing process.

Only after you are certain that your copy is perfect is it presented for signature or placed in a folder for protection until it is ready for signature and mailing. It is insulting to your employer to present material that has not been carefully proofread and corrected.

Everybody makes mistakes; the skill comes in when you can keep that a secret.

Every medical transcriptionist sees and hears a variety of popular errors that somehow made it out of the office or medical records department. So that you will not be the focus of humor, when you hear something odd, ask yourself, "Did I really hear what I thought I heard?"

Dictated: . . . history of intermittent claudication
Transcribed: . . . *history of intimate provocation*

Dictated: The proctoscopic examination revealed internal hemorrhoids
Transcribed: *The bronchoscopic examination revealed internal hemorrhoids*

Dictated: He was a 28-year-old, white male, obese
Transcribed: *He was a 28-year-old, white male, a beast*

Dictated: He had no dyspnea on exertion
Transcribed: *He had no dysmenorrhea on exertion*

Dictated: There were no bowel sounds.
Transcribed: *There were no foul sounds.*

Dictated: It was a well-healed incision, no soreness.
Transcribed: *It was a well-heeled incision, no soarness.*

Dictated: Lungs: Clear. There were no rales or rhonchi.
Transcribed: *Lungs: Clear. There were no rales or bronchi.*

5. No errors (C)

6. 199X (in other words, the year date for last year)

7. patient's / reading

8. The bladder was nicked when closing the wound. (The verbal phrase must logically and clearly refer to the subject of the sentence. The bladder did not close the wound.)

9. is sitting

10. accommodate / is increased

11. very angry or "mad as heck" or very upset or "mad as hell" (insert the quotes)

12. No errors (C)

13. and me

14. has discussed

15. *nor* the referring doctor *has*

16. *is listed* or change *diagnosis* to *diagnoses* and keep the *are listed*

17. has been tested

18. no errors (C)

19. numbness and swelling

20. H. influenzae or Haemophilus influenzae

21. were negative

22. For over a year, the patient has had chest pain if she lies on her left side.

23. Check the medical record to see if the patient is edentulous or the teeth are in poor repair; they can't be both.

24. whoever

25. An intravenous

26. was doing quite well

27. Number 4-0 (Don't begin a sentence with a figure.) You can recast the entire sentence to read as follows: The skin edges of both incisions were secured and reapproximated with 4-0 plain chromic catgut.

28. no errors (C)

29. in toto

30. His mother first noticed that he was not responding to loud noises when he was three weeks old. OR: When he was three weeks old, his mother noticed that he was not responding to loud noises.

◪ Answers to 7 – 2: Self-Study

At cystoscopy, there were multiple urethral polyps, small in caliber, and an irritated bladder neck. The ureteral orifices were normal, and the remainder of the bladder wall was not remarkable. I will have to presume that the bleeding is coming from the urethral polyps. I do not think this accounts for all this woman's symptoms, however.

I am returning her to your care and will follow her along for a while to see what we can do about the hematuria.

⊡ **Answers to 7 – 3: Self-Study**

PERFECT PUNCTUATION COMPANY
2526 LA MAL AVENUE
SAN VALLEY, CA 92014
(714) 555-7185

July 17, 199x

Northern Ohio Gas and Electric Company
Post Office Box 1831
Bay Village, OH 44140

Attention T. J. Thompson, Insurance Analyst

Gentlemen:

RE: Richard Wright

Mr. Richard Wright was seen in my office on July 9, 199x .

He was still having considerable pain in the right shoulder area
but there was full range of passive motion and he felt like he was
gradually improving, although he was not nearly as pain free as
before the recent surgery.

The surgical wound was well healed on inspection. There continued
to be considerable tenderness to palpation in the depths of the
surgical incision site. There was no swelling or increased heat
or redness and, as noted above, there was a full range of passive
motion of the right shoulder.

Because of the continuing rather excessive pain symptoms, x-rays
were reexposed and felt to be completely within normal limits.

I continue to have no good explanation for the patient's continuing
right shoulder symptoms, particularly in their present degree of
severity. It would seem to me that he would be much improved over
what he was prior to his recent surgery. I have asked him to use
the part as much as possible and to return in two weeks. Hopefully,
at that time, some consideration can be given to a return-to-work
date. Further reports will be forwarded as indicated.

Thank you for the pleasure of caring for this patient.

Very truly yours,

Patrick D. Quinn, M.D.

ref

7

Spelling, Word Division, and Using References

8

OBJECTIVES

After reading this chapter and working the exercises, you should be able to

1. identify and spell those medical terms with silent letters.
2. find medical terms by the use of cross references.
3. identify where English words and medical words are divided.
4. use the *Physicians' Desk Reference* as a drug speller and to identify generic and brand-named drugs.
5. locate references that are available to the transcriptionist.
6. develop English and medical spelling skills.
7. identify French and other unusual medical terms.
8. identify medical words that have two or more spellings.

• •

INTRODUCTION

This chapter is designed to increase your spelling, hyphenation, and capitalization skills. It will introduce you to the most common and helpful references for the medical transcriptionist, especially the medical dictionary, medical word books, and the *Physicians' Desk Reference* (PDR). At the end of the book there is a list of references for each transcribing category. (See Appendix C.)

Remember how hard it is to find the correct spelling of a word in the dictionary if you can't spell it to begin with? Appendix B (p. 392) contains a Sound and Word Finder Table. This will provide you with some phonetic clues so that you can locate words more easily both in the medical dictionary and in the regular dictionary. When you cannot find a word, look up the sound in the Sound and Word Finder Table and it will guide you to some possible letters or letter combinations with the same sound.

Example: The physician has dictated "kon-DRO-ma." Refer to the Sound and Word Finder Table and look under the K. Notice the clues given are *cho, co,* or *con.* Using your medical dictionary, locate the correct spelling of the term.

171

THE MEDICAL DICTIONARY

The medical transcriptionist's primary reference is, of course, the medical dictionary; no matter how expert you become, you will always need it. Because of this, it is important to obtain the most comprehensive and most recent edition (no more than ten years old). Since about 1,000 new medical words are coined each year, a medical dictionary's usefulness as a reference will diminish in time. A beginning transcriptionist must spend time becoming familiar with the arrangement of the dictionary because it will be an important asset in assuring accuracy.

The best dictionaries usually include word origins, phonetics, abbreviations, and anatomic illustrations for each medical term (Fig. 8–1). Numerous words are not spelled exactly as they sound, so learn to check the phonetic spelling to determine the correct word to use. Since there are some variations in reference books, we shall base our exploration of the medical dictionary on *Dorland's Illustrated Medical Dictionary,* published by W. B. Saunders Company. All answers to Self-Study exercises, Practice Tests, and Reviews are based on the 27th edition. If you have

another medical dictionary, follow along with this explanation as closely as you can.

Check the index for the tables and plates (illustrations) so that you will have a better idea of what anatomic pictures and lists are present. Look through and review the pertinent information in the tables themselves. If you have not had a formal course in medical terminology, check your dictionary for a listing of prefixes, suffixes, combining forms, and roots (i.e., "Fundamentals of Medical Etymology" at the beginning of the Dorland's dictionary) and become familiar with them.

In some dictionaries, there may also be a listing of the muscles, nerves, and arteries grouped together in one place.

CROSS REFERENCE

Many times the physician will dictate a word or combination of words that you cannot find when you consult your dictionary. An example is *"biferious pulse."* Since biferious is difficult to spell, it may be hard for you to find under the "B's," so the first step is

FIGURE 8–1. A typical word entry from a popular medical dictionary, Dorland's Illustrated Medical Dictionary, 27th edition. W. B. Saunders Company, Philadelphia, 1988.

to look under *"pulse,"* which is easy to spell. You will find that *"biferious"* is listed alphabetically under this heading. In other words, this term is located under the NOUN rather than the adjective. Many other medical terms can be found in similar fashion. This knowledge is very helpful for you since the noun is often much easier to spell than the adjective, and the adjective spelling may be what brought you to the dictionary in the first place. It should be mentioned, however, that in some medical phrases the adjective is not necessarily the first word, as in "biferious pulse." In Latin terms it is usually the second (e.g., "pulsus biferiens") (Fig. 8–2).

Some physicians use complete Latin terms to designate muscles and nerves. In these instances, consult the Table of Muscles or the Table of Nerves to get the correct spelling.

Here is a list of some frequently used nouns that have descriptive adjectives listed alphabetically under them in the dictionary.

pulse (puls) [L. *pulsus* stroke]   1. the rhythmic expansion of an artery which may be felt with the finger. The *pulse rate* or number of pulsations of an artery per minute normally varies from 50 to 100. See also *beat.*   2. a brief surge, as of current or voltage. **abdominal p.,** the pulse over the abdominal aorta. **abrupt p.,** a pulse which strikes the finger rapidly; a quick or rapidly rising pulse. **allorhythmic p.,** a pulse marked by irregularities in rhythm. **alternating p.,** pulsus alternans. **anacrotic p.,** one in which the ascending limb of the tracing shows a transient drop in amplitude, or a notch. **anadicrotic p.,** one in which the ascending limb of the tracing shows two small additional waves or notches. **anatricrotic p.,** one in which the ascending limb of the tracing shows three small additional waves or notches. **atrial liver p.,** a presystolic pulse corresponding to the atrial venous pulse, sometimes occurring in tricuspid stenosis. **atrial venous p., atriovenous p.,** a cervical venous pulse having an accentuated "a" wave during atrial systole, owing to increased force of contraction of the right atrium; a characteristic of tricuspid stenosis. **biferious p., bisferious p.,** pulsus bisferiens. **bigeminal p.,** a pulse in which two beats follow each other in rapid succession, each group of two being separated from the following by a longer interval, usually related to regularly occurring ventricular premature beats. **cannon**

FIGURE 8–2.   An example of a noun, *pulse,* showing some adjective entries associated with this noun. (From Dorland's Illustrated Medical Dictionary, 27th edition. W. B. Saunders Company, Philadelphia, 1988.)

8

aberration	deafness	immunity	ramus	treatment
abortion	degeneration	incision	rate	tremor
abscess	dermatitis	index	ratio	triangle
acid	diabetes	inflammation	reaction	tube
acne	diarrhea	jaundice	reflex	tubercle
agglutination	diet	joint	region	tuberculosis
alcohol	disease	keratitis	respiration	tuberculum
alopecia	duct	lamina	rule	tumor
anastomosis	ductus	law	serum	tunica
anemia	dysplasia	layer	shelf	tunnel
anesthesia	dystrophy	ligament	shock	typhus
aneurysm	edema	line	sign	ulcer
artery	embolism	maneuver	sinus	unit
atrophy	erythema	margin	sodium	urine
bacillus	facies	membrane	solution	vaccine
bacterium	factor	method	space	valve
bandage	fascia	microscope	speculum	vas
block	fever	muscle	spine	vein
body	fiber	nerve	splint	vena
bone	fissure	node	sprain	vertebra
bougie	fistula	nucleus	stimulant	virus
bursa	fold	oil	stomatitis	wave
canal	formula	operation	strain	wax
capsule	fossa	os	substance	zone
carcinoma	fracture	paralysis	sulcus	
cartilage	ganglion	pars	surgery	
cataract	gland	pericarditis	suture	
cavity	graft	phenomenon	symptom	
cell	gout	plane	syndrome	
center	granule	plate	system	
circulation	groove	plexus	tendon	
cirrhosis	heart	pneumonia	test	
clamp	hemorrhage	point	theory	
condyle	hernia	position	therapy	
conjunctivitis	hormone	pressure	tic	
corpus		process	tissue	
crisis		pulse	tongue	
culture			tooth	
cycle			tourniquet	
cyst			tract	

Using your dictionary, look up "syndrome." How many adjectives did you find as subheadings of this word?

NOTE: The same entity may be referred to as a disease or a syndrome (as Fabry's disease—Fabry's syndrome) or as a sign or a phenomenon (as Gower's sign—Gower's phenomenon). In some instances, the physician may have dictated a noun that does not list the adjective modifier you need. In this case, you will need to know the synonym for another choice. Here are some synonyms.

test (sign)	syndrome (disease)
phenomenon (sign)	procedure (operation)
test (reaction)	method (operation)

8–1: SELF-STUDY

Directions: Try the following exercises to get some experience using cross references.

What was dictated:	*Look under:*	*Spelling:*
Example:		
KRŌŌR-al ligament	ligament	crural
1. bi-PEN-ate muscle	_____	_____
2. pi″lo-MO-tor nerve	_____	_____
3. mi-en-TER-ik reflex	_____	_____
4. os per″o-NE-um	_____	_____
5. SHIL-erz test	_____	_____
6. lab″i-RIN-thīn symptom	_____	_____
7. HOR-nerz syndrome	_____	_____
8. de-KU-bi-tus paralysis	_____	_____
9. tik do-loo-ROO	_____	_____

Please turn to the end of the chapter for the answers to these problems.

8–2: PRACTICE TEST

Directions: Use your medical dictionary and locate the noun to see how to spell the adjective that has been dictated. If there is no listing, see if the adjective is listed to obtain the correct spelling.

1. pe-NAHRZ maneuver	_____	_____
2. sal″i-SIL-ik acid	_____	_____
3. WOS-er-man test	_____	_____
4. BAR-to-linz duct	_____	_____
5. vas spi-RA-le	_____	_____
6. dif″the-RIT-ik membrane	_____	_____
7. id″e-o-PATH-ik disease	_____	_____
8. SKIR-us carcinoma	_____	_____
9. TU-ni-kah ad″ven-TISH-e-ah	_____	_____
10. ALTZ-high-mers disease	_____	_____

The answers to these will be found in Appendix E at the back of your text.

MEDICAL WORD BOOKS

Medical word books are another tool for the medical transcriptionist. They are inexpensive, compact, and provide a simple method of locating a term quickly since the words are alphabetically arranged. However, since they do not have definitions, a good medical dictionary is needed if you need to learn whether the term is part of the anatomy, a disease, operation, pathology word, and so forth. Medical word books are

8

by no means a complete listing of medical terms, and you may still encounter a problem when a current new term or a slang expression is dictated that might not appear in any reference yet published. If you are using a general medical word book, read the preface so you will learn how to find the terms. If you know the term is a surgical word, refer to a surgical word book. There are specialty word books for surgery, pathology, radiology, drugs, abbreviations, and almost every specialty in medicine. Since the terms are well organized in these word books, the time needed to find a specific word is greatly reduced. Appendix C gives a comprehensive listing of all the word books under these headings:

1. Abbreviations Dictionaries/Medical

2. Immunology and AIDS

3. Pharmaceutical (shown marked with an asterisk)

4. Specialty References
   a. Cardiology
   b. Dermatology
   c. Gastroenterology
   d. Obstetrics and Gynecology
   e. Ophthalmology
   f. Oral and Maxillofacial Surgery
   g. Orthopedics
   h. Pathology
   i. Psychiatry
   j. Radiology
   k. Surgery

5. Spelling Books, Medical (shown marked with an asterisk)

WORD DIVISION

When typing letters and medical reports, it is preferable to eliminate hyphenation at the end of a line whenever possible. Unhyphenated words are easier to read, and hyphenation is time-consuming because the typist must come to a complete stop to decide where to divide the word. Dividing a word incorrectly is the same as misspelling it, and the error is very difficult to correct. Newspapers and magazines divide words in places that do not necessarily conform to grammatical rules, so do not use journalistic material for a reference. If a word division is imperative at the end of a typed line, follow the appropriate rule for either English words or medical terms. It is important to know your rules so you do not have to get the dictionary out routinely to find the proper place to divide a word.

BASIC RULES FOR DIVISION OF ENGLISH WORDS

RULE 8.1   English words may be divided only between syllables and in keeping with proper American pronunciation.

Examples
dex/ter/ous (not dexte/rous)
cel/lo/phane (not cell/ophane)
nom/i/na/tion (not nomin/ation)

NOTE: If you are unsure of the syllabication of a word despite your understanding of the rules for hyphenation, consult a dictionary. Although it is acceptable to divide a word at any syllable break shown in the dictionary, it is preferable to divide at certain points to obtain a more intelligible grouping of syllables.

RULE 8.2   If a one-vowel syllable appears in the middle of a word, divide after, not before, it.

Examples
organi/zation
regu/late
busi/ness
criti/cal

RULE 8.3   If two vowels appear together within the word, divide between them.

Examples
cre/ative
retro/active
valu/able

RULE 8.4   Divide a solid compound word between the elements of the compound.

Examples
time/table
home/owner
sales/person
gall/bladder
child/birth

RULE 8.5   Try to avoid dividing dates. If you must, divide dates between the day and the year but not between the month and the day.

8

Example
September 1, /1991 (Not: September/1, 1991 or
Sep/tember 1, 1991)

RULE 8.6   Divide names before the surname. Names preceded by long titles should be broken between the title and the name. Proper nouns are not divided.

Examples
Mary Margaret/Smith
Rear Admiral/John Wenworth
John D./Brown

RULE 8.7   Divide a hyphenated or compound word at the point of the hyphenation.

Examples
brother-/in-law
get-/together
cross-/reference

RULE 8.8   Divide a word with a prefix between the prefix and the root.

Examples
ante/natal
post/operative
trans/sacral
non/reactive

RULE 8.9   Divide a word between doubled consonants. Divide a word root that ends with a double consonant between the root and the suffix.

Examples
salpingo/oophorectomy
admit/ting
misspell/ing

BASIC RULES FOR DIVISION OF MEDICAL TERMS

RULE 8.10   Medical terms are *not* divided between syllables but are divided according to their component parts; that is, prefix, suffix, or root of the word. Whenever you have a choice, divide after a prefix or before a suffix rather than within the root word.

Examples
gono/coccus
ile/ostomy
naso/frontal

REMEMBER: Always refer to your medical or English dictionary when in doubt about hyphenation or division of a word. A misdivided word is a misspelled word.

BASIC RULES FOR AVOIDING DIVISION OF A WORD

RULE 8.11   Avoid dividing words with fewer than six letters.

Examples
pain
tumor

RULE 8.12   Avoid dividing words that leave confusing syllables at the beginning of the next line.

Example
encompass
encom-pass (incorrect)
en-compass (correct)

RULE 8.13   Do not divide one-syllable words.

Examples
weight
thought
strength

NOTE: Even when "ed" is added to some words, they still remain one syllable and cannot be divided.

Examples
passed
trimmed
weighed

RULE 8.14   Do not set off a one-letter syllable at the beginning or the end of a word.

Examples
amount (not a-/mount)
bacteria (not bacteri-/a)
ideal (not i-/deal)
piano (not pian-/o)

RULE 8.15 Do not divide a word unless you can leave a syllable of at least three characters (the last of which is the hyphen) on the upper line and you can carry a syllable of at least three characters (the last may be a punctuation mark) to the next line.

Examples
ad-ducent
de-capsulation
bi-lateral
criti-cal
radi-ator
accept-able

RULE 8.16 Do not divide names, other proper nouns, abbreviations, numbers, or contractions.

Examples
William/son (incorrect)
Ph.D.   UNESCO   f.o.b.   CMT   wouldn't
can't   200,000

NOTE: Write the contraction out and divide it in that manner.

Examples
would / not
could / not

RULE 8.17 Street addresses may be divided after the name of the street and before the word *street, avenue, circle,* and so on, but not between the number and the street name.

Examples
3821 Ocean / Street
821 East Hazard / Road
or 821 East/Hazard Road

NOTE: Avoid breaking these word groups whenever possible.

RULE 8.18 Do not divide identifying information from accompanying numbers.

Examples
2 cm
page 421

RULE 8.19 Do not divide a word that would change its meaning when hyphenated.

Examples

He re-infused the pump.	Ascitic fluid was rein-fused after ultrafil-tration.
Dr. Cho re-treated the inflamed area.	She retreated to Hawaii for a vacation.
I will re-collect the patient daily slips.	He had to recollect the operative procedure.
Meg re-marked the x-ray cassette.	Mrs. Avery remarked to me about the case.
Please re-sort the ledger cards.	She had to resort to turning the patient's account over to a collection agency.

RULE 8.20 Do not allow more than two consecutive lines to end in hyphens.

RULE 8.21 Do not divide at the end of the first line or the last full line in a paragraph.

RULE 8.22 Do not divide the last word on a page. (See also Chapter 6, page 131.)

 8-3: SELF-STUDY

Directions: Decide if each of the following words and word groups should be divided at the end of a line. If so, indicate the best division point. If necessary, refer to Rules 8.1 through 8.21 to complete this exercise.

RULE NO.

1. critical   criti/cal   8.2
2. Medical Assistant Jane Ever _____

3. Marie Carey Collins _____

4. radiator _____

5. 35 mg _____

6. preoperative _____

7. angiectasis _____

8. businessman _____

9. January 2, 1984 _____

10. 5 ft 10 in _____

11. clerk-typist _____

12. rested _____

13. acceptable _____

14. infra-axillary _____

15. president-elect _____

Please turn to the end of the chapter for the answers to these problems.

8

8–4: PRACTICE TEST

Directions: Decide if each of the following words and word groups should be divided at the end of a line. If so, indicate the best division point. If necessary, refer to Rules 8.1 through 8.21 to complete this exercise.

RULE NO.

1. eject _____

2. couldn't _____

3. page 590 _____

4. impossible _____

5. scheme _____

6. 7 o'clock _____

7. today _____

8. doesn't _____

9. 2480 Ames Drive _____

10. CHAMPUS _____

11. t.i.d. _____

12. shipped _____

13. around _____

14. 7,201,082,976 _____

15. John Jeffers, M.D. _____

16. 35-year-old _____

The answers to these will be found in Appendix E at the back of your text.

 ## 8–5: PRACTICE TEST

Directions: Divide the following medical terms at their most desirable point. Remember that medical words must be divided only where root elements have been combined.

Example: pre-mature rather than prema-ture.

1. claustrophobia _____
2. infraorbital _____
3. leukopenia _____
4. postoperative _____
5. posterolateral _____
6. tuberosity _____
7. acromion _____
8. metatarsus _____
9. myoplasty _____
10. bursitis _____
11. edema _____
12. viruses _____

The answers to these will be found in Appendix E at the back of your text.

ENGLISH SPELLING

A prudent transcriptionist will work hard to become a good speller. Although accurate spelling is an invaluable skill in any occupation, it is especially vital in the medical field. Few people feel secure and self-confident about their ability to spell accurately; therefore, unless you are one of those rare persons who remember when to double a consonant (acco*mm*odate or acco*m*odate, o*cc*asion or o*c*asion); whether to type *ie* or *ei*; whether to use *-able* or *-ible*; or whether to finish a word with *-ance* or *-ence*, you must be continually on the alert for these and other problem-causing syllables. Another difficulty is our own inability to recognize that we have a spelling problem. Never accept the spelling of a word given by the dictator or anyone else unless you know it is correct or have checked it in a reference source.

 ## 8–6: SELF-STUDY

SPELLING PRETEST

Directions: Before studying the spelling rules, try this spelling pretest to discover if you need assistance in this area. Each word is spelled in two ways, the correct way and the commonly misspelled way. See if you can decide which is correct. Write the letter of the correct spelling in the blank provided. Do not consult your references. After completing the pretest, refer to the answers at the end of this chapter on page 201.

1. (a) adaptable   (b) adaptible   —————
2. (a) advisable   (b) advisible   —————
3. (a) deniable   (b) denible   —————
4. (a) practicible   (b) practicable   —————
5. (a) inevitible   (b) inevitable   —————
6. (a) possable   (b) possible   —————
7. (a) digestable   (b) digestible   —————
8. (a) insensable   (b) insensible   —————
9. (a) forcable   (b) forcible   —————
10. (a) significant   (b) significent   —————
11. (a) indigent   (b) indigant   —————
12. (a) recieve   (b) receive   —————
13. (a) height   (b) hight   —————
14. (a) caffeine   (b) caffine   —————
15. (a) efficeint   (b) efficient   —————
16. (a) excede   (b) exceed   —————
17. (a) preceed   (b) precede   —————
18. (a) begining   (b) beginning   —————
19. (a) traveler   (b) traveller   —————

Spelling Rules

RULE   -able and -ible

Words usually end in *-able* when

1. The root is a *complete* word.

   Examples
   adapt   adapt*able*
   change   change*able*

2. The root is a *complete* word from which the *final e* has been dropped.

   Example
   advis*e*   advisable

3. The root ends in *i* or the original word ends in *y*. Change the *y* to an *i* and add *-able.*

   Examples
   apply   applicable   rely   reliable
   deny   deniable

4. The root ends in hard *c* (as in back) or hard *g* (as in big).

Examples
practicable   navigable

EXCEPTIONS TO THE ABOVE RULES:
affable   indomitable   malleable
amenable   inevitable   memorable
capable   inexorable   palpable
controllable   inflammable   portable
equitable   inscrutable   probable
formidable   inseparable   vulnerable
hospitable   intolerable

Words usually end in *-ible* when

1. The root is *not a complete* word.

   Examples
   audible   edible   possible

2. The root is a *complete* word that has *-ive* or *-ion* in one of its forms.

Example
digest   digestive   digestion   digest*ible*

EXCEPTIONS:
correct*able*   predict*able*

3. The root ends in *-ns* or *-ss*.

Examples
insens*ible*   admiss*ible*

EXCEPTION:
indispens*able,* which is related to dispens*ation.* If any form of the word has a long *a*, the word takes the *able* ending.

4. The root ends in soft *c* (as in reduce) or soft *g* (as in ginger).

Examples
forc*ible*   neglig*ible*

EXCEPTIONS TO THE ABOVE RULES:

collaps*ible*	flex*ible*
contempt*ible*	gull*ible*
convert*ible*	inflex*ible*
divis*ible*	irresist*ible*
discern*ible*	revers*ible*

NOTE: "-ible" words are rarer than "-able" words.

8–7: SELF-STUDY

Directions: Write the following words in solid form as you think they should be spelled with an *-able* or *-ible* ending. Then check your answers at the end of the chapter on page 202.

1. love   _____
2. manage   _____
3. agree   _____
4. adapt   _____
5. knowledge   _____
6. work   _____
7. force   _____
8. response   _____
9. change   _____
10. predict   _____
11. transfer   _____
12. move   _____
13. size   _____
14. notice   _____

8

RULE   -ant/-ance and -ent/-ence

1. When the suffix is preceded by *c* having the sound of *k*, or by *g* having a hard sound, use *-ant, -ance,* or *-ancy.*

Examples
significant   arrogant   applicant   elegance

2. When *c* has the sound of *s*, or *g* the sound of *j*, use *-ent, -ence,* or *-ency.*

Examples
indigent   innocence   reticent   diligent

3. If the suffix is preceded by a letter other than *c* or *g* and you are in doubt about the spelling, consult the dictionary, as there are no clear-cut rules.

8–8: SELF-STUDY

Directions: Write the following words in solid form as you think they should be spelled. Then check your answers at the end of the chapter on page 202.

	+-*ance* or -*ence*		+-*ant* or -*ent*
1. convalesc _____		7. persist _____	
2. neglig _____		8. excell _____	
3. assist _____		9. resist _____	
4. depend _____		10. recurr _____	
5. attend _____		11. differ _____	
6. clear _____		12. extravag _____	

RULE   ei and ie

1. This mnemonic (memory aid) will help you solve the *ie* or *ei* problem:

   I before *e* except after *c* or when sounded like *a*, as in n*ei*ghbor and w*ei*gh.

   Examples
   ie: chief, believe, relief, hygiene
   ei: receive, conceive, weigh, neighbor, vein

   EXCEPTIONS: financier, either, leisure, neither, seize, weird

2. In long *i* syllables, most words are spelled *ei*.

   Example
   height

3. In long *e* syllables, use *ei*.

   Examples
   caffeine, codeine, protein

4. Use *ie* after the letter *c* when *c* is pronounced like *sh.*

   Examples
   efficient, deficient

RULE   -cede, -sede, and -ceed

Supersede is the only word in the English language spelled with -*sede.* Only three words are spelled with -*ceed* (exceed, proceed, succeed). All others are spelled with -*cede* (precede, recede, and so forth).

RULE   Doubling the Consonant

1. Double the final consonant of a one-syllable word before adding a suffix beginning with a vowel, if the final consonant is preceded by a single vowel.

   Example
   pl*o*t, plo*tt*ed

   EXCEPTION: Before the plural ending -es, the final consonant remains single.

   Examples
   bus-es   gas-es

2. If the final consonant is preceded by another consonant or by two vowels, *do not double the final consonant.*

   Examples
   rea*c*t, reac*t*ing
   br*ie*f, brie*f*er
   l*oo*k, loo*k*ed
   la*u*d, lau*d*able

3. Double the final consonant of a word of more than one syllable before adding a suffix beginning with a vowel if the final consonant is preceded by a vowel and the word is accented on the last syllable.

   Examples
   begi*n*', begi*nn*ing
   refe*r*', refe*rr*ing, refe*rr*ed

   EXCEPTION: Reference.

4. When the accent does not fall on the last syllable or the final consonant is preceded by another consonant, do not double the final consonant.

Examples

*tra'*vel, trave*l*er
*prof'*it, profi*t*ed
*de'*sert, deser*t*ing
*can'*cel, cance*l*ing

5. Double the final *l* before a suffix even when the root word is not accented on the last syllable.

Examples

grave*ll*y   tonsi*ll*itis

Prefixes

1. Retain the consonant or vowel when attaching a prefix that brings identical letters into contact.

Examples

dissociation   reexcitation
salpingo-oophorectomy

NOTE: Doubling of an initial consonant does not occur as a result of adding a prefix except with Greek initial *rh*.

Examples

rhythm   arrhythmia

EXCEPTION: Biorhythm

2. Change the *d* in the prefix *ad-* to *c, f, g, p, s,* or *t* before words beginning with those consonants

Examples

afferent   accident   agglutination
appointment   assist   attend

3. Change:
con- to *co-* before vowels or *h*

Examples

coalesce
coaptation
coarctation
con- to *col-* before *l*

Example

collateral

con- to *com-* before *b, m,* or *p*

Example

commissurotomy

con- to *cor-* before *r*

Example

corrugation

4. Delete the *n* in the prefix *syn-* when it appears before *s*, change it to *l* before *l*, and change it to *m* before *b, m, p,* and *ph*.

Examples

systaltic   symphysis   symblepharon
symmetry

5. Change the *n* in the prefix *en-* to *m* before *b, p,* or *ph*.

Examples

engorgement   emphlysis

6. Change the *n* in the prefix *in-* to *m* before *b, p,* or *m*; change the *n* to *l* or *r* before words beginning with those consonants.

Examples

infiltration   insertion   irradiation
immersion

7. Change the *b* in the prefix *ob-* to *c* before words beginning with that consonant.

Examples

obtuse   occlude

 8–9: SELF-STUDY

Directions: Add a consonant, if needed, to each word below. If a second consonant is not needed, rewrite the word as is. Then check your answer at the end of the chapter on page 202.

1. facet___ed   _____
2. run___ing   _____
3. pin___ing   _____
4. brief___er   _____
5. transfer___ing   _____
6. inflam___ed   _____
7. inflam___ation   _____
8. cancel___ing   _____

9. profit___ed   _____
10. occur___ence   _____
11. concur___ence   _____
12. recur___ence   _____
13. prefer___ence   _____
14. refer___ence   _____
15. penicil___in   _____
16. tonsil___ectomy   _____

RULE Final Silent e

Words ending in silent *e* usually keep the *e* before a suffix beginning with a consonant, but drop the *e* before a suffix beginning with a vowel (-ing, -able, -er, -ed, -or, and so on).

Examples

pale, pale*ness*   use, us*able,* us*ing*
operate, opera*tion,* operat*or*

EXCEPTIONS:

1. After *c* or *g,* if the suffix begins with *a* or *o,* the *e* is kept.

Example

notice   noticeable

2. Keep the *e* if dropping it causes confusion with another word.

Example

dye   dyeing   (Not: dying)

3. If the word ends in *oe,* the *e* is kept.

Example

hoe   hoeing   (Not: hoeed or hooer)

8–10: SELF-STUDY

Directions: Write the following words in solid form as you think they should be spelled. Some dictionaries give two spellings of the same word, but usually the first one stated is preferable. Because of this inconsistency, there is all the more reason to consult a dictionary whenever in slightest doubt about a word. Check your answers at the end of the chapter on page 202.

1. accommodate + ed _____
2. manage + ment _____
3. argue + ing _____
4. improve + ment _____
5. aggravate + ion _____
6. acknowledge + ing _____
7. achieve + ment _____
8. commit + ment _____
9. develop + ment _____
10. excite + ment _____
11. supervise + or _____
12. survive + al _____

Following is a list of 150 frequently misspelled words. Read this list over carefully to become familiar with the words. Better yet, ask a friend, co-worker, or instructor to dictate some of these words to you, after you have studied them, to see how you might score. You can develop a similar spelling list for hard-to-spell medical terms and post it near your typing area for quick reference. Be sure that you place both English and medical words that cause you difficulties in your own reference notebook. Every time you misspell a word, concentrate on the area where the problem occurs and memorize some little device to help you remember it in the future. For example, to remember that *irresistible* is spelled *-ible* and not *-able,* you memorize "*I am irresistIble.*" If you have difficulty with principle and principal, remember princip*le* is a ru*le* (we follow certain spelling principles) and princip*al* is either an adjective meaning m*ain* or a noun meaning m*ain* person, thing, or amount.

Example: The principal diagnosis is pneumonia.

ONE HUNDRED AND FIFTY FREQUENTLY MISSPELLED WORDS

1. accommodate
2. accumulate
3. achievement
4. acknowledgment, acknowledgement
5. acquire
6. affect
7. aftereffect
8. allegedly
9. all right
10. among
11. apparent
12. arguing
13. argument
14. assistance
15. believe
16. beneficial
17. benefited, benefitted
18. canceling
19. cancellation
20. category
21. Caucasian
22. cigarette, cigaret
23. cite (to quote)
24. coming
25. commitment
26. comparative
27. conscientious
28. conscious
29. controversial
30. controversy
31. define
32. definitely
33. definition
34. describe
35. description
36. disastrous
37. effect

38. elicit
39. embarrass
40. enlargement
41. environment
42. exaggerate
43. except
44. existence
45. experience
46. explanation
47. fascinate
48. February
49. forty
50. fulfill
51. gauge
52. government
53. height
54. hindrance
55. hygiene
56. illicit
57. inasmuch
58. incidentally
59. indispensable
60. inflamed
61. inflammation
62. inoculate
63. insistence
64. insofar
65. interfered
66. iridescent
67. irresistible
68. its (it's)
69. judgment, judgement
70. led
71. license
72. likelihood
73. loose
74. lose

75. losing
76. maintenance
77. marriage
78. misspell
79. necessary
80. ninety
81. occasion
82. occur
83. occurred
84. occurrence
85. opinion
86. opportunity
87. particular
88. permissible
89. persistent
90. personal
91. personnel
92. persuade
93. possession
94. possible
95. practical
96. precede
97. preferable
98. prejudice
99. prepare
100. prescription
101. prevalent
102. principal (main or chief officer)
103. principle (rule)
104. privilege
105. probably
106. procedure
107. proceed
108. profession
109. professor
110. prominent
111. publicly

8

112. pursue
113. questionnaire
114. quiet
115. receive
116. receiving
117. recommend
118. referring
119. repetition
120. resistant
121. rhythm
122. seize
123. separate
124. separation

125. sieve
126. sight (to view)
127. similar
128. sincerity
129. site (a place)
130. studying
131. succeed
132. succession
133. suing
134. surprise
135. technique
136. than (conjunction of comparison)
137. then (at that time)

138. their (belonging to them)
139. there (in that place)
140. they're
141. thorough
142. to, too, two
143. transferable
144. transferred
145. unnecessary
146. usage
147. villain
148. vertical
149. visible
150. weird

8–11: PRACTICE TEST

Directions: Here are some "spelling demons." Each word is spelled here in two ways, the correct way and the commonly misspelled way. See if you can decide which is correct. Write the letter of the correct spelling in the blank provided. Do not consult your references.

1. (a) alright   (b) all right   _____
2. (a) supersede   (b) supercede   _____
3. (a) embarassed   (b) embarrassed   _____
4. (a) drunkeness   (b) drunkenness   _____
5. (a) irresistible   (b) irresistable   _____
6. (a) occurrance   (b) occurrence   _____
7. (a) ecstasy   (b) ecstacy   _____
8. (a) anoint   (b) annoint   _____
9. (a) occassion   (b) occasion   _____
10. (a) disappoint   (b) dissapoint   _____
11. (a) analize   (b) analyze   _____
12. (a) tyranny   (b) tyrrany   _____
13. (a) inoculate   (b) inocculate   _____
14. (a) cooly   (b) coolly   _____
15. (a) indispensable   (b) indispensible   _____
16. (a) superintendent   (b) superintendant   _____
17. (a) battalion   (b) batallion   _____
18. (a) perseverance   (b) perseverence   _____

19. (a) iridescent   (b) irridescent   _____

20. (a) reccomend   (b) recommend   _____

Scoring: If you are able to select 9 to 13 correct answers, you are far above the average speller. A score of 14 or more is considered superior. Check your answers in Appendix E at the end of this text.

MEDICAL SPELLING

Many medical terms of Greek derivation are difficult to spell. Those that start with a silent letter cause particular problems because we cannot locate them in the dictionary unless we know which phonetic sounds are likely to begin with a silent consonant.

Here is a list of some typical Greek word beginnings, along with their phonetic sounds and an example of a word in which each is used.

Spelling at Beginning of Word	Phonetic Sound	Example
pn	n	pneumonia (nu-MO-ne-ah)
ps	s	psychiatric (si″ke-AT-rik)
pt	t	ptosis (TO-sis)
ct	t	ctetology (te-TOL-o-je)
cn	n	cnemis (NE-mis)
gn	n	gnathalgia (nath-AL-je-ah)
mn	n	mnemonic (ne-MON-ik)
kn	n	knuckle (NUK-l)

Medical terms of Greek derivation may also have silent letters in the middle of the word. Notice the silent "g" in "phlegm" (flem) and the silent "h" in "hemorrhoid" (HEM-o-roid).

Furthermore, the *ch* combination makes the sound of *k,* as in *key,* and the *ph* combination makes the sound of *f,* as in *find.*

Two other Greek combinations are "ae" and "oe." In modern usage they often become simply "e." For example, "anaesthesia" is now written as "anesthesia" and "orthopaedic" as "orthopedic." However, when corresponding with the American Academy of Orthopaedic Surgeons (AAOS), use the "ae" spelling. The suffix "-coele" is now written as "-cele," as in the word "rectocele."

Some combinations of prefixes sound similar in dictation. Watch out for ante/anti, para/peri, inter/intra, hyper/hypo, super/supra. Refer to Chapter 10 and Appendix A for help with these troublemakers.

Lastly, there are six Greek suffixes that cause spelling problems for the beginning transcriptionist. They are -rrhagia (RA-je-ah), -rrhaphy (RHA-fe), -rrhexis (REK-sis), -rrhea (RE-ah), -rrhage (raj), and -rrhoid (royd). You will notice the double *r* but the sound of only one. Memorize these.

REMINDER: Refer to Appendix B, Sound and Word Finder Table, to provide you with some phonetic clues when you encounter the possibility of a silent letter.

8–12: PRACTICE TEST

Directions: The left column below indicates how certain words would sound when dictated. See if you can spell them correctly by using your medical dictionary as a reference. For help in looking up the words, refer to Appendix B, The Sound and Word Finder Table. Explanation of pronunciation: ā as in *nate,* ă as in *apple,* short stress mark (″), long stress is noted in capital letters.

Phonetic Sound	Remember the Silent	Spelling
soo″dō-lŭk-SĀ-shŭn	p	pseudoluxation
1. năth″ō-DĬN-ē-ah	_____	_____
2. tĕ-RĬJ-ē-ŭm	_____	_____
3. nū-MĂT-ĭk	_____	_____
4. NĒ-mē-ăl	_____	_____
5. NŎK-nē	_____	_____

6. dĭs-mĕn″ō-RĒ-ah   _____ _____

7. HEM-or-ij   _____ _____

8. DEN-she-ah PRE-koks   _____ _____

9. ki-RA-grah   _____ _____

10. kak-o-JU-se-ah   _____ _____

11. met-ro-REK-sis   _____ _____

12. men″o-met-ro-RA-je-ah   _____ _____

13. her-ne-OR-ah-fe   _____ _____

14. pi″o-nu″mo-ko″le-sis-TI-tis   _____ _____

15. u-SIT-e-ah   _____ _____

16. u-thah-NA-ze-ah   _____ _____

17. DI-ah-fram   _____ _____

The answers to these will be found in Appendix E at the back of your text.

8

MEDICAL WORDS SPELLED IN MORE THAN ONE WAY

Here are some common medical terms that have more than one spelling. The most popular and current spelling is seen in the left column, and the optional spelling is seen in the right column. Again, you might like to add these to your own reference book.

amnionitis	(am-ne-o-NI-tis)	amnitis
aneurysm	(AN-u-rizm)	aneurism
arthroclisis	(ar″thro-KLI-sis)	arthrokleisis
blastodisk	(BLAS-to-disk)	blastodisc
calices	(KAL-i-sez)	calyces
catalepsy	(KAT-ah-lep″se)	katalepsy
cesarean	(se-SA-re-an)	cesarian, caesarean, caesarian
contrecoup	(kon-tr-KOO)	contracoup
curet	(ku-RET)	curette
disk	(disk)	disc
dysfunction	(dis-FUNK-shun)	disfunction
endoderm	(EN-do-derm)	entoderm
fetal	(FE-tal)	foetal
fontanel	(fon″tah-NEL)	fontanelle
hygroma	(hi-GRO-mah)	hydroma (hi-DRO-mah)
leukocyte	(LU-ko-sīt)	leucocyte
liter	(LE-ter, LI-ter)	litre
orthopedic	(or″tho-PE-dik)	orthopaedic*
otoblenorrhea	(o″to-blen″o-RE-ah)	otoblennorrhea
proctencleisis	(prok″ten-KLI-sis)	proctenclisis
sclera	(SKLE-rah)	sklera
trephination	(tref″i-NA-shun)	trepanation (trep″ah-NA-shun)
venipuncture	(VEN-e-punk″tur)	venepuncture

ONE WORD, TWO WORDS, OR HYPHENATED WORDS

A common dilemma confronting the medical transcriptionist is the question of whether certain compound words are written as one word or two or are hyphenated. This problem occurs not only with English words but also with medical words. Try the following practice test to help brush up your word skills.

---

* An exception is in correspondence or manuscript pertaining to the American Academy of Orthopaedic Surgeons. The Academy still prefers the "ae" spelling of orthopedic.

8–13: PRACTICE TEST

Directions: Circle the correct word — or two words — in parentheses for each of the following sentences.

1. The four hospital visits cost $150 (altogether/all together).

2. We should learn how to operate the new word processors (altogether/all together).

3. At this hospital, (anyone/any one) is entitled to incentive pay when doing medical transcription.

4. The laboratory information is outdated, but type it into the chart note (anyway/any way).

5. Is there (anyway/any way) you can have the history and physical typed by 2 p.m.?

6. (Although/All though) it's Friday, we still have to put in some overtime.

7. Is it (alright/all right) to turn the discharge summary in a day late?

8. The cholecystectomy is planned for (someday/some day) in January.

9. She knows that (someday/some day) she will be given a raise.

10. The medical records and medical transcription supervisors are finally (already/all ready) to announce the new incentive policy.

11. The radiology report was (already/all ready) filed in the medical record when the physician asked for it.

12. Dr. Gordon should be able to see you (anytime/any time) in February.

13. The emergency room services are open for your use (anytime/any time).

14. He has certain clothes for (everyday/every day) wear and surgical gowns for work.

15. For (sometime/some time) now, he has been dictating his medical reports a day late.

16. The consultation reports were sent (sometime/some time) last week.

17. Her senior medical typists don't get (anymore/any more) pay raises.

18. Is there (anything/any thing) Dr. Avery can get you for your headache?

19. It took her (awhile/a while) to understand what the patient was complaining about.

20. Is there (anywhere/any where) we haven't looked for that missing patient's medical record?

21. This new medical position means (everything/every thing) to her.

22. Dr. Champion will take (anybody/any body) who wants to volunteer for this typing task.

The answers to these will be found in Appendix E at the back of your text.

 8–14: SELF-STUDY

Directions: The following self-test includes some of the more frequently encountered compound words in medical letters and reports. Indicate your choice by writing a letter on the blank. Check your answers at the end of the chapter on page 202. Medical or English dictionaries may not have some of those mentioned below. Refer to Appendix C, Spelling Books, English, for some excellent books on this subject.

			Answer
Example: (a) gallbladder	(b) gall-bladder	(c) gall bladder	a
1. (a) dip stick	(b) dipstick	(c) dip-stick	_____
2. (a) nosedrops	(b) nose drops	(c) nose-drops	_____
3. (a) finger tip	(b) finger-tip	(c) fingertip	_____
4. (a) fiber optic	(b) fiber-optic	(c) fiberoptic	_____
5. (a) hammertoe	(b) hammer toe	(c) hammer-toe	_____
6. (a) purse string (n.)	(b) pursestring (n.)	(c) purse-string (n.)	_____

7. (a) pursestring (adj.)   (b) purse-string (adj.)   (c) purse string (adj.)   _____

8. (a) cogwheel   (b) cog wheel   (c) cog-wheel   _____

9. (a) after load   (b) afterload   (c) after-load   _____

10. (a) chickenpox   (b) chicken pox   (c) chicken-pox   _____

11. (a) face lift   (b) facelift   (c) face-lift   _____

12. (a) cheekbone   (b) cheek bone   (c) cheek-bone   _____

13. (a) chin bone   (b) chin-bone   (c) chinbone   _____

14. (a) bed-rest   (b) bedrest   (c) bed rest   _____

15. (a) head-rest   (b) head rest   (c) headrest   _____

16. (a) follow-up (examination)   (b) followup (examination)   (c) follow up (examination)   _____

17. (a) follow up (on the case)   (b) followup (on the case)   (c) follow-up (on the case)   _____

18. (nervous) (a) break down   (b) breakdown   (c) break-down   _____

19. (a) mid dorsal   (b) mid-dorsal   (c) middorsal   _____

20. (a) reexamine   (b) re-examine   (c) re examine   _____

21. (a) pre operative   (b) preoperative   (c) pre-operative   _____

22. (a) postoperative   (b) post-operative   (c) post operative   _____

23. (a) nonmedical   (b) non medical   (c) non-medical   _____

24. (a) clearcut   (b) clear-cut   (c) clear cut   _____

25. (a) take down (of fistula)   (b) takedown (of fistula)   (c) take-down (of fistula)   _____

26. (a) herpes virus   (b) herpesvirus   (c) herpes-virus   _____

27. (a) footdrop   (b) foot-drop   (c) foot drop   _____

28. (a) bed sores   (b) bedsores   (c) bed-sores   _____

29. (a) down going   (b) down-going   (c) downgoing   _____

30. (a) lightheaded   (b) light headed   (c) light-headed   _____

31. (a) water hammer (pulses)   (b) waterhammer (pulses)   (c) water-hammer (pulses)   _____

32. (a) nailplate   (b) nail-plate   (c) nail plate   _____

33. finger nail   (b) finger-nail   (c) fingernail   _____

34. (a) lidlag   (b) lid lag   (c) lid-lag   _____

35. (a) pacemaker   (b) pace maker   (c) pace-maker   _____

36. (a) piggy back   (b) piggyback   (c) piggy-back   _____

37. (a) pig skin (graft)   (b) pig-skin (graft)   (c) pigskin (graft)   _____

38. (a) pigtail (catheter)   (b) pig tail (catheter)   (c) pig-tail (catheter)   _____

39. (a) seagull (bruit)   (b) sea-gull (bruit)   (c) sea gull (bruit)   _____

40. (a) sea fronds   (b) seafronds   (c) sea-fronds   _____

41. (a) zigzag   (b) zig zag   (c) zig-zag   _____

42. (a) ear drum   (b) ear-drum   (c) eardrum   _____

43. (a) ear wax   (b) ear-wax   (c) earwax   _____

44. (a) breastfeeding (b) breast-feeding (c) breast feeding _____

45. (a) breast bone   (b) breastbone   (c) breast-bone   _____

46. (a) checkup   (b) check-up   (c) check up   _____

47. (a) in patient   (b) inpatient   (c) in-patient   _____

48. (a) out patient   (b) outpatient   (c) out-patient   _____

FRENCH MEDICAL WORDS

French words are difficult to pronounce for English-speaking people because different sounds are given to the letters. Furthermore, some physicians do not attempt to use the French pronunciation but pronounce the word as if it were English. The following are some commonly used French medical terms with their pronunciation in French, with an occasional English version. Practice these words by repeating them aloud several times as you write them. To further enhance your spelling skills, ask someone to dictate them to you.

ballottement	(bah-LOT-maw) or (bah-LOT-ment)
bougie	(boo-ZHE) or (BOO-zhe, BOO-je)
bougienage	(boo-zhe-NAHZH)
bruit	(brwe) or (broot)
cafe-au-lait	(kah-FAY-o-LAY)
chancre	(SHANG-ker)
contrecoup, contracoup	(kon-tr-KOO)
cul-de-sac	(KUL-de-sahk)
curette, curet	(ku-RET)
debridement	(da-BRED-maw) or (de-BRIDE-ment)
douche	(doosh)
fourchette	(foor-SHET)
gastrogavage	(gas"tro-gah-VAHZH)
gastrolavage	(gas"tro-lah-VAHZH)
grand mal	(grahn MAHL)
lavage	(lah-VAHZH) or (LAV-ij)
milieu	(me-LOO)
peau d'orange	(po-do-RAHNJ)
perleche	(per-LESH)
petit mal	(pe-TE MAHL)
poudrage	(poo-DRAHZH)
rale	(rahl)
Roux-en-Y	(ROO-en-why)
tic douloureux	(tik doo-loo-ROO)
triage	(tre-AHZH)

8–15: SELF-STUDY

Directions: The following words are medical "spelling demons." Each term is spelled in two ways, the approved form and the common misspelling. See if you can select the correctly spelled medical word. Write the letter of the correct form in the blank provided. Check your answers at the end of the chapter on page 203.

1. (a) sequela   (b) sequellae   _____

2. (a) accomodation (b) accommodation _____

3. (a) inoculate   (b) innoculate   _____

4. (a) fascia   (b) fasia   _____

5. (a) sagittal   (b) saggital   _____

6. (a) currettage   (b) curettage   _____

7. (a) palliative   (b) paliative   _____

8. (a) inflamed   (b) inflammed   _____

9. (a) syphillis   (b) syphilis   _____

10. (a) flacid   (b) flaccid   _____

11. (a) inflamation   (b) inflammation   _____

12. (a) diptheria   (b) diphtheria   _____

13. (a) opthalmology   (b) ophthalmology   _____

14. (a) hemorrhoid   (b) hemorroid   _____

15. (a) supuration   (b) suppuration   _____

16. (a) arhenoblastoma   (b) arrhenoblastoma   _____

17. (a) cirrhosis   (b) cirhosis   _____

18. (a) cachexia   (b) cacexia   _____

19. (a) tonsilectomy   (b) tonsillectomy   _____

20. (a) catarrhal   (b) catarhal   _____

21. (a) transacral   (b) transsacral   _____

22. (a) sessile   (b) sesile   _____

23. (a) splenectomy   (b) spleenectomy   _____

24. (a) xiphoid   (b) ziphoid   _____

25. (a) menstruation   (b) menstration   _____

8

UNUSUAL MEDICAL TERMS

After mastering a beginning terminology course and embarking on a transcription career, you will probably be taken aback when you hear the physician or dictator giving you an unusual expression, such as "coffee-ground stools." The dictation may be quite clear, and you will probably type the expression out without difficulty but with question in your mind concerning what you "really" heard. Or it could be that the dictation is not too clear, and you forge ahead looking for the words in a medical or English reference. Chances are you will not find the expression. One hundred unusual terms commonly dictated in medical reports are given here to help you through this puzzling dictation.

TABLE 8–1. **UNUSUAL TERMS COMMONLY DICTATED IN MEDICAL REPORTS**

TERM	SPECIALIST/DEFINITION
acorn tipped catheter	urologist
Ambu bag	(a low-tech resuscitation tool in the emergency room)
angle of Louis	surgeon
argyle tube	surgeon
ash leaf spots (eye)	ophthalmologist
BABYbird respirator	respiratory system
banana blade knife	orthopedist
banjo-string adhesions	surgeon
basement membrane	nephrologist, ophthalmologist
Best clamps	surgeon
bikini bottom	orthopedist
Billroth II (procedure)	gastroenterologist/surgeon
Bird machine (on the Bird)	respiratory system

TABLE 8–1. *Continued*

TERM	SPECIALIST/DEFINITION
black doggie clamps	clamps
black heel	orthopedist
blowout fracture	orthopedist
blue bloaters	radiologist
bony thorax	orthopedist
brawny edema or brawny induration	skin (a general term)
bucket-handle tear	orthopedist
buffy coat	pathologist
CABG (pronounced "cabbage") refers to coronary artery bypass graft	cardiologist
CAT scan	radiologist
chain cystogram	urologist
charley horse	orthopedist
choked disc (or disk)	ophthalmologist
cigarette (or cigaret) drain	surgeon
clap (gonorrhea)	gynecologist/urologist
clergyman's knee	orthopedist
clog (clot of blood)	cardiovascular surgeon
coffee-ground stools	gastroenterologist
cogwheel rigidity or motion	hemologist
cottonoid patty	surgeon
COWS	refers to cold to the opposite, warm to the same —a mnemonic device used in otolaryngology for the Hallpike caloric stimulation response
crick (painful spasm in a muscle, usually in the neck)	orthopedist
Dandy scissors	surgeon
doll's eye movements	neurologist
fat pad	orthopedist
fat towels (wound towels)	surgeon
fern test (an estrogen test)	gynecologist
finger clubbing	pediatrician, orthopedist
fish-mouthed cervix	obstetrician/gynecologist

TERM	SPECIALIST/DEFINITION	TERM	SPECIALIST/DEFINITION
flashers and floaters (eye exam)	ophthalmologist	running off (diarrhea)	gastroenterologist
49er brace	orthopedist (a knee brace)	salmon flesh excrescences	—
frank breech position	obstetrician	sand (encrusted secretions about the eyes)	ophthalmologist
gallops, thrills, and rubs	respiratory system	saucerize (refers to suturing a cyst inside out so it will heal)	—
gimpy (lame)	orthopedist		
glitter cells	pathologist	scotty dog's ear	surgeon
goose egg (swelling due to blunt trauma)	orthopedist	seagull bruit	respiratory system, cardiologist
gull-wing sign	neurologist	shiner	black eye or hematoma of eye
guy suture	surgeon	shoelace suturing	surgeon
haircut (syphilitic chancre)	—	shotty nodes or shoddy nodes	a general term
hammock configuration	—	simian crease (seen in Down syndrome)	pediatrician
hanging drop test	pathologist		
hickey	dermatologist	skin wheals	dermatologist
His (bundle)	cardiologist	skinny needle or Chiba needle	surgeon
hot potato voice	otolaryngologist	sky suture	surgeon
jogger's nipples	orthopedist	sleep (inspissated mucus about the eyes)	a general term
joint mice	orthopedist		
Kerley's B (costophrenic septal lines)	radiologist	smile or smiling incision	surgeon
		smoker's face	a general term
Kerley's C lines	radiologist	snowball opacities	ophthalmologist
kick counts	obstetrician	snowbanks	ophthalmologist
lacer cock-up (splint)	orthopedist	snuff box	orthopedist
lemon squeezer (instrument)	vascular surgeon	steeple sign (on chest x-ray)	radiologist
Little lens	ophthalmologist	stick-tie	refers to suture ligature, transfixion suture, or a long strand of suture clamped on a hemostat
loose body	orthopedist		
Mill-house murmur	cardiologist		
mouse (periorbital ecchymosis)	ophthalmologist		
mouse units	laboratory	stonebasket	urologist
MUGA	cardiologist	stoved (of a finger) means stubbed	orthopedist
Mule vitreous sphere	ophthalmologist		
musical bruit	cardiologist	string sign	radiologist
Mustard procedure	vascular surgeon	sugar-tong plaster spling	orthopedist
octopus test	ophthalmologist	sugar-tongs (instrument)	orthopedist
outrigger (orthopedic)	orthopedist	"surf" test (surfactant test of amniotic fluid)	pathologist
ox cell hemolysin test	pathologist		
oyster (mass of mucus coughed up)	respiratory system	tailor's seat	orthopedist
		tennis elbow	orthopedist
pants-over-vest (technique)	surgeon	trick (of a joint) means unstable	orthopedist
parrot beak tear	orthopedist	trigger finger	orthopedist
patient flat lined ("expired" is preferred)	a general term	tumor plot	cardiologist
		two-flight dyspnea	respiratory system
peanut (a small surgical gauze sponge)	surgeon	two-pillow orthopnea	respiratory system
		walking pneumonia	respiratory system
PERLA or PERRLA	(pupils equal, regular, react to light and to accommodation)	weaver's bottom	orthopedist
		wet mount	pathologist
		wing suture	surgeon
piggyback prove	—	witches milk	neonatologist
pigtail catheter	cardiovascular surgeon	yoga foot drop	orthopedist
piles (hemorrhoids)	proctologist	ZEEP (zero end respiratory pressure)	pulmonologist
pill-rolling (tremor)	neurologist		
pink puffer (patient showing dyspnea but no cyanosis)	cardiologist	zit (comedo)	dermatologist
pins and needles (paresthesias)	neurologist		
pollywogs (cotton pledgets or sponges with pointed ends)	surgeon		
prep or prepped (from the word "prepared")	surgeon		
prostate boggy	urologist		
proudflesh (granulation tissue)	surgeon		
prune belly syndrome	endocrinologist		
pulmonary toilet	pulmonologist		
purse-string suture	surgeon		
rocker-bottom foot	orthopedist		
romied, from an acronym: R = rule, O = out, M = myocardial, I = infarction	cardiologist		
rooting reflex	pediatrician		
rubber booties	surgeon		
rugger jersey sign	—		
runner's rump	orthopedist		

SPELLING THE NAMES OF DRUGS

A drug has three different names: the *chemical name* is the long and often complicated formula for the drug; the *generic* (or nonproprietary) *name* is usually a short, single name; and the *brand name* is the proprietary or trade name of the drug and is copyrighted by the manufacturer. Popular drugs have several brand names because each manufacturer gives the drug a different identity. You can often spot a brand name by the superscript ® before or after it. Brand names always begin with a capital letter.

Look at the following list of everyday items to help you differentiate between the brand name for an item (capitalized) and the generic name for the same item (not capitalized).

Brand Name	Generic Name
Scotch tape	cellophane tape
Kleenex	facial tissue
Xerox	photocopy machine
Schwinn	bicycle

Now, look at the brand names and chemical name for a well-known tranquilizer, meprobamate. You will see that the same principles apply to drugs.

Brand Names
SK-Bamate Tablets
Deprol
Equanil
Milpath
Miltown

Chemical Name
2-methyl-2-*n*-propyl-1,3-propanediol dicarbamate

Generic Name
meprobamate

Notice that *only* the first letter of most brand-name drugs is a capital except for a few unusual exceptions, such as NegGram and pHisoHex. Most hyphenated brand names also have a capital letter after the hyphen, as in Ser-Ap-Es. A generic term is not capitalized. Some drug names can appear either capitalized or in lower case, such as the word penicillin. But if the physician dictates a certain type of penicillin, such as Penicillin G, the term should always be capitalized.

The fact that brand names for drugs are always capitalized and generic names are not presents a difficult problem to the beginning transcriptionist. Fortunately, help in the form of word books that specialize in listing only drug terms is available. Some books show whether a drug is generic or brand and what type of drug it is (narcotic, laxative, diet aide, hormone, and so forth). Using such books speeds locating the term since detailed drug information is not included. However, most physicians who belong to the American Medical Association receive the *Physicians' Desk Reference* (PDR) along with their membership. This reference book lists only those drugs that the pharmaceutical companies pay to have listed, and, therefore, not all drugs are shown. A complete list of drug reference books appears in Appendix B. Since most physicians refer to the PDR and have one in their office, we will emphasize how to use the book; any self-study or practice tests in this chapter are based on using it because of its availability.

The PDR is published annually by Medical Economics, Inc., in cooperation with the manufacturers whose products are described in the book. During the year, supplements are published to update the current edition until the next year's edition is released. The PDR is divided into seven different color-coded sections to facilitate use. These sections may vary in color designation in different editions, and the titles may also vary in wording. However, as a basis of discussion, the 1990 PDR consists of the following color-coded sections (only those sections preceded by an asterisk are used by the transcriptionist).

Section 1 (white)	Alphabetical Index by Manufacturer
*Section 2 (pink)	Alphabetical Index (brand names)
*Section 3 (blue)	Product (Drug) Category Index
*Section 4 (yellow)	Generic and Chemical Name Index
Section 5 (white)	Product Identification Section
*Section 6 (white)	Product Information Section (Therapeutic Indication)
Section 7 (green)	Diagnostic Products Information Section

It is important to become familiar with these seven sections, since not all drugs are listed in each one.

In addition to indicating the spellings of drugs, the PDR lists injectable materials used in radiographic procedures and the brand names of products used for laboratory and skin tests. The Alphabetical Index by Manufacturer is helpful when you are writing to a pharmaceutical firm to request drug samples for the physician. It gives current national and regional office addresses for each major drug firm.

When the physician dictates an unfamiliar drug name, refer first to the *Alphabetical Index* to see if you can find the proper spelling and capitalization. This is a listing of all the brand or trade names of drugs.

102 **Product Name Index**

Allerest Headache Strength Tablets (Fisons Consumer) .... ▣	Aminophylline Tablets (Duramed) 936	◆ Anbesol Liquid Antiseptic-Anesthetic - Maximum Strength (Whitehall) 435, 2294	◆ Aristocort Intralesional (Lederle) 414, 1142
Allerest 12 Hour Caplets (Fisons Consumer) .... ▣	Aminophylline Tablets (Geneva) 1003		Aristocort Syrup (Lederle)........ 1139
Allerest No Drowsiness Tablets (Fisons Consumer) .... ▣	Aminophylline Tablets & Oral Solution (Roxane) 1905	◆ Ancef Injection (Smith Kline &French) 430, 2084	◆ Aristocort Tablets (Lederle) .. 414, 1139 ◆ Aristocort Topical Cream (Lederle) 413, 1141
Allerest Sinus Pain Formula (Fisons Consumer) .... ▣	Aminoplex Capsules & Powder (Tyson) 2206	◆ Ancobon Capsules (Roche) 424, 1778	◆ Aristocort Topical Ointment (Lederle) 413, 1141
Allergenic Extracts, Diagnosis and/or Immunotherapy (Barry) 651	Aminosine Capsules (Tyson) ...... 2206 Aminostasis Capsules & Powder (Tyson) 2206	Android-5 Buccal (ICN Pharmaceuticals) .... 1060 Android-10 Tablets (ICN Pharmaceuticals) 1060	◆ Aristocort Topical Products (Lederle) .... 413, 1141 ◆ Aristo-Pak (Lederle) ....414 ◆ Aristospan Parenteral
Allerhist Extended Release Tablets and Elixir (Warner Chilcott) 2276	Aminotate Capsules (Tyson) ...... 2206 Aminoxin Tablets (Coenzymatic B₆) (Tyson) 2207	Android-25 Tablets (ICN Pharmaceuticals) .... 1060 Anectine Flo-Pack (Burroughs Wellcome)................767	Intra-articular 20 mg/ml (Lederle) .... 414, 1145 ◆ Aristospan Parenteral Intralesional 5 mg/ml (Lederle) 414, 1145
Allerphen 100 (Legere) .... 1192 Allopurinol Tablets (Geneva) 1003	Amitriptyline HCl Tablets (Biocraft) 680	Anectine Injection (Burroughs Wellcome)................767 Anestacon Solution (Webcon)............ 2277	Arlidin Tablets (Rorer Pharmaceuticals) 1861
Allopurinol Tablets (Lederle) .... 1134 Allopurinol Tablets (Mylan) .... 1522 Allopurinol Tablets (Par) 1576	Amitriptyline HCl Tablets (Geneva) 1003	◆ Anexsia 5/500 (Beecham Laboratories) 405, 656	◆ Armour Thyroid Tablets (Rorer Pharmaceuticals) 426, 1888
Allopurinol Tablets (Rugby) .... 1914 Allopurinol Tablets (Squibb) 2124	Amitriptyline HCl Tablets (Lederle) .... 1134 Amitriptyline HCl Tablets	◆ Anexsia 7.5/650 (Beecham	

If you cannot find the dictated drug name in the *Alphabetical Index,* check next to see if it is in the *Generic and Chemical Name Index* as a heading. If you find it in this section as a heading, you will know it is a generic name and is not capitalized.

Generic and Chemical Name Index 303

Amitriptyline Hydrochloride Tablets (Mylan) 1522	**AMPICILLIN** Ampicillin Capsules (Biocraft) 680	**ANTI-INHIBITOR COAGULANT COMPLEX** Autoplex T, Anti-Inhibitor	Fiogesic Tablets (Sandoz Pharmaceuticals) 1936
Amitriptyline Hydrochloride Tablets (Roxane) 1905	Ampicillin Capsules (Rugby)........ 1914 Ampicillin Capsules (Warner Chilcott) 2276	Coagulant Complex, Heat Treated (Hyland Division) 1052	Fiorinal Capsules (Sandoz Pharmaceuticals) .... 427, 1937 Fiorinal w/Codeine Capsule
Amitriptyline Hydrochloride Tablets (Warner Chilcott)........ 2276	Ampicillin for Oral Suspension (Warner Chilcott) 2276	**ANTIPYRINE** Aurafair Otic Solution	(Sandoz Pharmaceuticals)........ 427, 1937 Fiorinal Tablets (Sandoz
Chlordiazepoxide & Amitriptyline HCl Tablets (Lederle) 1134	Ampicillin Suspension (Biocraft) ....680 Ampicillin-Probenecid Suspension (Biocraft) 680	(Pharmafair) .... 1680 Auralgan Otic Solution (Wyeth-Ayerst) 2350	Pharmaceuticals) .... 427, 1937 Gelpirin Tablets (Alra Laboratories) ....608 Lortab ASA Tablets (Russ) .. 427, 1923
Chlordiazepoxide & Amitriptyline Hydrochloride Tablets (Mylan) 1522	Omnipen Capsules (Wyeth-Ayerst) .... 437, 2397 Omnipen for Oral Suspension	Tympagesic Otic Solution (Adria) 586	Meprobamate and Aspirin Tablets (Par) .... 1576 Methocarbamol and Aspirin
Chlordiazepoxide and Amitriptyline Tablets (Par) 1576	(Wyeth-Ayerst) .... 2397 Polycillin Capsules, Oral Suspension, and Pediatric	**ANTIVENIN (CROTALIDAE) POLYVALENT** Antivenin (Crotalidae)	Tablets (Par) .... 1576 Norgesic Forte Tablets (3M Riker) 416, 1254
Chlordiazepoxide/Amitriptyline HCl Tablets (Rugby) .... 1914 Elavil Injection (Merck Sharp & Dohme) 1374	Drops (Bristol-Myers Institutional) ....739 Polycillin-N Injection and in ADD-Vantage Vials	Polyvalent (equine origin) (Wyeth-Ayerst) .... 2344 **ANTIVENIN (MICRURUS FULVIUS)**	Norgesic Tablets (3M Riker) .. 416, 1254 Orphengesic (Orphenadrine Citrate with Caffeine and
Elavil Tablets (Merck Sharp & Dohme)........ 418, 1374 Endep Tablets (Roche Products) 425, 1818	(Bristol-Myers Institutional) ....739 Polycillin-PRB Oral Suspension (Bristol-Myers	Antivenin (Micrurus fulvius) (Wyeth-Ayerst) 2345	Aspirin) (Par) .... 1576 Oxycodone w/Aspirin Tablets (Barr) ....651 Percodan Tablets (DuPont
Etrafon Forte Tablets (4-25) (Schering) .... 428, 1975 Etrafon 2-10 Tablets (2-10) (Schering) 428, 1975	Institutional)................739	**APROBARBITAL** Alurate Elixir (Roche) 1775	Pharmaceuticals) 409, 928

Although some generic names have been adopted by drug manufacturers as brand names, use the generic form when transcribing unless the dictator wishes otherwise. At times the physician prescribes a generic drug instead of a brand-name drug because generic drugs are usually less expensive. Furthermore, in some medical writing, the dictator is asked to use generic names rather than to specify the brand. Some drug references use a format whereby brand and generic names appear capitalized. If in doubt about a generic name, check a good medical dictionary, which will list most generic drug names.

If you cannot clearly understand the name of the drug, it may be necessary to look it up under the *Product (Drug) Category Index* (see page 196), which lists drugs by their class, such as antihistamines, antibiotics, laxatives, and so forth. For example, if the physician dictates that the anorexic "DEX-ah-drene" was prescribed, you may look up "anorexics" and check the list to see if you can find a word that sounds like what was said; you will find "Dexedrine." Notice that this brand-name drug is capitalized.

If you have the brand name for the drug and you wish to find the generic name, you must look in the *Product Information Section.* Refer to Figure 8–3 (page 196) and you will see that the generic name of the drug is listed in parentheses below the brand name. This section is awkward to use because the drugs are listed alphabetically *after* the name of the drug company that manufactures them.

8

If, after checking all of these sections, you are still uncertain about what drug name was dictated, leave a space on the line and write a note to the dictator, describing how the drug name sounded. When the physician dictates a drug name that does not appear in the PDR, write it in the PDR in the place where it would normally appear, after you ascertain the correct spelling. Be sure to place it in your reference notebook as well, and be careful to indicate if it is a brand or generic name by using capital or lower case letters.

If the physician is prescribing an over-the-counter (OTC) drug for the patient and you have difficulty spelling the drug name, a number of references have been published, such as *Physicians' Desk Reference for Nonprescription Drugs,* published annually by Medical Economics, Inc.

For additional pharmaceutical references, see Appendix C at the end of this book.

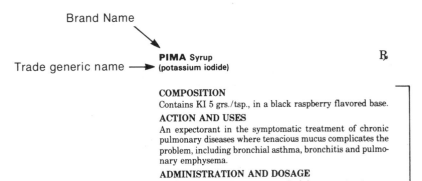

Brand Name →

Trade generic name → **PIMA** Syrup
(potassium iodide)   ℞

COMPOSITION
Contains KI 5 grs./tsp., in a black raspberry flavored base.

ACTION AND USES
An expectorant in the symptomatic treatment of chronic pulmonary diseases where tenacious mucus complicates the problem, including bronchial asthma, bronchitis and pulmonary emphysema.

ADMINISTRATION AND DOSAGE
Children—one half to one tsp. and adults one or two tsp. every 4-6 hours.

SIDE EFFECTS
May include gastrointestinal upset, metallic taste, minor skin eruptions, nausea, vomiting and epigastric pain. Therapy should be withdrawn.

PRECAUTIONS
In patients sensitive to iodides, in hyperthyroidism, and in rare cases iodine-induced goiter may occur.

HOW SUPPLIED
Plastic pints and gallons.

Information on composition of the drug, its action and uses, administration and dosage, and possible side effects. Precautions are given as well as in what form the drug is available.

FIGURE 8-3. A typical drug listing from the Product Information Section (white) of the Copyright Physicians' Desk Reference (PDR), 1990 edition, published annually by Medical Economics Company, Inc., Oradell, New Jersey.

8-16: PRACTICE TEST

Directions: To become better acquainted with the *Physicians' Desk Reference,* complete the following exercises:

1. Give the name of the section in the PDR that can help you to spell a brand-name drug.

   _____

2. Give the name of the section to locate drugs used as analgesics.

   _____

3. Here are some generic names for drugs. See if you can write in a brand name for each one.

                              Brand Name

   a. diazepam   _____

   b. allopurinol   _____

   c. belladonna ergotamine _____

   d. nylidrin   _____

   e. norethynodrel   _____

4. Here are some brand names. Give the generic names for each.

                   Generic Name

   a. Miltown   _____

   b. Norlestrin   _____

   c. Ascriptin   _____

   d. Coramine   _____

   e. Sanorex   _____

5. The physician has dictated a report mentioning the following drugs. Check to be sure that they are spelled correctly and make any necessary corrections.

   Drug Name Phonetics   *Spelling*

   a. EK-wa-nil   _____

   b. O-bi-trol   _____

   c. TEP-i-nil   _____

   d. be-LAD-e-nol Prep.   _____

   e. TEM-e-ril   _____

6. Here is a short exercise on sound-alike, look-alike drug names.
   a. The physician dictated something that sounded like Mesantoin, Mestonin, or Metatensin. You check the patient's record and see it is for hypertension. The one you want, therefore, is

   _____

   However, what would you do if the record was not available? _____

   b. Mrs. Bates' record shows that she has arthritis. The physician has dictated a word that sounds like Indocin or Lincocin. In checking the PDR, you find the word you want is

   _____

c. You are in the middle of typing a medical report and in referring to the patient's chart notes you find that the physician has scribbled in a medication that looks like Temaril, Demerol, or Tepanil. The patient is overweight. Which medication is written on the chart?

_____

The answers to these will be found in Appendix E at the back of your text.

8–17: PRACTICE TEST

Directions: Using your *Physicians' Desk Reference,* write the letter identifying the correct generic name and the letter identifying the correct product category with each of the following brand names.

Brand Name		Generic Name	Product Category
Motrin	_e,b_	a. clofibrate	a. sedative
1. Dalmane	_____	b. nortriptyline HCl	b. anti-inflammatory agent
2. Ilosone	_____	c. flurazepam	c. antilipidemic agent
3. Atromid-S	_____	d. desoximetasone	d. antidepressant
4. Topicort	_____	e. ibuprofen	e. antibiotic
5. Pamelor	_____	f. erythromycin estolate	f. steroid cream
6. Demerol	_____	g. cephalexine	g. antinauseant
7. Flagyl	_____	h. prochlorperazine	h. analgesic
8. Compazine	_____	i. meperidine HCl	i. amebicide
9. Keflex	_____	j. metronidazole	

The answers to these will be found in Appendix E at the back of your text.

8–18: PRACTICE TEST

Directions: Using your *Physicians' Desk Reference,* write in the generic name for each brand given.

Brand Name	Generic Name
1. Dymelor	_____
2. Benadryl	_____
3. Hygroton	_____
4. Dilantin	_____
5. Dramamine	_____
6. Gantrisin	_____
7. Tofranil	_____
8. Lomotil	_____
9. Pyridium	_____
10. Mellaril	_____

The answers to these will be found in Appendix E at the back of your text.

LABORATORY TERMINOLOGY AND NORMAL VALUES

A beginning medical transcriptionist may have difficulty when the physician dictates laboratory results. The sequence of numbers, the metric terms, the abbreviations, and the development of short-form expressions all sound like a foreign language. Normal laboratory values for many tests vary from one laboratory to another depending on the type of equipment used. Appendix D in this text gives approximate normal values so you will know whether the information dictated is abnormal or within normal limits. A self-study exercise is presented here to help you become more familiar with the terminology and numbers and thus overcome difficulty in transcribing such information.

8–19: SELF-STUDY

Directions: The physician has dictated the following sentences in some discharge summaries. Refer to Appendix D in this text, Laboratory Terminology and Normal Values, to help you obtain the answers. Read the statement, list the normal ranges, and then indicate whether the figure is high, low, or within normal limits (WNL).

	Normal Ranges	*High or Low*
Example: Laboratory data revealed a BUN of 16.	10.0 to 26.0 mg/dl	WNL
1. Glucose 107.		
2. Chloride 110.		
3. White blood count was 16,000,		
4. with 69% polys,		
5. 6% lymphs,		
6. 5% monocytes.		
7. SGPT 44.		
8. SGOT 38.		
9. The triglycerides were 646 mg/dl.		
10. (female) Hemoglobin and hematocrit were 15 and 42.2,	HGB	
11.	HCT	
12. with an MCV of 84,		
13. and MCHC of 35.2.		
14. Urinalysis was 1.020 for specific gravity with negative dipstick.		
15. Uric acid 7.7.		
16. Platelet count 74,000.		
17. LDH 232.		
18. Prothrombin times ranged from 17.2 to 19.9 seconds, with a 10- to 12-second control.		
19. (female, Wintrobe method) Blood sed rate was 25.		
20. Alkaline phosphatase 155.		
21. Total bilirubin 0.9.		
22. Total protein 6.7.		

23. Albumin 3.9. _____

24. Potassium 3.3. _____

25. The arterial gases showed a pO_2 of 75, _____

26.   and pCO_2 of 35. _____

27. CO_2 24. _____

The answers to this exercise may be found on page 203.

8-20: REVIEW TEST

Directions: The physician has dictated these 20 brand or generic drug names in a research paper. See if you can ascertain the correct spelling for each by referring to your *Physicians' Desk Reference.* Be sure to begin all brand names with a capital and all generic names in lower case. Type your answers on a separate sheet of paper.

Drug Name
Physician Dictated   *Phonetics*

  1. ibuprophen   eye-bu-PRO-fen
  2. diasapam   die-AS-a-pam
  3. nembutal   NEM-bu-tal
  4. xylocain   ZY-lo-kane
  5. lorasapam   lore-AS-a-pam
  6. alprasolam   AL-PRA-SO-lam
  7. dramamene   DRAM-ah-meen
  8. sekanol   SEK-oh-nal
  9. bensokain   BEN-zoe-kane
 10. klonadene   klo-NA-dene
 11. floorandrenolide   floor"an-DREN-o-līd
 12. surpasil   SER-pa-sil
 13. thorazene   THO-ra-zeen
 14. pentothal   PEN-to-thal
 15. zepharin   ZEF-ear-an
 16. milanta   my-LAN-ta
 17. libreeum   LIB-ree-um
 18. hexaklorafene   hex-ah-KLOR-oh-feen
 19. desonid   DES-o-nīd
 20. delantin   dy-LAN-tin

SPELLING WORD HUNT

The following article, which appeared as an editorial in *Cutis,* has 25 spelling errors. See if you can spot the incorrectly spelled words and list them on a separate sheet of paper with their correct spelling. Check your answers with those given at the end of this chapter on page 203.

PRURITIS

For some years I used to bet new groups of medical students that they could not correctly spell the medical word for itching. Only one lad in over ten years won the bet.

Burrough's solution, a commonly prescribed medium for wet compresses, is often mispelled. Electrodessication and curretage, the ubiquitous twins of dermatologic surgery, seem to confuse many. Innoculation is a medical teaser few seem to spell correctly.

Lichen sclerosis et atrophicus and condyloma lata are derived from Latin and with our de-Latinized educational system, I guess knowledge of their proper spelling is too much to ask.

As you can see your Editor is using his alloted space to ventilate his pet peeve—mispelling. In our youth-oriented culture, many educational leaders feel that spelling is merely a boring detail and that the "grasp of the concept" is all important. "Rap sessions" replace disciplined original essays. I disagree, but in a democracy we must accomodate all views.

There are three ways to avoid mispelling: 1. If you don't know how to spell a word, use an alternate. I personally find this much easier than hauling out the old dictionery; 2. Look it up in the dictionery. This takes time and is certainly an authoritarian method completely foreign to many of our younger set; 3. Who cares! Use it anyway. Someday our youngsters will run the goverment, which will supervise medical journals and mispelling will be so common we can all dispense with dictioneries. Practitioneers will not have to be bored by spelling and will have more time for goverment forms.

This, the 107th CUTIS Editorial, is devoted to spelling, and it is with the greatest personal pride that your Editor has never knowingly mispelled a word on this page. Burrough's is correctly spelled Burrow's; pruritis is puritus, and there are 25 spelling errors in this epistle.

John P. Mc Carthy, MD

Answers to 8–1: Self-Study*

1. muscle — bipennate
2. nerve — pilomotor
3. reflex — myenteric
4. os — peroneum
5. test — Schiller's
6. symptom — labyrinthine
7. syndrome — Horner's
8. paralysis — decubitus
9. tic — douloureux

Answers to 8–3: Self-Study

		Rule No.
1. critical	criti/cal	8.2
2. Medical Assistant Jane Ever	Medical Assistant/Jane Ever	8.6
3. Marie Carey Collins	Marie Carey/Collins	8.6
4. radiator	radi/ator	8.2, 8.3, 8.14
5. 35 mg	do not divide	8.18
6. preoperative	pre/operative	8.8, 8.9
7. angiectasis	angi/ectasis	8.3
8. businessman	business/man	8.4
9. January 2, 1984	January 2,/1984	8.5
10. 5 ft 10 in	do not divide	8.18
11. clerk-typist	clerk-/typist	8.7
12. rested	do not divide	8.12
13. acceptable	accept/able	8.1, 8.14
14. infra-axillary	infra-/axillary	8.7
15. president-elect	president-/elect	8.7

Answers to 8–6: Self-Study (Spelling Pretest)

1. a 8. b 15. b
2. a 9. b 16. b
3. a 10. a 17. b
4. b 11. a 18. b
5. b 12. b 19. a
6. b 13. a
7. b 14. a

* This exercise can be used with Dorland's or Taber's Medical dictionaries. If using Stedman's Dictionary, numbers 4, 6, and 11 are not listed under the noun. If using the pocket-size Dorland's dictionary, numbers 1, 3, 4, and 14 are not listed under the noun.

▣ Answers to 8–7: Self-Study

1. lovable
2. manageable
3. agreeable
4. adaptable
5. knowledgeable
6. workable
7. forcible
8. responsible
9. changeable
10. predictable
11. transferable
12. movable or moveable
13. sizable or sizeable
14. noticeable

▣ Answers to 8–8: Self-Study

1. convalescence
2. negligence
3. assistance
4. dependence
5. attendance
6. clearance
7. persistent
8. excellent
9. resistant
10. recurrent
11. different
12. extravagant

▣ Answers to 8–9: Self-Study

1. faceted or facetted
2. running
3. pinning
4. briefer
5. transferring
6. inflamed
7. inflammation
8. canceling
9. profited
10. occurrence
11. concurrence
12. recurrence
13. preference
14. reference
15. penicillin
16. tonsillectomy

▣ Answers to 8–10: Self-Study

1. accommodated
2. management
3. arguing
4. improvement
5. aggravation
6. acknowledging
7. achievement
8. commitment
9. development
10. excitement
11. supervisor
12. survival

▣ Answers to 8–14: Self-Study

1. (b) dipstick
2. (b) nose drops
3. (c) fingertip
4. (a) (c) depends on reference used
5. (a) (b) depends on reference used
6. (b) pursestring (noun)
7. (b) purse-string (adj.)
8. (a) cogwheel
9. (b) afterload
10. (a) chickenpox
11. All considered correct, depending on reference used
12. (a) cheekbone
13. (a) chin bone
14. (b) (c) depends on reference used
15. (c) headrest
16. (a) follow-up (adj.)
17. (a) follow up
18. (b) breakdown (noun)
19. (c) middorsal
20. (a) reexamine
21. (b) preoperative
22. (a) postoperative
23. (a) nonmedical
24. (b) clear-cut
25. (a) (b) depends on reference used
26. (b) herpesvirus
27. (a) footdrop
28. (b) bedsores
29. (c) downgoing
30. (a) lightheaded
31. (c) water-hammer (adj.)
32. (c) nail plate
33. (c) fingernail
34. (b) lid lag
35. (a) pacemaker
36. (b) piggyback
37. (c) pigskin (adj.)
38. (a) pigtail (adj.)
39. (a) seagull
40. (a) sea fronds
41. (a) zigzag
42. (c) eardrum
43. (c) earwax
44. (b) breast-feeding
45. (b) breastbone
46. (a) checkup
47. (b) inpatient
48. (b) outpatient

⌨ Answers to 8 – 15: Self-Study

1. a (sequela)
2. b (accommodation)
3. a (inoculate)
4. a (fascia)
5. a (sagittal)
6. b (curettage)
7. a (palliative)
8. a (inflamed)
9. b (syphilis)
10. b (flaccid)
11. b (inflammation)
12. b (diphtheria)
13. b (ophthalmology)
14. a (hemorrhoid)
15. b (suppuration)
16. b (arrhenoblastoma)
17. a (cirrhosis)
18. a (cachexia)
19. b (tonsillectomy)
20. a (catarrhal)
21. b (transsacral)
22. a (sessile)
23. a (splenectomy)
24. a (xiphoid)
25. a (menstruation)

14. 1.002 to 1.030 WNL
15. 2.2 to 7.7 mg/dl WNL
16. 150,000 to 350,000/ml Low
17. 80 to 120 units/ml High
18. 12.0 to 14.0 sec Outside of normal limits/High
19. 0 to 15 mm/hr High
20. 10 to 32 milliunits/ml High
21. 0.3 to 1.1 mg/dl WNL
22. 6.0 to 8.0 gm/dl WNL
23. 3.0 to 5.0 gm/dl WNL
24. 3.5 to 5.0 mEq/liter Low
25. 75 to 100 mm Hg WNL
26. 32 to 35 mm Hg WNL
27. 22 to 30 mmol/liter WNL

⌨ Answers to 8 – 19: Self-Study

1. 60 to 100 mg/dl High
2. 96 to 106 mEq/liter High
3. 4,200 to 10,000 High
4. 54 to 62% High
5. 25 to 33% Low
6. 3 to 7% WNL
7. 0 to 17 milliunits/ml High
8. 0 to 19 milliunits/ml High
9. 40 to 150 mg/dl High
10. HGB 12.0 to 16.0 gm/dl WNL
11. HCT 37 to 47 ml/dl WNL
12. 80 to 105 microns WNL
13. 32 to 36% WNL

⌨ Answers to Spelling Word Hunt

1. pruritus
2. Burow's
3. misspelled
4. electrodesiccation
5. curettage
6. inoculation
7. sclerosus
8. atrophicans
9. latum
10. allotted
11. misspelling
12. accommodate
13. misspelling
14. dictionary
15. dictionary
16. government
17. misspelling
18. dictionaries
19. practitioners
20. government
21. misspelled
22. Burow's
23. Burow's
24. pruritus
25. pruritus

8

Word Endings: Plurals, Nouns, and Adjectives

OBJECTIVES

After reading this chapter and working the exercises, you should be able to

1. explain the rules for making medical and English words plural.
2. identify adjective and noun endings.
3. construct plural and adjective endings of medical terms.

. . . .

INTRODUCTION

Word endings are emphasized in this textbook because they can cause problems for both the beginning and the experienced typist when transcribing medical documents. Some dictators tend to swallow up the endings of words as they dictate or may dictate a singular ending when the context of the sentence indicates a plural form should be used. Spelling of plural forms of Latin and Greek words do not follow English rules. Therefore, it is important to become familiar with these differences. You will also learn that some of the Latin and Greek words have been Anglicized to have English plural endings. Besides Latin and Greek endings, you will learn the difference between noun endings and adjective endings. In the examples and exercises presented, some of the most common words dictated in medical reports will be introduced so you can have experience in working with them.

VOCABULARY

Adjective: Words used to limit or qualify a noun.

> **Example:** This is a *well-developed* and *well-nourished young Hispanic* boy.

Noun: The name of a person, place, or thing (see Chapter 4, p. 82).

> **Example:** This is a well-developed and well-nourished young Hispanic *boy.*

Plural: A noun that refers to more than one.

> **Example:** No *x-rays* are available for review.

Singular: A noun that refers to only one.

> **Example:** No *x-ray* is available for review.

Suffix: A letter or group of letters added to the end of a word to give it grammatical function or to form a new word.

> **Example:** Diagn*osis:* Cellul*itis,* left arm.

PLURAL ENDINGS

Medical terms, as you know from previous study, stem mainly from Greek and Latin. The rules to make these words plural differ from the rules for forming English plurals. You will have to know these rules and the few variations. If the physician dictates a plural form that is unfamiliar to you, check it in the medical dictionary to make sure of the ending. In current usage, many terms have developed English plural endings, and it is good policy to use an English plural whenever one is available. There is a wide variation among physicians, however, and you will notice that some will dictate Latin or Greek endings even though English ones are acceptable.

FORMING PLURALS OF MEDICAL TERMS

The following are some rules for making medical terms plural.

RULE 9.1 When a word ends in *"um,"* change the *"um"* to *"a"* (pronounced ah).

9–1: SELF-STUDY

Directions: Read the following sentences and choose the correct singular or plural form. Then on the blank line type or handwrite the word you choose to reinforce spelling. Use your medical dictionary as a reference, if necessary. Check your answers with those given at the end of this chapter on page 215.

1. A culture (medium, media) was prepared. _____

2. The Table of Culture (Medium, Media) had a typographical error in the spelling of Mycoplasma. _____

3. The right and left (acetabulum, acetabula) showed mild degeneration. _____

4. Mark Evans had four (diverticulum, diverticula) noted during the colonoscopy. _____

5. The (ischium, ischia) on the left showed a fracture line on the x-ray. _____

6. The (bacterium, bacteria) in question were bacilli. _____

7. There was an infection of the maxillary (antrum, antra) on the left. _____

8. During cardiac catheterization, a thin, flexible tube was introduced into an artery and guided through the right (atrium, atria). _____

9. There was severe damage seen at the (hilum, hila) of the spleen. _____

10. The coronary and sinusoidal (ostium, ostia) were explored at surgery. _____

11. The nasal (septum, septa) was deviated to the right. _____

12. Pieces of bone were taken from the right and left crest of the (ileum, ilium, ilia). _____

13. The (labium, labia) majora pudendi is the greater lip of the pudendum. _____

RULE 9.2 When a word ends in *"a,"* form the plural by adding an *"e"* (variably pronounced ī, ē, or ā).*

9–2: SELF-STUDY

Directions: Read the following sentences and choose the correct singular or plural form. Then on the blank line type or handwrite the word you choose to reinforce spelling. Use

---

* Dictionaries do not agree on pronunciation.

your medical dictionary as a reference, if necessary. Check your answers with those given at the end of this chapter on page 216.

1. The patient's right shoulder (bursa, bursae) was injected with cortisone. _____

2. Both lung (pleura, pleurae) were filled with fluid. _____

3. The posterior pleura overlying the (aorta, aortae) was incised. _____

4. The remaining attachments of the muscle at the base of the (lamina, laminae) were removed. _____

5. The infant had congenital defects of the right and left (maxilla, maxillae). _____

6. Eyes: (Conjunctiva, Conjunctivae) clear; (sclera, sclerae) clear. _____

7. The fifth and sixth (vertebra, vertebrae) were fractured in the auto accident. _____

8. The (areola, areolae) of the right breast appeared red, inflamed, and warm to the touch. _____

9. The lacrimal (fossa, fossae) secrete the tears. _____

10. The posterior dorsal surface of the left (scapula, scapulae) had a mottled appearance on the x-ray film. _____

12. The left lower lobe had one very large (bulla, bullae) as well as two smaller moderate-sized (bulla, bullae), which were excised with the stapler. _____

9

RULE 9.3 When a word ends in *"us,"* change the *"us"* to *"i"* (pronounced ī).

EXCEPTIONS: plexus becomes plexuses
corpus becomes corpora

meatus stays meatus or becomes meatuses
syllabus becomes syllabuses or syllabi
viscus becomes viscera

 ## 9–3: SELF-STUDY

Directions: Read the following sentences and choose the correct singular or plural form. Then on the blank line type or handwrite the word you choose to reinforce spelling. Use your medical dictionary as a reference, if necessary. Check your answers with those given at the end of this chapter on page 216.

1. This patient was diagnosed as having pneumonia, as she has an acute inflammation and infection of the (alveolus, alveoli). _____

2. The tumor apparently originated at the left main (bronchus, bronchi) and extends peripherally. _____

3. Specimen consists of an irregular black (calculus, calculi) that measures 5 mm in maximum dimension. _____

4. A scraping from the skin lesion on the dorsal aspect of the left foot was sent for a test for (fungus, fungi). _____

5. Leg length was measured from the medial (malleolus, malleoli) to the crest of the (ileum, ilium, ilia). _____

6. After removal of the dumbbell cyst, the (glomerulus, glomeruli) of the left kidney did not function. _____

7. On testing the right knee, crepitation could be felt at both medial and lateral (meniscus, menisci). _____

8. The Gram stain showed a few gram-positive (coccus, cocci). _____

9. The cuboid bone of the (tarsus, tarsi) shows a slight fracture on x-ray film. _____

10. The (nucleus, nucleuses, nuclei) show atypism and hyperchromatism but no mitotic figures. _____

11. The tumor occurs in many (focus, focuses, foci) in the TURP specimen. _____

12. Sections reveal a placenta with mature chorionic (villus, villi), which have mild to moderate fibrinous deposits, hyalinization, and calcification. _____

RULE 9.4   When a word ends in *"is,"* change the *"is"* to *"es"* (pronounced ēz or ēs).

EXCEPTIONS: iris becomes irides
arthritis becomes arthritides
epididymis becomes epididy-
    mides
femoris becomes femora

 ## 9–4: SELF-STUDY

Directions: Read the following sentences and choose the correct singular or plural form. Then on the blank line type or handwrite the word you choose to reinforce spelling. Use your medical dictionary as a reference, if necessary. Check your answers with those given at the end of this chapter on page 216 to 217.

1. The rectal stump was considered to be quite adequate for (anastomosis, anastomoses). _____

2. (Diagnosis, Diagnoses): 1. Amyotrophic lateral sclerosis. 2. Ventilatory insufficiency. _____

3. An (ecchymosis, ecchymoses) was noted on examination of the right arm. _____

4. The x-ray film revealed an (exostosis, exostoses) on the distal end of the femur. _____

5. The patient's (prognosis, prognoses) is poor. _____

6. The body scan showed one bone and two liver (metastasis, metastases). _____

7. (Urinalysis, Urinalyses) are to be done on Mrs. James every two months. _____

8. It seems there are multiple (crisis, crises) that occur as a result of drug problems. _____

9. The right (testis, testes) was tender and swollen. _____

10. In 1989, two seborrheic (keratosis, keratoses) were removed from the 80-year-old patient. _____

11. After poliomyelitis, the patient's left (epiphysis, epiphyses) of the tibia were not affected, but the right distal (epiphysis, epiphyses) of the tibia was affected. _____

12. After suffering a stroke, Mr. McCreary had (paralysis, paralyses) of the entire left side of his body. _____

RULE 9.5 When a word ends in "ax" or "ix" change the "x" to "c" and add "es."

Examples
thorax becomes thoraces
calyx or calix becomes calyces or calices

RULE 9.6 When a word ends in "ex" or "ix," change the "ex" or "ix" to "ices."

Examples
appendix becomes appendices
apex becomes apices

RULE 9.7 When a word ends in "en," change the ending to "ina."

Example
foramen becomes foramina

RULE 9.8 When a word ends in "ma," change the ending to "mata."

Example
carcinoma becomes carcinomata

NOTE: With this ending, it is also permissible to add an "s" to the singular.

Example
carcinomas

RULE 9.9 When a word ends in "nx," change the "x" to "g" and add "es."

Example
phalanx becomes phalanges

RULE 9.10 When a word ends in "on," change the "on" to "a."

Examples
criterion becomes criteria
zygion becomes zygia

 9–5: SELF-STUDY

Directions: Read the following sentences and choose the correct singular or plural form. Then on the blank line type or handwrite the word you choose to reinforce spelling. Use your medical dictionary as a reference, if necessary. Check your answers with those given at the end of the chapter on page 217.

1. A Pap smear report stated minimal dysplasia of the (cervix, cervices). _____

2. A tendon of the (index, indexes, indices) finger was severed when his hand went through the glass door. _____

3. The patient's blood pressure of 200/100 was a symptom of her tumor of the adrenal (cortex, cortices) of the adrenal gland. _____

4. The (lumen, lumina) of the catheters had defects so they were returned to the manufacturer. _____

5. The male anatomy has two (epididymis, epididymes). _____

6. Obstruction of the (larynx, larynges) was caused by a benign growth. _____

7. Diagnosis: Multiple (chondroma, chondromata, chondromas) of the left tibia. _____

8. There were many (fibroma, fibromata, fibromas) that formed in the soft tissue of the upper thigh. _____

9. The child had many (exanthema, exanthemata, exanthemas) due to various food allergies. _____

10. Preoperative diagnosis: Hypermenorrhea, multiple (leiomyoma, leiomyomata, leiomyomas) versus adenomyosis. _____

11. The (phalanx, phalanges) or finger bones number 14 in each hand, three for each finger and two of the thumb. _____

12. The female anatomy has two fallopian tubes or (salpinx, salpinges). _____

13. There is widespread distribution of (ganglion, ganglia) throughout the body. _____

14. Two aneurysmoid (varix, varices) were seen on the arteriogram. _____

15. The pathology lab reported the presence of a well-differentiated benign thyroid (adenoma, adenomata, adenomas). _____

TO FORM PLURALS

IF THE SINGULAR ENDING IS	EXAMPLE	THE PLURAL ENDING IS	EXAMPLE
a	bursa	ae (pronounce ae as i)	bursae
us	alveolus	i	alveoli
um	labium	a	labia
ma	carcinoma	mata	carcinomata
on	criterion	a	criteria
is	anastomosis	es	anastomoses
ix	appendix	ices	appendices
ex	apex	ices	apices
ax	thorax	aces	thoraces
en	foramen	ina	foramina
nx	phalanx	ges	phalanges

Exceptions to Rules for Plural Endings

The words in the following list form plurals in irregular ways:

1. cornu becomes cornua

2. femur becomes femora

3. os, which has two meanings, becomes ora for mouths or ossa for bones

4. paries becomes parietes

5. pons becomes pontes

6. vas becomes vasa

NOTE: Add these to your personal notebook.

BASIC PLURAL RULES FOR ENGLISH WORDS

Many medical terms take English plurals by applying the basic rules for forming plurals of English nouns.

RULE 9.11   The plural is usually formed by adding "s" to the singular.

Examples
myelogram myelogram*s*   disease disease*s*

RULE 9.12   When a noun ends in "s," "x," "ch," "sh," or "z," add "es" to the singular.

Examples
stress stress*es*   helix helix*es*   patch patch*es*
mash mash*es*

RULE 9.13   When a noun ends in "y" preceded by a consonant, change the "y to "i" and add "es."

Examples
mammoplasty mammoplast*ies*
artery arter*ies*

RULE 9.14   When nouns ending in "o" are preceded by a consonant, in most cases "es" is added to the singular.

Examples
tobacco tobacco*es*   mulatto mulatto*es*
vertigo vertigo*es*   zero zero*es*

NOTE: In regard to this rule, many words are pluralized by simply adding an "s" to the singular.
albino albino*s*   ego ego*s*   embryo embryo*s*
impetigo impetigo*s*   placebo placebo*s*

EXCEPTIONS: comedo   comedone*s*
lentigo lentigine*s*   ambo ambone*s*

| RULE 9.15 Most nouns that end in "f" or "fe" are made plural by changing the "f" or "fe" to "ves." | **Examples**
scarf scar*ves*   life li*ves*
calf cal*ves*   knife kni*ves* |

9–6: SELF-STUDY

Directions: Practice these endings by changing the nouns to both foreign and English plurals. Fill in the blanks. Check your answers with those given at the end of this chapter on pages 217 to 218.

1. The head of the femur fits into the *acetabulum*. A human has two _____ or _____ .

2. An *antrum* is a cavity or chamber. The patient has fluid in three sinus _____ or _____ .

3. The *aorta* is one of the main arteries of the body. We do not have two _____ or _____ .

4. The *apex* is the top of an organ. We have several _____ or _____ in our anatomy.

5. Some books have an *appendix*. Many large reference books have several _____ or _____ .

6. *Areola* can pertain to the eye or breast. This patient has a rash on the _____ or _____ of both breasts.

7. *Axilla* means armpit. He had cysts of both _____ or _____ .

8. The first skin *biopsy* was taken from Mrs. Aver's arm, but the second and third _____ were taken from the knee and thigh.

9. She has basal cell *carcinoma,* but previously she had two other types of _____ or _____ of the thyroid and kidney.

10. *Comedo* is another word for blackhead. The teenager came in with many _____ or _____ .

11. The *conjunctiva* protects our eyes from dust and dirt. We have two _____ or _____ in our anatomy.

12. *Exanthema* is an eruptive disease. The baby brothers had _____ or _____ .

13. The thigh bone is called the *femur.* We have two _____ or _____ in our anatomy.

14. The wrist *fibroma* was removed, but the thigh still had three more _____ or _____ .

15. The *fibula* is the smaller of the two bones of the leg. We have two _____ or _____ .

16. A *fistula* is an abnormal passage. The patient had two anal

_____ or _____ .

17. *Foramen* means opening or passage. We have numerous

_____ or _____ throughout our skel-

etal anatomy.

Besides all the English, Latin, and Greek rules for pluralizing words, there are additional variances that a beginning medical typist should know. In units of measurement (inches or pounds), although the plural may sound right, actually the singular is correct.

Example

Dictated
"Mrs. Seitz weighs one hundred and twelve *pounds.*"

Transcribe
Mrs. Seitz weighs 112 *lb.*

Example

Dictated
"There *were* two milliliters drawn up in the syringe."

Transcribe
There *was* 2 ml drawn up in the syringe.

Example

Dictated
"Her height is five feet two *inches.*"

Transcribe
Her height is 5 ft 2 *in.*

If you interpose "of an" between 2 and inch you would not say 2 of an inches, would you? This works with any measurement and any decimal part thereof. Try it. If the number is one plus a fraction, the sentence should read, "one and a half *inches is* the length of the little finger." Note that the verb must be singular.

Some medical terms are commonly seen as plurals in all dictation. We have two eyes and two ears, but physicians commonly dictate:

Dictated
"Conjunctiva clear."

Transcribe
Conjunctivae clear.

Dictated
"Tympanic membrane intact."

Transcribe
Tympanic membranes intact.

Since heart sounds are multiple, physicians commonly dictate the word bruits, which is the plural form of bruit. The use of the word determines whether it is singular or plural.

Example
There is no bruit heard.   (singular)
There are no bruits heard.   (plural)

Some words can be singular or plural in use, i.e., biceps, triceps, data, series, none (means not one or not any). Some words are always plural in use, i.e., adnexa, feces, forceps, genitalia, measles, menses, scabies, scissors, tongs, tweezers. Some words are always singular when used, i.e., ascites, herpes, lues, news, physics, and so forth.

To form the plural of French words that end in *eau* and *eu,* add an *x.*

Examples
milieu (singular)   milieux (plural)
rouleau (singular)   rouleaux (plural)

To form the plural of Italian words that end in *o,* change the *o* to an *i.*

Example
virtuoso (singular)   virtuosi (plural)

NOUN ENDINGS

There are many more noun endings to medical terms than adjective endings. Take as an example the words *microscope, microscopic,* and *microscopy.*

1. The *-scope* on the end of microscope tells us two things about the word:
   a. it is a noun.
   b. it is an instrument.

2. The *-scopic* on the end of the word tells us two things:
   a. it is an adjective.
   b. it means pertaining to an examination.

3. The *-scopy* on the end tells us two things:
   a. it is a noun.
   b. it means the process of examining.

Notice how these endings have changed the meaning of the word. If the dictator slurs the ends of words, you can see how difficult it is to determine which way to spell the word unless you know the meaning of how the word is used in context. The following is a list of some of the most frequently used noun endings, their meanings, and an example of how each is used.

Suffix That Makes Word a Noun	Meaning	Example
-algia	pain	neuralgia
-ase	an enzyme	phosphatase
-asia, -asis, -esis, -osia, -osis, -ia,* -iasis	condition or state of	phlegmasia hypophonesis synarthrosis calcemia, cholelithiasis
-ation, -tion, -ion	act of	disarticulation
-ectomy	excision, the process of cutting out	hysterectomy
-emia	condition of the blood	leukemia
-er	agent	ultrasonographer
-gram	record tracing (record)	cardiogram
-graph	instrument to record	cardiograph
-graphy	process or action of recording	cardiography
-ician, -ist	one who specializes in, agent, one who practices	physician, allergist
-ism	condition or theory	mutism
-itis	inflammation	cystitis
-ity	expresses quality	clarity, obesity
-meter	instrument that measures	thermometer
-metry	process of measuring	optometry
-ologist	one who studies, specialist in disease of . . .	endocrinologist
-ology	study of, science of	endocrinology
-oma	tumor, a morbid condition	carcinoma
-or	denoting an agent, doer, a person; a quality or condition	objector error, horror
-pen, -penia	need, deficiency, poverty	leukopenia
-scope	an instrument for visual examination	cytoscope
-scopy	process, action, examination	cystoscopy
-stomy, -stomata, -ostomy	an artificial opening	colostomy, stomata
-tom, -tome	an instrument for cutting	microtome
-tomy, -otomy	a cutting into, incision	meatotomy
-um, -us	pertaining to	diverticulum, digitus
-y	process or action	acromegaly

* Many Greek nouns that end in -ia appear in English with a -y instead of -ia.

ADJECTIVE ENDINGS

As you recall from the vocabulary, a word that qualifies or restricts the meaning of a noun is called an adjective. Example: "A *small* cyst was present at the olecranon process." Medical terms can have either English or Latin adjective endings, and in certain instances, this can confuse the transcriptionist. For instance, *mucus* is a noun, whereas *mucous* is an adjective. Mucous is a kind of membrane, therefore an adjective, and mucus is its secretion, and therefore a noun. These words are pronounced exactly alike, so the good transcriptionist must see how the word is used in the sentence to determine its spelling.

In many instances, the medical dictionary does not list the adjective form. It is, therefore, vital to know the noun and be able to convert it to an adjective based on what you hear being dictated. For example, if the dictator says "HI-lar," you look in the dictionary and find the noun "hilum." You then recognize that "ar" has to fit on the root "hil" and come up with "hilar."

The following are the most common adjective endings with their literal translations and examples of how they appear in medical terms. You will notice that a few of these adjective endings are interchangeable with the noun forms (designated by asterisks).

Adjective Ending	Meaning	Example
-able, -ible	capable of, able to be, fit or likely	friable, digestible
-ac	characteristic of, relating to, affected by or having	cardiac
-al, -alis	of or pertaining to, belonging to	oral, brachialis†
-ar, -ary	pertaining to, belonging to, showing	ocular, elementary
-ate	possessing or characterized by, caused by	quadrate
-ery, -ary*	one who, that which, place where, relating to, engaging in or performing	surgery, capillary
-ic, -icus	dealing with, pertaining to, connected with, resembling	organic, cephalicus†
-id,	signifying state or condition, marked by, given to showing	viscid
-ive	having power to, having the quality of	palliative
-oid	like or resembling	sphenoid
-ory*	having the nature of	circulatory
-ous, -ose	to be full of, marked by, given to, having the quality of	squamous, adipose

* Many Greek nouns that end in -*ia* appear in English with a -*y* instead of -*ia*.

† These are Latin endings and can usually be found in the medical dictionary under the headings of veins, arteries, nerves, ligaments, and so forth.

9–7: SELF-STUDY

Directions: Now see if you can identify the following endings by indicating whether the word is an adjective or a noun. State whether the nouns have singular or plural endings. Adjectives are not found in singular or plural forms. Check your answers with those given at the end of this chapter on page 218.

	Adjective or Noun:	**Singular or Plural:**
derm*oid*	adjective	
lymph*omas*	noun	plural
1. sphygmomano*meter*		
2. arthr*algias*		
3. lumbosacr*al*		
4. mit*oses*		
5. cyto*penia*		
6. ent*opic*		
7. rhin*itis*		
8. annu*lar*		
9. glyc*emia*		
10. lapar*otomy*		
11. endotheli*um*		
12. progn*oses*		
13. lumb*ar*		
14. synech*ia*		
15. adip*ose*		
16. prolifer*ous*		
17. claudic*ation*		
18. radio*graph*		

9–8: REVIEW TEST

Directions: Make these nouns into plurals and then into adjectives. Use your English dictionary to help.

Noun	Greek or Latin Plurals	English Plural	Adjective
axilla	axillae	axillas	axillary
1. cranium			
2. focus			
3. caput			
4. pelvimeter			
5. prognosis			
6. lingua			
7. pelvis			
8. phalanx			

Directions: Make these adjectives into nouns by locating the noun in the dictionary. Then spell out the medical term that the physician dictated as an adjective.

The Physician Has Dictated an Adjective That Sounds Like:	The Spelling of the Adjective Is:	The Noun Is:
AN-u-lar	annular	annulus or anulus or anus
9. VIS-er-al		
10. kar″de-o-GRAF-ik		
11. kil-o-MET-rik		
12. sis″to-SKOP-ik		
13. in-FEK-shus		
14. an″es-THET-ik		
15. du″o-DE-nal		
16. kon″di-LO-mah-toid		
17. BRONG-ke-al		
18. FEE-kal		
19. AB-sessed		
20. her-PET-ik		

▣ Answers to 9–1: Self-Study

1. medium
2. media
3. acetabula
4. diverticula
5. ischium
6. bacteria, bacilli
7. antrum
8. atrium
9. hilum
10. ostia
11. septum
12. ilium
13. labia

Answers to 9-2: Self-Study

1. bursa

2. pleurae

3. aorta

4. lamina

5. maxillae

6. conjunctivae, sclerae. Rationale: Two eyes, so plural must be shown.

7. vertebrae

8. areola

9. fossae. Rationale: Two eyes, so plural must be shown.

10. scapula

11. bulla, bullae

Answers to 9-3: Self-Study

1. alveoli. Rationale: Lungs have many clusters of air sacs (alveoli).

2. bronchus

3. calculus

4. fungi. Rationale: Plural since pathologists test for more than one fungus.

5. malleolus, ilium

6. glomeruli. Rationale: A kidney has many filtering units (glomeruli), not just one unit.

7. menisci

8. cocci

9. tarsus

10. nucleuses and nuclei (both are plural forms). Rationale: The pathologist would be looking at more than one cell in a specimen.

11. focuses and foci (both are plural forms)

12. villi

Answers to 9-4: Self-Study

1. anastomosis

2. Diagnoses

3. ecchymosis

4. exostosis

5. prognosis

6. metastases. Rationale: Cancer cells have spread to two locations in the liver.

7. Urinalyses

8. crises

9. testis

10. keratoses

11. epiphyses, epiphysis

12. paralysis

Answers to 9–5: Self-Study

1. cervix. Rationale: Patient has a single cervix of the uterus.

2. index

3. cortex

4. lumina

5. epididymes

6. larynx

7. chondromata and chondromas (both are plural forms)

8. fibromata and fibromas (both are plural forms)

9. exanthemata, exanthemas (both are plural forms)

10. leiomyomata and leiomyomas (both are plural forms)

11. phalanges

12. salpinges

13. ganglia

14. varices

15. adenoma

Answers to 9–6: Self-Study

1. acetabulums or acetabula

2. antra or antrums

3. aortas or aortae

4. apexes or apices

5. appendixes or appendices

6. areolas or areolae

7. axillas or axillae

8. biopsies

9. carcinomas or carcinomata

10. comedos or comedones

11. conjunctivas or conjunctivae

12. exanthemata or exanthemas

13. femurs or femora

14. fibromata or fibromas

15. fibulas or fibulae

16. fistulas or fistulae

17. foramens or foramina

◪ Answers to 9–7: Self-Study

1. noun   singular

2. noun   plural

3. adjective

4. noun   plural

5. noun   singular

6. adjective

7. noun   singular

8. adjective

9. noun   singular

10. noun   singular

11. noun   singular

12. noun   plural

13. adjective

14. noun   singular

15. adjective. "Adipose" is generally used as an adjective but also can be used as a noun.

16. adjective

17. noun   singular

18. noun   singular

Antonyms, Eponyms, and Homonyms

OBJECTIVES

After reading this chapter and working the exercises, you should be able to

1. identify words that sound alike but have different meanings and different spellings.
2. define the difference between the terms "antonym," "homonym," and "eponym."
3. locate eponyms in the medical dictionary.

10

. . . .

INTRODUCTION

This chapter will introduce the "word demons" of medical language. We will discuss words that sound alike but are spelled differently and have different meanings (homonyms), words that have opposite meanings (antonyms), and words that derive from the name of a particular person because of research done in the medical field (eponyms). Distinguishing between these pairs of words can be confusing to the transcriptionist; a good deal of experience may be required to choose the correct term and to spell it properly. Homonyms are the most difficult of the "word demons" for many transcriptionists; hence a large part of the chapter is devoted to them.

Because heteronyms are not as troublesome for the majority of people, they are only briefly touched on in this chapter. Generally, heteronyms are problem words for the foreign-born individual trying to learn the English language. A heteronym is a word that has the same spelling as another but a different meaning and a different pronunciation. For example, let's take the word *tear*. It can mean a drop of water as from the eye, or it can mean to pull or rip something apart. Suppose you hear "the details are so *minute* that it takes more than a *minute* or two to dictate that paragraph in the operative report." Or "the doctor's interest was *peaked* as he saw the patient who looked a little *peaked*." Do you know the meaning of minute and peaked in these instances? There are literally hundreds of these words in the English language that are accepted daily.

219

VOCABULARY

antonym: A word, prefix, or suffix that means the opposite of another word.

eponym: The person for whom something is or is believed to be named; a name (as of a drug or a disease) based on or derived from an eponym.

heteronym: A word that has the same spelling as another but a different meaning and a different pronunciation.

homonym: A word that is similar in pronunciation but different in meaning and spelling. Also known as homophone.

homophone: See homonym.

ANTONYMS

An antonym is a whole word, a prefix, or a suffix that means the opposite of another word. To give an example from nonmedical English, *sad* is the antonym of *happy*. Sometimes these antonyms cause spelling trouble because of their similarities in sound. Here is a list of confusing antonyms, their meanings, and some examples. You will notice that the prefixes are shown with a hyphen following the component and that the suffixes have a hyphen preceding the component.

ANTONYM PAIRS

COMPONENT	MEANING	EXAMPLE
ab-	away from	abducent
ad-	to, near, toward	adducent
ecto-	without, outside	ectopic
ento-	within, inner	entopic
-ectomy	excision	cholecystectomy
-tomy	incision	cholecystotomy
hypo-	under, below	hypotension
hyper-	over, above	hypertension
macro-	large, long, great	macroscopic
micro-	small	microscopic

EPONYMS

Medical eponyms are adjectives used to describe specific operations, surgical instruments, diseases, and parts of the anatomy. Each of these words is the surname (or an adjective formed from the surname) of an individual who is prominently connected with the development or discovery of the disease, instrument, or surgical procedure. Currently, the American Medical Association recommends that an eponym not be used when a comparable medical term can be substi-

tuted for it. It is the dictator's responsibility to dictate the proper term, since in this instance the transcriptionist merely types what was heard.

An example of an eponym is "Buerger disease (or "Buerger's disease"). The comparable medical term is "thromboangiitis obliterans." It is important to note that more and more writers are making exceptions to the possessive rule by not showing the possessive ('s) with an eponym. In checking dictionaries and other reference books, you will find conflicting spellings, one showing the eponym with the possessive and one showing it without. These are alternative acceptable forms. Generally, when surgical and diagnostic instruments, materials, and solutions are dictated, there is no possessive. In summary, one may eliminate the possessive if the dictator does not use it or has no objection to its elimination.

Examples
Foley catheter
Gigli saw
Mayo scissors
Richard retractors

Many anatomic eponyms are now written in lower case, such as eustachian tube, fallopian tube, and so forth. Words derived from eponymic names (parkinsonism, addisonian, cushingoid facies, and so forth) should not be capitalized. See Chapter 4, page 83, for the rule on these words.

To find the medical term or definition that corresponds to an eponym, look up the second term, the *clue word,* as shown in the following italicized examples. These are just a few of the many thousands of medical eponyms. The paragraph on Cross References in Chapter 8, pages 172 to 174, will help you to locate others.

1. Abbe's *anemia*

2. Addison's *anemia*

3. Babinski's *reflex*

4. Bell's *palsy*

5. Bravais-jacksonian *epilepsy*

6. Bright's *disease*

7. Cheyne-Stokes *respiration*

8. Colles' *fracture*

9. Cooper's *ligament*

10. Dupuytren's *contracture*

11. Feleky's *instrument*

12. Hanot's *cirrhosis*

13. Highmore's *antrum*

14. Koch's *bacillus*

15. Laennec's *cirrhosis*

16. Romberg's *sign*

17. Skene's *glands*

18. Stensen's *duct*

10–1: SELF-STUDY

Directions: Match the following with their correct definitions. Check your answers with those on page 226 at the end of this chapter.

1. antonyms   ———   a. Words that have the same spelling but different meanings and different pronunciations.

2. eponyms   ———   b. Words that are opposite to each other in meaning.

3. homonyms   ———   c. Words that sound alike but are spelled differently and have different meanings.

4. heteronyms   ———   d. Words that have been derived from the surname of a person.

Do you remember what an acronym is, as mentioned in Chapter 4? Define it here. ———

ENGLISH HOMONYMS

Homonyms are words that are similar in pronunciation but different in meaning and spelling. Sometimes these are called "phonetic pairs." A few English examples are *hare* and *hair, weak* and *week,* and *too, two,* and *to.* If one of these words were dictated, knowing its meaning would help you decide how to spell it.

10

ENGLISH TROUBLESOME TWOSOMES

WORD	MEANING	EXAMPLE
advice (n)	counsel; recommendation	The advice that Dr. Blake gave was excellent.
advise (v)	to counsel; to notify	Dr. Blake will advise (influence) her to have surgery.
affect (v)	to influence (more psychological)	The medication prescribed might affect his stomach.
effect (v)	to bring about (more physiological)	The treatment did not effect (to bring about) any change.
effect (n)	a result	One effect (result) of physical therapy is more mobility of injured joints.
all ready (adj)	completely ready	The office was all ready to close when an emergency case came in.
already (adv)	by this time, previously	The physician was already gone when the call came in.
all together	in a group, collectively	By typing the same insurance forms all together, fewer errors will occur.
altogether	entirely, completely	The two medical cases are altogether different.
bare	uncovered; plain	For ultrasound, the area must be bare.
bear	to carry; an animal; to be directed	The physician prefers to bear the good news to the patient.
breath (n)	air taken into the lungs and then expelled; the act of breathing	The patient becomes out of breath when walking up a flight of stairs.
breathe (v)	to inhale and exhale air	The patient was able to breathe again easily.
cite (v)	to quote	You may cite the article as your reference.
sight (n)	vision	His sight was 20/20 on right and left.
site (n)	location	The site of the injury was the left leg.
complement (n or v)	complete, harmonize	The office has a full complement of staff members.
compliment (n or v)	praise, congratulate	Maria was complimented several times by her employer.

ENGLISH TROUBLESOME TWOSOMES

WORD	MEANING	EXAMPLE
elicit (v)	to draw forth	The physician tried to elicit the facts about the patient's condition.
illicit (adj)	unlawful	It is illicit to give out information about a patient without his written permission.
loose (adj)	not tightly bound	The patient complained of loose stools.
lose (v)	to suffer loss or deprivation	The patient began to lose weight.
principal (adj, n)	chief; main; leader	The patient's principal complaint was pain.
principle (n)	rule	Her knowledge of punctuation principles is questionable.
stationary (adj)	still, not moving	The patient's condition was stationary.
stationery (n)	writing paper	Please purchase some stationery at the store.
than (conj)	conjunction of comparison	A word processor is faster than an electric typewriter.
then (adv)	at that time	Proofread your work; then you can vouch for its accuracy.
their (adj)	of, belonging to, made, or done by them	Pat and Jo have done their homework.
there (adv)	at or in that place; toward	There are several laboratory tests to be performed.

10-2: PRACTICE TEST

Directions: Perhaps you are still a bit confused by English words that sound alike. Try this exercise to see how you score. For each of the following sentences, select the word within the parentheses that completes the sentence correctly. Mark through the incorrect word. (If both words are incorrect, mark through both words and write the correct word above them.) Note that some sentences have two sets of selections.

1. He will (advice, advise) anyone on their medical problems.

2. Please (lay, lei) the paper down on the examination table.

3. The medical assistant intended the remark as a (compliment, complement).

4. (Whose, Who's) dictionary is this on my desk?

5. (Your, You're) office is (too, two) far from the hospital.

6. The old medical building was (razed, raised) to make room for a new hospital.

7. With a great (serge, surge) the patient leaped (fourth, forth).

8. Tell the patient to (sight, cite) an example for you.

9. Ms. Drake had one (coarse, course) of radiation treatment following her left mastectomy.

10. Sitting (here, hear), I can (here, hear) you clearly.

11. Our stock of office (stationary, stationery) is almost exhausted.

12. The patient's rhinoplasty had a tremendous (affect, effect) on her social relationships.

13. The (affect, effect) of the new surgical procedure gave hope to millions of people.

14. The patient would prefer to come at 8 a.m. if an appointment is available (than, then).

15. Developing x-ray films is much faster (than, then) it was ten years ago.

16. The medical assistant quickly sorted the (correspondence, correspondents) for filing.

17. The surgery on Mr. Salazar lasted nine hours, and Dr. Cho performed another surgery on Mrs. Baker without a (brake, break).

18. The (principle, principal) reason for the trip was to search for a new hospital (sight, site).

19. The physician gave the medical assistant instructions to (accept, except) the subpoena when it was served.

20. A horizontal osteotomy was (affected, effected).

21. On general examination of the abdominal cavity, (they're, their, there) was no abnormality found.

22. (They're, Their, There) bringing in the accident case to the emergency room.

23. The tubes were traced out to the fimbriae to doubly identify (they're, their, there) anatomy.

The answers to these will be found in Appendix E at the back of your text.

MEDICAL HOMONYMS

Medical homonyms may prove somewhat tougher if you are not thoroughly versed in terminology or if the difficult word pairs have never been pointed out to you. Perhaps even now you are using an incorrect spelling of a word. Mastery of some of the more challenging ones can save you time and possibly embarrassment. Appendix A is a list of common homonyms, showing their pronunciation and meaning and the words that sound similar to them.

What if a word is dictated that sounds like pair-ah-NEE-al? Is it spelled p-e-r-o-n-e-a-l or p-e-r-i-n-e-a-l? Do you know their meanings and know which word to select because of how it is used in the sentence dictated? You will be confronted by homonyms throughout your career as a medical transcriptionist.

 ## 10–3: SELF-STUDY

Directions: The following components are used daily in dictation. See if you can match them up with their definitions.

1. ab-	_____	a. to eat or swallow
2. ad-	_____	b. small
3. ante-	_____	c. above, beyond (used in medical words)
4. anti-	_____	d. to, near, toward
5. -lysis	_____	e. before
6. -clysis	_____	f. from, away from
7. myo-	_____	g. loosening, destroying
8. myco-	_____	h. fungus
9. myelo-	_____	i. against
10. mio-	_____	j. above, beyond (used in English words)
11. peri-	_____	k. washing
12. para-	_____	l. marrow, spinal cord
13. -phasia	_____	m. close around
14. -phagia	_____	n. trachea, windpipe
15. super-	_____	o. to speak
16. supra-	_____	p. neck or neck-like structure
17. tracheo-	_____	q. muscle
18. trachelo-	_____	r. beside, beyond, near

Check your answers on page 226 and then tackle the next two assignments encompassing still more medical sound-alikes.

10–4: PRACTICE TEST

Directions: Let's do some vocabulary-building homonym exercises and enrich our mastery of medical terms. The following sentences are arranged in pairs. If you have difficulty completing the exercises, refer to Appendix A, Common Medical Homonyms, on pages 377–393. Select the word from the left column that is needed to complete correctly each sentence in the right column.

position
apposition
opposition

1. The physician was in _____ when Sally wanted to make a new policy in the office.

2. Successive layers in the cell walls were in _____ to each other.

3. Dry, sterile dressings were applied and a modified Jones _____ utilized, incorporating a dorsal plaster of paris splint.

aberration
abrasion

4. On examination, Miss Baker had a 1-cm _____ over the right patella.

5. The patient's illness showed an _____ in his condition.

dysphagia
dysphasia

6. The patient denies at any time any pain or tenderness in the neck, no _____, hoarseness, or enlargement of the thyroid gland.

7. After suffering a stroke, Mr. James had _____ for six months and then regained normal speech.

absorption
adsorption

8. The physician used a collagen suture material so there would be _____ into the tissues.

9. The bandage showed an _____ to the surface of the skin.

adherence
adherents

10. There are _____ to the cause of Martin Luther King.

11. The _____ of the bandage to the skin caused Mrs. Base to break out in a rash.

Select one word from the left column that is needed to correctly complete the sentence in the right column.

pectineal
perineal
perineum
peritoneum
peroneal
mucosa
mucous
mucus

12. The omentum was seen readily upon opening the _____.

13. The _____ membrane of the mouth showed irritation and redness.

abduction
addiction
adduction

14. Mrs. Cafers had an _____ to caffeine.

auscultation
oscillation
oscitation
osculation

15. During the physical examination, the physician performed _____ and percussion to hear the chest sounds.

alveolar
alveoli
alveolus
alveus
alvus

16. The physician referred to the _____, meaning the abdomen with its contained viscera.

afebrile
a febrile
febrile

17. The patient had a fever; the physician said he had _____ illness.

arteriosclerosis
arteriostenosis
atherosclerosis

18. The arteriogram showed narrowing of the arteries called _____. This is caused by hardening and loss of elasticity of the arterial walls indicating _____ .

scirrhous
scirrhus
serous
serious

19. The wound was draining _____ fluid.

rials
riles
rails
rales

20. On examination the patient's chest was clear of wheezes and _____ .

cortisone
corporal
cortisol
cortical

21. The dexamethasone suppression test (DST) revealed a 1400-hour _____ level of 1.8 μg/dl and a 2300-hour level of 0.9 μg/dl.

The answers to these will be found in Appendix E at the back of your text.

10–5: REVIEW TEST

Directions: The following sentences are arranged in groups. If you have difficulty completing the exercises, refer to Appendix A, Common Medical Homonyms, on pages 377–393. Select the word from the left column that is needed to correctly complete each sentence in the right column.

10

aura
aural
ora
oral

1. The ear is concerned with the acoustic or _____ sense.

2. Betsy Blake complained of having an _____ before her epileptic attacks.

3. Valium is an _____ medication.

4. The _____ serrata is the serrated margin of the retina in the anterior portion of the eyeball.

hypertension
Hypertensin
hypotension

5. Mr. Yoshida's blood pressure was 165/90, indicating _____ .

6. Mrs. Lockhard had a blood pressure reading of 100/60, which is a condition of _____ .

7. _____ is a drug that produces a rise in blood pressure.

amenorrhea
dysmenorrhea
menorrhea
menorrhagia
metrorrhagia

8. Her chief complaint was _____ , meaning absence of the menses.

9. One of Miss Mason's symptoms was abnormal uterine hemorrhage between periods, and this is called _____ .

antiseptic
asepsis
aseptic
sepsis
septic

10. The surgical instruments must be _____ at all times.

11. The laboratory report indicated pus-forming microorganisms in the blood, a condition of _____ .

palpation
palpitation

12. She has had no further episodes of _____ of the heart.

13. The physician examined the area by _____ and felt a small cyst.

dilation
dilatation

14. Because of hemorrhaging, Beth was advised to have a _____ and curettage.

15. The process of _____ is used when examining the eyes.

discrete
discreet

16. Breast exam reveals no _____ masses or abnormalities.

tract
track

17. He was seen in consultation by Dr. Friedman, who did an upper _____ endoscopy with no unusual findings.

regimen
regime

18. On this _____, it was noted his electrolytes remained normal.

introitus
enteritis

19. Preliminary pelvic examination showed a parous _____.

instillation
installation

20. Prior to the _____ of general anesthesia, a KUB was obtained.

▣ Answers to 10–1: Self-Study

1. b

2. d

3. c

4. a

An acronym is a word composed from the initial letters of other words.

▣ Answers to 10–3: Self-Study

1. f	10. b
2. d	11. m
3. e	12. r
4. i	13. o
5. g	14. a
6. k	15. j
7. q	16. c
8. h	17. n
9. l	18. p

Medical Chart Notes and Progress Notes

OBJECTIVES

After reading this chapter and working the exercises, you should be able to

1. explain the necessity of typing accurate notes on patient progress.
2. demonstrate the proper procedure for transcribing patient medical chart notes.
3. use the different methods employed in preparing medical chart notes.
4. recognize and correct any erroneous entry made into the medical record.
5. list the basic information to be found in patient notes.

• •

INTRODUCTION

Chart notes (also called progress notes) are the formal or informal notes taken by the physician when he or she meets with or examines a patient. These notes are a part of the patient's permanent medical record; as you recall from Chapter 1, medical records are a vital key in patient care. Although medical records are used mainly to assist the physician with care of the patient, they can be reviewed by attorneys, other physicians, insurance companies, or the court. It is essential that they be neat, accurate, and complete.

"Accurate" means that they are transcribed verbatim (exactly as dictated), and "complete" requires that they be dated and signed or initialed by the dictator. A new assistant can hardly insist that the physi-

cian sign or initial the records, but the assistant might overcome the physician's reluctance by making it easier to do so, as by typing a line at the end of each chart entry for the signature or initials. Then, at the end of the day, all the reports can be stacked on the physician's desk for signing. Another suggestion would be for the physician to sign the notes when the patient returns for a follow-up visit, since the previous notes are generally reviewed at this time anyway.

For a chart to be admissible as evidence in court, the party dictating or writing entries should be able to attest that they were true and correct at the time they were written. The best indication of that is the physician's signature or initials at the end of each typed note. The hospital will insist that the physician sign all dictated material and all entries he or she makes on

227

the patient's record; failure to do so could result in a loss of hospital staff privileges.

Furthermore, before copies of records leave the office, the originals must be checked for accuracy; and if they have not been signed before, they must be signed now. Any liability of the medical assistant, personally, is of small significance unless there are unusual circumstances such as negligence, willfulness, or malice. A physician cannot easily shift the blame to an assistant, because the faulty records are his or her responsibility as long as the proper procedure for release of information has been established. If a medical secretary or transcriptionist is at fault in recording improperly, the physician has the right to discharge him or her for inefficiency, and this is a peril for the careless assistant.

Most physicians handwrite daily progress entries into the patient's hospital medical record. In office or clinic situations some physicians never dictate chart notes, preferring to enter them into the patient's record in longhand. Although it is not essential that medical records be typed, it is best to do so. Obviously, typewritten notes are easier to read; and when more than one physician is involved in patient care, as in a large office or clinic, it is vital that all notes be easily read with no chance of misinterpretation. In this chapter, we are not concerned with longhand notes but with learning the process of taking chart notes from the transcribing equipment and typing them properly into the patient's record.

The physician should try to dictate as soon as he or she is finished seeing a patient and the details are still fresh in his or her mind. Some physicians have also found it helpful to dictate the notes with the patient present. This gives the physician the opportunity to ask for any details that may have been overlooked in the initial history taking; it also gives him or her an opportunity to reinstruct the patient on medication

---

INFORMATION REQUIRED FOR CASE HISTORY FILE

Date..

Patient.. Date of Birth.................... Age.............
(Mr., Mrs., Miss, Master) First Name Initial Last Name

Name of Husband, Wife or Parent.. Home Phone..........................

Home Address.. If Military, Serial No. Soc. Sec. No.............................

Patient Employed By:..
City or Town   Zip Code

Business Address..

Occupation.. Business Phone..........................

Husband or Wife Employed by:..

Business Address..
City or Town   Zip Code

Occupation.. Business Phone..........................

Name of nearest relative not named above (indicate relationship)..

Address..

Insured by:..Group No.............. Member No.....................

Recommended by:.. Former Physician..........................

If patient a minor Give name of person legally responsible:..

I hereby authorize and request the .... Insurance Company to pay the amount due me in my pending claim for medical expense Benefits directly to ....M.D.

Date.. Signature..........................

FIGURE 11-1. Example of a social data sheet.

Mary Neidgrinhaus   DOB: 06-11-9x   REF: Yuen Wong, M.D.

12-18-9x

HX: This 4½-year-old girl has been having URIs beginning in October, 1984. She has
         had several of these infections since that time and has been seen by another
         otolaryngologist who recommended that she have surgery including an adeno-
         tonsillectomy and bilateral myringotomies with tubes. The mother desired
         another opinion and the family doctor referred her to me.

ALLERGIES: <u>AMPICILLIN and SEPTRA</u>

<u>PX</u>:   Well-developed, well-nourished girl in no acute distress.

VS: Pulse: 84/min. Resp: 20/min. Temp: 98.8^{0} axillary.

HEENT: Eyes: PERRLA. EOMs normal. Ears: The rt TM was retracted and slightly injected.
         The left TM was retracted but not injected. Both canals were negative.
         Nose: The nasal septum was roughly in the midline. Mucous membrane lining
         somewhat pale and slightly swollen. Throat: Tonsils were +3 and very cryptic.
         Neck: There were tonsillar nodes palpable in both anterior cervical triangles.

CHEST: Lungs: Clear to auscultation. Heart: Regular rate and rhythm, no murmurs.

IMP: 1. Hypertrophy of tonsils and adenoids.
         2. Bilateral recurrent serous otitis media.

<u>RX</u>:   Dimetapp elixir, 4 oz, 1 t q.i.d.

mlo

                                                      _____
                                                      Gene M. Kasten, M.D.

DEC. 2 8 **199**x
         Rt ear improved; no change in the left. Mother still does not want surgery.

RX: Actifed syrup, 2 oz, ½ t q.i.d.

mlo

                                                      _____
                                                      Gene M. Kasten, M.D.

1-3-9x Mother telephoned Actifed "not helping." Called in
        Ceclor, 4 oz, 1t qid per Dr. Kasten. mlo

JAN.1 4 **199**x No improvement in left ear. Rt ear significantly the same as when last seen.
         Mother now approves surgical removal of the tonsils and adenoids and bilateral
         myringotomies with tube insertions.

mlo

                                                      _____
                                                      Gene M. Kasten, M.D.

   2-5-9x See copy of History & Physical dictated for View of the Lakes Memorial. mlo
   2-6-9x Pt admitted 3:30 PM mlo
   2-8-9x See letter to Dr. Wong. mlo

FIGURE 11-2. Example of typical unlined chart note paper. See note of December 18 to see how the "allergy" is handled.

11

or the purpose of tests and the expected results. An advantage to the patient is the ability to hear the same information repeated into the dictating machine, reinforcing what was previously discussed. The patient will also get another opportunity to ask questions that may have been forgotten, and he or she may even provide additional pieces of information. Lastly, patients get a better understanding of the amount of time spent in their physician's care.

The items dictated into a chart note will vary and may include all or only some of the following: an account of health history of the patient and family, the findings on physical examination, the signs or symptoms occurring while the patient is under observation, and the medication and treatments the patient receives or those recommended. This information may be set off by individual topics, such as the chief complaint (CC): the reason the patient is visiting the

PATRICK D. QUINN, M.D.
FAMILY PRACTICE
555 LAKE VIEW DRIVE
BAY VILLAGE, OHIO 44140

Name		Date
Legal Address		Tel. No.
Local Address		Tel. No.
Birthplace	Age Sex	Marital Status
Occupation Employer Address		Tel. No.
Nearest Relative, or Guardian (Relationship) Address		Tel. No.
Occupation Employer Address		Tel. No.
Referred by Address		Tel. No.
Insurance Company Address		Policy No./Type

PHYSICAL EXAMINATION

Height _____ Weight _____ T _____ P _____ General Appearance _____

Eyes _____ Vision Recorded on Sight Screener _____

Ears _____ Hearing: rt _____ lt _____

Teeth _____ Nose _____

Throat _____ Thyroid _____

Skin _____ Scars _____

Heart _____ BP _____

Lungs _____

Breasts _____

Abdomen _____

Rectum _____ Hernia _____

Extremities _____

Nervous System _____

Reflexes _____

Personality _____

Hygiene _____

Remarks _____

FIGURE 11-3. Example of medical office chart paper, initial visit.

doctor; the history (Hx) of the complaint; the treatment (Rx) recommended by the physician; and the physician's impression (Imp) or diagnosis (Dx) of the problem. Abbreviations are used very freely in office chart notes, and you might like to refer again to the list of abbreviations on pages 107 to 108. In addition, a brief general list is provided for you to refer to as you begin your assignments.

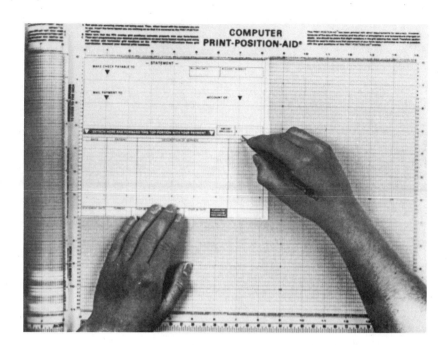

FIGURE 11-4. Positioning a lined, preprinted chart note sheet under a Print Position Aid (transparent grid template) for completion via computer or word processor. (Reproduced with permission from Computing Aids, P.O. Box 227, Needham, Massachusetts.)

The office transcriptionist will be working with dictated progress notes made when the patient is seen in the office, at home, or in the emergency room, with reference made to admissions and discharges from the hospital or a nursing facility. Telephone conversations made with the patient or with other physicians treating the patient may also be recorded.

NEW PATIENT, OFFICE

When a patient comes into the office for the initial visit, a chart is prepared. These charts will vary, just as physicians and their medical specialties vary. Therefore, we shall examine the broad methods of record preparation; you can easily apply these instructions to the method used where you work. There is really no "best" way to keep medical records other than that they be neat, accurate, complete, and timely (made as soon as possible after the patient leaves the office).

The patient will complete a social data sheet on the initial visit (Fig. 11-1). These data sheets, again, will vary according to the wishes of the individual physician or staff. This information is then used to prepare the accounting (ledger) file for the patient as well as to supply the initial information for the patient's chart. Some offices will transfer all of this information to the initial page of the medical record; others will take the barest minimum (complete name and birthdate, or age). Medical consultants often wish to have the name and telephone number of the referring physician. It will be important for you to learn exactly what information your employer wishes transferred from the social data sheet to this initial chart page.

Figures 11-2, 11-3, and 11-5 illustrate a variety of chart paper styles. You will notice that both lined and unlined paper are used. Some physicians have special paper printed for notes, others purchase chart paper from medical printing supply houses, and others prefer plain $8\frac{1}{2} \times 11$ inch typing paper. When typing via computer or word processor onto a lined sheet, you can locate your print positions easily and quickly with the use of a grid template. In addition to chart note sheets, grid templates can assist you in completing any style of preprinted form, i.e., insurance claim forms. See Figure 11-4.

After the initial information is transferred from the patient's social data sheet, the receptionist or the secretary will then date the chart paper using a date stamp, typewriter, or longhand. The date may be written out, abbreviated, or written in figures. The paper is then placed into a labeled file folder and presented to the physician at the time he or she sees the patient.

After seeing the patient, the physician will write the notes in the chart, dictate them to be transcribed into the chart, or dictate a separate document that will take the place of the chart entry. This document can be a formal history and physical report (which you will learn to prepare in Chapter 12), it may be a formal report to an attorney or workers' compensation company, or it may be a consultation report to the physician who referred the patient to the office (see Fig. 11-2, entry of 2-5-9x). If the dictator prefers not to make a chart entry and dictates a document, as just discussed, to take the place of the entry, you will transcribe the document and make a note of it in the patient's chart where the normal chart entry belongs.

11

Example

February 7, 199x   See note to Dr. Normington *mlo*

(also correct)

Feb. 7, 199x   See note to Dr. Normington mlo

You may type this entry or write it in longhand. Always follow *your* personal chart entry with *your* initials written in longhand.

ESTABLISHED PATIENT, OFFICE

Although the initial visit notes are usually lengthy, subsequent or follow-up notes may be as brief as one line, but they will vary according to the patient's complaint and type of visit to the office. For example, an entry for an established patient being seen in the office in follow-up to a hospitalization for a myringotomy could well read as follows *(note the 5-5 and 5-12 entries):*

Example

Again, a follow-up letter may be dictated to a referring physician at this point, rather than making a regular entry note. As new pages are added, be sure that the patient's name is typed on the top of the page. There is no reason why you cannot continue the notes to the back of the chart paper, and many offices do this to prevent the medical record from becoming bulky. Other physicians prefer to use one side of the chart paper only. The second and all subsequent pages of the progress notes are headed up with the patient's name. If you must continue a chart entry to the following page in the middle of an entry, be sure to type "continued" at the bottom of the beginning page and head up the following page with the date of the chart entry and the word "continued" as well as the patient's name.

Please see Figures 11–5 through 11–8 for different examples of medical office progress notes.

```
Tammy O. Beckley                              BD: 02-15-9x

                                              AGE:  3

5-1-9x        Sunday, 3 a.m., pt seen in ER complaining of pain, a.d./3 days.
              PX revealed fluid and pus.  Temp. 101.
ADVICE:       Myringotomy.
IMPRESSION:   Rt otitis media

tat                                           Jillian Cooke-Dieter
                                              Jillian Cooke-Dieter, M.D.

5-1-9x        Admit Mercy Hospital  tat
5-2-9x        Rt myringotomy with aspiration  tat
5-3-9x        Discharged 10:15 a.m.  tat

5-5-9x        No pain rt ear.  Pt progressing.  Rtn 1 week.  Temp 98.

tat                                           Jillian Cooke-Dieter
                                              Jillian Cooke-Dieter, M.D.

5-12-9x       Temp normal, no fluid, no pus, no pain.  Rtn PRN.

tat                                           J C-D
                                              Jillian Cooke-Dieter, M.D.
```

William A. Berry, M.D.

PATIENT NAME	AGE	CHART NUMBER
Stoffer, Grace W. (Mrs. William J.)	47	G-96390

JAN 23 199x

CC: Rectal bleeding, intermittent for 2 months.

After BM, bright red blood.

PX: No external hemorrhoids or fissures seen.

Internal hemorrhoids but none ulcerated on anoscopic exam.

Can see no bleeding.

On digital, at finger end, feels like fold or may be mass

above on rt, posterior rectal wall?

Rx: Return tomorrow for sigmoidoscopy and biopsy.

CBC ordered.   WAB/ref

JAN 24 199x

CC: Rectal bleeding, intermittent.

Possible mass on posterior rectal wall.

PE: Sigmoidoscopy to 15 cm. Unable to get beyond at 15 cm on

the left posterolateral wall of the rectum because of a

hemorrhagic area. Biopsy taken of this area.

No other areas seen.

Hx: Father had abnormalities of rectum, 1961.

Patient has no history of skin or scalp lesions.

Rx: Barium enema ordered.   WAB/ref

Rtn. in 4 days to discuss results of BE and biopsy.

JAN 28 199x

CC: Several more episodes of rectal bleeding, always following

a BM

Biopsy and BE essentially negative for source of bleeding

PE: Anoscopy: moderate hemorrhoidal tags.

Rx: Anusol HC suppositories, 1 morning and evening/ 6 days.

Call or return in 3-4 weeks.

February 15, 199X Telephone call, no symptoms. Will call if

episodes begin again.   WAB/ref

11

FIGURE 11-5. Example of typed chart notes using lined paper.

```
Flanaghan, Michael R.                        AGE:  82

03-17-9x

SUBJECTIVE:    Pt presented complaining of insomnia, weakness and
               shortness of breath.  Described Hx of progressive
dyspnea on exertion over a 2-3 year period.

OBJECTIVE:     BP:  150/110.  Pulse 120 and regular.  Visible neck
               vein distention at 45 degrees elevation; rales at both
lung bases.  Cardiac examination revealed an enlarged heart with PMI
felt at the midclavicular line.  Sounds were distant but a systolic
murmur was described.

     EKG:  Sinus tachycardia, left axis deviation and right bundle
           branch block.

     ECHO: Enlarged left ventricle and calcified and stenotic aortic
           valve.  Left ventricular hypertrophy also demonstrated.

ASSESSMENT:    Calcified aortic stenosis and congestive heart failure,

PLAN:          1.  Admit to hospital.
               2.  Treat with sodium restriction, digitalis and a
                   diuretic.


     mlo
                                   _____
                                   Joseph D. Becquer, M.D.
A
```

FIGURE 11-6. *A* and *B*, Sample chart entry using the SOAP (Subjective, Objective, Assessment, Plan) method.

These examples of chart entries that you have just examined are not intended to show *exactly* how to type entries but rather to indicate a variety of methods used by different transcriptionists. At this point, you will not be able to determine exactly how a chart is to be typed because your employer may have definite guidelines for you to follow. For now, and to practice, try to achieve a readable note. Do not run all the information together, but pull out the main topics. It is helpful if you do not bring the line of typing back to the left margin until the third line so that the date and topics will stand out clearly; the third and subsequent lines may be brought back to the left margin or blocked under the first two lines. (See Figures 11–6*A* and 11–8 for this method.)

TRANSCRIPTION HINTS

1. Date every entry with the month, day, and year. These may be spelled out, abbreviated, or made with a date stamp.

2. Single space and keep the margins narrow (not less than one-half inch, however). Double space between topics or major headings.

3. Make outline headings on all but very brief entries.

These headings will vary according to the physician's style. Some use the "SOAP" method (see Figures 11–6*A* and 11–6*B*):

a. S: This signifies *subjective.* "Subjective" means from the patient's point of view. This is the reason the patient is seeking care. It is the main problem requiring care (also called chief complaint).

b. O: This refers to *objective* or the physician's point of view and what is found on physical examination, x-ray film, or laboratory work: the clinical evidence.

c. A: This refers to *assessment* or what the examiner thinks may be or is wrong with the patient based on the information gathered above: the diagnosis.

d. P: This refers to *plan* or what the physician plans to do or advises the patient to do: laboratory tests, surgery, medications, referral to another practitioner, treatment, management, and so forth.

Another format choice could include:

a. CC: This refers to the CHIEF COMPLAINT (the same as "subjective" above).

b. Px: This refers to the PHYSICAL EXAMINATION also PE (the same as "objective" above).

c. Dx: This refers to the DIAGNOSIS, IMPRES-

OUTLINE FORMAT PROGRESS NOTES

Patient Name __Flanaghan Michael R.__   AGE: 82

Prob. No. or Letter	DATE	**S** Subjective	**O** Objective	**A** Assess	**P** Plans	Page ____1____

3-17-9X Patient presented complaining of insomnia, weakness and shortness of breath. Described Hx of progressive dyspnea on exertion over a 2-3 year period.

BP: 150/110. Pulse 120 and regular. Visible neck vein distention at 45 degrees elevation; rales at both lung bases. Cardiac exam revealed an enlarged heart with PMI felt at the midclavicular line. Sounds were distant but a systolic murmur was described.

EKG: Sinus tachycardia, left axis deviation and right bundle branch block.

ECHO: Enlarged left ventricle and calcified and stenotic aortic valve. Left ventricular hypertrophy also demonstrated.

Calcified aortic stenosis and congestive heart failure.

1. Admit to hospital.
2. Treat with sodium restriction, digitalis, and a diuretic.

JDB/mlo

Start each Progress Note (Subjective, Objective,   Assessment and Plans) at the appropriate   shaded column to create an outline form. Write
through the intervening columns to the right   margin of the page.

B   ANDRUS/CLINI-REC® PRIMARY CARE CHARTING SYSTEM, FORM NO. 26-7115-01, © 1976 BIBBERO SYSTEMS, INC., PETALUMA, CA.

FIGURE 11-6. *Continued*

```
Flanaghan, Michael R.                          AGE:  82

March 17, 199x
   HX:    Pt presented complaining of insomnia, weakness and shortness
          of breath.  Described Hx of progressive dyspnea on exertion
          over a 2-3 year period.

   PX:    BP: 110.  Pulse 120 and regular.  Visible neck vein distention
          at 45 degrees elevation; rales at both lung bases.  Cardiac
          examination revealed an enlarged heart with PMI felt at the
          midclavicular line.  Sounds were distant but a systolic murmur
          was described.

   EKG:   Sinus tachycardia, left axis deviation and rt bundle branch
          block.

   ECHO:  Enlarged left ventricle and calcified and stenotic aortic
          valve.  Left ventricular hypertrophy also demonstrated.

   DX:    1)  Calcified aortic stenosis
          2)  Congestive heart failure

   PLAN:  1)  Admit to hospital
          2)  Treat with sodium restriction, digitalis, diuretic



                                       Joseph D. Becquer, M.D./mlo
```

FIGURE 11-7. Sample chart entry using the HX, PX, DX method.

SION (IMP), or ASSESSMENT (the same as "assessment" above).

d. Rx: This abbreviation for *prescription* is used for the advice or plans for the patient (the same as "Plan" above). See Figure 11–5.

Other titles such as LAB or X-RAY may be used as headings. Multiple-physician practices, clinics, and hospitals often use the Problem-Oriented Medical Record (POMR) format, which is a problem list with corresponding numbered progress notes. Briefly this includes the following areas:

a. DATA BASE: the chief complaint, the history of this complaint, a review of the body systems, physical examination, and laboratory work.

b. PROBLEM LIST: a numbered list of every problem that the patient has that requires further investigation.

c. TREATMENT PLAN: numbered list to correspond with each item on the problem list.

d. NOTES: numbered progress notes to correspond with each item on the problem list.

4. Use abbreviations and symbols freely as the dictator wishes, but be sure that the abbreviations are standard. (Remember that the records could be viewed by persons outside the office.) Abbreviations save space, and notes should be as concise as possible. (See Chapter 1, page 10, concerning the use of abbreviations in hospital records.)

5. Use indentions to make topics stand out. Type the main topics in full caps.

6. Underline and type drug allergies in full caps; use a highlighting pen or underline with a red pen.

7. Initial the entry just as you initial any letter or other document that you type or transcribe.

8. Type a signature line or leave sufficient space for the dictator's signature or initials.

9. Check daily about the previous day's house calls, emergency room calls, and hospital admissions or discharges, so that the charts can be pulled and these entries made.

Please see Figures 11–6 and 11–7 again for typing format.

These are some common abbreviations found frequently in office chart notes. You may use these as well as those found in Chapter 5, pages 107 to 108, as you complete the following assignments.

pt	patient	PO	postoperative
Hx	history	pre	preoperative or prepartum
Px	physical or physical exam	FUO	fever of unknown origin
PE	physical or physical exam	H&P	history and physical
CC	chief complaint	TPR	temperature, pulse, respiration
Dx	diagnosis	inj	injection
Tx	treatment	anPX	annual exam
Rx	prescription or plan	CPX	complete physical exam
STAT	immediate	DKA	did not keep appointment
BP	blood pressure	DNS	did not show (keep appointment)
VS	vital signs	pre-op	preoperative
IMP	impression	consult	consultation
PH	past history	PG?	question of being pregnant
R/O	rule out		

11–1: SELF-STUDY

Directions: Retype the following material into chart note format, as illustrated in Figure 11–7.

The date is October 10, 199X. The patient is Anthony Frishman. Tony is now 12½ years old. He underwent bilateral triple arthrodesis in August 199X. He is out of his splints and doing well. His foot rests are a bit long and his feet are not touching them. He has no major complaints as far as his feet are concerned. Exam: He has a long c-curve to the right, which may be slightly increased clinically since last x-rayed in June 199X when it was twenty-five degrees. His feet are in neutral position as far as equinus. There is a slight varus inclination. X-rays: multiple views of his feet demonstrate fusion bilaterally of the triple staples. Diagnosis is limb girdle dystrophy. The plan is to return to clinic in one to two months for sitting SP spine x-ray. Also we will obtain pulmonary function test at that time. Karl T. Robrecht, M.D. (After you have completed this assignment; turn to the back of the chapter for a possible transcript.)

11–2: PRACTICE TEST

Directions: Retype the following information as an office chart note for your employer, Eugene W. Gomez, M.D. Use the current date, minimum chart note heading, and plain (unlined) 8½ × 11 inch paper.

The patient's name is Maryellen Mawson.

Note: this is a six year old who has had a three week history of polydipsia polyuria polyphagia and weight loss. the child has become progressively more lethargic over the past twenty four hours and twelve hours ago the parents noticed she was breathing rapidly. physical examination reveals; height one hundred twenty seven centimeters weight thirty three kilograms temperature ninety nine degrees fahrenheit pulse one hundred twelve and blood pressure ninety five over seventy. the child was semicomatose. she has dry mucous membranes but good skin turgor and full peripheral pulses. a stat lab report shows: sodium one hundred thirty eight milliequivalents per liter, potassium three point three milliequivalents per liter chloride ninety seven milliequivalents per liter and a total carbon dioxide of five milliequivalents per liter. blood glucose is seven hundred milligrams percent. plan is to admit stat to childrens hospital. (After you complete this, please see Appendix E for a possible transcript.)

11-3: REVIEW TEST

Directions: Carefully examine the examples of chart notes that have been illustrated and retype the following information as office chart notes for your employer, Laurel R. Denison, M.D. You may use the minimum chart note heading, plain (unlined) $8\frac{1}{2} \times 11$ inch paper, format of your choice, and standard abbreviations where applicable. Use today's date. Please notice that these are notes about several patients; therefore, each patient will have a separate sheet of paper.

1. *Gustavo deVargas.* Birthdate 3-3-34. Patient had onset of persistent vomiting five days ago. He does not appear seriously ill. The abdomen remains flat and there is no tenderness or rigidity; no masses are palpable; bowel sounds are scarce. X-ray of the abdomen yesterday revealed a four centimeter, ill-defined, round mass in the right upper quadrant and loops of small bowel containing air. Subsequent x-rays, including some taken today, revealed that this rounded mass persists, is quite well outlined on some of the x-rays, and is now in the left lower quadrant. There is small bowel distention in relation to the mass, which suggests that the mass is a loop of small bowel with gaseous distention proximal to it. It is questionable whether there is any gas in the colon. Rectal examination is negative. Impression: intestinal obstruction due to ingested foreign body. Advice: laparotomy.

2. *Mrs. Esther Conway.* Age 33. Patient complains of constant dribbling, wetting at night, uses fifteen pads a day. Urinalysis: specific gravity one point zero, few bacteria, few urates. Diagnosis: urinary incontinence. Patient is to return in four days for diagnostic testing.

3. *Robin Vincenti.* Age 27. Patient complains of having had the flu and headache, and of being tired. Unable to go to work today. Exam shows weakness of left hand. Hyperreflexia on the left. X-ray shows cardiomegaly and slight pulmonary congestion. Impression: post flu syndrome, transient ischemic attack; possible CVA. Patient to return in four days and may return to work in approximately one week.

4. *Marissa Weeks.* Age 17. CC: thrown from a horse. Px: numerous contusions, tenderness in thoracic region, x-ray ordered. Dx: compression fracture of "tee twelve." Rx: patient referred to Edward Harrison, orthopedic specialist.

5. *Bobby West.* Age 1 month. Make your entry showing a letter was dictated, rather than a chart entry made. See Self-Study 6–1, page 134, for the actual letter that was dictated and transcribed.

11-4: REVIEW TEST

Directions: Using the instructions you have just received, type the following information into the patients' charts that you previously prepared. Use a date four days from the date you used for Review Test 11–3.

1. *Gustavo deVargas.* Patient telephoned office today and agreed to laparotomy. He is to be admitted to Valley Presbyterian Hospital tomorrow afternoon at 3 for surgery the following day.

2. Secretary: Please make your own entry into the chart showing that Mr. deVargas was admitted to the hospital on the appropriate day.

3. *Robin Vincenti.* Chest clear to P&A. X-ray is clear and shows normal heart silhouette. Full use of left hand, no residual pain or weakness. Plans to return to work tomorrow.

4. *Mrs. Esther Conway.* Intravenous pyelogram and cystoscopy revealed multiple fistulae of bladder with two openings into urinary bladder and copious leakage into vagina. Continued to work. Diagnosis: multiple vesicovaginal fistulae. To be admitted to the hospital for repair.

5. Secretary: Please make your own entry into the chart for day of admission, four days from her last visit, into University Hospital for Mrs. Conway.

MAKING CORRECTIONS

Errors in handwritten chart notes are corrected as follows. Draw a line through the error, being careful not to obliterate it; make the correct notation either above or below the error, wherever there is room, and date and initial the entry. Do not write over your error, do not erase the error, do not try to "fix" the error, and do not attempt to blot it out with heavy applications of ink or self-adhesive typing strips.

Errors that are made while the entry is being typed are corrected just as you would correct any other typewritten material. Errors found subsequently are corrected in longhand following the above procedures. However, it is not necessary to date errors when they are made or discovered on the same day as they are entered; just correct and initial the error.

See Figure 11–8 for an example of chart notes with entry errors properly corrected. You will notice that these corrections are not dated, which indicates that they were made on the day of the entry.

 11–5: SELF-STUDY

Directions: In the following chart note, the entry of "left thoracotomy" should read "right thoracotomy." You discover the error on February 1, 199X. Please correct it.

Please look at the end of the chapter for the proper correction technique.

11

Brad Philman   Age 47

1-13-9X   Pt admitted to Good Sam for bronchoscopy and possible left
          thoracotomy and pleural poudrage. *ren*

TIME SAVER

When you have a stack of charts to do, it soon can become a nuisance to find the proper page in the chart, unfasten it (if fasteners are used), feed it into the typewriter, align it properly, and type the note. Then it must be removed, placed in the proper place in the chart, refastened, and returned to the dictator for approval and signature. Finally, it is returned to the files. If you are working on a computer, word processor, or some other piece of equipment that uses automatic paper feed, it may be difficult or impossible to insert individual sheets of paper.

There is, however, a handy solution to this problem. Several companies manufacture pressure-sensi-

tive paper for transcribing medical notes. This paper comes in a variety of forms as well as a continuous sheet of paper folded into an $8\frac{1}{2} \times 11$ inch box. The box is placed behind the typewriter or printer and the paper inserted. One then simply types the patient's name, the date, and the dictation, leaving a space at the end for the dictator's signature or initials. Each note is typed without removing any paper from the chart. Then, when the transcript is finished, the entire sheet is cut off and placed on the dictator's desk for signature. This makes it easier for the physician as well because individual charts do not have to be opened and signed. This is particularly helpful when dictation is sent out of the office and the medical records do not accompany it. Of course one does not

---

(Master) Norman Brockman   AGE: 4

February 22, 199x   The patient is a white male, age 4, who came in to see me
                    today with a history of yellow discharge in the right
ear, a fever and a sore throat of two days duration. His oral temperature wa
100°. The pharynx was infected, the tonsils inflamed, and there was crusted
purulent material seen in the right ear canal. The tympanic membrane was
normal.

DIAGNOSIS: Tonsillitis and otitis externa.

Medication: Erythrocin, 400 mg, q4H.

lr   24br   Michael R. Stearn, M.D.

February 22, 199x   After 24 h of therapy, the pt   was afebrile and comfort-
                    able. Temperature is 99.6°. The throat is slightly
infected. Secretions in the ear canal were dry and both TMs normal.

lr   Michael R. Stearn, M.D.

February 26, 199x   Follow-up exam showed him to be completely asymptomatic
                    and free of unusual physical findings. The drug was
stopped at this time.

lr   Michael R. Stearn, M.D.

July 6, 199x   Stepped on a piece of glass. Cleansed wound. Mother
                    said Norman had tetanus booster just six weeks ago in
Boyd Hosp.ER after a dog bite. Pt not to return unless problem develops.

jt   Michael R. Stearn, M.D.

November 11, 199x   Pt caught right index finger in car door 2 MRS days ago;
                    finger became inflamed, red, swollen yesterday.
Today there is seropurulent discharge present; no lymphangitis visible.
Distal phalanx is involved.

Advice: Hot compress to right hand t.i.d. To return in 24
                    hours if no change.

DIAGNOSIS: Cellulitis, right index finger, distal phalanx.

lr   Michael R. Stearn, M.D.

FIGURE 11-8. Example of a properly corrected chart note.

initiate this process without the consent of the dictator. Some physicians request that the pertinent medical records be available when the notes are signed in case they are needed for reference.

After approval, the notes are carefully separated at the perforation or cut apart with a paper cutter or scissors (Fig. 11-9A). The backing is peeled off each one and the note is then placed on the next blank space of the progress sheet so as not to obliterate information previously entered in the patient's chart (Fig. 11-9B). The charts will be stacked in the order in which they were dictated so it will be easy for the secretary or transcriptionist to locate the correct chart.

FIGURE 11-9. *A*, Transcriptionist demonstrating the ease with which the pressure-sensitive paper can be torn at the perforations. (Courtesy of Randi Hanks.) *B*, Secretary placing Time Saver labels into the chart. (Courtesy of March and Green.)

11-6: REVIEW TEST

Directions: Pretend that you are typing the following notes on pressure-sensitive paper. Don't forget to leave a little space between the notes so they can be cut apart, but do not cut your notes apart. Use today's date. Use the "SOAP" format for chart note #5. Your employer is Catherine R. Schultz, M.D.

1. *Lupe Morales.* Lump, right breast. Patient found this lump four weeks ago. It has increased in size rapidly, she says. She also has a lump under her right arm. Ordered mammograms. Diagnosis: Possible carcinoma of the breast.

2. *Adeline Pierson.* CC: pain and swelling over the right wrist. Hx: The patient states that while she was working as a waitress she was lifting and carrying a tray of dishes and it slipped, resulting in pain and swelling over the radial side of the distal radius of her right wrist. This was found to be a ganglion and was aspirated by another physician. However, it has recurred and is larger than before. She wishes this surgically removed. Her past general health has been good. She has had no serious illnesses and no surgeries. She takes no medications. Allergies: None known.

3. *Peter Barton.* PO follow-up. Incision looks good, some slight swelling and tenderness.

4. *Kellis McNeil.* CC: Right inguinal hernia. Hx: Patient first noticed that he had a right inguinal hernia because of pain there approximately one week ago. He presents with a very tender right inguinal ring. The hernia was reduced but readily protruded. PH: The patient had an umbilical hernia repair eight years ago. He had a hemorrhoidectomy four years ago. Drugs: Valium, 5 mg, t.i.d. Advise: Right herniorrhaphy.

5. *Arnott B. Weeks.* stiff finger joints. pt says more severe after sleeping or nonuse. general fatigue stopped, occurred again in last 2 weeks. stopped drinking, some weight loss. on exam there is swelling and pain around joints of fingers. symmetrical involvement. bp is one hundred forty four over eighty five pulse is sixty seven weight is one hundred seventy eight. x-ray: narrowed joint space, osteoporosis at joint. uric acid: four point two. rheumatoid arthritis. aspirin ten grains qid, phenylbutazone one hundred milligrams qid, number twenty eight. return one month.

⌨ Answers to 11–1: Self-Study

Anthony Frishman   AGE   12½

October 10, 199x

HX: Pt underwent bilateral triple arthrodesis in August, 199x. He is out of splints and doing well. His foot rests are a bit long and his feet are not touching them. He has no major complaints as far as his feet are concerned.

PX: He has a long C-curve to the right which may be slightly increased clinically since last x-rayed in June, 199x, when it was 25°. His feet are in neutral position as far as equinus. There is a slight varus inclination.

X-RAY: Multiple views of his feet demonstrate fusion bilaterally of the triple staples.

DX: Limb girdle dystrophy.

PLAN: 1. Return to Clinic in one-two months for sitting SP spine x-ray.
        2. Obtain pulmonary function test at that time.

ref

_____
Karl T. Robrecht, M.D.

⌨ Answers to 11–5: Self-Study

Brad Philman   Age 47

1-13-9X   Pt admitted to Good Sam for bronchoscopy and possible ~~left~~ *right* thoracotomy and pleural poudrage. *ren*   *2-1-9X ren*

"That's what you dictated, Doctor!"

By Dorothy Reid

All the following gems are quotations from the dictation of staff physicians at Memorial Mission Hospital in Asheville, N.C., where I supervise the transcription unit. I don't intend this to be critical of our fine staff. It just shows how things sometimes come out no matter who happens to be doing the dictating.

The left leg became numb at times and she walked it off.

Patient has chest pain if she lies on her left side for over a year.

Father died in his 90s of female trouble in his prostate and kidneys.

Both the patient and the nurse herself reported passing flatus.

Skin: Somewhat pale but present.

On the second day the knee was better, and on the third day it had completely disappeared.

The pelvic examination will be done later on the floor.

Patient stated that if she would lie down, within two or three minutes something would come across her abdomen and knock her up.

By the time she was admitted to the hospital her rapid heart had stopped and she was feeling much better.

Patient has bilateral varicosities below the legs.

If he squeezes the back of his neck for 4 or 5 years it comes and goes.

Patient was seen in consultation by Dr. Blank who felt we should sit tight on the abdomen, and I agreed.

Speculum was inserted between the eyes.

Dr. Blank is watching his prostate.

Discharge status: Alive but without permission.

Coming from Detroit, Mich., this man has no children.

At the time of onset of pregnancy the mother was undergoing bronchoscopy.

She was treated with Mycostatin oral suppositories.

Healthy appearing decrepit 69 year old white female, mentally alert but forgetful.

When you pin him down, he has some slowing of the stream.

Preparation of a History and Physical

OBJECTIVES

After reading this chapter and working the exercises, you should be able to

1. identify the various mechanical formats used to prepare a typewritten history and physical.
2. explain why certain information is obtained from the patient and recorded.
3. describe the many different ways of gathering and dictating vital medical data.
4. prepare a formal history and physical using a variety of acceptable styles.

12

INTRODUCTION

The primary purpose of the history and physical (H & P) is to assist the physician in making a diagnosis upon which he or she will base the patient's care and treatment. There are no precise rules for exactly how a history is taken down or a physical examination carried out, nor is there an exact format for recording the data gathered. These will vary just as the personalities of the dictators vary. However, most physicians, regardless of medical specialty, approach the evaluation of the patient in a similar fashion.

All patients, when initially seen, need to give the physician a complete history of their problems and be examined. How many questions they are asked, the types of questions, and body area emphasized are determined both by the patient's problem and by the

medical specialty involved. For instance, a patient with chest pain seeing a cardiologist will have far more attention paid to the chest than to the bladder and bowels. The patient with a hearing problem does not expect an extensive examination of the abdomen or extremities. However, when a patient is scheduled for a major operative procedure, or has symptoms that suggest a complex systemic illness, all body systems are examined to some extent.

You will need to know how to transcribe an H & P if you work in the word processing unit of a hospital or clinic. If you work in a private medical office for a surgical or medical specialist, you will also be required to type H & Ps. As with chart notes, some physicians will write their H & Ps in longhand. There is certainly no requirement that they be typed. However, because they are part of the patient's medical record, it is im-

245

portant that they be neat, readable, complete, and accurate.

Some physicians will dictate an H & P as the initial chart note entry, and surgeons will do an H & P on the preoperative visit with a patient, since the hospital will require this document to be in the patient's hospital record. This record performs an important function as a diary of what has happened to the patient in the past, a plan for care in the present, and an outline of how the patient may be helped in the future.

THE FORMATS

Several formats are used for typing an H & P. There is no "best" style or method, but each hospital, clinic, or medical office should adopt a standard outline. The responsibility for designing the format for the hospital belongs to the hospital forms committee. The hospital will generally accept the H & P prepared by the medical office assistant as long as it falls within the general guidelines of the styles that follow.

Just as we examined the three formats for letter set-up, we will now discuss the four formats, with variations, for H & P set-up. The actual wording of the outline itself may vary, too, but we will discuss that and the data that go into the report later. Keeping the facts in the proper sequence, spacing them properly, and typing them accurately make the work of transcribing interesting and challenging.

THE HISTORY

Usually the data for the history are obtained first. The following four examples and guides for typing histories are observed, when you are typing the physical examination as well. Always check with your employer for the preferred style.

Full Block Format Report Style (Fig. 12 – 1)

Statistical Data:	As determined by the medical facility.
Title:	*History* or *Personal History* centered on the page. Typed in all capital letters.
Main Topics:	Typed in all capital letters, followed by a colon. Underlined. On a line by itself. Begun on edge of left border.
Subtopics:	Capitalized.
Data:	Begun on the *same* line as subtopic. Single-spaced. All lines return to the left margin. Double space between the last line of one heading and the next heading.
Margins:	Narrow (one-half inch to three-quarter inch is appropriate).
Close:	Typed line for signature. Dictator's typed name. Transcriptionist's initials. Date of dictation (D). Date of transcription (T).
Variations:	1. No space below main topic. 2. Subtopics grouped after main heading in paragraph format. The subtopic title is typed in full caps or both upper and lower case. 3. Main topics not underlined.

de Mars, Verna Marie
Cortland M. Struthers, M.D.

                              HISTORY

CHIEF COMPLAINT:

Prolapse and bleeding after each bowel movement for the past 3-4 months.

PRESENT ILLNESS:

This 68-year-old white female says she usually has three bowel movements a day in small amounts, and there has been a recent change in the frequency, size and type of bowel movement she has been having. She is also having some pain and irritation in this area. She has had no previous anorectal surgery or rectal infection. She denies any blood in the stool itself.

PAST HISTORY:

ILLNESSES: The patient had polio at age 8 from which she has made a remarkable recovery. Apparently, she was paralyzed in both lower extremities and now has adequate use of these. She has no other serious illnesses.

ALLERGIES: ALLERGIC TO PENICILLIN. She denies any other drug or food allergies.

MEDICATIONS: None.

OPERATIONS: Herniorrhaphy, 25 years ago.

SOCIAL: She does not smoke or drink. She lives with her husband who is an invalid and for whom she cares. She is a retired former municipal court judge.

FAMILY HISTORY:

One brother died of cancer of the throat, another has cancer of the kidney.

REVIEW OF SYSTEMS:

SKIN: No rashes or jaundice.

HEENT: Unremarkable.

CR: No history of chest pain, shortness of breath, or pedal edema. She has had some mild hypertension in the past but is not under any medical supervision nor is she taking any medication for this.

GI: Weight is stable. See Present Illness.

OB-GYN: Gravida II Para II. Climacteric at age 46, no sequelae.

EXTREMITIES: No edema.

NEUROLOGIC: Unremarkable.

jrt   _____
D: 5-17-9x   Cortland M. Struthers, M.D.
T: 5-20-9x

FIGURE 12-1. Example of a history typed in full block format.

12

Modified Block Format Report Style (Fig. 12–2)

Statistical Data: As determined by the medical facility.

Title: *History* or *Personal History* centered on the page.
Typed in all capital letters.

Main Topics: Typed in all capital letters, followed by a colon.
Underlined.
Begun on edge of left border.

Subtopics: Indented three to five spaces under main topics.
Typed in full caps, followed by a colon.

Data: Begun on the *same* line as the topic or subtopic.
Tabulated 23 spaces from the left margin; use a block indent on a word processor.
(This is adequate space so that all data are blocked.)
Each line blocked under previous line.
Single spaced.
Double space between the last line of a topic and the next heading.

Margins: Narrow (one-half inch to three-quarter inch).

Close: Typed line for signature.
Dictator's typed name.
Transcriptionist's initials.
Date of dictation (D).
Date of transcription (T).

Variations:
1. No underlining.
2. Single space between subtopics.

12

de Mars, Verna Marie
Cortland M. Struthers, M.D.

                            HISTORY

CHIEF COMPLAINT: Prolapse and bleeding after each bowel movement for the past
                        3-4 months.

PRESENT ILLNESS: This 68-year-old white female says she usually has three bowel
                        movements a day in small amounts, and there has been a recent
                        change in frequency, size and type of bowel movement she has
                        been having. She is also having some pain and irritation in
                        this area. She has had no previous anorectal surgery or rectal
                        infection. She denies any blood in the stool itself.

PAST HISTORY:

    ILLNESSES: The patient had polio at age 8 from which she has made a remark-
                        able recovery. Apparently, she was paralyzed in both lower
                        extremities and now has adequate use of these. She has no other
                        serious illnesses.

    ALLERGIES: ALLERGIC TO PENICILLIN. She denies any other drug or food allergies.

    MEDICATIONS: None.

    OPERATIONS: Herniorrhaphy, 25 years ago.

    SOCIAL: She does not smoke or drink. She lives with her husband who is
                        an invalid and for whom she cares. She is a retired former
                        municipal court judge.

FAMILY HISTORY: One brother died of cancer of the throat, another has cancer
                        of the kidney.

REVIEW OF SYSTEMS:

    SKIN: No rashes or jaundice.

    HEENT: Unremarkable.

    CR: No history of chest pain, shortness of breath, or pedal edema.
                        She has had some mild hypertension in the past but is not under
                        any medical supervision nor is she taking any medication for this.

    GI: Weight is stable. See Present Illness.

    OB-GYN: Gravida II Para II. Climacteric at age 46, no sequelae.

    EXTREMITIES: No edema.

    NEUROLOGIC: Unremarkable.

jrt   _____
D: 5-17-9x   Cortland M. Struthers, M.D.
T: 5-20-9x

FIGURE 12-2. Example of a history typed in modified block format.

Indented Format Report Style (Fig. 12–3)

Statistical Data:	As determined by the medical facility.
Title:	*History* or *Personal History* centered on the page. Typed in all capital letters.
Main Topics:	Typed in all capital letters, followed by a colon. Underlined. Begun flush with the left margin.
Subtopics:	Typed in all capital letters, followed by a colon. Indented three to five spaces under main topics.
Data:	Begun on the *same* line as topic or subtopic.

First *and* second lines tabulated 23 spaces from the left margin.*

Third and *subsequent* lines brought back to the left margin (as long as they clear the outline—if too brief, block under first two lines). See Figure 12–3, data after "Social."
Single spaced.
Double space between topics.

Margins:	Narrow (one-half inch to three-quarter inch).
Close:	Typed line for signature. Dictator's typed name. Transcriptionist's initials. Date of dictation (D). Date of transcription (T).
Variations:	1. No underlining. 2. Do not indent subtopics.

---

* This varies to 27 spaces when formatting an operative report.

12

de Mars, Verna Marie
Cortland M. Struthers, M.D.

                              HISTORY

CHIEF COMPLAINT: Prolapse and bleeding after each bowel movement for the past 3-4
                   months.

PRESENT ILLNESS: This 68-year-old white female says she usually has three bowel
                   movements a day in small amounts, and there has been a recent
change in the frequency, size and type of bowel movement she has been having. She
is also having some pain and irritation in this area. She has had no previous anorectal surgery or rectal infection. She denies any blood in the stool itself.

PAST HISTORY:

   ILLNESSES: The patient had polio at age 8 from which she has made a remark-
                   able recovery. Apparently, she was paralyzed in both lower
extremities and now has adequate use of these. She has had no other serious illnesses.

   ALLERGIES: ALLERGIC TO PENICILLIN. She denies any other drug or food allergies.

   MEDICATIONS: None.

   OPERATIONS: Herniorrhaphy, 25 years ago.

   SOCIAL: She does not smoke or drink. She lives with her husband who is an
                   invalid and for whom she cares. She is a retired former municipal
                   court judge.

FAMILY HISTORY: One brother died of cancer of the throat, another has cancer of
                   the kidney.

REVIEW OF SYSTEMS:

   SKIN: No rashes or jaundice.

   HEENT: Unremarkable.

   CR: No history of chest pain, shortness of breath, or pedal edema. She
                   has had some mild hypertension in the past but is not under any
medical supervision nor is she taking any medication for this.

   GI: Weight is stable. See Present Illness.

   OB-GYN: Gravida II Para II. Climacteric at age 46, no sequelae.

   EXTREMITIES: No edema.

   NEUROLOGIC: Unremarkable.

                                              Cortland M. Struthers, M.D.
jrt
D: 5-17-9x
T: 5-20-9x

FIGURE 12-3. Example of a history typed using indented format.

Run-On Format Report Style (Fig. 12–4)

Statistical Data:	As determined by the medical facility.
Title:	*History* or *Personal History* centered on the page. Typed in all capital letters.
Main Topics:	Full caps, followed by a colon. Begun flush with the left margin.
Subtopics:	Upper and lower case, followed by a colon. Data continued within the paragraph.
Data:	Begun on the same line as the outline, a double space after the colon. Single spaced. Double space between topics.
Margins:	Narrow (one-half inch to three-quarter inch).
Close:	Typed line for signature. Dictator's typed name. Transcriptionist's initials. Date of dictation (D). Date of transcription (T).
Variations:	1. Single space between topics. 2. Subtopics begun on a separate line and typed in caps. 3. Main topic underlined and in full caps.

Run-on format uses much less space on the paper and takes less time to prepare because tabulations, underlining, and double spacing are lessened or eliminated entirely. It takes time to feed such information in and play it out again on automated equipment. Production and speed must not be sacrificed for format in this case.

Now we will briefly examine each part of the outline.

Statistical Data. This always includes the name of the patient and any other means of identification that the hospital, office, or clinic uses. It may include the patient's record number, age, room number, date of admission, referring physician, the dictator's name, and the names of anyone who is to receive a copy of the dictation. This material is often stamped on forms by use of an Addressograph or identification card issued at the time of admission.

Chief Complaint. (This is abbreviated *CC,* but do not use the abbreviation unless it is approved.) This is

a description of what brought the patient to the physician or the hospital in the first place. It is usually brief, may be specific or vague, and may be dictated in the patient's own words. If there is a list of complaints, they are usually dictated in the order of importance.

Present Illness. (Abbreviated *PI*). This is also called *History of Chief Complaint* or *History of Present Illness* (abbreviated *HPI*). The patient's problem is now discussed in detail with emphasis on duration and severity. The patient will relate the details he or she feels are significant, and the physician will inquire if they are related to other symptoms or events. If the patient has been treated by another physician for the same or a similar problem, this will be discussed, along with the possible diagnosis and treatment prescribed.

Past History. (Abbreviated *PH*). This section begins with the patient's childhood and includes all past medical history with reference to diseases, illnesses, surgical procedures, and accidents. This main topic is generally broken down into subtopics as follows:

Habits. The use of alcohol, tobacco, and drugs, both prescription and recreational use. Or the dictator may use a separate topic for drugs the patient may have taken recently or is currently taking and call this subtopic *Medications.*

Diseases. This includes both childhood and adult diseases and any complications that arose as a result.

Operations. All surgical procedures, dates, and sequelae are recorded. This subtopic may also be called *Surgeries.*

Allergies. This includes any reactions the patient may have to drugs, food, or the environment. (Many physicians direct the transcriptionist to underline in red [or type in all capital letters] a positive reply to a drug allergy.)

Social. The socioeconomic status of the patient, his or her occupation, profession, or trade, recreational interests, home environment, and marital status.

Gynecologic. (when the patient is a female). The number of pregnancies, deliveries, complications, living children, abortions, and sexual activity. The times of menarche and menopause are noted, along with any problems associated with the menses.

Prolonged investigation of any one or more of these topics is made, depending on the patient's chief complaint. Some dictators use some or all of the topics

```
de Mars, Verna Marie
Cortland M. Struthers, M.D.

                            HISTORY
CHIEF COMPLAINT:  Prolapse and bleeding after each bowel movement for the past 3-4
months.

PRESENT ILLNESS:  This 68-year-old white female says she usually has three bowel move-
ments a day in small amounts, and there has been a recent change in the frequency,
size and type of bowel movement she has been having.  She is also having some pain
and irritation in this area.  She has had no previous anorectal surgery or rectal
infection.  She denies any blood in the stool itself.

PAST HISTORY:  Illnesses:  The patient had polio at age 8 from which she has made a
remarkable recovery.  Apparently, she was paralyzed in both lower extremities and now
has adequate use of these.  She has had no other serious illnesses.  Allergies:
ALLERGIC TO PENICILLIN.  She denies any other drug or food allergies.  Medications:
None.  Operations:  Herniorrhaphy, 25 years ago.  Social:  She does not smoke or drink.
She lives with her husband who is an invalid and for whom she cares.  She is a retired
former municipal court judge.

FAMILY HISTORY:  One brother died of cancer of the throat, another has cancer of the
kidney.

REVIEW OF SYSTEMS:  Skin:  No rashes or jaundice.  HEENT:  Unremarkable.  CR:  No
history of chest pain, shortness of breath, or pedal edema.  She has had some mild
hypertension in the past but is not under any medical supervision nor is she taking
any medication for this.  GI:  Weight is stable.  See Present Illness.  OB-GYN:
Gravida II Para II.  Climacteric at age 46, no sequelae.  Extremities:  No edema.
Nuerologic:  Unremarkable.

jrt
D:  5-17-9x
T:  5-20-9x                                    _____
                                               Cortland M. Struthers, M.D.
```

FIGURE 12-4. Example of a history typed using run-on format.

listed; others group all of these data together in a brief paragraph entitled *Past History.* You will also notice that physicians list many negative replies to some of these items; for example, "the patient denies any allergies or drug sensitivities"; "there is no history of familial disease"; "the patient does not use drugs or alcohol."

Family History. The state of health of the patient's parents, siblings, and grandparents is discussed. If they are deceased, the age and cause of death are recorded. Inquiry is made concerning certain diseases that tend to be familial, such as tuberculosis, diabetes, epilepsy, carcinoma, and heart disease. The place and circumstances of the patient's birth might also be noteworthy.

Review of Systems. This is also called *Systemic Review, Functional Inquiry,* or *Inventory by Systems.* This is an oral review conducted in question-and-answer style with the patient, as stated, of all the body systems to make sure that nothing has been overlooked. The absence or presence of problems is noted. Again, a variety of methods is used for typing this

information. Generally, the physician will review by starting at the top of the body and going through the body systems, ending with the nervous or musculoskeletal system. He or she may dictate the data as a single paragraph with no headings or break it down into subtopics. The subtopics used are as follows, along with the abbreviations commonly used and accepted:

Skin. Includes eruptions, rashes, itches, discolorations.

Hair. Includes changes in its texture or distribution.

HEENT. This pertains to the *h*ead, *e*yes, *e*ars, *n*ose, and *t*hroat. Additional subtopics may be added, or a single, all-inclusive paragraph may be utilized.

Eyes. Will include vision problems such as glaucoma, scotoma, conjunctivitis, trachoma, pain, discharge, redness, fields, use of glasses.

Ears. Will include hearing loss, discharge, dizziness, syncope, tinnitus, pain, condition of the tympanic membranes.

Nose. Will include discharges, sense of smell, colds, allergies, epistaxis.

Mouth and Throat. Will include condition of teeth, dental hygiene, dentures, gums, difficulty in swallowing, hoarseness, thyroid, movement of the neck, position of the trachea.

CR (Cardiorespiratory). Includes dyspnea, orthopnea, shortness of breath, hemoptysis, edema, pneumonia, angina, tachycardia.

GI (Gastrointestinal). Includes appetite, indigestion, dysphagia, anorexia, vomiting, hematemesis, change in weight or diet, change of bowel habits, melena, flatus, diarrhea, constipation, jaundice.

GU (Genitourinary). Includes dysuria, nocturia, hematuria, urgency, frequency, pyuria, oliguria, venereal disease, incontinence, hesitancy, dribbling, discharge, lumbar pain.

GYN (Gynecologic). Includes menarche, flow, dysmenorrhea, menorrhagia, metrorrhagia, dyspareunia, leukorrhea, use of contraceptives, obstetric history, pregnancies, deliveries, abortions. *Gravida* followed by a number (either arabic or roman) refers to the number of pregnancies, including ectopics, hydatidiform moles, abortions, and normal pregnancies. *Para* followed by a number (either arabic or roman) refers to the number of deliveries after the 20th week of gestation (live or stillbirth, single or multiple, vaginal or cesarean) and does not correspond to the number of infants born.

NP (Neuropsychiatric). Includes syncope, headache, vertigo, pain, scotomata, paralysis, ataxia, convulsion, emotional state.

MS (Musculoskeletal). Includes pain, stiffness, limitation of movement, fractures.

Sometimes there is nothing noteworthy to add to the history in the systemic review (it was covered adequately in the history as related), so the dictator says, "systemic review is essentially negative." This expression is typed after the outline topic.

The actual structuring of the paragraphs is the responsibility of the transcriptionist, and therefore this basic understanding of a history will aid you. The physician may not dictate the outline, and you must be able to recognize each body part he or she is discussing so you can choose the appropriate topic or subtopic.

If the history continues to a second page, type the word *continued* in parentheses after the last typed line on the first page. On the second page, beginning at the left margin, repeat the statistical data from the first page and add the heading *History, page 2*.

Before you begin your first assignment, briefly review the illustrated histories.

---

12 **12–1: SELF-STUDY**

Directions: Retype the following data into history outline using the indented format and no variations. Remember to set your tab stop at 23 spaces. The patient's name and other statistical data can be set up as you desire. Be alert to topic changes and proper mechanics.

The patient is Geoffrey Paul Hawkins. The dictating physician is Paul R. Elsner, M.D. The tape was dictated yesterday. The patient's hospital ID number is 54-98-10. His chief complaint is abdominal pains and vomiting since 3 a.m. Present illness: This $11\frac{1}{2}$ year old white male, who was perfectly well yesterday and last evening, awoke from his sleep with vomiting at 3 a.m. today. This was followed by nausea, which has been severe, together with a little bile coming up, but no great amount of continued vomiting. There is severe, recurrent, doubling-up type cramping to time of admission at 10 o'clock. There has been no recent upper respiratory tract infection, no prior similar episode, no history of recurrent constipation or diarrhea. Patient's last bowel movement was yesterday and of normal quality. His mother reports that he eats sunflower seeds to excess and may have done so yesterday. Past history: Patient was born at home with midwife delivery, uncomplicated. He has had the usual immunizations for childhood. There has been no prior hospitalization, no tonsillectomy, no surgery, no fracture. He has had stitches a couple of times in the office. Family History: Mother is 35 and at the present time is under treatment for cancer of the breast. She reports that she had surgery and is on chemotherapy at the present time. She has not been given radiation. Father is age 40, living and well. There are two sisters, both older than the patient, both living and well. They both had appendectomies, one of which had ruptured. There are a maternal great niece, uncle and paternal grandmother who have had diabetes. There is no diabetes in the immediate family and no other history of familial disorders such as bleeding, anemia, tuberculosis, heart disease. Personal history: The patient has no known drug allergies, has not been on any medication at the present time. Grade six, but does poorly. Seems to be the class clown according to his mother. He has no hobbies. Systemic review: HEENT: There has been a muscle in one eye which has been off for years; Dr. McMannis is following this. His vision is good, hearing is normal. CR: No known murmurs. No chronic cough, no recent cough, no dyspnea. GI: no prior GI difficulty. No food allergies. No chronic or recurrent constipation. GU: No nocturia, no enuresis, no GU infection. NM: No history of head injury, no history of polio, paralysis, meningitis, or numbness.

Please turn to the end of the chapter to check your work. Pay close attention to format.

12–2: PRACTICE TEST

Directions: Retype the following data into a history outline using modified block format. Be alert to topic changes. Remember that the dictator might not follow the exact wording or format seen in the sample outlines.

The patient is Joseph R. Balentine. The report was dictated on 11-16-9X and transcribed the same day. The dictating physician is Benjamin B. Abboud. He requests that a copy be sent to Stuart L. Paulson, M.D. The patient's ID number is 423-12-22. His chief complaint: the patient is a 25 year old male complaining of recurring epistaxis. Present illness: the patient reports that yesterday he had onset of epistaxis in the left side of his nose. This was intermittent throughout the day and at 4:30 this morning, he came to the ER. Past History: Allergies: None. Bleeding History: None, except for PI. Illnesses: The patient had a collapsed lung about five years ago and subsequently had surgery, but does not know the exact etiology of the problem or the exact name of the surgery. Medications: None. Family History: Essentially unremarkable. Father, mother, siblings are all well and healthy. Review of Systems: Skin: no rashes or jaundice. HEENT: See PI. CR: See past history. No history of pneumonia, tuberculosis, chronic cough, or hemoptysis. No history of pedal edema. GI: Weight is stable. He denies any nausea, vomiting, diarrhea, or food intolerance. GU: no history of GU tract infections, dysuria, hematuria, pyuria. Endocrine: no polyuria or polydipsia. Neurologic: no history of psychiatric disorder.

A transcript for this appears in Appendix E.

Morris G. Heslop

527-98-6540

Room 631-A

March 7, 199x

HISTORY

CHIEF COMPLAINT: Acute onset, severe abdominal pain and indigestion.

PRESENT ILLNESS: This 41-year-old male patient presented to Fletcher Hills Memorial Emergency Room at approximately 12 o'clock on Friday, March 6, 199x, complaining of a gaseous feeling in his upper abdomen, radiating to the right side, and down to the right lower quadrant of the abdomen. The patient is a pilot for Atlantic-Pacific Airlines. Last night, approximately 6 p.m., he had a spaghetti dinner in Denver, Colorado, and was restless approximately 5-6 hours later, and while he did not have diarrhea, he felt bloating and indigestion, which was relieved to a very small extent by Maalox. He continued to have increasing discomfort in his upper abdomen with radiation to the back, between the shoulder blades, but there was no vomiting, diarrhea, or fever. He became quite sweaty and pale while flying and had the co-pilot take over.

PAST HISTORY:
Operations: The patient had a herniorrhaphy two years ago at Fletcher Memorial and an appendectomy as a teenager.
Allergies: None.
Habits: He does not smoke. The only alcohol intake is occasional wine with meals. No current drugs or medications.

FAMILY HISTORY: There is no family history of importance.

REVIEW OF SYSTEMS:
EENT: No double vision, no ringing of the ears. No headache.
GI: No weight change, no change in bowel habits or any blood in the bowel movements.
GU: No difficulty urinating, no blood in the urine.
CR: Denies any chest pain or radiation of any type of pain into his left hand or arm over to the shoulders.

PHYSICAL EXAMINATION

GENERAL: The patient is an alert, cooperative male, clutching at the right lower portion of his abdomen at times during the interview. He says that this is still uncomfortable. Pulse: 78 and regular. BP: 116/80. Temperature: 98.6. Afebrile.

HEENT: React to L&A, no AV nicking. Ears are normal. Pharynx is normal. No thyroid enlargement or bruit noted.

CHEST: Heart tones are normal.

ABDOMEN: On pressure in the epigastrium, he complains of little discomfort more to the right side of the abdomen and on pressure in the right lower quadrant he does wince. Bowel sounds are

(continued)

FIGURE 12-5. History and physical typed in run-on format, first page.

THE PHYSICAL EXAMINATION

A thorough physical examination (PX or PE) comprises an examination and complete assessment of all body systems. It is usually done after the history is taken and includes an inspection of the body, beginning with the head and concluding with the feet: cephalocaudal. An analysis of the subjective findings that were taken down during the history and review of systems indicates the extent of the physical examination of different body parts that is required. For example, extensive complaints in the cardiovascular system will result in intensive examination of the lungs and heart.

Four basic procedures are included in the complete PX:

1. Inspection: looking at the body.

2. Palpation: feeling various parts and organs.

3. Percussion: listening to the sounds produced when a particular region is tapped (percussed).

4. Auscultation: listening to body sounds.

The style and format for the PX are identical to those for the history. Be consistent and follow the same style you use for the history when typing the physical examination. The PX should be typed on a separate sheet of paper, but, again, in run-on format you simply continue on the same sheet. The first example is run-on format, showing you both a history and a physical.

Follow the same guidelines as illustrated in the history section for typing the physical examination.

History and Physical, Run-On Format

Examples of a combined history and physical in run-on format are shown in Figures 12–5 (page 256) and 12–6 (page 258). Please notice the preferred line-up when there is more than one diagnosis.

```
Morris G. Heslop
527-98-6540
Room 631-A
Physical Examination, Page 2

hypoactive, and there is no palpable liver, kidney, spleen.  There
is no rebound on percussion.  There is no inguinal hernia.

GENITALIA:  Testicles are normal.

RECTAL:  No heat and there is no blood in the bowel movements
on gross examination.  There is no diarrhea present.

NEUROMUSCULAR:  Biceps, triceps, Achilles, patellar reflexes are
normal.  Range of motion of all extremities is normal.  There is
no pedal edema and pedal pulses are normal.

DIAGNOSIS:  1.  Possible acute cholecystitis.
            2.  Possible food poisoning.
            3.  Possible early, penetrating ulcer.
            4.  Rule out pancreatitis.

PLAN OF DIRECTION:  X-rays, ulcer-type diet, EKG, two-hour urine
amylase.

                                    _____
                                    Frank O. Bodner, M.D.
cjt
D:  3-7-9x
T:  3-9-9x
```

FIGURE 12–5. *Continued*

Morris G. Heslop   March 7, 199x
527-98-6540

Room 631

HISTORY

CHIEF COMPLAINT: Acute onset, severe abdominal pain and indigestion.
PRESENT ILLNESS: This 41-year-old male patient presented to
Fletcher Hills Memorial Emergency Room at approximately 12 o'clock
on Friday, March 6, 199x, complaining of a gaseous feeling in his
upper abdomen, radiating to the right side, and down to the right
lower quadrant of the abdomen. The patient is a pilot for Atlantic-
Pacific Airlines. Last night, approximately 6 p.m., he had a
spaghetti dinner in Denver, Colorado, and was restless approximately
5-6 hours later, and while he did not have diarrhea, he felt bloating
and indigestion, which was relieved to a very small extent by
Maalox. He continued to have increasing discomfort in his upper
abdomen with radiation to the back, between the shoulder blades, but
there was no vomiting, diarrhea, or fever. He became quite sweaty
and pale while flying and had the co-pilot take over.
PAST HISTORY:
Operations: The patient had a herniorrhaphy two years ago at
Fletcher Memorial and an appendectomy as a teenager.
Allergies: None.
Habits: He does not smoke. The only alcohol intake is occasional wine
with meals. No current drugs or medications.
FAMILY HISTORY: There is no family history of importance.
REVIEW OF SYSTEMS:
EENT: No double vision, no ringing of the ears. No headache.
GI: No weight change, no change in bowel habits or any blood in the
bowel movements.
GU: No difficulty urinating, no blood in the urine.
CR: Denies any chest pain or radiation of any type of pain into his
left hand or arm over to the shoulders.

PHYSICAL EXAMINATION

GENERAL: The patient is an alert, cooperative male, clutching at
the right lower portion of his abdomen at times during the interview.
He says that this is still uncomfortable. Pulse: 78 and regular.
BP: 116/80. Temperature: 98.6. Afebrile.
HEENT: React to L&A, no AV nicking. Ears are normal. Pharynx is
normal. No thyroid enlargement or bruit noted.
CHEST: Heart tones are normal.
ABDOMEN: On pressure in the epigastrium, he complains of little
discomfort more to the right side of the abdomen and on pressure in
the right lower quadrant he does wince. Bowel sounds are hypoactive,
and there is no palpable liver, kidney, spleen. There is no rebound
on percussion. There is no inguinal hernia.
GENITALIA: Testicles are normal.
RECTAL: No heat and there is no blood in the bowel movements on
gross examination. There is no diarrhea present.
NEUROMUSCULAR: Biceps, triceps, Achilles, patellar reflexes are normal.
Range of motion of all extremities is normal. There is no pedal
edema and pedal pulses are normal.
DIAGNOSIS: 1) Possible acute cholecystitis 2) Possible food poisoning
3) Possible early, penetrating ulcer. 4) Rule out pancreatitis.
PLAN OF DIRECTION: X-rays, ulcer-type diet, EKG, two-hour urine
amylase.

ref D: 3-7-9x   T: 3-9-9x   Frank O. Bodner, M.D.

FIGURE 12-6. History and physical typed in run-on format.

Physical Examination, Full Block Format

Follow the same format as illustrated for you in typing the history. The statistical data are repeated on the new page, and the title *Physical Examination* is centered on the page, typed in full capital letters.

Figure 12–7 is an example of a physical examination typed in full block format. Note that the line-and-a-half spacing between topics and main topics takes extra time but saves space on the page.

Physical Examination, Modified Block Format

Follow the same method that was illustrated for the history typed in this style. The statistical information is repeated on the new page, and the title *Physical Examination* is centered on the page, typed in full capital letters. *Tabulate only 15 spaces from the left margin, rather than 23 as you did for the history.*

Figure 12–8 is an example of a physical examination typed in modified block format.

12

de Mars, Verna Marie
Cortland M. Struthers, M.D.

PHYSICAL EXAMINATION

GENERAL:

This is a 68-year-old, well-developed, well-nourished, slightly obese white woman in no acute distress. She is alert and oriented to time, place, and person.

VITAL SIGNS:

PULSE: 76/min. BP: 130/80. RESP: 12. TEMPERATURE: 99°.

HEENT:

EYES: Pupils equal and react to light and accommodation. EOMs intact. Sclerae white. Fundi not visualized.

EARS: Hearing and drums are normal.

MOUTH: The teeth are in poor repair. Several bridges are present. The tongue protrudes in the midline with some questionable deviation to the right. Uvula projects upward on elicitation of the gag reflex. No lesions of the mucous membranes.

NECK:

Supple with some limitation of motion to the right. No masses present. The carotid pulsations are equal with no bruit. There is no neck vein distention and no thyromegaly. The trachea is deviated slightly to the right.

CHEST:

No increase in AP diameter.

LUNGS: Clear to P&A.

HEART: Quiet precordium. Normal sinus rhythm without murmurs, rubs or gallops. Heart sounds appear normal and to split physiologically. No S-4 heard.

ABDOMEN:

Flat without scars. No organomegaly. Liver, lidneys, and spleen not palpable. Tympanic to percussion. The bowel sounds are normoactive.

PELVIC:

Deferred.

RECTAL:

On anoscopy, there is an exophytic, soft, easily movable mass encompassing one-half the circumference of the rectum directly at the dentate line. Full sigmoidoscopic examination to 25 cm was unremarkable.

EXTREMITIES:

Range of motion is within normal limits. No pedal edema. All pulses appear equal and full bilaterally. No evidence of chronic arterial or venous disease.

NEUROLOGICAL:

Cranial nerves II-XII appear grossly intact. There are no pathological reflexes demonstrated. Reflexes within normal limits.

IMPRESSION:

Rectal tumor.

jrt
D: 5-17-9x
T: 5-20-9x

_____
Cortland M. Struthers, M.D.

FIGURE 12-7. Example of a physical examination typed in full block format.

de Mars, Verna Marie
Cortland, M. Struthers, M.D.

PHYSICAL EXAMINATION

GENERAL: This is a 68-year-old, well-developed, well-nourished, slightly obese
                  white woman in no acute distress. She is alert and oriented to time,
                  place, and person.

VITAL SIGNS: PULSE: 76/min. BP: 130/80. RESP: 12. TEMPERATURE: 99°.

HEENT:

    EYES: Pupils equal and react to light and accommodation. EOMs intact. Sclerae
                  white. Fundi not visualized.

    EARS: Hearing and drums are normal.

    MOUTH: The teeth are in poor repair. Several bridges are present. The tongue
                  protrudes in the midline with some questionable deviation to the right.
                  Uvula projects upward on elicitation of the gag reflex. No lesions of
                  the mucous membranes.

NECK: Supple with some limitation of motion to the right. No masses present.
                  The carotid pulsations are equal with no bruit. There is no neck vein
                  distention and no thyromegaly. The trachea is deviated slightly to the
                  right.

CHEST: No increase in AP diameter.

    LUNGS: Clear to P&A.

    HEART: Quiet precordium. Normal sinus rhythm without murmurs, rubs or gallops.
                  Heart sounds appear normal and to split physiologically. No S-4 heard.

ABDOMEN: Flat without scars. No organomegaly. Liver, kidneys, and spleen not
                  palpable. Tympanic to percussion. The bowel sounds are normoactive.

PELVIC: Deferred.

RECTAL: On anoscopy, there is an exophytic, soft, easily movable mass encompassing
                  one-half the circumference of the rectum directly at the dentate line.
                  Full sigmoidoscopic examination to 25 cm was unremarkable.

EXTREMITIES: Range of motion is within normal limits. No pedal edema. All pulses
                  appear equal and full bilaterally. No evidence of chronic arterial
                  or venous disease.

NEUROLOGICAL: Cranial nerves II-XII appear grossly intact. There are no pathological
                  reflexes demonstrated. Reflexes within normal limits.

IMPRESSION: Rectal tumor.

jrt
D: 5-17-9x
T: 5-20-9x   _____
                                                  Cortland M. Struthers, M.D.

FIGURE 12-8.   Example of a physical examination typed in modified block format.

```
De Mars, Verna Marie
Cortland M. Struthers, M.D.
                         PHYSICAL EXAMINATION
GENERAL:        This is a 68-year-old, well-developed, well-nourished, slightly obese
                white woman in no acute distress.  She is alert and oriented to time,
place,and person.
VITAL SIGNS:    PULSE: 76/min.  BP: 130/80.  RESP: 12.  TEMPERATURE: 99°.
HEENT:
     EYES:      Pupils equal and react to light and accommodation.  EOMs intact.  Sclerae
                white.  Fundi not visualized.
     EARS:      Hearing and drums are normal.
     MOUTH:     The teeth are in poor repair.  Several bridges are present.  The tongue
                protrudes in the midline with some questionable deviation to the right.
Uvula projects upward on elicitation of the gag reflex.  No lesions of the mucous
membranes.
NECK:           Supple with some limitation of motion to the right.  No masses present.
                The carotid pulsations are equal with no bruit.  There is no neck vein
distention and no thyromegaly.  The trachea is deviated slightly to the right.
CHEST:          No increase in AP diameter.
     LUNGS:     Clear to P&A.
     HEART:     Quiet precordium.  Normal sinus rhythm without murmurs, rubs or gallops.
                Heart sounds appear normal and to split physiologically.  No S-4 heard.
ABDOMEN:        Flat without scars.  No organomegaly.  Liver, kidneys, and spleen not
                palpable.  Tympanic to percussion.  The bowel sounds are normoactive.
PELVIC:         Deferred.
RECTAL:         On anoscopy, there is an exophytic, soft, easily movable mass encompassing
                one-half the circumference of the rectum directly at the dentate line.
Full sigmoidoscopic examination to 25 cm was unremarkable.
EXTREMITIES:    Range of motion is within normal limits.  No pedal edema.  All pulses
                appear equal and full bilaterally.  No evidence of chronic arterial
                or venous disease.
NEUROLOGICAL:   Cranial nerves II-XII appear grossly intact.  There are no pathological
                reflexes demonstrated.  Reflexes within normal limits.
IMPRESSION:     Rectal tumor.


jrt                                          _____
D:  5-17-9x                                  Cortland M. Struthers, M.D.
T:  5-20-9x
```

FIGURE 12-9. Example of a physical examination typed in indented format.

Physical Examination, Indented Format

Follow the same format that was illustrated for the history typed in this style. The statistical data are repeated on the new page, and the title *Physical Examination* is centered on the page, typed in full capital letters. *Tabulate only 15 spaces from the left margin, rather than 23 as you did for the history.*

Please notice the subtopics under HEENT in Figure 12–9. Some medical transcriptionists group these

as a single paragraph after the main heading HEENT. This illustrated style shows you, however, that the subtopic format is more attractive and easier to read. The subtopics under "Chest" could also have been typed in paragraph form. In both cases, type the outline in full caps. Also notice that the third line under the topic "Extremities" is not brought back to the left margin but is blocked under the previous two lines. This is done to avoid a few words dangling in the margin.

THE OUTLINE

As we did with the history, we will briefly examine each part of the outline used in the physical examination. You will type the statistical data just as you did for this history and the heading *Physical Examination*. Now begin with the topics:

General. This includes the general appearance and nutritional state of the patient as well as age, height, weight, and race. It may include the emotional condition (euphoric, lethargic, distracted, well-oriented, agitated).

Vital Signs. Includes the temperature, pulse, respiration, and blood pressure. Most often, however, this information is included with the previous topic.

HEENT (or Head and Neck). This includes the head, eyes, ears, nose, and throat. After the main heading abbreviation, the individual subtopics are pulled out and typed in either outline or paragraph form, depending on the emphasis placed on all or each. The personal wishes of either the dictator or the transcriptionist will also determine which method is used; both methods were illustrated for you in the previous examples. These subtopics include the following:

Head. Includes shape, and color and texture of the skin and hair.

Eyes. Includes the sclerae, corneae, conjunctivae, fundi, reaction of the pupils to light and accommodation (PERLA or PERRLA), extraocular movements (EOMs), and visual acuity and fields.

Ears. Includes canals, ossicles, tympanic membranes (TMs), hearing, discharge.

Nose. Includes airway, septum, sinuses.

Mouth and Throat. Includes teeth, gums, lips, tongue, salivary glands, tonsils, dentures, palate, uvula, mucosa.

Neck. Includes contour, mobility, lymph nodes, thyroid size and shape, position of trachea, carotid pulses, neck vein distention.

The next main topic is the chest, which is often divided into the subtopics of heart and lungs.

Chest. Includes the shape, symmetry, expansion, breasts.

Lungs. Includes breath sounds, expansion, fields, resonance, adventitious sounds (rales, rhonchi, wheeze, rubs, stridor).

Heart. Includes rhythm (sinus rhythm), borders, silhouette, rate, murmurs, rubs, gallops, heaves, lifts, thrills, palpitation.

Abdomen. Includes the symmetry, shape, contour, bowel sounds, tenderness, rigidity, guarding, herniation, and palpation of the liver, spleen, and kidneys.

Genitalia (or Pelvic or Genitourinary). In the female, this includes external genitalia (vulva), Skene's and Bartholin's glands, introitus, vagina, cervix, uterus, adnexa, discharge, escutcheon. In the male, this includes prostate, testes, epididymis, penis, lesions, discharge.

Rectal. Includes anus, sphincter tone, perineum, hemorrhoids.

Extremities. Includes bones, joints, movement, color, temperature, edema, varicosities.

Neurologic. Includes reflexes, cranial nerves, orientation in all three spheres (time, place, person), signs (Babinski, Brudzinski, Hoffmann, Kernig, Romberg, Strunsky), station and gait.

Diagnosis (Impression, Assessment, or Conclusion). Includes a provisional or final diagnosis, which is the conclusion the examiner has reached based on the history he or she has taken down and the examination just concluded. Diagnostic studies may be ordered (such as x-rays, electrocardiogram, blood workup) before making a final diagnosis. These are generally typed in lined-up format when there is more than one diagnosis. See Figures 12–5 and 12–6.

NOTE: Do not use abbreviations in the diagnosis portion of this part of the medical record.

Treatment (or Recommendation). Includes the plan of treatment and may indicate surgery or some of the diagnostic studies mentioned above.

THE DATA

The physician may dictate the data in narrative form without topics or subtopics, or he or she may dictate the topics and subtopics for you. You will use the proper topic as soon as reference is made to it, no matter how it is dictated. For instance, the dictator may say: "The abdomen is scaphoid. There are no masses or rigidity." You will type:

ABDOMEN: Scaphoid, no masses or rigidity.

On the other hand, some records departments require everything in sentence form. In this case you would type:

ABDOMEN: The abdomen is scaphoid; there are no masses or rigidity.

Always ask your employer for preferred format and style.

In transcribing physical examinations you should be prepared to write a tactful note to the physician or your supervisor if the dictator leaves out a vital part of the examination; for example, a hysterectomy is the contemplated procedure and the pelvic examination was not dictated. Be alert to laboratory values so that you recognize where a decimal point belongs when it is not dictated. (Laboratory values are printed in Appendix D.)

12–3: PRACTICE TEST

Directions: Retype the following data into physical examination outline, using the indented format. Be careful to use the proper indentations and tab stops (15). (This is difficult to do when copying. When you are actually transcribing and can look at what you are typing, this format is easier to use.) This is the physical examination for the patient in Self-Study 12–1, Geoffrey Paul Hawkins.

The patient is a well-developed, well-nourished, white male who appears his age of eleven and a half. He is of moderately small stature but is well tanned from being in the sun. He appears to be in no acute distress but is quite apprehensive. The skin is warm and dry, well-tanned, no jaundice, no lesions. The pupils are round, regular and equal; react to light and accommodation. No icterus seen. Conjunctivae normal. Nose: septum straight. No lesions. The mouth and throat are benign. The tonsils are small and the teeth are in good repair. The neck is supple. The thyroid is not enlarged. There is no remarkable lymphadenopathy. Trachea is in the midline with no tug. Ears: drums pearly, hearing is good to spoken voice. The lungs are clear to percussion and auscultation. Heart: regular sinus rhythm, no murmurs heard. A-2 is louder than P-2. The abdomen is scaphoid with no scars. Patient indicates midepigastric tenderness. Peristalsis is audible and possibly slightly hyperactive but very close to average in intensity. There is some tenderness, mainly in the right upper quadrant. Both left and right lower quadrants appear to be soft with no rebound present. Equivocal Murphy punch tenderness is present. No CVA tenderness. Genitalia: testes down, no penile lesions. Rectal: There is stool in the ampulla. Sphincter tone is good. Patient complains of some tenderness in both vaults, but no masses found. Skeletal: No gross bone or joint anomalies. Neurologic: no motor or sensory loss found. Deep tendon reflexes active and equal. Toe signs down. Pedal pulses palpable. Impression: Abdominal pain, etiology unproved, but probable gastroenteritis. Rule out early appendicitis.

See Appendix E at the back of the book for the proper response to this assignment.

12–4: PRACTICE TEST

Directions: Retype the following data into physical examination outline, using modified block format. This is the patient you had for Practice Test 12–2, Joseph R. Balentine.

The patient is a well-developed, muscular, slightly pale, young man in somewhat acute distress, secondary to the apprehension and bleeding. Blood pressure is one hundred ten over seventy. Pulse is seventy four. Respirations are sixteen. HEENT: Head is normocephalic. Eyes are round, regular and equal and bilaterally react to light and accommodation. There is bilateral cerumen in the ears, TMs are normal. The right nasal cavity was somewhat congested to the nasopharynx. There is active bleeding from the left nasal cavity. There are no palpable nodes in the neck and the thyroid is in the midline. The chest is symmetrical; normal male breasts. The lungs are clear bilaterally, no rales or wheezes. There is a pneumonectomy scar, left anterolateral chest. The heart is normal in size. There is normal sinus rhythm, no murmurs, thrills or rubs. The abdomen is soft, no tenderness. The rectal exam is deferred. The extremities are symmetrical, no cyanosis, edema or deformities. There is normal range of motion. Reflexes are physiological. Pulses are two plus and equal bilaterally. There is no cranial or neurological deficit. The impression is left posterior epistaxis, recurrent.

See Appendix E at the back of the book for the proper response to this assignment.

12-5: PRACTICE TEST

Directions: Retype the following data into proper H & P form. The patient is Lily Mae Jenkins and the dictator is Philip D. Quince. He wants copies sent to Dr. Willow Moran and Dr. Gordon Bender. The patient's clinic number is 5980-A. Please use run-on format and today's date.

The chief complaint is right rectal bleeding, one day. Present illness: This ninety-year-old lady has been looking after her own personal affairs and living with her daughter for the last three years. Last night, she had a bowel movement that had some bright rectal blood mixed in with it. This morning, she had another bowel movement, and it consisted mostly of bright-red blood. She has a history of gallbladder disease, dating back over 50 years. She refused to have her gallbladder taken out but has been on a low fat diet ever since that time. Her daughter describes numerous gallbladder attacks, lasting for several days, consisting of severe, right upper quadrant pain. She has had occasional, intermittent right lower quadrant pain that does not seem similar to the gallbladder attacks. Past History: Operations: In 1967 she had enucleation of the left eye. She had surgery in 1976 for glaucoma in the right eye. Medical: 1966, Colles' fracture, right wrist. 1970's severe arthritis of her spine. Medications: patient is presently taking Peritrate, one capsule, b.i.d. Reserpine-A, one tablet every morning. Indocin, one tablet, t.i.d. She takes Bufferin prn for pain. She takes nitroglycerin, 2-3 tablets a week for chest pain and has done so for five years. Both of her parents lived until their nineties. She had six children: one died at age three as the result of injuries sustained in an automobile accident, one died at age 56 of carcinoma of the breast.

12

Otherwise, the family history is unremarkable. There are four children who are alive and well. Functional inquiry: HEENT: Hearing in her right ear is absent. Hearing in her left ear is decreased. There is an artificial eye in the left and there is only slight vision in her right eye if one comes exactly in the middle of her visual field. Patient has been edentulous for several years. Chest: Nonsmoker. CV: Patient has had angina for over five years and abnormal cardiograms for the last three. She is cold all of the time and is constantly bundling herself up in an effort to keep warm. GI: Her bowel movements have been normal. See history of present illness. GU: She has no history of any bladder or kidney infections, despite the fact that she had a history of kidney failure last year. NM: Patient has shooting, severe pains up her spine, which are relatively incapacitating, but she manages to keep going by just taking Bufferin. Physical examination: This is a ninety year old black woman in no obvious distress, who is hard of hearing, but can answer questions. HEENT: The ears: There is wax in both ears. The drums, beyond the wax, appear within normal limits. There is no hearing in the right ear and only slight hearing in the left. The left eye is artificial. The right eye is pinpoint. There is no scarring in the right eye, consistent with an iridectomy. She has a cataract in the right eye, as well. Nose is unremarkable. Mouth is edentulous. Neck: There are no carotid bruits. No jugular venous distention. Thyroid is palpable and unremarkable. Range of motion of the neck is generally slightly restricted. Chest is clear to percussion and auscultation. Heart: The apical beat is not palpable. There is some tenderness over the costochondral cartilages on the left side. The heart size is not enlarged to percussion. There is muffled heart sound. There is no third or fourth heart sound. There are no murmurs heard in the supine position. Breasts are palpable and there are no masses noted. Abdomen is soft. There are marked senile keratoses over the abdominal wall. There is some diffuse tenderness on deep palpation over the cecum in the right lower quadrant. There is no other tenderness noted or abnormal bowel sounds noted in the abdomen. Bowel sounds are within normal limits. Pelvic: Not done. Rectal: Full sigmoidoscopic examination to 25 cm revealed fresh blood in the sigmoid area with no obvious bleeding source noted. Extremities: There is essentially no motion in the back. Range of motion of the hips is within normal limits and painless. There is only a + 1 dorsalis pedis on the right; otherwise, there are no peripheral pulses present. There is marked coldness of both feet. Central nervous system: The patient's strength is within normal limits. The reflexes are within normal limits. Coordination is not tested. There is an involuntary shaking, consistent with the diagnosis of old Parkinson's disease. Impression: Acute gastrointestinal hemorrhage, etiology not yet diagnosed. Chronic cholecystitis. Severe osteoarthritis of spine. Arteriosclerotic heart disease with angina pectoris.

See Appendix E at the end of the book for the proper response to this assignment.

12-6: SELF-STUDY

Directions: Please answer the following questions by referring to the figures in this chapter. Answer here or on a separate sheet of paper.

USING FIGURE 12-1

1. Under the subtopic "Allergies": why is "allergic to penicillin" typed in capital letters and underlined? _____

2. Under the subtopic "Neurologic": what does "unremarkable" mean? _____

   _____

3. Under "GI": why is "Present Illness" capitalized? _____

4. Under "OB-GYN": what does "climacteric" mean? _____

USING FIGURE 12-6

5. Under "Present Illness": why is "between the shoulder blades" enclosed in commas?

   _____

6. Under "General": what does "afebrile" mean? _____

7. Under "Family History": what does it mean when it is said that "there is no family history of importance"? _____

8. Under "HEENT": what does "L&A" mean? _____

9. Under "Neuromuscular": why didn't the transcriptionist abbreviate that "NM"?

   _____

USING FIGURE 12-8

10. Under "Eyes": why is "sclerae" not written "sclera," "fundi" not written "fundus," and EOMs not written "EOM" or "eom"? _____

    _____

11. Under "Neurological": why are the roman numerals used to describe the cranial nerves two through twelve? _____

USING FIGURE 12-10

12. Under "Recommendation": why not use the standard abbreviation "T&A" instead of "tonsillectomy and adenoidectomy"? _____

USING FIGURES 12-7, 12-8, AND 12-9: ALL HAVE IDENTICAL MATERIAL

13. Which one is the most attractive? _____

14. Which one is easiest to read? _____

15. Which one was the easiest to type? (you have typed all three formats, so you should have an opinion on this one, too.) _____

Please look at the end of the chapter, page 272, for the answers to these questions.

12-7: REVIEW TEST

Directions: Retype the following data into proper H & P form. The patient is J. J. "Kip" Siegler. The physician is Felix Rios, M.D. Use today's date and full block format.

The chief complaint is right sided, abdominal pain, eight hours duration. The present illness is as follows: this is the first Brookside Hospital admission for this twenty-four year old unemployed carpenter who was in his usual state of excellent health until approximately eight hours prior to admission when he developed some high, transverse midepigastric abdominal pain following completion of a Chinese meal. The pain became progressively more intense and gradually, over the following four hours, localized in the right lower quadrant. One hour prior to admission, while preparing to come to the hospital, the patient had one episode of emesis. The patient denies any subsequent nausea and diarrhea but has been "constipated" for the past two days. The past medical history: Serious injuries: None. Surgery: None. Illnesses: None. Allergies: Assorted pollens, undetermined. Medications: None. Smoke: None. Alcohol: Very infrequently. Immunizations: None in the past four years. The father is deceased, age 21, apparent suicide. The mother is living and well, age 41. One sister, age 22, living and well. The patient is married and has one child and has been unemployed for the past six months. He spends most of his time refurbishing an old sailboat. Systemic review is unremarkable. On physical examination there is an alert, oriented, Caucasian male, in very mild abdominal distress, lying supine, with his right hip flexed. His temperature is one hundred one point two degrees, pulse is eighty eight, respirations twenty, blood pressure is one hundred thirty over seventy eight. The skin is warm and moist without pallor, icterus, or cyanosis. There are no acute lesions or petechiae. Tympanic membranes are clear. Pupils are equal and reactive to light. Conjunctivae are mildly injected. Nares, likewise mildly injected. Pharynx and mouth, likewise, very minimally injected, without evidence of purulent debris. The neck is supple without cervical adenopathy. The lungs are clear to auscultation and percussion. The heart rhythm is regular without murmurs or enlargement. The abdomen is somewhat protuberant with absent bowel sounds, with moderate tenderness and guarding in the right lower quadrant without rebound. There is also very mild tenderness in the right "See vee a" area. There are no apparent herniae determined in the supine position. Rectal: Prostate is normal. There is moderate to exquisite tenderness in the right anterior quadrant. Stool is brown, and hematest is negative. Genitalia: Patient is circumcised. Testicles are bilaterally descended, appear normal in size and shape. Extremities: No deformities or edema. Neurologic: Two plus deep tendon reflexes, bilaterally. Diagnosis: Acute appendicitis.

SHORT-STAY RECORD

When the patient is being admitted for 48 hours or less, a shortened form of the history and physical examination record is acceptable in most hospitals. This form is appropriate for many diagnostic procedures and minor operative procedures. The statistical data would be the same as required on the longer forms, but the description of the patient's condition and the physical examination would be considerably condensed.

Figure 12–10 is an example of a short-stay record set up in modified block format.

```
                                        Roland, Jamie T.
                                        543098

                                        June 8, 199x

Copy:  Robert R. Shoemaker, M.D.

                         SHORT-STAY RECORD

    HISTORY:             Patient is a 6-year-old male complaining of
                         frequent episodes of tonsillitis.  He has
                         missed several weeks of school this spring because
                         of infections.  He is a constant mouth breather.
                         He snores loudly at night.  He has constant
                         nasal obstruction.  There is no history of
                         earaches.

    PAST HISTORY:        There are no allergies.  Bleeding history:
                         None.  Operations:  None.  Illnesses:  None
                         Medications:  Vitamins, iron.  Has been on
                         Penicillin for resolution of symptoms.
                         Family History:  Noncontributory.

    PHYSICAL EXAMINATION: Skin:  No rashes.  EENT:  Ears:  TM and
                         canals appeared normal.  Nose:  Congested
                         posteriorly but not anteriorly.  Throat:
                         Very large cryptic tonsils meeting in the
                         midline.  Neck:  Numerous palpable nodes.

    CHEST:               Lungs:  Clear to percussion and auscultation.
                         Heart:  Not enlarged, normal sinus rhythm,
                         no murmurs.

    ABDOMEN:             Soft, nontender.

    EXTREMITIES:         Full range of motion.

    NEUROLOGICAL:        Completely normal.

    IMPRESSION:          Chronic hypertrophic tonsils and adenoids with
                         recurrent infections.

    RECOMMENDATION:      Tonsillectomy and adenoidectomy.


                                 Peter Anthony Nelson, M.D.

    sd
    D:  6-8-9x
    T:  6-8-9x
```

FIGURE 12–10. Example of a short-stay record typed in modified block format.

12

INTERVAL HISTORY

If the patient returns to the hospital within a month of being discharged and is suffering from the same complaint, a complete history and physical do not have to be written on the patient. However, an interval history (or interval note) is completed to describe what has happened to the patient since discharge. The complete statistical data are used, but the medical information is considerably briefer, with emphasis on the present complaint and interval history. The physical examination would include any new findings since the last examination and may also include a brief check on vital body systems. More extensive examination would be done in the area prompting the readmission to the hospital.

Figure 12–11 is an example of an interval history note.

Benita L. Martinez   March 17, 199x

09-74-12   William B. Dixon, M.D.

                        INTERVAL HISTORY

PRESENT COMPLAINT: This is a 45-year-old female who the first of
                        March had a Roux-en-Y gastrojejunostomy done
                        for a reflux bile gastritis. Postoperatively,
                        she did moderately well; however, she began
                        to evidence signs of anastomotic obstruction
                        which got persistently worse. Upper GI series
                        was done 4 days ago which showed an almost
                        complete obstruction of the anastomosis.
                        Patient is now being admitted for decompression
                        of her stomach and revision of the gastro-
                        jejunostomy.

PAST HISTORY: Regional family, see old chart.

PHYSICAL EXAMINATION: Well-developed, well-nourished, but nervous,
                        white female in no acute distress.

HEENT: Eyes: React to L&A. Ears: Canals and
                        membranes normal. Nose: Negative. Neck:
                        Supple with no masses, no enlargement of glands.
                        Thyroid: Not palpable.

LUNGS: Clear to percussion and auscultation.

HEART: Rhythm and rate normal. No murmurs. No
                        enlargements.

ABDOMEN: Recent bilateral, subcostal incision, well-
                        healed. No other abdominal masses.

PELVIC: Not done.

EXTREMITIES: Negative.

IMPRESSION: Gastrojejunal anastomotic obstruction.

ADVICE: 1. Decompression by Levin tube.
                        2. Re-resection and anastomose tomorrow.

                        _____
                        William B. Dixon, M.D.

mlo
D: 3-17-9x
T: 3-20-9x

FIGURE 12–11. Example of an interval history typed in modified block style.

◪ Answer to 12 – 1: Self-Study

```
Geoffrey Paul Hawkins
54-98-10
                                   HISTORY

CHIEF COMPLAINT:        Abdominal pains and vomiting since 3 a.m.

PRESENT ILLNESS:        This 11½-year-old white male, who was prefectly well yesterday
                        and last evening, awoke from his sleep with vomiting at 3 a.m.
today.  This was followed by nausea, which has been severe, together with a little
bile coming up, but no great amount of continued vomiting.  There is severe, recurrent,
doubling-up type cramping to time of admission at 10 o'clock.  There has been no recent
upper respiratory tract infection, no prior similar episode, no history of recurrent
constipation or diarrhea.  Patient's last bowel movement was yesterday and of normal
quality.  His mother reports that he eats sunflower seeds to excess and may have done
so yesterday.

PAST HISTORY:           Patient was born at home with midwife delivery, uncomplicated.
                        He has had the usual immunizations for childhood.  There has been
no prior hospitalization, no tonsillectomy, no surgery, no fracture.  He has had stitches
a couple of times in the office.

FAMILY HISTORY:         Mother is 35 and at the present time is under treatment for cancer
                        of the breast.  She reports that she has had surgery and is on
chemotherapy at the present time.  She has not been given radiation.  Father is age 40,
living and well.  There are two sisters, both older than the patient, both living and
well.  They both had appendectomies, one of which had ruptured.  There are a maternal
great niece, uncle and paternal grandmother who have had diabetes.  There is no diabetes
in the immediate family and no other history of familial disorders such as bleeding,
anemia, tuberculosis, heart disease.

PERSONAL HISTORY:       The patient has no known drug allergies, has not been on any
                        medication at the present time.  Grade six, but does poorly.  Seems
to be the class clown according to his mother.  He has no hobbies.

SYSTEMIC REVIEW:

    HEENT:              There has been a muscle in one eye which has been off for years;
                        Dr. McMannis is following this.  His vision is good, hearing is
                        normal.

    CR:                 No known murmurs.  No chronic cough, no recent cough, no dyspnea.

    GI:                 No prior GI difficulty.  No food allergies.  No chronic or
                        recurrent constipation.

    GU:                 No nocturia, no enuresis, no GU infection.

    NM:                 No history of head injury, no history of polio, paralysis,
                        meningitis, or numbness.

mlo                                      _____
D:  (yesterday's date)                        Paul R. Elsner, M.D.
T:  (today's date)
```

Note: Check to be sure that the format followed is that illustrated; that the outline is typed in full caps and underlined; that all first and second lines are blocked evenly and that third and subsequent lines are brought back to the left margin; and that subtopics are indented 3 to 5 spaces from the left margin. Check also the signature line. The assignment should be neat and attractive, with narrow margins.

12

Answers to 12–6: Self-Study

1. To call attention to it.

2. There were no abnormal findings.

3. Because it refers back to that major topic in the outline.

4. The "menopause" or end of her regular menstrual cycles.

5. It is a nonessential phrase.

6. The patient did not have a fever or elevated body temperature.

7. No one suffers from or has died of any diseases or conditions that are considered hereditary.

8. How the pupils react to light and accommodation.

9. It was not in keeping with the rest of the format where topics were spelled out in full. Also, one must presume that if the outline were dictated, the dictator did not say "NM" but "neuromuscular."

10. It is clear from the transcript that the dictator is referring to both eyes; therefore the plural form is necessary. English abbreviations are written in capital letters, not lower case letters as are Latin abbreviations.

11. This is the custom; one could call it tradition.

12. One must presume that the dictator did not say "T&A," and furthermore, it is, not a good idea to abbreviate items of this importance.

13. This is up to you.

14. All three are pretty easy, certainly easier than the run-on format. It is up to you.

15. This is up to you and what you enjoy doing.

12

Preparation of Miscellaneous Medical Reports

OBJECTIVES

After reading this chapter and working the exercises, you should be able to

1. identify the kind of information that appears in various medical reports.
2. prepare a discharge summary, operative report, pathology report, radiology report, consultation report, autopsy protocol, and medicolegal report.
3. list the kind of information that appears in a medicolegal report.
4. explain the differences in typing a medical report versus an autopsy protocol.

• •

INTRODUCTION

A variety of medical reports concerning patients may be transcribed by medical transcriptionists in the Word Processing Department or Medical Records Department of a hospital. On a few occasions, a physician may want his or her private secretary to transcribe some of these reports; and in some medical facilities, the department secretary will do the transcribing. For instance, the Pathology Department may have laboratory reports and autopsy reports transcribed right in the department. Consultation reports may be transcribed in the hospital or physician's office, and medicolegal reports are usually done in the private medical office. Private transcription agencies are prepared to do all kinds of medical typing and transcribing. Since you do not know where you will seek employment, it is necessary for you to be pre-

pared to type these different parts of the medical record.

Reports are sent to consultants who participated in the management of the patient, to insurance companies who wish background information on patients, to third-party carriers to justify bills, to referring physicians, and to the Social Security Administration for assessing a patient for total disability.

Accuracy and readability are the most important factors emphasized in reference to format. All headings and subheadings must follow the same format, so it is important to determine how you will set up the report before you begin typing. Topics of equal importance are given equal emphasis by using capital letters, lower case letters, spacing, underlining, centering, and so forth. The figures in this chapter will give you just a glimpse of possible headings, since each physician/dictator may choose different words to em-

13

273

Silverman, Elaine J.

80-32-11

July 16, 199x

DISCHARGE SUMMARY

ADMISSION DATE: June 14, 199x   DISCHARGE DATE: July 15, 199x

HISTORY OF PRESENT ILLNESS:
This 19-year-old black female, nulligravida, was admitted to the hospital
on June 14, 199x with fever of 102°, left lower quadrant pain, vaginal discharge, constipation, and a tender left adnexal mass. Her past history
and family history were unremarkable. Present pain had started 2 to 3
weeks prior to admission. Her periods were irregular, with the latest
period starting on May 30, 199x and lasting for 6 days. She had taken
contraceptive pills in the past, but had stopped because she was not
sexually active.

PHYSICAL EXAMINATION:
She appeared well-developed and well-nourished, and in mild distress. The
only positive physical findings were limited to the abdomen and pelvis. Her
abdomen was mildly distended, and it was tender, especially in the left lower
quadrant. At pelvic examination her cervix was tender on motion, and the
uterus was of normal size, retroverted, and somewhat fixed. There was a tender
cystic mass about 4-5 cm in the left adnexa. Rectal examination was negative.

ADMITTING DIAGNOSIS:
1. Probable pelvic inflammatory disease (PID).
2. Rule out ectopic pregnancy.

LABORATORY DATA ON ADMISSION:
Hb 8.8, Hct 26.5, WBC 8,100 with 80 segs and 18 lymph. Sedimentation rate
100 mm in one hour. Sickle cell prep + (turned out to be a trait). Urinalysis
normal. Electrolytes normal. SMA-12 normal. Chest x-ray negative, 2-hour
UCG negative.

HOSPITAL COURSE AND TREATMENT:
Initially, she was given cephalothin 2 gm IV q6h, and kanamycin 0.5 gm IM BID.
Over the next 2 days the patient's condition improved. Her pain decreased and
her temperature came down to normal in the morning and spiked to 101° in the
evening. Repeat CBC showed Hb 7.8, Hct 23.5. The pregnancy test was negative.
On the second night following admission she spiked to 104°. The patient was
started on anti-tuberculosis treatment, consisting of isoniazid 300 mg/day,
ethambutol 600 mg BID, and rifampin 600 mg daily. She became afebrile on the
sixth postoperative day and was discharged on July 15, 199x, in good condition.
She will be seen in the office in one week.

SURGICAL PROCEDURES:
Biopsy of omentum for frozen section; culture specimens.

DISCHARGE DIAGNOSIS:
Genital tuberculosis.

Surgeon _____
                    Harold B. Cooper, M. D.

mtf
d: 7-15-9x
t: 7-16-9x

FIGURE 13-1. Discharge Summary, report form, typed in full-block format. The absence of a letterhead and the final two notations on the left side of the page indicate that this report was prepared by a hospital transcriptionist. In paragraph four, "PID" was dictated and the transcriptionist spelled out the diagnosis and put the abbreviation in parentheses. In paragraph five, UCG means urinary chorionic gonadotropin.

phasize. The sequence of the topic words may also be reversed in some dictations. The general guideline to follow is to transcribe exactly the sequence that is dictated, trying to pick out the emphasis words for major headings and those requiring less emphasis as subheadings. In some institutions, forms with pre-printed headings require that you reformat the dictation so that it is typed in the sequence given on the forms.

DISCHARGE SUMMARIES

A discharge summary (clinical resume or final progress note) is required for each patient who is discharged from a hospital. It contains the same information that is found in the patient's history and physical with the addition of the admitting and discharge diagnoses; operations performed; laboratory and x-ray studies; consultations; hospital course; and, finally, the condition of the patient at the time of discharge with the medications on discharge, instructions for continuing care, therapy, and possibly a fol-low-up postoperative office visit date. The condition of the patient on discharge should be stated in terms that permit a specific measurable comparison with the condition on admission, avoiding the use of vague terminology, such as "improved." If a resident or intern (house staff physician) dictates the discharge summary, it is usually approved by the attending physician (attending staff physician). If authorized in writing by the patient or a legally qualified representative, a copy of the discharge summary should be sent to any known medical practitioner or medical facility responsible for follow-up care of the patient.

In the case of a patient's death, a summary statement should be added to the record either as a final progress note or as a separate resume. This final note should give the reason for admission, the findings and course in the hospital, and events leading to death.

Since the previous chapter discussed the history and physical in detail, we will not repeat the entire contents. However, Figure 13–1 gives an example of a complete discharge summary to show you its appearance, format, and content. The formats discussed will follow the four illustrated in Chapter 12.

13–1: SELF-STUDY

Directions: Retype the following data into discharge summary outline using the full block format. Pay careful attention to punctuation and capitalization. The patient's name and other statistical data may be set up as you desire. Note topic changes and proper mechanics. The location of the headings, admitting diagnosis and discharge diagnosis, may vary —occurring at the beginning of the report, in the natural order of dictation (as seen in Fig. 13–1), or at the end of the report — as specified by the individual facility. See page 246 for the full block format report style.

The patient is Marcia M. Bacon. The dictating physician is Henry R. Knowles, M.D. The summary was dictated on May 10 and transcribed on May 11. The patient's hospital ID number is 52-01-96. The patient's room number is 248-C. The date of hospital admission is May 7, 199X, and she was discharged on May 9, 199X. Admission diagnosis: Torn medial meniscus, left knee. Discharge diagnosis: Torn medial meniscus, left knee; chondromalacia of the medial femoral condyle. History of present illness: The patient injured her left knee on April 11, 199X, while playing tennis. She subsequently had difficulty with persistent effusion and pain in the left knee. An arthrogram prior to admission revealed a tear of the medial meniscus. Physical examination: absence of tenderness to palpation of any of the joint structures. There was approximately 30-55 cc of fluid within the joint. Range of motion was full. Laboratory data: admission hemoglobin was 15.9, hematocrit 47% with a white count of 7,400 with normal differential. Urinalysis was within normal limits. Chem panel 19 showed an elevated cholesterol of 379 mg%. Chest x-ray was reported as negative. Treatment and hospital courses: The patient was taken to the Operating Room on the same day as admission, at which time she underwent arthroscopy. This revealed that she had a tear of the medial meniscus. Arthrotomy was performed, with

13

medial meniscectomy. A chondral fracture was noted in the medial femoral condyle, measuring approximately 5 mm in greatest diameter. The edges of this were sheathed. Postoperatively, the patient's course was benign. There was no significant temperature elevation. She became ambulatory with crutches on the first postoperative day with no difficulty with straight leg raising. Disposition: The patient is being discharged home ambulatory with crutches and an exercise program. She is to be seen in the office in one week for suture removal. Condition at the time of discharge: Improved. Complications: None. Medications: None.

Please see the end of the chapter for a possible transcript of this assignment.

OPERATIVE REPORTS

Whenever a surgical procedure is done in the hospital, an outpatient surgical center, or in a clinic, an operative report should be dictated or written in the medical record immediately after surgery. It should contain a description of the findings, the technical procedures used, the specimens removed, the preoperative and postoperative diagnosis or diagnoses, the type of operation performed, and the name of the primary surgeon and any assistants. The body of the report is a narrative of the procedure and findings and contains the type of anesthetic, incision, instruments used, drains, packs, closure, and sponge count. The completed operative report should be authenticated by the surgeon and filed in the medical record as soon as possible after surgery. When there is a transcription or filing delay, a comprehensive operative progress note should be entered in the medical record immediately after surgery to provide pertinent information for other physicians who may be attending the patient.

See Figure 13–2 for an example of an operative report. Notice that the first paragraph is one long paragraph. Although this may seem awkward to you, this is how many surgeons dictate their operative records. However, some hospitals require that surgeons separate the report into subheadings, such as anesthesia, incision, findings, procedure, closure, and so forth. In designating suture material size, see Chapter 5, Rule 5.18, page 99.

13–2: PRACTICE TEST

Directions: Retype the following data into an operative report using the indented format and no variations. Set your tab stop at 27 spaces. The patient's name and other statistical data may be set up as you desire. Pay attention to proper mechanics and capitalization. Date the report January 4, 199X. See page 250 for the indented format.

The patient's name is John P. Dwight, and his hospital ID number is 86-30-21. The surgeon is Felix A. Konig. The patient's room number is 582-B. The preoperative and postoperative diagnosis is: otosclerosis, left ear. The operation is a left stapedectomy. The findings, otosclerosis, footplate. Under local anesthesia, the ear was prepared and draped in the usual manner. The ear was injected with two percent lidocaine and one to six thousand epinephrine. A stapes-type flap was elevated from the posterosuperior canal wall, and the bony overhang was removed with the stapes curet. The chorda tympani nerve was removed from the field. The incudostapedial joint was separated. The stapes tendon was cut. The superstructure was removed. The mucous membrane was reflected from the ear, stapes, and facial nerve promontory. The footplate was then reamed with small picks and hooks. A flattened piece of Gelfoam was placed over the oval window and a five millimeter wire loop prosthesis was inserted and crimped in the incus. The drum was reflected, and a small umbilical tape was placed in the ear canal. The patient tolerated the procedure well.

Please see Appendix E for a possible transcript of this test.

COLLEGE HOSPITAL
4567 BROAD AVENUE
WOODLAND HILLS, XY 12345

Patient: Elaine J. Silverman   Date: June 20, 199x

Hospital No.: 84-32-11   Room No.: 1308

OPERATIVE REPORT

PREOPERATIVE DIAGNOSIS: 1. Menorrhagia.
                            2. Chronic pelvic inflammatory disease.
                            3. Perineal relaxation.

POSTOPERATIVE DIAGNOSIS: 1. Menorrhagia.
                            2. Chronic pelvic inflammatory disease.
                            3. Perineal relaxation.

OPERATION: 1. Total abdominal hysterectomy.
                            2. Lysis of pelvic adhesions.
                            3. Bilateral salpingo-oophorectomy.
                            4. Appendectomy.
                            5. Posterior colpoplasty.

PROCEDURE: Under general anesthesia, the patient was prepared and
                    draped for abdominal operation. The abdomen was opened
through a Pfannenstiel incision, and examination of the upper abdomen was entirely
normal. Examination of the pelvis revealed an enlarged uterus. The uterus was
three degrees retroverted and adhered to the cul-de-sac. Both tubes and ovaries
were involved in an inflammatory mass, with extensive adhesions to the lateral
pelvic wall on both sides. The tubes revealed evidence of chronic pelvic inflammatory disease. The omentum was also attached to the fundus and to the left
adnexa. The omentum was dissected by means of blunt and sharp dissection; the
dissection was carried to each adnexa, freeing both tubes and ovaries by means
of blunt and sharp dissection. The uterus was found to be approximately two
times enlarged, after freeing all the adhesions. The uterovesical fold of peritoneum was then incised in an elliptical manner, bladder was dissected off the
lower uterine segment. The round ligament, infundibulopelvic ligament on each
side was identified, clamped, cut, and ligated. The uterine artery on each side,
was clamped, cut and doubly ligated. Paracervical fascia was developed. Heaney
clamps were placed on the cardinal ligaments, the cardinal ligaments cut, and
pedicles ligated. The vagina was circumscribed; the uterus, both tubes and
ovaries were removed from the operative field. The cardinal ligaments were then
sutured into the lateral angles of the vagina by means of interrupted sutures;
the vagina was then closed with continuous over-and-over stitch. The paracervical
fascia was sutured into place with interrupted figure-of-eight suture; the lateral
suture incorporated the stumps of the uterine arteries; the pelvis was then re-
peritonealized with continuous length of GI 2-0 atraumatic suture. Appendix was
identified, and appendectomy was done in the usual manner. The appendiceal stump
was cauterized with phenol and neutralized with alcohol. Re-examination at this
time of the pelvis revealed all bleeding well controlled. The abdominal wall
was then closed in layers, and the skin was approximated with camelback clips.
During the procedure, the patient received one unit of blood. Patient was then
prepared for vaginal surgery.

(continued)

FIGURE 13-2. Operative Report, report form, typed in indented format with the body of the report done in one or two large paragraphs.

Elaine J. Silverman   Page 2   June 20, 199x

Patient was placed in lithotomy position, prepared and draped. Posterior colpoplasty was begun, for repair of rectocele and perineal relaxation. The posterior vaginal mucosa was dissected from the perirectal fascia; the excess posterior vaginal mucosa was excised and perirectal fascia was brought together with continuous interlocking suture of 0 chromic. The posterior vaginal mucosa was closed with continuous interlocking suture of 0 chromic. Perineal body was closed with subcutaneous, subcuticular stitch. There was a correct sponge count. The patient withstood the operation well. Patient left the operating room in good condition.

Surgeon _____
Harold B. Cooper, M. D.

mtf
D: 6-20-9x
T: 6-22-9x

FIGURE 13-2 *Continued*

PATHOLOGY REPORTS

As a medical transcriptionist, you can specialize by typing pathology or radiology reports. Surgical pathology transcriptionists work in laboratories, in hospital medical laboratories, and in coroners' offices. There is a wide variety of job duties besides transcription and these can consist of giving reports via the telephone, filing, Systematic Nomenclature of Pathology (SNOP) and ICD-9-CM coding, keeping tumor and autopsy logs, typing statistical reports, delivering reports, labeling and filing specimens, and other miscellaneous laboratory tasks depending on the size of the work place and the number of pathologists on the staff. Some of the departments in the laboratory include histology, chemistry, hematology, microbiology/bacteriology, immunology, and blood bank.

When a surgical procedure is done to remove tissue or fluid from the body, these specimens may be examined by the pathologist to determine the nature and extent of the disease. In some instances, a pathologist may render his or her opinion even before the patient is sutured, as in the event of a malignancy, in which case more extensive surgery may be required. This tissue examination, or biopsy report, is called a pathology report or tissue report (Fig. 13-3). It consists of a *gross description* of the specimen submitted, which means the way the specimen looks with the naked eye before it is prepared for microscopic study. The *microscopic description* is the description of the tissue after it has been prepared and carefully examined under the microscope. The *diagnosis* is then given. Many times the gross descriptions (grosses) of all the surgical specimens are dictated, transcribed, and given to the pathologist, who then dictates the microscopic descriptions (micros). These are transcribed, and the completed pathology reports are given to the pathologist for signature. A copy of the report is given to each physician involved in the case and a copy is retained in the laboratory. The original is placed in the patient's medical record. Besides tissue and tumor reports, a pathology transcriptionist may type autopsy reports, forensic reports, and coroner reports. Pathology reports must be completed within 24 hours. Pathologists usually dictate in the present tense because they interpret the pathological findings as they look at the specimen. The history is in past tense, and the findings are in present tense.

In dictation involving pathology, it is often the non-

College Hospital
4567 Broad Avenue
Woodland Hills, XY 12345

PATHOLOGY REPORT

Date: June 20, 199x   Pathology No.   430211
Patient: Elaine J. Silverman Room No.   1308
Physician: Harold B. Cooper, M.D.
Specimen Submitted: Tumor, right axilla

GROSS DESCRIPTION: Specimen A consists of an oval mass of yellow fibro-
                            adipose tissue measuring 4 x 3 x 2 cm. On cut
                            section, there are some small, soft, pliable areas of
                            gray apparent lymph node alternating with adipose
                            tissue. A frozen section consultation at time of
                            surgery was delivered as NO EVIDENCE OF MALIGNANCY
                            on frozen section, to await permanent section for
                            final diagnosis. Majority of the specimen will be
                            submitted for microscopic examination.

                            Specimen B consists of an oval mass of yellow soft
                            tissue measuring 2.5 x 2.5 x 1.5 cm. On cut section,
                            there is a thin rim of pink to tan-brown lymphatic
                            tissue and the mid portion appears to be adipose
                            tissue. A pathological consultation at time of
                            surgery was delivered as no suspicious areas noted
                            and to await permanent sections for final diagnosis.
                            The entire specimen will be submitted for microscopic
                            examination.

RFW:mtf

MICROSCOPIC DESCRIPTION: Specimen A sections show fibroadipose tissue and nine
                            fragments of lymph nodes. The lymph nodes show areas
                            with prominent germinal centers and moderate sinus
                            histiocytosis. There appears to be some increased
                            vascularity and reactive endothelial cells seen.
                            There is no evidence of malignancy.

                            Specimen B sections show adipose tissue and 5 lymph
                            node fragments. These 5 portions of lymph nodes show
                            reactive changes including sinus histiocytosis.
                            There is no evidence of malignancy.

DIAGNOSIS: A & B: TUMOR, RIGHT AXILLA: SHOWING 14 LYMPH NODE
                            FRAGMENTS WITH REACTIVE CHANGES AND NO EVIDENCE OF
                            MALIGNANCY.

                            _____
                            Stanley T. Nason, M. D.

STN:mtf
D: 6-18-9x
T: 6-18-9x

FIGURE 13-3. Pathology Report, report form, typed in modified-block format with no variations.

medical term that puzzles the novice transcriptionist because it can be difficult to understand the mechanics behind the dictated words. A common phrase encountered and typed incorrectly is "The specimen is submitted in toto." This means that all of the specimen is submitted by the pathologist for further processing. Since many pathologic terms cannot be found in standard references, see Appendix C for a good reference if you do a great deal of transcription dealing with pathology.

13–3: PRACTICE TEST

Directions: Retype the following data into a pathology report using the modified format and no variations. Remember to double space between topics. Date the report June 6, 199X. See page 248 for modified format.

The patient's name is Joan Alice Jayne, and her hospital ID number is 72-11-03. The referring physician is John A. Myhre, M.D., and the pathologist is James T. Rodgers, M.D. The date the specimen was removed was June 6, 199X. The patient's room number is 453-A. Pathology number is 532009. Specimen(s): The specimen consists of a four point five centimeter in diameter nodule of fibro-fatty tissue removed from the right breast at biopsy and enclosing a central, firm, sharply demarcated nodule one centimeter in diameter. Surrounding breast parenchyma reveals dilated ductiles (microcystic disease). Frozen section impression: Myxoid fibroadenoma of breast. Microscopic and diagnosis: Myxoid fibroadenoma occurring in right parenchyma, the site of microcystic disease of right breast.

Please see Appendix E for a possible transcript of this test.

RADIOLOGY REPORTS

As mentioned previously, another way of specializing is to become a radiology transcriptionist for a group of radiologists or for the radiology department of a hospital. One can become certified as a radiology transcriptionist taking a test offered annually by the American Association for Medical Transcription. See Chapter 1 for their address if you wish to obtain further information.

An x-ray report is a description of the findings and interpretations of the radiologist who reviews the x-ray films taken of a patient (Fig. 13–4). These can be bone and joint films, soft tissue films, or special studies of the internal organs that require the patient to take contrast media (dyes) orally or by injection. These contrast media may be radiolucent (permitting the passage of some roentgen rays) or radiopaque (not permitting passage of roentgen rays). For assistance in spelling the types of contrast media used in the taking of x-ray films, refer to the back of the current PDR, which has a comprehensive reference list. When an examination of an organ by radioactive isotopes is done, it is called a "scan." Radiologists may change from present to past tense within the body of a report. As a rule, the procedure was performed (past tense),

and the findings are in the present tense. At some facilities each physician has a set of normal phrases or paragraphs logged into computer memory. The physician may choose to dictate the radiological examination and say, "add note N1," to access one of these phrases; if necessary, the phrase may be edited here and there depending on the case dictated.

Technology has produced methods to view structures in dimension (stereoscopy) or in layers (tomography). Through the use of x-rays with computers, a specific slice of the abdomen, chest, or head can be seen, and this is called computed tomography (CT scan). Using a dry photocopier with x-ray images, xeroradiography is available. A process for measuring temperature by photographically recording infrared radiations emanating from the body's surface is called thermography. Employment of high-frequency sound waves without use of x-ray can give a composite picture of an area, and this is called a sonogram or echogram. A system that produces sectional images of the body and does not employ x-rays is magnetic resonance imaging (MRI), also called nuclear magnetic resonance (NMR) (Fig. 13–5). It uses a band of radio frequencies and a range of magnetic field strengths, so information is obtained simultaneously from a large number of points in a volume. The information is

```
                        College Hospital
                        4567 Broad Avenue
                     Woodland Hills, XY 12345



                        RADIOLOGY REPORT

Examination Date:   June 14, 199x      Patient:      Elaine J. Silverman
Date Reported:      June 14, 199x      X-ray No.:    43200
Physician:          Harold B. Cooper, M.D.  Age:      19
Examination:        PA Chest, Abdomen   Hospital No.: 80-32-11

Findings:

PA Chest:          Upright PA view of chest shows the lung fields are clear,
                   without evidence of an active process.  Heart size is
                   normal.

                   There is no evidence of pneumoperitoneum.

IMPRESSION:        NEGATIVE CHEST.

ABDOMEN:           Flat and upright views of the abdomen show a normal gas
                   pattern without evidence of obstruction or ileus.  There
                   are no calcifications or abnormal masses noted.

IMPRESSION:        NEGATIVE STUDY.


                   Radiologist_____
                             Marian B. Skinner, M.D.

mtf
D:  6-14-9x
T:  6-14-9x
```

FIGURE 13–4. Radiology Report, report form, typed in modified-block format with no variations.

sorted out with computers using mathematical techniques similar to those used to form CT images.

Some facilities provide radiotherapy for treatment or palliation of malignancy, so radiotherapy summaries become part of the patient's medical record. Nuclear medicine diagnostic and therapeutic procedures require reports stating the interpretations, consultation, and therapy (specific preparation of the patient, identity, date, and amount of radiopharmaceutical used) (Fig. 13–6).

The radiology report includes the preliminary information at the top of the report and the type of x-ray films taken or the x-ray examination done. This is followed by the impression, or interpretation, of the radiologist. Because several x-ray examinations may be included in the same report, it is very helpful to have a general knowledge of how the various x-ray examinations are done in addition to knowing how to transcribe the terms correctly.

Some of the types of radiology reports dictated are the following:

aortogram
arteriogram
arthrogram
barium enema
bronchogram
cardioangiogram
cholangiogram
cholecystogram
cineradiogram
computed tomogram (CT scan)
cystogram
echogram
encephalogram
esophagram
fluoroscopy (chest, colon, gallbladder, and stomach)
hysterosalpingogram
intravenous cholangiogram (IVC)
intravenous pyelogram (IVP)
laminagram
lymphangiogram
magnetic resonance imaging (MRI)
myelogram, spinal
nephrotomogram
nuclear magnetic resonance (NMR)
pneumoencephalogram

Continued on page 284

```
                    XYZ Magnetic Imaging Center
                         4500 College Road
                       Woodland Hills, XY 12345
                          (013) 647-0980

                          INTERPRETATION
PATIENT:  Jeffrey Clauson                    AGE:  27
NUMBER:   4309x                              DATE:  August 30, 199x

MAGNETIC RESONANCE IMAGING, CERVICAL SPINE:

HISTORY:       Cervical radiculopathy

TECHNIQUE:     Sag. G.E. 600/30/23. M.R., 43 Nex, 5 mm., C.C.
               Sag. S.E. 500/24, M.R., 4 Nex, 5mm., C.C.
               Ax. S.E. 1000/30, H.R., 2 Nex, 5 mm., C.C.

FINDINGS:
```

The sagittal sequences cover from the lower posterior fossa to approximately T4-5. The axial sequence covered from the upper odontoid process through mid-T1.

There is mild reversal of the normal lordotic curve of the cervical spine.

The C2-3 and C3-4 interspaces are normal.

There is posterior osteophyte formation projecting broadly across the anterior aspect of the spinal canal at C4-5 level. On the sagittal sequences, this appears to contact the cord. There is no deformity identified with the cord to indicate compression. The foramina are patent.

The C5-6 level is unremarkable aside from some narrowing of the anterior subarachnoid space, probably a result of mild spurring and the effect of the reversal of the normal lordotic curve.

At C6-7 there are degenerative disk changes with disk space narrowing and osteophyte formation. There is no cord compression, although there is moderate left foraminal stenosis.

The C7-T1 level demonstrates moderate left foraminal stenosis.

There is either spur or disk bulge at the T1-2 level. This was only seen on the sagittal sequences. The abnormality appears to contact the cord but does not appear to cause any compression. There are no additional extradural abnormalities. There are no intradural extramedullary lesions. The cord is normal without abnormal intensity to indicate the presence of infarction or mass, and there is no evidence of a syrinx. This is mentioned in that the cerebellar tonsils project somewhat below the foramen magnum indicating the possibility of a Chiari I malformation.

```
IMPRESSION:  CEREBRAL SPONDYLOSIS AS DESCRIBED ABOVE.

             PROBABLE CHIARI I MALFORMATION.  NO CORD SYRINX.

                          Jason B. Iverson, M.D.
rmt
```

FIGURE 13-5. Magnetic resonance imaging (MRI), report form, typed in full-block format with no variations.

College Hospital
4567 Broad Avenue
Woodland Hills, XY 12345

RADIATION THERAPY CONSULTATION

Name: Theodore V. Valdez   Requested by: John L. Morris, M.D.

MR# 380780   Rm # 499   Date: 6/15/9x

HISTORY OF PRESENT MEDICAL ILLNESS: This is a 72-year-old who underwent decompressive laminectomy and Harrington rod placement in 1986 for angiosarcoma. Postoperative radiation therapy at Midway Hospital (Camarillo): 4025 cGy[1] in 23 fractions (175 cGy), 4 treatments per week, 2 to 1 PA to AP portals measuring 13 × 9 cm at 100 SSD on 8 Mv Linac, 5 HVL cord block at 3000 cGy. Dr. Davis estimates coverage T2 to T8. Myelogram and CT scan negative two years ago. However, developed cough and hemoptysis in past month. Chest x-ray and CT: right perihilar mass extending into mediastinum with multiple central and one anterior mediastinal mass with postobstructive infiltrate, bilateral pleural effusion. Bronchoscopy: 75% narrowing right upper lobe orifice to subsegments, 50% narrowing right lower lobe orifice. Bleeding at right upper lobe orifice. Draining right pleural effusion and sclerodesis with negative cytology. However, preliminary tissue diagnosis from right paratracheal area and mediastinoscopy: probable angiosarcoma.

PAST MEDICAL HISTORY: Hypertension.

SOCIAL HISTORY: 50 year tobacco habit.

PHYSICAL EXAMINATION: General: Well-developed male in no acute distress. No palpable adenopathy. Lungs: Clear. Heart: Regular rate and rhythm. Abdomen: Unremarkable. Extremities: Without circulatory collapse and edema. Neurologic: Without focal deficit.

ASSESSMENT: Recurrent metastatic angiosarcoma with postobstructive pneumonitis and hemoptysis.

PLAN: 4000 cGy[1] to symptom producing mediastinal disease. Initial 1000 cGy at 200 cGy fractions then oblique off previously irradiated spinal cord and boost with 250 cGy fractions. No plans for chemotherapy. Discussed radiation therapy procedures, risks, and alternatives with patient, emphasizing possible long-term risks to spinal cord, lung, and heart as well as increased potential for morbidity resulting from prior irradiation. He agrees with treatment as outlined.

Sincerely,

Barry T. Goldstein, M.D.
Radiology Medical Group, Inc.

mtf
D: 6-15-9X
T: 6-16-9x

13

FIGURE 13-6. Radiotherapy Report generated from a hospital, typed in report form and run-on format. (From Fordney, M. T., and Diehl, M. O.: Medical Transcription Guide. Do's and Don'ts. W. B. Saunders Company, Philadelphia, 1990.)

1. cGy means centigray, and the abbreviation can also be typed CGy.

retrograde pyelogram (RP)	sonogram	upper GI series	venogram
scan (blood and heart,	sialogram	ultrasonogram (bile	ventriculogram
bone, full body, brain,	stereoscopy	ducts, gallbladder,	xeromammogram
liver, lung, spleen,	thermogram	kidneys, liver, ovaries,	xeroradiogram
and thyroid)	tomogram	and uterus)	

13–4: SELF-STUDY

Directions: Retype the following data into a radiology report using the modified block format, indented paragraphs, and no variations. Remember to double space between topics as done in full block format. Date the report June 8, current year. See page 246 for full block format.

The patient's name is Donna Mae Weeser. Her x-ray number is 16-A2 and her hospital number is 52-80-44. This patient is age 46. The referring physician is George B. Bancroft, M.D., and the radiologist is Clayton M. Markham, M.D. The examination is mammography, right and left breasts. There are retromammary prosthetic devices in position. The anterior parenchyma is somewhat compressed. There is no evidence of neoplastic calcification or skin thickening demonstrated. No dominant masses are noted within the anteriorly displaced parenchyma. No increased vascularity is evident. Impression: mammography right and left breasts shows the presence of retromammary prosthetic devices in position. The demonstrated tissue appears within normal limits.

Please see the end of the chapter for a possible transcript of this assignment.

CONSULTATION REPORTS

Often the attending physician will seek the advice and opinions of a consulting physician. The consultant will dictate a report that will be incorporated into the patient's hospital record (Figs. 13–7 and 13–8). The physician may see the patient in consultation in the office, the emergency room, or in the hospital; then a report is dictated and sent to the referring physician. The report may contain the present history, past history, x-ray and laboratory studies, physical examination, impression, and comments on findings, prognosis, and the future course of treatment recommended. It may be dictated in letter form or report form with content and headings similar to a history and physical medical report.

13–5: PRACTICE TEST

Directions: Retype the following material into letter form. Use modified block format, indented paragraphs, mixed punctuation, and the current date. See page 248 for modified block format.

Estimate the number of words in the body of the letter and place your margins accordingly. Watch for proper paragraphing, placement, and mechanics.

The letter is from Margo A. Wilkins, M.D. and is to Glen M. Hiranuma, M.D., 2501 Main Street, Ventura, California 93003 and is in reference to Mrs. Hazel R. Plunkett.

Dear Dr. Hiranuma ¶Thank you for referring your patient Mrs. Hazel R. Plunkett for neurological consultation, evaluation, and treatment of chronic and recurrent headaches. ¶In the past, the patient has had episodes of probably typical migraine occurring perhaps six or eight times in her life. She remembers that her mother had a similar complaint. This

HAROLD B. COOPER, M.D.
6000 MAIN STREET
VENTURA, CALIFORNIA 93003

June 15, 199x

John F. Millstone, M.D.
5302 Main Street
Ventura, CA 93003

Dear Dr. Millstone:

RE: Elaine J. Silverman

     This 19-year-old woman was seen at your request. The patient was admitted to the hospital yesterday because of chills, fever, and abdominal and back pain.

     The history has been reviewed. A prominent feature of the history is the presence of intermittent, severe, shaking chills for four days with associated left lower back pain, left lower quadrant abdominal pain and fever to as high as 103 or 104 degrees. The patient has had hypertension for a number of years and has been managed quite well with Aldomet 250 mg twice a day.

     On examination her temperature at this time is 100.6 degrees. The pulse is 110 and regular. Blood pressure is 190/100. The patient has partial bilateral iridectomies, the result of previous cataract surgery. Otherwise, the head and neck are not remarkable. Lung fields are clear throughout. The heart reveals a regular tachycardia, heart sounds are of good quality. No murmurs heard and there is no gallop rhythm present. The abdomen is soft. There is no spasm or guarding. A well-healed surgical scar is present in the right flank area. There is considerable tenderness in the left lower quadrant of the left mid abdomen, but as noted, there is no spasm or guarding present. Bowel sounds are present. Peristaltic rushes are noted and the bowel sounds are slightly high pitched in character. The extremities are unremarkable.

     Diagnosis: I believe the patient has acute diverticulitis. She may have some irritation of the left ureter in view of the findings on the urinalyses. She appears to be responding to therapy at this time in that her temperature is coming down and also there has been a slight reduction in the leukocytosis from yesterday.

     I agree with the present program of therapy and the only suggestion would be to possibly increase the dose of gentamicin to 60 mg every eight hours, rather than the 40 mg q8h which she is now receiving.

     Thank you for asking me to see this patient in consultation.

                                        Sincerely,

                                        Harold B. Cooper, M.D.

mtf

13

FIGURE 13-7. Consultation Report generated from a medical office, letter form, typed in modified-block format with indented paragraphs and mixed punctuation.

COLLEGE HOSPITAL
4567 BROAD AVENUE
WOODLAND HILLS, XY 12345

HEMATOLOGY CONSULTATION

NAME: MORGAN, JENNIFER   CONSULTANT: B. JAMISON, M.D.

MR# 379764   RM# 388   REQUESTED BY: JOHN L. MORRIS, M.D.

DATE: 4/14/9x

_____

REASON FOR CONSULTATION: This is a 72-year-old white female with
known history of lymphoma who has developed a severe anemia.

HISTORY OF PRESENT ILLNESS: The patient had been treated by Dr.
Palma with Cytoxan, Procarbazine, Prednisone and Vincristine
since January, 199x when she presented with axillary adenopathy
that was biopsied and found to be diffuse histiocytic lymphoma.
Gallium scan at that time showed Stage VI involvement with liver
and spleen enlarg~~~~~robable involvement of the mediastinum
~~d periaortic ~~~~~nodes. The p~~~~~has been toler~~~
~~ her th~~~~~he was ~i~~~~~mother~

CONSULTATION CONTINUED...PAGE 2

PHYSICAL EXAMINATION

BP 100/60. Pulse 100 and regular. Respirations 24. Temperature
has been up to 100.4°.

GENERAL APPEARANCE: This is an obese, somewhat cushingoid, pale
elderly woman in no acute distress.

SKIN: Some senile purpura.

HEENT: Atraumatic. Nonicteric. Pupils equally reactive to
L&A. EOMI. Mouth without intraoral lesions.

NECK: Supple. Trachea midline. No palpable thyromegaly.

NODES: Bilateral axillary adenopathy and cervical adenopathy,
minimal, which is new.

NEUROLOGIC: A~~~~~ented times thr~~~~~focal signs.

ASSESSMENT: With the recurrence of adenopathy, it is probable
that the patient's present deterioration in terms of anemia,
weakness and low-grade fever, are on the basis of progressive
lymphoma.

The patient is presently to receive transfusion. Will also be
checking for possible blood loss or nutritional deficiency. Most
likely the patient will need restaging in terms of bone marrow
and gallium scan.   (continued)

FIGURE 13-8. Consultation Report generated from a hospital, report form, typed in run-on format.

```
Thank you for allowing me to see this pleasant lady.  Will follow
with you.


                                    _____
                                    BRIAN JAMISON, M.D.

BJ/mtf
D&T:  4/14/9x
```

FIGURE 13-8 *Continued*

would begin with loss in the field of vision; and then, approximately fifteen minutes thereafter, she would have a relatively typical, unilateral throbbing pain of a significant degree which would often incapacitate her. These headaches disappeared many years ago and have never returned. ¶However, for the last eight years approximately, the patient has had recurrent daily headaches, always right-sided, with associated pain beginning in the back of the neck with stiffness of the right side of the neck, radiating forward over the vertex to the right orbit, the nose, and the jaw. She also notes some pain in the right trapezius area. The pain tends to appear from 10 a.m. to noon, when she will take a Fiorinal, and often after she goes to sleep at night (at about 12:30 a.m.). She controls this pain by taking Fiorinal, one to four a day, and Elavil, 75 mg at bedtime. She estimates that the headaches occur approximately twice daily, are relatively short-lived but occasionally last a full day. The pain is dull and heavy, not throbbing, and worse at some times than at others. ¶On examination she was a quiet woman, not in acute distress, and somewhat dour; but she gave a careful and concise history. Her gait and station were normal. The head functions were basically intact. The fundi showed only modest arteriosclerotic changes. The temporal arteries were normal. Facial motility and sensation was normal. There was a significant right carotid bruit present which was persistent and which could be heard all along the course of the right carotid artery. It was not transmitted from the neck. There was moderate pain and tenderness at the insertion of the great muscles of the neck and the occiput, and palpation over this area consistently reproduced the patient's symptoms. She also had a persistent area of tenderness in the right trapezius muscle. Otherwise, power, size, and symmetry of the arms and legs were essentially normal. The deep tendon reflexes were brisk. There were no long tract or focal signs, and sensation was intact.

Impression: 1. Muscle contraction headaches, chronic. 2. Localized myositis, right side of neck, right shoulder girdle. 3. Right carotid bruit, silent, asymptomatic. ¶Comment: The findings were discussed in detail with the patient but no neurological studies were done. I suggested simple measures of physical therapy to the neck including the use of heat, hot packs, and massage and advised also that she purchase a cervical pillow on which to rest during the day. Motrin, 400 mg twice daily and Maolate, 400 mg at night were suggested in an attempt to provide anti-inflammatory and muscle relaxant properties. It may also be necessary to inject these tender areas which are quite well localized. This can be determined after thirty to sixty days on the treatment regimen outlined above. ¶The patient also has what seems to be a silent right carotid bruit. Certainly she is without symptoms. This should be brought to the attention of those who are caring for her, so that if transient ischemic attacks appear in the future, appropriate steps can be taken. I do not think that the right carotid bruit has anything to do with the patient's headaches, which are not vascular, and certainly there is no sign of cranial arteritis. ¶She was referred back to you for continuing medical service. Thank you for the opportunity of seeing this patient. Sincerely,

Please see Appendix E for a possible transcript of this test.

AUTOPSY PROTOCOLS

When a patient dies while in the hospital, permission may be requested from the next of kin to perform an autopsy or postmortem examination of the body to ascertain the exact cause of death. The complete protocol should be made part of the record within 90 days from death. Through autopsies much knowledge has been gained which assists in the diagnosis and treatment of disease. A visual and microscopic examination is done on every organ and related structure. When an organ is removed from a cadaver for purposes of donation, there should be an autopsy report that includes a description of the technique used to remove and prepare or preserve the donated organ. All states have laws that govern autopsies. When someone dies unattended or there is suspicion of a crime (such as violent death, unusual death, self-induced or criminal abortion, homicide, suicide, poisoning, drowning, fire, hanging, stabbing, exposure, starvation, and so forth), an autopsy may be ordered by the court, or it may become the responsibility of the coroner's office to determine the cause of death. The professionals associated with the coroner's office include the following: pathologist, forensic pathologist, forensic dentist, chemist, toxicologist, anesthesiologist, radiologist, odontologist, psychiatrist, and psychologist.

The written record of an autopsy is generally referred to as an autopsy protocol. In pathology, there are five forms: the narrative (in story form), the numerical (by the numbers), pictorial (hand drawings or anatomical forms), protocols based on sentence completion and multiple-choice selection, and problem-oriented protocols (a supplement to the Problem-Oriented Medical Record System).

Frequently a hospital autopsy protocol (Fig. 13–9) will contain the clinical history, which is a brief resume of the patient's medical history and course in the hospital prior to demise. It will include the patho-

logical diagnosis made at autopsy, a report of final summary, and the gross anatomy findings (visual examination of the organs of the body before any tissues are removed for preparation and examination). There will also be a microscopic examination (an examination of the particular organs through the microscope). An epicrisis or final pathological diagnosis is given at the end of the protocol. This is a critical analysis (actual finding) or discussion of the cause of disease after its termination.

In forensic pathology, an Autopsy Protocol may be organized under the following general guidelines:

1. External description

2. Evidence of injury
   a. External
   b. Internal

3. Systems and organs (cavities and organs)

4. Special dissections and examinations

5. Brain (and other organs) after fixation

6. Microscopic examination

7. Findings (diagnoses), factual and interpretative

8. Opinion or summary (conclusion), interpretative and opinion

9. Signature

Some autopsy protocol typing procedures are not necessarily seen in other types of medical dictation and transcription. Since autopsy records may possibly be entered into a court of law to relate information about the cause of death, the essential element is clarity so that interpretation of typed material is accurately understood. Because of this, more words tend to be spelled out and abbreviations are kept to a minimum. Many states require that military time be used when documenting the time a body is brought in for autopsy (Example: 1400 hours). If a person was last seen before midnight, the pathologist dictates "found over the date of January 1, 199X." If the person was last seen after midnight, the pathologist stated "found over the hour of 9:00 a.m. or 0900." Note that ciphers are used in stating the nonmilitary time. Units of measurement may be spelled out, such as pounds, inches, and grams. Quote marks (") are never used to indicate

inches but are used when indicating a marking on the body (Example: tattoo device of the words "J. J., Tramp"). Temperature is typed "88 degrees Fahrenheit." Numbers may be typed as "2 fresh punctures" or "two (2) stab wounds."

Numbers may be typed numerically and then spelled out in brackets any time clarity needs to be

```
                              College Hospital
                              4567 Broad Avenue
                           Woodland Hills, XY 12345


                              AUTOPSY REPORT


Silverman, Patricia M.

College Hospital

June 21, 199x

                        This is an autopsy on a prematurely born female
                        infant weighing 2 lb  12 oz.  The body measures
15.25 inches in length.  The body has not been embalmed prior to this
examination.

EXTERNAL EXAMINATION:   The head, neck and chest are symmetrical.  The
                        abdomen is soft.  The external genitalia are
normal female.  The extremities are symmetrical and show no evidence of
developmental abnormality.

INTERNAL EXAMINATION:

   ABDOMINAL CAVITY:    The abdominal cavity is opened and the liver is
                        enlarged extending 4.0 cm below the costal margin
in the right midclavicular line.  The spleen appears enlarged.  The intestinal
coils are freely dispersed and contain gaseous fluid.  All other organs are
in normal position.

   PLEURAL CAVITIES:    The pleural cavities are opened revealing the left
                        lung to be collapsed and lying  in the left pleural
cavity.  The right lung is partially expanded and the pleura is smooth and
glistening in both pleural cavities.

   MEDIASTINUM:         The mediastinum contains a moderate amount of thymic
                        tissue.

   PERICARDIAL SAC:     The pericardial sac is opened containing a few cubic
                        centimeters of serous fluid.  The heart is normal in
position and appears to be average in size.

   HEART:               The heart weighs approximately 10 gm.  Thorough
                        search of the heart fails to show any evidence of
congenital abnormality.  The foramen ovale has a thin membrane over the surface.
The ductus arteriosus is noted and patent.  There is no septal ventricular
defect.  All valves are competent.  There is no rotation of the heart.  The
pulmonary artery is noted and appears normal.  A few subendocardial and subepi-
cardial petechiae and ecchymoses are noted.


(continued)
```

FIGURE 13-9. Hospital Autopsy Protocol, report form, typed in indented format with no variations.

Patricia M. Silverman
Page 2
June 21, 199x

INTERNAL EXAMINATION: (continued)

LUNGS: The lungs weigh together 33 gm. The left lung
                          and the right lung sink in water, then slowly rise
to the surface. The lungs are subcrepitant and atelectatic. This is
particularly noted in the left lung. The bronchi contain a small amount of
frothy mucus. The cut surfaces of the lungs are beefy and atelectatic.
There are no cysts or tumors. The findings are consistent with hyaline
membrane disease and pulmonary atelectasis.

LIVER: The liver weighs approximately 75 gm. The liver
                          appears enlarged and is reddish-brown and soft. The
cut surface is reddish-brown and soft. There is no gross evidence of bile
duct blockage. The gallbladder, cystic duct and common bile duct are not
remarkable.

PANCREAS: The pancreas appears average in size weighing approxi-
                          mately 1.5 grams. The pancreas is yellowish-white
and soft on the cut surface. There is no gross evidence of cystic disease.

SPLEEN: The spleen weighs approximately 4 gm. and is
                          bluish-purple. The spleen on cut surface is
reddish-brown and soft.

ADRENAL GLANDS: The adrenal glands weigh together approximately 4.5
                          gm. The adrenal glands are soft and tan and the
cortical portion is distinct from the medullary portion. There is no gross
evidence of hemorrhage, cysts or tumors. Both adrenals are similar.

KIDNEYS: The kidneys weigh together approximately 13 gm.
                          The capsule strips with ease leaving a faint fetal
lobulation and a reddish-brown soft surface. The cut surface shows the
cortex and medulla, both of which are distinct and in average proportions.
The parenchyma is reddish-brown, moist and soft. Both kidneys are similar
in appearance and consistency. The ureters are not remarkable.

URINARY BLADDER,   These organs are grossly not remarkable.
UTERUS, TUBES
AND OVARIES:

GASTROINTESTINAL   The esophagus is examined as well as the stomach.
TRACT: There is no evidence of reduplication, ulcer or
                          tumor. The small and large bowel are not remarkable.

BRAIN: The brain weighs approximately 230 gm. The brain
                          is slightly edematous. A few petechiae are observed.
On sectioning the brain anterior to posterior, the brain tissue is soft and
somewhat edematous. The fluid in the ventricles is clear and watery. The
cerebellum and cerebrum are symmetrical and grossly not remarkable. There is
no gross evidence of hemorrhage or tumor.

(continued)

FIGURE 13-9 *Continued*

```
Patricia M. Silverman
Page 3
June 21, 199x


INTERNAL EXAMINATION: (continued)

    SKELETAL SYSTEM:     Not remarkable.

GROSS ANATOMICAL DIAGNOSIS:  1)  Prematurity, 2 lb 12 oz.
                             2)  Pulmonary atelectasis.
                             3)  Hyaline membrane disease.




                         Chief Pathologist_____
                                           Stephen M. Choi, M. D.

mtf
D:  6-20-9x
T:  6-21-9x
```

FIGURE 13-9 *Continued*

emphasized. Metric terms are seen as abbreviations (Examples: 0.5 cm, 200 ml, 3 × 3 mm). Forensic dentists work closely with forensic pathologists. They describe bite marks by size, shape, and location. They swab for saliva to determine blood type. They make impressions or molds of the mark and photograph and make impressions of the suspect's dentition.

There are instances when two medical examiners are involved and the reference initials at the closing of the protocol must be shown (Example: MB:DVW:mtf). Only general guidelines for typing protocols are stated here. Each county has different practices and must meet various legal requirements.

 ## 13-6: REVIEW TEST

Directions: Retype the following material into a hospital autopsy protocol using the full block format with variation number 1. The patient's name and other statistical data may be set up as you desire. Use a current date and correct punctuation. The dictator is Dr. Susan R. Foster, chief pathologist. See page 246 for full block format.

13

I performed an autopsy on the body of Phyllis B. Dexter, Patient No. 65-43-90, at the College Hospital. ¶ Clinical Diagnosis: Congenital heart defect.

General Examination: The body is that of a well developed and well nourished newborn female infant, having been embalmed prior to examination through a thoracic incision and cannulization of the heart. The recorded birth weight is 7 lb 2 oz. ¶ Thorax opened: Considerable blood is present around the heart incident to the embalming procedure, and two incisions in the cardiac muscle are evident but the valves and great vessels do not appear to have been injured by the embalming procedure. Examination discloses a massive heart lying transversely in the midanterior thorax, the distended right ventricle exceeding in volume the ventricular mass. Examination discloses no enlargement of the ductus arteriosus or any significant deviation of the size of the great vessels. On exploration of the heart there is found to be a completely imperforate pulmonary artery at the level of the pulmonary valve, all three cusps of which appear to be adequately formed but fused by scar tissue slightly proximal to the free margins of the cusps. It is impossible to probe the existence of any opening in this area. The right heart is markedly hypertrophic, approximating three times the muscle mass of the normal infant heart. There is no evidence of an interventricular defect. There is a sacculation adjacent to the valve of the inferior vena cava as it enters the inferior right auricle and in the dome of this sacculated area the foramen ovale is demonstrated. The foramen is unusually small in diameter (estimated to be no more than 4 mm in diameter) and this is covered by a plica. It would appear that the pressure of the distended right auricle would further compromise the capacity of the foramen to transmit blood. In the absence of any interventricular defect, this would be the only way that blood could get from the right to the left side of the heart. The lungs are heavy and poorly serrated and the bronchial tree contains some yellowish fluid which, in the absence of feeding by mouth, must be assumed to be aspirated vernix. ¶ Abdomen Opened: The stomach contains some bloody mucus but no evidence of formula. The liver and abdominal viscera appear entirely negative throughout. ¶ Head: Not opened. ¶ Cause of Death on Gross Findings: Massive chylous pericardial effusion, etiology not established but presumptively related to defect in formation of thoracic duct tissue. Microscopic: Sections of the thymus gland revealed a generally normal histological architecture for the thymus of the newborn, epithelial elements still being distributed through the lymphoid tissues. Certainly no tumor is present in the thymic tissue. The pulmonary tissues are poorly expanded although the bronchi appear open. There is a general vascular congestion of pulmonary tissue and some apparent extravasation of blood into the poorly expanded alveoli. In addition, there are deposits of hyaline material on the surfaces of some of the air spaces that would indicate the existence of hyaline membrane disease. The liver shows marked congestion and a rather active hematopoiesis. The heart muscle is not remarkable and the epicardial surface does not appear thickened or unusual. The kidney tissue exhibits some punctate hemorrhages in the parenchyma consistent with anoxia. ¶ Microscopic Diagnosis: Renal hemorrhages incident to anoxia.

MEDICOLEGAL REPORTS

Medicolegal reports originate from medical offices and hospitals, but when from the latter, they generally come from the Medical Records Department, which makes copies or abstracts of record entries rather than transcribing them (Fig. 13–10). The prudent physician responds to a request for medical information with a prompt and complete report and, in doing so, assists his or her patient in supporting claims for damages (probably including the physician's own bill),

facilitates the attorney's representation of a client, and can often spare himself or herself a trip to court. Usually a report of this type involves an accident case or workers' compensation case. The report is a legal document and is admissible as evidence in a court of law. Sometimes the attorney will abstract data from the report and incorporate the information into a formal document presented to the physician for signature and subsequent notarization. Accuracy is essential.

The properly prepared medicolegal report follows a

familiar format and is typed on the physician's letterhead stationery.

Patient Identification. The patient must be identified in the first paragraph. Include the patient's name, age, date of birth, or both, and address. If the patient is a child, he or she should be identified as the son or daughter of his or her parents, whose names should also be included.

CLARENCE F. STONES, M.D.
3700 OCEAN DRIVE
OXNARD, CALIFORNIA 93030

October 20, 199x

Aetna Casualty and Surety Company
3200 Roosevelt Boulevard
Oxnard, CA 93030

Re: Injured - Howard P. Winston
     Date of Injury - July 27, 199x
     Employer - College Chemistry Co.
     Case No. - 450-33-0821

Dear Madam or Sir:

EXAMINATION AND REPORT

HISTORY: This 43-year-old white male was working with a
                     chemical pump. It slipped and fell forward.
He over-corrected and fell. The pump fell on the patient, striking him
in the occiput area. The approximate weight of the pump was 325 lb
and was rolled off by a friend. He was knocked unconscious. He attended
a meeting the following day in San Mateo. The pain occurred a day later
in San Mateo. Three days later the pain was intense in the right shoulder
and elbow. He went to Dr. John Garrett for physiotherapy. The left side
then began to give him trouble also. He had a pressure type of pain in
the left elbow which was relieved by codeine. He entered the College
Hospital in Oxnard under Dr. Garrett's service. The right leg, and later
the right thigh, began getting numb. A myelogram was followed by fusion
at C 5-6 and C 6-7. He wore a brace for six months. He still has right
shoulder pain, neck pain with radiation into the right thumb and right
mastoid. In June, 199x, he was admitted to the Community Hospital in
Ventura, California. The left eye began drooping and there was no pupil
dilatation. He was improved one week later. A myelogram and brain scan
were performed. There was pain on the left side, with pain into the
rectum with spasms. He states that he fell several times. The surgery
was postponed because of the eyes and the sudden loss of equilibrium.

FAMILY HISTORY: The father died of burns in a fire in 1940. The
                     mother died of kidney disease at age 82. He has
two brothers and one sister, living and well. He is widowed. His wife
had cancer of the uterus. He has four children, alive and well. There is
no history of diabetes and no accidents.

ALLERGIES: Penicillin and tetanus.

PHYSICAL EXAMINATION: Blood pressure 122/78; pulse 84 and regular.

    GENERAL: The patient is cooperative and oriented to time
                     and place.

    HEENT: Head: Normal size and shape; no facial asymmetry.
                     He shows no evidence of elevated intra-cranial
pressure. Extraocular muscles intact. Pupils are equal and react briskly (continued)

FIGURE 13-10. Medicolegal Report, report form, typed in indented format with no underlining and mixed punctuation.

Howard P. Winston
Page 2
October 20, 199x

PHYSICAL EXAMINATION: (continued)

to light. At first one gets the impression that there might be a Horner's
syndrome on the left side because of inconstant ptosis of the right eyelid,
but this is not truly present.

    NEUROLOGICAL EXAM: The patient walks with sparing of the left leg.
                             There is no true paralysis present.

    REFLEXES: The right biceps and triceps are slightly reduced
                             on the left side, but present.

    SENSORY: There is evidence of patchy hyperesthesia in the
                             right upper extremity but following no particular
                             dermatomal pattern.

    CEREBELLAR FUNCTION: Intact. Lower cranial nerves within normal limits.
                             There were no pathological reflexes elicited.

The remaining exam was deferred.

OPINION AND COMMENT: The patient continues to have slight dysfunction
                          principally in the left lower extremity and right
upper extremity. It would seem to me that the pupillary abnormality, which
he experienced in June of 1977, merits some investigation including
arteriography. For his cervical disk problems, I would think that conservative treatment is warranted.

                              Very truly yours,

                              Clarence F. Stones, M.D.

mtf

FIGURE 13-10 *Continued*

Date of Accident or Injury. The date of the accident or injury must be noted, including the time of day, if known. (The physician should check the date of the accident given by the patient's attorney against the medical record. If they fail to agree, telephone the patient to clarify the discrepancy.)

History. The history of the accident, injury, or illness is described. Use the patient's own words, including quotes whenever possible. Be as detailed and complete as possible, listing all the facts.

Present Complaints. The patient's present complaints at the time of the first visit are recorded. (Sometimes these are referred to as subjective complaints.)

Past History. The past history should be described, along with any pre-existing defects or injuries that might affect the present accident.

Physical Findings. The physical findings on examination are recorded in detail. (These are sometimes referred to as objective findings.)

Laboratory or X-Ray Findings. Laboratory or x-ray findings should be included in the report. In some instances photocopies of x-ray, electrocardiograph, or operative reports should be made available. Consultation notes should also be photocopied and submitted with the medicolegal report.

Diagnosis. The diagnosis (or diagnoses in the case of multiple injuries) should be detailed.

Prescribed Therapy. The prescribed therapy must be described in detail. Each visit to the office should be listed, including any physical therapy treatments or medications prescribed.

Patient's Disability. The patient's disability should be outlined, describing work restrictions and including the dates of total or partial disability. The date the patient will be permitted to return to work is given.

Prognosis. The prognosis is of paramount importance to the attorney and thus to the patient. The settlement may depend on the physician's estimate of continued pain and whether there will be future permanent disability.

Physician's Statement. The physician's statement of fees for services rendered is an integral part of the report to an attorney. The statement should be itemized by date and service, making sure the statement correlates in detail with the dates of treatment mentioned in the report. The preparation of a report for an attorney is time-consuming, and the physician is entitled to charge a fee. Documents requiring extensive research of hospital records and consultants' reports merit higher fees.

Although many cases are settled out of court, the few that go to trial justify painstaking care in preparation of the medical report. Remember that the value of a detailed document cannot be overemphasized when the physician is asked to testify in a trial three or four years after an injury.

13-7: REVIEW TEST

Directions: Retype the following data into an industrial accident report form and prepare an envelope. Use letterhead paper. Use indented format, with no underlining, mixed punctuation, and the current date. Watch for proper paragraphing, placement, punctuation, and mechanics.

The letter concerns the patient George R. Champion and was dictated by Dr. James C. Taylor of 4320 Main Street, Ventura, California 93003. It is to be sent to an attorney, Ralph J. Claborne of 165 Cedar Street, Ventura, California 93003. Use a current date.

Dear Mr. Claborne. My patient Mr. George R. Champion was seen on September 14, 199X. History of injury: Mr. Champion was hit on the back of the head by a lettuce crate in April of 199X. He saw stars but was not knocked unconscious. Present complaints: The patient says he can see for an instant then the left eye blurs and also itches. He has had this problem since his accident in April, 199X. When he is working and turns to the left he cannot see things out of that side since they are fuzzy. He can look at an object to the left and five seconds later it is gone. Physical examination: Visual acuity uncorrected: right eye, 20/80; left eye, 20/40. Manifest refraction: right eye, $+1.75D = 20/30$ Jaeger 1; left eye, $+2.50 = 20/30$ Jaeger $1-$. Visual field: full centrally. Motility: Near point of convergence $= 8$ cm; Near point of accommodation $= 3.5D$. Prism cover test: Distance $=$ no shift; Near $= 8$ prism diopters exophoria. Cycloplegic refraction: right eye $= +2.50 + 0.50 \times 30 = 20/25 - 2$; left eye: $= +3.25 + 0.75 \times 125 = 20/20 - 1$. Slit-lamp examination revealed abnormal cornea, conjunctiva, iris and lens. Ocular tension was 11 mm Hg both eyes by applanation. Retinal examination revealed a normal optic disc, macula, vessels and periphery with direct and indirect ophthalmoscopy. Diagnosis: Compound hyperopic astigmatism with early presbyopia. Comments: I feel that this patient's focusing reserve was suddenly decreased by his accident when he was hit on the head. His basic problem of farsightedness coupled with a general weakness after the accident overcame his focusing reserve and caused his symptoms. I feel that glasses of the

13

proper strength will enable him to see and focus. His problem of poor convergence and exophoria at near were also brought into prominence by the weakness he had after the accident. His age (38) means that he would have had symptoms within the next five or seven years due to his farsightedness. Recommended treatment: Glasses to be worn all the time. Eye exercises for convergence problem if the glasses do not relieve his symptoms. Disability: The condition is now stationary and permanent; and with the proper glasses, he should be able to resume his normal work load. Very truly yours.

PSYCHIATRIC REPORTS

Psychiatry is one of the specialties of clinical medicine. It is a diverse field, and the language involves abnormal psychology, human behavior, and treatment terminology. Patients are referred to as clients. In a hospital setting, clients include the mentally disabled and developmentally disabled (DD), formerly referred to as mentally retarded.

For the mentally disabled client, an admission note might include a presentation of the problem, stating the vital signs, current medications, allergies, medication taken in the last four hours, present illness, psychological history, mental status examination, physical status examination, and a provisional diagnosis. Additional reports on the mentally disabled client might include a psychiatric evaluation, psychological evaluation, social history evaluation, rehabilitation therapy evaluation, discharge summary, and a treatment planning conference. The last is a program to establish goals of treatment and track the progress the client is making under the treatment, with the ultimate goal of being placed back into society as a full-functioning person.

The reports for a developmentally disabled client might include a medical history, review of systems, release summary, and a clinical record documentation system, which is equivalent to a treatment planning conference for a mentally disabled client. The reports are more detailed because these clients can be so low functioning that even the most basic self-care skills cannot be performed on admission. The facility staff attempts to teach these skills to the highest potential of each client as a goal.

A report dictated by a clinical psychologist would not necessarily contain a physical examination of the body systems or the medications but might describe motor skill problems. The main heading might be entitled psychological evaluation, and subheadings might be given as follows: purpose of the report, psychosocial history, results of the psychological assessment, mental status examination, test results, impressions, diagnosis, and recommendations.

Because so many clients have legal problems (divorce, marriage, adoption procedures, negligence, physical abuse, disability, and so forth), legal terminology is widely used. Since some clients may be seen for chemical abuse, drugs could be referred to by slang or street terms, and it is often these terms that puzzle the novice transcriptionist. These terms change from day to day and the list is constantly enlarged. Most transcriptionists prepare lists of these slang terms for reference to assist in typing up the reports. Since many of the words encountered in psychiatric reports do not appear in the standard English dictionary or medical dictionary, special reference books are available to assist you in typing such reports. The *Diagnostic and Statistical Manual of Mental Disorders, Third Edition, Revised* (DSM-III-R) is used for the psychiatric diagnosis for the mentally disabled. This is an excellent reference book for the transcriptionist since all mental diagnoses are given along with their code numbers. However, for developmentally disabled clients, the *International Classification of Diseases, 9th Edition, Clinical Modification* (ICD-9-CM) is used followed by the etiology. If the psychiatrist wishes, the DSM-III-R is also used for the diagnosis. Refer to the last paragraph in Figure 13–11 to see how the diagnoses and code numbers might be typed. Spanish-speaking developmentally disabled clients may have families that request information about the patient and in those instances the report may be generated in Spanish. It is, therefore, important to have on hand Spanish-English medical and legal dictionaries. See Appendix B for a list of the reference books needed when typing psychiatric reports.

Reports that contain information about a person's mental stability are very confidential. In fact, sometimes the information contained in the report is not divulged to the client. To obtain medical information, the signatures of the physician and the client are required on a special release of information form. If the client is developmentally disabled, the signatures of the physician and the guardian are needed. If authorized in writing by the client or his or her legally qualified representative and the psychiatrist in charge of

GUIDELINES	Date of Report: 11-9-9x Date Dictated: 11-14-9x Date Typed: 11-15-9x PSYCHIATRIC EVALUATION	Unit 99

A. PSYCHIATRIC HISTORY
1. Identification data
2. Source of information
3. Chief complaint
4. History of present illness (focus on recent illness, and include emotional behavior)
5. History of past psychiatric episodes
6. Relevant medical/surgical/trauma/medication history
7. Developmental history (if applicable)
8. Educational/Vocational
9. Relevant family history
10. Relevant social history

B. MENTAL STATUS EXAM
11. Attitude/Cooperation
12. General appearance (include speech)
13. Motor activity
14. Orientation
15. Mood and affect
16. Mental content
17. Memory
18. Fund of general knowledge
19. Cognition and comprehension
20. Abstraction ability
21. Counting and calculating
22. Judgement
23. Insight regarding illness
24. Patient strengths
25. Suicide, homicide, dangerousness

C. SUMMARY OF PSYCHIATRIC ASSESSMENT
26. Narrative summary (including Risk Potential)
27. Diagnosis (DSM III R)
28. Preliminary Treatment Plan
29. Prognosis
30. Signature and Title

PSYCHIATRIC HISTORY:

1. This 17-year-old, single, Hispanic male patient was admitted to XYZ Hospital on 11-8-9x on a temporary conservatorship 5353 from XYZ County. His birth date is 9-24-72. There is no religious preference. His mother is Mary Sanchez. Her address is 300 East Date Street, Woodland Hills, XY 12345, (013) 999-9999.

2. Information obtained by interviewing the patient and reviewing the accompanying papers from XYZ Medical Center. The patient speaks only Spanish. The interview had to be done through an interpreter. His information is not very reliable.

3. "I don't know why they sent me here."

4. July was admitted to XYZ Medical Center on August 26, 199x because of bizarre behavior for five days. According to the report five days prior to admission, he smoked marijuana dipped in PCP. He also smoked cocaine. He demonstrated bizarre behavior such as running nude in the streets, sticking his fingers into light sockets and receiving electric shocks, crawling under a car and trying to set it on fire. He was not sleeping. He laughed and cried inappropriately. He broke a restraint in the hospital. The drug screening test on August 26, 199x showed a positive cocaine and negative for PCP and other drugs. Peabody test in Spanish revealed his IQ was about 76. Beery developmental test of visual motor integration did not suggest organicity. He was treated with Haldol and discharged to his mother on 9-22-9x; however, he was readmitted to XYZ Medical Center on 9-24-9x on a 5150. His mother stated that after discharge from the hospital he was fearful and childish. He presented bizarre behavior such as collecting household articles, painting the walls, attempting to play with medicine bottles, refusing to eat or sleep, walking around the house nude, collecting piles of objects in his room, attempting suicide by jumping off an apartment building. He laughed and cried inappropriately. His mother stated that he did not take street drugs and he took only Haldol and Cogentin. However, on one occasion he went to the store without supervision. At the XYZ Medical Center he was confused, disorganized and disoriented. It was difficult for him to attend to a conversation or to concentrate. He was not able to function in school. He needs close supervision and care. He had been in physical restraints many times because of assaultive behavior. He also banged the walls and screamed. He was treated with Haldol 10 mg t.i.d. A long-term hospitalization was

SANCHEZ, Pedro J.   999999-9   U. 99

☐ Continued

EVALUATION REPORT
PSYCHIATRIC
Confidential Client/Patient Information
See W & I Code Section 5328

MH 5702 (Revised 7/87)
CRDM Reference 2410

FIGURE 13-11. Pages 1 and 4 of a psychiatric evaluation on a developmentally disabled client, typed in full-block format with no variations. At the end of the report, note the typing of the diagnoses and the code numbers. GAF means Global Assessment of Functioning Scale.

State of California—Health and Welfare Agency   Department of Mental Health

Date of Report: 11-9-9x
Date Dictated: 11-14-9x
Date Typed: 11-15-9x

Unit 99—PSYCHIATRIC EVALUATION

SUMMARY OF PSYCHIATRIC ASSESSMENT: (Continued)

26. Pedro's father deserted the family when Pedro was 11 years old. Around that time he stopped going to school after finishing sixth grade. The reason for that was not clear, but it is well known that people with mild mental retardation cannot go further than the sixth grade. He lived with his grandmother after his mother left Honduras four years ago. About eight months ago, he came to the United States to live with his mother because his grandmother was unable to handle him. He had been using cocaine and PCP for six or seven months. It was felt that his first hospitalization at XYZ Medical Center was due to PCP, Organic Mental Disorder. At this time, he appears retarded with residual symptoms of psychosis such as flat and inappropriate affect, loose associations, poverty of thoughts, no intention to go to school and he needs constant supervision for daily living activities.

27. Axis I: 298.90   Psychotic Disorder, NOS.
                           (Rule out 292.90 PCP, Organic Mental Disorder)
                 305.90   Psychoactive Substance Abuse, NOS.
    Axis II: V71.09   No diagnosis.
                           (Rule out Mental Retardation)
    Axis III: No somatic disorder.
    Axis IV: 5   Severe.
    Axis V: GAF on admission 25; highest GAF last year unknown.

28. Structured environment, special educational program, unit milieu, individual therapy, group therapy, and chemotherapy.

29. Guarded.

30.

_____, M. D.
Dan W. Stewart, M. D.

mtf

Page 4   SANCHEZ, Pedro J.   999999-9   U. 99   ☐ Continued Page _____

CONTINUATION PAGE

☒ Assessment (Specify: __Psychiatric_____)
☐ Team Conference (Specify: _____)
☐ Consultation (Specify: _____)
☐ Other (Specify _____)

MH 5705

FIGURE 13-11 *Continued*

the case, a copy of the report is sent to the referring medical practitioner or medical facility responsible for follow-up care of the patient. Psychiatric information can be sent to a placement facility if a client is to live in the community in a residential facility. This gives the receiving facility information regarding treatment and medication. At times, the court system may subpoena the medical records.

13–8: OPTIONAL TEST

Directions: Retype the following data into a psychiatric report form. Use letterhead paper. Use full block format with variation No. 1, mixed punctuation, and the current date. Watch for proper paragraphing, punctuation, placement, and mechanics.

The letter concerns the patient Tu Anh Dao, and was dictated by Dr. Stephen B. Salazar of 5028 South Broadway, Woodland Hills, CA 90217. It is to be sent to Department of Social Services Disability Evaluation Unit, 15 Kenneth Street, Woodland Hills, CA 90217.

Head this report Psychiatric Social Survey. Presenting Problem: This 29 year old Vietnamese male was seen today at the request of the Department of Social Services Disability Evaluation Unit. Questions regarding mental status appearance simple repetitive tasks interests and daily activities and ability to relate and interact with public and co-workers were raised. The interview was conducted in the living room of the home in which he lives and has lived for the last three or four years. The claimant resides in this home with his mother and his 11 year old younger sister. His mother and an interpreter were present in the room during the interview. The interview lasted one hour. The claimant was very quiet and at some points hardly audible. He declined to answer questions quite often during the interview. Several times during the interview the mother interrupted and gave answers to him. He seemed to show some pressure of speech and memory difficulties during the interview. History: The history revealed that Mr. Dao was born in Hanoi Vietnam where he went to school up to the eighth grade. At the eighth grade he dropped out and began to farm doing rice farming. At age 26 he moved to Santa Monica. After arriving in Santa Monica he worked in a restaurant which he cannot name as a dishwasher for two or three months but he quit because the job in the first place was part time and temporary. He then worked for two years as a gardener and quit this job because of health problems he was always feeling sick. He also worked for one or two months as a carpenter but he quit because he did not have the money to buy the tools. In 1990 he was admitted to College Hospital where he had surgery and was in the hospital for one or two months during the winter of the year. He claims that the surgery was neurological although it could have been rather than on the brain an inner ear surgery due to vertigo and tinnitus problems. There is no history of any other hospitalizations. The claimant is the oldest son of five children he has two sisters and two brothers they are all living in the United States. Environment: The claimant has lived in his present house for one and a half years with his mother and his 10 year old sister. He states that he wakes at 8 or 9 am. He walks around in the yard for awhile and then he eats breakfast he does not eat lunch but does eat dinner. He said that during this time his appetite is good and he eats because he is hungry. Once a week he leaves the house to see a doctor who checks for the surgery and his neurological problems. He states that he had a ringing in the left ear which was partially a result of the surgery. He has not done any kind of work since the head surgery and he has not done anything around the house. He reports difficulty with memory. He rarely does anything with friends except when they come over to visit him and only leaves the house to walk around the yard or go to the doctor appointments. He is able to dress himself and bathe himself but does not do any chores of any kind around the house. He states that his mother cooks for him and he has never cooked for himself and he does not do anything around the yard either. His grooming showed him to be wearing a shirt slacks with no shoes or socks and he was clean shaven his hair styled and neatly brushed. He reports going to bed around 1 or 2 am. Most of his day is spent listening to the radio and watching television. While showing that he could ambulate he had significant difficulty walking on his toes; he was unable to do this but he was able to walk on his heels and his gait appeared to be normal. There was no significant psychomotor retardation noted. Mental status: The mental status reveals a 29 year old Vietnamese male who appears to be of average height and weight. He denied any paranoid ideations or auditory or visual hallucinations. He was oriented to time place and date and he was able to do 1 to 20 forward and backwards without any difficulty. He refused to do serial 7's although he was able to subtract 7 from 10 correctly. He showed difficulty with memory although he could remember that he had lived in the house that he lives in now for the last year and a half. He denied any headaches or visual difficulties or aura that might indicate seizure activity. He did have an affect of sadness and depression. When asked what he would change about himself he stated that he would change his bad health to good health. He has no goals at the present time. He is on no medication at the present time and he does not have a history of drug or alcohol use or abuse. He denied sleep or appetite problems or crying. There does appear to be some anhedonia. Medications: The claimant is taking no medications at the present time. Provisional Diagnosis: Axis I. Transient situational depression due to surgery mild to moderate. Axis II. Rule out organic brain syndrome. Observations and recommendations: Because there were no medical reports sent with this individual it would be recommended that there be a review to see if there actually was a surgery at College Hospital and what was the purpose of the surgery and what an update may be on his neurological function. In fact I would recommend a neurological evaluation to see if the depression emanates from the surgery itself or from some emotional disturbance. There is no indication that Mr. Dao could handle his own funds and it is recommended that a payee be appointed if he is approved for disability. Thank you for the consultation. Very truly yours

▣ Answer to 13 – 1: Self-Study

Bacon, Marcia M.
52-01-96
Room No. 248-C

DISCHARGE SUMMARY

ADMISSION DATE: May 7, 199X   **DISCHARGE DATE**: May 9, 199X

ADMISSION DIAGNOSIS:
Torn medial meniscus, left knee; chondromalacia of the medial femoral condyle.
or 1)   2)   *or* 1)
                                                              2)

DISCHARGE DIAGNOSIS:
Torn medial meniscus, left knee; chondromalacia of the medial femoral condyle.

HISTORY OF PRESENT ILLNESS:
The patient injured her left knee on April 11, 199X, while playing tennis. She subsequently had difficulty with persistent effusion and pain in the left knee. An arthrogram prior to admission revealed a tear of the medial meniscus.

PHYSICAL EXAMINATION:
Absence of tenderness to palpation of any of the joint structures. There was approximately 30-55 cc of fluid within the joint. Range of motion was full.

LABORATORY DATA:
Admission hemoglobin was 15.9, hematocrit 47% with a white count of 7,400 with normal differential. Urinalysis was within normal limits. Chem panel 19 showed an elevated cholesterol of 379 mg%. Chest x-ray was reported as negative.

TREATMENT AND HOSPITAL COURSE:
The patient was taken to the Operating Room on the same day as admission, at which time she underwent arthroscopy. This revealed that she had a tear of the medial meniscus. Arthrotomy was performed, with medial meniscectomy. A chondral fracture was noted in the medial femoral condyle, measuring approximately 5 mm in greatest diameter. The edges of this were sheathed. Postoperatively, the patient course was benign. There was no significant temperature elevation. She became ambulatory with crutches on the first postoperative day with no difficulty with straight leg raising.

DISPOSITION:
The patient is being discharged home, ambulatory, with crutches, and an exercise program. She is to be seen in the office in one week for suture removal.

CONDITION AT THE TIME OF DISCHARGE:
Improved.

COMPLICATIONS:
None.

MEDICATIONS:
None.

Surgeon _____

(student's initials)
D: 5-10-*year*   Henry R. Knowles, M.D.
T: 5-11-*year*

13

◪ Answer to 13 – 4: Self-Study

This assignment is to be set up using modified block format and no variations.

RADIOLOGY REPORT

Examination Date:	June 8, 199X	Patient:	Donna Mae Weeser
Date Reported:	June 8, 199X	X-ray No.:	16-A2
Physician:	George B. Bancroft, M. D.	Age:	46
Examination:	Mammography, right and left breasts	Hospital No.:	52-80-44

XEROMAMMOGRAPHY,
RIGHT AND LEFT BREASTS: There are retromammary prosthetic devices in position. The anterior parenchyma is somewhat compressed. There is no evidence of neoplastic calcification or skin thickening demonstrated. No dominant masses are noted within the anteriorly displaced parenchyma. No increased vascularity is evident.

IMPRESSION: Mammography right and left breasts shows the presence of retromammary prosthetic devices in position. The demonstrated tissue appears within normal limits.

Radiologist _____
                        Clayton M. Markham, M. D.

(student's initials)
D: 6-8-year
T: *(current date)*

13

Composing Business Letters and Making Travel Arrangements

OBJECTIVES

After reading this chapter and working the exercises, you should be able to

1. discuss the importance of the ability to compose a good business letter.
2. identify the various types of letters that a secretary in a private office should be able to write.
3. compose a letter for your employer's signature.
4. compose letters for your own signature under a variety of circumstances.
5. recognize and use the rules for writing effective business letters.
6. test the various aids available to writers of business letters.
7. make travel arrangements, including hotel accommodations, transportation, and itineraries.

14

• •

INTRODUCTION

This chapter is for the medical office assistant who wishes to perform some executive secretarial tasks for an employer. Many assistants are unable, reluctant, or unskilled in doing duties other than those that they are specifically directed to undertake. This chapter is not for the reluctant. It *is* for you if you are willing to shoulder some extra responsibility.

In the business world, an executive secretary can share in much of an employer's work load; in contrast, the medical secretary may find the scope somewhat limited. After all, one cannot help practice medicine. But you *can* relieve your physician-employer of many nonmedical business chores.

The area of responsibility that you can assume in a private physician's office is that of handling the office correspondence. As an office secretary, you probably

303

will be responsible for opening, marking, and routing the mail that arrives in the office. Under your employer's direction, some of this mail can be returned to you for reply, either over the physician's signature or over yours. The mail that you will handle over your own signature may be collection letters to patients about overdue accounts, orders for supplies and instruments, the making or confirmation of appointments or hospital admissions, requests for information, inquiries to insurance companies, and the making of travel arrangements for your employer.

The type of mail that you might compose for your employer's signature can range from letters requiring very limited responsibility, such as acknowledgment of professional announcements, to those of great responsibility, such as replying to an insurance company's request for patient data, writing certificates of return to work, making reports about treatment to compensation carriers, and transmitting medical or laboratory results to a patient or another physician. There is no limit concerning the types of letters that you may be asked to write, provided that you can demonstrate the skill to do the work competently. As you can readily see, you will enhance your value to a prospective employer if you have a good command of English and the ability to express yourself well on paper.

THE ART OF LETTER WRITING

Entire texts are written about the art of letter writing, and business students spend semesters or years devoted to acquiring this skill. Assuming you already have some skill in letter writing, this chapter will try to redirect and enhance your skills. If you find that you are not an effective correspondent, you might consider a special course in business writing. Many community colleges offer this course in the evening because of the special needs of employed persons.

WRITING BETTER SENTENCES

Good business writing depends on clarity. If the basic element used to convey meaning—the sentence—is unclear, the entire message may be difficult to understand. Good sentence structure requires the application of all the rules of English grammar and the avoidance of certain particularly common errors.

Let us examine some of the common problem areas.

Sentence Fragments

A sentence is a group of words that expresses a complete thought and must contain a subject (usually a noun) and predicate (usually a verb). Any combination of words that does not fulfill these conditions is not a sentence and should be avoided in good business English.

Examples

Accommodations are required for Dr. Varney so please advise me about.

I want to bring to your attention.

Run-On Sentences

When two sentences are run together without any connecting word (such as *although, therefore,* or *and*) or punctuation (a semicolon, dash, or colon) to divide them, they may be difficult to understand.

Example

Dr. Broughton is out of town, therefore I am replying to your letter.

Each phrase could stand alone as a separate sentence. Therefore, the phrases should be separated by a word or by some form of punctuation stronger than a comma. The example could be corrected in any of the following ways:

Dr. Broughton is out of town; therefore, I am replying to your letter.

Dr. Broughton is out of town. Therefore, I am replying to your letter.

Because Dr. Broughton is out of town, I am replying to your letter.

Parallel Structure

Always express coordinate elements within a sentence or within a list in similar grammatical forms. Match nouns with nouns, infinitives with infinitives, verbs with verbs, adjectives with adjectives, and so on.

Example

Learning to write is a challenge and interesting.

Here writing is described with an adjective (interesting) and a noun (challenge). It would be better to use two adjectives and change the sentence to read as follows:

Learning to write is challenging and interesting.

Examine the lack of coordinate elements in the following example:

Example

The purpose of this study:

1. To enhance communication between members of the team.

2. So that we can provide a retrospective study of care.

3. To be able to strengthen the transcriptionist's role.

   IMPROVED: The following are examples of the purpose of this study:

1. *To enhance* communication between members of the team.

2. *To provide* a retrospective study of care.

3. *To strengthen* the transcriptionist's role.

Dangling Construction

The most awkward and sometimes embarrassing errors in writing often result from poor sentence construction. Sometimes certain kinds of phrases and clauses, usually occurring at the beginning of a sentence, do not agree logically with the subject. These constructions are referred to as "dangling."

To correct a dangling construction, make the subject of the sentence the doer of the action expressed in the troublesome phrase or clause. If that is not at all feasible, rework your sentence completely to make it logical. Examine these "danglers" and a possible restructure of the sentence.

Example

She has protruding eyes which have been present all her life.

IMPROVED: All her life she has had protruding eyes.

Example

Having met his wife's aunt, a family dinner was planned.

IMPROVED: A family dinner was planned to celebrate meeting his wife's aunt.

Example

Upon leaving the building, the door caught my coat.

IMPROVED: The door caught my coat as I left the building.

Unnecessary or Repetitious Words

Eliminate unnecessary phrases and useless words from your sentences.

Wordy	Concise
I have taken the liberty of writing at the present time	I am writing now
In view of the fact that	Since
Additional reports will be issued from time to time in the future	Additional reports will be issued periodically
It is the hope of the undersigned	I hope

Notice the unnecessary phrases and useless words italicized in the following examples:

1. Give this your prompt *and speedy* attention

2. Your letter arrived *in this office*

3. We will have an opening *coming up*

4. The device was circular *in shape*

5. We will convert *over* to

6. My *personal* opinion

7. My *actual* experience

Substitute the words in the second list below for those in the first list:

Avoid	Use
converse	talk
fully cognizant of	know
the writer	I
relative to	about
in regard to	about
in connection with	about
will you be so kind as to	please
are in need of	need
in the amount of	for
in the event that	if
under date of	on
in the near future	soon
a substantial segment	many
interrogate	question
due to the circumstance	because

 14–1: SELF-STUDY

Directions: Type your answers on a separate piece of paper. Restructure the following sentences to avoid run-on structure.

1. Please retype this, it is your responsibility.

2. Remodeling is taking place in the Emergency Room, therefore reroute all patient traffic to Ward B until further notice.

3. The new chief-of-staff will take over the first of next month, furthermore there will be many new physicians added to the active staff roster.

Rewrite the following to maintain parallel structure:

4. To be accurate and meet your production level is important here.

5. Pull the patient's record, notifying the doctor of the emergency, then give the record to the doctor and be sure to relate any information you have received.

6. Please observe the following:
   a. Enter your department number on each requisition.
   b. Use the preprinted requisitions.
   c. If the preprinted requisition is not available for the products you require, refer to the Inventory Stock Catalogue and enter the appropriate stock number.

7. Duties of the custodian of records:
   a. to keep accurate records
   b. correcting must be made in the proper way
   c. be sure the records are signed or initialed
   d. don't let unauthorized persons see the records without a release

8. Rules for taking phone calls:
   a. If the person is talking, don't interrupt him/her
   b. Remember to pick up the phone as soon as it rings
   c. Ask the name of the person calling
   d. In transferring calls, be sure to get the right extension
   e. Be sure to answer with your name and the department's name

Eliminate the dangling construction in the following sentences:

9. I saw many new flowers jogging through the parking lot.

10. While on vacation, my dog stayed at my mother's house.

11. Her first and only child was born at age 44.

12. The record was finally returned floating through the department.

Strike through the unnecessary words that take up space and add nothing to the ideas expressed. (You may write directly on the page.)

13. Mrs. Benson just recovered from an attack of pneumonia.

14. Your letter arrived at a time when we were on vacation.

15. The water is for drinking purposes only.

16. The consultation fee is the sum of twenty dollars.

17. The color of the new typewriter is beige.

18. We will return the equipment at a later date.

19. The file is made out of steel.

20. We are now engaged in building a new medical wing.

21. The report describes the patient's medical records during the period from May 1990 to May 1991.

22. The operative procedure lasted up to eight hours in duration.

23. The new word processor is smaller in size.

24. The patient's disability will last a period of eight weeks.

25. The physician is actively providing professional services to many government employees.

Correct the grammar in the final sentences by adding, eliminating, or changing words.

26. I feel the nursing personnel as well as pulmonary medicine staff will benefit from the information and instructions.

27. The Advisory Committee and Management Department would like to express their thanks for the time you gave to present the material to us.

28. When operating a postage meter, you should remember the following:
    a. The date should be changed daily.
    b. The amount of postage set on the meter should be checked before the envelope is stamped.
    c. The meter should be reset to zero.
    d. All unused postage metered tapes and envelopes should be saved for refund with application for the refund made within a year.
    e. Mail should be deposited on the date shown or postage may be forfeited.
    f. If an error is made by the meter (poor ink, incorrect postage amount) a request for a full refund should be made and no further postage should be imprinted until the problem has been corrected.
    g. Hand Stamp should be written in large red letters on both the front and back of a bulky envelope.

29. For this reason, that the medical record might be the physician's only witness in court, that record must be absolutely correct.

30. By writing one, learns to write.

(Please check the end of this chapter for possible editing of these problems.)

GETTING STARTED

One of the major hurdles in writing is getting through the agonizing stage of deciding what to say and getting started. Some people, expecting to produce simultaneously a well-planned, well-written, polished, and finely typed letter, try in vain to organize their thoughts and compose on their typing or word processing equipment.

Let us be realistic. Organize your thoughts on scratch paper before you begin. Plan carefully. The extra steps you take to rough draft your thoughts are not wasted because you will have the letter more than half-written before you actually start to compose it.

Make an outline to cover the following points:

1. WHY: Formulate a clear idea of the reason for the message. Clearly state your purpose for writing.

2. WHO: Know the audience to whom you are writing and how that audience should be approached.

3. WHAT: List all information to be conveyed. List the secondary or supporting topics that go with the central idea. Be careful about details.

4. REACTION: Describe how you expect the recipient to react, your desired action or desired attitude.

Using your outline, list exactly what you want to say; be concise and specific. Remember that you want to convey a particular message without confusion or excess verbiage. A concise letter avoids anything that the reader already knows. However, sometimes it is necessary to "remind" the reader of certain things before continuing with new information. If you are writing to order an item, jot down all of the pertinent information to describe it, and add any questions you have concerning its operation, warranty, cost, or delivery. If you are making an appointment for a patient, state the exact day of the week, date, and time that you expect the patient, including any directions to explain specifically how the arrangements may be changed if the patient is dissatisfied with them.

COMPOSING

When you know exactly what you need to say, you must organize your material in an orderly fashion and learn how to express yourself well. Let us see how this plan works with the outline:

1. WHY: The patient wants an appointment.

2. WHO: An established office patient.

14

3. WHAT: The exact time, day, and date.

4. PLUS (details): Notification to bring his x-ray films with him; we will change the date if it is not convenient.

5. REACTION: The patient will arrive on the proper date with the x-ray films or reply that the arrangements are not satisfactory.

Here is a letter following our outline:

Dear Mr. Johnson: [1]An appointment has been reserved [2]for you with [3]Dr. Beem on Friday, May 11, 199X, at 3:30 p.m. [4]Please bring your x-ray films from Dr. Bowers' office with you. I hope these arrangements are convenient for you; if not, [5]please telephone the office. Sincerely,

Since Mr. Johnson is an established patient in our office, we probably have built a friendly rapport with

him. Therefore, this rather cold, formal letter may be made more personal without sacrificing our basic plan.

Dear Mr. Johnson: We are looking forward to seeing you again on Friday, May 11, 199X, at 3:30 p.m. Dr. Beem would like you to bring your x-ray films from Dr. Bowers' office with you for this appointment. I hope these arrangements are convenient; if not, please telephone me. Sincerely,

Finally, reread the letter and see if it covers clearly and exactly what you wish to say. Make sure you have followed your outline and have omitted nothing. Read your document as if you were the person receiving it. Do you have any questions? No. (Good!) Yes. (Rewrite!) Be sure you have written clear, correctly worded sentences. Use proper letter mechanics and type it attractively.

14-2: PRACTICE TEST

Directions: Write an outline for a letter using the following information. You will not write the letter, only the outline.

Dr. Berry has received a request from one of his patients who wishes to have a copy of her medical record. He has agreed to make an abstract of this record and meet with the patient to discuss the abstract and answer any questions. He has set a fee of $40 for the conference and the abstract. You are to let the patient know how he is going to respond to her request and make a tentative appointment for the conference.

See Appendix E for a possible outline.

Planning and Writing Paragraphs

A good way to form paragraphs is to use the technique of striving for a two- or three-paragraph letter because most letters require only three paragraphs. If a letter has more than three paragraphs, it might not be poorly constructed but it probably does need tightening up. However, check the letter to see if anything is lacking. (Quite often the missing element is the personal touch—the extra something that communicates feeling to the reader.)

Therefore, the letter should have three characteristics:

1. One subject

2. Two aspects, feeling and thinking

3. Two or three paragraphs including a beginning, a middle, and an end

Start by taking out the excess verbiage. One fault of poor letters is complexity. Often this is caused by burying the main point, the main idea, deep in dates of prior correspondence, invoice numbers, identification numbers, and so on. The cure for this is simple: Use a subject line. This lets you get right down to business in the main part of the letter. It allows you to make your point early, clearly, and concisely.

Another frequent cause of complexity is trying to cover more than one subject in one letter. The remedy for this is to write two letters. If this is inconvenient, write one letter as if it were two and use the final paragraph to sum up the substance of both subjects.

Your paragraphs should be concise and courteous. Try this method: Write an opening paragraph that states the problem or makes the point; use a second paragraph that elaborates or provides detail; and sum up or state in the final paragraph what has to be done. Of course, very brief paragraphs may be joined.

Opening Paragraph

Write a topic sentence that states the main idea to be developed. Place the topic sentence at or near the beginning of the letter.

Transitions

Use connective phrases such as *however, therefore, nevertheless, for this reason, in fact, in contrast,* and so on to achieve transitions within or between paragraphs. You do not want an abrupt change in shifting to the next sentence or next paragraph.

Second Paragraph

Give details in sequence (chronological or locational) or use enumerations such as first, second, third, and so on. Remember that this paragraph elaborates and provides all the necessary details for the reader.

Final Paragraph

State clearly the results, reaction, action, or desired attitude. If you followed your plan for outlining your letter, this will coincide with that plan.

The Beginning

1. Get right in and say what you want to say. Be concise, yet complete and courteous.

2. Avoid beginning a letter with *I* or *We.*
   NOT: I would like to order a #14 Jackson bronchoscope.
   BUT: Please send a #14 Jackson bronchoscope, catalog number . . .

3. Avoid trite openings.
   NOT: In reference to your correspondence of July 14 inviting me . . .
   BUT: Thank you for the invitation to attend . . .

4. In writing for another person, use an impersonal tone or place the other's name foremost.
   NOT: I am glad to inform you that the results of your tests . . .
   BUT: This letter is to inform you that the results of your tests . . .

   NOT: I want to make reservations for Dr. and Mrs. Kirsch . . .
   BUT: Dr. and Mrs. Kirsch would like reservations for . . .

   NOT: I submitted the report on . . .
   BUT: The report was submitted on . . .

NOTE: In general, avoid using the passive voice verb construction, as illustrated in the last example, because it is wordy and sometimes unclear. Exception: The reason outlined in item 4.

A good balance of active and passive voice can be pleasant but will depend on where you wish to place your emphasis in writing.
   NOT: The surgery was performed by Dr. Augustus. (passive)
   BUT: Dr. Augustus performed the surgery. (active)
   NOT: He was released for return to his regular employment by Dr. Berry. (passive)
   BUT: Dr. Berry released him for regular employment. (active)

Notice in the last example of passive voice that it not only takes longer to say what you want to say but it also might appear that Dr. Berry is the employer.

5. Use a positive approach. Discuss what can be done instead of what cannot.
   NOT: We are unable to give you an appointment on the date you requested.
   BUT: Dr. Elsner will be pleased to see you at 10:30 a.m. on . . .

6. Avoid words that antagonize, such as *overlooked, failure, neglected, forgot, careless, mistake.*
   NOT: We do not understand your failure to pay this bill.
   BUT: We are certain that your nonpayment of this bill is an oversight.

7. Use a subject line when appropriate. This device lets you get right down to business in the main part of the letter.

Examples
Re: Frich pacemaker model Z-141

Subject: Final notice

The Body of the Letter

8. Use simple, natural language similar to your everyday conversation. Avoid unnecessary words and phrases. (See page 305.)
   NOT: Enclosed herewith please find my check in the amount of $25 for payment . . .
   BUT: Enclosed is my $25 payment.

9. Be sure you tell the reader all he or she needs to know to act or respond. You must remember to support your theme, and any secondary ideas should be related to the main one. Point the recipient toward a required action or attitude.

14

10. Use courteous language: *please, thank you, I appreciate.*

11. Use short and interesting sentences; vary the construction of your sentences.

12. Avoid favorite words or expressions and be sure that you are not "cute" or flip.
NOT: It *certainly* was nice to hear from you last week and I *certainly* appreciate . . .
BUT: It was nice to hear from you last week and I appreciate . . .

13. Do not confuse the reader with abrupt moves from one idea to the next.

14. Use words your reader will understand, and avoid using technical terms when writing to patients or to other people outside of your profession.
NOT: Dr. Berry wants you to come in for your test NPO, midnight.
BUT: Please do not eat or drink anything after midnight.

Closing

15. Acknowledge a favor if there was one.

Example
Thank you for the invitation to participate.

16. Make an appropriate apology if necessary.

Example
We are sorry for any inconvenience this delay may have caused.

However, don't "overapologize" or pass the blame to someone else.
NOT: I don't know how I could have made such an awful mistake, and I promise I will never let it happen again.
BUT: I am sorry that my negligence inconvenienced you.

17. Create a feeling of cooperation and good will.
We are looking forward to seeing you in the office on Friday, May 19, at 3:30 p.m.

18. Avoid the "ing" endings.
NOT: Hoping to hear from you, Trusting this will give you time, Thanking you in advance, Looking forward to payment,
BUT: We look forward . . .

19. Thank only after the fact. Do not thank in advance.
NOT: Thank you for taking care of this immediately.
BUT: Your cooperation in attending to this will be appreciated.

Review the Final Product

20. Be sure that your grammar, spelling, and punctuation are accurate.

21. Scrutinize for clarity, content, and tone.

22. Review your plan and check to see that it is complete.

23. Be prepared to revise, rewrite, and eliminate redundant phrases; change the positions of sentences; correct the grammar.

24. Seek criticism and accept it gracefully.

25. Check for attractiveness. The way that the letter looks is almost as important as the message that it carries.

The following are examples of some of the letters the secretary may write for his or her signature.

A Letter of Apology
Dear Mrs. Steiner: ¶ Thank you for returning the letter which I inadvertently sent to you. ¶ I appreciate its prompt return, and I hope that I did not inconvenience you. ¶ Your letter is enclosed. Sincerely,

A Letter of Acknowledgment
(When your employer is away from the office for several days, you are expected to acknowledge the mail that would ordinarily receive the employer's prompt attention.)
Dear Dr. Knape: ¶ Dr. Berry is out of the city and is not expected in the office for ten more days. ¶ Your letter will be brought to his attention immediately upon his return to work. Sincerely.

Canceling an Appointment
Dear Professor Steele: ¶ Dr. Berry asked me to cancel all his appointments for Monday, September 8, 199X, because of an unexpected surgery scheduled. ¶ Therefore, it is necessary to cancel your three o'clock appointment that day. I am sorry for the inconvenience. ¶ Please telephone the office so that I can arrange a new appointment for you. Sincerely,

Requesting a Fee from an Insurance Company
Dear Mr. Tomlinson: ¶ Thank you for your check for $25 as payment toward the completion of the Request for Medical Information on Mr. Silas Trotter. ¶ The fee in this office for these medical reports is $50. We will be happy to complete the form and return it to you as soon as we receive the full fee. Sincerely,

NOTE: If you often have to write letters of this kind, it is a good idea to type a form letter with blanks in appropriate places. You can photocopy your original and fill in the blanks to meet the circumstances or use the "merge" feature on the word processor.

Gentle Collection Letter

(Precise instruction regarding payment is a very important part of collection letters.) Dear Mrs. Lincoln: ¶ Your attention is specifically directed to the enclosed statement for $36. This amount represents the balance due on your account for professional services rendered by Dr. Berry in February of this year. ¶ No further payments can be anticipated from your insurance company and this balance, therefore, remains your personal responsibility. ¶ We would greatly appreciate payment in full within the next ten days. Sincerely,

Less Gentle Collection Letter

Dear Mrs. Dobe: ¶ Your attention is invited to the balance of $85 that is due for professional services rendered you by Dr. Berry in August, 199X. ¶ Although five months have elapsed since these services were rendered, no payment has been received on this account nor have you communicated with the office regarding your plans for payment. ¶ We feel that we have been very patient and lenient in handling this account but now must insist that some arrangements be made to take care of the balance. Unless this account is paid in full prior to February 5, 199X, it will be necessary for us to initiate other means to secure collection. Sincerely,

NOTE: Even though you may copy these collection letters and personalize them to match the circumstances, do not turn them into form letters, since a more personal note may result in better cash flow.

Letter to an Insurance Company

Dear Sir or Madam: RE: Edna Mae Wright, Policy #782-A. ¶ On March 29, 199X, Dr. Berry submitted to your firm a medical report on the above-named patient. This claim of $175 was for services rendered by Dr. Berry on March 15 and 16, 199X. ¶ Neither Mrs. Wright nor Dr. Berry has heard from you regarding this matter. A photocopy of the original claim form is enclosed. ¶ Please send us a check as soon as possible. Sincerely,

14–3: SELF-STUDY

Directions: Your employer, William A. Berry, M.D., has asked you to write the following letter for your signature. Make your outline first. Then compose your letter following the appropriate rules. You will use Dr. Berry's letterhead stationery and identify yourself properly as his secretary. (See Chapter 6, page 126.) Use today's date, modified block format, and mixed punctuation.

Dr. Berry has made arrangements for one of his patients, Mr. Ray Littlefield, to see another physician, Paul R. Vecchione, in consultation. You may invent the necessary information to write Mr. Littlefield who knows that these arrangements were to be made.

Check the end of the chapter for a possible outline and letter.

14–4: REVIEW TEST

Directions: Follow the directions given with Self-Study 14–3 and compose letters for your signature for the following situations. (When each individual letter is complete, ask yourself the questions listed below.)

1. Is it attractive? Check it quickly for appearance.

2. Have you used proper letter mechanics for modified block format with mixed punctuation?

3. Did you need or use a reference line?

4. Did you use a pleasant opening or closing paragraph?

5. Is your main point quickly introduced?

6. Are any details missing? Will the recipient know exactly how to respond?

7. Did you notice any misspelled words or improper use of grammar or punctuation marks?

8. Was the letter precise or could fewer words have been used to say what was said?

14

After you have thoroughly checked your letter, retype it if necessary.

1. Dr. Berry has agreed to address the high school PTA in his community concerning the increased use of alcohol by young adults. Write the program chairman, inventing the necessary data. Part of Dr. Berry's presentation will be the screening of a film entitled "More Than a Few Beers," and he will be prepared for a question-and-answer period.

2. Dr. Berry's engraved stationery is ordered from a neighboring community. You need to order paper and envelopes. Invent all the necessary information to complete this assignment. Be sure to be precise; cover all details. You may wish to review Chapter 6, page 123 Item 1 and Item 2 concerning the details of office and hospital stationery.

3. Dr. Berry received a letter from a surgeon's office indicating that an operative report was enclosed. You carefully checked the contents of the envelope and discovered that the report had not been included. Write a letter to the surgeon's office concerning this oversight. Invent the necessary information to complete this assignment.

4. A former patient, Mrs. Bertha Wilson, has written that she will be in town next month and would like to see Dr. Berry for an examination and an ECG. Please write to give her an appointment inventing the necessary data.

Sample Letters

The following are examples of some types of letters that the secretary may compose for his or her employer's signature:

Unable to Attend a Staff Meeting
Dear Dr. Benson: ¶ Please excuse me from attending the Round Valley Hospital Medical Staff Meeting next Wednesday evening. ¶ I am taking a postgraduate class at the university, and the final examination is scheduled for the same evening. Respectfully, William A. Berry, M.D.

Letter Concerning Laboratory Test Results
Dear Mr. Swan: ¶ Enclosed are copies of the results of the urinalysis and biochemical survey that I ordered at Community Hospital. These values are entirely normal. ¶ I will look forward to seeing you again if you have any further problems. Sincerely, William A. Berry, M.D.

Excuse from Physical Education Class
TO WHOM IT MAY CONCERN: ¶ Since March 18, Angela Marsi has been a patient in this office with an upper respiratory infection requiring the use of antibiotics. ¶ Today I released her to return to school, but I would like her to be excused from physical education classes for one more week. Sincerely, William A. Berry, M.D.

Letter to Compensation Carrier
Dear Mr. Thompson: RE: Toni Wilden, File 0713. ¶ An exploration of the right shoulder has been scheduled on Ms. Wilden at Center City Hospital next Wednesday at 7:30 a.m. ¶ Her convalescence will require 2-3 days in the hospital and absence from work for about three weeks. ¶ Thank you for allowing me to continue with her care. Sincerely, William A. Berry, M.D.

Return to Work
Dear Mr. Girard: ¶ Mr. Samuel Gordon was seen today in final examination after his surgery of May 17, 199X. ¶ His wound is well healed; he has no complaints referable to his cardiorespiratory system; he seems in excellent physical condition. ¶ In my opinion, he should be able to resume his normal work load, with no restrictions, on June 10, 199X. Sincerely, William A. Berry, M.D.

Letter of Congratulations
Dear Dr. Kirkham: ¶ My staff and I would like to express our sincere congratulations to you on your new partnership with Dr. John Champe in the practice of thoracic surgery. ¶ We wish you success and happiness in your new association. Sincerely, William A. Berry, M.D.

Dismissal of a Patient Who Does Not Pay His Medical Bill
Dear Mr. Shamkne: ¶ The records in our office indicate a long-overdue balance on your account totaling $278. ¶ My staff assures me that every reasonable effort to arrange some mutually agreeable plan of payment has failed to prompt any sign of cooperation on your part. ¶ Thus I am forced to conclude that the best interests both of this office and of you will be served by the adoption of the following conditions:

1. Unless your debt is paid in full by April 6, 199X, you will be discharged finally and fully as a patient.

2. Your clinical records will be closed for forwarding by our staff to any physician of your choice. Fail-ure on your part to name a new physician or to advise us of your selection in writing will be your responsibility, not ours. Yours very truly, William A. Berry, M.D.

14–5: REVIEW TEST

Directions: Your employer, Dr. Berry, hands you some mail and asks you to reply to it for his signature; on some letters, he may have made a brief suggestion to guide you. Attempt to make these letters sound as though he dictated them. The relationship between your employer and the recipient will determine the salutation and tone. Use letterhead stationery. Here are the letters and notes for your reply and his signature. Use the current date, full block format, and mixed punctuation.

1. He received a letter from a physician friend who has a cabin on the lake. The friend has invited him to spend the following three-day weekend there, fishing. Dr. Berry asks you to send his regrets because he is on call that weekend and has a patient entering the hospital Sunday afternoon. Invent the necessary information to complete the assignment.

2. Dr. Berry receives a formal announcement from Frank R. Curtis, M.D., a new physician opening his office in the same medical complex, for the practice of family medicine. Dr. Berry asks you to send a note of congratulations. Invent the address.

3. There is a note to you that reads: "I referred Mrs. Dorothy Winters to Dr. John Briton for consultation about three weeks ago, and I have not received a consultation report from him about her. She had a lump in her right breast. Please write him to inquire about her progress." Invent any necessary information to complete this assignment.

ABSTRACTING FROM PATIENTS' CHARTS

Many routine requests for medical information on patients can be handled by the secretary. The physician may review the record first, noting that there is nothing unusual, and then ask you to reply for his or her signature. This request from another physician, hospital, insurance company, lawyer, employer, or compensation carrier must always be accompanied by a signed release from the patient authorizing the physician to release this information (Fig. 14–1 and Figs. 1–3 and 1–4).

Examine the chart note on Mr. Dow (Fig. 14–2). Then read the letter and see how the secretary has included all the pertinent information in the reply (Fig. 14–3).

REFERENCE MATERIALS

Because there are many kinds of reference materials to assist you in writing letters, a partial list is provided in Appendix C. Additionally, you should start your own file of sample letters that you have written, to be adapted or combined to meet individual situations.

A good dictionary, a punctuation and grammar book, a style manual, and a thesaurus should be in your desk library. Because we have discussed all of these except the thesaurus in previous chapters, we will discuss it now.

Thesaurus means *treasury* in Greek, and a real treasure it can be for you. A dictionary is used to find the meaning of a word, and a thesaurus is used to find an alternative word to express the same idea (synonym). Or you may have a negative idea that you wish to make positive; the thesaurus also contains antonyms.

Every synonym listed is not an exact substitute for the word you might want, however, and care must be taken to see that the word not only fits the context of the sentence but that it is also a word that you could use comfortably.

For instance, if you decide that you want to use another word for *stolen* in the sentence *My dress was stolen,* you look for *steal* in the thesaurus. There you find that many synonyms are given but not all are applicable to *stolen* as expressed in the sentence: The dress could not have been *robbed, abducted, embezzled, purloined, plundered, swindled,* or *plagiarized.* Furthermore, the slang expressions *pinched, carried off,* and *ripped off* might even carry an additional

14

RECORDS RELEASE

Date ....1-25-9x....

To ....William A. Berry, M.D.....
DOCTOR OR HOSPITAL

....3933 Navajo Road, San Diego, CA 92119....
ADDRESS

I hereby authorize and request you to release

To ....Quality Life Assurance Society....

....Box 2187, New York, NY 10001....
ADDRESS

The complete medical records in your possession concerning my illness

and/or treatment during the period from ....9-1-9x.... to ....1-15-9x....

Signed ....*Michael T. Dow*....
PATIENT OR NEAREST RELATIVE

....*Maryellen Dow*....
WITNESS
Relationship ....spouse....

FIGURE 14-1. Authorization to release medical information.

Michael T. Dow
AGE: 41

REF: Frank R. Evans, M.D.
911 Washington
San Diego, CA 92101
800-5981

9-1-9x   Patient complains of dyspnea on exertion, malaise of
6 weeks duration. Chest x-ray from Dr. Evans' office
reveals left lower lobe infiltrate. Suggest bilateral bronchography to rule out bronchiectasis.

jt
_____
William A. Berry, M.D.

9-3-9x   *Bilateral bronchograms, Centre City Hosp. jt*
9-4-9x   *Left lower lobectomy. jt.*

9-15-9x   See letter to Dr. Evans.

10-11-9x   Incision is well-healed. No complaints referable to
CR system. Pain free. Pt. to return to work Monday,
October 14 with no restrictions.

jt
_____
William A. Berry, M.D.

12-10-9x   Pt. seen in final follow-up. No problems. Need not
return. See letter to Dr. Evans.

jt
_____
William A. Berry, M.D.

FIGURE 14-2. Patient's chart note.

William A. Berry, M.D.

3933 Navajo Road
San Diego, California 92119

463-0000

January 28, 199x

Quality Life Assurance Society
Medical Department
Box 2187
New York, NY 10001

Gentlemen:

RE: Michael T. Dow

Mr. Dow was first seen on September 1, 199x, complaining
of dyspnea on exertion and malaise of six weeks duration.
A chest x-ray revealed a left lower lobe infiltrate.

After bilateral bronchograms on September 3, 199x, the diagnosis
of bronchiectasis was confirmed, and a left lower lobectomy
was performed on September 4, 199x.

The patient was released to return to work on October 14,
199x, and was last seen in the office on December 10, 199x,
and released from further care.

A copy of the operative report and pathology report is enclosed.

Sincerely yours,

William A. Berry, M.D.

jt

Enclosures

FIGURE 14-3. Letter composed by the secretary for her employer's signature, based on information in the patient's chart.

meaning that you do not intend. However, you also find the word *taken; taken* fits what you want to say and you are comfortable with it.

A thesaurus may be arranged alphabetically, like a dictionary, or you may have to look up the "idea" of the word and use cross references. Definitions usually are not given. You will need to explore your thesaurus to see how it is organized. There are programs available for use with word processing equipment that contain a thesaurus. (Often these are in combination with a spelling-check program.) When composing a document, you may instantly bring up a list of substitute words for the particular word for which you need a choice.

 14-6: SELF-STUDY

Directions: You will need a thesaurus for the following assignment. This assignment is to help you become familiar with using a thesaurus as a reference source for achieving variety in word usage.

Using a thesaurus as a reference, type three to five words that can be substituted for the following overworked words:

1. know

2. awful

3. tell

4. nice

5. think

Please check the end of the chapter for possible responses.

14–7: REVIEW TEST

Directions: As you can see from Self-Study 14–6, the word choices are very broad but become very limiting when they are to be substituted into the context of a complete thought. In the following exercises, there will be more than one word that needs a substitute and you will need to be sure that each substitute word fits the context of what you wish to say. Often, it is necessary to change other words in the sentence to make the new word fit properly. Retype each of the following sentences, substituting your alternate word or words for those underlined. *You should write two complete sentences for each target sentence.* You may adjust the sentence to fit your needs.

Example
How much did you <u>get</u> from that <u>game</u> you played?
Possible rewrites:
How much did you <u>obtain</u> from that <u>contest</u> you *entered?*
How much did you <u>receive</u> from that <u>match</u> you *made?*

1. She <u>needs</u> to <u>ask</u> her boss for a raise.

Please see the end of the chapter for some possible responses to this. Continue with the rest of the exercise without assistance of other than your thesaurus.

2. It is <u>difficult</u> to <u>know</u> how to complete <u>certain</u> office tasks.

3. Please <u>arrange</u> for your <u>group</u> to be <u>on time</u>.

4. Please <u>excuse</u> my <u>delay</u> in <u>answering</u> your request.

5. It gives me <u>great pleasure</u> to welcome you.

6. We, as a <u>rule</u>, do not <u>employ inexperienced</u> secretaries.

14

TRAVEL ARRANGEMENTS

The secretary may be asked by the physician to formulate and expedite arrangements for a vacation or travel to a medical convention held in the United States or abroad. A worry-free trip depends on systematic and prudent planning to eliminate the frustrating problems that haphazard arrangements can bring. No matter what the distance or duration of the trip, the secretary should be able to set it up when the physician announces his or her plans.

The secretary must see that applications for attendance at out-of-town seminars or continuing medical education (CME) courses are made as soon as the location is announced. Upon receiving written confirmation, the secretary should make travel and hotel arrangements. Any delay or procrastination in initiating reservations may mean the physician will be unable to stay at the hotel where the convention is being held, and it might affect the chance of securing the most direct transportation.

General information on the physician's travel preferences can be accumulated in a permanent travel file folder to help you plan any trip. This would include the following:

1. Name of a reputable travel agent

2. Employer's credit card numbers

3. Car rental preference

4. Travel:
   a. Preferred method of travel (air, rail, or car) to specific destinations
   b. Class of travel
   c. Airline seating choice (window or aisle)

5. Hotel:
   a. Who exactly the reservations are for
   b. Type of accommodations required. (Specific features desired such as bed size; suite; studio; connecting rooms; views of garden, pool, terrace, ocean, and so on.)
   c. Price rate range desired

To the general information, the secretary can then add the more specific information, such as:

1. Destination

2. Preferred route. Any side trips or tours?

3. Date and time for departure and arrival

4. Number in party

5. Approximate hotel arrival and departure time

6. Date and time preferred for arrival. (Which is more important—at destination or departure from homes?)

When you have gathered all your information, your next step is to call your travel agent, primarily a central source of information for tours, carriers, and accommodations. A travel agent can sell tickets or make reservations, but the service to you is free because the commission is paid by the tour operator, by the hotel, or by the carrier. Most travel agencies have computers providing current information on airline fares and schedules, both domestic and international, and on hotel availability with addresses and telephone numbers. The computer gives information on weather conditions in all parts of the world, train reservation information, special tour packages featuring discounts, and money rate of exchange. In addition to figuring out schedules, making reservations, and centralizing ticket purchases, a travel agent can help you with many small details: arrange for visas, insurance, car rentals, special meals or dietary preferences, airline aisle or window seating choice, and tickets to special events. A valuable agent will usually be familiar with the area your employer is visiting.

To make plane or rail reservations, your travel agent can select from all possible lines out of the city. You provide the specific details; the agent will make and confirm the reservations and mail or deliver the tickets. Tickets may be charged on a credit card. If airline tickets are mailed to the office, the secretary promptly checks arrival and departure dates and times against the information he or she has on the itinerary work sheet to see that they have been made as requested. If your employer wishes to rent a car upon arrival at the destination, the travel agent can reserve one. (Please note: It is necessary to have a valid driver's license as well as a nationally recognized credit card—for example, VISA, MasterCard, Carte Blanche, and American Express—in order to rent a car.)

The agent will give you the details concerning arrangements for picking the car up at the airport or rail terminal. If your employer does not want a rental car, you need to know about other available means of transportation. The travel agent can tell you if there is hotel limousine, bus, or taxi service and the methods for obtaining these vehicles.

Hotel reservations can also be made by the travel agent, but many secretaries prefer to write or telephone for these themselves, particularly for a business trip. As a convenience to travelers, most hotel/motel chains have toll-free 800 numbers that can be used to make reservations and check on them. If arrival time is to be after 6 p.m., it is necessary to tell this to the reservation clerk. Sometimes a deposit must be made to assure that the room will be reserved. If the physician is attending a convention, the assistant needs to convey this to the hotel reservation clerk to obtain special group rates since rooms are held specifically for people attending the convention. In fact, you may be turned down for reservations if you fail to mention the fact that your employer is attending a convention. Provide the following additional information in your letter to the hotel for accommodations: the names of all persons staying in the room, the type of accommodations desired, the date and approximate time of arrival, and the date of departure. Send a deposit or credit card number and ask for written confirmation.

When you have completed all the arrangements, the travel agent may computer-generate an itinerary, which you may use to prepare a complete travel itinerary and present it and a copy to your employer (keep a copy for yourself) with the tickets and hotel confirmation. The itinerary will include:

1. Departure date, time, airlines, class, flight number, including connecting flights. This may also include seating arrangements when you are able to obtain them in advance.

2. Arrival time (if in another time zone, indicate the time zone). You can give approximate air time, information concerning meals, inflight movies when available.

3. Transportation arrangements: bus, taxi, rental car.

4. Hotel arrangement, including address and telephone number.

14

5. Return date, time, airlines, class of travel, flight number.

This information should be attractively typed so that it is easy to read (Fig. 14–4).

Your copy of the itinerary is put in the travel folder for future reference. Some secretaries make a check-off sheet to be sure that they have not overlooked any detail of the travel plans (Fig. 14–5).

```
                          ITINERARY
                            for
                  Dr. and Mrs. William A. Berry
                       June 1-5, 199x

       DEPARTURE:    Buttergold Airlines, Flight 792, Non-stop
                     Leaves:    7:05 a.m. Breakfast will be served on board
                     Arrives:   11:45 a.m. (their time).
                               (Flying time:  3 hours, 40 minutes)

       CAR RENTAL:   Lo-Rate Cars. Booth located near baggage pickup.
                     199x Odyssey is reserved. $28/day, unlimited mileage.
                     Confirmation attached.

       HOTEL:        Saint Ann's Inn, 321 Main Street.
                     Phone 222-500-8438
                     Confirmation attached.

       RETURN:       Buttergold Airlines, Flight 251, Non-stop
                     Leaves:    3:15 p.m.  Supper will be served on board
                     Arrives:   6:00 p.m. (our time)

       Have a good time!

       Arrangements: Fiesta International Travel Service.  231-2548.
```

FIGURE 14–4. Sample itinerary.

14

Travel Arrangements:

_____ Call covering physician's office to be sure he or she will be available to take calls from the doctor's patients.

_____ Cross off the time in the appointment book.

_____ Call for airline reservations. Airlines preferred _____

_____ Write the hotel.

_____ Arrange for car rental. Agency preferred _____

       Credit card # _____

_____ Check driver's license. Expiration date _____

_____ Purchase traveler's checks. Numbers _____

_____ Notify answering service of dates and name of covering physician.

_____ Type itinerary. Copies to _____

_____ Confirm airline reservation.

_____ Confirm hotel reservation.

_____ Confirm car rental.

_____ Obtain names and phone number of anyone the doctor may be visiting while out of the city _____

FIGURE 14–5. Sample check sheet.

14–8: REVIEW TEST

Directions: Your employer, Dr. Claire Duennes, is flying to Mexico City for the International Congress of Family Physicians. She will have five days in Mexico City, including the arrival day, and three of them will be taken up with the meeting.

1. Please write a letter to make hotel reservations for Dr. Duennes. The convention is being held in the Pan Americas Hotel, 387 Avenida Juarez, Mexico City, Mexico, D.F., and she would like to stay there. She plans to arrive as early in the day as possible (so she can do some sightseeing before the meeting begins). Invent any other data you need to do the assignment properly.

2. Prepare a travel itinerary for Dr. Duennes, inventing all the data you need to complete it properly so you will not have to consult a local travel agent. She is not concerned about the return time or arrival to her home city.

WE HOPE YOU HAVEN'T BEEN USING THESE RULES!*

1. Make sure each pronoun agrees with their antecedent.

2. Just between you and I, case is important.

3. Verbs has to agree with their subjects.

4. Watch out for irregular verbs which have crope into English.

5. Don't use no double negatives.

6. A writer must not shift your point of view.

7. When dangling, don't use participles.

8. Join clauses good like a conjunction should.

9. Don't write a run-on sentence you got to punctuate it.

10. About sentence fragments.

11. In letters reports and articles use commas to separate items in a series.

12. Don't use commas, which are not necessary.

13. Its important to use apostrophe's correctly.

14. Check to see if you have any words out.

15. Don't abbrev.

16. In the case of a letter, check it in terms of jargon.

17. As far as incomplete constructions, they are wrong.

18. About repetition, the repetition of a word might be real effective repetition—take, for instance, the repetition of words in Lincoln's Gettysburg Address.

19. In my opinion, I think that an author when he is writing should not get into the habit of making use of too many unnecessary words that he does not really need in order to put his message across.

20. Last but not least, lay off clichés.

▣ Answers to 14–1: Self-Study

1. Please retype this; it is your responsibility.

2. Remodeling is taking place in the Emergency Room; therefore, reroute all patient traffic to Ward B until further notice.
   Remodeling is taking place in the Emergency Room, so reroute all patient traffic to Ward B until further notice.

3. The new chief-of-staff will take over the first of next month; furthermore, there will be many new physicians added to the active staff roster.
   The new chief-of-staff will take over the first of next month, and there will be many new physicians added to the active staff roster. (Or write two separate sentences.)

---

* With permission of THE READER'S DIGEST, March, 1963, "Pardon, Your Slip is Showing."

14

4. To be accurate and to meet your production levels is important here.
   It is important here to be accurate and to meet your production levels.

5. Pull the patient's record; notify the doctor of the emergency; give the record to the doctor; relate any information you have received.

6. (Change the final line only.) (3) Refer to the Inventory Stock Catalogue and enter the appropriate stock number if the preprinted requisition is not available for the products you require.

7. The following is a list of the duties of the custodian of records:
   a. to keep accurate records
   b. to make corrections in the proper way
   c. to be sure that records are signed or initialed
   d. to obtain a release before you permit unauthorized persons to see the records.

8. (The order on this one needs changing too.)
   Rules for taking phone calls:
   a. Pick up the phone as soon as it rings
   b. Answer with your name and that of the department
   c. Ask for the name of the person calling
   d. Refrain from interrupting the caller
   e. Transfer to the right extension.

9. Jogging through the parking lot I saw many new flowers.

10. My dog stayed at my mother's house while I was on vacation.

11. She was 44 when her first and only child was born.

12. The record, which has been throughout the department, finally was returned.

13. an attack of

14. at a time

15. purposes

16. the sum of/change the twenty dollars to $20

17. color of the

18. at a/date

19. made out of

20. engaged in

21. during the period

22. in duration

23. in size

24. a period of

25. actively

26. I feel *that* the nursing personnel as well as *the* pulmonary medicine staff will benefit from the information and instructions.

27. The *members of the* Advisory Committee and Management Department would like to express their thanks for the time you gave to present the material to us.

28. (In this one, we need to eliminate several "shoulds" as well as rewrite using parallel construction.)
   When operating a postage meter, remember the following:
   a. Change the date daily.
   b. Check the amount of postage set before stamping the envelope.
   c. Reset the meter to zero.
   d. Save all unused postage metered tapes and envelopes for a refund.
   e. Make application for the refund within a year.
   f. Deposit the mail on the date shown or postage may be forfeited.
   g. Make a request for a full refund if an error is made by the meter (poor ink, incorrect postage amount). A request for a full refund should be made and no further postage imprinted until the problem has been corrected.
   h. Write "HAND STAMP" in large red letters on both the front and back of a bulky envelope.

29. The medical record may be the physician's only witness in court. For this reason, the medical record must be completely accurate.

30. By writing, one learns to write. (Just put the comma in the right place!)

■ Answers to 14–3: Self-Study

WHO: Obtain patient's complete name and address.
WHY: Dr. Berry asked me to arrange for a consultation for patient with Dr. Paul Vecchione.
WHAT/WHEN: Give patient complete date, time, place, and reason for visit.
REACTION: Patient will call me to make any changes if necessary.

Today's date, 199X

Mr. Ray Littlefield
1234 Songbird Lane
Cradle Valley, CA 90000

Dear Mr. Littlefield:

Dr. Berry asked me to let you know that your consultation with Paul R. Vecchione, M.D., has been arranged. His office is in the same medical complex as Dr. Berry's office, Suite 210. Dr. Vecchione will be pleased to see you:

                Monday, July 1
                10 a.m.
                Suite 210
                476-8974

Please let me know if you have any questions or if this appointment is not suitable. I will be happy to make any adjustment to fit your schedule.

                        Sincerely yours,

                        (Ms.) Your name, Receptionist

There are many acceptable variations on this assignment. The important areas to consider are as follows:

- *does the patient know why he is seeing another physician*
- *who is this doctor*
- *where is he located*
- *exactly when is this appointment*
- *what does he do if he can't make it then*
- *whom does he call if he has a problem about this*
- *does the letter look attractive*
- *is the letter error free*

14

▣ Answers to 14–6: Self-Study

Here are some possible word choices:

1. KNOW: perceive, discern, recognize, see, comprehend, understand, realize, appreciate, experience, be aware of.

2. AWFUL: terrific, tremendous, horrible, dreadful, fearful.

3. TELL: describe, narrate, explain, inform, advise, state.

4. NICE: delicate, fine, pleasing, attractive, accurate.

5. THINK: presume, understand, reason, reflect, speculate.

◖ Answer to First Question on 14–7: Review Test

1. She wants to propose that her boss give her a raise.

2. She finds it necessary to request a raise from her boss.

Notice that there are many substitute words for "needs" and "ask." However, one would *not* say: It is a *requirement* to *implore* her boss for a raise.

14

Typing Reports, Memos, Minutes, and Agenda

OBJECTIVES

After reading this chapter and working the exercises, you should be able to

1. explain proper report format.
2. type an agenda for a meeting.
3. record, prepare, and type minutes for a meeting in correct format.
4. prepare an intraoffice memo for your employer's signature.

. . . .

INTRODUCTION

This chapter will explain in detail the format for reports other than medical reports regarding patient care. Refer to Chapter 12 for information on preparing a history and physical and Chapter 13 for preparing miscellaneous medical reports. Here we will discuss how to type hospital protocols and memos as well as how to prepare and type an agenda and how to record and type minutes for a meeting. Formats enhance written communication; however, we cannot overlook the most important aspect of composing such documents, and that is readability or communication effectiveness.

TYPING HOSPITAL PROTOCOLS

Hospital protocols are also known as hospital reports or hospital policies. Each section of a hospital has departmental policies and procedures. Since each in-

stitution has variances, only general guidelines on format, headings, and subheadings will be stated. Hospital protocols have individual headings for the topics and titles. These will vary just as the nature of the report will vary. The originator of a report may or may not formulate the title for the transcriptionist, so he or she should be able to extract the title from the paragraph itself by pulling out the main idea and composing a brief heading for that section. The hospital or institution will usually have a special format, and often special paper, for typing these documents.

Headings and Format

The format will follow outline form using the full block, modified block, or indented style. If there is more than one paragraph under a specific title, paragraph just as you would in a full block letter: double space and begin the new paragraph flush with the left margin. A policy (protocol) should be headed with the

15

323

title of the policy and its identifying number. Headings should be consistent throughout the report and follow simple guidelines:

1. Title: centered on the page and typed in full capital letters. It may be underlined if you desire.

2. Main topics: full caps underlined.

3. Subtopics: full caps not underlined.

4. Minor topics: upper-case and lower-case underlined.

5. Page one: If the protocol is for a department in the hospital, e.g., emergency room, the page might be shown as ER-1; radiology department may be shown as RD-1, and so forth.

Listing

The following rules apply to listing in memos, reports, minutes, or policies.

1. Lists may be introduced with serial numbers or letters of the alphabet followed by a period or parentheses. Bullets (•) are also appropriate substitutes for numbers or letters.

2. Lists are typed in block format under the beginning of each line, and typing is not brought back under the number, letter, or bullet.

3. Lists do not need to be complete sentences but should be terminated with periods.

4. Lists should have parallel construction and be grammatically consistent, e.g., each line beginning with a verb: *type, list spell, space;* each line beginning with a noun or pronoun: *who, what, when, where;* each line being a complete sentence.

Multipage Reports

If a hospital protocol, policy, or report continues to more than one page, the word *continued* may be typed at the bottom of the completed page. The subsequent page or pages begin an inch from the top of the page with the title of the document, the page number (the second page might be shown as ER-2 for emergency room, RD-2 for radiology department, and so forth), and any other important data (the policy number, for instance).

Closing Format

Figures 15–1 and 15–2 illustrate a simple report or policy closing format typed using full block format. The typist should identify every report or policy she or he prepares with a two- or three-letter identification, i.e., initials. Hospital protocols or policies are approved by hospital committees and revised from time to time.

MEMORANDA

The purpose of the memo (plural: memoranda) is to send information to one or more people within the office, company, department, or hospital, quickly and economically, in any situation in which written communication is appropriate. Memos provide permanent or temporary records of announcements, instructions, appointments, and so on. A special format is used for writing memos, and composing a memo is very much like composing a letter. First, identify what you want to say and why you are saying it. Second, think of your reader. Design the memo in such a way that the information you want to communicate is easy to absorb and in such a form that the reader will be able to make use of the information easily. As in all business writing, the message should be clear, concise, correct, and complete.

Following are the elements used in setting up the format for the memo, with an explanation for each. The first four headings are typed on the actual memorandum. (Please see Figure 15–3 for the completed memo format.) Preprinted forms, made of less expensive paper than letter stationery, are usually available but if not, use plain paper and type in the headings.

To: A list of all the names of the persons or departments for routing of the memo. The memo can go from one person to another, or each staff member can receive a copy of the memo. You indicate distribution by writing "please route" on a single copy of the memo with staff names under the list or by making a copy for each person or department.

From: Writer or dictator. The originator usually does not sign the memo but may initial it next to his or her name or at the bottom of the memo.

Date: Date of origination.

Subject: A subject line will appear in the heading, telling the reader what the memo is about; thus the reader can get right to the main point. The accuracy of the subject line is extremely important. Be specific enough to keep the reader from having to wade through the first paragraph to see what the announcement refers to or guess what it should be filed under.

MR-1

XYZ Medical Center
30 South Main Street
Woodland Hills, XY 12345

MEDICAL RECORD PROCEDURES

SUBPOENAS

Medical records shall only be removed from the hospital jurisdiction in accordance with court order, subpoena, statute, or upon the approval of the Hospital Administrator.

Only those individuals specifically authorized by the Director of Medical Records may accept subpoenas for medical records.

No subpoena will be accepted by medical record personnel for cases in which the hospital is a party to the action unless specifically authorized to do so by the Administrator. These subpoenas must be served upon the Administrator, or his designee in the case of his or her absence. The subpoenaed medical records will be given to the Administrator to be placed in a controlled environment.

If it appears necessary to remove medical records from the hospital's jurisdiction as under court order, subpoena, or statute, an effort will be made to ascertain if it would be acceptable to send copies of the record as opposed to removing the original medical record.

CONTINUING EDUCATION AND INSERVICE

Medical Record Department personnel shall be encouraged to participate in educational programs, professional associations, organizational meetings and pertinent correspondence courses related to their duties. Educational achievement shall be documented.

FILING OF INCOMPLETE MEDICAL RECORDS

No medical record shall be filed until it is complete except on order of the Medical Record Committee.

LIST OF COMMONLY USED ABBREVIATIONS, ACRONYMS, AND SYMBOLS

A list of approved abbreviations, acronyms, and symbols for use in the medical record will be maintained in the Medical Record Department. This list shal be approved by the medical staff.

MICROFILMING MEDICAL RECORDS

Charts will be microfilmed after a reasonable period of time depending upon the filing space available for completed medical records. The process of microfilming will be performed by the Medical Record Microfilm Clerk. Records will be screened to ensure accurate patient identification prior to microfilming. Each processed microfilm roll will be reviewed to assure readability of the film prior to the destruction of the original records.

Approved ———————————————————   Policy Number 90-100

Effective date: June 1, 199x   Revised:

Reviewed: Revised:

15

FIGURE 15–1.   An example of a page from a hospital policy and procedure manual illustrating full block format. Wording and content of hospital policies and procedures varies from institution to institution.

ALVARADO HOSPITAL MEDICAL CENTER

DEPARTMENT OF NURSING SERVICES

Date:

Approved:

Page: 1 of

PROCEDURE:

Reviewed/
Revised by:

Date:

FIGURE 15-2. Sample format for a hospital procedure or policy. (From Fordney, M. T., and Diehl, M. O.: Medical Transcription Guide. Do's and Don'ts. W. B. Saunders Company, Philadelphia, 1990.)

15

MEMORANDUM

DATE: September 22, 199x
TO: Joan M. Abbott
           Shirley N. Andrews
           Marilyn P. Dorley

FROM: Michael Jones, M. D. *mJ*

SUBJECT: Office Procedure Manual

It has come to my attention that when someone is sick or leaves on
vacation, it is difficult to know how to complete certain tasks in
the office. Therefore, I would like each of you to work on a procedure manual for your specific job in this office outlining from
A to Z exactly what tasks you perform and how to carry them out.

The following activities should be listed.
        1. Daily duties.
        2. Weekly duties.
        3. Monthly duties.
        4. Quarterly duties.
        5. Yearly duties.
        6. Stat duties.

Please have this ready by November 22.
        sna

FIGURE 15–3. Sample memorandum, vertical style.

Closing Elements: The memo is completed with the typist's initials a double space after the last line of the body of the memo. It is not necessary to type the author's initials, but one should do so if it is the custom in the organization. A typed signature line is not used, nor does the author/dictator sign the memo. (There is a trend toward omitting the FROM line in favor of a typed signature at the close of the memo. If you choose this less formal approach, the author may initial or sign the memo here.) Even though the memo is not signed by the author, it should always be submitted to him or her for approval before being distributed. Some writers will initial their memo after their name on the FROM line. Reference initials, enclosures, and copy notations should be handled exactly as they are in a letter: reference initials are typed two blank lines below the closing, then the enclosure line, followed by the copy notation, followed by the postscript, in that order, one or two blank lines below one another.

Continuations: If the memo continues to an additional page or pages, begin typing one inch down from the top of the page and type in your headings: name of the addressee, date, and page number. Triple space and continue with the body of the memo.

15–1: PRACTICE TEST

Directions: The following is a handwritten note from your employer. Please complete the memo with his name as the originator. Your employer is William A. Berry, M.D., and the other women in the office are Mary Connors, CMT, Sue Marcos, RN, and Joan Taylor, CMA-A. Your name and title (office manager) should also be listed as one of the recipients.

5/7/9X

please compose a memo for my signature to be distributed to all the staff concerning use of the new photocopy machine. I want everyone to receive a copy of the operation & upkeep of the machine. Each staff member should be thoroughly familiar with operation. The machine is to be used only for reproducing billing statements, making copies of insurance claim forms, & to make copies of chart documents when required. Office correspondence should be typed with a carbon copy whenever possible but a photocopy of the original will be made for outside copies. There will be no personal use of the machine without my permission, please. HAB

15

AGENDA

The agenda is prepared before a meeting and establishes the order of business of the meeting and the items to be discussed or the plan of activities. It may be mailed to the membership before the meeting or distributed as the meeting begins. The secretary will be able to use a copy to assist in taking notes and preparing the minutes.

The format of the agenda should be functional and easy to read. These goals are achieved by using layout techniques such as centered headings, columnar lists for agenda items, and white space between items. The agenda should be typed, double spaced, and kept to one page if possible. Roman numerals are often used to number the items. The following information may be included in a formal agenda:

1. The name, date, and time of the meeting (centered on the page).

2. The location of the meeting.

3. Call to order.

4. Roll call and/or introduction of members and/or board of directors.

AGENDA

TEAM MEDICAL MANAGEMENT PROGRAM

May 9, 199X

I.   Call to Order

II.   Roll Call and introduction of guests

       James Morgan, M.D., representative from
       Bayville Hospital

III.   Approval of Minutes of April 14, 199X

IV.   Officers' Reports

          Treasurer's report

V.   Committees

          1. Bylaws Committee
          2. Membership Committee
          3. Nominating Committee
          4. Credentials Committee

VI.   Old Business
          1. Attendance
          2. Proposed changes in meeting time or day
          3. Special project funding

VII.   New Business
          1. Health Fair (Dr. Dunn)
          2. Evaluation of treadmill (Dr. Patton)
          3. Discussion of 199X vacation schedules (Dr. Majur)

VIII. Announcements

          Position open at Desert View Community. See Ron Miller.

          Next meeting: Wednesday, June 18, 3 p.m., Board Room
          (subject to approval today)

IX.   Adjournment

FIGURE 15–4. Sample of a formal agenda. (From Fordney, M. T., and Diehl, M. O.: Medical Transcription Guide. Do's and Don'ts. W. B. Saunders Company, Philadelphia, 1990.)

15

Team Medical Management Program Agenda

May 9, 199X

☐ Call to order
☐ Roll call
☐ Approval of minutes of last meeting
☐ Reports of officers
☐ Reports of committees
☐ Old Business
   • Attendance
   • Changes in meeting time/day
   • Special project funding
☐ New Business
   • Health Fair
   • Treadmill
   • Vacation schedules
☐ Announcements
☐ Adjournment

FIGURE 15–5. Sample of an informal agenda with squares introducing main headings and bullets introducing subheadings. (From Fordney, M. T., and Diehl, M. O.: Medical Transcription Guide. Do's and Don'ts. W. B. Saunders Company, Philadelphia, 1990.)

5. Introduction of guests and/or new members.

6. Reading and approval of the minutes of the previous meeting.

7. Officers' reports. This is the main topic, and the individual reports are listed as subtopics.

8. Committee reports. This is the main topic, and the individual committee reports are listed as subtopics.

9. Old business. Unfinished business from the previous meeting is included. *Old business* is the main topic, and the individual topics constituting old business are listed as subtopics.

10. New business. This is the main heading, and the individual topics (when known) constituting new business are listed as subtopics. Additional space is allowed at this point so that new topics may be added shortly before the meeting (at the president's discretion) or during the meeting itself.

11. Announcements. Often includes when and where the next meeting will be held.

12. Adjournment.

Figure 15-4 provides a sample formal agenda, and Figure 15–5 provides a sample informal agenda.

15–2: SELF-STUDY

Directions: Referring to Figure 15–4, use that format, with Roman numerals, and type an agenda that might have been prepared before this meeting took place.

MINUTES

Minutes are the taking of notes or making a brief summary of a meeting. They become the official documentation when approved by the members of the organization. A standardized form can be used to fill in information as the meeting is conducted. Basically, it would follow the items in the agenda for the meeting. Minutes are usually taken by the recording secretary, although anyone attending the meeting may take minutes. It is helpful to have the minutes of the previous meeting, a list of the membership, and the agenda for the meeting. The detail with which the notes are taken (or tape recorded) is determined by the organization and the business conducted. Depending on the policy of the organization, discussions

Desert View Hospital   Mirage, Arizona

SAFETY COMMITTEE

<u>MINUTES</u>

<u>DATE</u>:

A meeting of the Safety Committee was called to order at 2:05 p.m.
on August 22, 199x, in the Board Room.

<u>MEMBERS PRESENT</u>:

Jack Herzog, Terri Peters, Bobbi Lee, Rita Hardin, Bob Duncan, Roland
Wolf, Joan Yubetta, Carolyn Rath, Pam Hollingsworth, and Dave Leithoff.

<u>MEMBERS ABSENT</u>:

Absent and excused were Peter Hulbert, Mary Harreld and Carolyn Germano.

<u>MINUTES</u>:

The minutes of the previous meeting were read. Bobbie Lee's name was
added to the list of members present for the July 26 Safety Committee
Meeting. The minutes were then approved as corrected.

<u>ROTATION OF MEMBERSHIP</u>:

A discussion was held concerning rotation of membership. It was
suggested that Doreen Black be admitted as a member of the committee.
It was also suggested that each member take turns inviting one guest
with Bob Duncan bringing the first guest. Jack Herzog will contact the
departments not represented at the Safety Committee.

<u>ELECTRICAL SAFETY PROGRAM</u>:

Joan Yubetta suggested that an electrical safety program be started.
Rita Hardin reported that electrical cords are not being taped down.

<u>FIRE DRILLS</u>:

Dave Leithoff reported that there had been no fire drill in a month and
suggested that there should be one by the end of September.

<u>FIRST AID</u>:

Terri Peters reported a total of 36 injuries for the month of August.
Back injuries were down to five for August. There were seven falls,
three cuts, and one foreign body.

It was suggested by Bob Duncan and Terri Peters that a form be designed
for reporting scratches, puncture wounds, etc.

<u>BEVERAGE SPILLING</u>:

It was suggested that Bobbi Lee put an article in the Capsule on the
spilling of beverages. It was further suggested that <u>spill</u> stations be
set up in key places in the hospital. Bob Duncan will bring this up in
the cabinet meeting.

<u>ADJOURNMENT</u>:

There being no further business, the meeting was adjourned at 4:15 p.m.
by Bob Duncan, Chairperson.

Respectfully submitted,

Dave Leithoff, Recording Secretary

lro

FIGURE 15-6. Sample minutes from a meeting typed in full block format.

15

are summarized and speakers are cited. Format is flexible but can be done as follows:

Title. The heading is usually centered on the page and typed in full capital letters. It is optional to underline it.

Date, Time, and Place. Date, time, and place of the meeting may be part of the heading or part of the report itself. The presiding officer is identified with the *call to order* or adjournment notation.

Names of the Members. Names of the members present as well as members absent are listed in the minutes. If roll is taken, that sheet may be attached to the minutes. The names are usually listed in alpha-betical order. List the names and include appropriate titles and other identifying information of any ex offi-cio members or guests in attendance.

Format. The format should be consistent from meeting to meeting and secretary to secretary. The events should be reported in the order in which they occurred during the meeting. Outline format should be followed using the full block, modified block, or indented style. The titles of the sections follow those of the agenda used at the meeting itself. Roman numerals are often used to introduce the titles of each section. Generally, headings (with or without numbers) should be typed flush with the left margin. Single space the material under the headings and double space between headings. The headings are typed ei-

---

TITLE CENTERED AND TYPED IN FULL CAPS

I. Main Topic (first item) (Capitalize the first letter of each important word.)
  A. Secondary heading (Capitalize the first letter and any
  B. . . .   proper nouns here and at all
  C. . . .   other levels.)
  D. . . .
    1. Third level heading
    2. . .
    3. . .
    4. . .
      a. Fourth level heading
      b. . . . .
        (1) Fifth level heading
        (2). . . .
        (3). . . .
          (a) Sixth level heading
          (b). . . .
II. Main Topic (second item) (You will have to backspace once
  A. . . .   to allow for the roman numeral —
  B. . . .   for balance.)
  C. . . .
    1. . . .
    2. . . .
  D. . . .
    1. . . .
    2. . . .
    3. . . .
III. Main Topic (third item) (You will have to backspace twice on this line for balance.)

The major headings and subdivisions may be a single word or phrase; long phrases or clauses; complete sentences; or any combination of sentences, phrases, and single words.

Between-line spacing is as follows:
  After title: triple-space.
  Main topic: double-space before and after each one.
  Subdivision items: single-space.
  Very brief outline: double-space all.

Indenting is as follows:
  Roman numerals: align to the left margin
  Division under each topic: set tab stops for four-space indent
  Second line: begin the second line of an item directly under the first letter of that line

FIGURE 15–7. Outline mechanics. (From Fordney, M. T., and Diehl, M. O.: Medical Transcription Guide. Do's and Don'ts. W. B. Saunders Company, Philadelphia, 1990.)

ther in full capitals and underlined or with just the initial letter of the main words capitalized and the entire heading underlined.

The following items should be included: approval of minutes of the previous meeting; records of all officer and committee reports; records of all motions, seconds, and so forth; action on any unfinished business; record of new business; announcements, including the date, time, and place of the next meeting; and the time of adjournment.

If the minutes continue to more than one page, the word *continued* may be typed at the bottom of the completed page. The subsequent page or pages begin an inch from the top of the page with the title of the minutes, the page number, and any other important data.

Listing. See *Listing* under Typing Reports and Policies at the beginning of this chapter.

Closing. The salutation *Respectfully submitted* followed by a triple space and the originator's name closes the minutes. The typist identifies the preparation of the document with a two- or three-letter identification, i.e., initials, and a double space at the end, flush with the left margin.

Distribution. The minutes should be typed as soon as possible after the meeting and a copy distributed to all members (those present at the meeting and those absent) unless it is the custom to read the minutes at the following meeting. Some committees or organizations have a special distribution list that will include anyone who needs to be aware of the proceedings. See Figure 15–6 for a sample of minutes.

OUTLINES

Outlines are traditionally set up as shown in Figure 15–7. Remember that you must have at least two divisions or subdivisions in each set or a set cannot be made. Roman numerals, Arabic numerals, and letters of the alphabet are combined to identify different heading levels. A period and a double space follow each number or letter of the alphabet except at the levels where the parentheses are used, at which point you double space after the closing parenthesis. The outlines are indented so that successive levels are obvious. One must leave space to backspace from the main topics to accommodate the width of the Roman numerals. It is helpful to use the decimal tab set to align these numerals properly.

15–3: PRACTICE TEST

Directions: The following is from a section of the hospital's cardiovascular laboratory procedure manual. Type it in proper full block format with careful attention to main headings, subheadings, and additional heading levels. Refer to Figure 15–1. You will begin by typing page CV-15 and the second page will be CV-16. It will be entitled Holter Monitor. At the end of the procedure, put in the approved signature line; the effective date will be the current date. The policy number is 90-202.

Objective: To obtain a magnetic tape record of a patient's electrocardiographic activity over a 24-hour period. Equipment: 1. Holter monitor. 2. Battery. 3. Tape. 4. Patient cable. 5. Universal cable. 6. ECG machine. 7. ECG electrodes. 8. 2 × 2 pads, alcohol, and Redux paste. 9. Transpore tape. 10. Patient diary. 11. Shaving prep kit. Procedure: 1. Verify the physician's order by checking the medical chart. 2. Assemble all equipment and bring to the patient's bedside. 3. Introduce yourself to the patient and thoroughly explain what you are about to do. 4. Verify the patient's identity by checking the patient's I.D. bracelet. 5. Have the patient remove all clothing covering his or her chest. 6. Locate the necessary anatomical landmarks and prepare the five areas as follows: a. Shave all hair. b. Cleanse the area with alcohol. c. Scrub the cleansed area with Redux paste. d. Remove the Redux paste with alcohol. 7. Attach the electrodes to the patient's chest: a. 2nd rib space on the right side of the sternum. b. 2nd rib space on the left side of the sternum. c. over the xiphoid process. d. Right V4 - Right mid-clavicular at the 5th intercostal space. e. Left V4 - Left mid-clavicular at the 5th intercostal space. 8. Attach the electrode cables to the patient: a. White - right arm. b. Brown - left arm. c. Black - V1. d. Green - right leg. e. Red - left leg. 9. Tape the electrode cables in a loop on the patient's abdomen allowing the cable to hang free. 10. Place a tape in the Holter monitor unit. 11. Place a battery in the Holter monitor unit. 12. Attach the recorder to the belt or shoulder strap (patient's preference). 13. Plug Universal cable into recorder. 14. Connect RA, LA, RL, LL, and V1 from ECG machine to Universal cable. 15. Connect patient cable to recorder. 16. Run a short strip on the ECG machine to verify the quality of the tracing (L1, L2, L3, AVR, AVL, AVF, and V1). 17. Disconnect Universal cable from recorder unit. 18. Set time on recorder and start Holter monitor. 19. Record starting time in the patient diary and explain the importance of the diary to the patient. 20. If an outpatient, remind the patient of the importance of returning in 24 hours. 21. After 24 hours, record ending time in the patient's diary. 22. Remove the cable from the recorder. 23. Remove the cable and electrodes from the patient. 24. Prepare the tape for scanning. Care of Equipment: 1. Exercise caution when handling unit to avoid dropping. 2. Instruct patient not to bathe, shower, or go swimming while attached to the unit. 3. Clean recording heads and capstan with alcohol after each patient use. Important Points: 1. Proper preparation of the patient's chest is important to a good recording. 2. Run a short strip with the ECG machine to insure that the electrodes are placed correctly. 3. Make sure the patient thoroughly understands the importance of the diary.

▣ Answer to 15 – 2: Self-Study

AGENDA
SAFETY COMMITTEE MEETING
August 22, 199X

   I.   Call to Order
  II.   Roll Call and Introduction of Guests
 III.   Approval of Minutes of July 26, 199X
  IV.   Rotation of Membership
   V.   Electrical Safety Program
  VI.   Fire Drills
 VII.   First Aid
VIII.   Beverage Spilling
  IX.   New Business (this might be included on the agenda in the event someone at the meeting might want to discuss some new problem to work on.)
   X.   Adjournment

15

Manuscripts and Abstracts

OBJECTIVES

After reading this chapter and working the exercises, you should be able to

1. define words concerned with the typing and editing of manuscripts and abstracts.
2. type a manuscript, abstract, or speech in correct format.
3. locate reference books available on these subjects.

● ●

INTRODUCTION

Because of ever-changing surgical techniques, new drugs, and modern equipment, a physician must continue his or her education. Physicians share the information they gain in their practice, in research, and in study by writing and lecturing about their discoveries and observations. The transcriptionist may be asked to assist the physician in the preparation of these articles and speeches by helping to assemble the material and by typing and editing the manuscript. If the article is published, the transcriptionist may help with corrections by checking the galley proofs.

In this chapter you will learn how to help the physician with his or her research and how to type the manuscript properly. Each medical journal or magazine has different guidelines for the preparation of an abstract or manuscript. Therefore, it is important for you to have these instructions on hand before attempting to do the final typing. Many times these instructions are sent to an author after an abstract has been submitted and accepted. These guidelines also appear in journals and magazines, so you may clip these out of a current issue of any journal in question. A list of useful references is given in Appendix C to assist you in proofreading and typing manuscripts. Because proofreading has been discussed in Chapter 7, we will occasionally make reference to that chapter.

VOCABULARY

Abstract: A brief statement of each part of a book, article, speech, court record, or case record as it leads up to the conclusion.

Bibliography: A list of the books, articles, and literary works used or referred to by an author. Each entry includes the name of the author, the title, the publisher, and the date of publication.

Book Review: A critical report and evaluation, as in a newspaper or magazine, of a current book.

16

335

Epitome: A short statement of the main points of a book, report, incident, and so forth.

Footnote: A note of reference at the bottom of the manuscript page or within the context of the manuscript.

Galley proof: Printer's proof sent in uncut sheets to permit correction of errors before the type is made up into pages.

Heading: A word or words set above or at the beginning of the text to identify text divisions, paragraphs, and so forth; usually set in a different typeface in books.

Legend: A description or key to explain an illustration or photograph.

Manuscript: A handwritten or typewritten document or paper, such as an author's copy of his or her work, as submitted to a publisher or printer.

Margin: The blank space around the typed area on a manuscript page.

Proofread: To read and mark corrections on a manuscript, galley proof, or page proof.

Reprint: An edition (booklet or pamphlet) of a printed work that is a verbatim copy of the original.

Summary: A statement that abbreviates the contents of the article as a whole.

Synopsis: A statement giving a brief, general review or condensation; a summary.

RESEARCH OF A PROFESSIONAL REPORT

One of the important steps in writing a paper is thoroughly researching the subject; a medical transcriptionist can help an employer in this if he or she knows where to go for help and what to look for. The reference librarian of your local library can help you locate articles in the *Cumulative Index Medicus,* the *Current List of Medical Literature,* and the *Cumulative Index to Hospital Literature,* or you can obtain information from computer systems, such as MEDLARS (Medical Literature Analysis and Retrieval System) or AIM-TWX (Abridged Index Medicus teletype).

PREPARING A MANUSCRIPT

The proper format of a typed manuscript will be shown on the following pages. The manuscript begins with a title page and a table of contents. These may be optional, depending on whether the paper is to be given as a lecture or submitted to a publisher. A professional report also contains a list of acknowledgments, a body, illustrations or figures with legends, and a bibliography. You will notice that on pages 337 to 345 the margins and positions of each typed line are given to you.

The first (or rough) draft may be triple spaced to allow space for corrections and revisions. Paper of different colors may be used to distinguish between first, second, and final drafts. If you make a photocopy of the manuscript, the physician can cut out and rearrange paragraphs or sentences, and you will be spared much extra retyping. If prepared on a word processor or computer, the edited manuscript can then be easily manipulated into a final draft.

The final draft is double spaced in manuscript format on white $8\frac{1}{2} \times 11$ inch bond paper. This enables the editor who receives the manuscript to make any additional corrections and to insert instructions to the printer. Type on one side of the paper only, and make a photocopy of the original.

If the manuscript is submitted to a journal for publication, the letter of transmittal should contain a statement of its estimated length. To determine the length of a manuscript, add the number of words in six lines. Divide this number by six, to get the average number for one line. Then multiply the average by the number of lines on the page but disregard the lines that have no more than two or three words. The result is the average number of words on one page. To obtain the estimated length for the whole manuscript, multiply the average number of words per page by the total number of pages.

The pages of the body of the manuscript should be numbered. Generally, the first page is not numbered. Beginning with page 2, the numbers should be in the upper right hand corner of the sheet about one-half inch from the top and one inch from the right margin; or they can be centered at the top of the page and typed with a hyphen on each side (-2-). When using a word processor, the margins may be less than one inch owing to "headers" in the software program.

FIGURES AND ILLUSTRATIONS

If photographs or illustrations are used in the manuscript, these should be attached to separate sheets. It is important to cite these in the body of the manuscript by stating "see Figure 16-1" meaning the first illustration in the sixteenth chapter. Permission must be obtained for the use of a photograph from the person photographed or, if the illustration is borrowed from another source, from the publisher of the original picture.

Text continued on page 342

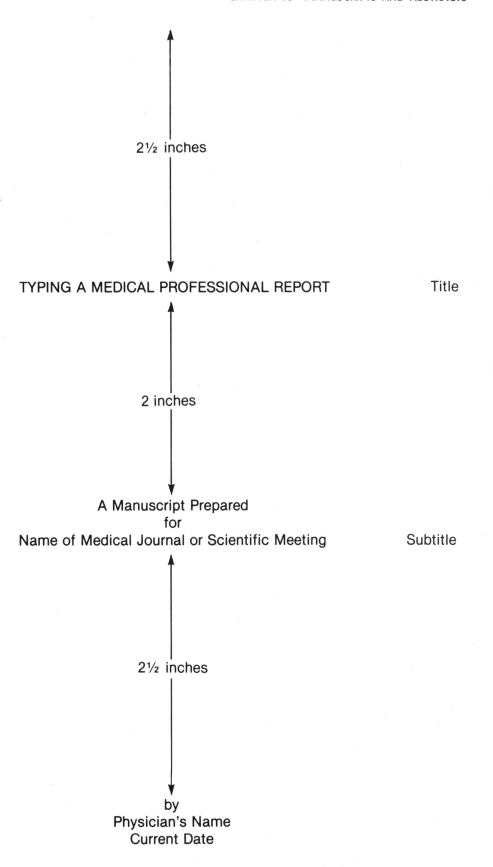

2½ inches

TYPING A MEDICAL PROFESSIONAL REPORT   Title

2 inches

A Manuscript Prepared
for
Name of Medical Journal or Scientific Meeting   Subtitle

2½ inches

by
Physician's Name
Current Date

16

Center the Table of Contents on the page.

TABLE OF CONTENTS

Triple space

Page

TITLE PAGE 0

TABLE OF CONTENTS 0

BODY OF MANUSCRIPT 0

    Margins 0
    Headings 0
    Footnotes 0

BIBLIOGRAPHY 0

3 spaces

16

2 inches

Main Heading   TYPING A MEDICAL PROFESSIONAL REPORT

◄ Triple space

This is your manuscript typing guide and will help you prepare a

◄ Double space

1 or 1½
inch   ➤   manuscript for your physician. Always double space the body of the
margin

manuscript and indent five or ten spaces at the beginning of each

paragraph. Make a carbon copy of each page and retain it for your

records. The left margin should be 1 or 1½ inches, and the right

margin should be one inch.

Triple space ➤   1-inch margin ➤

Underline   ➤ Title Page
or all caps
and no underline

A title page is not necessary for most manuscripts submitted for

publication. If you need to type a title page, refer to page 337 for

proper format.

Underline   ➤ Table of Contents
or all caps
and no underline

The table of contents is a list of headings of the major parts of the

manuscript. It is required by some, but not all, publishers. When

required, it is composed after the entire manuscript has been com-

pleted so that correct page numbers can be inserted. Notice that the

entire table of contents has been centered vertically on page 338.

16

1-inch
margin

339

—2— ◄ Page Number

Underline ➤ <u>Margins</u>

The body of the manuscript is typed double spaced on 8½ x 11 inch paper. It should have 1-inch top, bottom, and side margins, except for a 2-inch top margin on the first page. If a manuscript is bound, it requires extra space on the left for the binding; therefore you would leave a 1½-inch margin. Direct quotations of four or more lines are single-spaced and indented, without quotation marks, five spaces from each margin. Numbered items are listed numerically and indented five spaces from each margin, single spaced with double spacing between each item.

Try to keep the right margin as even as possible, and divide words according to proper word division guidelines. Do not have two consecutive end-of-line hyphenations and do not end a page with a hyphenated word. You may type two or three spaces beyond the desired right margin to avoid word division.

<u>Headings</u>

The titles of the main divisions of the body of the manuscript are called headings. These headings should appear in the table of contents. Main headings are usually centered on the page and typed in all capital letters. There are two kinds of subheadings: side headings and paragraph headings.

Side Heading   ➤ <u>Side Headings</u>

These indicate major divisions of the main topic. Type them even with the left margin, with the main words starting with a capital

16

letter. Underline them and follow with double spacing. Triple space before a side heading and double space after it.

Paragraph Heading ➤ <u>Paragraph Headings</u>. If the paragraph needs to be divided further, paragraph headings may be used. The main words of the heading are begun with a capital letter, indented, underlined, and followed by a period. Do not underline the period.

<u>Footnotes</u>

When original material has been used in a manuscript, credit must be given in a footnote. It is not necessary that it be a direct quotation. Footnotes may be typed in the following ways: 1) Typed at the bottom of the page on which the reference has been made, 2) typed in the copy directly below the statement referred to and separated by two solid lines, or 3) typed on a separate sheet listed together at the end of the chapter or report. The format for footnotes is usually determined by the publisher. Footnotes are numbered consecutively throughout the report. If a footnote is to be included at the bottom of the typed page, allowance of space must be made. Allow one-half inch (three lines) for each 2-line footnote. A footnote should never be continued on another page. Here is an example of a direct quotation which illustrates how the footnote would appear if typed directly below the statement.

A manuscript submitted to an editor, publisher, or printer should be carefully and attractively typed.[1]

16

1. Sarah Augusta Taintor and Kate M. Monro, *The Secretary's Handbook,* The Macmillan Company, New York, New York, 1969, p. 435.

Look below to see how a footnote would appear if credit is given at the bottom of the typed page. Footnotes placed on the page should be set off from the last line of the text by a 1½ to 2 inch underline. The underline is preceded by a single space and followed by a double space. Each footnote is single spaced (with the first line indented); a double space is left between footnotes. If the article was presented at a scientific meeting, the information regarding the name of the medical society and the date of the meeting should be included in a footnote. For assistance in properly placing your footnotes at the bottom of your typed page, refer to Chapter 6, Figure 6-5, page 133 and make up a guide sheet. You can also place a light pencil mark about ½ inch above the bottom margin for each footnote that should appear on the bottom of the page. The pencil mark will remind you to type the footnotes. Adapt the left margin for a bound manuscript.

---

1. Sarah Augusta Taintor and Kate M. Munro, *The Secretary's Handbook,* The Macmillan Company, New York, New York, 1969, p. 435.

Any one of a number of special expressions may be used in referring to a previously cited work to avoid repeating the original footnote in whole. Here is a key to these and to other special terms used in manuscript preparation.

Term	Meaning
c., cir.	about
ca., circa	about

cf.	compare
do.	ditto
e.g.	for example
et al.	and elsewhere, or and others
et seq.	and the following
f. or ff.	following. Used after a page number to indicate that the next page or pages are also referred to.
ibid.	in the same place. Refers to a book, article, etc., cited in a reference immediately preceding.
i.e.	that is
l.	line
ll.	lines
loc. cit.	in the place cited. Refers to exactly the same place in a book, article, etc., cited in an earlier reference, but not the one immediately preceding. (For the latter reference you would use "ibid.")
n.b.	note well
op. cit.	in the work cited. Refers to a book, article, etc., cited in a reference not immediately preceding.
sic	thus. Used to emphasize that an unlikely looking expression or spelling is really the one meant.
q.v.	which see
viz.	namely

16

Underline ➤ Bibliography

A bibliography is a list of the sources of information on the topic discussed in the entire manuscript. It can be a list of the works of an author or of the literature pertaining to a particular subject. Bibliographical entries differ from footnotes in that they are arranged in alphabetical order by the surnames of the authors. If the author is not known, the title of the reference is used. The following page is an example of a typed bibliography, which shows format and spacing. It also gives ten different bibliographic examples.

16

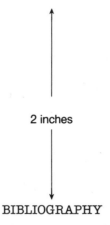

2 inches

BIBLIOGRAPHY

Item ◄ Triple space

1   Follis, Joan L., and Marilyn T. Fordney, <u>Medical Office Procedures</u>
      <u>Worktext</u>, Syllabus, Ventura College, Ventura, California, 1977.

2   Franks, Richard, <u>Simplified Medical Dictionary</u>, Medical Economics/
      Delmar Publishers, Albany, New York, 1977.

3   Frederick, Portia M., and Mary E. Kinn, <u>The Medical Office Assistant,</u>
      <u>Administrative and Clinical</u>, W. B. Saunders Company, Philadel-
      phia, Pennsylvania, 1988.

4   Lessenberry, D. D. et al., <u>College Typewriting</u>, South-Western Publish-
      ing Company, Cincinnati, Ohio, 1975.

5   Lessenberry, D. D., S. J. Wanous, C. H. Duncan, and S. E. Warner,
      <u>College Typewriting, Self-Paced Activities — An Individualized</u>
      <u>Approach</u>, 9th edition, South-Western Publishing Company,
      Cincinnati, Ohio, 1976.

6   "Manuscript," <u>The World Book Encyclopedia</u>, 1970, XIII, p. 130.

7   Murphy, Lucie Spence, "Techniques On Writing The Medical Article,"
      <u>Medical Record News</u>, American Medical Record Association,
      Chicago, Illinois, LIV, No. 6 (April, 1970), pp. 38–43.

8   <u>Oxnard Press Courier</u>, May 23, 1985, p. 15.

9   Swindle, Robert E., "Individualized Instruction in Business Commu-
      nication," <u>Journal of Business Education</u>, Volume XL (May,
      1973), pp. 335–336.

10   <u>United States Goverment Printing Office Style Manual</u>, Washington,
      D.C., U.S. Government Printing Office, 1984.

16

Items Illustrated

1. Unpublished manuscript
2. One-author book
3. Two-author book
4. A book written by a number of authors
5. Book with subtitle and a four-author book
6. Encyclopedia
7. Bound volume of a periodical with page reference
8. Newspaper
9. Bound volume of a professional journal citing volume and page
10. Public document

A legend is written for each of the figures and these are typed on a separate sheet of paper, double spaced and numbered to correspond to each figure. Place the author's name, the title of the manuscript, and the number of the figure on the back of each photograph or illustration. Black-and-white glossy photographs reproduce best. Some journals will accept color photographs. Charts and line drawings should be done in India ink on heavy white bond paper.

EDITING AND PROOFREADING

The entire manuscript should be proofread several times to check for clarity of meaning, spelling, punc-tuation, grammar, and other mechanics before it is submitted for publication. If the manuscript has been accepted by the publisher, it will be typeset into galley proofs. These are sent to the author for final corrections, deletions, and additions. The galley proof is carefully matched with the original manuscript to be sure nothing has been omitted and then returned to the publisher to be made into page proofs. Formal proofreading signs and symbols are used on manuscript, galley proof, and page proof. You learned to use these in Chapter 7, page 156.

16–1: PRACTICE TEST

Directions: A rough draft of a manuscript page appears on page 347. Retype this draft as it would appear in final manuscript form. You will notice formal proofreading corrections and errors in spelling and punctuation. The title of the manuscript is "Cocktails can cause cardiac complications."[1] The author is Roger Balor, M.D., Mount Sinai Hospital and Mount Sinai School of Medicine of the City University of New York, New York City. Dr. Balor wishes to submit this manuscript to *Modern Medicine* in Chicago, Illinois, for publication. Prepare a title page.

At the bottom of your typed page, place a footnote to indicate that some of the material for this paper came from an abstract that appeared in the *Quarterly Journal for the Study of Alcoholism,* volume 34, pages 774–785, 199X. The paper was written by George J. Sanna, M.D., University Hospital, in Boston, Massachusetts.

16

ABSTRACT PREPARATION

An abstract is a brief statement of each major part of a report. It shows the reader how the various items in the report lead up to the conclusion. An abstract may also be called a summary or an epitome. Abstracts give the information contained in the article in as brief a fashion as possible.

Many medical and scientific journals include an abstract at the beginning of each major article that they publish. The abstracts may be collected and reissued on a regular basis. Some journals reissue abstracts of articles that originally appeared in other publications; others publish only abstracts of their own articles. See Figure 16–1 for an example of an abstract.

Some physicians routinely prepare abstracts of articles that they find of interest. If the transcriptionist is able to help with this task, the physician may also dictate an abstract and have you transcribe it. The

¶ Prolonged, heavy ingestion of alcohol by certain individuals, even though they are well-nourished, may result in cardiac abnormalities that are clinically evident or electrocardiographically, or both. Electrocardiographic abnormalities in these patients may indicate the stet developmental stages of cardiomyopathy, a process that may be reversed if the patient abstains from ingestion of alcohol. ¶ Cardiac abnormalities in well-nourished alcoholics may include resting tachycardia sinus tachycardia or bradycardia premature ventricular contractions premature atrial contractions paroxysmal atrial fibrillation or a rhythm varying between sinus rhythm with frequent premature beats and atrioventricular dissociation. First-degree atrioventricular block may be also found. ¶ Notched or tall P waves may be present on the electrocardiogram. In addition, the QRS complex may show some abnormality, as may the S-T segment and T wave. T-wave abnormalities may consist of diminished wave amplitudes, diphasic waves, or frank wave inversion. Some patients may have enlarged hearts. ¶ The electrocardiograms of 50 randomly chosen well-nourished alcoholics were studied and compared with those from 50 nonalcoholic controls. No subject in either group had any known heart disease. ¶ The electrocardiogram was considered to be within normal limits in 36 alcoholic patients but was clearly abnormal in 4 others. Only one control patient had an abnormal electrocardiogram.

abstract is typed on a card on which the periodical, author, title, volume, date of publication, and page numbers are indicated. If abstract cards are kept, it is not necessary to clip and file the actual article.

Abstracts can be found in the following journals.

1. *American Journal of Medical Sciences*
2. *American Journal of Medicine*
3. *Biological Abstracts*
4. *Chemical Abstracts*
5. *Current Contents*
6. *Excerpta Medica*
7. *Journal of the American Medical Association*
8. *New England Journal of Medicine*
9. *Nutrition Abstracts and Reviews*
10. *Physiological Reviews*
11. *Postgraduate Medicine*

16

AM J DISEASES OF CHILDREN—CHICAGO

Red Blood Cell δ-Aminolevulinic Acid Dehydrase Activity

P. I. NIEBURG et al (F. A. OSKI, 750 E Adams St, Syracuse, NY 13210)
Am J Dis Child 127:348-350 (March) 1974

Twenty children had simultaneous measurements of blood lead and red blood cell δ-aminolevulinic acid dehydrase (RBC-ALAD) activity, and then received chelation treatment with edetic acid. The inhibition of RBC-ALAD activity was found to be highly correlated with the amount of lead excreted in the urine. In this study, the measurement of RBC-ALAD appeared to be superior to the measurement of blood lead in identifying those children with an increased burden of chelatable lead. The measurement of the degree of inhibition of red blood cell δ-aminolevulinic acid dehydrase activity may be a useful indicator for the detection of children with increased lead absorption.

FIGURE 16-1. An abstract that appeared in JAMA 227:1489, 1974.

A physician may be asked to write an abstract of his or her original article when submitting the article to a journal for publication. The contents of an abstract consist of the following:

1. Surname of the author, with initials or first name

2. Affiliations of the author, if any

3. Title of the article

4. Title of the journal

5. The year, volume, and page numbers of the journal

6. Text (body of the abstract)

If the author writes the abstract, it is signed "author's abstract." If another person writes the abstract, it is signed by that person followed by the name of the institution with which he or she is associated. In some instances an abstract may be published without a signature.

16-2: SELF-STUDY

Directions: Type the following material in abstract form on a plain sheet of $8\frac{1}{2} \times 11$ inch paper for submission to the *Journal of the American Medical Association.*

The title of the abstract is "Treatment of Pain in Hemophilia" by R. A. Binder et al., Georgetown University Hospital, Washington, D.C. 20007. The complete article appeared in the *American Journal of Diseases of Children,* volume 127, pages 371-373, March 199X issue.

Aspirin alters platelet function, causing impairment of ~~large~~ *small* vessel

hemostasia and prolongation of bleeding time. Therefore, aspirin should

be *avoided* in those who have a tendency to bleed. In this st*u*dy, a standardized

~~time~~ bleeding, using the template ~~method~~, was used to screen a number of *stet*

common analgesics and anti-inflammatory agents (propoxyphene hydrochloride,

salicylate choline, pentazocine hydrochloride, prednisone, and codeine)

in ③ patients with hemophilia A and ⑩ normal volunteers. A comparison of

the bleeding time, before and after ingestion of these drugs, showed no

major differences. These ag*e*nts are suggested for ~~treatment~~ *therapy* in those

p*a*tients with pain & inflammation who are known to have hemophilia.

16–3: PRACTICE TEST

Directions: A rough draft of a manuscript page appears below. Retype this draft as it would appear in final manuscript form, using a plain sheet of 8½ × 11 inch paper. You will notice formal proofreading corrections and errors in spelling and punctuation. Pay special attention to placement of side headings and paragraph headings. The title of the manuscript is "Categories of Tumors." The author is Joan T. Bennett, M. D., XYZ Medical Center, Philadelphia, Pennsylvania. Dr. Bennett wishes to submit this manuscript to the *Journal of the American Medical Association* in Chicago, Illinois for publication. Prepare a title page on a plain sheet of 8½ × 11 inch paper. See Appendix E for answers to this test after you have completed it.

> *Categories of Tumors*
>
> ¶ There are ~~many~~ several categories of tumors. Epithelial tumors is the topic of interest. 1. Epethelial tumors. These tumors arise from the coelomic mesothelium which is capable of differentiating into both benign and malignant tumors. The transition from benign to malignant is not abrupt there is an (borderline or
> *tr* intermediate) category. Distinguishing benign borderline or malignant tumors is important in
> *#* terms of (tx &) prognosis. Epithelial malignancies represent 82% of all ovarian malignancies. a. The predominant cell types are: (1) Serous (a) One out of 3 serous tumors is malignant. (b) Serous cancers are more (then) (3X) as common as the mucinous variety (& 7X) as common as the endometrioid variety. (c) Serous cyst-adenoma carcinoma the most common type of ovarian cancer tends to be bilateral in 35%–50% of cases. (2) Mucinous (a) One out of 5 mucinous tumors are malignant. (b) Mucinous tumors are bilateral in 10%–20% of cases. (3) Endometrioid (a) The microscopic pattern is similar to primary carcinoma of the endometrium. (b) Areas of endometriosis in the ovary may be present. (c) The prognosis is much

Illustration continued on following page

16

> *better (then) that of the serous (+) mucinous carcinomas. b. The prognosis for each stage of epithelial ovarian tumors is linked to the grade of the tumor; poorly differentiated tumors have a poor prognosis. Long=term survival of patients with border-line or well=differentiated cancers after primary surgery is common ⊙*

SPEECHES

If the paper is prepared for a lecture, double space it and use large type so the speech can be read easily. At the bottom of each page in the lower right hand corner type the first two or three words that appear at the beginning of the next page.

BOOK REVIEWS

A physician may be asked to do a book review that is an evaluation of a current publication, highlighting its good and bad points. These reviews are published in magazines, journals, or newspapers.

16–4: PRACTICE TEST

Directions: Complete the following statements by filling in the blanks.

1. The page in a manuscript that contains the report title, for whom the manuscript is prepared, the name of the author, and the date of the manuscript is called the _____ .

2. A manuscript title is typed in _____ letters on the title page.

3. When a manuscript is submitted to a journal for publication, a _____ should accompany it stating the estimated length.

4. The table of contents page indicates the topics in the manuscript and the _____ of each topic.

5. The body of the manuscript is generally typed with _____ spacing or _____ format.

6. Quoted material within a report is normally typed with _____ spacing.

7. References used to cite the source of quoted material are called _____ .

8. Footnotes are typed with _____ spacing within the footnote and _____ spacing between footnotes.

9. Give the abbreviations for the following terms used in footnotes and in the manuscript.
   a. and elsewhere, or, and others _____
   b. in the same place _____
   c. in the work cited _____
   d. that is _____
   e. for example _____

10. The _____ identifies sources or references quoted within the manuscript.

16

11. When there are three or more authors of a single work, the bibliographic entry gives the name of the first author, followed by the phrase _____.

12. Indicate the top, bottom, and side margins in inches for the manuscript, and provide the correct location of the page number.

	Top	*Bottom*	*Left*	*Right*	*Page Number*
a. Unbound report: Page 1	_____	_____	_____	_____	_____
Other pages	_____	_____	_____	_____	_____
b. Left-bound report: Page 1	_____	_____	_____	_____	_____
Other pages	_____	_____	_____	_____	_____

Answers to this test may be found in Appendix E.

◨ Answers to 16–2: Self-Study

TREATMENT OF PAIN IN HEMOPHILIA

R. A. Binder, et al. (Georgetown University Hospital, Washington, D.C. 20007), <u>American Journal of Diseases of Children</u>, 127: 371-373 (March) 1984.

Aspirin alters platelet function, causing impairment of small vessel hemostasia and prolongation of bleeding time. Therefore, aspirin should be avoided in those who have a tendency to bleed. In this study, a standardized bleeding time, using the template method, was used to screen a number of common analgesics and anti-inflammatory agents (propoxyphene hydrochloride, salicylate choline, pentazocine hydrochloride, prednisone, and codeine) in three patients with hemophilia A and ten normal volunteers. A comparison of the bleeding times, before and after ingestion of these drugs, showed no major differences. These agents are suggested for therapy in those patients with pain and inflammation who are known to have hemophilia.

16

Applying for a Transcribing Position

OBJECTIVES

After reading this chapter and completing the assignments, you will be able to

1. list prospective employers.
2. compose a cover letter to accompany your resume.
3. prepare a resume.
4. identify temporary jobs in your locale.
5. prepare for an interview.
6. explain professionalism.

. . . .

INTRODUCTION

Now that you have learned the basic transcription skills, you are ready to hunt for a job and start your new career. There are many factors to consider in beginning your job search: typing your resume, locating prospective employers, and preparing for the interview. We will discuss some traditional attitudes to guide those of you seeking a first job, and we will give some pointers to those of you already working but planning to change jobs.

PREPARE YOUR RESUME

A resume is a personal statement of "you." There is no exact format to be followed, but usually a resume is

chronological or functional, or sometimes a combination of the two. A *chronological* resume is arranged historically (Fig. 17–1), stating recent experiences first, along with the dates and descriptive data on each job. A *functional* resume highlights the qualifications or various duties that an individual can perform (Fig. 17–2). This format is appropriate for you in that you will be applying for a specific job in a specific field, and when your resume is geared specifically to a certain job it is more likely that you will be successful in obtaining that position. A functional resume is also appropriate for those who have breaks in their work experience. The *combination* format emphasizes job skills as well as dates and places of employment (Fig. 17–3). The examples shown will give you a few suggestions for organization as well as format.

A one-page resume is ample for a beginning tran-

17

353

CURRICULUM VITAE

NAME: Joan M. Seymour

ADDRESS: 4011 Jefferson Street
Belmont, XY 12345

TELEPHONE: (013) 487-2399

EDUCATION:

College: Ventura Community College   Ventura, California   9-87 to 6-89

High School: Oxnard High School   Oxnard, California   9-83 to 6-87

WORK EXPERIENCE:

John D. Avers, M.D., 403 Sea St., Oxnard, CA 93030   013/200-3921   7-89 to 6-90

   <u>Position</u>
   Medical Secretary. Made appointments; handled telephone, billing, and insurance form
      completion; purchased supplies, filed and typed correspondence.

PROFESSIONAL AFFILIATIONS:

Member of the American Association for Medical Transcription, Modesto, California.
Member of the American Association of Medical Assistants, Chicago, Illinois.

REFERENCES:
Available upon request.

FIGURE 17–1. An example of a chronological resume. The statements of birthdate, height, weight, marital status, and physical condition have been omitted to conform to the Civil Rights Act of 1964, enforced by the Equal Employment Opportunity Commission (EEOC).

scriptionist, but someone in mid-career may require two or three pages. However, even if you have enough for two or three pages, it is wise to try and condense it to one page. Even if you are not actively looking for a job, keep a few carefully prepared resumes on hand in case an opportunity arises unexpectedly.

Your resume should be professionally typed or printed on white bond paper. (Or, if you wish to catch the eye of a prospective employer, try using off-white paper.) Handwritten resumes are never acceptable. Carefully check your resume for spelling, punctuation, and typographical errors. If you have someone else proofread your resume, they may spot typographical errors and give you additional suggestions. Even one misspelled word or typographical error could discourage a prospective employer and negate your opportunity for an interview. Use wide, neat margins and balance the information well to produce an attractive page. If you need several copies of the resume, have it reproduced on a copy machine that produces excellent photocopies or have it printed professionally. If using a computer, generate it via a laser printer for a professional appearance and highest quality.

The title for your resume can be Resume, Personal Data Sheet, Biographical Sketch, or Curriculum Vitae. The body of the resume should begin with your name, address, and telephone number. The Civil Rights Act of 1964 allows you to exclude your age, birthdate, marital status, height, weight, and physical condition but sometimes listing these can enhance getting a job. However, if you do wish to indicate your age, use your birthdate so that your resume will be current for more than one year.

The second major subject of your resume should be your educational background. Include high school, college, and any business school that you may have attended. If you have received any awards or scholastic honors, these should also be included.

Following your education, list your work experience. Begin with your latest place of employment and end with your first position. Include summer, full-time, part-time, and temporary jobs as well as volunteer work and be sure to list past job accomplishments. Describe briefly the duties that you had in each position. It is not necessary to state reasons why you left a job; this question may be asked during the interview or may appear on a job application form. Job hopping or gaps of several months between jobs will be scrutinized; if you wish, this can be dealt with during an interview. References may be listed, or you may state, "References furnished upon request." Choose references from former employers and teachers, a family physician, or a professional friend. Always ask permission to use the names of your references on your resume. Indicate what your relationship is/was with each reference, i.e., former (or current) instructor, employer, supervisor, friend for _____ years, and so forth.

When applying for a position as a transcriptionist, list your typing skill in words per minute and your transcription speed in lines or characters per hour. Remember to list all business machines you know how to operate. State your membership in professional organizations, along with any offices or chairmanships held. It is optional for you to mention hob-

bies or special interests, since this is irrelevant material. However, if you are fluent in another language, be sure to insert this information on your resume. A current photograph of yourself included with the resume is helpful to the interviewer when trying to recall an applicant. It, too, is optional, however.

Cover Letters

If you are sending your resume to a prospective employer, it is important to compose a cover letter that is attractive and flawlessly typed. It should be composed for a specific job opening and should contain information not already in your resume or information that you may want to highlight and bring to the interviewer's attention (Fig. 17-4). The letter should be

```
BIOGRAPHICAL SKETCH
Personal Details

Name:      Harriet B. Stacy
Address:   5301 Upland Street
           Chatsworth, XY 12345
Telephone: 013/430-2199

Education

Oxnard Community College   Oxnard, California    Attended 9-87 to 6-89
St. Mary's High School     Ventura, California   Attended 9-83 to 6-87

Work Experience

William A. Berry, M.D.  June 1989 - August 1990.
Duties: Receptionist, transcriptionist, insurance clerk.

Skills

Typing: 65 wpm. Transcription: 100 lines/hr. Excellent editing and
composition skills. Pleasant telephone voice. Conversational Spanish.

(A functional resume does not list specific jobs or specific dates. It is
organized to highlight the qualifications of the applicant. Stress selected
skill areas, such as typing words per minute, transcription speed, editing
skills, writing skills, operating types of equipment, and so forth. If you
have had previous jobs, you can emphasize or play down past job duties.)

References

Mrs. Lynn D. Lamb   431 J Street, Oxnard, California 913/320-1200 (teacher)
John F. Camp, M.D.  320 Main Street, Ventura, Calif. 013/430-4300 (former employer)

(List two or three. You may include former employers, teachers, former business
associates, or other professional persons. Do not use relatives as a reference.)
```

FIGURE 17-2. An example of a functional resume.

```
                    PERSONAL DATA SHEET


                    Carmen F. Espinoza
                    42 Colonia Dirve
                    Oxnard, California 93030
                    (013) 499-2399


EDUCATION:          Justin College, Oxnard, California, Graduated  1990
                    with an A.A. degree.

                    Emory High School, Oxnard, California, Graduated 1988,
                    Diploma awarded.

WORK EXPERIENCE:    James Henson, 211 Mary Street, Oxnard, California
                    Telephone:  013/480-2311.  Employed from 2-90 to 8-90
                    as a clerk.

SKILLS:             Type 50 words per minute.
                    Knowledge of medical terminology.
                    Excellent speller.
                    Able to transcribe.
                    Able to speak Spanish fairly well.
                    Excellent proofreader.
                    (List those skills that would be of value in the
                    employment you are seeking.)

REFERENCES:         Furnished upon request.
```

FIGURE 17-3. An example of the combination-format resume. Personal data may be excluded, if you wish, as a result of the Civil Rights Act of 1964, enforced by the EEOC.

addressed to an individual, if possible, and mailed with the resume. Both letter and resume should contain your name, address, and telephone number. Ask for an interview before you close your letter.

PROSPECT SOURCES

First of all, tell everyone you know—friends, relatives, and professional contacts—that you are now available for work. Remember, most jobs are not advertised. When you visit a medical facility on business, let the staff members know that you are looking for a position and would appreciate any leads. Make frequent visits to hospitals and large medical clinics and check the personnel bulletin board. Openings are listed in this manner before they are publicized. Provide your instructor or school placement office with your resume so that they will have it handy and be truly knowledgeable about your background if they are contacted by a prospective employer. School counselors may give you a lead on where to look for a job. Go to the personnel offices of local hospitals, medical clinics, transcription businesses, and word processing centers and complete a job application to be filed in the event that an opening occurs in the future. Some large private medical buildings will permit you to leave resumes with the switchboard operator or pharmacist. Check with your local medical society to see if it has a provision for supplying you with leads. Consult the telephone directory or medical society roster for sources, and make a blind mailing of your resume to possible prospects. In the *Yellow Pages* of your telephone directory, physicians are listed under "Physicians and Surgeons," and typing services are generally listed under "Secretarial Services." The state employment department may have a list of available jobs, and there is no charge for their service. If you use a professional employment agency, you must be prepared to pay a fee if they place you. Join a chapter of the American Medical Record Association, American Association of Medical Assistants,

Inc., or American Association for Medical Transcription. By attending meetings and receiving their professional magazines and bulletins, you may hear of a job opportunity. Place a notice in your local chapter newsletter that you are looking for a job. Contact the national headquarters of each association for further information about local chapters.

American Association of Medical Assistants, Inc.
20 North Wacker Drive, Suite 1575
Chicago, IL 60606

American Association for Medical Transcription
P.O. Box 576187
Modesto, CA 95357
Telephone: 800-982-2182
Fax: 209-551-9317

American Health Information Management
  Association
875 North Michigan Avenue, Suite 1850
Chicago, IL 60611

If you plan to work in Canada, contact the following resources:

Canadian Association of Medical Transcriptionists
P.O. Box 396
Vancouver, BC, Canada V5Z 4C9

Ontario Medical Secretaries' Association
250 Bloor Street East, Suite 600
Toronto, Ontario, Canada M4W 1G6

Canadian Medical Association
P.O. Box 8650
Ottawa, Ontario, Canada K1G 0G8

Canadian Health Record Association
250 Ferrand Drive, Suite 909
Don Mills, Ontario, Canada M3C 3G8

Medical Office Assistants' Association of British
  Columbia
c/o British Columbia Medical Association
115-1665 West Broadway Street
Vancouver, BC, Canada V6J 1X1

```
Your present address
City, State, Zip code
Date of typing this letter



John Doe, M. D. or
Personnel Director
Street Address
City, State, Zip code

Dear Dr. Doe:

1st paragraph - Tell how you heard of the position.  Tell why you are
writing by naming the position, medical transcriptionist.

2nd paragraph - State one or two qualifications you consider to be of
greatest interest to the doctor or hospital.  Explain why you are
interested in his or her practice, location, or type of work.  If you
have past experience or special training, be sure to mention this.

3rd paragraph - Refer the reader to the resume or application form
enclosed.

4th paragraph - End the letter by asking for an interview and suggesting
a date and time or that you will call for an appointment.  If this letter
is to request further information about the job opening, enclose a
self-addressed, stamped envelope as a courtesy.  The closing should not
be vague but should give the reader a specific action to take.

Sincerely,

(your handwritten signature)

Type your name

Enclosure
```

FIGURE 17-4. Suggested content for a cover letter to accompany a resume.

TEMPORARY JOBS

There could be reasons why you want to work temporarily or as a permanent part-time employee. It may be difficult to decide exactly where you want to work, or perhaps you have small children at home and are unable to work full time. You may need income to meet monthly bills while you are waiting for a full-time position. As a medical transcriptionist, you can work for various employers or for one particular office or hospital, doing overflow work. With the proper equipment, transcribing can be done in your home. Because the need for transcriptionists is so great, most communities can use part-time transcriptionists.

Usually you can find this type of work from the sources we mentioned previously, or you can be hired by a company that places you. Some of these national companies are Kelly Services; Manpower Incorporated; TOP Services; Western Temporary Services, Incorporated; and Olsten Temporary Services. Some have branch offices in foreign countries as well. Your community may have other local and regional temporary employment firms. Look in the *Yellow Pages* of your phone directory under the heading "Employment-Temporary." There are some advantages in applying to such a company, since it will screen you, test your skills, place you into a job category or categories, and have incentive plans to encourage you to remain with it instead of taking a full-time job. Obtain a typing speed certificate while you are still in school to avoid taking a typing test under stress. Rather than being isolated in one office, you can have the experience of working in many offices and learning a variety of procedures. There is less chance that routine work will become boring or stale. Work schedules are flexible, and if you are called for a job and cannot report that day or week, you are not obliged to take the job. If a business has to cut costs, it tends to use "temporaries" rather than hire permanent employees to handle short-term increases in work load. Physicians whose offices are near resort areas may have to handle seasonal peak volumes of work and will need temporary help. Temporary firms do not encourage it, but if an employer wishes to hire you full time, there can be allowances in the contract for you to accept such a position.

Because medical transcription is a specialized and technical position, a "temporary" with medical transcribing skills can often command higher wages than other employees who receive close to minimum wage. Workers' compensation insurance is provided through temporary agencies, but group health insurance is not. Fringe benefits are likely to be cash bonuses for long or exceptional service or for recruiting other employees to the temporary employment firm. Some firms offer their employees profit-sharing plans and paid vacations. If travel is an objective, you can obtain work through national and international firms and work out of any of their branches. In some cases, retesting may not be required.

PREPARE FOR THE INTERVIEW

To prepare for an interview, find out as much as you can about the job and the organization to which you are going for the interview. If it has a personnel office, ask if you can be permitted to read the job description for the position you are applying for. Brush up on any technical jargon or terminology associated with the medical specialty of the physician. If you visit an office for an application and are asked to remain for an interview, make an appointment so you can prepare for it.

One way to prepare yourself for an interview is by role playing. A panel might interview you, so do not get all set up for a one-to-one interview and be startled by a three-to-one. Get in front of a mirror and ask yourself questions so that you will be prepared for the answers and will not stumble on words (or give a friend a list of questions to ask you). Use a tape recorder and then replay the tape to see how you sounded when you asked yourself the questions. Here are some questions for role playing that may be of some help. See if you can answer them spontaneously and honestly.

Example

Employer: "If you get this job, how will you want me to assist you in your work?

Job candidate: "I would expect you to help me learn your policies and procedures, and then I'd ask for help if I didn't understand something." This type of answer would indicate to the employer a job candidate's ability to work on his or her own and willingness to seek advice when he or she needs it.

1. Tell me something about yourself.

2. What is your major weakness?

3. Why do you want to work for me? Or for us?

4. Why do you think you would like this job?

5. What special qualifications do you have that make you feel you will be successful?

6. What have you done that shows initiative and willingness to work?

7. Will you be able to work overtime?

8. What salary do you expect?

9. How did you obtain your last job and why did you leave it?

10. What does success mean to you?

11. What type of person do you like to work for?

12. How is your health?

13. Do you like routine work?

14. What do you plan to be doing five years from now?

15. Have you any plans to further your education?

When asked a question, reply in a manner that will bring out your strong points and assets. Do not reply immediately; *think* carefully and be alert to the reply you know the interviewer wishes to hear, but be aware of your handicaps, and be ready to emphasize your best qualities. For instance, if the interviewer notes that your typing speed is not high, you might emphasize that your accuracy is very high if that is the case. If you are short on practical experience, point out your excellent school record. This is the one time when you may be completely frank about your qualifications without being a boaster or braggart. Do not sell yourself short or make negative statements about yourself. Do not discuss personal problems. Be enthusiastic and *ask* for the position if you want it. For questions that a prospective employer cannot ask, refer to the section on Application Blanks.

THE INTERVIEW

Arrive early to allow time for parking, finding the proper office, relaxing, and catching your breath. Take a pen, note pad, and your resume.

Dress carefully for the interview. Remember all the truisms about "first impressions." Since you do not know the attitude of the interviewer, you should always be appropriately attired. If a woman, wear a clean skirt, dress, or tailored suit and nylon stockings with low-heeled pumps. If a man, wear a clean dark gray or navy suit, plain socks, and well-shined shoes. Men should avoid a lot of facial hair, long hair, earrings, and heavy aftershave lotion. Women should style their hair in a conservative and becoming manner and wear jewelry sparingly. They should avoid heavy makeup, low-cut necklines, sleeveless dresses, strong perfume, and dark or bright nail polish. Do not smoke or chew gum. Use a suitable deodorant. Try to eliminate nervous habits, such as thumping your fingers on the table, wringing your hands, or clicking the lid on a pen. Do not take anyone with you to the interview. Make up a checklist of questions on a note pad or 3 × 5 cards so you do not forget to ask the interviewer any questions you may have about the position. Once you are introduced to the interviewer, make a point to remember his or her name, and refer to the name in your conversation. Look the interviewer in the eye when answering questions, being careful not to avert your eyes. Maintaining eye contact implies sincerity.

Some jobs have fringe benefits about which you may have questions. Here are several pertinent ones. However, be careful not to appear too interested in benefits.

1. What is the salary? (If the interviewer does not bring up salary, you are entitled to ask what he or she can offer.)

2. What are the duties of this job?

3. Does the firm encourage or provide continuing education for its employees?

4. Will the employer pay tuition for courses I take?

5. What are the opportunities for advancement?

6. What types of insurance plans are available? Does this facility contribute to them? Group health insurance, pension, or profit sharing?

7. What are the starting and quitting times?

8. Is there an incentive pay program?

9. Is there often overtime required? Will I be paid for it?

10. How long must I work before I am eligible for paid vacation time?

11. How many paid sick days will I earn?

12. Do you have a company cafeteria? How much time are employees allowed for lunch? Coffee breaks?

13. What kind of equipment will I be using?

14. How and when can I qualify for a raise?

15. What is your ceiling salary for my job description?

16. Are there any dress restrictions that employees must observe?

17. Do you pay for membership fees in professional organizations?

If the job is offered to you at the time of the interview and you are not sure you want it, you might ask, "May I have some time to think it over?" or "How soon do you need to know?" This will give you time to think about the job before you commit yourself.

Portfolio

When going for an interview, take along a document file or portfolio. A portfolio gives the interviewer the impression that the applicant is organized and serious about getting the job. It should contain your resume,

```
                    4021 Madison Road
                    El Cajon, XY 12345
                    January 10, 199x



          Harris M. Peterson, M. D.
          3200 Main Street
          La Mesa, XY 12346

          Dear Dr. Peterson:

          Thank you for giving me so much time yesterday to discuss
          the medical transcribing position in your office.

          I hope that you will give me the opportunity to prove my
          ability as I feel that I can perform the work to your
          satisfaction; I am very eager to try.

          Please let me hear from you in the near future (486-3200).

          Sincerely yours,



          (Mrs.) Jane Simon
```

FIGURE 17-5. An example of a thank-you letter after an interview.

school diplomas, transcripts, work samples, alphabetical notebook of words, letters of recommendation, names and addresses of references, and anything related to your prior experiences that is relevant to your current job campaign. This information may be placed in a manila envelope or report folder with a transparent cover.

After the Interview

Immediately following the interview, write a thank-you note to the interviewer, thanking him or her for the interview. Restate your interest in the position and ask for consideration for employment (see Figure 17-5, which will give you an idea of how the letter should appear and what it should contain).

APPLICATION BLANKS

Read the application form entirely before you begin. Use a pen to complete the form, and follow the directions carefully, such as "Please print," "Complete in your own handwriting," or "Put last name first." This does indicate your ability to follow instructions. Copy from your resume. This will help you to be accurate and consistent. Make the form look exceptionally neat. When you leave, this paper may be all that is left to represent you. Complete all the blanks and if they

do not apply, put in "NA" (not applicable). Be sure to sign the form. Now reread the form all the way through, word for word, to catch possible errors of omission or commission. You do not want to have to explain or apologize during the interview for a mistake. If a question appears on an application form regarding salary, a proper answer might be "negotiable" or "flexible" so that this can be discussed during an interview. You want to avoid overpricing or underpricing yourself. Before the interview, do some research to see if the salary (when offered) is acceptable. In negotiating a salary, you may decide to accept a salary that is lower than you want with an understanding that after a three- to six-month period your work will be evaluated for an increase of pay.

If you are an immigrant or alien, you will need to establish citizenship with a birth certificate or a Social Security card and your identity by a driver's license with a photo. If you have a document that establishes both identity and authorization to work, take it with you when you apply for a job, i.e., a U.S. passport, a naturalization certificate, an alien registration card. Employers must conform to the Immigration Reform and Control Act of 1986 and will request documents from you or they can be fined, imprisoned, or both, for repeated violations.

There are many questions that may be considered discriminatory when applying for a job. A prospective employer cannot ask the following:

17

1. Your age

2. Date of birth

3. Birthplace

4. Ethnic background

5. Religious beliefs

6. Native language

7. Maiden name

8. Marital status

9. Date of marriage

10. Whether your spouse is employed

11. How much your spouse earns

12. If female, whether you are pregnant

13. If female, whether you have had an abortion

14. The number of dependent children living with you

15. To explain all the gaps in your employment record (i.e., to find out if you have taken time off to have children)

16. Whether you have any physical or emotional defects (but an interviewer can ask whether you have any job-related defects)

If a question is asked about why you left a previous employer and you had some difficulty in that position, you can state "for personal reasons." This can then be discussed in further detail if the interviewer wishes to know the particulars.

PROFESSIONALISM

The dictionary says professionalism is the conduct, aims, or qualities that characterize or mark a profession. Because professionalism is intangible, it is difficult to put into words, but "you know it when you see it." Professional means more than being proficient at medical transcription. It is that extra effort you take in retyping a sloppy report (even when you are paid on production) or looking up a word when you are not sure of the spelling. Other qualities shared by true professionals are having enthusiasm for work, being courteous and dependable, having the right attitude, and being able to get along with others. As a professional, you want to reflect an image and convey a message that you are bright, alert, capable, and top-notch; so look the part. Professionals are self-confident, honest, and fair in their dealings with others.

An important aspect of professionalism is a willingness to continue learning even after long experience.

To keep abreast of new medical terms, techniques, and procedures, consider joining a chapter, the national association, or both, of the American Association for Medical Transcription (AAMT). Participate in their continuing medical education program by becoming certified. Refer to Chapter 1 for details regarding the requirements to become a certified medical transcriptionist (CMT). Categories of membership include active, associate, institutional, and student.

Aim for personal and professional success.

TIPS FOR HOLDING A JOB

Here are some suggestions on how to keep that good job now that you have landed it.

1. Be punctual in reporting for work.

2. Report fit and alert, being absent only when absolutely necessary.

3. Be well groomed at all times; dress attractively and appropriately.

4. Do not criticize your employer. If you do not like where you are working, find another employer.

5. If there are job assignments you do not particularly care for, accept your share of the responsibility for these without complaints. Every job will have its good and bad points.

6. Stay within the time limit for coffee breaks and lunch period.

7. Limit personal phone calls made or received to those that are absolutely necessary.

8. If you are not busy, offer to assist someone else who is.

9. Social visits with other employees should occur only after or before working hours.

10. Keep your personal problems to yourself.

11. Always do the job the boss's way. Later, when your experience and skills are established, your ideas and suggestions will be welcomed, but not in the beginning.

12. Keep a learning attitude. Stay flexible and adjust to new changes.

JOB EVALUATION

During our many years of teaching, a number of students have asked how a medical transcription supervisor evaluates their performance after they are hired.

17

Usually employers have a job description, which lists the job responsibilities for each employee. It assists managers, supervisors, and others in recruiting, supervising, and evaluating individuals in their positions. Figure 17–6 is a model job description for a medical transcriptionist that was developed by the American Association for Medical Transcription. It is not a complete list of specific duties and responsibilities but is to be used as an aid in developing a job description by employers for their medical transcriptionist. Evaluation of the relative and comparable worth of a beginning medical transcriptionist may affect your career growth within an organization and involves a number of factors. First, does the employer have a job evaluation plan? This is foremost because, without job evaluation, there is no valid way to determine the relative worth of different positions within an organization. The relative worth of any position is determined by what the employee actually does. To compare position levels based only on job titles is misleading. The title "medical secretary" may cover different levels of responsibility ranging from "medical typist," "medical transcriptionist," "insurance specialist," or "administrative or executive medical assistant." You might be asked to write a job description listing some of the following:

1. What do you actually do when working and, if you transcribe, how much do you accomplish per day?

2. What are your most complex duties performed?

3. What skills and experience are required? Since hired, have your skills improved?

4. To what extent, or in what areas, is independent judgment required?

5. What is the likelihood and impact of errors? Since hired, have your errors diminished in frequency?

6. With whom do you interact? Is the interaction positive or negative, compatible or incompatible?

7. What physical effort or manual dexterity is required?

8. What unusual working conditions exist?

9. What supervisory responsibilities are involved?

The employer must also have developed quantity (productivity) standards and quality standards. Your transcripts will be carefully scrutinized during your probationary period to see if you measure up to these standards and if you are meeting the turnaround time. In addition, your supervisor may take into account your independent action, whether your attendance at work was perfect or whether you missed work days owing to illness, or if you stayed overtime to transcribe STAT reports without complaints.

SELF-EMPLOYMENT OR FREELANCING

After sufficient transcription experience, you may wish to be your own boss and have a flexible work schedule. This means full-time commitment, a lot of hard work, and long hours to develop a number of clients. Estimate how much money you will need in the start-up months, taking into consideration equipment, overhead, taxes, and final profit. Some transcriptionists work from their homes in the beginning, thereby reducing the overhead. However, working at home involves a certain amount of self-discipline. Time management is essential, so map out a schedule. When you are the boss, you are responsible for everything—advertising, billing, bookkeeping, obtaining clients, and so forth. It is wise to have a cushion of money to run your business for six months to a year before you quit your regular job. One of the most common reasons that businesses fail is they are undercapitalized from the beginning. It usually takes at least a year before you make any real profit, so be patient. If you are weak in accounting, take a bookkeeping course. Attend seminars on starting a business offered by financial institutions, universities, community colleges, or private institutions. Set up detailed financial records from day one, even if you intend to hire an accountant. Get expert advice. Consult a lawyer or accountant or both about the best way of legally setting up your business and the tax pros and cons of each option.

Equipment to consider would be a typewriter, transcription equipment, phone answering machine, FAX machine, typewriter table, filing cabinet, and a calculator. Investigate transcription equipment that has the capacity to handle standard and minicassettes or microcassettes. Thoroughly explore current equipment available and talk to those already using the equipment about maintenance (service contracts), purchase, and lease options. To handle a large volume of transcription and expand your service, a word processor and a direct phone-in line would be considered as well as faxing documents back to clients. A large percentage of clients like this method because of convenience and the rapid turnaround time in furnishing reports. Some companies have equipment that emits a beep for purposes of confidentiality if someone comes on the line. Since this equipment is more expensive as far as purchase and upkeep, investigate possible loan sources: commercial and savings banks, government-sponsored small business loans, finance companies, family, and friends. Obtaining loans from individual investors or venture capital can mean a percentage of the business or profits going to the investor, depending on the contractual agreement. Low-interest government Small Business Ad-

Text continued on page 367

American Association for Medical Transcription

AAMT Model Job Description:

Medical Transcriptionist

The *AAMT Model Job Description* is a practical, useful compilation of the basic job responsibilities of a medical transcriptionist. It is designed to assist human resource managers, department managers, supervisors, and others in recruiting, supervising, and evaluating individuals in medical transcription positions.

The *AAMT Model Job Description* is not intended as a complete list of specific duties and responsibilities. Nor is it intended to limit or modify the right of any supervisor to assign, direct, and control the work of employees under supervision. The use of a particular expression or illustration describing duties shall not be held to exclude other duties not mentioned that are of a similar kind or level of difficulty.

AAMT gratefully acknowledges Lanier Voice Products Division, Atlanta, Georgia, for funding the development of the *AAMT Model Job Description: Medical Transcriptionist.*

For additional information, contact AAMT, P.O. Box 576187, Modesto, California 95357. Telephone 209-551-0883 or 800-982-2182. FAX 209-551-9317.

FIGURE 17–6. AAMT Model Job Description: Medical Transcriptionist. This is a practical, useful compilation of the basic job responsibilities of a medical transcriptionist. It is designed to assist human resource managers, department managers, supervisors, and others in recruiting, supervising, and evaluating individuals in medical transcription positions. This is not intended as a complete list of specific duties and responsibilities, nor is it intended to limit or modify the right of any supervisor to assign, direct, and control the work of employees under supervision. The use of a particular expression or illustration describing duties shall not be held to exclude other duties not mentioned that are of a similar kind or level of difficulty. (From the American Association for Medical Transcription, Modesto, CA, Copyright 1990.)

17

Illustration continued on following page

AAMT MODEL JOB DESCRIPTION: MEDICAL TRANSCRIPTIONIST

Position Summary: Medical language specialist who interprets and transcribes dictation by physicians and other healthcare professionals regarding patient assessment, workup, therapeutic procedures, clinical course, diagnosis, prognosis, etc., in order to document patient care and facilitate delivery of healthcare services.

Knowledge, skills, and abilities:
1. Minimum education level of associate degree or equivalent in work experience and continuing education.
2. Knowledge of medical terminology, anatomy and physiology, clinical medicine, surgery, diagnostic tests, radiology, pathology, pharmacology, and the various medical specialties as required in areas of responsibility.
3. Knowledge of medical transcription guidelines and practices.
4. Excellent written and oral communication skills, including English usage, grammar, punctuation, and style.
5. Ability to understand diverse accents and dialects and varying dictation styles.
6. Ability to use designated reference materials.
7. Ability to operate designated word processing, dictation, and transcription equipment, and other equipment as specified.
8. Ability to work independently with minimal supervision.
9. Ability to work under pressure with time constraints.
10. Ability to concentrate.
11. Excellent listening skills.
12. Excellent eye, hand, and auditory coordination.
13. Certified medical transcriptionist (CMT) status preferred.

Working conditions:
General office environment. Quiet surroundings. Adequate lighting.

Physical demands:
Primarily sedentary work, with continuous use of earphones, keyboard, foot control, and where applicable, video display terminal.

17

AAMT MODEL JOB DESCRIPTION: MEDICAL TRANSCRIPTIONIST

Job responsibilities:	Performance standards:
1. Transcribes medical dictation to provide a permanent record of patient care.	1.1 Applies knowledge of medical terminology, anatomy and physiology, and English language rules to the transcription and proofreading of medical dictation from originators with various accents, dialects, and dictation styles. 1.2 Recognizes, interprets, and evaluates inconsistencies, discrepancies, and inaccuracies in medical dictation, and appropriately edits, revises, and clarifies them without altering the meaning of the dictation or changing the dictator's style. 1.3 Clarifies dictation which is unclear or incomplete, seeking assistance as necessary. 1.4 Flags reports requiring the attention of the supervisor or dictator. 1.5 Uses reference materials appropriately and efficiently to facilitate the accuracy, clarity, and completeness of reports. 1.6 Meets quality and productivity standards and deadlines established by employer. 1.7 Verifies patient information for accuracy and completeness. 1.8 Formats reports according to established guidelines.
2. Demonstrates an understanding of the medicolegal implications and responsibilities related to the transcription of patient records to protect the patient and the business/institution.	2.1 Understands and complies with policies and procedures related to medicolegal matters, including confidentiality, amendment of medical records, release of information, patients' rights, medical records as legal evidence, informed consent, etc. 2.2 Meets standards of professional and ethical conduct. 2.3 Recognizes and reports unusual circumstances and/or information with possible risk factors to appropriate risk management personnel. 2.4 Recognizes and reports problems, errors, and discrepancies in dictation and patient records to appropriate manager. 2.5 Consults appropriate personnel regarding dictation which may be regarded as unprofessional, frivolous, insulting, inflammatory, or inappropriate.
3. Operates designated word processing, dictation, and transcription equipment as directed to complete assignments.	3.1 Uses designated equipment effectively, skillfully, and efficiently. 3.2 Maintains equipment and work area as directed. 3.3 Assesses condition of equipment and furnishings, and reports need for replacement or repair.

© Copyright 1990. AAMT.

Continues

17

AAMT MODEL JOB DESCRIPTION: MEDICAL TRANSCRIPTIONIST	
Job responsibilities:	**Performance standards:**
4. Follows policies and procedures to contribute to the efficiency of the medical transcription department	4.1 Demonstrates an understanding of policies, procedures, and priorities, seeking clarification as needed. 4.2 Reports to work on time, as scheduled, and is dependable and cooperative. 4.3 Organizes and prioritizes assigned work, and schedules time to accommodate work demands, turnaround-time requirements, and commitments. 4.4 Maintains required records, providing reports as scheduled and upon request. 4.5 Participates in quality assurance programs. 4.6 Participates in evaluation and selection of equipment and furnishings. 4.7 Provides administrative/clerical/technical support as needed and as assigned.
5. Expands job-related knowledge and skills to improve performance and adjust to change.	5.1 Participates in inservice and continuing education activities. 5.2 Provides documentation of inservice and continuing education activities. 5.3 Reviews trends and developments in medicine, English usage, technology, and transcription practices, and shares knowledge with colleagues. 5.4 Documents new and revised terminology, definitions, styles, and practices for reference and application. 5.5 Participates in the evaluation and selection of books, publications, and other reference materials.
6. Uses interpersonal skills effectively to build and maintain cooperative working relationships.	6.1 Works and communicates in a positive and cooperative manner with management and supervisory staff, medical staff, co-workers and other healthcare personnel, and patients and their families when providing information and services, seeking assistance and clarification, and resolving problems. 6.2 Contributes to team efforts. 6.3 Carries out assignments responsibly. 6.4 Participates in a positive and cooperative manner during staff meetings. 6.5 Handles difficult and sensitive situations tactfully. 6.6 Responds well to supervision. 6.7 Shares information with co-workers. 6.8 Assists with training of new employees as needed.
© Copyright 1990. AAMT.	

17

ministration (SBA) loans and loans to physically challenged individuals are available to those who qualify.

Call local competitors and obtain information on range of fees regarding character count, line count, page count, stroke count, or hourly rates so you have an idea of what to charge as a fee for your work. Research your market area to see who will use your services in the community, such as physicians' offices (orthopedists, cardiologists, and so on), hospitals (medical record, pathology, or radiology departments), clinics, nurse practitioners, and so forth. You can find work by substituting for transcriptionists who are ill, on vacation, or overloaded. Other professionals in search of transcriptionists are chief residents going into private practice, new physicians in town, a physician appointed to head an association, or physicians who are changing offices or adding colleagues. Send prospective clients a letter (Fig. 17–7). Your major responsibility is convincing clients that

---

```
                          LETTERHEAD


     DATE


     Client's Name
     Address
     City, State, ZIP Code

     Dear_____:

     For__years, I have worked as a medical transcriptionist for _____.
     I am now establishing my own business.  Perhaps your office or hospital
     has an overload or your medical transcriptionist is ill or planning a
     vacation.  Maybe you have a manuscript you need typed for a medical journal
     or need a personnel manual, grant proposal or research paper typed.

     You can be assured of the following:

      1.  Consultation rendered at no charge.
      2.  Accurate, complete, and speedy medical transcription.  All work is proofread.
      3.  Courier service (pick up and delivery available).  Your transcripts will be
          delivered to you on the day and at the hour you specify.  Special RUSH pick
          up when required.
      4.  Low competitive rates.
      5.  Premium pay for overtime work eliminated on in-house transcription.
      6.  In-house office space and equipment requirements reduced, or eliminated.
      7.  Confidentiality of work guaranteed.
      8.  Personal, professional, dependable service provided on a temporary "fill-in"
          basis.
      9.  Service available 24 hours a day, 7 days a week, including holidays.
     10.  Call-in dictation from any location available.
     11.  Retyping of a report at no charge, if you are not satisfied with the tran-
          script.

     My business equipment includes _____typewriter or word processor and
     transcription equipment adaptable to standard, micro- and mini- cassettes.

     Professional references will be supplied on request.  I am a Certified Medical
     Transcriptionist (CMT) and a member of the American Association for Medical
     Transcription.

     I welcome the opportunity to speak with you personally about this new service
     and will call you to set up an appointment in the near future.  If you need my
     services immediately, please call_____ and leave a message.  Please keep my
     telephone number on file in case you need my services in the future.

     Sincerely,
```

FIGURE 17–7. Example of a letter to prospective clients.

```
                              LETTERHEAD


        DATE


        Client's Name
        Address
        City, State, ZIP code

        Dear_____:

        This is to confirm my conversation with you yesterday regarding
        transcription of your medical reports.

        I agree to deliver completed transcripts to your office the day
        after pick up of the dication.  The rate is $_____ per page
        with proration applied to those pages with less than half a page.

        Please call me anytime you need my service.  I look forward to
        transcribing for you.

        Sincerely yours,



        Note:  You may wish to make the second paragraph specific by stat-
        ing "I agree to pick up dication on ___Tuesday___ and deliver on
        ___Thursday___."
```

FIGURE 17–8. Example of a letter outlining terms of an agreement.

your service is better than the competition, stressing dependability; efficient service; professional, prompt turnaround of quality work; direct phone-in line, courier service (pick up and delivery); and so forth. Misunderstandings about agreements can occur, so put everything in writing. If you change the terms of the agreement, write a letter outlining the new terms (Fig. 17–8). Some self-employed medical transcriptionists consider a standard page as 30 single-spaced lines. First pages are counted as a whole page, even when the letter or report is half a page. The final page of the work is prorated—anything under 15 lines is a half page, and anything over 15 lines is considered a full page. The monthly statement to the client should consist of a detailed record of patients' names, date of each report, and number of pages or hours depending on how you structure your fees (Fig. 17–9). You might want to establish a minimum charge. In trying to obtain a client, you might state the following:

"My charge is computed on a per-page level, as this is quicker for you to check and for me to compute. I am currently charging _____ cents a line on full, single-spaced pages. This works out to $_____ a full page for billing purposes."

If someone who is self-employed gets too much work and asks you to pitch in, you are subcontracting. The self-employed individual will pay you so much per line, per page, or hourly and keep a percentage. Payment should be made at the time of delivery of the work to the self-employed individual, since you, the subcontractor, are not dealing directly with the client.

As an independent (self-employed) contractor who establishes a business at home, you get a few dozen deductions for a home office. Obtain the Internal Revenue Service Publication No. 587 entitled "Business Use of Your Home." Each year you must pay a self-employment tax on net income. You also have to make estimated tax payments quarterly once your net income amounts to $500 or more. To avoid headaches at tax time, retain all receipts and keep careful, complete records of income and expenses.

LETTERHEAD

Date

Client's Name
Address
City, State, ZIP code

BILLING STATEMENT

Tapes	Patient's Name	Report* Code No.	Pickup Date	Delivery Date	Pages or Hours	Balance Due
1	Mary Brown	3	11-22-9x	11-23-9x	13.5 pages	
2	Sue Morse	4	11-22-9x	11-23-9x	4.0 pages	
3						
4						
5						
6						
TOTALS		2			17.5	$

RATE: $____per full singlespaced page (equals____cents per line).

TERMS: *Terms should be stated on the billing statement, such as payable on delivery, net 30, net 15 days from inovice, end of month, payment due within 15 days of invoice, and so forth.*

*Report Code No.   1 = Chart note   5 = Letter
                   2 = Consultation   6 = Operative Report
                   3 = Discharge Summary   7 = Other
                   4 = History and Physical

FIGURE 17-9. Example of a monthly billing statement to a client.

NEW BUSINESS CHECKLIST

1. Decide what address you will use, since you may wish to obtain a post office box number instead of using your home address.

2. Obtain a business license from the business license section of your city hall. Regulations vary in each city licensing office. You might have to obtain a home occupation permit from the planning department and have it signed by your landlord if you are renting. The city may have guidelines on hours of business, pedestrian and vehicular activity, noise, and so forth in the residential area.

3. File a fictitious business name (Doing Business As—DBA) at the county clerk's office by obtaining the proper form for completion. If you use your given name, you do not have to file a fictitious business name.

4. Publish the fictitious name in a local newspaper.

5. Contact the Internal Revenue Service (IRS) for an employer identification number and/or tax

17

information. Obtain the booklet *Tax Guide for Small Business* No. 334 to determine business expenses that are deductible. Depending on how you set up your business, some possible tax breaks are as follows: depreciation of office equipment; declaring a room of your home as an office; subscriptions to professional publications; dues to professional associations; expenses associated with your automobile; telephone, photocopying, office supplies (stationery, books, typewriter ribbons, and so on); promotion and advertising (postage, meals with business associates, and so on); and any expenses pertaining to meetings, conventions, workshops, or seminars (registration fees, lodging, meals, transportation, parking, and so forth).

6. If you have no employees, contact the Franchise Tax Board for the form used for estimating state withholding taxes for yourself. This must be filed quarterly. If you build up your business and have employees, obtain the proper forms and information for employees (state income tax, and state disability and unemployment insurance).

7. Obtain the insurance that you need: health insurance, disability insurance, life insurance, liability insurance, worker's compensation (if you have employees), and so forth. Insurance is available to protect you against loss of material called "Release of Information Insurance" or "Errors and Omissions Insurance" with a "Hold Harmless" clause. You might want to consider a retirement IRA or Keogh plan.

8. Contact the telephone company for phone equipment. Do this early because there is often a delay in hook-up. You might consider using your existing telephone number and switching to a business listing. This allows you to be listed in the *Yellow Pages* of your telephone directory.

9. Open a bank account. If you want your telephone number on your checks, put the checks on hold until the telephone is confirmed.

10. Order business cards, stationery, billing forms, and reference books.

11. Begin to advertise your business by some of the following methods: newspaper, radio, flyers, announcements, signs, word of mouth, and letters to prospects (hospitals, clinics, and physician's offices).

There are some additional points to consider if you are ready to expand to a location outside of your home.

1. Check the zoning of the location at your city hall's planning department or, if you are in the county, the county's planning department. Sign a lease contingent on proper zoning and on meeting all federal, state, county, and city building safety and health requirements. Inquire about parking and sign restrictions at the planning department. Find out if you need any permits (building permit, certificate of occupancy, health permit, and so forth). City and county offices may require a sign permit for new signs and changes on old ones.

2. If you have opened an office at a location, make a deposit for water, gas, and electricity. Rent, renovation, and janitorial or trash services must be considered.

3. Call the assessor's office and ask to be put on the mailing list for business property tax (inventory tax).

4. Contact the various inspectors: health, building and safety, and sign to have all completed work inspected and the necessary permits signed off.

HOW TO LEAVE A JOB

After working several years for one employer, some transcriptionists may wish to change jobs for a different environment. For instance, working in a hospital setting is certainly different from working in a physician's office for one or two dictators. Factors beyond your control can arise, such as pregnancy, a spouse's transfer to another location, and so forth. Before considering such a move, it is important to consider all aspects of your total compensation and working environment. It is also wise to obtain a new position before leaving your present one, giving at least two weeks' notice, depending on the hospital or office policy. You can complete the form on page 371 to discover your true earnings before contemplating a move.

If you know of a well-qualified person to take your place, suggest his or her name to your supervisor. This will communicate to your employer that you see the situation from his or her viewpoint. Make it easy for the replacement to step in. No one is indispensable, yet some employees want their presence to be missed so much that they destroy any helpful guides for the new employee. You will be thought of more kindly and will leave a good impression if you leave information that might be helpful to the new employee. Clean out your work station so that someone else does not have to finish the job before he or she moves in. If you do not like your employer, keep the negative thoughts to yourself and do not make derogatory remarks to your peers. Do not neglect any of your responsibilities or skip any last-minute commitments.

DIRECT COMPENSATION:
Salary $_____
Bonuses   _____
Paid Vacation   _____
Sick Pay   _____
Incentive Compensation   _____

EMPLOYEE BENEFIT PLANS FULLY OR PARTIALLY
PAID BY EMPLOYER – INSURED:
Medical/Dental Insurance $_____
Group Term Life Insurance   _____
Additional Accidental Death and Dismemberment _____
Long-term Disability   _____
Workers' Compensation Insurance   _____
Federal Unemployment Insurance   _____
State Unemployment Insurance   _____

EMPLOYEE BENEFIT PLANS – UNINSURED:
Medical Reimbursement $_____
　　Free Medical Care for Employee
　　Free Medical Care for Family

RETIREMENT CONTRIBUTIONS:
Pension Plan $_____
Profit Sharing Plan   _____
FICA (social security) – Employer Paid   _____

MISCELLANEOUS:
Mileage Allowance $_____
Uniform Allowance   _____
Continuing Medical Education   _____
　　(tuition, registration fees, dues)

TOTAL COMPENSATION $_____

Remember to say "thank you" to your supervisor, employer, or both, and to those who helped you in some way or made your job easier and more pleasant. Let your supervisor know what you are doing as your career progresses. Your paths may cross again directly or indirectly. Perhaps he or she will be in a position to recommend you for a job in the future. Keep your record unblemished, since it may have taken you several years to build up your reputation. Be courteous. Be thoughtful. Be professional.

17–1: ASSIGNMENT

Directions: Prepare your resume by selecting one of the formats shown in Figures 17–1, 17–2, and 17–3. Rough draft it first and let your instructor read through it. Then do a final draft after the constructive criticism.

17–2: SELF-STUDY

Directions: The following advertisement appeared in your local newspaper. Compose a cover letter to go with your resume. Refer to Figure 17–4 for guidance in organizing your thoughts.

17

FULL TIME

Job No. Description

1311   Medical transcriptionist. Working in medical records. A thorough knowledge of medical termi-
         nology with fast, accurate typing required. CMT preferred. Excellent incentive pay program and
         fringe benefits. Send resume or call Personnel Dept., St. Anne's Hospital, 4021 Main Street,
         Oxnard, CA 93030 013/480-2349.

17-3: ASSIGNMENT

Directions: Type a list of where you could go for temporary jobs in your locale. Then meet at least three people who have a job that you would like. Obtain their name, place of employment, job title, and any special skills they needed to obtain the job. Type and hand this list in to your instructor.

17-4: TIMED TYPING TEST

Take a timed typing test to see what your typing speed is at the end of the course. Your instructor may also wish to time you with familiar work as well as unfamiliar work. Compare this typing speed with the typing speed you had when you did Timed Typing Test 1-1 in Chapter 1. If you know how many words you transcribe within a given amount of time or how many words you type a minute, this may let you know where you stand when you are compared with an experienced transcriptionist or typist. On the following pages are some timed typing segments. One or more of these can be dictated by the instructor to obtain a timed transcription rate or they can be used by simply looking at them while typing to obtain typing speed and accuracy.

Directions

1. Type the copy line for line, making a return at the end of each printed line. Do not type the numbers.

2. Time yourself for five minutes. When the time is up, finish the line you are on and mark the spot.

3. The number in the right margin next to this line tells you how many words you just typed according to the average word-length formula. Write that number down.

4. Now go to the quick-scoring chart in Chapter 1 and follow the directions at the bottom of it to obtain your typing speed and grade.

Good luck with your resume, and much success and happiness in your exciting new career!

Answers will vary, so no key is provided for Assignments 17-1 through 17-4.

17

TIMED TYPING #1

Jackson, Howard T.   3
1932-01-4321   6
                         DISCHARGE SUMMARY   9
ADMISSION DATE: December 11, 199x   DISCHARGE DATE: December 15, 199x 24
HISTORY OF PRESENT ILLNESS: 29
This patient is a 57-year-old white, married female admitted here on   43
a "hold" because of developing gross confusion and disorganized   56
behavior and was reported grabbing at people. She has a long   68
history of chronic alcoholism and was last treated at College   80
Hospital last summer. She was there for two months in September   93
and October of 1983. According to both she and her husband, she   106
has been totally dry since then. There is considerable confusion   119
as to what might be the cause of her "disorganized behavior."   131
However, her husband reports that they had just moved to a new   143
location, and his wife had been working very hard packing and   155
was also quite disappointed in the move. It was only a few days   169
later that she became disordered. She was admitted through College   183
Hospital since she had returned there. They did do a blood alcohol   197
level on her, but we do not know what it was.   206
Her course in the IPU was uneventful. She was treated with a few   219
small doses of Haldol here and there, but apparently after her   231
first day she became asymptomatic. There were never any delusions   244
or hallucinations. She consistently denied getting into any alcohol   258
since last July. She was placed in seclusion once on the day of   271
admission for irrational disturbed behavior.   280
She is being discharged on no psychotrophic medication. She will   293
continue to take other medication associated with her high blood   306
pressure. These medications are Dyazide, Corgard, Nitrostat, and   319
Apresoline and are prescribed by a private physician. Accordingly,   333
she is not given a mental health follow-up either.   343
DISCHARGE DIAGNOSIS: 347
Organic mental disorder of a mixed type.   355

                                                                            358

                         John B. Cooper, M. D.   363
(student's initials)   364
D: 12-21-*year*   366
T: 12-22-*year*   367

17

Kathryn T. Sloan   TIMED TYPING #2   3
527-98-6541   5
Room 543-A   7

HISTORY   8

CHIEF COMPLAINT: This 56-year-old white female under therapy for   21
metastatic carcinoma of the breast had an episode of vomiting and   34
diarrhea for the past 3-4 days prior to admission.   44
PRESENT ILLNESS: The patient developed some rib pain and right   57
leg and groin pain this past summer. Evaluation by Dr. Small   69
revealed metastatic carcinoma of the breast. The patient began   82
combination chemotherapy two weeks ago with Cytoxan, 5-FU, and   95
Methotrexate. She is also on Megace, 40 mg, q.i.d. Because of   107
persistent pain of the right leg, the patient has been receiving   120
radiation therapy. She finished up her radiation about a week ago.   133
However, towards the end of that course, she had significant   145
diarrhea and anorexia.   149
In the past 4-5 days, she developed first diarrhea followed by   161
nausea and vomiting. She was unable to keep anything down. This   174
continued over the weekend and she was brought to the hospital.   187
The patient did not note any blood in her emesis or in the stools.   200
She had abdominal cramps with it but no severe pain. She continues   213
to have some heartburn and indigestion and has a previous history   226
of hiatal hernia.   229
PAST HISTORY, REVIEW OF SYSTEMS, FAMILY HISTORY AND SOCIAL HISTORY: 242
One is referred to old charts.   248

PHYSICAL EXAMINATION   252

GENERAL: BP 130/80. Pulse 90 and regular. Respirations 18. The   265
patient is an obese, middle-aged woman who appears more acutely ill.   279
SKIN: No significant dermatoses.   285
HEENT: Atraumatic and nonicteric. Pupils equally reactive to   297
light and accommodation. Extraocular muscles intact. Funduscopic   310
examination shows discs to be flat. Mouth and throat show dry   322
mucous membranes.   325
NECK: Supple.   328
NODES: No significant peripheral lymphadenopathy.   338
BREASTS: The right breast has a healing lumpectomy scar. It is   351
nontender without signs of recurrence. Left breast is pendulous   364
and without masses.   368
LUNGS: Clear to percussion and auscultation.   377
HEART: Regular rhythm without significant gallops, rubs or murmurs.   391
ABDOMEN: Soft, nontender and nondistended. No shifting dullness   404
or organomegaly.   407
RECTAL: Examination to be performed.   414
PELVIC: Examination performed by Dr. Small within the past several   427
months and was unremarkable.   432
EXTREMITIES: Without edema, cyanosis or clubbing. No calf tenderness.   446
NEUROLOGIC: Without focal signs.   452

17

ASSESSMENT: 454

1)   Nausea, vomiting and diarrhea; possible gastroenteritis; rule   467
     out toxic effect to radiation or chemotherapy; rule out peptic   480
     ulcer disease; rule out structural lesion such as bowel   492
     obstruction.   495

2)   Metastatic carcinoma of the breast to bone. Patient is   507
     presently on therapy.   512

   514

                 William B. Smith, M. D.   519

(student's initials)   520

D: *Current Date*   522

T: *Current Date*   524

TIMED TYPING #3

RADIOLOGY REPORT   3

Examination Date:	May 14, 19--	Patient:	Curt Dowdy	16
Date Reported:	May 14, 19--	X-ray No.:	43201	28
Physician:	John Doe, M. D.	Age:	25	39
Examination:	PA & Lateral chest	Hospital No.:	48-91-02	51

Findings: 53

PA AND LATERAL CHEST: 57
Patchy and confluent infiltrate is present in the left lower   69
lobe compatible with acute pneumonia. Additional infiltrate   81
may be present at the right base medially. Both lungs appear   93
mildly hyperinflated with bilateral apical bleb and bulla   104
formation. Heart size appears top normal with left ventricular   116
prominence. Moderate gaseous distention of bowel loops beneath   128
the slightly elevated left hemidiaphragm is identified. There   140
are no bony abnormalities.   145
CONCLUSIONS: 147
1) Patchy and partially confluent left lower lobe pneumonia.   159
Additional infiltrate may be present at the right base medially.   172
2) Underlying mild COPD with bilateral apical bleb and bulla   184
formation.   186
3) Heart size top normal with left ventricular prominence.   198
4) Slight elevation of the left hemidiaphragm.   207
5) Moderate gaseous distention of bowel loops noted in the left   220
central and upper abdomen.   225

   227

                 Marian B. Skinner, M. D.   232

17

(student's initials)   233

D: *Current Date*   235

T: *Current Date*   237

TIMED TYPING #4

PATHOLOGY REPORT   3

Date: June 20, 19--   Pathology No. 432011   15
Patient: Elaine B. Cox   Room No.   140A   26
Physician: John Temple, M. D.   33
Specimen Removed: Appendix   38
GROSS DESCRIPTION: 41
The specimen consists of a quite distorted vermiform appendix   53
in two parts; the larger part consists of a proximal 4 cm of   65
the appendix and a mass about its distal end approximating   77
3.5 x 2.5 x 2.0 cm while the separate second portion of tissue   89
appears to be derived from the area appearing possibly as peri-   102
appendiceal abscess within desmoplastic inflammatory tissue.   114
The proximal appendix averages 1 cm in diameter and expands   126
at the site of the periappendiceal mass in the center of which   138
it appears to double back on itself so that the distal half of   150
this portion on being cut across shows two appendiceal cross   162
sections, side by side. Throughout this length the appendix   174
does not appear inflamed although its lumen appears compressed   186
as if by edema, and its wall thickened as if by edema. In the   198
separate portion of tissue, there is a shaggy, hemorrhagic,   210
irregular central cyst-like, or abscess-like area surrounded   222
by a varying thickness of desmoplastic tissue extending into   234
mesenteric fat. Multiple representative sections are made.   246
MICROSCROPIC DESCRIPTION: 251
Sections reveal segments of appendiceal wall and mesoappendix   263
which are extensively and diffusely infiltrated with acute   274
inflammatory cells with areas of abscess formation surrounded   286
by a rim of histiocytes and fibroblasts. A considerable number   298
of eosinophils are detected in these sections. Negative for   310
specific inflammation or malignancy.   317
DIAGNOSIS: 319
Vermiform appendix: Acute, necrotizing hemorrhagic appendicitis 332
with periappendiceal abscess formation.   340
                                                                  341
                        Alan Blackstone, M. D.   345
(student's initials)   346
D: Current Date   347
T: Current Date   349

17

Common Medical Homonyms

The following words are commonly encountered in medical transcription. You will notice that they are in alphabetical sequence with the homonyms listed indented below each word. Phonetics are shown and the stress point of the word is capitalized. Abbreviated definitions are listed so that you do not have to refer to your medical dictionary unless you wish a more detailed meaning.

abduction *addiction* *adduction* *subduction*	ab-DUK-shun	A drawing away from the midline.
aberrant *afferent* *efferent* *inferent*	ab-ER-ant	Wandering or deviating from the normal course.
aberration *abrasion* *erasion* *erosion* *operation*	ab″er-A-shun	Deviation from the usual course.
abrasion *aberration* *erasion* *erosion* *operation*	ah-BRA-zhun	Denudation of skin.
absorption *adsorption* *sorption*	ab-SORP-shun	The uptake of substances into tissues.
addiction *abduction* *adduction*	ah-DIK-shun	Dependence on a drug or some habit.
adduction *abduction* *addiction*	ah-DUK-shun	A drawing toward the midline.
adherence *adhered to* *adherent* *adherents*	ad-HĒR-ens	The act or quality of sticking to something.
adsorption *absorption* *sorption*	ad-SORP-shun	To collect in condensed form on a surface.

A

377

affect *effect*	af-FEKT	To have an influence on; the feeling experienced in connection with an emotion.
afferent *aberrant* *efferent*	AF-er-ent	Conveying toward a center.
alveolar *alveolate* *alveoli* *alveolus* *alveus* *alvus* *areolar*	al-VE-o-lar	Pertaining to an alveolus.
alveoli *alveolar* *alveolate* *alveolus* *alveus* *alvus* *areolar*	al-VE-o-li	Plural of alveolus.
alveolus *alveolar* *alveolate* *alveoli* *alveus* *alvus* *areolar*	al-VE-o-lus	A small saclike dilatation.
alveus *alveolar* *alveolate* *alveoli* *alveolus* *alvus* *areolar*	AL-ve-us	A trough or canal.
alvus *alveolar* *alveolate* *alveoli* *alveolus* *alveus* *areolar*	AL-vus	The abdomen with its contained viscera.
amenorrhea *dysmenorrhea* *menorrhagia* *menorrhea* *metrorrhagia*	ah-men"o-RE-ah	Abnormal stoppage of the menses.
antiseptic *asepsis* *aseptic* *sepsis* *septic*	an"tĭ-SEP-tik	Preventing decay or putrefaction.

A

aphagia *abasia* *aphakia* *aphasia*	ah-FA-je-ah	Abstention from eating.
aphakia *aphagia* *aphasia*	ah-FA-ke-ah	Absence of the lens of the eye.
aphasia *abasia* *aphakia* *aphagia*	ah-FA-ze-ah	Loss of the power of expression by speech, writing, or signs.
apposition *opposition*	ap"o-ZISH-un	The placing of things in juxtaposition or proximity.
arrhythmia *erythema* *eurhythmia*	ah-RITH-me-ah	Variation from the normal rhythm of the heartbeat.
arteriosclerosis *arteriostenosis* *atherosclerosis*	ar-te"re-o-skle-RO-sis	A disease characterized by thickening and loss of elasticity of arterial walls.
arteriostenosis *arteriosclerosis* *atherosclerosis*	ar-te"re-o-ste-NO-sis	The narrowing or diminution of the caliber of an artery.
atherosclerosis *arteriosclerosis* *arteriostenosis*	ath"er-o"skle-RO-sis	Deposits of yellowish plaques containing cholesterol and lipoid material formed on the inside of the arteries.
aural *aura* *ora* *oral*	AW-ral	Pertaining to or perceived by the ear.
auscultation *oscillation* *oscitation* *osculation*	aws"kul-TA-shun	The act of listening for sounds within the body.
bare *bear*	ber	Naked.
border *boarder* *quarter*	BOR-der	A rim, margin, or edge.
bowel *bile* *vowel*	BOW-el	The intestine.
breath *breadth*	breth	The air taken in and expelled by the expansion and contraction of the thorax.
breathe *breed*	brēth	To take air into the lungs and let it out again.
bronchoscopic *proctoscopic*	brong"ko-SKOP-ik	Pertaining to bronchoscopy or to the bronchoscope.

A

bruit *brute*	brwe, broot	A sound or murmur heard in auscultation.
calculous *calculus* *caliculus* *callus* *callous*	KAL-ku-lus	Pertaining to, of the nature of, or affected with calculus.
calculus *calculous* *caliculus* *callus* *callous*	KAL-ku-lus	Any abnormal stony mass or deposit formed in the body.
callous *calculous* *calculus* *callus* *talus*	KAL-us	Pertaining to a hardened, thickened place on the skin.
callus *calculous* *calculus* *callous* *talus*	KAL-us	A hardened, thickened place on the skin; formation of new bone between broken ends of a bone.
cancellous *cancellus* *cancerous*	KAN-sĕ-lus	Of a reticular, spongy, or lattice-like structure.
cancellus *cancellous* *cancerous*	kan-SEL-us	Any structure arranged like a lattice.
cancer *canker* *chancre*	KAN-ser	Malignant tumor.
cancerous *cancellous* *cancellus*	KAN-ser-us	Pertaining to cancer.
canker *cancer* *chancre*	KANG-ker	Ulceration, chiefly of the mouth and lips.
carbuncle *caruncle* *furuncle*	KAR-bung-kl	A cluster of boils; furuncles.
carpus *carpal* *corpus*	KAR-pus	The wrist.
caruncle *carbuncle* *furuncle*	KAR-ung-kl	A small fleshy eminence, whether normal or abnormal.
chancre *cancer* *canker*	SHANG-ker	The primary sore of syphilis.

A

cirrhosis *cillosis* *psilosis* *sclerosis* *serosa* *xerosis*	sir-RO-sis	A degenerative disease of the liver.
coarse *course* *force*	kors	Not fine or microscopic; rough or crude.
contusion *concussion* *confusion* *convulsion*	kon-TU-zhun	A bruise.
cord *chord* *cor*	kord	Any long, rounded, flexible structure. Also spelled chord and chorda.
corneal *cranial*	KOR-ne-al	Pertaining to the cornea of the eye.
corpus *carpus* *copious* *core* *corps* *corpse*	KOR-pus	A human body; the body (main part) of an organ.
cranial *corneal*	KRA-ne-al	Pertaining to the cranium (skull).
cytology *psychology* *sitology*	si-TOL-o-je	The study of cells.
diaphysis *apophysis* *diastasis* *diathesis* *epiphysis*	di-AF-ĭ-sis	Shaft of a long bone.
diathesis *diaphysis* *diastasis*	di-ATH-ĕ-sis	A predisposition to certain diseases.
dilatation *dilation*	dil-ah-TA-shun	A dilated condition or structure.
dilation *dilatation*	di-LA-shun	The process of dilating or becoming dilated.
dysphagia *dysbasia* *dyscrasia* *dysphasia* *dysplasia* *dyspragia*	dis-FA-je-ah	Difficulty in swallowing.

A

dysphasia *dysbasia* *dyscrasia* *dysphagia* *dysplasia* *dyspragia*	dis-FA-ze-ah	Impairment of the faculty of speech.
dysplasia *dysbasia* *dyscrasia* *dysphagia* *dysphasia* *dyspragia*	dis-PLA-se-ah	Abnormality in development of tissues or body parts.
dyspragia *dysphagia* *dysphasia* *dysplasia*	dis-PRA-je-ah	Painful performance of any function.
dyspraxia *dystaxia*	dis-PRAK-se-ah	Partial loss of ability to perform coordinated acts.
ecchymosis *achymosis* *echinosis* *echomosis*	ek″ĭ-MO-sis	A bruise.
effect *affect* *defect*	e-FEKT	The result; to bring about.
efferent *aberrant* *afferent*	EF-er-ent	Conveying away from a center.
elicit *illicit*	e-LIS-it	To cause to be revealed; to draw out.
embolus *bolus* *embolism* *thrombus*	EM-bo-lus	A blood clot carried in the bloodstream.
endemic *ecdemic* *epidemic* *pandemic*	en-DEM-ik	A disease native to a particular region.
enervation *denervation* *innervation*	en″er-VA-shun	Lack of nervous energy; removal or section of a nerve.
enteric *icteric*	en-TER-ik	Pertaining to the small intestine.
epidemic *ecdemic* *endemic*	ep″ĭ-DEM-ik	The rapid spreading of a contagious disease.
erythema *arrhythmia* *erythremia* *eurhythmia*	er″i-THE-mah	Redness of the skin due to a variety of causes.

eschar *a scar* *escharotic* *scar*	ES-kar	A slough produced by a thermal burn or by gangrene.
everted *inverted*	e-VER-ted	Turned outward.
facial *basal* *fascial* *faucial* *racial*	FA-shal	Pertaining to the face.
fascial *facial* *falcial* *fascia* *fashion* *faucial*	FASH-e-al	Pertaining to fascia.
fauces *facies* *feces* *foci* *fossa* *fossae*	FAW-sēz	The throat.
fecal *cecal* *fetal* *focal* *thecal*	FE-cal	Pertaining to or of the nature of feces.
fetal *fatal* *fecal*	FE-tal	Pertaining to a fetus.
flexor *flexure*	FLEK-sor	Any muscle that flexes a joint.
flexure *flexor*	FLEK-sher	A bent position of a structure or organ.
fundi *fungi*	FUN-di	Plural of fundus, a bottom or base.
furuncle *carbuncle* *caruncle*	FU-rung-k'l	A boil.
gastroscopy *gastrostomy* *gastrotomy*	gas-TROS-ko-pe	Inspection of the stomach with a gastroscope.
gastrostomy *gastroscopy* *gastrotomy*	gas-TROS-to-me	Artificial opening into the stomach.
gavage *lavage*	gah-VAHZH	Feeding by stomach tube.
glands *glans*	glands	Groups of cells that secrete or excrete material not used in their metabolic activities.

glans *glands*	glanz	Latin for gland.
hypercalcemia *hyperkalemia* *hypocalcemia*	hi″per-kal-SE-me-ah	An excess of calcium in the blood.
hyperinsulinism *hypoinsulinism*	hi″per-IN-su-lin-izm″	Excessive secretion of insulin by the pancreas; insulin shock.
hyperkalemia *hypercalcemia* *hyperkinemia* *hypokalemia*	hi″per-kah-LE-me-ah	Abnormally high potassium concentration in the blood.
hypertension *Hypertensin* *hypotension*	hi″per-TEN-shun	High blood pressure.
hypocalcemia *hypercalcemia* *hyperkalemia*	hi″po-kal-SE-me-ah	Reduction of the blood calcium below normal.
hypokalemia *hypercalcemia* *hyperkinemia* *hyperkalemia*	hi″po-ka-LE-me-ah	Abnormally low potassium concentration in the blood.
hypoinsulinism *hyperinsulinism*	hi″po-IN-su-lin-izm	Deficient secretion of insulin by the pancreas.
hypotension *hypertension*	hi″po-TEN-shun	Low blood pressure.
icteric *enteric* *mycteric*	ik-TER-ik	Pertaining to or affected with jaundice.
ileum *ilium*	IL-e-um	Part of the small intestine.
ilium *ileum*	IL-e-um	The flank bone or hip bone.
illicit *elicit*	i-LIS-it	Illegal.
infarction *infection* *infestation* *infraction* *injection*	in-FARK-shun	The formation of an infarct.
infection *infarction* *infestation* *inflection* *inflexion* *in flexion* *injection*	in-FEK-shun	Invasion of the body by pathogenic microorganisms.
infestation *infarction* *infection* *injection*	in-fes-TA-shun	Invasion of the body by small invertebrate animals, such as insects, mites, or ticks.

injection *infarction* *infection* *infestation* *ingestion*	in-JEK-shun	Act of forcing a liquid into a part or an organ.
innervation *enervation*	in"er-VA-shun	The distribution of nerves to a part.
insulin *inulin*	IN-su-lin	Protein formed by the islet cells of Langerhans in the pancreas.
inulin *insulin*	IN-u-lin	A vegetable starch.
inverted *everted*	in-VERT-ed	Turned inside out or upside down.
keratitis *keratiasis* *keratosis* *ketosis*	ker"ah-TI-tis	Inflammation of the cornea.
keratosis *keratitis* *keratose* *ketosis*	ker"ah-TO-sis	Any horny growth, such as a wart or a callosity.
ketosis *keratitis* *keratosis*	ke-TO-sis	Abnormally high concentration of ketone bodies in the body tissues and fluids.
laceration *maceration* *masturbation*	las"er-A-shun	Act of tearing; wound made by tearing.
lavage *gavage*	lah-VAHZH	The irrigation or washing out of an organ.
lipoma *fibroma* *lipomyoma* *lymphoma*	lĭ-PO-mah	A benign tumor composed of mature fat cells.
lithotomy *lithotony*	lith-OT-o-me	Incision of an organ for removal of a stone.
lithotony *lithotomy*	lith-OT-o-ne	Creation of an artificial vesical fistula that is dilated to extract a stone.
liver *livor* *sliver*	LIV-er	A large gland of dark-red color in the upper part of the abdomen on the right side.
livor *liver*	LIV-or	Discoloration.
lymphoma *lipoma*	lim-FO-mah	Any neoplastic disorder of the lymphoid tissue.
maceration *laceration* *masturbation*	mas"er-A-shun	The softening of a solid by soaking.
mastitis *mastoiditis*	mas-TI-tis	Inflammation of the mammary gland, or breast.

A

mastoiditis *mastitis*	mas"toi-DI-tis	Inflammation of the mastoid antrum and cells.
masturbation *laceration* *masceration*	mas"tur-BA-shun	Production of orgasm by self-manipulation of the genitals.
menorrhagia *menorrhea* *metrorrhagia*	men"o-RA-je-ah	Excessive uterine bleeding at menstruation time.
menorrhea *amenorrhea* *dysmenorrhea* *menorrhagia* *metrorrhagia*	men"o-RE-ah	The normal discharge of the menses.
metacarpal *metatarsal*	met"ah-KAR-pal	Pertaining to the metacarpus.
metastasis *metaphysis* *metastases* *(plural)* *metastasize* *metastatic*	mĕ-TAS-tah-sis	The transfer of disease from one site to another not directly connected with it.
metastasize *metastases* *metastasis* *metastatic*	me-TAS-tah-size	To form new foci of disease in a distant part by metastasis.
metastatic *metastases* *metastasis* *metastasize*	met"ah-STAT-ik	Pertaining to metastasis.
metatarsal *metacarpal*	met"ah-TAR-sal	Pertaining to the metatarsus.
metrorrhagia *menorrhagia* *menorrhea*	me"tro-RA-je-ah	Uterine bleeding at irregular intervals sometimes being prolonged.
mucoid *Mucor* *mucosa* *mucosal*	MU-koid	Resembling mucin.
mucosa *mucosal* *mucosin* *mucous* *mucus*	mu-KO-sah	A mucous membrane.
mucosal *mucosa* *mucous* *mucus*	mu-KO-sal	Pertaining to the mucous membrane.
mucous *mucosa* *mucosal* *mucus*	MU-kus	The adjective that means pertaining to mucus.

mucus *mucosa* *mucosal* *mucous*	MU-kus	The noun that means a viscid watery secretion of mucous glands.
myogram *myelogram*	MI-o-gram	A recording or tracing mode with a myograph.
necrosis *narcosis* *nephrosis* *neurosis*	ne-KRO-sis	Death of tissue.
nephrosis *necrosis* *neurosis* *tephrosis*	ne-FRO-sis	Any disease of the kidney.
neurosis *necrosis* *nephrosis* *urosis*	nu-RO-sis	Disorder of psychic or mental constitution.
obstipation *constipation* *obfuscation*	ob"sti-PA-shun	Intractable constipation.
oral *aura* *aural*	O-ral	Pertaining to the mouth.
oscillation *auscultation* *oscitation* *osculation*	os"i-LA-shun	A backward and forward motion; vibration.
oscitation *auscultation* *excitation* *oscillation* *osculation*	os"i-TA-shun	The act of yawning.
osculation *auscultation* *escalation* *oscillation* *oscitation*	os"ku-LA-shun	To kiss; to touch closely.
palpation *palliation* *palpillation* *palpitation*	pal-PA-shun	The act of feeling with the hand.
palpitation *palliation* *palpation* *papillation*	pal"pĭ-TA-shun	Regular or irregular rapid action of the heart.
parasthenia *paresthesia*	par"as-THE-ne-ah	A condition of organic tissue causing it to function at abnormal intervals.
paresthesia *pallesthesia* *parasthenia* *paresthenia*	par"es-THE-ze-ah	An abnormal sensation, such as burning or prickling.

A

parietitis *parotitis* *parotiditis*	pah-ri″ĕ-TI-tis	Inflammation of the wall of an organ.
parotiditis *parietitis* *parotitis*	pah-rot″ĭ-DI-tis	Inflammation of the parotid gland.
parotitis *parietitis* *parostitis* *parotiditis*	par″o-TI-tis	Inflammation of the parotid gland.
parous *Paris* *pars* *porous*	PA-rus	Having brought forth one living offspring.
pedicle *medical* *particle* *peduncle* *pellicle*	PED-ĭ-k′l	A footlike or stemlike structure.
perineal *pectineal* *peritoneal* *peroneal*	per″i-NE-al	Pertaining to the perineum.
perineum *peritoneum*	per″i-NE-um	The region at the lower end of the trunk between the thighs.
peritoneum *perineum*	per″i-to-NE-um	The serous membrane lining the abdominal walls.
peroneal *pectineal* *perineal* *peritoneal* *peronia*	per″o-NE-al	Pertaining to the fibula or outer side of the leg.
pleural *plural*	PLOOR-al	Pertaining to the pleura.
prostate *prostrate*	PROS-tāt	A gland in the male that surrounds the neck of the bladder and the urethra.
prostrate *prostate*	PROS-trāt	Lying flat, prone, or supine.
psychology *cytology* *sitology*	si-KOL-o-je	The science dealing with the mind and with mental and emotional processes.
pyelonephrosis *pyonephrosis*	pi″e-lo-nĕ-FRO-sis	Any disease of the kidney and its pelvis.
pyonephrosis *pyelonephrosis*	pi″o-nĕ-FRO-sis	Suppurative destruction of the parenchyma of the kidney.
pyrenemia *pyoturia* *pyuria*	pi″rĕ-NE-me-ah	The presence of nucleated red cells in the blood.
pyuria *paruria* *pyorrhea* *pyoturia* *pyrenemia*	pi-U-re-ah	The presence of pus in the urine.

radical *radicle*	RAD-ĭ-kal	Directed to the source of a morbid process, as radical surgery.
radicle *radical*	RAD-ĭ-k′l	Any one of the smallest branches of a vessel or nerve.
recession *resection*	re-SESH-un	The act of drawing away or back.
reflex *efflux* *reflux*	RE-fleks	A reflected action; an involuntary muscular movement.
reflux *efflux* *reflex*	RE-fluks	A backward or return flow.
resection *recession*	re-SEK-shun	Excision of a portion of an organ or other structure.
rhonchi *bronchi* *ronchi*	RONG-kī	Plural of rhonchus, a rattling in the throat; a dry, coarse rale.
scar *a scar* *eschar* *scarf*	skahr	A mark remaining after the healing of a wound.
scirrhous *cirrhosis* *cirrus* *scirrhus* *sclerous* *serious* *serous*	SKIR-us	Pertaining to a hard cancer.
scirrhus *cirrhosis* *cirrus* *scirrhous* *sclerous* *serious* *serous*	SKIR-us	Scirrhous carcinoma.
sedentary *sedimentary*	SED-en-ter″e	Sitting habitually.
sedimentary *sedentary*	sed-ĭ-MEN-ter-e	Of, having the nature of, or containing sediment.
separation *suppression* *suppuration*	sep-ah-RA-shun	Break; division; gap.
sepsis *antiseptic* *asepsis* *aseptic* *septic* *threpsis*	SEP-sis	The presence in the blood of pathogenic microorganisms or their toxins.

A

septic *antiseptic* *asepsis* *a septic* *aseptic* *sepsis* *septal* *septile* *skeptic*	SEP-tik	Owing to decomposition by microorganisms.
serosa *cirrhosis* *xerosis*	se-RO-sah; se-RO-zah	Any serous membrane (tunica mucosa); tunica serosa; the chorion.
serous *cirrus* *scirrhous* *scirrhus* *sclerous* *sera* *serious* *serose*	SE-rus	Pertaining to serum.
sight *cite* *cyte* *side* *site* *slight*	sīt	The act of seeing; a thing seen.
stasis *bases* *basis* *station* *status* *staxis*	STA-sis	A stoppage of the flow of blood.
staxis *stasis*	STAK-sis	Hemorrhage.
stroma *soma* *stoma* *struma* *trauma*	STRO-mah	The supporting tissue of an organ.
struma *stoma* *stroma*	STROO-mah	Goiter.
suppression *separation* *suppuration*	sŭ-PRESH-un	The sudden stoppage of a secretion, excretion, or normal discharge.
suppuration *separation* *suppression* *susurration*	sup″u-RA-shun	The formation of pus.
sycosis *psychosis*	si-KO-sis	A disease marked by inflammation of the hair follicles; a kind of ulcer on the eyelid.

A

tenia *taenia* *Taenia* *tinea*	TE-ne-ah	A flat band or strip of soft tissue.
thenar *femur* *thinner*	THE-nar	The mound on the palm at the base of the thumb.
thrombus *embolus*	THROM-bus	A blood clot that remains at the site of formation.
tinea *linea* *linear* *taenia* *Taenia* *tenia*	TIN-e-ah	Ringworm.
trachelotomy *tracheophony* *tracheotomy*	tra″ke-LOT-o-me	The surgical cutting of the uterine neck.
tracheophony *trachelotomy* *tracheotomy*	tra″kĕ-OF-o-ne	A sound heard in auscultation over the trachea.
tracheotomy *trachelotomy* *tracheophony*	tra″ke-OT-o-me	Incision of the trachea through the skin and muscles of the neck.
tympanites *tympanitis*	tim″pah-NI-tēz	Distention of the abdomen due to gas or air in the intestine or in the peritoneal cavity.
tympanitis *tenonitis* *tinnitus* *tympanites*	tim″pah-NI-tis	Inflammation of the middle ear.
ureter *urethra* *urethral* *ureteral*	u-RE-ter	The tube that conveys the urine from the kidney to the bladder.
ureteral *ureter* *urethra* *urethral*	u-RE-ter-al	Pertaining to the ureter.
urethra *ureter* *ureteral*	u-RE-thrah	The canal conveying urine from the bladder to the outside of the body.
urethral *ureter* *ureteral* *urethra*	u-RE-thral	Pertaining to the urethra.
urethrorrhagia *ureterorrhagia*	u-re″thro-RA-je-ah	A flow of blood from the urethra.

A

uterus
  ureter
  urethra
  urethral
	U-ter-us	The womb.

vagitis *vagitus*	va-JI-tis	Inflammation of the vagal nerve.
vagitus *vagitis*	vah-JI-tus	The cry of an infant.
vagus *valgus*	VA-gus	The tenth cranial nerve.

valgus
  vagus
  varus
  vastus
	VAL-gus	Bent outward, twisted, as in knock-knee (genu valgum).

variceal *varicella*	var″ĭ-SE-al	Pertaining to a varix, an enlarged artery or vein.
varicella *variceal*	var″ĭ-SEL-ah	Chickenpox.

varicose
  verrucose
  very close
  very coarse
	VAR-ĭ-kos	Pertaining to a varix, an enlarged artery or vein.

variolar *variola*	vah-RI-o-lar	Pertaining to smallpox.
venous *Venus*	VE-nus	Pertaining to the veins.
Venus *venous*	VE-nus	The goddess of love and beauty in Roman mythology; the planet second from the sun.

verrucose
  varicose
  verrucous
  vorticose
	VER-oo-kōs	Rough; warty.

verrucous
  varicose
  verrucose
  vorticose
	VER-oo-kus	Rough; warty.

vesical
  fascicle
  vesica
  vesicle
  vessel
	VES-ĭ-kal	Pertaining to the bladder.

vesicle
  fascicle
  vesica
  vesical
  vessel
	VES-ĭ-k′l	A small bladder or sac containing liquid.

vessel
  vesical
  vesicle
	VES-′l	A tube or duct containing or circulating a body fluid.

A

villous *villose* *villus*	VIL-us	Shaggy with soft hairs.
villus *villose* *villous*	VIL-lus	A small vascular process or protrusion.
viscera *visceral* *viscus*	VIS-er-ah	Plural of viscus.
viscus *discus* *vicious* *viscera* *viscose* *viscous*	VIS-kus	Any large interior organ in any one of the three great cavities of the body.
womb *wound*	wōom	The uterus.
wound *womb*	wōond	An injury to the body caused by physical means.
xerosis *cirrhosis* *serosa*	ze-RO-sis	Abnormal dryness.

A

APPENDIX B

Sound and Word Finder Table

The following are some common examples of how English and medical terms sound phonetically together with clues as to how they would be spelled to help you locate them in the medical dictionary. If you cannot find a word when you look it up, refer to this table and use another combination of letters that has the same sound.

If the phonetic sound is like . . .	Try the spelling as in . . .	Examples
a in fat	ai	pl*ai*d
	al	h*al*f
	au	dr*au*ght
a in sane	ai	p*ai*n
	ao	g*ao*l
	au	g*au*ge
	ay	p*ay*, x-r*ay*, T*ay*-Sachs
	ue	s*ue*de
	ie	p*ie*dra
	ea	br*ea*k
	ei	v*ei*n
	eigh	w*eigh*
	et	sach*et*
	ey	th*ey*, p*ey*ote
a in care	ai	*ai*r, cl*air*voyant
	ay	pr*ay*er
	e	th*e*re
	ea	w*ea*r
	ei	th*ei*r
a in father	au	*au*ral, *au*ricle, *au*scultation
	e	s*e*rgeant
	ea	h*ea*rt
a in ago	e	ag*e*nt
	i	san*i*ty
	o	c*o*mply
	u	foc*u*s
	iou	vic*iou*s
aci in acid	acy	*acy*stia
ak	ac	*ac*cident
	ach	*ach*romatic
	acr	*acr*omegaly

Copyright © 1991 by W.B.S. All rights reserved. ISBN 0-7216-3479-6

ark	arch	*arch*icyte
b in big	bb	ru*bb*er
	pb	cu*pb*oard
bak sound in back	bac	*bac*teremia
bee	by	pres*by*opia
ch in chin	c	*c*ello
	Cz	*Cz*ech
	tch	sti*tch*
	ti	ques*ti*on
	tu	den*tu*re, fis*tu*la
d in do	dd	pu*dd*le
	ed	call*ed*
die	di	*di*agnosis, *di*arrhea
dis	dis	*dis*charge
	dys	*dys*pnea
dew	deu	*deu*teropathy
	dew	*dew*lap
	du	*du*ra
e in get	a	*a*ny
	ae	*ae*sthetic
	ai	s*ai*d
	ay	s*ay*s
	e	*e*dema
	ea	h*ea*d
	ei	h*ei*fer
	eo	l*eo*pard
	ie	*frie*nd
	oe	r*oe*ntgen
	u	b*u*rial
e in equal	ae	h*ae*moglobin
	ay	qu*ay*
	ea	l*ea*n
	ee	fr*ee*
	ei	dec*ei*t
	eo	p*eo*ple
	ey	k*ey*
	i	hem*i*cardia
	ie	s*ie*ge
	oe	am*oe*ba
	y	tracheotom*y*
e in here	ea	*ea*r
	ee	ch*ee*r
	ei	w*ei*rd
	ie	b*ie*r
ek	ec	l*ec*totype, *ec*zema
	ek	*ek*phorize
er in over	ar	li*ar*
	ir	elix*ir*
	or	auth*or*, lab*or*

B

	our	glam*our*
	re	ac*re*
	ur	aug*ur*
	ure	meas*ure*
	yr	zeph*yr*
eri, ere, aire	ery	*ery*throcyte, *ery*thema
ex	ex	*ex*travasation
	x	*x*-ray
f in fine	ff	cli*ff*
	gh	lau*gh*, slou*gh*
	lf	ha*lf*
	ph	*ph*ysiology, pro*ph*ylactic
fizz	phys	*phys*ical
floo, flu	flu	*flu*oride, *flu*oroscopy
g in go	gg	e*gg*
	gh	*gh*ost
	gu	*gu*ard
	gue	prolo*gue*
gli in glide	gly	*gly*cemia
grew	grou	*grou*p
guy (also see jin)	gy	*gy*necomastia
h in hat	g	*G*ila monster
	j	San *J*oaquin Valley fever
	wh	*wh*o, *wh*ooping cough
he	he	*he*matoma
	hae	*hae*matology
	(British	
	spelling)	
hi in high	hy	*hy*drocele
i in it	a	us*a*ge
	e	*E*nglish
	ee	b*ee*n
	ia	carr*ia*ge
	ie	s*ie*ve
	o	w*o*men
	u	b*u*sy
	ui	b*ui*lt
	y	lar*y*ngeal, n*y*stagmus
i in kite	ai	gu*ai*ac
	ay	*ay*e
	ei	h*ei*ght, m*ei*osis
	ey	*ey*e
	ie	t*ie*
	igh	n*igh*
	is	*is*land of Langerhans
	uy	b*uy*
	y	m*y*ograph
	ye	r*ye*

B

ik or ick	ich	*ich*thyosis
ink	inc	*inc*ubator
j in jam	d	gra*d*ual
	dg	ju*dg*e
	di	sol*di*er
	dj	a*dj*ective
	g	re*g*ister, fun*g*i
	ge	ven*ge*ance
	gg	exa*gg*erate
jin	gyn	*gyn*ecology
k in keep	c	e*c*zema
	cc	ac*cc*ount
	ch	*ch*ronic, ta*ch*ycardia
	ck	ta*ck*
	cq	a*cq*uire
	cu	bis*cu*it
	lk	wa*lk*
	qu	li*qu*or
	que	pla*que*
key	che	*che*motherapy
	chy	ec*chy*mosis
ko	cho, co	*cho*lecyst, *co*lon
kon	chon	*chon*droma
	con	*con*dyloma
kw sound in quick	ch	*ch*oir
	qu	*qu*intuplet
l in let	ll	ca*ll*
	sl	i*sl*e
la in lay	lay	*lay*ette
	le	*le*i
lack	lac	*lac*rimal
loo	leu	*leu*kocyte
	lew	*lew*isite
m in me	chm	dra*chm*
	gm	phle*gm*
	lm	ba*lm*
	mb	li*mb*
	mm	ha*mm*er toe
	mn	hy*mn*
mass	mac	*mac*erate
mix	myx	*myx*edema
n in no	cn	*cn*emial
	gn	*gn*athic
	kn	*kn*ife
	mn	*mn*emonic
	nn	ti*nn*itus
	pn	*pn*eumonia

B

ng in ring	ngue	to*ngue*
new	neu	*neu*rology
	pneu	*pneu*mococcus
o in go	au	m*au*ve
	eau	b*eau*
	eo	y*eo*man
	ew	s*ew*
	oa	f*oa*m
	oe	t*oe*
	oh	*oh*m
	oo	br*oo*ch
	ou	sh*ou*lder
	ough	d*ough*
	ow	r*ow*
o in long	a	*a*ll
	ah	Ut*ah*
	au	fr*au*d
	aw	th*aw*
	oa	br*oa*d
	ou	*ou*ght
off	oph	ex*oph*thalmos, *oph*thalmology
oi in oil	oy	b*oy*
oks	occ	*occ*iput
	ox	*ox*ygen
oo in tool	eu	l*eu*kemia
	ew	dr*ew*
	o	m*o*ve
	oe	sh*oe*
	ou	gr*ou*p
	ough	thr*ough*
	u	r*u*le, t*u*laremia
	ue	bl*ue*
	ui	br*ui*se
oo in look	o	w*o*lffian
	ou	w*ou*ld
	u	p*u*ll, t*u*berculosis
ow in out	ou	m*ou*th
	ough	b*ough*
	ow	cr*ow*d
p in put	pp	ha*pp*y
pack	pach	myo*pach*ynsis, *pach*yderma
pi in pie	py	nephro*py*osis
r in red	rh	*rh*abdocyte
	rr	be*rr*y
	rrh	ci*rrh*osis, hemo*rrh*oid
	wr	*wr*ong, *wr*ist
re in repeat	rhe	*rhe*ostosis
	ri	mala*ri*a
	rrhe	oto*rrhe*a

rew	rheu	*rheu*matism
	rhu	*rhu*barb
rom	rho	*rho*mboid
rye	rhi	*rhi*noplasty
s in sew	c	*c*yst, fo*c*i
	ce	ri*ce*
	ps	*p*sychology
	sc	*sc*iatic, vi*sc*era
	sch	*sch*ism
	ss	mi*ss*
	sth	i*sth*mus
sh in ship	ce	o*ce*an
	ch	*ch*ancre
	ci	fa*ci*al
	s	*s*ugar
	sch	*Sch*wann's cell
	sci	fa*sci*a
	se	nau*se*ous
t in tea	pt	*pt*erygium, *pt*osis
zh sound in azure	ge	gara*ge*, massa*ge*, curetta*ge*
	s	vi*s*ion
	si	fu*si*on
	zi	gla*z*ier
zi	zy	*zy*goma, *zy*gote, en*zy*me
(rhymes with sigh)	x	*x*iphoid, *x*anthoma
zz	ss	sci*ss*ors
	zz	bu*zz*

As an additional spelling aid, here is a group of letter combinations that can cause problems when you are trying to locate a word.

If you have tried . . .	Then try . . .
pre	per, pra, pri, pro, pru
per	par, pir, por, pur, pre, pro
is	us, ace, ice
ere	ear, eir, ier
wi	whi
we	whe
zi	xy
cks, gz	x
tion	sion, cion, cean, cian
le	tle, el, al
cer	cre
si	psi, ci
ei	ie
dis	dys
ture	teur
tious	seous, scious
air	are, aer
ny	gn, n
ance	ence
ant	ent
able	ible
fizz	phys

B

APPENDIX C

Reference Materials and Publications

Abbreviations Dictionary/General

Crowley, Ellen T., and Helen E. Sheppard (eds.), *Reverse International Acronyms, Initialisms, and Abbreviations Dictionary.* Detroit, Gale Research Company, 1985.

Paxton, John (ed.), *Everyman's Dictionary of Abbreviations.* Totowa, NJ, B & N Imports, 1986.

Spillner, Paul, *World Guide to Abbreviations,* vols. 1–3, ed. 2. New York, S-Z. Bowker, 1973.

Abbreviations Dictionary/Medical

The Charles Press Handbook of Current Medical Abbreviations. Philadelphia, The Charles Press Publishers, 1985.

Davis, Neil M., *Medical Abbreviations: 4200 Conveniences at the Expense of Communications and Safety.* Huntingdon Valley, PA, Neil M. Davis Associates, 1987.

Delong, Marilyn Fuller, *Medical Acronyms and Abbreviations.* Oradell, NJ, Medical Economics Books, 1989.

Garb, Solomon, et al., *Abbreviations and Acronyms in Medicine and Nursing.* New York, Springer Publishing Company, 1976.

Hughes, Harold K., *Dictionary of Abbreviations in Medicine and Health Sciences.* Lexington, MA, Heath, 1977.

Jablonski, Stanley, *Dictionary of Medical Acronyms and Abbreviations.* St. Louis, MO, C. V. Mosby Company, 1987.

Jenners, Pauline, and Ann Wesson, *Think Metric,* U.S.A. Dubuque, IA, Educulture, 1975.

Keller, J. J., *The Modernized Metric System Explained.* Neenah, WI, J. J. Keller & Associates, 1974.

Kerr, Avice, *Medical Hieroglyphs, Abbreviations and Symbols.* Downey, CA, Enterprise Publications, 1970.

Logan, Carolynn, and M. Katherine Rice, *Logan's Medical and Scientific Abbreviations.* Philadelphia, J. B. Lippincott Company, 1987.

Medical Abbreviations: A Cross Reference Dictionary. Lansing, MI, The Special Studies Committee of the Michigan Occupational Therapy Association, 1977.

Medical Abbreviations Handbook. Oradell, NJ, Medical Economics Books, 1983.

Mitchell, Sara Lu, *Davis's Book of Medical Abbreviations: A Deciphering Guide.* Philadelphia, F. A. Davis Company, 1991.

Quick Directory of Medical Abbreviations. Darien, CT, Miller & Fink Corporation, 1977.

Roody, Peter, et al., *Medical Abbreviations and Acronyms.* New York, McGraw-Hill Book Company, 1977.

Schattner, Robert L., *Acronymal Dictionary with Abbreviations.* Thorofare, NJ, Slack Incorporated, 1988.

Schertel, A., *Abbreviations in Medicine.* New York, S. Karger, 1984.

Sloane, Sheila B., *Medical Abbreviations and Eponyms.* Philadelphia, W. B. Saunders Company, 1985.

Sloane, Sheila B., *The Medical Word Book.* Philadelphia, W. B. Saunders Company, 1982.

Steen, Edwin B., *Medical Abbreviations,* ed. 5. Philadelphia, W. B. Saunders Company, 1984.

Stylebook/Editorial Manual of the American Medical Association. Littleton, MS, Publishing Sciences Group, 1976.

Venolia, Jan, *Write Right!* Woodland Hills, CA, Periwinkle Press, 1980.

Antonyms, Eponyms, Homonyms, Syndromes, and Synonyms

Chapman, Robert L., *Roget's International Thesaurus,* ed. 4. New York, Harper & Row, Publishers, 1984.
Fernald, James C., *English Synonyms and Antonyms with Notes on the Correct Use of Prepositions.* Darby, PA, Arden Lib., 1981.
Megalini, Sergio I., *Dictionary of Medical Syndromes,* ed. 2. Philadelphia, J. B. Lippincott Company, 1981.
Rodale, J. I., *The Synonym Finder.* Emmaus, PA, Rodale Press, 1978.
Webster's New Dictionary of Synonyms. Springfield, MA, G & C Merriam Company, 1973.
Webster's Synonyms, Antonyms, and Homonyms. Alhambra, CA, Dennison, 1974.

Career Development

American Association for Medical Transcription Journal. Modesto, CA, American Association for Medical Transcription, quarterly.
American Association for Medical Transcription Newsletter. Modesto, CA, American Association for Medical Transcription, bimonthly.
Analysis: Civil Service Classification of Medical Transcriptionist. Modesto, CA, American Association for Medical Transcription, 1981.
Dennis, Robert Lee, and Jean Monty Doyle, *The Complete Handbook for Medical Secretaries and Assistants.* Boston, Little, Brown & Company, 1978.
Fordney, Marilyn T., and Joan M. Follis, *Administrative Medical Assisting.* Albany, New York, Delmar Publishers, Inc., 1989.
Health Professions Institute, *Perspectives on the Medical Transcription Profession.* Modesto, CA, 1988.
Kinn, Mary E., *The Administrative Medical Assistant.* Philadelphia, W. B. Saunders Company, 1988.

Certification

The AAMT Test Guide. Modesto, CA, American Association for Medical Transcription, 1982.

Composition

Andrews, William D., and Deborah C. Andrews, *Write For Results.* Boston, Little, Brown & Company, 1982.
Blumenthal, Lassor A., *Successful Business Writing.* New York, Putnam Publishing Group, 1985.
Brogan, John A., *Clear Technical Writing.* New York, McGraw-Hill Book Company, 1973.
Funk and Wagnalls Standard Desk Dictionary. New York, Harper & Row, 1984.
Hodges, John C., *Harbrace College Handbook.* Orlando, FL, Harcourt Brace Jovanovich, 1986.
Random House Dictionary of the English Language. New York, Random House, 1987.
Ross-Larson, Bruce, *Edit Yourself—A Manual for Everyone Who Works with Words.* New York, W. W. Norton and Company, 1982.
Secretary's Portfolio of Letters Most Often Used in a Physician's Office. West Nyack, NY, Parker Publishing Company, 1968.
Skillin, Marjorie E., and Robert M. Gay, *Words into Type.* Englewood Cliffs, NJ, Prentice-Hall, 1974.

Editing

Plotnik, Arthur, *The Elements of Editing,* Macmillan Publishing Company. New York, NY, 1982.

English Handbooks (Grammar, Punctuation, and General Clerical Information)

Branchaw, Bernadine P., and Joel P. Bowman, *SRA Reference Manual for Office Personnel,* Chicago, SRA Science Research Associates, 1986.
Clark, James L., and Lyn Clark, *How 4: A Handbook for Office Workers.* Belmont, CA, Kent Publishing Company, 1985.
Flesch, Rudolf, *Look It Up.* New York, Harper & Row, 1977.

Fordney, Marilyn, and Marcy Diehl, *Medical Transcription Guide: Do's and Don'ts,* Philadelphia, W. B. Saunders Co., 1990.

Hodges, John C., *Harbrace College Handbook.* Orlando, FL, Harcourt Brace Jovanovich, 1986.

House, Clifford R., and Kathie Sigler, *Reference Manual for Office Personnel.* Cincinnati, South Western Publishing Company, 1981.

Irmscher, W. F., *The Holt Guide to English: A Comprehensive Handbook of Rhetoric, Language, and Literature.* New York, Holt, Rinehart and Winston, 1981.

Johnson, Edward, *Handbook of Good English.* New York, Facts on File Publisher, 1983.

Klein, A. E., *The New World Secretarial Handbook.* Cleveland, William Collins-World Publishing Company, 1973.

Longyear, Marie M., *The McGraw-Hill Style Manual: Concise Guide for Writers and Editors.* New York, McGraw-Hill Book Company, 1982.

Perrin, P. G., and J. W. Corder, *Handbook of Current English.* Glenview, IL, Scott Foresman & Company, 1975.

Sabin, William A., *The Gregg Reference Manual.* New York, McGraw-Hill Book Company, 1985.

Shaw, Harry, *Punctuate It Right!* New York, Harper & Row, 1986.

Shertzer, Margaret D., *The Elements of Grammar.* New York, Macmillan Publishing Company, 1986.

Strumpf, Michael, and Auriel Douglas, *Painless Perfect Grammar.* New York, NY, Monarch Press, 1985.

Stylebook/Editorial Manual of the American Medical Association. Littleton, MS, Publishing Sciences Group, 1976.

Eponyms

See Antonyms, Eponyms, Homonyms, Syndromes, and Synonyms.

Foreign Dictionaries

Robb, Louis A., *Diccionario De Terminos Legales.* Mexico, Editorial LIMUSA, 1989. (Order from Bernard Hammill, Spanish-English Books, 10977 Santa Monica Boulevard, Los Angeles, CA 90025.)

Torres, Ruiz, *Diccionario De Terminos Medicos.* Madrid, Spain, 1989. (Distributor: Gulf Publishing Company, Book Division, P. O. Box 2608, Houston, TX 77001.)

Homonyms

See Antonyms, Eponyms, Homonyms, Syndromes, and Synonyms.

Humor and Games for Medical Typists and Transcriptionists

Pitman, Sally C. (ed.), *The eMpTy Laugh Book.* Modesto, CA, American Association for Medical Transcription, 1981.

Tank, Hazel (ed.), *The Puzzlement for Medical Transcriptionists.* Modesto, CA, American Association for Medical Transcription, 1981.

Insurance

Fordney, Marilyn T., *Insurance Handbook for the Medical Office,* ed. 3. Philadelphia, W. B. Saunders Company, 1989.

Law and Ethics

American Medical Association, *Judicial Council Opinions and Reports.* Chicago, American Medical Association, 1976.

American Medical Association, *Medicolegal Forms with Legal Analysis.* Chicago, American Medical Association, 1973.

Bander, Edward J., and Jeffrey J. Wallach, *Medical Legal Dictionary.* Dobbs Ferry, NY, Oceana Publishing, 1970.

Black, Henry Campbell, *Black's Law Dictionary.* St. Paul, MN, West Publishing Company, 1979.

Brody, Howard, *Ethical Decisions in Medicine.* Boston, Little, Brown and Company, 1981.

Ehrlich, Ann, *Ethics and Jurisprudence.* Champaign, IL, The Colwell Company, 1983.

Flight, Myrtle R., *Law, Liability, and Ethics for Medical Office Personnel.* Albany, Delmar Publishers, Inc., 1988.

Hayt, Emanuel, *Medicolegal Aspects of Hospital Records.* Berwyn, IL, Physician's Record Company, 1977.

Heller, Marjorie K., *Legal P's and Q's in the Doctor's Office.* Bayside, NY, Lawyer's Bookshelf, 1981.

Holder, Angela Roddey, *Medical Malpractice Law.* New York, John Wiley & Sons, 1978.

Huffman, Edna K., *Medical Record Management.* Berwyn, IL, Physician's Record Company, 1985.

Kapp, Marshall B., *Legal Guide for Medical Office Managers.* Chicago, IL, Pluribus Press, Inc., 1985.

Lewis, Marcia A., and Carol D. Warden, *Law and Ethics in the Medical Office Including Bioethical Issues,* ed. 2. Philadelphia, F. A. Davis Company, 1988.

Scott, Walter L., *Medicolegal Glossary.* Oradell, NJ, Medical Economics, 1989.

Medical Dictionaries

Blakiston's Gould Medical Dictionary. New York, McGraw-Hill Book Company, 1979.

Churchill's Medical Dictionary, Churchill Livingstone Fulfillment Center, Naperville, IL, 1989.

Critchley, Macdonald, *Butterworth's Medical Dictionary.* Woburn, MA, Butterworth's Publishers, 1980.

Dorland's Illustrated Medical Dictionary, ed. 27. Philadelphia, W. B. Saunders Company, 1988.

Franks, Richard, and H. Swartz, *Simplified Medical Dictionary.* Oradell, NJ, Medical Economics Books, 1977.

Glossary of Hospital Terms. Chicago, American Medical Record Association, 1974.

Gomez, Joan, *Dictionary of Symptoms.* Briarcliff Manor, NY, Stein & Day, 1983.

Hinsie, Leland E., and Robert J. Campbell, *Psychiatric Dictionary.* New York, Oxford University Press, 1970.

Isler, Charlotte, *Isler's Pocket Dictionary: A Guide to Disorders and Diagnostic Tests.* Oradell, NJ, Medical Economics Books, 1984.

Melloni, Biagio John, and Gilbert M. Eisner, *Melloni's Illustrated Medical Dictionary.* Baltimore, Williams & Wilkins Company, 1985.

Miller, Benjamin F., and Claire B. Keane, *Encyclopedia and Dictionary of Medicine, Nursing, and Allied Health,* ed. 3. Philadelphia, W. B. Saunders Company, 1983.

Pyle, Vera, *Current Medical Terminology.* Modesto, CA, Prima Vera Publications, 1985.

Scott, Walter L., *Medicolegal Glossary.* Oradell, NJ, Medical Economics Books, 1989.

Stedman's Medical Dictionary. Baltimore, Williams & Wilkins Company, 1981. (Software available.)

Thomas, Clayton L. (ed.), *Taber's Cyclopedic Medical Dictionary.* Philadelphia, F. A. Davis Company, 1985.

Urdang, Laurence, and Helen H. Swallow, *Mosby's Medical and Nursing Dictionary.* St. Louis, C. V. Mosby Company, 1986.

Wakeley, Sir Cecil, *The Farber Medical Dictionary.* Philadelphia, J. B. Lippincott Company, 1975.

White, Wallace F., *Language of the Health Sciences.* New York, John Wiley & Sons, 1977.

Medical Records

Gordon, B. L., *Simplified Medical Records System.* Acton, MA, Publishing Sciences Group, 1975.

Hospital Medical Records: Guidelines for Their Use and Release of Medical Information. Chicago, American Medical Association, 1972.

Medical Record Departments in Hospitals: Guide to Organization. Chicago, American Hospital Association, 1972.

Mosier, Alice, and Frank J. Pace, *Medical Records Technology.* Indianapolis, Bobbs-Merrill Company, 1975.

Medical Terminology

Austrin, Miriam G., *Young's Learning Medical Terminology Step by Step.* St. Louis, C. V. Mosby Company, 1983.

Bradbury, Peggy F., *Transcriber's Guide to Medical Terminology.* Garden City, NY, Medical Examination Publishing Company, 1973.

Chabner, Davi-Ellen, *The Language of Medicine, A Write-In Text Explaining Medical Terms.* Philadelphia, W. B. Saunders Company, 1985. (Cassettes available.)

Cohen, Alan Y., *Medicine/Biology Terminology Cards* (1,000 flash cards). Springfield, OH, Visual Education Association, 1978.

DeLorenzo, Barbara, and Doris Fedun, *Medical Terminology,* vol. I, A-L and vol. II, M-Z. Thorofare, NJ, Slack Incorporated, 1988.

C

Dunmore, Charles W., and Rita M. Fleischer, *Medical Terminology: Exercises in Etymology.* Philadelphia, F. A. Davis Company, 1985.

Fisher, J. Patrick, *Basic Medical Terminology.* Indianapolis, Bobbs-Merrill Company, 1983. (Cassettes available.)

Frenay, Sister Agnes, *Understanding Medical Terminology.* Haverford, PA, Catholic Hospital Association, 1984. (Transparencies available.)

Gross, Verlee E., *Mastering Medical Terminology: Textbook of Anatomy, Diseases, Anomalies and Surgeries with English Translation and Pronunciation.* Simi Valley, CA, Halls of Ivy Press, 1969.

Gross, Verlee E., *The Structure of Medical Terms.* Simi Valley, CA, Halls of Ivy Press, 1973.

Gylys, Barbara A., and Regina Masters, *Medical Terminology and Advanced Medical Terminology.* Philadelphia, F. A. Davis Company, 1985. (Software program and user's manual.)

Gylys, Barbara A., and Mary Ellen Wedding, *Medical Terminology: A Systems Approach.* Philadelphia, F. A. Davis Company, 1988.

Kinn, Mary E., *Medical Terminology Review Challenge.* Albany, Delmar Publishers, Inc., 1987.

LaFleur, Myrna Weber, and Winifred K. Starr, *Exploring Medical Language.* St. Louis, C. V. Mosby Company, 1985. (Computer software available.)

Leonard, Peggy, *Building a Medical Vocabulary.* Philadelphia, W. B. Saunders Company, 1988. (Cassettes and computer software available.)

Prendergast, Alice, *Medical Terminology: A Text/Workbook.* Reading, MA, Addison-Wesley Publishing Company, 1983.

Smith, Genevieve Love, and Phyllis E. Davis, *Medical Terminology, A Programmed Text.* New York, John Wiley & Sons, 1981. (Cassettes available.)

Sormunen, Carolee, *Terminology for Allied Health Professionals.* Cincinnati, South-Western Publishing Company, 1985. (Cassettes available.)

Sorrells, Sally (Ingmire), *Medical Vocabulary from A to Z.* Mountain View, CA, Western Tape, 1981. (Cassettes available.)

Wroble, Eugene M., *Terminology for the Health Professions.* Philadelphia, J. B. Lippincott Company, 1982.

Medical Terminology Guides

Current Procedural Terminology. Chicago, American Medical Association, 1977.

Rimer, Evelyn H., *Harbeck's Glossary of Medical Terms.* Brisbane, CA, San Francisco, WEB Offset, 1967.

Stegeman, Wilson, *Medical Terms Simplified.* St. Paul, MN, West Publishing Company, 1975.

Strand, Helen R., *An Illustrated Guide to Medical Terminology.* Baltimore, Williams & Wilkins Company, 1968.

Pharmaceutical

Beebe, Judy, *Instant Drug Index.* Palo Alto, CA, William Kaufmann, Inc. (This is a word book for quick and easy location of spelling of drug names and no descriptive data, with updates available spring and fall of each year; published new edition approximately every two years.)

Billups, Norman F., *American Drug Index.* Philadelphia, J. B. Lippincott Company. (Annual publication.)

DeLorenzo, Barbara, *Pharmaceutical Terminology,* Thorofare, NJ, Slack Incorporated, 1988. (This is a word book for quick and easy location of spelling of drug names and no descriptive data listed.)

Griffith, H. Winter, M. D., *Complete Guide to Prescription and Nonprescription Drugs.* Tucson, AZ, H. P. Books, Inc., 1987.

Hospital Formulary. Washington, D.C., American Society of Hospital Pharmacists, 1978.

Kastrup, Erwin K., and Bernie R. Olin, III, *Facts and Comparisons.* Philadelphia, J. B. Lippincott Company, updated monthly.

Lewis, Arthur J., *Modern Drug Encyclopedia and Therapeutic Index.* New York, The Yorke Medical Group, The Dun-Donnelly Publishing Corporation, 1973.

Medi-Spell Transcriber's Bulletin, P. O. Box 2546, Mission Viejo, CA 92690 (published quarterly list of current drugs).

National Drug Code Directory, vols. 1 and 2. Washington, D.C., U.S. Government Printing Office, 1980.

National Formulary XIV (NF). Washington, D.C., American Pharmaceutical Association, 1975.

Patterson, H. Robert, Edward A. Gustafson, and Eleanor Sheridan, *Falconer's Current Drug Handbook.* Philadelphia, W. B. Saunders Company, 1984–1986.

Physicians' Desk Reference for Nonprescription Drugs. Oradell, NJ, Medical Economics Books (annual publication).

Physician's Desk Reference for Ophthalmology. Oradell, NJ, Medical Economics Books (annual publication).

Physician's Desk Reference: The Indices. Oradell, NJ, Medical Economics Books (annual publication).

Physician's Desk Reference to Pharmaceutical Specialties and Biologists (PDR). Oradell, NJ, Medical Economics Books (annual publication).

Physician's Desk Reference for Radiology and Nuclear Medicine. Oradell, NJ, Medical Economics Books (annual publication).

Shirkey, Harry C., *Pediatric Dosage Handbook.* Washington, D.C., American Pharmaceutical Association, 1980.

Squire, Jessie E., and Jean M. Welch, *Basic Pharmacology for Nurses.* St. Louis, C. V. Mosby Company, 1977.

Turley, Susan M., *Understanding Pharmacology.* Modesto, CA, Health Professions Institute, 1988.

The United States Pharmacopoeia (U.S.P.). Rockville, MD, The Pharmacopoeia of the United States of America, 1984. (Annual supplements.)

Physically Challenged

Many catalogues give information on what is available on tape, what has been put into braille, or what is printed in a large typeface. The large-print books are done by the American Printing House for the Blind and various volunteer groups throughout the United States. However, for the severely physically challenged, taped books are essential. If no source can be found, inquiries can be made by sending the name of the book, author, copyright date, and publisher to one of the following. They will tell you if the book is available and, if so, where to obtain it.

Mr. Carl Lappin, IMRO Director
American Printing House for the Blind
P. O. Box 6085
Louisville, KY 40206

Mr. Fred Sinclair, Consultant
Clearinghouse-Depository for the Handicapped Student
State Department of Education
721 Capitol Mall
Sacramento, CA 95814

Other references for the physically challenged are:

American Association for Medical Transcription, Visually-Impaired MT Committee, c/o Frances Holland, 635 West Grace, Apt. 306, Chicago, IL 60613.

American Association of Medical Assistants, Inc., *AAMA Guided Study Course: Anatomy, Terminology and Physiology* (cassettes), 20 North Wacker Drive, Chicago, IL 60606.

American Foundation for the Blind, 15 West 16th Street, New York, NY 10011 (annual catalogue of publications).

American Printing House for the Blind, P. O. Box 6085, Louisville, KY 40206 (large-print books, books on tape, books put into braille).

Bowe, Frank G., *Personal Computers and Special Needs* (1984), Sybex, Inc., 2021 Challenger Dr., No. 100, Alameda, CA 94501.

Chabner, Davi-Ellen, Audio tapes to *The Language of Medicine.* W. B. Saunders Company, Independence Square West, Philadelphia, PA 19106-3399.

Clearinghouse-Depository for the Handicapped Student, State Department of Education, 721 Capitol Mall, Sacramento, CA 95814 (for information on large-print books, books on tape, and books put into braille).

Diehl, Marcy O., and Marilyn T. Fordney, *Medical Transcribing Techniques and Procedures,* ed. 1 on cassettes from Recording for the Blind, Inc., 5022 Hollywood Boulevard, Los Angeles, CA 90027.

Fisher, J. Patrick, *Basic Medical Terminology* (cassettes). The Bobbs-Merrill Educational Publishing Company, 4300 West 62nd Street, Indianapolis, IN 46268.

Gross, Verlee E., *Mastering Medical Terminology* (braille). Braille Institute, 1150 East Fourth Street, Long Beach, CA 90802.

Hollander, Charles S., *Patient's Guide to Vision Rehabilitation for the Partially Sighted.* Sight Improvement Center, Inc., 25 West 43rd Street, New York, NY 10036.

Leonard, Peggy C., *Audio Tapes for Building a Medical Vocabulary.* W. B. Saunders Company, Independence Square West, Philadelphia, PA 19106-3399.

McWilliams, Peter, *Personal Computers and the Disabled.* New York, Doubleday, 1984.

Pyle, Vera, *Current Medical Terminology* (braille), Mrs. Gerri Beeson, Volunteer Services Director, Oklahoma Library for the Blind and Physically Handicapped, 1108 N. E. 36th Street, Oklahoma City, OK 73111.

Raised Dot Computing Newsletter (monthly newsletter to keep you up to date on new products; available in print or on audiocassette), 408 South Baldwin Street, Madison, WI 53703.

Russell, Phillip C., *Dynamic Job Interviewing for Women* (braille), Federally Employed Women, P. O. Box 251, Port Hueneme, CA 93041.

C

Sensory Aids Foundation, 399 Sherman Avenue, Palo Alto, CA 94306 (quarterly journal, research sensory aids, job opportunities, information on latest equipment).

Smith, Genevieve L., and Phyllis E. Davis, *Audio Cassettes for Medical Terminology.* Delmar Publishers, Inc., 2 Computer Drive, West, Box 15015, Albany, NY 12212-5015.

Proofreading

Dewar, Thadys J., and H. Frances Daniels, *Programmed Proofreading.* Cincinnati, South-Western Publishing Company, 1982.

Preston, Sharon, *Proofreading.* Mountain View, CA, Western Tape, 1977.

References for the Handicapped

See Physically Challenged.

Self-Employment and Freelancing

Adams, Paul, *The Complete Legal Guide for Your Small Business.* New York, John Wiley & Sons, 1982.

Boos, Patricia, *Typing . . . A Way to Your Own Business.* Bowie, MD, The Seasons Publishing Company, 1981.

DeMenezes, Ruth, *You Can Type for Doctors At Home!* Thousand Oaks, CA, Claremont Press, 1981.

Murray, Jean Wilson, *Starting and Operating a Word Processing Service.* Babylon, NY, Pilot Books, 1983.

Strickland, Lois, *How to Start a Manuscript Typing Business in Your Home* (1983), 513 Polk Street, Manchester, TN 37355.

Wisely, Rae, and Gladys Sanders, *The Independent Woman: How to Start and Succeed in Your Own Business.* Los Angeles, Houghton Mifflin Company, 1981.

Specialty References

Cardiology

Health Professions Institute, *Cardiology Words and Phrases: A Quick Reference Guide.* Modesto, CA, Health Professions Institute, 1989.

Littrell, Helen E., *Cardiovascular and Pulmonary Terminology.* Thorofare, NJ, Slack Incorporated, 1988.

Dermatology

Leider, Morris, and Morris Rosenblum, *A Dictionary of Dermatological Words, Terms, and Phrases.* West Haven, CT, Dome Laboratories, 1976.

Gastroenterology

Health Professions Institute, *Gastrointestinal Words and Phrases: A Quick Reference Guide.* Modesto, CA, Health Professions Institute, 1989.

History and Physical

Dirckx, John H., M. D., *A Nonphysician's Guide to the Medical History and Physical Examination.* Modesto, CA, Prima Vera Publications, 1987.

Immunology and AIDS

McIntyre, Maureen, and Diane K. Cartwright, *AIDS Related Terminology.* 1484 Old Forest Road, Pickering, Ontario, Canada LIV 1N9

Laboratory

See Pathology

C

Neurology

See Psychiatry

Obstetrics and Gynecology

Hughes, Edward C., *Obstetric-Gynecologic Terminology with Section on Neonatology and Glossary of Congenital Anomalies.* Philadelphia, F. A. Davis Company, 1972.

Littrell, Helen, *Obstetric and Gynecologic Terminology,* Thorofare, NJ, Slack Incorporated, 1990.

Oncology

De Lorenzo, Barbara, *Oncologic Terminology with AIDS Related Terms.* Thorofare, NJ, Slack Incorporated, 1988.

Ophthalmology

Cassin, Barbara, and Sheila Solomon, *Dictionary of Eye Terminology.* Gainesville, FL, Triad Publishing Company, 1984.

DeLorenzo, Barbara, and Doris Fedun, *Ophthalmic Terminology.* Thorofare, NJ, Slack Incorporated, 1988.

Stein, Harold A., Bernard J. Slatt, and Penny Cook, *Manual of Ophthalmic Terminology.* St. Louis, C. V. Mosby Company, 1982.

Oral and Maxillofacial Surgery

American Society of Oral Surgeons: The Oral and Maxillofacial Surgery Procedural Terminology with Glossary. Chicago, American Society of Oral Surgeons, 1975.

Orthopedics

Blauvelt, Carolyn T., and Fred R. T. Nelson, *A Manual of Orthopaedic Terminology.* St. Louis, C. V. Mosby Company, 1985.

Cittadine, Thomas J., *Orthopedic Terminology.* Thorofare, NJ, Slack Incorporated, 1988.

Gold Coast Chapter of AAMT, *A Guide to Pathology Terminology.* Fort Lauderdale, FL, Gold Coast Chapter of AAMT, 1984.

Health Professions Institute, *Orthopedic Words and Phrases: A Quick Reference Guide.* Modesto, CA, Health Professions Institute, 1988.

Pathology

Bennington, James L., *Encyclopedia and Dictionary of Laboratory Medicine and Technology.* Philadelphia, W. B. Saunders Company, 1983.

DeLorenzo, Barbara, *Clinical Laboratory Science Terminology.* Thorofare, NJ, Slack Incorporated, 1991.

Pathology Words and Phrases. Modesto, CA, Health Professions Institute, 1988.

Shaw, Diane, *Pathophysiologic Terminology.* Thorofare, NJ, Slack Incorporated, 1991.

Sloane, Sheila B., and John L. Dusseau, *A Word Book in Pathology and Laboratory Medicine.* Philadelphia, W. B. Saunders Company, 1984.

Tietz, Norbert W. (ed.), *Clinical Guide to Laboratory Tests.* Philadelphia, W. B. Saunders Company, 1983.

Wallach, Jacques B., *Interpretation of Diagnostic Tests: A Handbook Synopsis of Laboratory Medicine.* Boston, Little, Brown & Company, 1986.

Willatt, E. Murden, *Medical Spelling Handbook, Book 1: Pathology.* Bellaire, TX, Medical Spelling Handbooks Publishing Company, 1970.

Psychiatry

American Psychiatric Association, *DSM-III-R Diagnostic and Statistical Manual of Mental Disorders.* Washington D.C., American Psychiatric Press, Inc., 1987.

Campbell, Robert J., *Psychiatric Dictionary.* New York, Oxford University Press, 1989.

D'Onofrio, Mary Ann, and Elizabeth D'Onofrio, *Psychiatric Words and Phrases.* Modesto, CA, Health Professions Institute, 1990.

International Classification of Diseases Adapted Ninth Revision Clinical Modification (ICD-9-CM), vols. 1, 2, and 3. 1978, ICD-9-CM. P. O. Box 999, Ann Arbor, MI 48106.

Littrell, Helen, *Neurologic and Psychiatric Terminology.* Thorofare, NJ, Slack Incorporated, 1991.

Stone, Evelyn M., *American Psychiatric Glossary.* Washington, D.C., American Psychiatric Press, Inc., 1988.

C

Pulmonary

See Cardiology.

Radiology

Chernok, Normal B., *Radiology Typist's Handbook*. Flushing, NY, Medical Examination Publishing Company, 1970.

DeLorenzo, Barbara, *Radiologic Terminology*. Thorofare, NJ, Slack Incorporated, 1990.

Ehlert, Theodora, *Handbook for Medical Secretaries*. Cleveland, Picker Corporation.

Etter, Lewis E., *Glossary of Words and Phrases Used in Radiology, Nuclear Medicine and Ultrasound*. Springfield, IL, Charles C Thomas, 1970.

Goldman, Myer, and David Cope, *A Radiographic Index*. Littleton, MA, PSG Publishing Company, 1987.

Radiology Words and Phrases. Modesto, CA, Health Professional Institute, 1990.

Roentgenographic Anatomical Terminology. Wilmington, DE, E.I. DuPont De Nemours and Company.

Sloane, Sheila B., *A Word Book in Radiology With Anatomic Plates and Tables*. Philadelphia, W. B. Saunders Company, 1988.

Surgery

Chernok, Normal B., *Surgical Typist Handbook*. Garden City, NY, Medical Examination Publishing Company, 1972.

Coleman, Frances, *Guide to Surgical Terminology*. Oradell, NJ, Medical Economics Books, 1978.

McMillan, Sam, *Surgical Terminology*. Thorofare, NJ, Slack Incorporated, 1991.

Smith, E. J., and Y. R. Smith, *Smiths' Reference and Illustrated Guide to Surgical Instruments*. Philadelphia, J. B. Lippincott Company, 1982.

Szulec, Jeanette, and Z. A. Szulec, *Syllabus for the Surgeon's Secretary*. Detroit, The Medical Arts Publishing Company, 1980.

Tessier, Claudia, *The Surgical Word Book*. Philadelphia, W. B. Saunders Company, 1981.

Willatt, E. Murden, *Medical Spelling Handbook, Book 2: Surgery*. Bellaire, TX, Medical Spelling Handbooks Publishing Company, 1970.

Spelling Books, English

Flesch, Rudolf, *Look It Up: A Deskbook of American Spelling and Style*. New York, Harper & Row, 1977.

Gilman, Mary Louise, *One Word, Two Words, Hyphenated?* National Shorthand Reporters Associations, Vienna, Virginia, 1988.

Horowitz, Edward, *Words Come in Families*. New York, A & W Publishers, 1979.

Lewis, Norman, *Correct Spelling Made Easy*. New York, Dell Publishing Company, 1987.

Lewis, Norman, *Instant Spelling Power*. New York, Amsco College Publications, 1976.

Spelling Books, Medical

American Medical Association, *Current Medical Information and Terminology,* ed. 5. Chicago, American Medical Association, 1981.

Bolander, Donald O., and Rita Bisdorf, *Instant Spelling Medical Dictionary*. Mundelein, IL, Career Publishing Institute, 1970.

Byers, Edward E., *Ten Thousand Medical Words, Spelled and Divided for Quick Reference*. New York, McGraw-Hill Book Company, 1972.

Campbell, Linda C., *The Anatomy Word Book*. Modesto, CA, PrimaVera Publication, 1988.

Carlin, Harriette L., *Medical Secretary Medi-Speller: A Transcription Aid*. Springfield, IL, Charles C Thomas, 1973.

Cole, Kathleen, and William R. Cole, *Mosby's Medical Speller*. St. Louis, C. V. Mosby Company, 1983.

Coleman, Frances, *Guide to Surgical Terminology*. Oradell, NJ, Medical Economics Books, 1978.

Cooper, Elsa Swanson, *The Language of Medicine: A Guide for Stenotypists*. Oradell, NJ, Medical Economics Books, 1977.

DDC Medical Speller. Dictation Disc Company, 240 Madison Avenue, New York, NY 10016.

DeLorenzo, Barbara, and Doris Fedun, *Medical Terminology,* vol. 1 A–L, vol. 2 M–Z. Thorofare, NJ, Slack Incorporated, 1988. (A book to help you with medical words and phrases.)

Doyle, John M., and Rita G. Doyle, *Spelling Reference for Business and School*. Reston, VA, Reston Publishing Company, 1976.

Emery, Donald W., *Variant Spellings in Modern American Dictionaries*. Urbana, IL, National Council of Teachers of English, 1973.

Franks, Richard, and H. Swartz, *Simplified Medical Dictionary.* Albany, Medical Economics/Delmar Publishers, 1977. (This book can help you locate a word if you know how the word ends and how the beginning is pronounced. The terms are categorized by their prefixes, suffixes, and roots, so you can seek out the word with minimal effort.)

Glossary of Hospital Terms. Chicago, IL, American Medical Record Association, 1974.

Hafer, Ann, *The Medical and Health Sciences Word Book.* Boston, Houghton Mifflin Company, 1982.

Johnson, Carrie E., *Medical Spelling Guide.* Springfield, IL, Charles C Thomas, 1966.

Kreivsky, Joseph, and Jordon L. Linfield, *The Bad Speller's Dictionary.* New York, Random House, 1974.

Lee, Richard V., and Doris J. Hofer, *How to Divide Medical Words.* Carbondale, IL, Southern Illinois University Press, 1972.

Lorenzini, Jean W., *Medical Phrase Index.* Oradell, NJ, Medical Economics Books, 1989.

Magalini, Sergio I., and Euclid Scrascia, *Dictionary of Medical Syndromes.* Philadelphia, J. B. Lippincott Company, 1981.

Mullins, Nancy L. (ed.), *Mosby's Medical Speller.* St. Louis, C. V. Mosby Company, 1983.

Pease, Roger W., Jr. (ed.), *Webster's Medical Speller.* Springfield, IL, G & C Merriam Company, 1975.

Prichard, Robert W., and Robert E. Robinson, *Twenty Thousand Medical Words.* New York, McGraw-Hill Book Company, 1972.

Pyle, Vera, *Current Medical Terminology.* Modesto, CA, PrimaVera Publications, 1988.

Rice, Elaine P., *Phonetic Dictionary of Medical Terminology: A Spelling Guide.* Baltimore, Williams & Wilkins, 1985.

Rimer, Evelyn Harbeck, *Harbeck's Glossary of Medical Terms.* Brisbane, CA, San Francisco WEB Offset, 1967.

Shaw, Diane, *Anatomy and Physiology Glossary.* Thorofare, NJ, Slack Incorporated, 1990.

Sloane, Sheila B., *The Medical Word Book,* ed. 2. Philadelphia, W. B. Saunders Company, 1982.

Tessier, Claudia J., *The Surgical Word Book.* Philadelphia, W. B. Saunders Company, 1981.

Thomas, Clayton L., *Taber's Medical Word Book With Pronunciations.* Philadelphia, F. A. Davis Company, 1990.

Willeford, Jr., George, *Webster's New World Medical Word Finder.* Englewood Cliffs, NJ, Prentice-Hall, 1987.

Willey, Joy, *Glossary of Medical Terminology for the Health Professions.* Thorofare, NJ, Slack Incorporated, 1988. (Terms included are not easily found in other standard reference books.)

Style Manuals/Medical and General

American Medical Association, *Style Book/Editorial Manual of the American Medical Association.* Littleton, MA, Publishing Sciences Group, 1976.

American Psychological Association: Publication Manual. Washington, D.C., American Psychological Association, 1974.

Barclay, William R., et al., compiled for American Medical Association, *Manual for Authors and Editors: Editorial Style and Manuscript Preparation.* Los Altos, CA, Lange Medical Publications, 1981.

The Chicago Manual of Style. Chicago, University of Chicago Press, 1982.

Council of Biology Editors Committee on Form and Style: CBE Style Manual. Washington, D.C., American Institute of Biological Sciences, 1974.

Ebbitt, Wilma R., and David Ebbitt, *Writer's Guide and Index to English.* Glenview, IL, Scott Foresman and Company, 1982.

Fordney, Marilyn and Marcy Diehl, *Medical Transcription Guide: Do's and Don'ts.* Philadelphia, W. B. Saunders Company, 1990.

Huth, Edward J., M. D., *Medical Style and Format—An International Manual for Authors, Editors, and Publishers.* Philadelphia, Institute for Scientific Information Press, 1987.

Preston, Sharon. *Proofreading.* Mountain View, CA, Western Tape, 1977.

Schramm, Dwane, *Typing Term Papers and Reports.* Mountain View, CA, Western Tape, 1974.

Strunk, William, Jr., and E. B. White, *The Elements of Style: With Index.* New York, Macmillan Publishing Company, 1979.

Tessier, Claudia, and Sally C. Pitman, *Style Guide for Medical Transcription.* Modesto, CA, American Association for Medical Transcription, 1985.

Trelease, S. F., *How to Write Scientific and Technical Papers.* Cambridge, MA, MIT Press, 1969.

Webster's Standard American Style Manual, Springfield, MA, Merriam-Webster, 1985.

Typing and Transcription

American Association for Medical Transcription, Modesto, CA.
   Exploring Transcription Practices: General Medicine Module, 1985
   Exploring Transcription Practices: Surgery Transcription, 1987
   Exploring Transcription Practices: Radiology Transcription, 1989

Diehl, Marcy O., and Marilyn T. Fordney, *Sound Tapes to Accompany Medical Typing and Transcribing Techniques and Procedures.* Philadelphia, W. B. Saunders Company, 1980.

Health Professions Institute, Modesto, CA.
Beginning Medical Transcription, 1989
Cardiology Transcription, 1989
GI Transcription, 1989
Orthopedic Transcription, 1988
Radiology Transcription, 1988
Pathology Transcription, 1988

Novak, Mary Ann, *Hillcrest Medical Center: Beginning Medical Transcription Course.* Cincinnati, South-Western College Division, 1989.

Word Division

Byers, Edward E., *Ten Thousand Medical Words, Spelled and Divided for Quick Reference.* New York, McGraw-Hill Book Company, 1972.

Hafer, Ann, *The Medical and Health Sciences Word Book.* Boston, Houghton Mifflin Company, 1982.

Lee, Richard B., and Doris J. Hofer, *How to Divide Medical Words.* Carbondale, IL, Southern Illinois University Press, 1972.

Pease, Roger W., Jr. (ed.), *Webster's Medical Speller.* Springfield, MA, G & C Merriam Company, 1975.

Silverthorn, J. E., and Devern J. Perry, *Word Division Manual.* Cincinnati, South-Western Publishing Company, 1970.

Willeford, George, Jr., *Webster's New World Medical Word Finder.* Englewood Cliffs, NJ, Prentice-Hall, 1987.

The Word Book II. Boston, Houghton Mifflin Company, 1983.

Zoubek, C. E., and G. A. Condon, *Twenty Thousand Words.* New York, McGraw-Hill Book Company, 1985.

Writing, Scientific/Technical

Alvarez, Joseph A., *Elements of Technical Writing.* Albany, Academic Press, 1986.

Brogan, John A., *Clear Technical Writing.* New York, McGraw-Hill Book Company, 1973.

Dagher, Joseph P., *Technical Communication: A Practical Guide.* Englewood Cliffs, NJ, Prentice-Hall, 1978.

Ehrlich, Eugene H., and Daniel Murphy, *Art of Technical Writing: A Manual for Scientists, Engineers, and Students.* Scranton, PA, Apollo Editions, 1969.

King, Lester S., *Why Not Say It Clearly: A Guide to Scientific Writing.* Boston, Little, Brown & Company, 1978.

Mitchell, John H., *Writing for Technical and Professional Journals.* Ann Arbor, MI, Books Demand UMI, 1968.

Skillin, Marjorie, and Robert Gay, *Words Into Type.* Englewood Cliffs, NJ, Prentice Hall, 1974.

Trelease, Sam F., *How to Write Scientific and Technical Papers.* Cambridge, MA, MIT Press, 1969.

Laboratory Terminology and Normal Values

Because normal values vary from one laboratory to another depending on types of equipment, the figures listed below are approximate.

Hematology

Complete Blood Count (CBC)

WBC (White blood count or cells)		4,200 – 10,000 (also typed 4.2 thousand)
RBC (red blood count or cells)	Males	4.6 to 6.2 million/ml
	Females	4.2 to 5.4 million/ml
HGB (hemoglobin)	Males	14.0 to 18.0 gm/dl
	Females	12.0 to 16.0 gm/dl
HCT (hematocrit)	Males	40 to 54 ml/dl
	Females	37 to 47 ml/dl

Indices

MCV (mean corpuscular volume)	80 to 105 microns
MCH (mean corpuscular hemo-globin)	27 to 31 UUG
MCHC (mean corpuscular hemoglobin concentration)	32 to 36%

Differential

polys (polymorphonuclear neutrophils) referred to as: Segs, Stabs, Bands	54 to 62%
lymphs (lymphocytes)	25 to 33%
eos or eosin (eosinophils)	1 to 3%
mono (monocytes)	3 to 7%
baso (basophils)	0 to 0.75%

Morphology

aniso (anisocytosis)
poik (poikilocytosis)
macro (macrocytic)
micro (microcytic)
hypochromia

platelets	150,000 to 350,000/ml
reticulocytes	25,000 to 75,000/ml

Coagulation Group

ESR or Sed Rate (sedimentation rate)	Wintrobe method:	Males	0 to 5 mm in 1 hr
		Females	0 to 15 mm in 1 hr
	Westergren method:	Males	0 to 15 mm in 1 hr
		Females	0 to 20 mm in 1 hr

D

PT (prothrombin time)	12.0 to 14.0 sec
PTT (partial thromboplastin time)	35 to 45 sec
fibrinogen	200 to 400 mg/dl
bleeding time Duke method	1 to 5 min
Ivy method	Less than 5 min
coagulation time (Lee-White)	5 to 15 min
Factor VIII	50 to 150% of normal

Blood Chemistry

A/G ratio (albumin/globulin ratio)	1.1 to 2.3
albumin	3.0 to 5.0 g/dl
BUN (blood urea nitrogen)	10.0 to 26.0 mg/dl
Ca (calcium)	8.5 to 10.5 mg/dl
cholesterol	150 to 250 mg/dl
creatinine	0.7 to 1.5 mg/dl
electrolytes	
bicarbonate, serum (bicarb)	23 to 29 mEq/liter
chlorides (cl)	96 to 106 mEq/liter
GGTP (gamma-glutamyl trans-peptidase)	8.0 to 35.0 milliunits/ml
K (potassium)	3.5 to 5.0 mEq/liter
magnesium, serum	1.5 to 2.5 mEq/liter
Na (sodium)	136 to 145 mEq/liter
phosphate	3.0 to 4.5 mg/dl
globulin	1.5 to 3.7 g/dl
glucose	60 to 100 mg/dl
immunoglobulins, serum	
IgA	60 to 333 mg/dl
IgD	0.5 to 3.0 mg/dl
IgE	greater than 500 ng/ml
IgG	550 to 1900 mg/dl
IgM	45 to 145 mg/dl
iron, serum	75 to 175 μg/dl
lipids, serum, total	450 to 850 mg/dl
liver functions	
acid phosphatase (ACP)	0 to 7.0 milliunits/ml
alkaline phosphatase, serum (ALP)	10 to 32 milliunits/ml
bilirubin	0.3 to 1.1 mg/dl
LDH (lactate dehydrogenase)	80 to 120 units/ml
SGOT (serum glutamic-oxaloacetic transaminase)/AST (aspartate aminotransferase)	0 to 19 milliunits/ml
SGPT (serum glutamic-pyruvic transaminase)/ALT (alanine-aminotransferase)	0 to 17 milliunits/ml
total protein	6.0 to 8.0 g/dl
triglycerides, serum	40 to 150 mg/dl
uric acid	2.2 to 7.7 mg/dl

Serology

ANA (antinuclear antibody)	negative
CRP (C-reactive protein)	negative
RA latex (rheumatoid arthritis)	negative
RPR (rapid plasma reagin)	negative
VDRL (Venereal Disease Research Laboratory)	nonreactive

Radioassay Thyroid Functions

T_3 uptake (tri-iodothyronine)	25 to 38%
T_4 (thyroxine)	4.4 to 9.9 μg/dl
TSH (thyroid-stimulating hormone)	0 to 7 microunits/ml

Blood Gases

O_2 (oxygen)	15 to 24 vol. %
CO_2 (carbon dioxide)	22 to 30 mmol/liter
PO_2 or pO_2 (oxygen partial pressure)	75 to 100 mm Hg
PCO_2 or pCO_2 (carbon dioxide partial pressure)	32 to 35 mm Hg

Urinalysis

Routine

color	yellow, straw, or colorless
sediment	clear or cloudy
sp.gr. (specific gravity)	1.002 to 1.030
pH	4.5 to 8.0 (acid or alkaline)
nitrite	negative
protein or albumin	negative
glucose	negative
acetone or ketones	negative
blood, occult	negative
bilirubin	0.02 mg/dl
urobilinogen	0.1 to 1.0 Ehrlich units/dl

Microscopic

RBC/hpf (red blood cells per high-powered field)	
WBC/hpf (white blood cells per high-powered field)	
epithelial cells/hpf	few or moderate
bacteria/lpf (low-powered field)	few or moderate
casts/lpf	negative
crystals/lpf	few
mucus	few or moderate
amorphous	few

Answers to Practice Tests

E

Answers to 3–3: Practice Test

1. No commas; everything here is essential.
2. Place a comma after *prostate.* The phrase that follows is nonessential and simply adds further information.
3. Enclose *who is a senior this year* in commas. This is nonessential. *Pat,* as a one-word appositive, is not enclosed in commas.
4. No commas; everything here is essential. We must answer the question *"which* children?"
5. Enclose *Ralph Birch* in commas. It is a nonessential appositive.
6. The phrase *not to operate* is essential and so is not enclosed in commas. It answers the question *"which* decision?" However, there is a comma after *hasty* to set off *if you ask me,* a parenthetical expression.
7. Enclose *which is a carbon* in commas because it is nonessential.
8. No commas; everything here is essential. We need to know *when* to contact the anesthesiologist.
9. Enclose *my textbook* in commas as a nonessential appositive.
10. Enclose *Bright's disease* in commas; it is a nonessential appositive.
11. Place a comma after *Charles,* to set off the nonessential appositive *the new resident.*
12. No commas; everything here is essential. We need to know *which* patients.
13. No commas; everything here is essential.
14. Place a comma in front of *however* to show that it is nonessential. Be sure that you do not enclose *who fail to attend the meeting* because it is essential. We need to know *which* staff members.
15. Enclose the nonessential *not the receptionist* in commas.
16. Place a comma after *furthermore.* It is a parenthetical expression.
17. No commas; *Ethel Clifford* is an essential appositive.
18. Place commas around *your patient* because it is a nonessential appositive.

Answers to 3–5: Practice Test

1. No commas. Everything is essential and there is no introductory phrase.
2. No commas. Everything is essential and there is no introductory phrase.
3. Enclose the nonessential appositive, *the pathologist,* in commas.
4. Enclose the nonessential appositive, *a girl,* in commas.
5. Place a comma after *furthermore,* a parenthetical expression.
6. Place a comma after *opportunity,* the final word of an introductory phrase.
7. Place a comma after *safe,* the final word of an introductory phrase.
8. Place an optional comma after *lunch,* the final word of a short introductory phrase.
9. Place a comma after *home,* the final word of an introductory phrase.
10. No commas. Everything is essential and there is no introductory phrase. Do not separate the subject from the verb with a comma after *word.*

Answers to 3–7: Practice Test

1. i—comma after *time.*
2. i—comma after *well.*
3. d—comma after *week.*
4. There are no commas in this sentence.
5. i—comma after *Hospital.*
6. There are no commas.

7. g and j—commas around *M.D.* and *Arizona*.

8. e—commas around *1989*.

9. f—optional comma after *group*.

10. d and h—commas after *examination* and *well-developed*. Note: There is no comma between *well-nourished and white,* the last modifier in the set.

11. h—comma after *effort* and *breath*. (The second comma is optional.)

12. a and e—commas around *with your concurrence* and *July 1;* a comma after 199x.

13. d—comma after *Jones* Note: No comma after *this* because it is the first part of the phrase.

14. c or d, g, b—commas after *know, Briggs, M.D.,* and *partner*.

15. e, a. Notice that the expression *which required intravenous antibiotics* simply adds information and does not qualify as being essential. Commas around *199x* and a comma after *bronchopneumonia*.

Answers to 3–8: Practice Test

September 16, 199x   1. date

Tellememer Insurance Company
25 Main Street, Suite R
Albuquerque, NM 87122   2. city, state

Gentlemen:

RE: Ron Emerson

I understand from Mr. Emerson that the insurance company feels
that the charges for my services on June 30, 199X, are excessive.   3/4. date

Mr. Emerson was seen on an early Sunday morning with a stab
wound in his chest, which had penetrated his lung producing
an air leak into his chest wall. In addition, he had a laceration   5. introductory
of his lung.

After consultation and review of his x-rays, his laceration was   6. introductory
repaired. He was observed in the hospital for two days to be
sure that he did not have continuing hemorrhage or collapse
of his lung.

I feel that the bill given to Mr. Emerson is a fair one. We
received, on July 31, 199X, a Tellememer Insurance Company check   7. nonessential
for $40, and I feel that your payment of $40 is unreasonable.
It is doubtful that one could get a plumber to come out early   8/9. date
Sunday morning to fix a leaky pipe for $40, and Mr. Emerson's   10. compound
situation, in my opinion, was much more serious than would be   11. compound
encountered by a plumber.   12/13. parenthetical

We will bill Mr. Emerson for the remainder of the $200 balance
on his account, but I want you to know that we feel that your   14. compound
payment is insufficient. If he feels that the bill is excessive,   15. introductory
we would be glad to submit to arbitration through the County
Medical Society Fee Committee. If this fails, I suggest we   16. introductory
seek help through the New Mexico Insurance Commission.

Sincerely yours,   17. close

William A. Berry, M.D.   18. degree

rl

Enclosed: X-ray report; history and physical report

Copy: Mr. Ron Emerson

Answers to 3–11: Practice Test

1. Rule d. Semicolon after *yet.*
2. Rules a and c. Period after *Mr.* and semicolon after *disease.*
3. Rules g and b. Colon after *follows.* Decimal point after *$650.*
4. Rules g, a, f. Colon after *staff,* periods after *Dr., A., Dr., R., Jr., Mrs.* Semicolons after *resident, director, supervisor.*
5. Rule h. Colon after *man.*
6. Rules b and e. Decimal point after *101;* semicolon after *nausea.*
7. Rule b. Decimal point after the zero in *0.5%.*
8. Rule c. Semicolon after *normal.*
9. Rule e. Semicolon after *normal.*
10. Rule i. Colons after *diagnosis* and *discharge.*

Answers to 3–13: Practice Test

1. Mrs. Gail R. Smith-Edwards was hospitalized this morning. She is the 47-year-old woman Dr. Blake admitted with a self-inflicted knife wound. Her blood pressure was 60/40. *(sixty over forty)*

   Rule c, a or b, a, j

2. Barbara Ness' happy-go-lucky personality was missed when she was transferred from Medical Records.

   Rule e, a, optional h (quotes around "happy-go-lucky")

3. Glen Mathews, the well-known trial lawyer, and the hospital's Chief-of-Staff, Dr. Carlton Edwards, will appear together (if you can believe that) on TV's latest talk show tonight. It's the only subject on the hospital's "gabfest." *Note:* Make sure your period is placed within the quotes.

   Rule a, e, c, i, e, f, e, h

4. I want a stamped, self-addressed envelope enclosed with this letter and sent out with today's mail.

   Rule a, e

5. Dr. Davis said his promotion was a good example of being "kicked upstairs." He obviously didn't want to leave his job in the X-ray Department. *Note:* Make sure your period is placed within the quotes.

   Rule h, f, b

6. Haven't you ever seen a Z-fixation? Bobbi-Jo will be happy to explain it to you.

   Rule f, b, c

7. We're all going to the CCU at 4 o'clock for instructions on mouth-to-mouth resuscitation.

   Rule f, f, a

E

8. Right eye vision: 20/20
   Left eye vision: 10/400
   Right retinal examination: Normal
   Left retinal examination: Inferior retinal detachment

   Rule j

9. You were seen on September 24 at which time you were having some stiffness at the shoulders which I felt was due to a periarthritis (a stiffness of the shoulder capsule); however, x-ray of the shoulder was negative.

   Rule i, b

10. After he completed the end-to-end anastomosis, he closed with #1 silk through-and-through, figure-of-eight sutures.

    Rule a, a, a

11. Dr. Chriswell's diagnosis bears out the assumption that the red-green blindness is the result of an X-chromosome defect.

    Rule e, a or d, b

12. After his myocardial infarction (MI), his blood test showed high level C-reactive protein.

    Rule i, b

Answers to 3–15: Practice Test

1. She inadvertently sterilized the Smith-Petersen nail instead of the V-medullary. (Needs 3 marks)
2. She has had no further spells, but she did have two episodes (prior to this one) several years ago. (Needs 4 marks)
3. The patient presents as a well-developed, asthenic, elderly, extremely bright, and oriented Caucasian female. She is fully alert and able to give an entirely reliable history; however, she is somewhat anxious and concerned over her present condition. (Needs 9 marks)
4. The patient has just moved to this community from Anchorage, Alaska, where he was engaged in the lumber industry. He had an emergency appendectomy performed at some remote outpost in January 1986. According to the patient, he has always felt like "something's hung up in there." Roentgenograms taken July 17, 199X, failed to reveal anything unusual. (Needs 12 marks)
5. He is a 35-year-old, well-developed, well-nourished black truck driver, oriented to time, place, and person. (Needs 10 marks)
6. The X-chromosome defect resulted in her ovarian aplasia, undeveloped mandible, webbed neck, and small stature: Morgagni-Turner syndrome. (Needs 7 marks)
7. Vital signs: Blood pressure: 194/97; pulse: 127; respirations: 32, regular, and gasping. General: Healthy-appearing male, looking his stated age, in moderately severe respiratory distress, with slightly dusky-colored lips. (Needs 17 marks)

Illustration continued on following page

Answers to 3–17: Practice Test

William A. Berry, M.D.

3933 Navajo Road
San Diego, California 92119

———
463-0000

August 13, 199x

John D. Mench, M.D.
455 Main Street
Bethesda, MD 20034

Dear Dr. Mench:

Re: Debra Walters

This letter is to bring you up to date on Mrs. Walters who was first seen in my office on March 2, 199x, at which time she stated that her last menstrual period had started August 29, 199x. Examination revealed the uterus to be enlarged to a size consistent with an estimated date of confinement of June 5, 199x.

The pregnancy continued uneventfully until May 19, at which time the blood pressure was 130/90. Hygroton was prescribed, and the patient was seen in one week. The blood pressure at the next visit was 150/100 and additional therapy in the form of Ser-Ap-Es was prescribed in addition to other antitoxemic routines. The blood pressure stabilized between 130 and 140/90.

The patient was admitted to the hospital on June 11, 199X, with ruptured membranes, mild preeclampsia, and a few contractions of poor quality. Intravenous oxytocics were started; and after two hours of stimulation, there was no change in the cervix, with that structure continuing to be long, closed, and posterior. The presenting part was at a -2 to a -3 station, and the amniotic fluid had become brownish-green in color, suggesting some degree of fetal distress.

Consultation was obtained, and it was recommended that a low cervical cesarean section be performed. A female infant was delivered by cesarean section. It was noted at the time of delivery that the cord was snugly wrapped around the neck of the baby three times, and this might have contributed to the evidence of fetal distress, as evidenced by the color of the amniotic fluid.

The patient's postoperative course was uneventful, and she and the baby were discharged home on the fifth postpartum day.

Sincerely yours,

William A. Berry, M.D.

mlo

Answers to Let's Have a Bit of Fun (Chapter 3)

1. b
2. b
3. a
4. a
5. a
6. b

7. b
8. both
9. a
10. b
11. b

Answers to 4–2: Practice Test

1. <u>t</u>he <u>r</u>ight <u>r</u>ev. <u>m</u>ichael <u>t</u>. <u>s</u>quires led the invocation at the graduation ceremony for greenlee <u>c</u>ounty's first paramedic class. (Right is an unusual title.)
2. <u>n</u>anci <u>h</u>olloway, a 38-year-old <u>c</u>aucasian female, is scheduled for a cesarean section tomorrow.
3. <u>t</u>he internist wanted him to have meprobamate so he wrote a prescription for <u>m</u>iltown. (Meprobamate is generic, and Miltown is a brand name.)
4. <u>j</u>ohnny <u>t</u>emple had chickenpox, red measles, and <u>g</u>erman measles his first year in <u>s</u>chool.
5. <u>u</u>nfortunately, the patient in <u>icu</u> whom <u>d</u>r. <u>b</u>erry saw this morning has <u>h</u>odgkin's disease.
6. <u>t</u>he pathology report showed a <u>c</u>lass IV malignancy on the <u>p</u>ap smear. (Pap is an unusual abbreviation.)
7. <u>s</u>ome patients have been very sick with <u>k</u>aposi's sarcoma, the rare and usually mild skin cancer that seems to turn fierce with <u>aids</u> victims.
8. <u>t</u>he <u>m</u>ustard procedure is often used to reroute venous return in the atria. (Mustard is an eponym.)
9. <u>t</u>he young man was an alert, asthenic, <u>i</u>ndochinese male who was well-oriented to time and place.
10. <u>t</u>he gynecologist wrote a prescription for <u>f</u>lagyl for the patient with <u>t</u>richomonas vaginalis. (Flagyl is the brand name for a drug.)
11. <u>p</u>lease note on <u>m</u>rs. <u>s</u>tefandatter's chart that she is allergic to phenobarbital. (Phenobarbital is a generic drug name.)
12. <u>d</u>r. <u>c</u>ollier recommended a combination of penicillin G (2,000,000 to 5,000,000 units, t.i.d.) and an aminoglycoside, such as <u>g</u>entamicin (3–5 mg/kg/day), for our patient with endocarditis.
13. <u>b</u>arbara, our <u>lpn</u>, is the new membership chairman for the local <u>now</u> chapter; she asked me to join.
14. <u>t</u>he <u>od</u> victim was brought to the <u>er</u> by his roommate.
15. <u>r</u>honda <u>k</u>eller, <u>m</u>r. <u>z</u>immer's executive secretary, spoke to the <u>aama</u> about good telephone manners.

Answers to 4–4: Practice Test

William A. Berry, M.D.

3933 Navajo Road
San Diego, California 92119

———————

463-0000

<u>m</u>ay 6, 199X

<u>m</u>rs. <u>a</u>drianne <u>l</u>. <u>s</u>hannon
316 <u>r</u>owan <u>r</u>oad
<u>c</u>learwater, <u>f</u>lorida 33516   *FL is the correct abbreviation*

<u>d</u>ear <u>m</u>rs. <u>s</u>hannon:

<u>d</u>r. <u>b</u>erry asked me to write to you and cancel your
appointment for <u>f</u>riday, <u>m</u>ay 15. <u>w</u>e hope this will not
inconvenience you, but <u>d</u>r. <u>b</u>erry has made plans to
attend the <u>a</u>merican <u>c</u>ollege of <u>c</u>hest <u>p</u>hysicians meeting
in <u>k</u>ansas <u>c</u>ity at that time. <u>i</u> have tentatively re-
scheduled your appointment for <u>m</u>onday, <u>m</u>ay 18, at
10:15 a.m.

<u>b</u>y the way, you might be interested to know that <u>d</u>r.
<u>b</u>erry has been asked to read the paper that he wrote,
entitled "<u>t</u>he <u>i</u>ns and <u>o</u>uts of <u>e</u>mphysema." <u>i</u> believe
that you asked him for a copy of this article the last
time you were in the office.

<u>s</u>incerely yours,

(<u>m</u>s.) <u>l</u>averne <u>s</u>hay
<u>s</u>ecretary

E

William A. Berry, M.D.

3933 Navajo Road
San Diego, California 92119

463-0000

<u>m</u>arch 3, 199X

<u>s</u>tate <u>c</u>ompensation <u>i</u>nsurance <u>f</u>und
<u>p</u>. <u>o</u>. <u>b</u>ox 2970
<u>w</u>innet<u>k</u>a, <u>i</u>llinois 60140   *IL is the correct abbreviation*

<u>a</u>ttention <u>r</u>alph <u>b</u>yron, <u>i</u>nspector

<u>g</u>entlemen:

<u>r</u>e: <u>j</u>ames <u>r</u>. <u>g</u>orman

<u>t</u>he above-referenced patient was seen today for pre-surgical examination in the office. <u>h</u>e has an acute upper respiratory infection with a red left ear and inflamed tonsils.   <u>t</u>herefore, his surgery was cancelled, and he was placed on <u>k</u>eflex, 250 mg every six hours.

<u>m</u>r. <u>g</u>orman's surgery was rescheduled for <u>m</u>arch 15 at <u>m</u>ercy <u>h</u>ospital. <u>h</u>e will be rechecked in the office on <u>m</u>arch 14.

<u>v</u>ery truly yours

<u>w</u>illiam <u>a</u>. <u>b</u>erry, <u>m</u>. <u>d</u>.

<u>r</u>ef

E

Answers to 5–2: Practice Test

1. On September 26, 1990, she had a left lower lobectomy.
2. Two sutures of 000 (or 3-0) cotton were placed so as to obliterate the posterior cul-de-sac. (Notice hyphens in the expression "cul-de-sac.")
3. He smoked $1\frac{1}{2}$ (or 1 1/2) packs of cigarettes a day. (leave out the word "and")
4. There was a tear in the iris at about 6 o'clock. (See Rule 5.12.)
5. The resting blood pressure is 76/40.
6. Please mail this to Dr. Ralph Lavton at 10 Dublin Street, Bowling Green, Ohio 43402. (Ten Dublin Street is also correct.)
7. We had 7 admissions Saturday, 24 Sunday, and 3 this morning. (See Rule 5.11.) (a.m. is used only with the time of day.)
8. In the accident, the spine was severed between C4–5. ($C_{4\text{-}5}$ also correct; C4 and C5 also correct; C-4 and C-5 also correct.)
9. The child was first seen by me in the X-ray Department on the evening of May 11, 1990. (Military or European dating is not used in narrative copy except in military documents prepared in the military service.)
10. I recommend a course of cobalt-60 radiation therapy. (Notice the hyphen.)

Answers to 5–4: Practice Test

1. He has a Grade I arteriosclerotic retinopathy and a Grade IV hypertensive retinopathy.
2. She was a Gravida V Para I Abortus IV and denied venereal disease but gave a history of vaginal discharge. (Note that there are no commas separating gravida, para, or abortus. These words may also be typed in lower case letters, although many dictators prefer the use of capital letters.)
3. I can see only 15-20 patients a day. (15 to 20 also correct.) (See Rule 5.10.)
4. Please order 12 two-gauge needles. (twelve 2-gauge also correct.)
5. Use only one-eighth teaspoonful. (Notice the hyphen.) (See Rule 5.5.)
6. The dorsalis pedis pulses were 2+ and equal bilaterally.
7. The ear was injected with 2% Xylocaine and 1:6000 Adrenalin.
8. Please check the reading in V_4 again. (V-4, V4 also correct.)
9. This is her third C-section.
10. She quickly advanced from a Stage II to a Stage IV lymphosarcoma.

E

Answers to 5–7: Practice Test

1. Hemoglobin (*Hb* would be incorrect) on July 27 (*7-27* or *7/27* would be incorrect) was 11.2 gm; hematocrit (*hct* would be incorrect) was 37.
2. Did you know that the postal rates were 25 cents (not *25¢*) for the first ounce (not *oz*) and 20 cents for each additional ounce to mail something first class in 1989? (*First Class* also correct.)
3. The protein was 65 mg%.
4. Electromyography shows a 3+ sparsity in the orbicularis oris.
5. An estimated 0.2 cc of viscid fluid was removed from the middle ear cavity. (Please notice the zero in front of the decimal point.)
6. He entered the ER at 4 a.m. (*AM* also correct) with a temperature of 99°F.
7. There was a reduction of the angle to within a two-degree difference. (*2-degree* also correct; *2°* also correct.)
8. Take 50 mg/day. (*50 mg per day* also correct.)
9. I then placed two 4 × 4 sponges over the wound.
10. The TB skin test was diluted 1 : 100.
11. Drainage amounts to several cubic centimeters a day. (*cc's, ccs,* and *cc* all incorrect.)

Answers to 6–6: Typing Practice Test

See the letter on page 424 properly prepared. The numbers in the margin refer to the comments below.

1. This is the correct placement of the reference line. However, it would also be correct to place it a double space under the salutation.
2. This is the appropriate paragraph break. To begin your second paragraph with "She brought the x-ray films . . . " is very weak.
3. Notice the insert of the "afterthought postscript." This would be the appropriate place to insert it when we have a rough draft. It is not incorrect to use it as a P.S. at the end of your document. It is just better at this place in the letter and the dictator appears better organized.
4. This is the appropriate paragraph break. However, it would be correct to attach it to either paragraph 2 or 4. It is attractive to have this one-sentence paragraph in the middle of the letter, however, and when we do have a choice like this, it is nice to take the option for appearance.
5. We hope this has now become an obvious paragraph break.
6. The parentheses at the end of this sentence are not the only way to handle this last comment. A comma at the end of "health" would also be appropriate. This is the correct paragraph break.
7. This final paragraph could have been joined to paragraph 6 since we are talking about "seeing" the patient in both. It does, however, make a nice balance with the one-line paragraph 3.
8. This enclosure line becomes necessary when the postscript has been eliminated and the data inserted into the body of the letter. If you left the postscript, it would appear here and the enclosure notice would be redundant.

Answers to 6–6: Typing Practice Test

E

Jon L. Mikosan, M.D.
6244 Applegate Road
Milwaukee, WI 53209

May 1, 199X

Ian R. Wing, M.D.
2261 Arizona Avenue, Suite B
Milwaukee, WI 53207

RE: Mrs. Elvira Martinez   (1)

Dear Dr. Wing:

I saw your patient Mrs. Elvira Martinez in consultation in my office today. She brought the x-rays from your office with her. She was afebrile today but, on questioning, admitted a low-grade fever over the past few days.   (2)

I removed the fluid, as seen on your film of April 30, from the right lower lung field, and she felt considerably more comfortable. On thoracentesis, there was 50 cc of straw-colored fluid. I am enclosing a copy of the pathology report on the fluid; as you can see, it is negative.   (3)

Her history is well known to you so I will not repeat it.   (4)

On physical examination, I found a well-developed, well-nourished white female with minimal dyspnea. There was no lymphadenopathy. Breath sounds were diminished somewhat on the right; there was dullness at the right base; the left lung was clear to percussion and auscultation. The remainder of the examination was negative.   (5)

Because of her history of chronic asthma, I suggested she might consider bronchoscopy if this fluid reaccumulates. Because she is a heavy smoker, I insisted she stop smoking completely. If she does not, she will not enjoy continuing good health (although I have no idea of the actual prognosis).   (6)

Mrs. Martinez has been returned to you for her continuing care. I will be glad to see her again at any time you think it necessary.

Thank you for letting me see this pleasant lady with you.   (7)

Sincerely yours,

Jon L. Mikosan, M.D.

your initials

Enclosure: Pathology report   (8)

Answers to 6-7: Typing Practice Test

The markings are a facsimile for proper placement on the #10 envelope.

— horizontal line

1.

NOAM L FLICKENGER MD
435 N MICHIGAN AVE
CHICAGO IL 60611

middle of envelope

SPECIAL DELIVERY or Special Delivery is typed under the postage area leaving plenty of room for stamp or meter impression placement.

— —

2.

MR STEVEN R MADRUGA
PO BOX 9982
PHILADELPHIA PA 19101

3.

ATTN MRS SYLVIA FARQUAR
OCCIDENTAL LIFE INSURANCE CO
1150 S OLIVE SUITE 16
LOS ANGELES CA 90015

Be sure that the "attention line" is positioned properly.

4.

MS MARIJANE N WOODS
MGR DESERT REALTY   (also MANAGER DESERT
2036 E CAMELBACK RD   REALTY)
PHOENIX AZ 85018

Be sure that the "confidential" notation is placed under the return address area in the upper left hand corner of the envelope.

Answer to 7–4: Practice Test

```
                                    September 15, 199X


    Carroll W. Noyes, M.D.
    2113 Fourth Avenue, Suite 171
    Houston, TX 77408
                            RE:  Erma Hanlyn
    Dear Dr. Noyes:

    I first saw Erma Hanlyn, your patient, on July 18, 199X, with a
    history of a thyroid nodule since March of this year.  This
    35-year-old woman had it diagnosed at Alvarado Hospital where
    they urged her to have surgery, I guess.

    She gave a history that the nodule was quite tender when she
    was seen there, and that she was on thyroid when they took her
    scan.  However, when I saw her, the tenderness was gone.  I
    could not feel any nodule.

    We have had her stay off the thyroid so that we could get an
    accurate reading, and on September  8, 199X, we had another
    scintigram done at Piikea General Hospital which revealed a
    symmetrical thyroid; it was free of any demonstrable nodules.
    All of the tenderness is gone and she feels well.  She is
    elated over the fact that she has avoided surgery.

    In my opinion, Mrs. Hanlyn probably had a thyroiditis when
    she was seen at Alvarado, and the radioactive iodine that she
    was given for the test is responsible for the cure.

    Thank you very much for letting me see her with you, and I will
    be happy to see her again at any time you or she feel it is
    necessary.

                            Sincerely,



                            Kwei-Hay Wong, M.D.

    student's initials
```

Answers to 8–2: Practice Test

1. maneuver	Pinard's	6. membrane	diphtheritic
2. acid	salicylic	7. disease	idiopathic
3. test	Wassermann	8. carcinoma	scirrhous or scirrhus
4. duct or gland	Bartholin's	9. tunica	adventitia
5. vas	spirale	10. disease	Alzheimer's

Answers to 8–4: Practice Test

1. eject	do not divide	8.11, 8.14
2. couldn't	do not divide or spell out could not	8.16
3. page 590	do not divide	8.18
4. impossible	im / possible or impos/sible	8.8, 8.9
5. scheme	do not divide	8.10, 8.13
6. 7 o'clock	do not divide or spell out seven / o'clock	8.18
7. today	do not divide	8.11
8. doesn't	do not divide or spell out does not	8.16
9. 2480 Ames Drive	2480 Ames / Drive	8.17

E

10. CHAMPUS	do not divide	8.16
11. t. i. d.	do not divide	8.16
12. shipped	do not divide	8.13
13. around	do not divide	8.14
14. 7,201,082,976	do not divide	8.16
15. John Jeffers, M.D.	do not divide or John / Jeffers, M.D.	8.6
16. 35-year-old	35- / year-old or 35-year / old	8.7

Answers to 8 – 5: Practice Test

1. claustrophobia	claustro / phobia	7. acromion	acro / mion
2. infraorbital	infra / orbital	8. metatarsus	meta / tarsus
3. leukopenia	leuko / penia	9. myoplasty	myo / plasty
4. postoperative	post / operative	10. bursitis	burs / itis or bur / sitis
5. posterolateral	postero / lateral	11. edema	do not divide
6. tuberosity	tuber / osity	12. viruses	vi / ruses

Answers to 8 – 11: Practice Test

1. b (preferred) (all right)	8. a (anoint)	15. a (indispensable)
2. a (supersede)	9. b (occasion)	16. a (superintendent)
3. b (embarrassed)	10. a (disappoint)	17. a (battalion)
4. b (drunkenness)	11. b (analyze)	18. a (perseverance)
5. a (irresistible)	12. a (tyranny)	19. a (iridescent)
6. b (occurrence)	13. a (inoculate)	20. b (recommend)
7. a (ecstasy)	14. b (coolly)	

Answers to 8 – 12: Practice Test

	Remember the Silent	Spelling
1.	g	gnathodynia
2.	p	pterygium
3.	p	pneumatic
4.	c	cnemial
5.	k	knock-knee
6.	rh	dysmenorrhea
7.	rr	hemorrhage
8.	a	dentia praecox
9.	i	cheiragra
10.	e	cacogeusia
11.	rh	metrorrhexis
12.	rh	menometrorrhagia
13.	rh	herniorrhaphy
14.	p	pyopneumocholecystitis
15.	e	eusitia
16.	e	euthanasia
17.	g	diaphragm

Answers to 8 – 13: Practice Test

1. altogether	6. Although	11. already	16. sometime	21. everything
2. all together	7. all right	12. any time	17. any more	22. anybody
3. anyone	8. some day	13. anytime	18. anything	
4. anyway	9. someday	14. everyday	19. awhile	
5. any way	10. all ready	15. some time	20. anywhere	

Answers to 8–16: Practice Test

1. Alphabetical Index (pink) Brand names
2. Drug (Product) Category Index, also known as Drug, Chemical, and Pharmacological Index
3. a. Valium
   b. Zyloprim or Lopurin
   c. Bellergal
   d. Arlidin
   e. Enovid
4. a. meprobamate
   b. norethindrone acetate and ethinyl estradiol
   c. aspirin-Maalox
   d. nikethamide NF
   e. mazindol
5. a. Equanil
   b. Obetrol
   c. Tepanil
   d. Belladenal
   e. Temaril
6. a. Metatensin. If the medical record was not available, the transcriptionist should flag it with a note to the dictator on what it sounded like.
   b. Indocin
   c. Tepanil

NOTE: Some generic names have been adopted by drug manufacturers as brand names, but the generic form is to be used when transcribing reports. You might also point out that some generic names may sound like a brand name but may be spelled differently (example: *adrenaline* with an "e" on the end is the generic and *Adrenalin* without an "e" is the brand name).

Answers to 8–17: Practice Test

1. Dalmane — c, a
2. Ilosone — f, e
3. Atromid-S — a, c
4. Topicort — d, f
5. Pamelor — b, d
6. Demerol — i, h
7. Flagyl — j, i
8. Compazine — h, g
9. Keflex — g, e

Answers to 8–18: Practice Test

1. Dymelor — acetohexamide
2. Benadryl — diphenhydramine HCl
3. Hygroton — chlorthalidone
4. Dilantin — phenytoin sodium
5. Dramamine — dimenhydrinate
6. Gantrisin — sulfisoxazole diolamine
7. Tofranil — imipramine HCl
8. Lomotil — diphenoxylate HCl
9. Pyridium — phenazopyridine HCl
10. Mellaril — thioridazine

Answers to 10–2: Practice Test

1. advise
2. lay
3. compliment
4. Whose
5. Your, too
6. razed
7. surge, forth
8. cite
9. course
10. here, hear
11. stationery
12. effect
13. effect
14. then
15. than
16. correspondence
17. break
18. principal, site
19. accept
20. effected
21. there
22. They're
23. their

Answers to 10–4: Practice Test

1. opposition	8. absorption	15. auscultation
2. apposition	9. adsorption	16. alvus
3. position	10. adherents	17. a febrile
4. abrasion	11. adherence	18. arteriostenosis, arteriosclerosis
5. aberration	12. peritoneum	19. serous
6. dysphagia	13. mucous	20. rales
7. dysphasia	14. addiction	21. cortisol

Answer to 11–2: Practice Test

Maryellen Mawson   Age: 6

(Today's date)   This is a 6-year-old who has had a 3-week history of polydipsia, polyuria, polyphagia,
and weight loss. The child has become progressively more lethargic over the past
24 hours and 12 hours ago, the parents noticed she was breathing rapidly.

PX: Height: 127 cm. Weight: 33 kg. Temp: 99°F. Pulse: 112. BP: 95/70.
The child was semicomatose. She has dry mucous membranes but good skin turgor and full
peripheral pulses.

STAT Lab: Sodium: 138 mEq/L. Potassium 3.3 mEq/L. Chloride: 97 mEq/L. Total CO_2: 5 mEq/L.
Blood glucose: 700 mg%.

PLAN: Admit STAT to Childrens Hospital.

(student's initials)   Eugene W. Gomez, M.D.

Answer to 12–2: Practice Test

Joseph R. Balentine
423-12-22
Copy: Stuart L. Paulson, M.D.

HISTORY

CHIEF COMPLAINT: The patient is a 25-year-old male complaining of recurring
epistaxis.

PRESENT ILLNESS: The patient reports that yesterday he had onset of epistaxis
in the left side of his nose. This was intermittent throughout
the day, and at 4:30 this morning, he came to the ER.

PAST HISTORY:
ALLERGIES: None.
BLEEDING HISTORY: None, except for PI.
ILLNESSES: The patient had a collapsed lung about five years ago and
subsequently had surgery but does not know the exact
etiology of the problem or the exact name of the surgery.
MEDICATIONS: None.
FAMILY HISTORY: Essentially unremarkable. Father, mother, siblings are all
well and healthy.

REVIEW OF SYSTEMS:
SKIN: No rashes or jaundice.
HEENT: See PI.
CR: See Past History. No history of pneumonia, tuberculosis,
chronic cough, or hemoptysis. No history of pedal edema.
GI: Weight is stable. He denies any nausea, vomiting, diarrhea, or
food intolerance.
GU: No history of GU tract infections, dysuria, hematuria, pyuria.
ENDOCRINE: No polyuria or polydipsia.
NEUROLOGIC: No history of psychiatric disorder.
mlo
D:11-16-9X
T: 11-16-9X   Benjamin B. Abboud, M.D.

(You should check to be sure that the format is that indicated: block format. Check to be
sure that all lines are blocked. Main topics are typed in full caps and underlined. Subtopics

are indented 3–5 spaces and typed in full caps. You may double space between main topics and subtopics, single space between subtopics. Be sure that the copy notation is made at either the top or the bottom. Patient and ID number of patient at top of page. Assignment should be neat, attractive, with narrow margins.)

E

Answer to 12–3: Practice Test

Geoffrey Paul Hawkins
54-98-10
PHYSICAL EXAMINATION

GENERAL: The patient is a well-developed, well-nourished, white male
                    who appears his age of 11½. He is of moderately small stature
but is well-tanned from being in the sun. He appears to be in no acute distress but is quite
apprehensive.

SKIN: Warm and dry, well-tanned, no jaundice, no lesions.

HEENT:
    EYES: Pupils are round, regular and equal; react to light and
                    accommodation. No icterus seen. Conjunctivae normal.
    NOSE: Septum straight. No lesions.
    MOUTH & THROAT: Benign. The tonsils are small and the teeth are in good repair.
    NECK: Supple. The thyroid is not enlarged. There is no remarkable
                    lymphadenopathy. Trachea is in the midline with no tug.
    EARS: Drums pearly, hearing is good to the spoken voice.

HEART: Regular sinus rhythm, no murmurs heard. A-2 is louder than P-2.

ABDOMEN: Scaphoid with no scars. Patient indicates midepigastric
                    tenderness. Peristalsis is audible and possibly slightly
hyperactive but very close to average in intensity. There is some tenderness, mainly in
the right upper quadrant. Both left and right lower quadrants appear to be soft with no
rebound present. Equivocal Murphy punch tenderness is present. No CVA tenderness.

GENITALIA: Testes down, no penile lesions.

RECTAL: There is stool in the ampulla. Sphincter tone is gone. Patient
                    complains of some tenderness in both vaults, but no

masses found.

SKELETAL: No gross bone or joint anomalies.

NEUROLOGIC: No motor or sensory loss found. Deep tendon reflexes active
                    and equal. Toe signs down. Pedal pulses palpable.

IMPRESSION: 1. Abdominal pain, etiology unproved, but probably
                       gastroenteritis.
                    2. Rule out early appendicitis.

mlo
D: *(date)*
T: *(date)*   _____
                                         Paul R. Elsner, M.D.

This is a physical examination that is to be set up in indented format. Check to be sure that all first and second lines are blocked evenly and that third and subsequent lines are brought back to the left margin. Be sure that main topics are full caps and underlined, subtopics indented and typed in full caps. The student may elect to type the subtopics in paragraph form. Check "Abdomen" to be sure that it is a main topic. Dictator did not specify it as obviously as other parts of the outline. Be sure that the patient I.D. number is repeated after the name as on Self-Study 12–1. Standard abbreviations may be used throughout the transcript. No abbreviations are to be used in the Diagnosis (Impression) data.

Answer to 12–4: Practice Test

```
Joseph R. Balentine
423-12-22
Copy: Stuart L. Paulson, M.D.
```
                               PHYSICAL EXAMINATION

GENERAL:	The patient is a well-developed, muscular, slightly pale, young man in somewhat acute distress, secondary to the apprehension and bleeding.
VITAL SIGNS:	BP: 110/70. Pulse: 74. Respirations: 16.
HEENT:	
HEAD:	Normocephalic.
EYES:	Round, regular and equal and bilaterally react to light and accommodation.
EARS:	There is bilateral cerumen in the ears; TMs are normal.
NOSE:	The right nasal cavity is somewhat congested to the nasopharynx. There is active bleeding from the left nasal cavity.
NECK:	There are no palpable nodes in the neck and the thyroid is in the midline.
CHEST:	Symmetrical.
BREASTS:	Normal male.
LUNGS:	Clear bilaterally, no rales or wheezes. There is a pneumonectomy scar, left anterolateral chest.
HEART:	Normal in size. There is normal sinus rhythm, no murmurs, thrills or rubs.
ABDOMEN:	Soft, no tenderness.
RECTAL:	Exam is deferred.
EXTREMITIES:	Symmetrical, no cyanosis, edema, or deformities. There is normal range of motion. Reflexes are physiological. Pulses are 2+ and equal bilaterally.
NEUROLOGICAL:	No cranial or neurological deficit.
IMPRESSION:	Left posterior epistaxis, recurrent.

```
mlo
D: 11-16-9X
T: 11-16-9X          _____
                         Benjamin B. Abboud, M.D.
```

(Check the main topics carefully since the dictator did not dictate the outline, just the data. Be sure that you made a copy notation. It was not repeated in the directions; it was hoped that you would pick it up from the history.)

Answer to 12–5: Practice Test

Copies: Be sure that the copies are designated properly to Willow Moran, M.D. and Gordon Bender, M.D. (These are given as Dr. Willow Moran and Dr. Gordon Bender in the directions. By now, you should be able to make the proper title change.)
Topics and Subtopics: Check these carefully as all were not "dictated." The Review of Systems is called the "Functional Inquiry" in this exercise.
Continuation: Be sure that the first page is marked "continued" and the second page carries all the vital patient data. (See Figure 12–6)
Impression: These should be numbered 1 through 4 although the "dictator" failed to designate them in other than individual sentences.

E

Lily Mae Jenkins
5980-A
Copies: Willow Moran, M.D.
    Gordon Bender, M.D.

HISTORY

CHIEF COMPLAINT: Right rectal bleeding, one day.

PRESENT ILLNESS: This 90-year-old lady has been looking after her own personal affairs and living with her daughter for the last three years. Last night, she had a bowel movement that had some bright rectal blood mixed in with it. This morning, she had another bowel movement, and it consisted mostly of bright-red blood. She has a history of gallbladder disease, dating back over 50 years. She refused to have her gallbladder taken out but has been on a low-fat diet ever since that time. Her daughter describes numerous gallbladder attacks, lasting for several days, consisting of severe, right upper quadrant pain. She has had occasional, intermittent right lower quadrant pain that does not seem similar to the gallbladder attacks.

PAST HISTORY: Operations: In 1967, she had enucleation of the left eye. She had surgery in 1976 for glaucoma in the right eye. Medical: 1966, Colles' fracture, right wrist. 1970's, severe arthritis of her spine.

MEDICATIONS: Patient is presently taking Peritrate, 1 capsule, b.i.d. Reserpine-A, 1 tablet q a.m. Indocin, 1 tablet, t.i.d. She takes Bufferin p.r.n. for pain. She takes nitroglycerin, 2–3 tablets per week for chest pain and has done so for 5 years.

FAMILY: Both of her parents lived until their nineties. She had 6 children: 1 died at age 3, the result of injuries sustained in an automobile accident, 1 died at age 56 of carcinoma of the breast. Otherwise, the family history is unremarkable. There are 4 children who are alive and well.

FUNCTIONAL INQUIRY: HEENT: Hearing in her right ear is absent. Hearing in her left ear is decreased. There is an artificial eye in the left and there is only slight vision in her right eye if one comes exactly in the middle of her visual field. Patient has been edentulous for several years.
CHEST: Nonsmoker.
CV: Patient has had angina for over five years and abnormal cardiograms for the last three. She is cold all of the time and is constantly bundling herself up in an effort to keep warm.
GI: Her bowel movements have been normal. See History of Present Illness.
GU: She has no history of any bladder or kidney infections, despite the fact that she had a history of kidney failure last year.
NM: Patient has shooting, severe pains up her spine, which are relatively incapacitating, but she manages to keep going by just taking Bufferin.

PHYSICAL EXAMINATION

GENERAL: This is a 90-year-old black woman in no obvious distress, who is hard of hearing but can answer questions.

HEENT: Ears: There is wax in both ears. The drums, beyond the wax, appear within normal limits. There is no hearing in the right ear and only slight hearing in the left. Eyes: The left eye is artificial. The right eye is pinpoint. There is no scarring in the right eye, consistent with an iridectomy. She has a cataract in the right eye, as well. Nose: Unremarkable. Mouth: Edentulous. Neck: There are no carotid bruits. No jugular venous distention. Thyroid is palpable and unremarkable. Range of motion of the neck is generally slightly restricted.

CHEST: Clear to percussion and auscultation. Heart: The apex beat is not palpable. There is some tenderness over the costochondral cartilages on the left side. Heart size is not enlarged to percussion. There is muffled heart sound. There is no third or fourth heart sound. There are no murmurs heard in the supine position. Breasts: Palpable and there are no masses noted.

ABDOMEN: Soft. There are marked senile keratoses over the abdominal wall. There is some diffuse tenderness on deep palpation over the cecum in the right lower quadrant. There is no other tenderness noted or abnormal bowel sounds noted in the abdomen. Bowel sounds are within normal limits.

PELVIC: Not done.

RECTAL: Full sigmoidoscopic examination to 25 cm revealed fresh blood in the sigmoid area with no obvious bleeding source noted.

(continued)

E

Lily Mae Jenkins
5980-A
Physical Examination, page 2

EXTREMITIES: There is essentially no motion in the back. Range of motion of the hips is within normal limits and painless. There is only a +1 dorsalis pedis on the right; otherwise, there are no peripheral pulses present. There is marked coldness of both feet.

CNS: The patient's strength is within normal limits. The reflexes are within normal limits. Coordination is not tested. There is an involuntary shaking, consistent with the diagnosis of old Parkinson's disease.

IMPRESSION: 1. Acute gastrointestinal hemorrhage, etiology not yet diagnosed.
              2. Chronic cholecystitis.
              3. Severe osteoarthritis of spine.
              4. Arteriosclerotic heart disease with angina pectoris.

(student's initials)
D: *(today's date)*
T: *(today's date)*   _____
                                        Philip D. Quince, M.D.

Answer to 13–2: Practice Test

This assignment is to be set up using indented format with no variations.

1	Date: January 4, 19-- Dwight, John P.
5	86-30-21
	Room No. 582-B
	OPERATIVE REPORT
	<u>PREOPERATIVE DIAGNOSIS:</u> Otosclerosis, left ear.
10	
	<u>POSTOPERATIVE DIAGNOSIS:</u> Otosclerosis, left ear. *(or Same)*
	<u>OPERATION:</u> Left stapedectomy.
15	<u>FINDINGS:</u> Otosclerosis footplate.
	<u>PROCEDURE:</u> Under local anesthesia, the ear was prepared and
	draped in the usual manner. The ear was injected
	with 2% Xylocaine and 1:6,000 Adrenalin. A stapes-type flap was elevated
	from the posterosuperior canal wall, and the bony overhang was removed with
20	the stapes curet. The chorda tympani nerve was removed from the field. The
	incudostapedial joint was separated. The stapes tendon was cut. The
	superstructure was removed. The mucous membrane was reflected from the ear,
	stapes, and the facial nerve promontory. The footplate was then reamed
	with small picks and hooks. A flattened piece of Gelfoam was placed over
25	the oval window and a 5 mm wire loop prosthesis was inserted and crimped in
	the incus. The drum was reflected and a small umbilical tape was placed in
	the ear canal. The patient tolerated the procedure well.
	Surgeon _____
	Felix A. Konig, M.D.
30	*(student's initials)*
	D: *1-4-year*
	T: *(current date)*
	Line 11: Some physicians dictate "same" for the postoperative diagnosis. Although it is not incorrect to type it, the preferred style is to spell out the diagnosis again.
	Line 18: Adrenalin is the brand and epinephrine is the generic name; Xylocaine is the brand name for lidocaine.

Answer to 13–3: Practice Test

This assignment is to be set up using modified block format and no variations.

PATHOLOGY REPORT

DATE: June 6, 199–   PATHOLOGY NO. 532009

PATIENT: Joan Alice Jayne   ROOM NO.   453-A

PHYSICIAN: John A. Myhre, M. D.   HOSPITAL NO.   72-11-03

SPECIMEN(S):   The specimen consists of a 4.5 cm in diameter nodule of fibro-fatty tissue removed from the right breast at biopsy, and enclosing a central, firm, sharply demarcated nodule 1 cm in diameter. Surrounding breast parenchyma reveals dilated ductiles (microcystic disease).

FROZEN SECTION IMPRESSION: Myxoid fibroadenoma of breast.

MICROSCOPIC AND DIAGNOSIS: Myxoid fibroadenoma occurring in right parenchyma, the site of microcystic disease of right breast.

Pathologist _____
                    James T. Rodgers, M.D.

(student's initials)
D: 6-6-year
T: (current date)

Answer to 13–5: Practice Test

This assignment is to be set up using modified block format with indented paragraphs and mixed punctuation.

Letterhead

Current Date

Glen M. Hiranuma, M.D.
2501 Main Street
Ventura, CA 93003

                              RE: Mrs. Hazel R. Plunkett

Dear Dr. Hiranuma:

Thank you for referring your patient Mrs. Hazel R. Plunkett for neurological consultation, evaluation, and treatment of chronic and recurrent headaches.

In the past, the patient has had episodes of probably typical migraine occurring perhaps six or eight times in her life. She remembers that her mother had a similar complaint. This would begin with loss in the field of vision; and then, approximately fifteen minutes thereafter, she would have a relatively typical, unilateral throbbing pain of a significant degree which would often incapacitate her. These headaches disappeared many years ago and have never returned.

However, for the last eight years approximately, the patient has had recurrent daily headaches, always right-sided, with associated pain beginning in the back of the neck with stiffness of the right side of the neck, radiating forwards over the vertex to the right orbit, the nose, and the jaw. She also notes some pain in the right trapezius area. The pain tends to appear from 10 a.m. to noon, when she will take a Fiorinal, and often after she goes to sleep at night (at about 12:30 a.m.). She controls this pain by taking

Illustration continued on following page

Fiorinal, one to four a day, and Elavil, 75 mg at bedtime. She estimates that the headaches occur approximately twice daily, are relatively short-lived, but occasionally last a full day. The pain is dull and heavy, not throbbing, and worse at some times than at others.

On examination she was a quiet woman, not in acute distress, and somewhat dour; but she gave a careful and concise history. Her gait and station were normal. The head functions were basically intact. The fundi showed only modest arteriosclerotic changes. The temporal arteries were normal. Facial motility and sensation were normal. There was a significant right carotid bruit present, which was persistent and could be heard all along the course of the right carotid artery. It was not transmitted from the neck. There were moderate pain and tenderness at the insertion of the great muscles of the neck and the occiput, and palpation over this area consistently reproduced the patient's symptoms. She also had a persistent area of tenderness in the right trapezius muscle. Otherwise, power, size, and symmetry of the arms and legs were essentially normal. The deep tendon reflexes were brisk. There were no long tract or focal signs, and sensation was intact.

Impression:　1.　Muscle contraction headaches, chronic.
　　　　　　　 2.　Localized myositis, right side of the neck, right shoulder girdle.
　　　　　　　 3.　Right carotid bruit, silent, asymptomatic.

RE: Mrs. Hazel R. Plunkett
Page 2
(Current Date)

Comment: The findings were discussed in detail with the patient, but no neurological studies were done. I suggested simple measures of physical therapy to the neck including the use of heat, hot packs, and massage and advised also that she purchase a cervical pillow on which to rest during the day. Motrin, 400 mg twice daily and Maolate, 400 mg at night were suggested in an attempt to provide anti-inflammatory and muscle relaxant properties. It may also be necessary to inject these tender areas which are quite well localized. This can be determined after 30 to 60 days on the treatment regimen outlined above.

The patient also has what seems to be a silent right carotid bruit. Certainly she is without symptoms. This should be brought to the attention of those who are caring for her, so that if transient ischemic attacks appear in the future, appropriate steps can be taken. I do not think that the right carotid bruit has anything to do with the patient's headaches, which are not vascular, and certainly there is no sign of cranial arteritis.

She was referred back to you for continuing medical service. Thank you for the opportunity of seeing this patient.

Sincerely,

Margo A. Wilkins, M.D.

(student's initials)

Answer to 14–2: Practice Test

WHY:	Dr. Berry has received her request and has agreed to make an abstract of her record.
	He wishes to meet with her and discuss the abstract.
	He wishes to answer any questions she may have.
WHO:	Obtain complete name and address of patient.
WHAT:	Find out how much time Dr. Berry wishes to save for the conference.
	$40 fee for the conference and abstract.
	Choose a date and time for the conference.
REACTION:	Patient is to call if the plans are suitable or make new arrangements.

(and a special note for myself:
FOLLOW-UP: Be sure abstract is dictated and transcribed in time for the conference.)

Answer to 15–1: Practice Test

```
                              MEMO

   DATE:     May 7, 199x

   TO:       Your name, Office Manager
             Mary Connors, CMT
             Sue Marcos, RN
             Joan Taylor, CMA-A

   FROM:     Dr. Berry

   SUBJECT:  Use of Photocopy Equipment

   Attached is a brochure outlining in detail our new photocopy equipment. Please become
   familiar with its operation and upkeep.

   The machine is to be used only for the following:

      1.       To reproduce billing statements.
      2.       To make copies of completed insurance claims.
      3.       To make copies of chart documents when required.
      4.       To make copies of correspondence leaving the office. (In-house copies are to be
               typed on carbon sheets whenever possible.)

   Please ask me for permission for any personal use of the machine.

   (your initials)
```

Answers to 15–3: Practice Test

HOLTER MONITOR   CV-15

OBJECTIVE:
To obtain a magnetic tape record of a patient's electrocardiographic activity over a 24-hour period.

EQUIPMENT:
1. Holter monitor.
2. Battery.
3. Tape.
4. Patient cable.
5. Universal cable.
6. ECG machine.
7. ECG electrodes.
8. 2×2 pads, alcohol, and Redux paste.
9. Transpore tape.
10. Patient diary.
11. Shaving prep kit.

PROCEDURE:
1. Verify the physician's order by checking the medical chart.
2. Assemble all equipment and bring to the patient's bedside.

E

3. Introduce yourself to the patient and thoroughly explain what you are about to do.
4. Verify the patient's identity by checking the patient's I.D. bracelet.
5. Have the patient remove all clothing covering his or her chest.
6. Locate the necessary anatomical landmarks and prepare the five areas as follows:
    a. Shave all hair.
    b. Cleanse the area with alcohol.
    c. Scrub the cleansed area with Redux paste.
    d. Remove the Redux paste with alcohol.
7. Attach the electrodes to the patient's chest.
    a. 2nd rib space on the right side of the sternum.
    b. 2nd rib space on the left side of the sternum.
    c. Over the xiphoid process.
    d. Right V4 — Right mid-clavicular at the 5th intercostal space.
    e. Left V4 — Left mid-clavicular at the 5th intercostal space.
8. Attach the electrode cables to the patient:
    a. White — right arm.
    b. Brown — left arm.
    c. Black — V1.
    d. Green — right leg.
    e. Red — left leg.
9. Tape the electrode cables in a loop on the patient's abdomen allowing the cable to hang free.
10. Place a tape in the Holter monitor unit.
11. Place a battery in the Holter monitor unit.
12. Attach the recorder to the belt or shoulder strap (patient's preference).
13. Plug Universal cable into recorder.
14. Connect RA, LA, RL, LL, and V1 from ECG machine to Universal cable.
15. Connect patient cable to recorder.
16. Run a short strip on the ECG machine to verify the quality of the tracing (L1, L2, L3, AVR, AVL, AVF, and V1).
17. Disconnect Universal cable from recorder unit.
18. Set time on recorder and start Holter monitor.
19. Record starting time in the patient diary and explain the importance of the diary to the patient.
20. If an outpatient, remind the patient of the importance of returning in 24 hours.
21. After 24 hours, record ending time in the patient's diary.
22. Remove the cable from the recorder.
23. Remove the cable and electrodes from the patient.
24. Prepare the tape for scanning.

CARE OF EQUIPMENT:
1. Exercise caution when handling unit to avoid dropping.
2. Instruct patient not to bathe, shower, or go swimming while attached to the unit.
3. Clean recording heads and capstan with alcohol after each patient use.

IMPORTANT POINTS:
1. Proper preparation of the patient's chest is important to a good recording.
2. Run a short strip with the ECG machine to insure that the electrodes are placed correctly.
3. Make sure the patient thoroughly understands the importance of the diary.

Approved: _____. Policy Number 90-202

Effective date: (current date)   Revised:
Reviewed: Revised:

Answer to 16–1: Practice Test

E

COCKTAILS CAN CAUSE CARDIAC COMPLICATIONS

A Manuscript Prepared

for

Modern Medicine

Chicago, Illinois

by

Roger Balor, M.D.

Mount Sinai Hospital and Mount Sinai School of Medicine

of the City University of New York

New York City, New York

Current Date

E

COCKTAILS CAN CAUSE CARDIAC COMPLICATIONS[1]

Prolonged, heavy ingestion of alcohol by certain individuals, even though they are well nourished, may result in cardiac abnormalities that are evident clinically or electrocardiographically, or both. Electrocardiographic abnormalities in these patients may indicate the early developmental stages of cardiomyopathy, a process that may be reversed if the patient abstains from ingestion of alcohol.

Cardiac abnormalities in well-nourished alcoholics may include resting tachycardia, sinus tachycardia or bradycardia, premature ventricular contractions, premature atrial contractions, paroxysmal atrial fibrillation, or a rhythm varying between sinus rhythm with frequent premature beats and atrioventricular dissociation. First-degree atrioventricular block also may be found.

Notched or tall P waves may be present on the electrocardiogram. In addition, the QRS complex may show some abnormality, as may the S-T segment and T wave. T-wave abnormalities may consist of diminished wave amplitudes, diphasic waves, or frank wave inversion. Some patients may have enlarged hearts.

The electrocardiograms of 50 randomly chosen, well-nourished alcoholics were studied and compared with those from 50 nonalcoholic controls. No subject in either group had any known heart disease.

The electrocardiogram was considered to be within normal limits in 36 alcoholic patients but was clearly abnormal in four others. Only one control patient had an abnormal electrocardiogram.

---

1. George J. Sanna, M.D., Quarterly Journal for the Study of Alcoholism, 34: 774-785, 1984.

Answer to 16-3: Practice Test

CATEGORIES OF TUMORS

A Manuscript Prepared

for

Journal of the American Medical Association

Chicago, Illinois

by

Joan T. Bennett, M.D.

XYZ Medical Center

Philadelphia, Pennsylvania

Current Date

CATEGORIES OF TUMORS

There are many categories of tumors. Epithelial tumors is the topic of interest.

1. Epithelial tumors. These tumors arise from the coelomic mesothelium, which is capable of differentiating into both benign and malignant tumors. The transition from benign to malignant is not abrupt; there is an intermediate or borderline category. Distinguishing benign, borderline, or malignant tumors is important in terms of treatment and prognosis. Epithelial malignancies represent 82% of all ovarian malignancies.

   a. The predominant cell types are:

   (1) Serous

       (a) One out of three serous tumors is malignant.

       (b) Serous cancers are more than three times as common as the mucinous variety and seven times as common as the endometrioid variety.

       (c) Serous cystadenoma carcinoma, the most common type of ovarian cancer, tends to be bilateral in 35%–50% of cases.

   (2) Mucinous

       (a) One out of five mucinous tumors is malignant.

       (b) Mucinous tumors are bilateral in 10%–20% of cases.

Illustration continued on following page

E

(3) Endometrioid

(a) The microscopic pattern is similar to primary carcinoma of the endometrium.

(b) Areas of endometriosis on the ovary may be present.

(c) The prognosis is much better than that of the serous and mucinous carcinomas.

b. The prognosis for each stage of eipthelial ovarian tumors is linked to the grade of the tumor; poorly differentiated tumors have a poor prognosis. Long-term survival of patients with borderline or well-differentiated cancers after primary surgery is common.

Answers to 16–4: Practice Test

1. title page
2. capital
3. letter of transmittal
4. page number
5. double spacing or manuscript format
6. single
7. footnotes
8. single spacing within the footnote and double spacing between footnotes
9. a. et al.
   b. ibid.
   c. i.e.
   d. e.g.
10. bibliography
11. et al.
12.

	Top	Bottom	Left	Right	Page Number
a. Unbound report:					
Page 1	2″	1″	1″	1″	none
Other pages	1″	1″	1″	1″	upper right or centered at top of page
b. Left-bound report:					
Page 1	2″	1″	1½″	1″	none
Other pages	1½″	1″	1½″	1″	upper right or centered at top of page

APPENDIX F

Performance Evaluation Sheets for Review Tests

F

Directions

The time element and accuracy criteria should be given to the student by the instructor before beginning each review test. The Performance Evaluation Sheet for each review test should be removed from the textbook. The instructor or monitor of the review test should check off each item as the student completes each task. At the end of the test, the Performance Evaluation Sheet should be attached to the top of the completed test. The instructor will fill in the student's grade and indicate whether the test has been successfully completed or if the student needs to repeat the test. The test and Performance Evaluation Sheet is returned to the student so he or she can see the results.

PERFORMANCE EVALUATION SHEET FOR REVIEW TEST 3-9

PERFORMANCE OBJECTIVE

Task: Place a comma or commas where needed in the sentences in this review test.
Conditions: Use an electronic typewriter or word processing computer and plain typing paper.
Standards: Time: _____ minutes
Accuracy: _____

NOTE: The time element and accuracy criteria may be given to you by your instructor.

PERFORMANCE EVALUATION CHECKLIST

_____ Read each sentence and determined which punctuation rule was applicable and inserted commas where appropriate.

_____ Proofread review test after typing for spelling and typographical errors.

_____ Completed the procedure within _____ minutes.

COMMENTS: _____

_____

Name _____

Grade _____   Successful completion _____

Date _____   Need to repeat _____

F

PERFORMANCE EVALUATION SHEET FOR REVIEW TEST 3-16

PERFORMANCE OBJECTIVE

Task: Place punctuation marks where needed in the sentences in this review test.
Conditions: Use an electronic typewriter or word processing computer and plain typing paper.
Standards: Time: _____ minutes
Accuracy: _____

NOTE: The time element and accuracy criteria may be given to you by your instructor.

PERFORMANCE EVALUATION CHECKLIST

_____ Read each sentence and determined which rule was applicable and inserted appropriate punctuation.

_____ Proofread review test after typing for spelling and typographical errors.

_____ Checked the placement and spacing of all punctuation marks.

_____ Completed the procedure within _____ minutes.

COMMENTS: _____

_____

Name _____

Grade _____   Successful completion _____

Date _____   Need to repeat _____

PERFORMANCE EVALUATION SHEET FOR REVIEW TEST 5-9

PERFORMANCE OBJECTIVE

Task: Type sentences and phrases using symbols, numbers, abbreviations, and capitalization, and place punctuation marks where needed in the sentences in this review test.
Conditions: Use an electronic typewriter or word processing computer and plain typing paper.
Standards: Time: ____ minutes
Accuracy: _____

NOTE: The time element and accuracy criteria may be given to you by your instructor.

PERFORMANCE EVALUATION CHECKLIST

____ Read each sentence and determined which rule was applicable.

____ Inserted punctuation where appropriate.

____ Checked the placement and spacing of all punctuation marks.

____ Proofread review test after typing for spelling and typographical errors.

____ Completed the procedure within ____ minutes.

COMMENTS: _____

_____

Name _____

Grade _____   Successful completion _____

Date _____   Need to repeat _____

PERFORMANCE EVALUATION SHEET FOR TYPING REVIEW TEST 6–8

PERFORMANCE OBJECTIVE

Task: Type a letter for the physician's signature using modified block format and open punctuation.

Conditions: Use an electronic typewriter or word processing computer and letterhead typing paper.

Standards: Time: _____ minutes

Accuracy: _____

NOTE: The time element and accuracy criteria may be given to you by your instructor.

PERFORMANCE EVALUATION CHECKLIST

_____ Assembled materials: stationery, references, and typing accessories.

_____ Used letterhead paper.

_____ Dated the letter.

_____ Typed in modified block format.

_____ Attractive placement of letter on sheet.

_____ Margins even and equal.

_____ Properly identified the person to whom the letter is being sent.

_____ Used proper address format for the inside address.

_____ Placed the salutation.

_____ Placed the reference line.

_____ Used open punctuation.

_____ Inserted capitalization and abbreviations where appropriate in the body of the letter.

_____ Checked the placement and spacing of all punctuation marks.

_____ Inserted proper paragraphing in the body of the letter.

_____ Inserted a page 2 heading.

_____ Page 2 heading placed properly.

_____ Placed the complimentary close and signature line.

_____ Inserted proper enclosure notation.

_____ Inserted typist's reference data.

_____ Proofread review test after typing for spelling and typographical errors while the letter remained in the typewriter.

_____ Prepared an envelope using United States Postal Service's approved format.

_____ Attached the envelope to the letter in presentation format ready for signature.

_____ Completed the procedure within _____ minutes.

COMMENTS: _____

_____

Name _____

Grade _____   Successful completion _____

Date _____   Need to repeat _____

PERFORMANCE EVALUATION SHEET FOR REVIEW TEST 8-20

PERFORMANCE OBJECTIVE

Task: Type in the correct spelling for 20 dictated drug names.
Conditions: Use an electronic typewriter or word processor.
Standards: Time: _____ minutes
Accuracy: _____

NOTE: The time element and accuracy criteria may be given to you by your instructor.

PERFORMANCE EVALUATION CHECKLIST

_____ Assembled materials: stationery, references, and typing accessories.

_____ Proofread review test after typing for spelling and typographical errors while the review test remained in the typewriter.

_____ Completed the procedure within _____ minutes.

COMMENTS: _____

_____

Spelling errors _____   Typo errors _____   Answer errors _____

Name _____

Grade _____   Successful completion _____

Date _____   Need to repeat _____

F

PERFORMANCE EVALUATION SHEET FOR REVIEW TEST 9-8

PERFORMANCE OBJECTIVE

Task: On a separate sheet of paper, hand write or type in the correct spelling of the Latin and English plurals and adjectives for the 8 given words. Then hand write or type in the correct spelling of the adjectives and nouns for the 12 given words.

Conditions: Use a pen, pencil, or an electronic typewriter or word processor.

Standards: Time: _____ minutes

Accuracy: _____

NOTE: The time element and accuracy criteria may be given to you by your instructor.

PERFORMANCE EVALUATION CHECKLIST

_____ Assembled materials: stationery, references, and typing accessories.

_____ Proofread review test after typing for spelling and typographical errors while the review test remained in the typewriter.

_____ Completed the procedure within _____ minutes.

COMMENTS: _____

_____

Spelling errors _____   Typo errors _____   Answer errors _____

Name _____

Grade _____   Successful completion _____

Date _____   Need to repeat _____

PERFORMANCE EVALUATION SHEET FOR REVIEW TEST 10-5

PERFORMANCE OBJECTIVE

Task: Hand write or type in the correct homonym by selecting a word from the left column that is needed to correctly complete each sentence in the right column.

Conditions: Use a pen, pencil, or an electronic typewriter or word processor.

Standards: Time: _____ minutes

             Accuracy: _____

NOTE: The time element and accuracy criteria may be given to you by your instructor.

PERFORMANCE EVALUATION CHECKLIST

_____ Assembled materials: stationery, references, and typing accessories.

_____ Proofread review test after typing for spelling and typographical errors while the review test remained in the typewriter.

_____ Complete the procedure within _____ minutes.

COMMENTS: _____

_____

Spelling errors _____   Typo errors _____   Answer errors _____

Name _____

Grade _____   Successful completion _____

Date _____   Need to repeat _____

PERFORMANCE EVALUATION SHEET FOR REVIEW TEST 11-3

PERFORMANCE OBJECTIVE

Task: Type chart notes for the physician's signature using a format of your choice.
Conditions: Use an electronic typewriter or word processing computer and plain typing paper.
Standards: Time: _____ minutes
Accuracy: _____

NOTE: The time element and accuracy criteria may be given to you by your instructor.

PERFORMANCE EVALUATION CHECKLIST

_____ Assembled materials: stationery, references, and typing accessories.

Chart Note	Date	Patient's Name	Format	Reference Line	Signature Line	No Errors	Errors As Marked	Score
1								
2								
3								
4								
5								

_____ Inserted capitalization and abbreviations where appropriate.

_____ Checked the placement and spacing of all punctuation marks.

_____ Proofread review test after typing for spelling and typographical errors while the chart notes remained in the typewriter.

_____ Ready for signature.

_____ Completed the procedure within _____ minutes.

COMMENTS: _____

_____

Name _____

Grade _____   Successful completion _____

Date _____   Need to repeat _____

PERFORMANCE EVALUATION SHEET FOR REVIEW TEST 11–4

PERFORMANCE OBJECTIVE

Task: Type chart notes for the physician's signature using a format of your choice.
Conditions: Use an electronic typewriter or word processing computer and plain typing paper.
Standards: Time: _____ minutes
            Accuracy: _____

NOTE: The time element and accuracy criteria may be given to you by your instructor.

PERFORMANCE EVALUATION CHECKLIST

_____ Assembled materials: stationery, references, and typing accessories.

Chart Note	Date	Patient's Name	Format	Reference Line	Signature Line	No Errors	Errors As Marked	Score
1								
2								
3								
4								
5								

_____ Inserted capitalization and abbreviations where appropriate.

_____ Checked the placement and spacing of all punctuation marks.

_____ Proofread review test after typing for spelling and typographical errors while the chart notes remained in the typewriter.

_____ Ready for signature.

_____ Completed the procedure within _____ minutes.

COMMENTS: _____

_____

Name _____

Grade _____   Successful completion _____

Date _____   Need to repeat _____

PERFORMANCE EVALUATION SHEET FOR REVIEW TEST 11–6

PERFORMANCE OBJECTIVE

Task: Type chart notes for the physician's signature using a format of your choice.
Conditions: Use an electronic typewriter or word processing computer and plain typing paper.
Standards: Time: ____ minutes
Accuracy: _____

NOTE: The time element and accuracy criteria may be given to you by your instructor.

PERFORMANCE EVALUATION CHECKLIST

____ Assembled materials: stationery, references, and typing accessories.

Chart Note	Date	Patient's Name	Format	Reference Line	Signature Line	No Errors	Errors As Marked	Score
1								
2								
3								
4								
5								

____ Inserted capitalization and abbreviations where appropriate.

____ Checked the placement and spacing of all punctuation marks.

____ Proofread review test after typing for spelling and typographical errors while the chart notes remained in the typewriter.

____ Ready for signature.

____ Completed the procedure within ____ minutes.

COMMENTS: _____

_____

Name _____

Grade _____   Successful completion _____

Date _____   Need to repeat _____

PERFORMANCE EVALUATION SHEET FOR REVIEW TEST 12-7

PERFORMANCE OBJECTIVE

Task: Type a History and Physical report for the physician's signature using a full block report format.

Conditions: Use an electronic typewriter or word processing computer and plain typing paper.

Standards: Time: _____ minutes
Accuracy: _____

NOTE: The time element and accuracy criteria may be given to you by your instructor.

F

PERFORMANCE EVALUATION CHECKLIST

_____ Assembled materials: stationery, references, and typing accessories.

_____ Dated the reports.

_____ Typed in full block report style.

_____ Margins even, equal, correct size.

_____ Inserted main topic headings.

_____ Inserted subtopic headings.

_____ Inserted capitalization and abbreviations where appropriate.

_____ Checked the placement and spacing of all punctuation marks.

_____ Inserted proper paragraphing.

_____ Inserted a page 2 heading.

_____ Used a separate page for each part of the report: History and Physical.

_____ Placed the signature lines for both the History and the Physical.

_____ Inserted typist's identifying sign-off data for both the History and the Physical.

_____ Proofread review test after typing for spelling and typographical errors while the History and then the Physical remained in the typewriter.

_____ Ready for signature.

_____ Completed the procedure within _____ minutes.

COMMENTS: _____

_____

Name _____

Grade _____   Successful completion _____

Date _____   Need to repeat _____

PERFORMANCE EVALUATION SHEET FOR REVIEW TEST 13-6

PERFORMANCE OBJECTIVE

Task: Type a hospital autopsy protocol into report form for the physician's signature using full block report format, with variation number 1 and the current date.

Conditions: Use an electronic typewriter or word processing computer and plain typing paper.

Standards: Time: _____ minutes

Accuracy: _____

NOTE: The time element and accuracy criteria may be given to you by your instructor.

PERFORMANCE EVALUATION CHECKLIST

_____ Assembled materials: stationery, references, and typing accessories.

_____ Used plain paper.

_____ Dated the report.

_____ Typed in full block report format.

_____ Typed variation number 1, no line space between main headings.

_____ Placed attractively on sheet.

_____ Provided even and equal margins.

_____ Identified the patient properly.

_____ Inserted the name of the hospital.

_____ Inserted capitalization and abbreviations where appropriate in the body of the report.

_____ Checked the placement and spacing of all punctuation marks.

_____ Inserted *(continued)* at the bottom of page 1.

_____ Inserted proper paragraphing in the body of the report.

_____ Inserted a page 2 heading.

_____ Page 2 heading placed properly.

_____ Placed the signature line.

_____ Inserted typist's reference data.

_____ Proofread review test after typing for spelling and typographical errors while the report remained in the typewriter.

_____ Completed the procedure within _____ minutes.

COMMENTS: _____

_____

Name _____

Grade _____   Successful completion _____

Date _____   Need to repeat _____

PERFORMANCE EVALUATION SHEET FOR REVIEW TEST 13-7

PERFORMANCE OBJECTIVE

Task: Type an industrial accident into report form for the physician's signature using indented format, with no underlining, mixed punctuation, and the current date.
Conditions: Use an electronic typewriter or word processing computer and plain typing paper.
Standards: Time: _____ minutes
Accuracy: _____

NOTE: The time element and accuracy criteria may be given to you by your instructor.

PERFORMANCE EVALUATION CHECKLIST

_____ Assembled materials: stationery, references, and typing accessories.

_____ Used plain paper.

_____ Dated the report.

_____ Typed in indented format.

_____ Placed attractively on sheet.

_____ Provided even and equal margins.

_____ Identified properly the person to whom the report is being sent.

_____ Used proper address format for the inside address.

_____ Placed the salutation.

_____ Placed the reference line.

_____ Used mixed punctuation.

_____ Inserted capitalization and abbreviations where appropriate in the body of the letter.

_____ Checked the placement and spacing of all punctuation marks.

_____ Inserted proper paragraphing in the body of the report.

_____ Inserted a page 2 heading.

_____ Page 2 heading placed properly.

_____ Placed the complimentary close and signature line.

_____ Inserted typist's reference data.

_____ Proofread review test after typing for spelling and typographical errors while the report remained in the typewriter.

_____ Prepared an envelope using United States Postal Service's approved format.

_____ Attached the envelope to the report in presentation format ready for signature.

_____ Completed the procedure within _____ minutes.

COMMENTS: _____

_____

Name _____

Grade _____   Successful completion _____

Date _____   Need to repeat _____

PERFORMANCE EVALUATION SHEET FOR OPTIONAL TEST 13-8

PERFORMANCE OBJECTIVE

Task: Type a psychiatric report for the physician's signature using full block report format with variation number 1, mixed punctuation, and the current date.

Conditions: Use an electronic typewriter or word processing computer and letterhead or plain typing paper.

Standards: Time: _____ minutes
Accuracy: _____

NOTE: The time element and accuracy criteria may be given to you by your instructor.

PERFORMANCE EVALUATION CHECKLIST

_____ Assembled materials: stationery, references, and typing accessories.

_____ Used letterhead or plain paper.

_____ Dated the report.

_____ Typed in full block report format.

_____ Typed variation number 1, no line space between main headings.

_____ Placed attractively on sheet.

_____ Provided even and equal margins.

_____ Identified properly the person to whom the report is being sent.

_____ Used proper address format for the inside address.

_____ Placed the salutation.

_____ Placed the reference line.

_____ Inserted the name of the hospital.

_____ Used mixed punctuation.

_____ Inserted capitalization and abbreviations where appropriate in the body of the report.

_____ Checked the placement and spacing of all punctuation marks.

_____ Inserted (*continued*) at the bottom of page 1.

_____ Inserted proper paragraphing in the body of the report.

_____ Inserted a page 2 heading.

_____ Page 2 heading placed properly.

_____ Placed the complimentary close and signature line.

_____ Inserted typist's reference data.

_____ Proofread review test after typing for spelling and typographical errors while the report remained in the typewriter.

_____ Prepared an envelope using United States Postal Service's approved format.

_____ Attached the envelope to the report in presentation format ready for signature.

_____ Completed the procedure within _____ minutes.

COMMENTS: _____

_____

Name ————————————————

Grade ————————————————   Successful completion ——————————

Date ————————————————   Need to repeat ———————————————

F

PERFORMANCE EVALUATION SHEET FOR REVIEW TEST 14-4

PERFORMANCE OBJECTIVE

Task: Compose and type letters for your signature using a modified block format and mixed punctuation.

Conditions: Use an electronic typewriter or word processing computer and letterhead paper.

Standards: Time: _____ minutes

Accuracy: _____

NOTE: The time element and accuracy criteria may be given to you by your instructor.

PERFORMANCE EVALUATION CHECKLIST

_____ Assembled materials: stationery, references, and typing accessories.

_____ Dated the letters.

_____ Typed in modified block format.

_____ Attractive placement of letters on sheet.

_____ Margins even and equal.

_____ Identified the person to whom the letter is being sent.

_____ Placed the salutation.

_____ Used mixed punctuation.

_____ Inserted capitalization and abbreviations where appropriate in the body of the letter.

_____ Checked the placement and spacing of all punctuation marks.

_____ Inserted proper paragraphing in the body of the letter.

_____ Used letterhead paper.

_____ Placed the complimentary close and signature line.

_____ Inserted typist's reference data.

_____ Proofread review test after typing for spelling and typographical errors while the letter remained in the typewriter.

_____ Ready for signature.

_____ Completed the procedure within _____ minutes.

COMMENTS: _____

_____

Concise _____ Too wordy _____ Chose appropriate or inappropriate words _____
Sentence fragments _____ Run-on sentences _____ Parallel structure _____
Dangling construction _____ Unnecessary or repetitious words _____
Spelling errors _____ Grammar errors _____

Name _____

Grade _____   Successful completion _____

Date _____   Need to repeat _____

PERFORMANCE EVALUATION SHEET FOR REVIEW TEST 14-5

PERFORMANCE OBJECTIVE

Task: Compose and type letters for your employer's signature using a full block format and mixed punctuation.
Conditions: Use an electronic typewriter or word processing computer and letterhead paper.
Standards: Time: _____ minutes
                          Accuracy: _____

NOTE: The time element and accuracy criteria may be given to you by your instructor.

PERFORMANCE EVALUATION CHECKLIST

_____ Assembled materials: stationery, references, and typing accessories.

_____ Dated the letters.

_____ Typed in full block format.

_____ Attractive placement of letters on sheet.

_____ Margins even and equal.

_____ Identified the person to whom the letter is being sent.

_____ Placed the salutation.

_____ Used mixed punctuation.

_____ Inserted capitalization and abbreviations where appropriate in the body of the letter.

_____ Checked the placement and spacing of all punctuation marks.

_____ Inserted proper paragraphing in the body of the letter.

_____ Used letterhead paper.

_____ Placed the complimentary close and signature line.

_____ Inserted typist's reference data.

_____ Proofread review test after typing for spelling and typographical errors while the letter remained in the typewriter.

_____ Ready for signature.

_____ Completed the procedure within _____ minutes.

COMMENTS: _____

_____

Concise _____ Too wordy _____ Chose appropriate or inappropriate words _____
Sentence fragments _____ Run-on sentences _____ Parallel structure _____
Dangling construction _____ Unnecessary or repetitious words _____
Spelling errors _____ Grammar errors _____

Name _____

Grade _____   Successful completion _____

Date _____   Need to repeat _____

PERFORMANCE EVALUATION SHEET FOR REVIEW TEST 14-7

PERFORMANCE OBJECTIVE

Task: Compose and type the following sentences substituting an appropriate word or words as found in your thesaurus for the target words.

Conditions: Use an electronic typewriter or word processing computer and plain typing paper.

Standards: Time: _____ minutes

Accuracy: _____

NOTE: The time element and accuracy criteria may be given to you by your instructor.

PERFORMANCE EVALUATION CHECKLIST

_____ Assembled materials: paper, thesaurus.

_____ Chose appropriate words. Sentence _ 2 _ 3 _ 4 _ 5_ 6

_____ Chose inappropriate word or words _____

_____ Used unnecessary or repetitious words. See sentence _____

_____ Spelling errors. See sentence _____

_____ Grammar errors. See sentence _____

_____ Punctuation errors. See sentence _____

_____ Sentence fragment. See sentence _____

COMMENTS: _____

_____

Name _____

Grade _____   Successful completion _____

Date _____   Need to repeat _____

F

PERFORMANCE OBJECTIVE

Task: Compose and type letters using proper letter format.
Conditions: Use an electronic typewriter or word processing computer and letterhead paper.
Standards: Time: _____ minutes
Accuracy: _____

NOTE: The time element and accuracy criteria may be given to you by your instructor.

PERFORMANCE EVALUATION CHECKLIST

_____ Assembled materials: stationery, references, and typing accessories.

_____ Dated the letter.

_____ Typed in proper letter format.

_____ Attractive placement of letter on sheet.

_____ Margins even and equal.

_____ Identified the person to whom the letter is being sent.

_____ Placed the salutation.

_____ Inserted capitalization and abbreviations where appropriate in the body of the letter.

_____ Checked the placement and spacing of all punctuation marks.

_____ Inserted proper paragraphing in the body of the letter.

_____ Used letterhead paper.

_____ Placed the complimentary close and signature line.

_____ Inserted typist's reference data.

_____ Proofread review test after typing for spelling and typographical errors while the letter remained in the typewriter.

_____ Ready for signature.

Itinerary:

_____ Included details of hotel accommodations.

_____ Included details of car rental (if desired).

_____ Included details of snacks, meals, movies, time zone changes when appropriate.

_____ Identified names of airlines and flight number.

_____ Included details of departure and arrival times both leaving and returning.

_____ Prepared itinerary attractively.

_____ Completed the procedure within _____ minutes.

COMMENTS: _____

_____

Concise _____ Too wordy _____ Chose appropriate or inappropriate words _____
Sentence fragments _____ Run-on sentences _____ Parallel structure _____
Dangling construction _____ Unnecessary or repetitious words _____
Spelling errors _____ Grammar errors _____

Name _____

Grade _____   Successful completion _____

Date _____   Need to repeat _____

Index